AF539485

MICROF

# MICROFINANCE

A.N. Sarkar

Published by

PUBLISHERS & DISTRIBUTORS (P) LTD

7/22, Ansari Road, Darya Ganj, New Delhi-110002
Phones : +91-11-40775252, 23273880, 23275880, 23280451
Fax : +91-11-23285873
Web : www.atlanticbooks.com
E-mail : orders@atlanticbooks.com

Branch Office
5, Nallathambi Street, Wallajah Road, Chennai-600002
Phones : +91-44-64611085, 32413319
E-mail : chennai@atlanticbooks.com



Printed in India at Nice Printing Press, A-33/3A, Site-IV, Industrial Area, Sahibabad, Ghaziabad, U.P.

# Contents

# Introduction

Microfinance, according to Otero, "is the provision of financial services to low-income poor and very poor self-employed people". These financial services, according to Ledgerwood, generally include savings and credit but can also include other financial services such as insurance and payment services. Schreiner and Colombet have defined microfinance as "the attempt to improve access to small deposits and small loans for poor households neglected by banks". Therefore, microfinance involves the provision of financial services such as savings, loans and insurance to poor people living in both urban and rural settings who are unable to obtain such services from the formal financial sector. The terms microcredit and microfinance are often used interchangeably, but it is important to highlight the difference between them because both the terms are often confused. Microcredit refers to small loans, whereas microfinance is appropriate where non-Government organizations (NGOs) and Microfinance Institutions (MFIs) supplement the loans with other financial services (savings, insurance, etc.). Therefore, microcredit is a component of microfinance in that it involves providing credit to the poor, but microfinance also involves additional non-credit financial services such as savings, insurance, pensions and payment services.

Microfinance is widely acknowledged to be a sound and well-tested institutional mechanism to extend financial services to low-income clients, including consumers and the self-employed, who traditionally lack access to banking and related services. In more concrete terms, it is a movement whose object is a world in which as many poor and near-poor households as possible have permanent accesses to an appropriate range of high quality financial services, including not just credit but also savings, insurance, and fund transfers. Those who promote microfinance generally believe that such access will help poor people out of poverty. Microcredit emphasizes the provision of credit services to low income clients, usually in the form of small loans for supporting to develop micro-enterprise and income-generating activities. The use of the term 'microcredit' is often associated with an inadequate amount of the value of savings for the poor. In most cases, the provision of savings services in 'microcredit' schemes simply involves the collection of compulsory deposit amounts that are designed only to collateralize those loans. Additional voluntary savings may collect but the clients have restricted access to their enforced savings. These savings become the main source of capital in the financial institutions, called microfinance institutions.

There are several benefits of microfinance, especially to fund the unbankables. In essence, the benefits of microfinance help manage the assets of the poor and generate income. Through microfinance institutions such as credit unions, financial non-governmental organizations and even commercial banks, poor people can obtain small loans and safeguard their savings. A microfinance initiative can promote larger poverty-reduction movements by increasing the financial knowledge of an average citizen. The other benefits of microfinance projects are that they allow low-income families to save their money, as most of the poor live day-to-day with the little money that they earn and cannot afford to save. Poor people need such alternatives in order to turn their savings into large lump sums or receive large sums and repay monthly with low interest rates. Banks and other money-lending institutions have high interest rates and simply would not extend loans to poor people with little or no assets or employment. Microfinance helps the poor people save funds or get an access to loans over a period of time with low interest rates. Also, the poor could solve their own issues by working together as a community and this creates trust and social capital in their communities. It also leads to stability and growth in their households, as well as their communities.

There are seemingly two ways in which the needs of the poor are not being met by microfinance in several instances. Firstly, the poor need to store savings for the long run, such as for their retirement, widowhood or for their children, but they are unable to save enough money to meet these needs. Secondly, the poor people's ability to save fluctuates with time and so they may not be able to save at any fixed rate. These two shortcomings create financial difficulties for the poor and they often get excluded or exclude themselves. Poor people have to take a risk to turn their savings into large lump sum of money because there is no perfect system that would protect their deposits. Linked to this, there are a large number of implementation and institutional issues that would need to be addressed for a comprehensive understanding on microfinance, largely for the benefit of the financial institutions and other cooperative/collaborative agencies/functionaries that are either directly or indirectly involved in the planning, execution, management and regulation of microfinance as an industry.

The Task Force on Supportive Policy and Regulatory Framework for Micro-Finance, constituted by NABARD (National Bank for Agriculture and Rural Development) defines microfinance as "the provision of thrift, saving, credit and financial services and products of very small amounts to the poor in rural, semi-urban and urban areas for enabling them to raise their income levels and improve their standard of living". The emphasis of support under microfinance is on the poor in 'pre-micro-enterprise' stage for building up their capabilities to handle larger resources. This perception is quite significant, keeping in view the limitations of any approach of micro-enterprise development to help the poorest of the poor in self-employment. The Task Force has not specified limit for the 'small' amount of financial services envisaged. Services of microfinance are being provided by various MFIs.

Building an inclusive financial sector has gained growing global recognition and momentum in bringing to the fore the need for development strategies that touch all lives, instead of a select few. The overall strategy for financial inclusion, especially amongst the poor and disadvantaged segments of the population should comprise ways and means to effect improvements within the existing formal credit delivery mechanism, as well as an evolution of new models for extending outreach, and a leverage on technology solutions to facilitate large-scale inclusion. Only two to five percent of the 500 million poorest households in the world have access to institutional credit, of which, women receive a disproportionately small share of credit from formal banking institutions. The Women's Self-Help Group movement is bringing about a profound transformation in rural areas of India.

Microfinance Institutions thus play a significant role in facilitating inclusion, as they are uniquely positioned in reaching out to the rural poor. Many of them operate in a limited geographical area, have a greater understanding of the issues specific to the rural poor, enjoy greater acceptability amongst the rural poor and have flexibility in operations providing a level of comfort to their clientele. Though MFIs advocate embeddedness of microfinance under the broad parameters of financial inclusion, there are certain implicit challenges, and associated issues linked to this would need to be considered. These include legal and gender issues, increasing accessibility of the poor, rate of interest, unbalanced geographical growth, choice of productive activities, assessment of demand, subsidy, capacity building, records maintenance, auditing, transparency, absenteeism policy, absence of proper database, low outreach, loan default and poor recovery regime, low education level, language barrier, late payments, and geopolitical factors.

The concept of microfinance involves informal and flexible approach to the credit needs of the poor. There is no single approach or model that fits in all the circumstances. Therefore, a number of microfinance models emerged in different countries/ states according to the suitability to their local conditions. Broadly, the microfinance delivery methods can be classified into the following six groups: Grameen Bank Model, Joint Liability Group Model, Individual Lending Model, the Group Approach

Model, Village Banking Model, and Credit Unions and Co-operative Model. In India and elsewhere, there is a wide variety of institutions in public as well as private sector which provide microfinance to the poor. These institutions can be broadly divided into two types. First type is the traditional formal financial institutions, while the second type is Microfinance Institutions. The former type of institutions comprise commercial banks, regional rural banks and co-operative banks. They provide microfinance services in addition to their general banking activities and are referred to as microfinance service providers. On the other hand, MFIs are different types of financial institutions whose main financial activity is providing microfinance only. Many of these institutions are NGOs, Mutually Aided Co-operative Societies (MACS) and Non-Banking Financial Companies (NBFCs). In case of traditional financial institutions both private and public ownership are found, but the MFIs are mainly in the private sector.

Microfinance has its root in Bangladesh, where experimenting with microloans for the rural poor started in the 1970s. From there, the concept spread rapidly across the globe. In 1976, Muhammad Yunus launched the research project to provide microcredit and banking services to the poor people. In addition to that, microcredit programme is based on unique mechanism such as group lending, social collateral and distinctive payment methods. It is not based on checking credit history, income sources and bank balances but works on character-based lending and thus managed to give loans to those who lack credit histories. It is also useful for those who have no access to conventional finance. In 1983, Muhammad Yunus formally established a Grameen bank which has become a milestone in the development of the microfinance industry. The objective of this bank is to give small loans at affordable rates of interest to poor people, especially women. The high number of clients and regular repayments are impressive achievements for the bank. The microcredit programme has not been restricted to Bangladesh as the similar activities are also under way in different parts of the world, including Indonesia (1972), India (1990s) and, more importantly, in Latin America (1990s) where microcredit operations were rapidly developed. Today, most borrowers still live in rural South Asia and the East Asia and Pacific (EAP) regions. Over a period of a couple of decades, microfinance has expanded also in Latin America and the Caribbean (LAC), in Eastern Europe and Central Asia (EECA), and in Sub-Saharan Africa. The expansion of microfinance was accompanied by a shift from group to individual lending. Because group lending is more difficult to apply in urban areas, and wealthier borrowers prefer individual contracts, individual lending is predominantly used in these cases.

Microfinance industry is one of the fastest growing set of finance-driven initiatives aimed at alleviating poverty, contributing to economic growth and supporting future growth through financial inclusion. A growing number of MFIs are attempting to build the human capital entrepreneurs in order to improve the livelihood of their clients and help further their mission of poverty reduction. Increased household income, access to health care and education, and better living conditions are just a few ways in which microfinance and complimentary services are helping the poor and underserved population around the world. United Nations' Millennium Development Goals (MDGs), in the context of microfinance, are centred on the reduction of extreme poverty, promotion of gender equality and empowerment of women and the development and implementation of strategies for decent and productive work for the youth.

It is hoped that MFIs will assist in the achievement of these goals as they are a viable tool used in eradicating poverty, and improving social and economic welfare of the people. The concept has become a top agenda item at the international fora and thus the UN has enlisted microfinance as one of the surest ways of meeting the MDGs if it is carefully implemented through sustainable institutions. Over the past 30 years, microfinance has grown to a $30 billion industry involving over 3,000 organizations. Half of these MFIs, however, have nothing more than anecdotal stories about the impact of MF on poverty. The connection between MF and poverty eradication is far from resolved. Measuring the mission impact is a crucial issue facing every MFI. They serve the dual goals of financial return and social mission achievement.

Microfinance has a very important role to play in development according to proponents of MF. Based on the studies, UNCDF states that MF plays three key roles in development, viz. it helps very poor households meet basic needs and protect against risks; is associated with improvements in household economic welfare; and helps to empower women by supporting women's economic participation, and so promotes gender equity. Otero—the great proponent of MF—illustrates various ways in which microfinance, at its core, combats poverty. He states that it creates access to productive capital for the poor, which together with human capital, addressed through education and training, and social capital, achieved through local organization building, enables people to move out of poverty. By providing material capital to a poor person, his/her sense of dignity is strengthened to empower the person to participate in the economy and society.

A livelihood security approach to MF aims for a holistic analysis and understanding of the root causes of poverty and how people cope with it. Very often several parts of the world identify livelihood shocks such as natural disasters and drought, tsunami, the social, political and economic context, and people's livelihood resources like education and local infrastructure as factors affecting people's livelihood security. Therefore, when analyzing the impact the MF is having on livelihood security, as is the objective of this book, a holistic analysis of people's livelihood security must be conducted, rather than just focusing on the material/economic impact of MF on the livelihood of the poor. The world at large has experienced that poverty and livelihood security consist of economic and social conditions. Therefore, when analyzing the impact of MF, social impact must be assessed. A wider social impact assessment is important for an organization's internal learning process, as an MFI would be aware of the full range of changes associated with its efforts, and use these to improve its performance. Hence, we must consider social impact to relate to human capital such as nutrition, healthcare and education, as well as social networks. The impact must be assessed on each of these issues if a true picture of the impact of MF on the livelihood support system for sustenance is to be obtained with a reasonable degree of authenticity.

In making such an effort, one must in particular move beyond individual or household analysis to include community, market/economy and national/state levels, if the wider effects of MF interventions are to be understood properly. Impacts at household level are more crucial for recognizing MF impact, especially in socio-economic terms. Health and education are two key areas of non-financial impact of microfinance on a household level. Wright has stated on the basis of some research that has been conducted on the impact of MF interventions on health and education that nutritional indicators seem to improve where MFIs have been working. Littlefield, et al. acknowledged the sparse specific evidence of the impact of MF on health but where studies have been conducted, they conclude: "Households of microfinance clients appear to have better nutrition, health practices and health education than comparable non-client households."

Measuring mission impact is a crucial issue facing every MF Institution. MFIs serve to achieve the dual goals of financial return and social mission achievement. The techniques for measuring financial return are well understood. A controversy persists, however, about what are the true impacts of MF on poverty—the level of social mission achievement. Over the past several years, MF has been under increased scrutiny as the global development community has gradually realized that MF is not the once acclaimed anti-poverty silver bullet. Three of the most significant criticisms of MF that the domains of popular news media, practitioners, and academia have put forward, are the following: Some MFIs are profiting greatly from lending to impoverished clients; the unjust profiting of MFIs can lead borrowers to stop repaying their loans; and it is unclear whether microfinance truly succeeds in lifting people out of poverty.

Over the past several decades, microfinance, i.e. credit targeted toward small-scale entrepreneurial activities of the poor who may otherwise lack access to financing, has become a pillar of economic development policies. In recent years, there has been a concerted effort to expand such programmes with the goal of alleviating poverty, and promoting development. Between 1997 and 2006, access to MF grew by up to 29 percent a year, reaching a scale at which macroeconomic considerations become relevant. The Microcredit Summit Campaign, as of 2010, reported 3,552 institutions serving 155 million borrowers, which, including borrowers and their households, impacted 533 million people, roughly the size of Latin America. For various countries, MF loans represent a significant fraction of their GDP. Despite the growth and prevalence of MF and its importance in academic and policy circles, quantitative analyses of these programmes are almost exclusively limited to micro evaluations. The macroeconomic effects of economy-wide MF have still been largely unexplored.

Poverty alleviation has been one of the key development challenges over the decades. One of the identified key constraints facing the poor is lack of access to formal sector credit. It will facilitate them to take advantage of economic opportunities to increase their level of output, and hence move out of poverty. Credit is considered to be an essential input to increase productivity, mainly land and labour. It is believed that credit boosts income levels, increases employment at household level and thereby alleviates poverty. Credit enables poor people triumph over their liquidity constraints and helps them undertake some income-generating activities. The MF impact on poverty alleviation is a keenly debated issue as we have seen, and it is generally accepted that it has not lived up in general to its expectation. However, when implemented and managed carefully, and when services are designed to meet the needs of clients, MF has had positive impacts, not just on clients, but also on their families and the community as a whole. There is however a need for greater assessment of these wider impacts if the true value of MF to development is to be understood. One such tool for measuring wider impact is a livelihood security analysis based on a livelihood framework which analyzes how a project impacts the livelihood of beneficiaries. Key challenges facing MFIs today that are affecting their impact on poverty alleviation were seen to be an over-emphasis on financial sustainability over social objectives, and a failure of many MFIs to work with the poorest in society. Therefore, there is a greater need for MFIs to carefully design services that meet the needs of the poor and this can only be done when MFIs understand their needs and the context within which the poor are working. If MFIs are to meet their overall development objectives then they need to ensure financial sustainability and outreach of financial services designed to meet the needs of those deprived of such services.

Microcredit is the most well-known aspect of MF and has been able to spread rapidly around the globe because variable quality of institutions offers little financial downside for clients. However, managing this expansion of credit services, and building upon it to offer other products like savings and insurance, has been approached very differently by countries around the world. If an MFI is mismanaged, or goes bankrupt, the customer's situation is left unchanged. Products like savings, pensions, and insurance for the poor have been less welcomed by regulators and the traditional financial sector because of the added responsibilities of such products. MFIs which offer such products must be subject to prudential regulation to ensure their solvency so that customer deposits or other obligations are not lost, damaging the financial situation of the client. Here, we will briefly view the development, structure, and result of four approaches from Bolivia, Cambodia, Bangladesh and the Philippines. Improving the access of low-income producers and the poor to basic financial services is viewed as an ingredient of the World Bank's efforts to promote economic growth and reduce poverty. The World Bank's approach emphasizes a market-driven approach in which the financial sustainability of financial intermediaries becomes paramount. In many cases that market approach is possible because of the use by MFIs of group lending and other techniques to offset borrowers' lack of collateral. The World Bank's overall strategy for helping countries develop micro, rural and small and medium enterprise (SME) finance includes a number of key measures in the overall legal and regulatory framework in building up institutional capacity and in the introduction of financial systems infrastructure.

Various aspects of MF and micro-enterprises have been discussed in literature. However, a few empirical studies conducted with valid database have quantified the MF impact on poverty; only some have focused on the relation between MF and socio-economic indicators; a few have concentrated on the sustainability and profitability; and few others have estimated the return to capital invested in micro-enterprises. MF surely brings some changes, which could be positive or negative on individuals, households and institutions. Some studies focused on the growth of income and expenditures of the borrowers due to MF. Hulme and Mosley, for example, analyzed the impact of MF on poverty alleviation using sample data for Indonesia, India, Bangladesh and Sri Lanka and found that growth of income of borrowers always exceeds that of control group and the increase was larger for better-off borrowers.

Micro-enterprise refers to any economic unit engaged in the production and distribution of goods and services at household level. It is primarily of self-employed nature, employing him/her in the enterprise and sometimes some family members. The enterprise runs on little amount of capital investment at a fixed market centre or mobile business locations. This sector is identified with features like reliance on indigenous resources, family ownership of enterprises, small scale of operation, labour-intensive, adapted technology, and minimum skill. Micro-enterprise, therefore, is particularly suitable for poor communities.

Micro-economic enterprises play a vital role in poverty reduction in both rural and urban areas, and reinforce urban-rural linkages for economic and social development in Nepal. The linkages are essential not only for utilization of local resources but also in acting as agents for the flow of goods and services between urban and rural areas. Their roles are important since they possess the features like self-employment generation, employment to poor and women, use of local resources, meeting basic needs of the poor, traditional enterprise/skill and craftsmanship, labour intensive, self-satisfaction on the job, entrepreneurship and innovative and fair income distribution among the poor.

In developing countries, such as India, China, Bangladesh, Indonesia, Sri Lanka, etc. there are nearly 90 percent of the people who lack access to financial services from the institutions, either for cridit or saving purpose. The situation is more critical for the poor who do not have any assets. In micro-enterprises generally there is need for small capital but it is still difficult for the poor people to manage even that small quantity of capital. Resultantly, this lack of capital hinders the growth of micro-enterprise. Entrepreneurship is one of the commonly used terms in business, management, economics and other related fields. Entrepreneurship means innovation, creativity, leadership, profit maximization or starting of a new business. It helps in the process to increase economic growth, employment generation, and increase national income. Among several agencies, the MFIs in particular promote, in a proactive and imaginative manner, the development of entrepreneurship and growth of micro-enterprises by extending customized financial services to the stakeholders.

MFIs support two types of micro-entrepreneurs: one is potential micro-entrepreneur, and the second an existing micro-entrepreneur. The micro-entrepreneurs mean the creation and the existing entrepreneurs mean the expansion of that entrepreneurship. The MFIs assist potential micro-entrepreneurs by providing financing and training to enable them to start a business activity. This help to potential micro entrepreneurs is for pro-poor mostly. The objective of targeting the poor is to enable them to start their own business, help them to increase their revenues and reduce their level of poverty. MFIs also provide services to existing micro-entrepreneurs. Other financial services available to the existing micro-entrepreneurs are money transfer using mobile banking to facilitate their transfers and other financial operations; and micro-insurance to insure their business operations and the unexpected events that affect the smooth functioning of the business, like the sickness or the death of the micro-entrepreneur. The MFIs also offer non-financial services to existing micro-entrepreneurs enabling them to expand and develop their activities and their skills as well as to empower them. The nonfinancial services provided to existing micro-entrepreneurs include managerial training, technical assistance, and analysis of the sector of activity.

Microfinance has been globally established as a leading development tool to combat poverty, and more specifically, it aims at economically empowering the poor and releasing their entrepreneurial potential. It was not prominent before 1970s, but after its emergence in Bangladesh, it expended very rapidly in the world. From this modest beginning, more than 3,000 MFIs now operate around the world, with the Microfinance Summit Campaign Report estimating that they serve 128.2 million poor people in developing countries. However, with the creeping commercialization of the MF sector, most discussion now rotates around profitability, sustainability and risk minimization. It is being increasingly, forcefully argued that the commercialization allows greater opportunity for MFIs to fulfil their social objectives which increase access to a range of demand driven MF products and services to the poor. Commercialization offers a win-win position in increasing outreach and sustainability while delivering social benefits.

MF is promoted as a mechanism for triggering or sustaining social and economic development by supporting entrepreneurial activities. MF can have multiple spin-off benefits, including the potential to be a component of poverty reduction strategies, thus contributing to the Millennium Development Goals (MDGs). Whilst clients who use MF services differ according to age, income, ethnicity and whether they access MF services as individuals or in groups, its typical MF clientele in many parts of the world have been resource-poor female entrepreneurs. MF programmes contribute to the achievement of MDGs by giving low-income rural women and men a chance to develop both their on- and off-farm income-generating activities. An increase in women's income has been shown to have positive effects for children's nutrition, education and well-being, which also supports other MDGs. Although responding to major development challenges cannot be based solely on simply improving access to financial services, MF is an effective tool if used in conjunction with other development approaches and policies. In this regard MF institutions themselves are quite diverse—ranging from large commercial banks—to smaller NGOs.

Maintaining gender equity is the cornerstone for remarkable achievements in innovative MF initiatives and micro-entrepreneurial ventures in several parts of the world. Gender broadly refers to social, economic and cultural roles and relations between women and men, taking into account the different responsibilities of women and men in a given culture or location and in different population groups (children, aged people, ethnic groups, etc.). 'Gender mainstreaming' is a process by which an MFI considers gender equality issues in all its activities, programmes and policies. Promoting gender-sensitive entrepreneurship via MFIs puts the onus on the institution itself to be gender sensitive. But, what do we exactly mean by 'gender sensitive'? Being gender sensitive would mean that the gender-based differences between men and women clients/staff are acknowledged and transparent. Once acknowledged, staffs from MFIs take into consideration how such differences affect the ability of MF clients to avail of microfinance services, and how such differences affect their entrepreneurial activities. Gender sensitivity in microfinance institutions would also imply that the institution acknowledges gender-based constraints that affect women in their entrepreneurship activities and plan services accordingly. At the very least, an MFI can try to ensure that it does not worsen or perpetuate inequalities between women and men by ignoring gender-based constraints, or expecting women's business to operate exactly like men's. MFIs should consider how their services can help women to operate in an often 'male-dominated' business world. Promoting gender-sensitive entrepreneurship via MFIs does not mean a focus only on women. Instead the MFI needs to examine the relative conditions of men and women. Without comparing women and men, and indeed different categories of women clients, it is not possible to highlight and address gender-based inequalities.

Littlefield, et al. have stated that access to MFIs can empower women to become more confident, more assertive, and likely to take more part in family and community decisions and better able to confront gender inequities. To compliment this statement,

Hulme and Mosley have argued that MF projects can reduce the isolation of women as when they come together in groups they have an opportunity to share information and discuss ideas and develop a bond that was not there previously. Knowledge about gender issues amongst those involved in providing MF services will vary depending on the type of MFI. While the staff of many NGOs involved in MF may have a comparative advantage regarding knowledge of gender issues, the lack of business skills among staff within the NGO sector may also limit their ability to sustainably deliver MF services to poorer clients. The heterogeneity of MFIs (and MF clients) poses challenges for the delivery of MF in a manner that is gender equitable.

In this context, gender sensitivity can be considered both in terms of programmes and policies to see whether services that MFIs offer to their male and female clients are appropriate and respond to their needs as well as the gender issues in the actual organizational structure and functioning of the MFI. Gender refers to the social, economic and cultural roles and relations between women and men, taking into account different responsibilities of women and men in a given culture or location and in different population groups (children, aged people, ethnic groups, etc.). Gender mainstreaming is a process by which an MFI considers gender equality issues in all its activities, programmes and policies. So, rather than having the focus only on women, the relative conditions of men and women in access to financial services and improving their entrepreneurial activities, are examined in order to highlight differences. Once such differences are identified, something can be done about these inequalities, or links to other organizations that can help redress inequalities.

Women made up 66 percent of MF clients funded by the US Agency for International Development (USAID) in 2004. USAID targets women at a higher rate than men because of the empirical evidence that "cash surpluses controlled by women are more likely to be invested in the well-being of children and the household than are surpluses controlled by men", as well as the "higher rates of social and economic exclusion" that women experience. The Microcredit Summit Campaign (MSC) estimated that the number of very poor women with access to microloans reached 55.6 million in 2004 (www.microcreditsummit.org). This represented 83.5 percent of the poorest clients and not the total clients. The MSC recognizes that it has failed to report on total women clients to date, and expects to remedy that soon. In many MFIs, women have become preferred clients because increase in their income benefits their families through improved nutrition, health, education and well-being, and that they have higher repayment rates, and they work better in the group lending programmes that make reaching the poor efficient.

At many levels, the MF industry has embraced best practices in reaching women clients, but understanding of how best to provide services for women could be much deeper within many MFIs. As the industry grows, even basic knowledge about the nature of women's businesses and the best ways to provide financial services to support them is sometimes ignored or lost in the face of new contexts and new pressures. It is important to emphasize here that neither women nor men (nor poorer women and men) are a homogeneous group, and should not be treated as such in MF programmes. Women that are 'targeted' for MF can be widowed, single, newly married, pregnant, young girls, those living with HIV/AIDS, unemployed, employed, rural, urban, etc. Likewise, men can be categorised by their marital status, age, income level, ethnicity, health status and so on. The different categories of women (and men) often have different needs for financial services. For example, savings are very important for both low-income women and men. Savings can provide a safety net for single mothers or women who face an uncertain future. On the other hand, in many parts of Asia, whilst women are often considered better at saving, rather than focus only on women, it would be better to encourage men in savings groups for more harmonious household financial management.

The expansion of MF since 1990s has significantly increased women's access to facilities for small loans and savings. This increased access to MF has been seen as contributing not only to poverty reduction and financial sustainability, but also to a series of 'virtuous spirals' of economic empowerment, increased well-being and social and political empowerment for women themselves, thereby addressing goals of gender equality and empowerment. Some of the dimensions of and interlinkages among the various virtuous impact spirals identified in the literature are shown in Figure 1. First, increasing women's access to MF services can lead to their economic empowerment (the linkages in the centre of the figure). Women's roles in household financial management may improve, in some cases enabling them to access significant amounts of money in their own right for the first time. This might enable women to start their own economic activities, invest more in existing activities, acquire assets or raise their status in household economic activities through their visible capital contribution. Increased participation in economic activities may raise women's incomes or their control of their own and household income.

The Microfinance Institutions (Development and Regulation) Draft Bill 2011, represents a step forward in the Government of India's engagement with the MF Sector. It defines MF services broadly as financial services in small amounts including microcredit, collection of thrift, remittances, pensions, insurance and so on—and brings all organizations—except cooperatives only accepting deposits from their members, under the purview of one regulator—the Reserve Bank of India (RBI). It was felt that regulations of the Bill should take into account the concerns of the poor while promoting the MF sector. There are also ongoing discussions on how to bridge the two kinds of gaps in the sector—development gap (financial exclusion of large sections of the population)—and regulation gap.

In the last two decades, many developing countries have witnessed a rapid growth of MF activities. The trends on the investment side have included increasing attention from socially responsible and capital market investors. From an institutional set-up, commercial banks are downscaling, MFIs are moving up market and convergence is happening between the so-called finance for growth and finance for all. Recognizing that MF is more and more integrated in the mainstream financial system brings calls for regulation to set up the rules of the game in this industry. The general tendency towards regulation is even reinforced by MFI's own self-interest. Since regulation remains a precondition for deposit mobilization in many countries, more MFIs seek to transform into regulated entities to access cheap and local currency deposits. Regulation opens also the door to a variety of funding opportunities and helps to reduce the overreliance on subsidies. Donors and MF practitioners are well aware that micro-lenders need to prepare for the day when subsidies disappear as donors choose to move on. Understanding how regulation affects performance matters. On one hand, costs of designing and enforcing regulatory policies to address the specific challenges of MF are substantial. On the other hand, complying with supervisory requirements is costly. An MFI acquires permission to lend through registration. Each legal structure, such as the one for MF institution, has different and unique formation requirements and privileges.

Although the regulation of MFI Sector has been of recent origin, the regulation per se of banking sector is established, well documented and evaluated over the years. The following are accepted as attended advantages and benefits of regulation and supervision of banks/MFIs: (i) Protect the interest of the depositors; (ii) Put in place prudential norms, standards and practices; (iii) Provide sufficient information about the true risks faced by the banks/MFIs; (iv) Promote systemic stability and thereby sustains public confidence in the banks/MFIs; (v) Prevent a bank's/MFI's failure/potential dangers through timely interventions; (vi) Penalise the violations, misconducts, non-compliance to the norms of behaviour; (vii) Provide invaluable advisory inputs for problem-solving and overall improvement of the banks/MFIs; (viii) Promote safe, strong and sound banking/MF system and effective banking/MF policy; and, (ix) Promote and enhance orderly economic growth and development.

The insufficient provision of financial services to micro and small enterprises has been identified as a common problem in many parts of the world, including countries whose financial systems are well developed. Traditionally, micro-enterprises have relied on informal mechanisms, such as moneylenders and rotating savings and cooperative associations (ROSCAs) in order to finance their operations. Due to high administrative cost, inadequate collateral, and lack of trained personnel, banks mostly decline to serve this sector. Over the last ten years, however, a large number of MFIs have emerged in order to deliver financial services to this sector. As MF has become increasingly popular among many developing countries, the international financial community has had an increased interest in the regulation and supervision of MFIs. Today, thousands of MFIs operate in countries around the world; however, the majority of these institutions are still not subject to government regulation. The theoretical discussion of the role and effects of the regulation of MFIs is at an early stage and there is limited empirical work on the subject. Furthermore, the theoretical and empirical literature does not address the question, whether the regulated MFIs will still be able to serve the same client base, or will they be forced to behavc like banks, i.e. lend to larger size enterprises by increasing the size of the loans that go beyond the absorptive capacity of micro-enterprises.

As MFIs expand their outreach and increase their assets, and as more MFIs become regulated entities that can capture savings deposits, clear articulation of the functions of their boards of directors is essential for effective governance. Governance is a process by which a board of directors, through management, guides an institution in fulfilling its corporate mission and protects the institution's assets. Fundamental to good governance is the ability of individual directors to work in partnership to balance strategic and operational responsibilities. Effective governance occurs when a board provides proper guidance to management regarding the strategic direction for the institution, and oversees management's efforts to move in this direction. The interplay between board and management centers on this relationship between strategy and operation, both of which are essential for the successful evolution of the institution. In exercising their governance responsibilities, board members must consider the perspectives of numerous external actors. Depending on the legal status of the MFI, these actors can include providers of capital such as donors, governments, depositors or other financial institutions; regulatory bodies like the superintendence of banks; and other stakeholders, including clients, employees, and shareholders. In its governance role, the board also is accountable to all these stakeholders and must assess continually which of these are the most important for the institution.

Governance is about achieving corporate goals. Governance of MFIs has only recently surfaced as an essential component of long-term institutional success. Its importance is highlighted by the juncture at which we find MF—a field poised to become part of national financial systems with links to international financial markets. At no other time has the competence and commitment of governance bodies of MFIs appeared more pressing. In the MF field, governance has assumed increasing importance for several reasons. First, as MFIs grow in their outreach, the size of their assets, as reflected in their portfolio, also grows considerably. Ensuring effective management of this growth requires added input and involvement by a board. Additionally, increasing numbers of MFIs are becoming regulated and assuming the responsibilities and challenges of a regulated entity. Capturing deposits from savers and investors is perhaps their most important challenge and requires the greatest oversight. Finally, MFIs are operating in increasingly competitive markets, and maintaining or increasing market share has become an important component of their strategic objective.

Good governance leads to a number of positive consequences, including trust, clear vision, mission, and direction, relevant values, connection to the stakeholders, and sustainable financial stability. The perception of Kofi Annan, former UN Secretary-General, and the United Nations about good governance may be stated as follows: "Good governance is perhaps the single most important factor in eradicating poverty and promoting development". The following are identified to be some of the contemporary and emerging issues relating to good governance aspects and organizational structure issues relating to microfinance industry: The dual mission: balancing social impact with financial objectives, ownership of MFIs, public ownership vis-à-vis government corporate structure, nonprofit NGO corporate structure, profit-oriented corporate structure; credit union corporate structure, fiduciary responsibility of MFIs, risk assessment capacity in MFIs, board membership modality,

Government structure, legal procedures, and issues for future research, and issues of dealing with difficult situations.

MFI is thematically a financial institution specializing in banking services for low-income groups or individuals. It provides services to small-balance accounts that would not normally be accepted by traditional banks, and offers transaction services for amounts that may be smaller than the average transaction fees charged by mainstream financial institutions. The industry is in need of an objective set of criteria that acts as a proxy for the maturity of MFIs. Access to credit can play a pivotal role in economic growth. Banks and lending institutions provide the services that allow people to save and invest available assets and resources, which further support and strengthen to take up economic activity. Within underdeveloped communities, the role of MFIs provides the credit access and financial services needed to develop income-generating businesses along with self-employment opportunities. MFIs provide small-scale financial services to poor people who are otherwise "excluded from the formal banking sector" and standard financial systems. Operating merely in developing and emerging countries, they have specialized in offering loans of minor scale to enable individuals to start small productive businesses and enhance entrepreneurship. Especially in rural areas of developing countries, the development of financial systems is often poor; sometimes they have not fully emerged at all. In this case, MFIs often represent a first opportunity for the local population to participate in financial systems and to benefit from access to business and capital.

MFIs vary in size and function with some organizations focusing entirely on microfinancing, while others working as extensions of large investment banks. People living in underdeveloped areas such as Asia, Latin America, Kosovo and countries within the Sub-Saharan region can access financial resources through the services provided by MFIs. Within any society, financial services provide a means for people and businesses to obtain credit and manage available assets on a continuous basis. Access to financial services enables existing businesses to grow and in the process provides the starting capital for starter businesses. MFIs provide these services within communities that have limited resources and few avenues for economic development. People within these communities can use microloans to develop small businesses based on their existing knowledge base and skill sets. In all such cases, mobilization of diverse sources of finance for capitalizing the financial institutions—in one form or the other is vital, especially to support the sustainable growth of micro-enterprises.

MFIs can play a significant role in facilitating inclusion, as they are uniquely positioned in reaching out to the rural poor. Many of them operate in a limited geographical area, have a greater understanding of the issues specific to the rural poor, enjoy greater acceptability amongst the rural poor and have flexibility in operations providing a level of comfort to their clientele. There are several legal forms of MFIs. However, firm data regarding the number of MFIs operating under different forms is not available. It is roughly estimated that there are about 1,000 NGO-MFIs and more than 20 Company MFIs. Further, in Andhra Pradesh, nearly 30,000 cooperative organizations are engaged in MF activities. However, the Company MFIs are major players accounting for over 80% of the microfinance loan portfolio.

Most poor people manage to mobilize resources to develop their enterprises and their dwellings slowly over time. Financial services could enable the poor to leverage their initiative, accelerating the process of building incomes, assets and economic security. However, conventional finance institutions seldom lend down-market to serve the needs of low-income families and women-headed households. They are very often denied access to credit for any purpose, making the discussion of the level of interest rate and other terms of finance irrelevant. Therefore, the fundamental problem is not so much of unaffordable terms of loan as the lack of access to credit itself. This lack is attributable to practical difficulties arising from the discrepancy between the mode of operation followed by financial institutions and the economic characteristics and financing needs of low-income households. For example, commercial lending institutions require that borrowers have a stable source of income out of which principal and interest can be paid back according to the agreed terms. However, the income of many self-employed households is not stable, regardless of its size. A large number of small loans are needed to serve the poor, but lenders prefer dealing with large loans in small numbers to minimize administration costs. They also look for collateral with a clear title—which many low-income households do not have. In addition, bankers tend to consider low income households a bad risk imposing exceedingly high information monitoring costs on operation.

Over the last ten years, however, successful experiences in providing finance to small entrepreneurs and producers demonstrate that poor people, when given access to responsive and timely financial services at market rates, repay their loans and use the proceeds to increase their income and assets. This is not surprising since the only realistic alternative for them is to borrow from informal market at an interest much higher than market rates. Community banks, NGOs and grass-roots-savings and credit groups around the world have shown that these micro-enterprise loans can be profitable for borrowers and for the lenders, making MF one of the most effective poverty-reducing strategies. To the extent that microfinance institutions become financially viable, self-sustaining, and integral to the communities in which they operate, they have the potential to attract more resources and expand services to clients. Despite the success of microfinance institutions, only about 2 percent of world's roughly 500 million small entrepreneurs are estimated to have access to financial services.

Although there is demand for credit by poor and women at market interest rates, the volume of financial transaction of MFIs must reach a certain level before their financial operation becomes self-sustaining. In other words, although microfinance offers a promising institutional structure to provide access to credit to the poor, the scale problem needs to be resolved so that it can reach the vast majority of potential customers who demand access to credit at market rates. To be successful, financial intermediaries that provide services and generate domestic resources must have the capacity to meet high performance standards. They must achieve excellent repayments and provide access to clients. And they must build towards operating and financial self-sufficiency and expanding client reach. In order to do so, microfinance institutions need to find ways to cut down on their administrative costs and also to broaden their resource base. Cost reductions can be achieved through simplified and decentralized loan application, approval and collection processes, for instance, through group loans which give borrowers responsibilities for much of the loan application process, allow the loan officers to handle many more clients and hence reduce costs.

MFIs can broaden their resource base by mobilizing savings, accessing capital markets, loan funds and effective institutional development support. A logical way to tap capital market is securitization through a corporation that purchases loans made by microenterprise institutions with the funds raised through the bonds issuance on the capital market. Savings facilities make large-scale lending operations possible. On the other hand, studies also show that the poor operating in the informal sector do save, although not in financial assets, and hence value access to client-friendly savings service at least as much access to credit. Savings mobilization also makes financial institutions accountable to local shareholders. Therefore, adequate savings facilities both serve the demand for financial services by the customers and fulfil an important requirement of financial sustainability to the lenders. MFIs can either provide savings services directly through deposit taking or make arrangements with other financial institutions to provide savings facilities to tap small savings in a flexible manner.

One way of expanding the successful operation of MFIs in the informal sector is through strengthened linkages with their formal sector counterparts. A mutually beneficial partnership should be based on comparative strengths of each sector. Informal sector microfinance institutions have comparative advantage in terms of small transaction costs achieved through adaptability and flexibility of operations. They are better equipped to deal with credit assessment of the urban poor and hence to absorb the transaction costs associated with loan processing. On the other hand, formal sector institutions have access to broader resource-base and high leverage through deposit mobilization. Therefore, formal sector finance institutions could form a joint venture with informal sector institutions in which the former provide funds in the form of equity and the later extends savings and loan facilities to the urban poor. Another form of partnership can involve the formal sector institutions refinancing loans made by the informal sector lenders. Under these settings, the informal sector institutions are able to tap additional resources as well as having an incentive to exercise greater financial discipline in their management. MFIs could also serve as intermediaries between borrowers and the formal financial sector and on the lent funds backed by a public sector guarantee. Business-like NGOs can offer commercial banks ways of funding micro-entrepreneurs at low cost and risk, for example, through leveraged bank-NGO-client credit lines. Under this arrangement, banks make one bulk loan to NGOs and the NGOs package it into large number of small loans at market rates and recover.

MF has been spread around the world as a popular poverty reduction strategy. In 1997, the Microcredit Summit Campaign was launched with the goal of servicing 100 million of the world's poorest households. This is in line with the Millennium Development Goals, agreed to at the United Nations Millennium Summit, which set a challenging goal of halving the absolute poverty in the world by 2015. MF has a high potential to contribute to these MDGs. As of December 2000, about 1600 MFIs reported to the Microcredit Summit that more than 19 million of the poorest households around the world have access to financial services. However, this leaves 81 million of the world's poorest people to be reached before the Campaign target of 100 million is achieved. If only 10 percent of the 1580 MFIs that reported to the Microcredit Summit could be scaled up to serve an average of 500,000 very poor households each, then the shortfall of 81 million could be overcome. However, without capital to cover its operations, to finance its lending operations, and to leverage financial resources from commercial institutions, it is unlikely that MFIs would be able to achieve this objective. Many pioneering MFIs all over the world have proved that they can deliver financial services to individuals and businesses that otherwise would not have access to financial services. However, for many of these MFIs, the dependence on donor funds increasingly constitutes an obstacle to growth, and thus they are now turning to other, commercial sources of funds.

Broadly, the various mechanisms to mobilize financial resources to capitalize the MFIs, among others, may include donor and government grants and soft loans, savings, raising private sector capital, non-bank, non-profit NGO MFIs, membership-based CFIs, postal savings banks, development finance institutions, specialized banking institutions, and commercial banks.

In India, there is a wide variety of institutions in public as well as private sector which provide MF to the poor. These institutions can be broadly divided into two types. First type is the traditional formal financial institutions, while the second type is MFIs. The traditional financial institutions comprise commercial banks, regional rural banks and co-operative banks. They provide MF services in addition to their general banking activities and are referred to as MF service providers. On the other hand, MFIs are different type of financial institutions whose main financial activity is providing MF only. Many of these institutions are NGOs, Mutually Aided Co-operative Societies (MACS) and Non-Banking Financial Companies (NBFCs). In case of traditional financial institutions both private and public ownership are found but the MFIs are mainly in the private sector. These financial institutions use a hierarchical network starting from the apex wholesale level to the retail level financial institutes. The retail level banks and MFIs borrow funds from apex financial institutions and use their branch network to provide MF at the doorstep of poor people. There is, however, a great scope of improvement of the present system by reforming the existing management information systems (MIS), and going in for aggressive web marketing.

Thus, MF is a highly researched area of development finance; and yet the success stories and several challenges confronted by the implementing agencies as well as the beneficiaries/stakeholders are not properly documented. This has been the compulsion and motivation behind writing this book.

Bearing in mind the historic backdrop, evolutionary development as well as recent advancement in the knowledge creation, impact generation, innovations in MF development programme initiative and the roles played by various MF institutions at local, country, regional and global level, it was thought appropriate to make a comprehensive treatise on the subject in the form of a book entitled, *Microfinance*. The thematic concepts and the content of the book have a universal appeal for all forms of industries, including the banking, and non-banking financial institutions, and medium, small and micro-enterprises.

The book will prove immensely useful and interesting to the readers and practitioners, especially the bankers, NBFIs, financial service industries, insurance industries, corporate leaders, business planners and analysts, financial investors, social scientists, social workers and activists, policymakers, research scholars, lawyers and dedicated workers in the field of eco-industries, lead NGOs and international business communities at large.

**A.N. Sarkar**

# 1

# Microfinance: The Concept, Achievements and Emerging Implementation and Institutional Issues

Microfinance is widely acknowledged to be a sound and well-tested institutional mechanism to extend financial services to low-income clients, including consumers and the self-employed, who traditionally lack access to banking and related services. More broadly, it is a movement whose object is a world in which as many poor and near-poor households as possible have permanent accesses to an appropriate range of high quality financial services, including not just credit but also savings, insurance, and fund transfers. Those who promote microfinance generally believe that such access will help poor people out of poverty. Micro-credit emphasizes the provision of credit services to low-income clients, usually in the form of small loans for supporting develop micro-enterprise and income generating activities. Use of the term 'micro-credit' is often associated with an inadequate amount of the value of savings for the poor. In most cases, the provision of savings services in 'micro-credit' schemes simply involves the collection of compulsory deposit amounts that are designed only to collateralize those loans. Additional voluntary savings may collect but the clients have restricted access to their enforced savings. These savings become the main source of capital in the financial institutions; called microfinance institutions.

Microfinance is one of the products of new developmental thinking and policy-making. It is a unique amalgamation of industrial (including financial) and institutional reforms in the present scenario of development economics. For the developing countries like India it has come as a breakthrough in the philosophy and practices of poverty eradication, economic empowerment and inclusive growth. Yet given the enormity of economic compulsions and complexities in these countries, microfinance is an unfinished agenda. The main objective of this chapter, therefore, is to shift the focus from mere financial access to poverty eradication and people's empowerment, sifting the 'performance' of Microfinance Institutions (MFIs) from their 'popularity' (The Microfinance Gateway, 'What is Microfinance?': available at http://www.microfinancegateway.org/section/faq). Microfinance, by implication, therefore, is considered to be a potent tool for socio-economic development and can be clearly distinguished from charity. Families who are destitute, or so poor they are unlikely to be able to generate the cash-flow required to repay a loan, should be recipients of charity. Others are best served by financial institutions. Modern microfinance was born as a response to the frustrated development resulting from subsidised rural credit in the 1950s and 1960s (Adams and Fitchett, 1992; Adams and Mehran, 2003). Thus, learning from history is inherent in its philosophy and not necessarily philanthropy. However, the importance of learning from banking history is generally unexplored in the microfinance literature, though some exceptions do exist.

The benefits of microfinance are that it helps to manage the assets of the poor and generates income. Through microfinance institutions such as credit unions, financial non-governmental organizations and even commercial banks poor people can obtain small loans and safeguard their savings. The limitations of microfinance are that through this savings plan participants are losing money by having to pay a fee. The user can also pay back their loans whenever they chose therefore encouraging a borrower to have various outstanding loans. The lender is also vulnerable in that there is no guarantee of the loan being repaid in the given arranged time frame, and the consequences to defaulting are not defined. When looking at a microfinance initiative, there are three main benefits and limitations for the model. These are based on a basic microfinance initiative, though they can be applied to many variations. When looking at the three benefits and limitations, they revolve around three key ideas—poverty, mistrust, and promoting change.

A microfinance initiative wishes to address these issues in a positive way. For example, microfinance can be an alternative programme to address poverty reduction where the tools needed to raise an individual or a family out of poverty is given to them directly. In a microfinance project these tools include money primarily, and may also be accompanied with a savings programme, and financial help. Along with poverty reduction, a microfinance initiative can aim to avoid a general sense of mistrust between the citizens and their national banks. The money in this case, is not coming from a bank, but rather within the community which allows those participating to foster social capital and community cohesion. Last but not least, a microfinance initiative can promote larger poverty reduction movements by increasing the financial knowledge of the average citizen. The other benefits of microfinance projects are that it allows low-income families to save their money; most of the poor live day to day with the little money that they earn and cannot afford to save. Poor people need such alternatives in order to turn their savings in to large lump sums or receive large sums and pay monthly with low interest rates. Banks and other moneylending institutions have high interest rates and simply won't extend loans to poor people with little or no assets or employment. Microfinance helps the poor people get access or save funds over a period of time with low interest rates. Also, the poor could solve their own issues by working together as a community and this creates trust and social capital in their communities. It also leads to stability and growth in their households, as well as their communities.

There are seemingly two ways in which the needs of the poor are not being met by microfinance in several instances. Firstly, the poor need to store savings for the long run; such as for their retirement, widowhood or their heirs but the examples such as saving up, down and through do not directly meet these needs. Secondly, the poor's ability to save fluctuates with time and so they may not be able to save the fixed rate of saving. These two shortcomings are difficult for the poor and they often get excluded or exclude themselves (Rutherford, 2009). Poor people have to take a risk to turn their savings in to large lump sum of money because there is no perfect system that would protect their deposits. Linked to this, these are a large number of implementation and institutional issues that would need to be addressed for a comprehensive understanding on microfinance, largely for the benefit of the financial institutions and other cooperative/collaborative agencies/functionaries that are either directly or indirectly involved in the planning, execution, management and regulation of microfinance as an industry.

This chapter is accordingly dedicated to discuss some of the key and emerging issues concerning the future growth perspectives of MFIs with focus on the modalities of mobilizing the financial resources to capitalize the MFIs in a self-sustaining manner. The aspects covered in the paper, *inter alia*, include: Modality for broad-basing the financial resources for MFIs, demand for microfinance services, supply of microfinance services and competition for MFIs, raising capital for microfinance using diversified sources of funding, innovative microfinancing mechanisms, international initiatives, financial performance of MFIs in India, institutional providers of rural finance and microfinance services, government's role in rural finance, microfinance to support SME finance programmes or agencies etc. The future challenges of execution of microfinance programmes in the special context of India are also elaborated to have an insight into the pathways to evolve new implementation strategies and guidelines for the future.

## 1. Microfinance: The Concept and the Process

Before we understand the concept of microfinance, it would be worthwhile to understand the term micro-credit as the two terms are closely related to each other. Poor people need micro-credit for various and different purposes. It may be to meet the major household expenses; emergency needs or even basic livelihood support. There are two main systems of micro-credit (Chauhan, 1990). One is formal financial institutions, banks and co-operatives, which provide micro-credit to the poor people under different schemes for livelihood support or helping them to start micro-enterprises. The other is informal system comprising traditional moneylenders, pawnbrokers and trade specific lenders. Both the systems have their own positive and negative aspects.

The positive aspects of formal financial system are that under this system, micro-credit is available at low rate of interest with easy and periodical repayments and moratorium period. The most important aspect of this type of credit is that it is available for income generating activities. But at the same time micro-credit from formal financial system is not easily available. The system requires collateral or security. It has complex legal and operational procedures, involving lot of paper work. Since the process of credit disbursement is time consuming, many times credit is not available in time. Finally, there is a stigma attached to the poor people so that the bankers do not think them credit-worthy and feel that the recovery rate is unsatisfactory. But this may not necessarily be true. The other positive aspects of informal system of micro-credit are that the credit disbursement is easy and relatively quick. No collateral is required and there is least paper work. Credit can be given for any activity, especially for consumption and emergency purposes. Credit is generally given for non-productive purposes as well. But at the same time there is very high interest rate in informal micro-credit system. Exploitation is also attached with this system. Moneylender takes repayment at one time only.

Based on these two systems of micro-credit, we can define micro-credit as the "provision wherein debtor takes money either from formal or informal sources of credit on unilaterally decided terms by the creditor". If we combine together positive aspects of both the systems like, low rate of interest, easy and periodical repayments with moratorium period, credit for income generating activities, easy process of disbursement, no collateral or security and less paper work, etc., we come closer to understanding the concept of microfinance. The 'Task Force on Supportive Policy and Regulatory Framework for Micro-Finance' constituted by NABARD (National Bank for Agriculture & Rural Development) defines "microfinance as the provision of thrift, saving, credit and financial services and products of very small amounts to the poor in rural, semi-urban and urban areas for enabling them to raise their income levels and improve their standard of living" (NABARD, 1999a). The emphasis of support under microfinance is on the poor in 'pre-micro-enterprise' stage for building up their capabilities to handle larger resources. This perception is quite significant, keeping in view the limitations of any approach of micro-enterprise development to help the poorest of the poor for self-employment (Awasthi, 1994 & 1996). The Task Force has not specified limit for the 'small' amount of financial services envisaged. Services of microfinance are being provided by various MFIs. In India, the Task Force mentioned above, has classified these MFIs under three categories as mentioned below:

*Not-for-Profit MFIs*: These include Societies registered under Societies Registration Act 1860 or similar State Acts, Public Trusts registered under the Indian Trust Act 1882 and Non-Profit Companies registered under Section 25 of the Companies Act 1956.

*Mutual Benefit MFIs*: Such as State Credit Co-operatives, National Credit Co-operatives and Mutually Aided Co-operative Societies (MACS).

*For-Profit MFIs*: Bodies like Non-Banking Financial Companies (NBFCs) registered under the Companies Act 1956 and Banks which provide microfinance along with their other usual banking services could be termed as microfinance service providers of this type.

The Task Force terms microfinance as the provision of thrift, credit and other financial services and products of very small amounts to the poor in rural, semi-urban or urban areas for enabling them to raise their income levels and improve living standards. The Task Force emphasizes that microfinance will cover not only consumption and production loans, but also loans for other credit needs such as housing and shelter.

Microfinance is a provision of a broad range of financial services such as savings, credit, insurance and payment services to the poor or low-income group who are excluded from the normal banking sectors (Ledgerwood, 1999). Microfinance is a development approach that provides financial as well as social intermediation. The financial intermediation includes the provision of savings, credit and insurance services, while social intermediation involves organising citizens' groups to voice their aspirations and raise concerns for consideration by policy-makers and develop their self-confidence (Robinson, 2002).

However, Conroy (2002) stated that microfinance is the provision of a broad range of financial services such as deposits, loans, payment services, money transfers, and insurance to poor and low-income households and their micro-enterprises. The term evolved from the concepts of "micro-credit" and "micro-enterprise" financing, to include the importance of savings as well as borrowing. Although the terms are used interchangeably, microfinance represents the field as a whole, while the other two terms are more technical and refer only to credit provision (Maria, 2004). The World Bank defines microfinance as ".... Small-scale financial services—primarily credit and savings—provided to people who farm or fish and who operate small enterprises or micro-enterprises where goods are produced, recycled, repaired, or sold; who provide services; who work for wages or commissions; who gain income from renting out small amounts of land, vehicles, draft animals, or machinery and tools; and to other individuals and groups at the local levels of developing countries, both rural and urban" (Robinson, 2001).

Microfinance activities usually involve giving small loans to customers for working capital, group guarantees, compulsory savings, insurance and access to repeat loans for a larger amount based on repayment performance. Microfinance is one of the important components required to get sustainable micro-enterprise besides technical support, training, technology, input supplies and market access. Many clients around the world benefited from these services. A survey conducted by the Micro-credit Summit Campaign (Sam-Daley-Harris, 2009) reported that about 3,552 MFIs provide financial services to more than 154 million clients around the world and more than 106 million of them were the poorest borrowers (Daley-Harris,

2009). This achievement is the fulfilment of a goal set a decade ago (Table 1).

**Table 1:** Progress of Microfinance from 1997 to 2007

| Year | Number of Institutions | Total Number of Client Reached (millions) | Number of Poorest Client Reported (millions) |
|---|---|---|---|
| 1997 | 618 | 13.5 | 7.6 |
| 1998 | 925 | 20.9 | 12.2 |
| 1999 | 1,065 | 23.6 | 13.8 |
| 2000 | 1,567 | 30.7 | 19.3 |
| 2001 | 2,186 | 54.9 | 26.8 |
| 2002 | 2,572 | 67.6 | 41.6 |
| 2003 | 2,931 | 80.9 | 54.8 |
| 2004 | 3,164 | 92.3 | 66.6 |
| 2005 | 3,133 | 113.3 | 81.9 |
| 2006 | 3,316 | 133.0 | 92.9 |
| 2007 | 3,552 | 154.8 | 106.6 |

*Source:* Sam-Daley-Harris, 2009.

Table 1 shows the progress of microfinance from 1997 until 2007. The table shows that the number of microfinance institutions was increased about 83 percent from only 618 institutions in 1997 to 3,552 institutions in 2007. Meanwhile, the Consultative Group to Assist the Poor (CGAP) estimated that MFIs in Asia have about 41 million loan accounts and 98 million deposit accounts.

Microfinance has been hailed as one of the most effective tools for combating poverty through loans, grants, insurance and other financial products offered to the poorest of the global poor around the world. As an international development strategy, it represents a major shift from governmental "top-down" to private "bottom-up" approaches and has revolutionized the approach to poverty alleviation and economic development. It also continues to be a model of social entrepreneurship, bringing creative business and financial strategies and tools to complex social and economic problems, as well as a wedge for empowerment of women and other disadvantaged citizens in some societies. To expand finance and sustain microfinance, however, microfinance institutions are becoming sophisticated financial institutions that structure, distribute and then finance a growing array of financial products and services to the global poor, which require increasingly sophisticated financing strategies as the global capital markets and leading financial institutions become the funding sources for microfinance institutions. At the same time, microfinance institutions are confronting fundamental changes in their operating environment and therefore their basic financial and business models. Certain microfinance institutions now confront shifting missions from non-profit idealistic non-governmental organizations to profit-seeking, growth and distribution focused financial firms; increasing regulation of the microfinance institutions as banks, insurers or regulated financial entities; financial asset and product risk as the amount and complexity of the financial products grows; and the rapidly expanding opportunities and disintermediation challenges of internet/mobile telephony finance as an extension or replacement of microfinance institutions in accessing and serving the global poor.

The Asian Development Bank (2000) defines microfinance as the provision of broad range of services such as savings, deposits, loans, payment services, money transfers and insurance to poor and low income households and their micro-enterprises. This definition of microfinance is not restricted to the below poverty line people but it includes low income households also. The Micro-Financial Sector (Development and Regulation) Bill, 2011 defines microfinance as the provision of financial assistance and insurance services to an individual or an eligible client either directly or through a group mechanism for an amount, not exceeding rupees fifty thousand in aggregate per individual for small and tiny enterprise, agriculture, allied activities (including for consumption purposes of such individual); or an amount not exceeding rupees one lakh fifty thousand in aggregate per individual for housing or other prescribed purposes. The eligible clients which may get financial assistance under this scheme may be landless labourers and migrant labourers; artisans and micro-entrepreneurs; disadvantaged cultivators of agricultural land including oral lessees, tenants, and sharecroppers; and farmers owning not more than two hectares of agricultural land.

Microfinance may be defined as "provision of thrift, the wide network of the organized banking system deep credit and other financial services and products of very into rural areas. Market and the government both failed to small amounts to the poor in rural, semi-urban or urban provide credit access to the poor. In fact the failure of areas, for enabling them to raise their income levels and institutional initiatives of rural credit and to the improve living standards." At present, a large part of weaknesses of the exploitative informal system of credit microfinance activity is confined to credit only. Women gave birth to Microfinance institutions. No doubt, constitute a vast majority of users of micro-credit and microfinance has been successful in providing credit savings services with access to the poor. But in recent times the role of microfinance has become controversial.

Microfinance in its modern form is a relatively new industry, not just in India, but worldwide. Globally, needy individuals have traditionally lacked access to the financial services provided by banks, regardless of the sum of money involved. One of the primary reasons for this is the significant transaction costs associated with servicing client accounts. Another major reason is that the poor lack assets that can be used as collateral to secure loans, providing banks with little recourse against defaulting borrowers. As a result of being denied access to credit services from formal banking and lending institutions, impoverished individuals' access to credit was limited to either traditional development programmes—which were criticized for failing to reach the world's neediest—or to moneylenders known for their predatory lending practices.

Modern microfinance developed as a solution to the poor's need for access to credit. The industry materialized in the 1970's in response to the "widespread perception that traditional development programmes, funded by international agencies such as the World Bank largely failed to reach the worlds poorest or to improve their life chances". Furthermore, research shows that not only were these programmes failing to reach their intended recipients, they actually undermined the developmental goals they were intended to carry out. Microfinance was established to provide a mechanism for putting money "directly into the hands of the poor" in a manner that would immediately impact their economic prospects. Given its goal of providing credit solutions to an under-served population, microfinance clearly started with an altruistic slant. In its initial phases, microfinance involved a standard procedure. Money would be lent to the needy; the principal amount would then be collected, with interest, and the proceeds from the collected payment would be contributed to a pool of capital that would be re-lent to other borrowers. It was intended that borrowers would use the loaned money to fund small entrepreneurial enterprises, which would hopefully provide them with an ongoing source of income. A micro-lender may, for example, loan a borrower enough money to cover the cost of a goat. Upon purchasing the goat, the borrower would be able to produce and sell the goat's milk. The profits from these sales would allow the borrower to maintain a constant income stream. Thus, rather than providing the borrower with temporary relief from financial distress, the microloan was intended to provide the borrower with an enduring source of financial support.

In the initial phases of microfinance, government agencies were the primary providers of productive credit to the needy. These lending programmes, heavily subsidized by international donors, were criticized due to their large loan losses and the lending organizations' frequent need to recapitalize, or put new money into their business, in order to continue operations. This led to microfinance in its modern form, rooted primarily in the private sector, as a market-based solution that quickly became viewed as an integral part of the financial system. Traditionally, microfinance programmes possessed two features that drove their success. First, impoverished people, particularly women, had excellent repayment rates that were often better than the formal financial sectors of most developing countries. Second, the poor were willing and able to pay interest rates that allowed [micro lenders] to cover their costs.

Thus, micro-lenders were able to function sustainably while reaching a large number of clients. Throughout the 1990s and into the 2000s, microfinance was viewed as a tool of socio-economic development, and was operated overwhelmingly as a non-profit enterprise, concentrated in developing countries throughout South Asia, Africa, and Latin America. Efforts to establish and implement microfinance were lauded worldwide. One of the most exalted figures in microfinance is Muhammad Yunus, the founder of the Grameen Bank of Bangladesh and one of the industry's pioneers. The Grameen Bank arose out of a study conducted by Yunus, then a professor at the Chittagong University in Bangladesh, in which he interviewed impoverished residents of villages surrounding the University in order to better understand their experiences with poverty. He concluded that the reason people were poor was that they lacked access to credit at reasonable interest rates and under appropriate conditions. Yunus attempted, unsuccessfully, to convince traditional banks to lend small amounts of money to the needy. The inability of traditional banks to provide adequate financing led him to conclude that "specialized financial institutions" were needed to provide these loans. Such institutions would need to be willing to provide loans to the impoverished individuals on terms and conditions that were appropriate for them. Yunus established the Grameen Bank using a model that was quite distinct from the traditional banking model. Strict qualification criteria were established to ensure a focus on the needy. In order to provide incentives for repayment; the bank implemented an innovative lending scheme in which borrowers were required to form groups of five and accept joint responsibility for repayment of loans. The ability to access future credit was conditioned upon repayment of each group member's loan (Yunus, 1989).

Another unique feature of the Grameen Bank's model was that small loans were repaid in weekly installments over the period of one year. Furthermore, rather than require borrowers to travel to the bank for service, Grameen Bank workers traveled to the borrowers' homes to provide service. This innovative framework distinguished the Grameen Bank from its peers in its ability to address the specific needs of the poor. Under this model, the Bank began in 1976 as a research project that served one local village and soon spread to neighbouring villages. In 1983, the government of Bangladesh recognized the Grameen Bank as an independent bank. The bank grew rapidly, expanding both in loan coverage and volume. In 2006, the organization and its founder were jointly awarded the Nobel Peace Prize, placing the microfinance industry in the international spotlight. Today, the Bank boasts that it is owned by the poor whom it serves with borrowers owning 90 percent of its shares and the Bengali Government owning the remaining 10 percent. While the Grameen Bank appears to have preserved its philanthropic roots by maintaining a structure that functions primarily to serve the needy, not every microfinance institution (MFI) can say the same. Over time, the industry's rapid growth has coincided with a shift from operations being funded primarily by the state or charitable donations to being largely dominated by the private sector. With this has come a shift from nonprofit to for-profit business models. While this transformation has occurred worldwide, it is especially salient in India.

## 2. Evolution of Microfinance

The concept of providing financial services to low income people is very old. Many informal credit groups have been operating in many countries for several years like the susus in Nigeria and Ghana, chit funds and Rotating Savings and Credit Associations (ROSCAs) in India, tontines in West Africa, pasanaku in Bolivia, hui in China, arisan in Indonesia, paluwagan in Philippines, etc. It is believed that initially, the informal financial institutions emerged in Nigeria dating back in the fifteenth century. Such type of institutions started establishing in Europe during the eighteenth century when in 1720 the first loan fund targeting poor people was founded in Ireland (Seibel, 2005). In 1847, some credit co-operatives were created in Germany which served 1.4 million people by 1910. In 1880s the British controlled government of Madras in South India tried to use the German experiment to address poverty in India. This effort resulted in membership of more than nine million poor to credit co-operatives by 1946. During the same time the Dutch colonial administrators constructed a co-operative rural banking system in Indonesia which eventually became Bank Rakyat Indonesia (BRI), now one of the largest Microfinance Institutions (MFIs) of the world (Schwiecker, 2004). In the 1970s, a paradigm shift started to take place. The failure of subsidized government or donor driven institutions to meet the demand for financial services in developing countries led to several new approaches. Bank Dagan Bali (BDB), established in Indonesia in 1970, was the earliest bank to institute commercial microfinance (Schwiecker, 2004). In 1973, ACCION International, a USA based NGO, disbursed its first loan in Brazil at commercial interest rate to start a micro-enterprise. One year later in 1974, the Self-Employed Women's Association of India (SEWA) started a bank to provide loans to poor women.

In 1976, Muhammad Yunus, a professor of Economics at Chittagong University, Bangladesh initiated an experimental research project of providing credit to the rural poor. He gave a small loan of 856 Taka ($27) from his pocket to 42 poor bamboo weavers and found that small loans radically changed the lives of these people and they were able to payback the loans with interest. The success of this idea led Yunus to establish Grameen Bank in 1983 in Bangladesh. This programme showed astonishing growth rates in Bangladesh, particularly during the 1980s and 1990s. It encouraged social innovators and organizations all over the world to begin experiments with different microfinance delivery methods to bring financial services to the poor. It is now adopted worldwide in the countries of different continents. Many international NGOs, such as Foundation for International Community Assistance (FINCA), Americans for Community Cooperation in Other Nations (ACCION), Freedom from Hunger, Opportunity International, Co-operative for Assistance and Relief Everywhere (CARE), Consultative Group for Assisting the Poor (CGAP), etc. are promoting microfinance programme for creating new businesses and combating poverty in a sustainable way. Over the past few decades, microfinance has been experimented in many developing countries. Bank Rakyat Indonesia (BRI) in Indonesia, Bancosol in Bolivia, Bank for Agriculture and Agricultural Co-operatives (BAAC) in Thailand, Grameen Bank, and Bangladesh Rural Advancement Committee (BRAC) of Bangladesh, NABARD in India, Amannah Ikhtiar Malaysia (AIM) of Malaysia, Agriculture Development Bank of Nepal (ADBN), K-Rep in Kenya and Mibanco in Peru have yielded encouraging results in alleviating poverty and empowering the poor through microfinance.

Many international NGOs, such as Foundation for International Community Assistance (FINCA), Americans for Community Cooperation in Other Nations (ACCION), Freedom from Hunger, Opportunity International, Co-operative for Assistance and Relief Everywhere (CARE), Consultative Group for Assisting the Poor (CGAP), etc. are promoting microfinance programme for creating new businesses and combating poverty in a sustainable way. Over the past few decades, microfinance has been experimented in many developing countries. Bank Rakyat Indonesia (BRI) in Indonesia, Bancosol in Bolivia, Bank for Agriculture and Agricultural Co-operatives (BAAC) in Thailand, Grameen Bank, and Bangladesh Rural Advancement Committee (BRAC) of Bangladesh, NABARD in India, Amannah Ikhtiar Malaysia (AIM) of Malaysia, Agriculture Development Bank of Nepal (ADBN), K-Rep in Kenya and Mibanco in Peru have yielded encouraging results in alleviating poverty and empowering the poor through microfinance.

In India, the history of microfinance dates back to establishment of Syndicate Bank in 1921 in private sector. During the early years, Syndicate Bank concentrated on raising micro-deposits in the form of daily/weekly basis and sanctioned micro-loans to its clients for shorter period of time. But microfinance came to limelight only when Dr Yunus gave it a mass movement in Grameen Bank experiment. Microfinance can be called a novel approach to provide saving and investment facility to the poor around world. Improved access and efficient provision of savings, credit, and insurance facilities in particular can enable the poor to gradually increase their consumption, manage their risks better, gradually build their asset base, develop their business, enhance their income earning capacity, and enjoy an improved quality of life. In India, microfinance mainly operates through Self-Help Group (SHGs), Non-Government Organizations (NGOs), and Credit Agencies. It provides poor people with the means to find their own way out of poverty. It put the power squarely in their hands, giving them a larger stake in their own success than one—time donation of food, goods, or cash.

The microfinance initiative in private sector in India can however be traced to the initiative undertaken by Shri Mahila SEWA (Self-Employed Women's Association) Sahakari Bank set up in 1974 by registering as an Urban Cooperative Bank at Ahmedabad City of Gujarat State. The main aim of SEWA bank was to provide banking services to the poor women employed in the unorganized sector. In the midst of the apparent inadequacies of the formal financial system to cater to the financial needs of the rural poor, National Bank for Agriculture and Rural Development (NABARD) sponsored an action research project related to formation of credit groups in 1987 through an NGO called MYRADA at Karnataka state.

Encouraged by the results of field level experiments in group based approach for lending to the poor, NABARD launched a Pilot Project in 1991-92 in partnership with Non Governmental Organizations (NGOs) for promoting and grooming self-help groups (SHGs) of homogeneous members and making savings from existing banks and within the existing legal framework. Steady progress of the pilot project led to the mainstreaming of the SHG-Bank Linkage Programme (SBLP) in 1996 as a normal banking activity of the banks with widespread acceptance. The Reserve Bank of India (RBI) set the right policy environment by allowing savings bank accounts of informal groups to be opened by the formal banking system. Launched at a time when regulated interest rates were in vogue, the banks were expected to lend to SHGs at the prescribed rates, but the RBI advised the banks not to interfere with the management of affairs of SHGs, particularly on the terms and conditions on which the SHGs disbursed loans to their members. This has laid the foundation stone of self-governance of the SHGs. The SHGs grown to federation and culminated to NGO-MFIs but the issues of governance remained unresolved. With the emergence of specialized Microfinance Institutions (MFIs) as a provider of financial services to the poor rural and semi urban folks with their unique dual mission 'to serve the poor' and '*remain financially sustainable*', Non-Banking Finance Companies (NBFCs) took the lead as an integral part of their business enhancement programme and successfully increase their client outreach through this business model. Section 25 companies (under Indian Companies Act 1956) and the Mutually Aided Cooperative Societies (MACS) were the latest entrants to this programme and concentrating in the truly remote areas with very less or no presence of commercial banks.

The initiatives of the Government for poverty alleviation could not succeed to the desired level, may be due to the fact that they do not take cognizance of power of the poor to deal with their own problems. Government tries to help them by way of subsidies and other help but these initiatives hardly reduce their poverty levels and are not a long-term solution. This section of society if given with guidance, power of capital and productive assets can emerge as the successful entrepreneur. This can easily be achieved by empowering them with power of micro-credit. The poor do not have any worthy asset base. Hence they have to be provided with mortgage free loan (Akula, 2008). It has been proved beyond doubt from Grameen Bank experiment. The system of microfinance was introduced about 28 years back with an organization of Grameen Bank in Bangladesh by a famous economist Prof. Mohammed Yunus. He observed that most villagers were unable to obtain credit at reasonable rates. So he began to lend them money from his own pocket, allowing the villagers to buy materials for projects like weaving bamboo tools and making pots (*The New York Times*, 1997). Ten years later, Dr. Yunus had set up Grameen Bank as a project in one of the village in Bangladesh in 1976 to assist poor families by providing credit to them. Today microfinance has been widely spread all over the world as an effective tool to poverty eradication. It is found that microfinance has reached about 80 million households and about, 20000 microfinance Institution are operating in developing countries of Asia, Africa, Europe and Latin America.

As is the case in many other countries, microfinance in India was traditionally operated under a non-profit model. The origins of microfinance in India can be traced back to the early 1970s when the Self-Employed Women's Association of the State of Gujarat created an urban cooperative bank, with the objective of offering banking services to impoverished women employed in rural parts of the state. The industry evolved in the 1980s around self-help groups (SHGs), which are "informal bodies that would provide their clients with much-needed savings and credit services". India's microfinance sector grew rapidly, evolving into a multibillion dollar industry. Like other countries that have embraced the industry, the foundation of India's microfinance industry rests on the failure of state-owned financial institutions to extend credit to the poor as well as the disappointing performance of government programmes intended to alleviate poverty by providing those in need with resources for self-employment. The industry operates on the assumption that "the core of poverty lies in the realm of the 'economic' and credit (debt) is an effective tool that helps the poor tackle the problem of deprivation, improve their welfare and social acceptance and credibility". In India, "the industry has grown under two different systems of patronage". The first system, linked to the National Bank for Agriculture and Rural Development (NABARD), has the patronage of the state as well as formal banking institutions. A parallel system is funded exclusively through the private sector. Due to the government's lack of involvement; the latter system traditionally functioned outside of any formalized legal or regulatory framework.

Microfinance began in India in the 1990s as a way of alleviating poverty, by encouraging income generating activities by poor households. Since then, the outreach of microfinance institutions (MFIs) in India has crossed 30 million poor households as at the end of March 2010. This is very commendable. However, there are two issues need to be addressed—how to reduce interest rates and the net impact of micro-credit. In this regard we may cite the example of BASIX (headquartered in Hyderabad, Andhra Pradesh), which is working with over a million poor households. For the first five years since inception in 1996, BASIX took the approach of primarily delivering micro-credit to its customers. After five years of pursuing this approach, BASIX carried out an impact assessment the year 2001. The results of this were rather disappointing. Only 52 percent of the customers, who had received at least three rounds of micro-credit from BASIX, showed a significant increase in their income (compared to a control group), 25 percent reported no change in income levels and 23 percent reported decline in their income levels. BASIX then carried out a detailed study of those who had had no increase or even a decline in income and found that the reasons for this could be clubbed into three factors (Basix—2000: 'Equity for Equity'—Available at http://www.basixindia.com/micro_finance_in_inda.asp); namely (1) Un-managed risk in their lives and livelihoods; (2) Low productivity, in terms of poor yields and higher costs, and (3) Unfavourable terms in input and output market transactions.

It was observed from the BASIX study that there is a need for risk mitigation, yield enhancement, cost reduction, and bringing rural producers together for better bargaining at the market place. Hence in 2002, BASIX revised its strategy, to provide a comprehensive set of 23 livelihood promotion services to rural poor households. BASIX reaffirmed that credit is a necessary but not sufficient condition for livelihood promotion. Its revised "Livelihood Triad" Strategy included provision of financial services beyond credit—such as insurance; provision of agricultural, livestock and non-farm enterprise development services; and institutional development services for producer organizations.

### *2.1 Role and Activities of Microfinance*

- *Micro-credit*: It is a small amount of money loaned to a client by a bank or other institution. Micro-credit can be offered, often without collateral, to an individual or through group lending.
- *Micro savings*: These are deposit services that allow one to save small amounts of money for future use. Often without minimum balance requirements, these savings accounts allow households to save in order to meet unexpected expenses and plan for future expenses.

- *Micro insurance*: It is a system by which people, businesses and other organizations make a payment to share risk. Access to insurance enables entrepreneurs to concentrate more on developing their businesses while mitigating other risks affecting property, health or the ability to work.
- *Remittances*: These are transfer of funds from people in one place to people in another, usually across borders to family and friends. Compared with other sources of capital that can fluctuate depending on the political or economic climate, remittances are a relatively steady source of funds.

### 2.2 Focus on Financing the Poor

The post-nationalization period in the banking sector, circa 1969, witnessed a substantial amount of resources being earmarked towards meeting the credit needs of the poor. There were several objectives for the bank nationalization strategy including expanding the outreach of financial services to neglected sectors. As a result of this strategy, Credit came to be recognized as a remedy for many of the ills of the poverty. While the objectives were laudable and substantial progress was achieved, credit flow to the poor, and especially to poor women, remained low. This led to initiatives that were institution driven that attempted to converge the existing strengths of rural banking infrastructure and leverage this to better serve the poor. The pioneering efforts at this were made by National Bank for Agriculture and Rural Development (NABARD b & c), which was given the tasks of framing appropriate policy for rural credit, provision of technical assistance backed liquidity support to banks, supervision of rural credit institutions and other development initiatives.

### 2.3 Rise of Self-Help Groups

This lead to the rise of Self-Help Groups and more formal SHG Federations coupled now with SHG Bank Linkage have made this a dominant form of microfinance in addition to microfinance institutions (MFI). The policy environment in India has been extremely supportive for the growth of the microfinance sector in India. Particularly during the International Year of Micro-credit 2005, significant policy announcements 18 from the Government of India (GoI) and the Reserve Bank of India (RBI) have served as a shot in the arm for rapid growth. SHGs have spread rapidly due to their ease of replication. SHG Bank Linkage has provided the capacity for SHGs to increase their capital base to fund more members and bigger projects. Today, it is estimated that there are at least over 2 million SHGs in India. In many Indian states, SHGs are networking themselves into federations to achieve institutional and financial sustainability. Cumulatively, 1.6 million SHGs have been bank-linked with cumulative loans of ₹ 69 billion. In 2004-05 alone, almost 800,000 SHGs were bank-linked.

While no definitive date has been determined for the actual conception and propagation of SHGs, the practice of small groups of rural and urban people banding together to form a savings and credit organization is well established in India. In the early stages, NGOs played a pivotal role in innovating the SHG model and in implementing the model to develop the process fully. In the 1980s, policymakers took notice and worked with development organizations and bankers to discuss the possibility of promoting these savings and credit groups. Their efforts and the simplicity of SHGs helped to spread the movement across the country. State governments established revolving loan funds which were used to fund SHGs. By the 1990s, SHGs were viewed by state governments and NGOs to be more than just a financial intermediation but as a common interest group, working on other concerns as well. The agenda of SHGs included social and political issues as well. The spread of SHGs led also to the formation of SHG Federations which are a more sophisticated form of organization that involve several SHGs forming into Village Organizations (VO) / Cluster Federations and then ultimately into higher level federations (called as Mandal Samakhya (MS) in AP or SHG Federation generally). SHG Federations are formal institutions while the SHGs are informal. Many of these SHG federations are registered as societies, mutual benefit trusts and mutually aided cooperative societies.

## 2.4 SHG Bank Linkage Model in India

A most notable milestone in the SHG movement was when NABARD launched the pilot phase of the SHG Bank Linkage programme in February 1992. This was the first instance of mature SHGs that were directly financed by a commercial bank. The informal thrift and credit groups of poor were recognized as bankable clients. Soon after, the RBI advised commercial banks to consider lending to SHGs as part of their rural credit operations thus creating SHG Bank Linkage. The linking of SHGs with the 19 financial sector was good for both sides. The banks were able to tap into a large market, namely the low-income households, transactions costs were low and repayment rates were high. The SHGs were able to scale up their operations with more financing and they had access to more credit products.

The institutionalization of self-help groups (SHGs) and their recognition by the banking system as a saving and effective credit delivery mechanism in 1990s was an important step in financial inclusion of the relatively less banked or unbanked rural areas. More so, because it was built on a premise that the SHG mechanism would instil credit discipline in the members and one day empower them to become individual clients of banks. What followed was a proliferation of the SHG-Bank Linkage Programme (SHG-BLP) to unprecedented heights. After the pilot testing phase from 1992 to 1995, the Reserve Bank of India advised banks that lending to SHGs should be treated as a normal banking activity in 1996. This led to the second phase (mainstreaming) of the programme as banks started financing SHGs on a relatively larger scale. During 1998-99, there was a quantum jump in the number of SHGs that had availed of loans from the banking system to 18,678 from 5,719 during 1997-98 (Fig. 1).This was the beginning of the growth and expansion phase (see graphic). As on March 31, 2009 42.24 lakh SHGs had loans outstanding with the banking system, which included 9.77 lakh SHGs under Swaranjayanti Gram Swarozgar Yojana (SGSY). The loan outstanding to the banking system, of non-SGSY SHGs, was INR 16,818 crore.

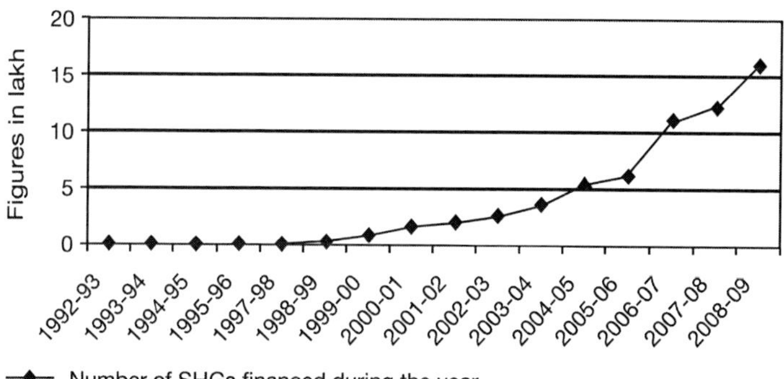


*Source:* Pankaj Kumar and Ramesh Golait (2009).

**Fig. 1:** Growth of SHG-Bank Linkage Programme during 1992-93 to 2008-09

### *2.4.1 Focus on Women Empowerment*

Microfinance programmes not only give women and men access to savings and credit, but reach millions of people worldwide bringing them together regularly in organized groups. Although no 'magic bullet', they are potentially a very significant contribution to gender equality and women's empowerment, as well as pro-poor development and civil society strengthening. Through their contribution to women's ability to earn an income these programmes have potential to initiate a series of 'virtuous spirals' of economic empowerment, increased well-being for women and their families and wider social and political empowerment. Microfinance services and groups involving men also have potential to question and significantly change men's attitudes and behaviours as an essential component of achieving gender equality. Majority of microfinance programmes focus women with a view to empower them. There are varying underlying motivations for pursuing women empowerment. Some argue that women are amongst the poorest and the most vulnerable of the underprivileged and thus helping them should be a priority. A more feminist point of view stresses that an increased access to financial services represent an opening/opportunity for greater empowerment.

Such organizations explicitly perceive microfinance as a tool in the fight for the women's rights and independence.

Finally, keeping up with the objective of financial viability, an increasing number of microfinance institutions prefer women members as they believe that they are better and more reliable borrowers. Self-help groups intermediated by micro-credit have been shown to have positive effects on women, with some of these impacts being ripple effects. They have played valuable roles in reducing the vulnerability of the poor, through asset creation, income and consumption smoothing, provision of emergency assistance, and empowering and emboldening women by giving them control over assets and increased self-esteem and knowledge (Zaman, 2001). Several recent assessment studies have also generally reported positive impacts (Simanowitz and Walker, 2002). Microfinance is gathering momentum to become a significant force in India. The self-help group (SHG) model with bank lending to groups of (often) poor women without collateral has become an accepted part of rural finance. With traditionally loss-making rural banks shifting their portfolio away from the rural poor in the post-reform period, SHG-based microfinance, nurtured and aided by NGOs, have become an important alternative to traditional lending in terms of reaching the poor without incurring a fortune in operating and monitoring costs. The government and NABARD have recognized this and have emphasized the SHG approach and working along with NGOs in its initiatives. In spite of the impressive figures, the supply side of microfinance in India is still presently grossly inadequate to fill the gap between demand and supply but it holds the promise to act as a great opportunity for the financial sector and the economy as a whole.

The linkage project envisages active involvement of NGOs who play a crucial role in formation, nurturing, stabilising and guiding the SHGs into cohesive and dynamic groups inculcating the habits of thrifts and credit management and ultimately establishing linkage with the banks. Under the SHG-bank linkage programme, three linkage models have broadly emerged. Under the first model, banks directly link SHGs without the intervention of the NGOs. In the second model, banks provide credit to SHGs and NGOs act as Self Help Promoting Institutions (SHPIs). Under the third model, NGOs act both as SHPIs and financial intermediaries for channelising credit from banks to SHGs. The SHG-Bank Linkage Programme implemented by commercial banks, RRBs and cooperative banks has emerged as the major microfinance programme in the country. Under the SHG-Bank Linkage Programme, as on March 31, 2009, 61,21,147 SHGs held savings bank accounts with total savings of ₹ 5,545.62 crore as against 50,09,794 SHGs with savings of ₹ 3,785.39 crore as on March 31, 2008. Thus more than 8.06 crore poor households were associated with banking agencies under the SHG- Bank Linkage Programme. The Table 2 clearly shows the progress under SHG Bank Linkage programme in India.

**Table 2:** Progress under SHG-Bank Linkage Programme during 2002-2009

| Year | New SHGs financed by banks Banks loan | | | | | Bank loan |
|---|---|---|---|---|---|---|
| | During the year | | Cumulative during the year | | | Cumulative amount |
| | No. | Growth (%) | No. | Amount | Growth (%) | |
| 2002-03 | 2,55,882 | 29 | 7,17,360 | 1,022.34 | 87 | 2,048.68 |
| 2003-04 | 3,61,731 | 41 | 10,79,091 | 1,855.53 | 81 | 3,904.21 |
| 2004-05 | 5,39,365 | 49 | 16,18,456 | 2,994.25 | 62 | 6,898.46 |
| 2005-06 | 6,20,109 | 15 | 22,38,565 | 4,499.09 | 50 | 11,397.55 |
| 2006-07 | 11,05,749* | — | 28,94.505 | 6,570.39 | — | 12,366.49 |
| 2007-08 | 12,27,770* | 11 | 36,25,941 | 8,849.26 | 35 | 16,999.90 |
| 2008-09# | 16,09,586* | 31.1 | 42,24,338 | 12,256.51 | 38.5 | 22,679.85 |

* From 2006-07 onwards, data in respect of number of SHGs financed by banks and bank loans are inclusive of SHGs financed under the Swarnajayanti Gram Swarozgar Yojana (SGSY) and the existing groups receiving repeat loans. Owing to this change, NABARD discontinued compilation of data on cumulative basis from 2006-07. As such data from 2006-07 onwards are not comparable with the data of the previous years (NABARD, 2008).

\# Provisional.

*Source:* Government of India (GOI), 2009.

As on March 31, 2009, commercial banks had the maximum share of SHG savings with savings of 35,49,509 SHGs (58 percent) amounting to ₹ 2,772.99 crore (50 percent); this was followed by RRBs with savings bank accounts of 16,28,588 SHGs (26.6 percent) and savings amount of ₹ 1,989.75 crore (35.9 percent) and cooperative banks with savings bank accounts of 9,43,050 SHGs (15.4 percent) and savings amount of ₹ 782.88 crore (14.1 percent). The share of the Swarnajayanti GramSwarozgar Yojana (SGSY) in SHG savings accounts was 15,05,581 SHGs, forming 25 percent of the total SHGs having savings accounts in banks. During 2008-09, the average savings per SHG with all banks increased from ₹ 7,556 as on March 31, 2008 to ₹ 9,060 as on March 31, 2009, varying between a high of ₹ 12,218 per SHG with RRBs and a low of ₹ 7,812 per SHG with commercial banks. As on March 31, 2009, the share of women SHGs in total SHGs with savings bank accounts was 48,63,921, accounting for 79.46 percent as compared to the previous year's share of 79.56 percent. During 2008-09, banks financed 16,09,586 SHGs, including repeat loans to existing SHGs, as against 12,27,770 SHGs during 2007-08—a growth of 31.1 percent (number of SHGs). As on March 31, 2009, 42,24,338 SHGs had outstanding (cumulative) bank loans of ₹ 22,679.85 crore as against 36,25,941 SHGs with outstanding bank loans of ₹ 16,999.90 crore as on March 31, 2008. This included 9, 76,887 SHGs (6.5 percent) with outstanding bank loans of ₹ 5,861.72 crore (21.7 percent) under the SGSY as against 9,16,978 SHGs with outstanding bank loans of ₹ 4,816.87 crore as on March 31, 2008. Commercial banks had the maximum share of around 70 percent of outstanding bank loans to SHGs followed by RRBs with a share of 23 percent and cooperative banks with the balance. As on March 31, 2009, the average bank loan outstanding per SHG was ₹ 53,689 as against ₹ 46,884 as on March 31, 2008. It varied from a high of ₹ 57,037 per SHG in the case of commercial banks to a low of ₹ 31,460 per SHG in the case of cooperative banks (NABARD, 2008; Puhazhendhi, 2012).

### *2.5 The Role of JLG*

Table 3 reports the results of a household sample in the period of the year 2009-10 before the AP crisis. The survey was conducted over a sample of 1,25,000 households at the district level, all across the country. The statistics show (a) what fraction of households in a given income category borrow, and (b) the source of their borrowings (Table 3).

**Table 3:** Mode of Households Borrowing (2009-2010)

| Category | HH Count (%) | Annual Income (₹ '000) | Source of Borrowing | | | | |
|---|---|---|---|---|---|---|---|
| | | | Friends and Family | Money-lender | SHG/ MFI | Bank | Any |
| Rich-I | 0.3 | 1,367 | 0.4 | 0.2 | 0.1 | 18.0 | 20.1 |
| Rich-II | 0.6 | 834 | 3.3 | 2.8 | 0.6 | 16.8 | 20.1 |
| High middle income-I | 5.6 | 479 | 9.9 | 8.6 | 2.1 | 22.8 | 30.9 |
| High middle income-II | 8.8 | 292 | 10.4 | 8.2 | 1.9 | 20.0 | 32.7 |
| High middle income-III | 9.5 | 209 | 11.8 | 7.8 | 2.3 | 14.2 | 32.2 |
| Middle income-I | 16.3 | 148 | 16.5 | 10.2 | 4.1 | 12.9 | 36.5 |
| Middle income-II | 10.2 | 108 | 20.9 | 13.1 | 6.0 | 10.4 | 40.4 |
| Low middle income-I | 22.4 | 77 | 21.5 | 14.6 | 7.0 | 7.3 | 42.1 |
| Low middle income-II | 19.3 | 49 | 24.7 | 14.3 | 7.7 | 5.2 | 42.6 |
| Poor-I | 5.2 | 31 | 29.5 | 14.1 | 7.0 | 4.6 | 46.1 |
| Poor-II | 1.8 | 19 | 30.0 | 13.3 | 6.7 | 3.1 | 44.9 |
| Overall | 100.0 | | 20.6 | 12.6 | 5.8 | 9.3 | 39.9 |

The Centre for Monitoring Indian Economy (CMIE) runs a system named Consumer Pyramids, which is a household survey database with a panel of 1,25,000 households measured every quarter. Information about borrowing by these households in fiscal year 2009-10 is reported in this table. The last column in the table shows the fraction of households in each income group who have borrowing. This varies from a fifth of the richest to a bit less than a half of the poorest. The role of banks peaks at 22.8 percent of households with a mean annual income of

₹ 4,79,000. It steadily peters away when dealing with lower incomes, down to 3.1 percent for the poorest. SHG and MFIs have come to play an important role starting from average annual income of ₹ 1,48,000 (6%) with a maximal role of 7.7 percent at a mean annual income of ₹ 49,000.

*Sources:* Household income data is from http://goo.gl/gOkeO and sources of borrowing data from http://goo.gl/yPX6U. Around 40 percent of the households in the sample have outstanding borrowings compared to 45 percent in the case of the poorest households that have outstanding loans. These borrowings are recorded as being friends and family, moneylender, SHG/MFIs, or banks. The role of banks peaks at 22.8 percent of the households that have a mean annual income of ₹ 4,79,000. However, banks cater less and less as a source of borrowing for households with lower incomes, coming down to 3.1 percent for the poorest.

For these low-income households, SHG and MFIs have come to play an important role starting from average annual income of ₹ 1,48,000 (6%) with a maximal role of 7.7 percent at a mean annual income of ₹ 49,000. This is higher than the 5.2 percent of the households that have loans outstanding to banks at the same income level. MFIs have thus established a significant presence in the space of household lending and have come to occupy a place in the credit industry between the formal sector banking channel and the informal sector moneylenders. The MFI sector has thus made remarkable inroads in the field of lending to the poor in just a few years compared with the banking sector, which has attempted to be in this field for over 50 years. These developments have largely taken place in the last decade. While MFIs are drawn from a medley of organizational forms, including non-profit organizations (NGOs, trusts) and for-profit firms, it is the for-profit firms that have dominated this growth in credit off-take of recent years (Srinivasan, 2010). These developments reflect important institutional innovations in Indian finance (Thorat, 2007). On the funding side, MFIs cannot raise money through deposits from the public. Originally, funding came from concessional aid and continues to come largely from banks under their priority sector lending (PSL) targets. The scaling up of the industry and its ability to make a difference to the economy on a meaningful scale is now critically about its ability to grow well beyond charitable motivations and shift to sustainable for-profit business models.

### 2.6 Role of Regulation in Finance

For laws, agencies and the private sector to operate in an optimal fashion, it is important to fully articulate the conceptual framework under which a government intervention is applied. This requires clearly answers to four key questions:

(a) What is market failure and what would go wrong with pure laissez faire?

(b) What are the interventions through which market failure will be addressed?

(c) How does this understanding of market failure and required interventions translate into law, and into the day-to-day engagement of financial regulatory agencies with the industry?

(d) How will supervision be done so that the 40,000 foot perspective of laws and regulations will actually be enforced on the ground?

The allegations made against the microfinance industry in the AP crisis involve problems relate to mis-selling, usurious interest rates and unfair debt collection practices. It can be argued that the resolution of such problems should have been left to forces of competition in the market. But this requires that consumers are alike and rational and that they have access to all information about services and service providers (Zingales, 2009).

It is universally recognized that unregulated finance leads to suboptimal outcomes and that one of the three pillars of financial regulation must be consumer protection (Campbell et al., 2011). In the field of microfinance, the problems of consumer skills are acute—the poor require complex products but would often find it difficult to understand complex products. Gabaix and Laibson (2006) show how it is optimal for a firm to "shroud" fees for goods when the market has a mixture of myopic and aware investors. In such markets it can be shown that competitive market forces do not arrive at the lowest cost or optimal service for the consumer. In microfinance these assumptions about the consumer's ability to differentiate between competing products and services can be exacerbated by the lack of financial awareness and literacy amongst the poor micro-borrowers. It is therefore unlikely that the resolution of the problems of the microfinance sector can be achieved solely through the market forces of competition.

The sector has suffered a loss of confidence in the public view and a key role that regulation plays is to bolster and restore trust (Zingales, 2009). In the field of financial regulation, a three-part classification is useful: (a) Consumer protection where the focus is to protect the rights and interests of the consumer of financial products and services; this focuses on the interfaces between financial firms and households. (b) Micro-prudential regulation where the focus is to monitor and reduce the probability of failure of individual financial firms so as to avoid the adverse impact on consumers. (c) Systemic risk, which aims to curtail the risk that the financial system as a whole collapses. This three-part framework is useful for analysing problems and proposed interventions in the field of microfinance, as it is for all parts of finance.

### *2.6.1 Regulatory Targets in the MFI Business*

India's MFIs are in the business of being credit providers with obligations on two fronts: the consumer at one end (which we call MFI-consumer linkage) and the formal financial sector at the other end (MFI-funding linkage) from whom MFIs obtains resources. These two linkages impose two different sets of obligations on the MFI. In the case of the MFI-funding linkage, there is a broad range of possible firms/entities that fund MFIs. These include donors (with gifts), banks and other financial firms (with loans), private equity firms, and the public equity market (with equity). All these are sophisticated financial participants. There is no difficulty with consumer protection in order to protect the interests of these sources of funds. The only role of regulation lies in ensuring high quality and truthful disclosures by MFIs to their shareholders and lenders.

However, the situation is very different in the linkage between a MFI and consumers. There are three roles that a MFI can play in the domain of MFI-consumer linkage that helps define their obligations to the consumer: (a) that of a credit provider with business processes to assess credit risk of non-collateralized retail consumers, along with processes to disburse and collect payments cost-effectively to this consumer base; (b) that of a distributor of other financial products; and (c) that of an agency that promotes awareness about financial services. These roles help define the following obligations on a MFI: (a) truth and transparency in the distribution of financial services, (b) adherence to fair collection practices, and (c) ensuring that the consumer is aware of all the alternatives before they make their choice.

### *2.6.2 Consumer Protection and Credit Recovery Issue*

Regulation can be readily visualised when there is a clear demarcation between those who have rights and those who have obligations. In standard financial contracts such as fixed deposits or insurance, the consumer has rights while the service provider has obligations. In the case of credit, the consumer (borrower) has obligations and the service provider (the lender) has rights. However, the borrower does have some rights, including being presented contracts that have clarity about the terms under which the loan is made, the definition of default, and their liabilities in case of default. Universally, legislation defines the rights of the borrower; regulation defines a code of conduct and practices under which debt collection can be undertaken and how recovery is to be done when the borrower defaults. However, this becomes complicated when credit is given through a JLG structure. Numerous studies have demonstrated the complexity of the joint-liability contract and the impact it has on group member behaviour (Besley and Coate, 1995; Ghatak, 1999; Gangopadhyay et al. 2005; Bhole and Ogden, 2010; Baland et al. 2011). In the AP crisis, for example, one of the allegations was coercive debt recovery practices. However, given that the first recourse to good credit performance was at the level of the group, the application of coercion might have been by the group leaders or other group members rather than the credit officer of the MFI. The code of conduct, therefore, needs to account for more than just the link between the service provider (the MFI as the lender) and the consumer (the borrower who is an individual in a Joint Liability Group (JLG). There are two more links to account for, which are (a) the link between the member of the JLG and the JLG itself, and (b) the link between the MFI and the other members of the JLG when one member defaults. To the extent that the loan is being made based on the strength of the credit quality of the group, there needs to be legal clarity on what are the rights of the lender and the obligations of the JLG when a member of the group defaults.

The other concern for regulation that is unique when the JLG is involved is the link between the member and other members of the JLG. Group leaders or other members of the JLG have far greater access to the borrower member than the MFI. This is a part of the strength of the JLG that enables the comfort about credit performance from the individual. This, however, becomes a concern for consumer protection. The group could more efficiently inflict damage in the process of debt collection or debt recovery than the MFI or their employees. The consumer protection mandate of the regulation must, therefore, have a provision for grievance redressal for the individual borrower against the MFI as well as the JLG or specific members of the JLG through which they obtained the loan. In summary, financial regulation applied to MFIs that is motivated by consumer protection needs to explicitly include protection at several levels: (a) the rights of the borrower against the MFI, (b) the rights of the JLG against the MFI, and (c) the rights of the individual borrower against the JLG, either individual members like the group leader or as a whole.

### *2.6.3 Unique Micro-Prudential Regulation Issues*

MFIs lend to households and present no risk to households if they fail. Hence, regulators do not need to worry about the failure of an MFI from the consumer protection perspective. There is, however, a concern about the implications of lending to MFIs for financial firms that lend to MFIs. This, in turn, requires a careful analysis of the mechanisms of failure of the

MFI. The credit risk associated with lending to a JLG differs in important ways from that associated with lending to an individual, for two reasons: The first issue relates to correlated defaults associated with homogeneous credit quality. It can be argued that there will always be a higher degree of homogeneity when lending to members in a group—whether the members are from the same cultural background, physical location, risk preferences, political preference, etc. The commonality of these factors in a group can lead to correlated changes in the level of default, as was seen in the case of willful defaults among micro-borrowers of the same community in the Kolar district in 2007. These defaults occurred simultaneously in all the MFIs that were operating in this district at the time.

MFIs have modified their business models to reduce this concentration risk. However, not all factors of homogeneity can be directly observed. Databases required to analyse these issues—at the group level and not just at the individual level —are not available at present. Credit bureaus currently collect repayment history at the level of individuals, and not groups. Complex dynamics can arise from the interplay between multiple individuals and multiple groups. If there are different groups (perhaps across different MFIs) who share some similar members, it is possible that a default of a member or a set of members can generate default across different groups. This, in turn, may adversely affect the default experience across MFIs depending upon the contractual implications of member default and JLG default to the MFI. The second path through which the JLG structure of lending could enhance the systemic risk for the MFI industry is because a group could be an easier channel for obtaining political interference. On one hand, the JLG can engender better credit behaviour from their members but on the flip side, they can lead to political mobilization that hampers a sound credit culture. These arguments suggest that the regulation of the credit business that is implemented using the JLG structure does involve different considerations. These unique features influence our thinking about the three pillars of financial regulation, namely, consumer protection, micro-prudential regulation and systemic risk.

*2.6.4 Review of Existing Policy Responses*

Two key efforts in proposing a framework for the Indian microfinance industry after the 2010 AP legislation was passed are the Malegam Report (2011) and the Microfinance Institutions (Development and Regulation) Bill, 2011, Planning Commission, GOI. Both focus heavily on micro-prudential norms and corporate governance issues for MFIs. We now analyse these efforts from the conceptual framework of the previous sections.

*2.6.4.1 The Malegam Committee Report*: The Malegam Committee Report (RBI, 2011) was initiated by RBI. Being the regulator of both NBFCs and banks, RBI had a twofold interest in this issue since several MFIs with large exposure to the AP defaults were structured as NBFCs and their collapse would affect bank portfolios since banks were the largest source of funding to NBFCs. The Malegam Committee report has consequently narrowly focused on the question of NBFC-MFI. It starts with a definition of NBFC-MFI and lays down conditions related to net worth and assets that it had to satisfy as a NBFC-MFI. The report requires NBFC-MFIs to maintain a capital-adequacy ratio and provisions for loan losses. NBFC-MFIs are also required to follow certain corporate governance norms.

A key gap in these recommendations is that they apply only to NBFCs, which are only 45 percent of MFIs by number (Srinivasan, 2010). Another problem is the focus on the prudential aspects of the MFI business. Even if all of these rules were in place before October 2010, they could not have protected the small consumer from the alleged malpractice of MFIs. The recommendations also seem to worry more about ensuring that bank-lending under PSL targets is done smoothly, and less about providing an enabling framework for microcredit as a whole. The approach of the committee as contained in the report towards consumer protection has been to prescribe conditions on who can be consumers of MFI and the manner in which MFIs can lend. The report goes on to stipulate rules on (a) the purpose for which MFIs can disburse loans (i.e. 75 percent of the loans may be disbursed only for productive purposes),

(b) pricing of loans and the quantities and rates that can be charged (a margin cap of 26 percent, which is the difference between the amount charged to the borrower and the cost of funds to the MFI), (c) location—where sanctioning and disbursement of loans can take place, and (d) individuals who can be consumers (an individual cannot be a member of more than two groups and has to have annual household income of less than ₹ 50,000).

These initiatives do not add up to a comprehensive approach to consumer protection. These conditions severely limit who can be consumers of microfinance and lead to a restrictive definition of financial exclusion—the very problem that MFIs were successful in solving—while not necessarily ensuring better credit processes. The report does mention the setting up of a credit information bureau and an ombudsman. The responsibility of arbitration, however, is left to the manager of a lead bank in each district that may not provide adequate protection against malpractices.

*2.6.4.2 The Microfinance Institutions (Development and Regulation) Bill, 2011*: The Microfinance Institutions (Development and Regulation) Bill, 2011, has been drafted with the objective to provide a regulatory structure for the microfinance industry. In a nutshell, the bill views MFIs as "extended arms of banks and financial services". However, rather than drawing upon existing regulation in these areas, it proposes to: (a) create advisory councils to guide the development of the industry, (b) place registration and micro-prudential functions on RBI, and (c) create a new redressal mechanism for handling consumer grievances. A careful legal analysis of this bill reveals certain areas of concern. The first is about the clarity of objectives. Regulation is not an end; it is the means to an end. Until the problem is clearly stated, the rationale underlying the bill will not be clear to the judiciary and to the regulated industry. In addition, the lack of clarity about market failures that motivate government intervention tends to obscure the process through which law is drafted.

The bill envisages deposit-taking by MFIs. However, it implies that these same fixed deposits would be then lent to micro-borrowers who could be depositors themselves. This would mean that the savings of the poor would be lent to risky credit products. Great care needs to be exercised here, particularly given the problems that have been experienced in India with cooperative banks and deposit-taking NBFCs. Even if it were felt that MFIs should become banks, the appropriate legal apparatus for this should be within the Banking Regulation Act and not a new parallel legislation. The bill envisages the field of microfinance as interacting with an array of government bodies: the central government, RBI, National Bank for Agriculture and Rural Development (NABARD), and microfinance development council and the State Advisory councils. The resulting scenario will involve friction between multiple government agencies through overlapping jurisdictions. This will inevitably lead to a loss of accountability since nobody is clearly responsible for a well-defined outcome. The bill envisages a fiscal function: a tax (in the form of a reserve fund) imposed upon the industry, which is to be earmarked for the purpose of funding MFIs. This is a questionable idea at many levels. Efficiency demands raising resources through income tax and the goods and services tax; levying charges on an industry should be avoided. In addition, it is not clear that the government can play a useful role as a venture capitalist or as a lender to this industry.

The bill has not provided a measure of the cost that will be faced by the government (or RBI and the other agencies in their regulatory capacity) in performing the tasks envisaged in the Bill. Such calculations would help improve the ability of the Ministry of Finance and Parliament in assessing the benefits versus the costs of enacting the legislation. The draft bill leaves many concerns on issues of rule of law (Roy et al., 2011). The bill makes any violation to be a criminal offence. At the same time, consumers are visualized as having no recourse to civil or criminal courts without the RBI's permission. There is no skilled judicial appeals mechanism (such as the Securities Appellate Tribunal) where orders can be appealed.

### 2.7 Challenges Ahead for Microfinance in India

An evaluation of SHGs carried out by the regional offices (ROs) of the Reserve Bank revealed that there was scope for improvement in the area of maintenance of books of accounts. It also brought out that rotation of group leaders was generally not followed by SHGs. However, other best practices like strict adherence to attendance of group meetings, recording minutes of the meetings and prompt repayment of bank loans were being followed. The momentum of growth in the microfinance sector has brought into focus the importance of regulating the sector to function in an efficient and orderly manner. There would be need for greater transparency in their functioning and for facilitating their reach to un-banked population of the country. Interest rates in the microfinance sector have to be significantly higher than in the banking sector reflecting the much higher cost of doing business. This attracts criticism but it is important to remember that most microfinance institutions charge rates which are much lower than rates charged by moneylenders. Borrowers stand to benefit from the experience of microfinance institutions as these provide competition to moneylenders (Planning Commission, 2006).

Over the past two decades, institutions that make micro-loans to low-income borrowers in developing and transition economies have focused increasingly on making their operations financially sustainable by charging interest rates that are high enough to cover all their costs. They argue that doing so will best ensure the permanence and expansion of the services they provide. Sustainable (i.e. profitable) microfinance providers can continue to serve their clients without needing ongoing infusions of subsidies, and can fund exponential growth of services for new clients by tapping commercial sources, including deposits from the public. MFIs on average have higher returns on assets than commercial banks do, but MFIs produce lower returns on equity for their owners. The median return on MFI owners equity in 2006 was moderate—12.3 percent, roughly 4 percent lower than the return for banks (Rosenberg et al., 2009). In this, there have been incidents of state governments imposing restrictions on microfinance institutions in a manner which does not reflect an appreciation of the realities on the ground. Excessive regulation and control of this sector may be particularly dangerous as it can prevent the development of a healthy and competitive microfinance sector which could compete with usurious money-lenders (Planning Commission, 2006).

## 2.8 Role of Information Technology in Microfinance Transactions

Microfinance is not only about credit. It is as much about thrift (or savings), remittance services and micro-insurance. In a way, even credit may be looked at as one's own savings made available at advance. There is need to put in place a workable system, technologically and managerially, for collecting savings from the poor in small amounts, at regular intervals and at their doorstep. In the case of the urban poor, in particular, it is observed that they suffer from high income drain on account of many avoidable practices. There is, as such, a great need for plugging this income drain through diverting their resources to savings. The economically active urban poor may be encouraged to own 'debit card' and banks may introduce ATM machines in the residential colonies of the poor. Besides this, the urban wage earners separated from their rural families require to send money home. NBFC-MFI network could devise a mechanism to deliver the money at their doorstep. There are, similarly, many upcoming technologies suitable for the rural poor. 'Gramteller', a rural ATM could be explored for their successful usability in rural areas. Introduction of (bio-metric) smart cards is also expected to revolutionize the microfinance sector and bring down the transaction costs.

ICTs can be effectively used to provide information about microfinance organizations and their services. Though many web sites provide information on microfinancing, there is dearth of information on the terms and conditions, institutions that provides microfinance, etc. This information can be provided both in English and also in other Indian languages. ICTs can be effectively utilised to monitor the various Micro-Finance activities. The various schemes implemented by the Department of Rural Development are monitored physically through various impact assessment studies. RURALSOFT (http://ruralsoft.nic.in.)

is software used to monitor the schemes on a monthly basis. At present assessments are done only up to district or block level because of the consolidated data. Details that truly reflect the success of the schemes are not currently captured because of non-availability of ICT infrastructure in rural areas and the information about individual beneficiaries. The information required to assess the schemes at the grassroot level can be out sourced to the self-help groups. This information can be fed into the Rural soft for detailed monitoring of the schemes.

ICTs can be used to provide access to wider markets and better prices. ICTs can be used to enhanced the economic returns for the microfinance activities by providing access to global markets at better prices. At present 'RURALBAZAR' (http://ruralbazar.nic.in) the application software has been conceptualized to assist market needs of products produced by rural people. It offers internet web to show case their products to the world. It appears some of the states like Tamil Nadu, Goa and Tripura have successfully adopted the software. However, efforts should be made to ensure quality of the products produced by rural producers and to provide logistic support like appropriate packages and timely delivery to the products.

### 3. Distinctive Features of the Business of Microfinance

Micro-credit is at the heart of many microfinance business models, and has a number of distinctive features. Product design, client profile and labour-intensive underwriting methodologies give micro-credit a unique risk profile. Effective credit risk management thus requires different tools and analyses than for conventional retail lending. Some of the more distinctive features of micro-credit include:

(a) *Micro-borrowers*: A micro-credit provider usually caters to low-income clients, both the underemployed and the entrepreneur with an often informal family business (e.g. petty traders). Borrowers are typically concentrated in a limited geographic area, social segment or entrepreneurial undertaking. Loans are usually very small, short-term, and unsecured, with more frequent repayments and higher interest rates than conventional bank loans. Many providers require higher interest rates to offset higher operational costs involved in the labour-intensive micro-lending methodology.

(b) *Credit risk analysis*: Loan documentation is generated largely by the loan officer through visits to the borrower's business and home. Borrowers often lack formal financial statements, so loan officers help prepare documentation using expected cash flows and net worth to determine the amortization schedule and loan amount. The borrower's character and willingness to repay is also assessed during field visits. Credit bureau data are not always available for low-income clients or for all types of microfinance providers, but when they exist, are used as well. Credit scoring, when used, complements rather than supplants the more labour-intensive approaches to credit analysis.

(c) *Use of collateral*: Micro-borrowers often lack collateral traditionally required by banks, and what they have to pledge is of little value for the financial institution but are highly valued by the borrower (e.g. TV, furniture). Where the lender does take some sort of collateral, it is for leverage to induce payment rather than to recover losses. In the absence of collateral, underwriting depends on a labour-intensive analysis of the household's repayment capacity and the borrower's character.

(d) *Credit approval and monitoring*: Because micro-lending tends to be a highly decentralized process, credit approval by loan committees depends heavily on the skill and integrity of loan officers and managers for accurate and timely information.

(e) *Controlling arrears*: Strict control of arrears is necessary given the short-term nature, lack of collateral, high frequency of payments (e.g. weekly or bi-weekly), and contagion effects of micro-loans. Traditionally, monitoring is primarily in the hands of loan officers as the knowledge of the client's personal circumstances is important for effective collections.

(f) *Progressively increasing lending*: Customers who have limited access to other financing are usually dependent upon ongoing access to credit. Micro-lending uses incentive schemes to reward good borrowers with preferential access to future, larger loans (sometimes with favourable repayment schedules and lower interest rates), which raises the risk of over-indebtedness, particularly where credit information systems are absent or deficient. This feature also affects interest rate risk management, as microfinance customers expect rates to decline as the customer's track record grows, regardless of changes in the general level of interest rates.

(g) *Group lending*: Some micro-lenders use group lending methodologies, where loans are made to small groups of people who cross guarantee other members of the group. Peer pressure also helps to ensure high repayment levels, as the default of one group member could adversely affect the availability of credit to others.

(h) *Contagion effects*: Tight control of arrears and peer pressure has driven traditionally sound repayment rates in most jurisdictions to date. However, the quality of individual loan portfolios can deteriorate quite rapidly, due in part to the unsecured or under-secured nature of micro-loans as well as so-called contagion effects, where borrowers who notice increasing delinquency in the institution may stop paying if they believe the institution will be less likely to offer future loans due to credit quality problems.

(i) *Currency-related risks*: Occasionally micro-lenders lend in a currency other than that of a borrower's repayment source (e.g. sale of goods or services), so foreign currency fluctuations may affect the borrower's ability to repay. While not unique to micro-credit, micro-borrowers may be less able to appreciate the nature of this exposure, much less take measures to mitigate it.

(j) *Political influences*: Micro-credit and microfinance in general, may be seen as a political tool in some countries, tempting politicians to demand forbearance or forgiveness of loans to poor customers during times of economic stress. This might affect repayment culture of microfinance borrowers.

The dynamics of microfinance assets and liabilities also differ from those of commercial banking, affecting liquidity and interest rate risk management. On the asset side, loan repayment is often driven by expectations of repeat loans over time, transforming short-term loan portfolios into long-term, fixed-rate assets. Illiquidity of such assets is heightened by the fact that there are few established securitization markets available for microcredit portfolios. Microfinance institutions also tend to grow rapidly, particularly in their early stages. In this situation, they may lack a cushion of unencumbered, high-quality liquid assets to enable them to withstand a range of stress events, since most funds are designated to support loan growth.

On the liability side, data on the historical volatility of deposits in ODTIs may not be available to allow for meaningful gap analysis. In addition, ODTIs tend to have less certain access to backup sources of liquidity from local banks, although lack of bank liquidity lines may be mitigated by the existence of a local wholesale lender or government programme set up to provide funding to the microfinance sector. ODTIs are also vulnerable to disruptions in commercial borrowings due to delays or changes in policies of public (government) and private (donors and lenders) funders. Nonetheless, borrowing from international lenders may be a stable source of liquidity depending on individual relationships and contract terms.

### *3.1 Demand for Micro-credit*

In terms of demand for micro-credit or micro-finance, there are three segments, which demand funds. They are:

1. At the very bottom in terms of income and assets are those who are landless and engaged in agricultural activities on a seasonal basis, and manual labourers in forestry, mining, household industries and construction. This segment requires, first and foremost, consumption credit during those months when they do not get labour

work, and for contingencies such as illness. They also need credit for acquiring small productive assets, such as livestock, using which they can generate additional income.

2. The next market segment is small and marginal farmers and rural artisans, weavers and those self-employed in the urban informal sector as hawkers, vendors, and workers in household micro-enterprises. This segment mainly needs credit for working capital, a small part of which also serves consumption needs. This segment also needs term credit for acquiring additional productive assets, such as irrigation pump-sets, bore-wells and livestock in case of farmers, and equipment (looms, machinery) and worksheets in case of non-farm workers.
3. The third market segment is of small and medium farmers who have gone in for commercial crops such as surplus paddy and wheat, cotton, groundnut, and others engaged in dairying, poultry, fishery, etc. Among non-farm activities, this segment includes those in villages and slums, engaged in processing or manufacturing activity, running provision stores, repair workshops, tea shops, and various service enterprises. These persons are not always poor, though they live barely above the poverty line and also suffer from inadequate access to formal credit.

## 4. Growth of Microfinance in India

Poverty alleviation has been one of the guiding principles of the planning process in India. Government has considerably enhanced allocation for the provision of education, health, sanitation and other facilities which promote capacity building and well-being of the poor. The Indian government puts emphasis on providing financial services to the poor and under-privileged since independence. The commercial banks were nationalized in 1969 and were directed to lend 40 percent of their loan at concessional rate to priority sector. The priority sector included agriculture and other rural activities and weaker section of society in general was to provide resources to help the poor to start their micro-enterprise to attain self-sufficiency. The government of India had also launched various poverty alleviation programmes like Small Farmers Development Scheme (SFDS) 1974-75, Twenty-Point Programme (TPP) 1975, National Rural Development Programme (NRDP) 1980, Integrated Rural Development Programme (IRDP) 1980, Rural Landless Employment Guarantee Programme (RLEGP) 1983, Jawahar Rozgar Yojna (JRY) 1989, Swarna Jayanti Gram Swarojgar Yojana (SGSY) 1999 and many other programmes. But none of these programmes achieved their desired goal due to poor execution and malpractices on the part of government officials. Public funds meant for poverty alleviation are being misappropriated or diverted through manipulation by the locally powerful or corrupt (Mehta, 1996a and b, 1998).

To supplement the efforts of micro-credit government of India had started a very good scheme, viz. Integrated Rural Development Programme (IRDP) in 1980. But these supply side programmes (ignoring demand side of economy) achieved little. It involved the commercial banks in giving loan of less than ₹ 15,000, to socially weaker section. In a period of nearly 20 years the total investment was around ₹ 250 billion to roughly 55 million families. But it was far from realizing its desired goal. The problem with IRDP was that its design incorporated a substantial element of subsidies (25-50 percent of each family's project cost) and this resulted in extensive malpractice and mis-utilisation of funds. This situation led bankers to view the IRDP loan as motivated handout and they largely failed to follow up with borrowers. The net result is that estimates of repayment rates in IRDP ranged from 25-33 percent. The two decades of IRDP experience in the 1980s and 1990s affected the credibility of micro-borrowers in the view of bankers and ultimately, hindered access of the less literate poor to banking services. This act of government had a serious long-term impact on development of micro-entrepreneurship among the underprivileged of the society. Thus a very good and potential programme which once claimed to be the world's largest microfinance programme failed due to poor execution and political interference. The mid-term appraisal of the ninth plan had indicated that these programmes presented a matrix of multiple programmes without desired linkages (Mehta, 1996a and b, 1998). The programmes suffered from critical investments, lack of bank credit, overcrowding in certain projects and lack of market linkages. The programmes were basically subsidy driven and ignored the process of social intermediation necessary for success of self-employment programmes. A one-time provision of credit without follow up action and lack of a continuing relationship between borrowers and lenders also contributed to the failure of the programmes. The planning commission constituted a committee in 1997 to review the effectiveness of self-employment and wage employment programmes. The committee recommended the merger of all self-employment programmes. It also recommended a shift of importance from individual beneficiary approach to a group based approach. It emphasized the identification of activity clusters in specific areas and strong training and marketing linkages.

The government of India accepted the recommendations of the committee. On 1st April 1999 a new programme called Swarnajayanti Gram Swarojgar Yojana (SGSY) was launched by amalgamating programmes like IRDP (Integrated Rural Development Programme) and a number of allied programmes such as TRYSEM (Training of Rural Youth for Self-Employment), DWCRA (Development of Women and Children in Rural Areas), SITRA (Supply of Improved Toolkits to Rural Artisans), GKY (Ganga Kalyan Yojana) and MWS (Million Wells Schemes). This is a holistic programme covering all aspects of self-employment such as formation of Self-Help Groups (SHGs), training, credit, technology, infrastructure and marketing. The programme aims at establishing a large number of micro-enterprises in rural areas. SGSY is a credit-cum-subsidy programme. It lays emphasis on activity 146 clusters. This programme has got tremendous response from the beneficiaries. The number of SHGs under this programme is about 2.25 million with an investment of ₹ 14,403 crore, profiting over 6,697 million people (Wikipedia).

Similarly, the entire network of primary cooperatives and RRBs, established to meet the need of the rural sector in general and poor in particular, has proved a colossal failure. Saddled with burden of directed credit and a restrictive interest regime, the position of the RRBs deteriorated quickly while cooperatives suffered from the malaise of mismanagement, privileged leadership and corruption born of excessive state patronage (Sinha, 2000, 2003).

The microfinance initiative in the private sector in India can be traced back to initiative undertaken by Shri Mahila SEWA (Self-Employed Women's Association) Sahakari Bank in 1974 for providing banking services to the poor women employed in the unorganized sector in Ahmedabad in Gujarat. This Bank was established at the initiative of 4000 self-employed women workers who contributed a share of ₹ 10 each with a specific objective of providing credit to these women so as to empower them and free them from vicious circle of debt. Currently SEWA Bank has over 318,594 account holders with total working capital of ₹ 1291.89 million (March, 2009). MYRADA (Mysore Rehabilitation and Development Agency) of Karnataka was another NGO to start in 1968 to foster a process of ongoing change in favour of the rural poor. While the objective is to help the poor help themselves, MYRADA achieves this by forming Self-Help Affinity Groups (SHGs) and through partnership with NGOs and other organization in 1984-85. At present it is managing 18 projects in 20 backward districts of Karnataka, Tamil Nadu and Andhra Pradesh. These initial initiatives had a much localized operation and were limited to their members only. Hence it failed to take the shape of a mass movement.

In India, initially many NGO microfinance institutions (MFIs) were funded by donor support in the form of revolving funds and operating grants. But it is only after intervention of National Bank for Agriculture and Rural Development (NABARD) in 1992 in the field of micro-credit, the movement of microfinance got a boost in India. In India around 70 percent of landless and marginal farmers did not have a bank account and 87 percent of poor had no access to credit from a formal source (NCAER Rural Financial Access Survey 2003). The share of formal financial sector in total rural credit was 56.6 percent compared to informal finance at 39.6 percent and unspecified source at 3.8 percent (RBI Report 1992). There is a huge potential of microcredit in rural India. The Reserve Bank of India has advocated for financial inclusion of majority of population for economic development of our country. Access to affordable financial services specially credit and insurance enlarges livelihood opportunities of poor. Apart from social and political empowerment, financial inclusion imparts formal identity and provides access to the payment system and to saving safety net like deposit insurance. Hence financial inclusion is considered to be critical for achieving inclusive growth (Thorat, 2007).

### *4.1 Present Status of Implementation of Microfinance in India*

Ever since micro-credit first began to capture public attention 25 years ago, it has been proclaimed a tool of extraordinary power to lift poor people, particularly women, out of poverty, by providing access to credit to better fund business endeavours. Along the way, micro-credit expanded into microfinance, which consists of offering a variety of financial products to poor customers, including savings products, pension products, insurance products, and credit for non-business expenditures. This full suite of financial products for the poor is thought to provide them greater opportunity to improve their financial situation, prepare for the future, and offset financial risk; much like the traditional finance sector does for wealthier clients. The microfinance environment in India currently consists primarily of micro-credit, with other products not offered due to regulation or not offered widely due to other circumstances. Micro-credit in India is delivered through two channels, microfinance institutions (MFIs) and self-help groups linked to banks (SHG-Linkage programme). Recent statistics show that MFIs, consisting of both for-profit and non-profit entities, reach 31.4 million customers with a total outstanding loan portfolio of 208 billion. MFIs mostly offer only credit through joint liability groups (JLGs), where group liability is substituted in place of collateral. Some MFIs are starting to offer individual lending options, sometimes using gold or other possessions as collateral. The vast majority of MFIs do not offer savings, insurance, or pension products due to regulatory restrictions. Microfinance sector has traversed a long journey from micro savings to micro-credit and then to micro-enterprises and now entered the field of micro insurance, micro pension. Financial institutions in the country continue to play a leading role in the microfinance programme for nearly two decades now. They have joined hands proactively with informal delivery channels to give microfinance sector the necessary momentum. The data for the year 2010-11 along with a few preceding year have been presented and reviewed under two models of microfinance (i) SHG-Bank Linkage model (ii) MFI-Bank Linkage model (Table 4).

**Table 4:** Overall Progress of under SHG-Bank Linkage Programme

| | Particulars | 2008-2009 | | 2009-2010 | | 2010-2011 | |
|---|---|---|---|---|---|---|---|
| | | No. of SHGs | Amount | No. of SHGs | Amount | No. of SHGs | Amount |
| SHG Saving with Banks as on 31st March | Total SHGs No. | 61.21 | 5545.62 | 69.53 | 6198.71 | 74.62 | 7016.30 |
| | Of which SGSY groups | 15.06 | 1563.38 | 16.94 | 1292.62 | 20.23 | 1817.12 |
| | All women SHGs | 48.64 | 4434.03 | 53.10 | 4498.66 | 60.98 | 5298.65 |
| Loan Disbursed to SHGs during the year | No. of SHGs extending Loans | 16.10 | 1225.51 | 15.87 | 14453.3 | 11.96 | 14547.73 |
| | Of which SGSY | 2.65 | 2015.22 | 2.67 | 2198 | 2.41 | 2480.37 |
| | All women SHGs | 13.75 | 10527.38 | 12.94 | 12429.37 | 10.17 | 12622.33 |
| Loan outstanding Against SHGs as on 31st March | Total SHGs No. Linked | 42.24 | 22679.84 | 48.51 | 28038.28 | 47.87 | 31221.17 |
| | Of which SGSY Groups | 9.77 | 5861.72 | 12.45 | 6251.08 | 12.86 | 7829.39 |
| | All women SHGs | 32.77 | 18583.54 | 38.98 | 23030.36 | 39.84 | 26123.75 |

*Source:* Status of Microfinance in India Report: 2010-11, NABARD.

The SHGs-Bank Linkage programme has received wide acceptance among multiplicity of stakeholders, civil society organizations, bankers and the international communities. Around 1.2 million new SHGs had credit link with banks and bank loans of ₹ 14,547 crore (including repeat loan) was disbursed to these SHGs in the financial year 2010-11. During same period 7.46 million SHGs maintained saving account with banks. On an average, the amount of saving per SHGs was ₹ 9,405.00 as compared to the amount of credit of ₹ 65,180.00 in 2010-11. During the same period 471 MFIs were provided loans by banks to the tune of ₹ 8,448 crore. Under the MFI-Bank Linkage Programme number of MFIs disbursed loans by Banks is less than previous years but amount of loan is much higher than the previous years. The growth is also higher than corresponding growth under the SHGs-Bank Linkage Programme in 2010-11 (Table 5). This is due to proactive role of the MFIs in micro-credit and professional management of funds from banks.

**Table 5:** Overall Progress of under MFI-Bank Linkage Programme

| | 2008-2009 | | 2009-2010 | | 2010-2011 | |
|---|---|---|---|---|---|---|
| | No. of MFIs | Amount | No. of MFIs | Amount | No. of MFIs | Amount |
| Loans Disbursed by Banks To MFIs | 581 | 3732.33 | 691 | 8062.74 | 471 | 8448.96 |
| Loans outstanding against MFIs as on 31st March | 1951 | 5009.09 | 1513 | 10147.54 | 2315 | 13730.62 |

*Source:* Status of microfinance in India report 2010-11, NABARD.
N.B: In the table the amount is in ₹ crore and number in lakhs.

The SHG-Linkage programme, headed by the National Bank of Agriculture and Rural Development (NABARD), reaches 98.1 million customers with a total outstanding loan portfolio of 306 billion. The programme offers savings options as well. NABARD is currently reviewing the SHG-Linkage programme, and soon intends to launch SHG-II, which is said to include new features such as voluntary savings (rather than mandatory), mechanisms for graduating customers to higher individual or small group loans, and a more sustainable mechanism for handholding of SHGs in the initial stages.

### *4.1.1 Multi-Agency Institutional Linkage in Microfinance Delivery Systems*

Micro-Finance services are geographically skewed in India, with the Southern states showing much higher penetration of services compared to Northern states. Recent regulation from RBI has set minimum capital requirements by geography to encourage institutions to open in under-penetrated regions. Though the availability of micro-credit has expanded over the last decade, many challenges exist for the decade ahead. We must identify a way to bring the full suite of microfinance products to the poor, so that they will have better opportunity to improve their own circumstance. We also must refine the micro-credit model to account for outstanding issues surrounding regulatory jurisdiction, customer protection, and stable funding opportunities for the industry.

In the development strategy adopted by independent India, institutional credit was perceived as a powerful instrument for enhancing production and productivity and for alleviating poverty. The growth of institutional credit is given in Table 5. The formal view was that lending to the poor should be a part of the normal business of banks. To achieve the objectives of production, productivity and poverty alleviation, the stance of policy on rural credit was to ensure that sufficient and timely credit was reached as expeditiously as possible to as large a segment of the rural population at reasonable rates of interest. The strategy devised for this purpose comprised:

- Expansion of the institutional structure,
- Directed lending to disadvantaged borrowers and sectors, and
- Interest rates supported by subsidies.

The institutional vehicles chosen for this were cooperatives, commercial banks and Regional Rural Banks. Between 1950 and 1969, the emphasis was on the promoting of cooperatives. Regional Rural Banks were set up in 1976 as low cost institutions mandated to reach the poorest in the credit-deficient areas of the country. It may not be wrong to say that RRBs are perhaps the only institutions in the Indian context which were created with a specific poverty alleviation—microfinance—mandate. The proportion of borrowings of rural households from institutional sources increased from 8 percent in 1951 to more than 60 percent at present (Table 6). This significant increase in the credit flow from institutional sources gave rise to a strong sense of expectation from the state agencies. But this could not be sustained due to loan defaults by the borrower. End result was a disturbing growth in over dues, which not only hampered the recycling of scarce resources of banks, but also affected profitability and viability of financial institutions.

**Table 6:** Share of Rural Household Debt by Source, India, 1951- 2010 (%)

| Credit Agency | 1951 | 1961 | 1971 | 1981 | 1991 | 2010 |
|---|---|---|---|---|---|---|
| Cooperatives and Commercial Banks | 5.7 | 10.3 | 24.4 | 58.6 | 58.8 | 52.8 |
| Government and other formal sources | 3.1 | 5.5 | 5.5 | 4.6 | 7.5 | 7.8 |
| All Institutional Agencies | 8.8 | 15.8 | 31.7 | 63.2 | 66.3 | 60.6 |
| Professional and Agriculturist Moneylenders | 68.6 | 62.0 | 36.1 | 16.1 | 17.5 | 18.2 |
| Traders | | 7.2 | 8.4 | 3.1 | 2.2 | 4.8 |
| Landlords | | 7.6 | 8.6 | 4.0 | 4.0 | 5.7 |
| Relatives and Friends | 14.4 | 6.4 | 13.1 | 11.2 | 4.6 | 4.4 |
| Other Sources | 8.2 | 0.8 | 2.1 | 2.4 | 2.3 | 4.6 |
| All Non-Institutional Agencies | 91.2 | 84.0 | 68.3 | 36.8 | 30.6 | 37.7 |
| Sources not specified | 0 | 0.2 | 0 | 0 | 3.1 | 1.7 |
| Total | 100 | 100 | 100 | 100 | 100 | 100 |

*Note:* In 1951, landlords and traders are lumped together within "other sources".

*Source:* All-India Rural Credit Survey for 1951, All-India Debt and Investment Survey for the others.

It is found that the share of "exploitative" sources (professional moneylenders, landlords and agriculturist moneylenders) in rural credit fell from an average of over 75 percent in 1951-1961 to less than 25 percent in 1991. The share of formal sector lending more than doubled between 1971 and 1991 but it declines after that due to liberalization policy and financial sector reforms. The object of this narrative is manifested in two facts. They are:

- That right from the time of independence, the concern of development policymakers has been to find ways and means to finance the poor and reduce the burden upon them.
- Between the concern of the policymakers and the quality of the effort, however, there has been a gap. The efforts made were not able to achieve the success envisaged for a variety of reasons mainly, defects in policy design and infirmities in implementation.

The consequences flowing from these facts are:

(i) That the banking system—was not able to internalize lending to the poor as a viable activity but only as a social obligation—something that had to be done because the authorities wanted it.

(ii) In banking language loans to the poor were part of social sector lending and not commercial lending; the poor were not borrowers, they were beneficiaries; poor beneficiaries did not avail of loans they availed of assistance.

(iii) The attitude was that the poor can never be bankable, that commercial principles cannot be applied in lending to the poor and what the poor require are not loans but charity. Once this mindset hardened it became more and more difficult for commercial bankers to accept that lending to the poor could be a viable activity. Traditionally, the formal sector Banking Institutions in India have been serving only the needs of the commercial sector and providing loans for middle and upper income groups. Following risks are generally perceived by the formal sector financial institutions:

- Credit Risk
- High transaction and service cost
- Absence of land tenure for financing housing
- Irregular flow of income due to seasonality
- Lack of tangible proof for assessment of income
- Unacceptable collaterals such as crops, utensils and jewellery.

As far as the formal financial institutions are concerned, there are Commercial Banks, Housing Finance Institutions (HFIs), NABARD, Rural Development Banks (RDBs), Land Development Banks, Land Development Banks, and Co-operative Banks (CBs). As regards the Co-operative Structures, the Urban Cooperative Banks (UCB) or Urban Credit Cooperative Societies (UCCS) are the two primary co-operative financial institutions operating in the urban areas. The Government has taken several initiatives to strengthen the institutional rural credit system. The rural branch network of commercial banks have been expanded and certain policy prescriptions imposed in order to ensure greater flow of credit to agriculture and other preferred sectors. The informal financial sources generally include funds available from family sources or local moneylenders. The local moneylenders charge exorbitant rates, generally ranging from 36 percent to 60 percent interest due to their monopoly in the absence of any other source of credit for nonconventional needs. Thus microfinance in India has emerged in the seventies to provide poor people access to credit and free them from the clutches of moneylenders.

### *4.1.2 Focus on SHG- Bank Linkage Programme*

Microfinance is emerging as a powerful instrument for poverty alleviation in the new economy. In India, Microfinance scene is dominated by Self-Help Group (SHGs)-Bank Linkage Programme as a cost effective mechanism for providing financial services to the "Unreached Poor" which has been successful not only in meeting financial needs of the rural poor women but also strengthen collective self-help capacities of the poor, leading to their empowerment. Rapid progress in SHG formation has now turned into an empowerment movement among women across the country. The SHG-Bank Linkage Programme started as an Action Research Project in 1989. In 1992, the findings led to the setting up of a Pilot Project. The pilot project was designed as a partnership model between three agencies, viz. the SHGs, Banks and Non-Governmental Organizations (NGOs). The SHG Bank Linkage Programme which started in 1992 has grown exponentially over two decades and around 74.62 lakh SHGs are linked to different Banks up to 2011. Of these nearly 65 percent have direct credit link with bank. Out of these 74.62 lakh SHGs 60.98 lakh are women SHGs. The overall progress under microfinance from the period 2006-07 to 2010-11 is presented in Table 7.

**Table 7:** The Overall Progress under Micro-Finance, 2007-08 to 2010-11

| Sl. No. | Particulars | 2007-08 | | 2008-09 | | 2009-10 | | 2010-11 | |
|---|---|---|---|---|---|---|---|---|---|
| | | No. of SHGs (in Lakh) | Amount (Cr.) | No. of SHGs (in Lakh) | Amount (Cr.) | No. of SHGs (in Lakh) | Amount (Cr.) | No. of SHGs (in Lakh) | Amount (Cr.) |
| 1. | Saving of SHGs with Bank | 50.90 | 3785.4 | 61.21 | 5545.62 | 69.53 | 6198.71 | 74.62 | 7016.3 |
| | | | | (22.21) | (46.5) | (13.6) | (11.8) | (7.3) | (13.2) |
| 2. | Bank Loans disbursed to SHGs | 12.28 | 8849.3 | 16.09 | 12253.5 | 15.89 | 14453.3 | 11.96 | 14547.7 |
| | | | | (31.1) | (38.5) | (–1.4) | (17.9) | (–24.6) | (0.01) |
| 3. | Bank Loans Outstanding with SHGs | 36.25 | 16999.9 | 42.24 | 22679.8 | 48.51 | 28038.3 | 47.87 | 31221.17 |
| | | | | (16.5) | (33.4) | (14.8) | (23.6) | (–1.3) | (11.4) |

*Source:* NABARD (2011).
*Note:* Figures in parentheses are percentages.

Table 8 shows that, though savings of number of SHGs with the bank is increasing over the years the growth rate of SHGs in percentage terms is declining from 22.21 in 2009 to 7.3 in 2011. Regarding the amount of savings it has a significant growth during 2008 to 2009 (46.5 percent) but after that it declines. Regarding bank loan disbursement to SHGs it shows a declining trend and in terms of number of SHGs became negative in 2011. The cause may be non-repayment of loan. With regard to bank loan outstanding the growth in amount is declining, which is a good sign.

**Table 8:** Position of Women SHGs (in Lakh)

| Particulars | Year | Total SHGs | Women SHGs | % of Women SHGs to Total SHGs |
|---|---|---|---|---|
| Saving Linked of SHGs | 2010 | 69.53 | 53.1 | 76.37 |
| | 2011 | 74.62 | 60.98 | 81.72 |
| | % Growth | (7.32) | (14.84) | |
| Bank Loans disbursed to SHGs | 2010 | 15.87 | 12.94 | 81.54 |
| | 2011 | 11.96 | 10.17 | 85.03 |
| | % Growth | (–24.64) | (–21.41) | |
| Bank Loans Outstanding with SHGs | 2010 | 48.51 | 38.97 | 80.33 |
| | 2011 | 47.87 | 39.84 | 83.23 |
| | % Growth | (–1.32) | (2.23) | |

*Source:* NABARD (2010).

Table 8 shows that in terms of percentage growth bank loans disbursed to women SHGs is declining from 2010 and negative in 2011. But percentage of women SHGs to total SHGs is showing an increasing trend in all the three cases. Again it is observed from the data (NABARD) that, with regard to amount of saving with banks percentage of women SHGs has increased from 1.46 percent in 2009-10 to 17.8 percent in 2011. But as regards to the growth in amount of loan disbursement to SHGs, the data shows a continuous declining trend from 40.8 percent in 2008-09 to 18.1 percent in 2009-10 and 1.6 percent in 2010-11. By achieving percentage growth in loan outstanding is gradually declining from 39.4 percent in 2008-09 to 13.4 percent in 2010-11, it is showing a positive aspect about microfinance in India.

The SBL approach involves the formation of self-help groups (mainly of women). These women regularly save money that is placed in a local (generally public sector) bank account. Many studies have shown that creation of a safe avenue for savings (on which interest is earned) is an attractive feature of SHGs, which has led to significant promotion of savings (NABARD,

2002, Hashemi et al. 1996; Rajasekhar, 2000a and b). This is supported by the data presented in Table 4 which signifies the growth of women SHGs in relation to total. The SHG has a set of byelaws devised and agreed by the members themselves. These include rules for monthly savings, lending procedures, periodicity and timing of meetings, penalties for default, etc. Meticulous accounts and records are maintained.

The SHG itself functions like a small bank. The group lends money to its members. After a certain period (six months to a year) of disciplined functioning, it becomes entitled to a loan from the bank where it has an account. A number of studies document the positive economic impact of SHGs on indicators such as average value of assets per household, average net income per household, employment and borrowing for income generation activities (Puhazhendi and Badatya, 2002; Harper, 2002). It has been shown that SHGs help inculcate the banking habit in rural women (Varman, 2005).

Through a number of impact analyses it has been proved at the international level that microfinance programmes contribute to the achievement of several impact aspects of the Millennium Development Goals (MDG). The microfinance Linkage Banking Programme (LBP) in India was launched by the National Bank for Agricultural and Rural Development (NABARD) at a national level in 1996. It links Self-Help Groups (SHG) with financial institutions with the aim of providing about one third of the rural poor with improved access to financial services by 2008. Despite the existence of a relatively deep and diversified infrastructure of financial institutions the majority of the rural population in India, especially poorer households and women, do not have an appropriate access to financial services offered through the formal banking sector. This contributes to a low utilisation of the potential for income and employment generating activities with negative consequences for economic growth and the reduction of poverty, which is especially high in rural areas with about 27 percent of the population (= nearly 200 million people). Most Indian banks used to be of the opinion that there was a serious obstacle to linking the poor to the formal banking system, mainly due to the high costs involved in managing small credit amounts without the usual collateral.

The strategy of the LBP of (i) building new and/or strengthening existing SHGs and (ii) encouraging the members of the groups to save on a regular basis and to conduct financial transactions among each other with interest, has been extraordinarily successful and has resulted in the largest microfinance programme worldwide. The rapidly expanding programme is meanwhile covering over one million SHGs (115,000 groups in March 2000) and reached out to about 16 million rural households by March, 2004. More than 35,000 branches of 560 different banks are implementing the programme together with more than 3,000 Self-Help Promoting Institutions (SHPI) in a nationwide approach. The LBP is supported by German Technical Cooperation through the 'Rural Financial System Development Programme'. The focus is on strengthening the quality and viability of financial services under SHG Linkage Banking as well as capacity building through which contributions are made to structural changes in the LBP. In the framework of an assessment study on the impact of the LBP on the MDGs commissioned by the Rural Finance System Development Programme in cooperation with NABARD, the major results of already existing impact studies with relevance for the MDGs were to be summarized as a first step. The review of available reports on the LBP revealed that in the context of this study three impact studies are relevant for summarization providing useful information on impact aspects of several MDGs. Two studies carried out by the Department of Economic Analysis and Research of NABARD in the years 2000 and 2002 investigated mainly the impact of the LBP on incomes, poverty reduction and several aspects of living conditions of SHG member households. The third impact study carried out by the NGO MYRADA in 2002 had its major emphasis on the empowerment of women members of SHGs. Overall 865 members of nearly 300 SHGs located in thirteen states participated in the three studies.

The results of the impact studies indicate that considerable socio-economic benefits are accruing from the fast growing LBP to small-scale farmers, rural micro-entrepreneurs and landless labourers. The improved access of SHG members to sustainable microfinance services as well as the group approach and related human capacity building processes contribute with cross cutting outcomes in several direct and indirect ways to most impact aspects of MDGs 1 to 6. In groups effectively linked to banks at least one basic saving and lending product is generally being offered to SHG members. Most SHG members substantially increase their saving rates. In borrowing patterns a shift can be observed over time from consumption loans to loans for income generating purposes. Increased savings and capital formation improve the self-financing capacities and even out the household's cash flow. Generally higher risk absorption capacities and decreased vulnerability can be assumed. The access to formal financial services also contributes to a strongly reduced dependency on informal moneylenders with positive effects on the reduction of capital costs.

The improved access to financial services benefits households and individuals in maintaining, intensifying and diversifying their economic activities, also in the non-agricultural sector, with positive effects on income and employment generation. According to the overall study results average net income increases of more than ₹ 6,000 or by about 32 percent to nearly ₹ 25,000 are realized per household. With the income increases substantial contributions are made to poverty alleviation. The share of households living below the poverty line is reduced from about 50 percent in the pre-SHG situation to about 31 percent in the post-SHG situation. Thus, nearly 20 percent of all sample SHG members are able to raise their income levels above the poverty line (MDG 1). The financial services and their impact on incomes also raise the capacities of the beneficiaries of the programme to increase their household expenditure for basic needs such as better nutrition (MDG 1) as well as for education (MDG 2) and health (MDGs 4 to 6).

With about 90 percent, a very high share of microfinance clients of the LBP is women. Participation in Linkage Banking SHGs contributes substantially to human capacity building and empowers women to become more self-confident and competent; they are also likely to participate more in family decision-making. It also promotes communication as well as cooperation among group members and improves the capacities for problem solving. The involvement of women in political bodies remains, however, even on village level still on a low level (MDG 3). In terms of various assessed parameters linkage models involving non-government organizations (NGO) as SHPI often perform better than the model 'SHGs formed and financed by banks'. The extent and quality of training seems to partly explain the differential impact across linkage models. Sustainability of the Linkage Banking approach is well established in many SHGs and can be verified through the better performances of older groups than those of the more recently formed groups in the different impact aspects investigated in the studies. There are clear indications that with increasing age of the SHGs the performances in respect of poverty reduction are further improving.

### *4.1.3 Contribution of Financial Institutions in Microfinance Sectoral Growth*

Commercial Banks in India are the major players to deliver microfinance in the form of SHG-Bank Linkage Programme (SBLP) through their vast network of 60000 plus branches in the rural and semi-urban areas. Out of the total loan outstanding (INR 17,000 crore) in this programme as on March 31, 2008, share of Commercial Banks alone stood at 67.5 percent (INR 11,475 crore). Regional Rural Banks and Co-operative Banks share the rest 32.5 percent (NABARD, 2008). Gross loan portfolio of MFIs during the same period was at INR 5954 crore (Sa-Dhan, 2008). The following tables (Tables 9 and 10) can best explain the growth of this sector during the last two years (2006-07 and 2007-08).

**Table 9:** Progress under Microfinance (Loan Outstanding)

(INR in crores)

| Financial Institutions | 2006-07 | 2007-08 | Growth (%) |
|---|---|---|---|
| Commercial Banks (Public sector and Private Sector) | 8760 | 11475 | 31 |
| RRBs and Co-operative Banks | 3606 | 5525 | 53 |
| MFIs (including NBFCs) (Gross Loan) | 3456 | 5954 | 72 |
| Total | 15822 | 22954 | 45 |

*Sources:* 1. NABARD—Microfinance Status 2006-07 and 2007-08.
2. Sa-Dhan—Bharat Microfinance, 2008.

**Table 10:** Progress under Microfinance (Client outreach)

(Number in lakhs)

| Financial Institutions | 2006-07 | 2007-08 | Growth (%) |
|---|---|---|---|
| Commercial Banks (Public sector and Private Sector)—No. of SHGs* | 18.93 | 23.79 | 26 |
| RRBs and Co-operative Banks—No. of SHGs | 10.02 | 12.47 | 24 |
| MFIs (including NBFCs) (Number of Client) | 100 | 114 | 14 |

* Av. number of members of SHGs in Commercial Banks and RRBs. are 14.

*Sources*: 1. NABARD—Microfinance Status 2006-07 and 2007-08.
2. Sa-Dhan—Bharat Microfinance, 2008.

Gross loan portfolios of the MFIs are increasing at a faster rate (72%) than commercial banks (31%) and RRBs (53%) which is reverse in case of client outreach and commercial banks again proved their robustness by increasing their client outreach at a rate of 26 percent on Year-to-Year basis compared to MFIs (14%).

In India, the history of microfinance dates back to establishment of Syndicate Bank in 1921 in private sector. During the early years, Syndicate Bank concentrated on raising micro-deposits in the form of daily/weekly basis and sanctioned micro-loans to its clients for shorter period of time. But microfinance came to limelight only when Dr. Yunus gave it a mass movement in Grameen Bank experiment. Microfinance can be called a novel approach to provide saving and investment facility to the poor around world. Improved access and efficient provision of savings, credit, and insurance facilities in particular can enable the poor to smoothen their consumption, manage their risks better, gradually build their asset base, develop their business, enhance their income earning capacity, and enjoy an improved quality of life. In India, microfinance mainly operates through Self-Help Group (SHGs), Non-Government Organizations (NGOs), and Credit Agencies. It provides poor people with the means to find their own way out of poverty. It put the power squarely in their hands, giving them a larger stake in their own success than one-time donation of food, goods, or cash. The initiatives of Government for poverty alleviation could not succeed to the desired level, may be due to the fact that they do not take cognizance of power of the poor to deal with their own problems. Government tries to help them by way of subsidies and other help but these initiatives hardly reduce their poverty levels and are not a long-term solution.

This section of society if given with guidance, power of capital and productive assets can emerge as the successful entrepreneur. This can easily be achieved by empowering them with power of microcredit. The poor do not have any worthy asset base. Hence they have to be provided with mortgage free loan (Akula, 2008). It has been proved beyond doubt from Grameen Bank experiment. The system of microfinance was introduced about 28 years back with an organization of Grameen Bank in Bangladesh by a famous economist Prof. Mohammed Yunus. He observed that most villagers were unable to obtain credit at reasonable rates. So he began to lend them money from his own pocket, allowing the villagers to buy materials for projects like weaving bamboo tools and making pots (*New York Times*, 1997). Ten years later, Dr. Yunus had set up Grameen Bank as a project in one of the village in Bangladesh in 1976 to assist poor families by providing credit to them. Today microfinance has been widely spread all over the world as an effective tool to poverty eradication. It is found that microfinance has reached about 80 million households and about, 20000 microfinance Institutions are operating in developing countries of Asia, Africa, Europe and Latin America.

As is the case in many other countries, microfinance in India was traditionally operated under a non-profit model. The origins of microfinance in India can be traced back to the early 1970s when the Self-Employed Women's Association of the State of Gujarat created an urban cooperative bank, with the objective of offering banking services to impoverished women employed in rural parts of the state. The industry evolved in the 1980s around self-help groups (SHGs), which are "informal bodies that would provide their clients with much-needed savings and credit services". India's microfinance sector grew rapidly, evolving into a multibillion dollar industry.

Like other countries that have embraced the industry, the foundation of India's microfinance industry rests on the failure of state-owned financial institutions to extend credit to the poor as well as the disappointing performance of government programmes intended to alleviate poverty by providing those in need with resources for self-employment. The industry operates on the assumption that "the core of poverty lies in the realm of the 'economic' and credit (debt) is an effective tool that helps the poor tackle the problem of deprivation, improve their welfare and social acceptance and credibility". In India, "the industry has grown under two different systems of patronage". The first system, linked to the National Bank for Agriculture and Rural Development (NABARD), has the patronage of the state as well as formal banking institutions. A parallel system is funded exclusively through the private sector. Due to the government's lack of involvement; the latter system traditionally functioned outside of any formalized legal or regulatory framework.

#### *4.1.4. Regional inequalities in the SHG-bank linkage programme*

The growth and progress has shown wide regional disparities. The Southern region has been commanding the progress as indicated by the following Table 11. Southern region accounted for 22,80,911 SHGs until 31 March 2009. Total loan outstanding for the region was ₹ 1551.5 million that constitutes 65.8 percent of the total loan outstanding, which is more than the combined share of all the regions that accounts for 34.2 percent.

If criterion of average loan is taken, analysis shows that average loan per SHG in southern region is ₹ 65,378, which is more than that of in any other region. As far as other regions are concerned, Eastern region seems to have been performing well, having 22.1 percent of total SHGs in India, which is almost equal to combined total share of rest of the regions (Excluding southern region). Progress of the regions in this context can be better indicated by attaching population of the region to the number of the SHGs in that region. The last column of the table shows number of SHGs per lakh (100 thousands) population,

**Table 11:** Region-wise spread and growth of SHGs (as on 31 March 2009)

| Regions | | | | Share (%) in total | | |
|---|---|---|---|---|---|---|
| | No. of SHGs | Loan outstanding to SHG (₹) | Average loan per SHG (₹) | No. of SHG | Loan of SHG (₹)s | SHGs per Lakh population |
| Northerm | 166511 | 67892 | 40773 | 3.9 | 3.0 | 289 |
| N. Eastern | 117812 | 49931 | 42381 | 4.2 | 2.2 | 615 |
| Eastern | 933489 | 302300 | 32384 | 22.1 | 13.3 | 543 |
| Central | 332116 | 204533 | 61585 | 7.9 | 9.0 | 279 |
| Western | 393499 | 155115 | 39419 | 9.3 | 6.8 | 535 |
| Southern | 2280911 | 1491214 | 65378 | 53.99 | 65.8 | 1217 |
| All India | 4224338 | 2267984 | 53689 | 100.00 | 100.00 | 596 |

*Source*: NABARD, status of microfinance in India 2008-09.

which again shows the dominance of the Southern region. It has 1,271 SHGs, even the national level average is less than half the average of the Southern region and the average of the Central region is almost one-fifth of the average of the southern region. The progress of other regions is not equitable, all regions other than Southern and Central account for even less than 10 percent on both the counts, i.e. number of SHGs and loan to SHGs. This shows the inadequacy of both the spread of SHGs and the credit flow to these regions.

The discussion is further extended by analyzing interstate aspects in the light of above analysis. Variations are visible at this level also as shown in the following table. In Table 12 apart from percentage share, the spread and quantum of finance are taken as the indicators of progress of the SHG-bank linkage programme. Spread is measured as number of SHGs per lakh population and finance as average loan (in thousand ₹) to SHGs. Southern region which is ranked the most successful region shows Andhra Pradesh (1,691 SHGs) has almost double the number of SHGs than as Karnataka (867 SHGs). In eastern region also Odisha (1,204 SHGs) has noticed remarkable progress which keeps it in the group of the most successful states with Andhra Pradesh, Kerala, etc. Other states in the same region like Bihar and Jharkhand have witnessed a poor coverage. States in the northern region have remained least covered states where no state has even one percent share of the total SHGs at India level. Similarly, in northeastern region the progress has been led by Assam and Tripura while other states register minimal progress in this region.

*4.1.4.1 SGHs spread in the light of prevailing poverty*: The prime objective of SHG-Bank linkage programme was to provide the poor with enhanced access to the banking; these poor are landless labourers, artisans, marginal farmers and people like hawkers and small vendors. In the light of prevailing poverty SHG-bank, linkage programme can be better analyzed. Table 12 links the spread of poverty and SHGs in the various regions. It is quite evident that the progress of SHGs is not satisfactory in the Eastern and Central region where despite a higher poverty ratio and higher portion of total poor, the share of the region is not very high. In the Central region particularly, it is far below what is required. The Southern region has the lion's share in the spread of SHGs. Northern and northern regions are better off, having a comparable share as shown by the almost equal proportion of total poor and total SHGs in the regions.

**Table 12:** Spread of Poverty and SHGs in Different Regions

| Regions | Proportion of total poor | Proportion of total SHGs |
|---|---|---|
| Northern | 7.4 | 6.6 |
| North Eastern | 2.6 | 3.4 |
| Eastern | 29.0 | 19.3 |
| Central | 32.1 | 11.7 |
| Western | 13.1 | 10.8 |
| Southern | 15.3 | 48.2 |
| All India | 100.0 | 100.0 |

*Source*: RBI Bulletin, 2009.

Another indicator used is the correlation between SHG spread that is measured in terms of SHG per lakh (100 thousands) population and poverty ratio shows a negative co-relation of –0.22 shows that the SHG movement is not commensurate with high prevailing poverty. Rather the movement has remained successful in states where incidence of poverty is comparatively less. Figure 2 shows SHG movement in the context of poor in the regions. Only Southern and North Eastern regions recorded equitable progress of SHG-bank linkage programme, and other regions showed sluggish progress. This is another evidence of the regional disparities in the bank linkage programme. The implication that emanates from the above discussion is that there is considerable disparity amongst the various regions of India with respect to SHG-bank linkage programme. Some regions are really lagging behind and more efforts should be put forth in these regions so that objective of 100 percent financial inclusion can be achieved.

### *4.1.5 Source of Funds of the MFIs*

Microfinance institutions (MFIs) have three main sources to fund their growth: debt, equity, and deposits (for those allowed to mobilize deposits). In this review, we will focus on the role of debt financing and our current knowledge about this source of funds for MFIs. For the past three years, debt comprised over one-third of the total funding of MFIs, increasing by 7 billion USD during the same period. However, by 2010, the share of debt shrank and volumes remained constant as investors retreated from markets that experienced internal crises as well as those affected by the global financial crisis.

Figure 2 shows the funding structure of MFIs according to their region and charter type. In most regions debt represented at least one-third of the funding sources of MFIs. NBFIs and especially NGOs are reliant on debt as a source of funding since deposit mobilization for these institutional types tends to be more limited, with the exception of Africa. The category/variable-wise variability of the Funding structure of MFIs in the region during 2010 is shown in Fig. 3.

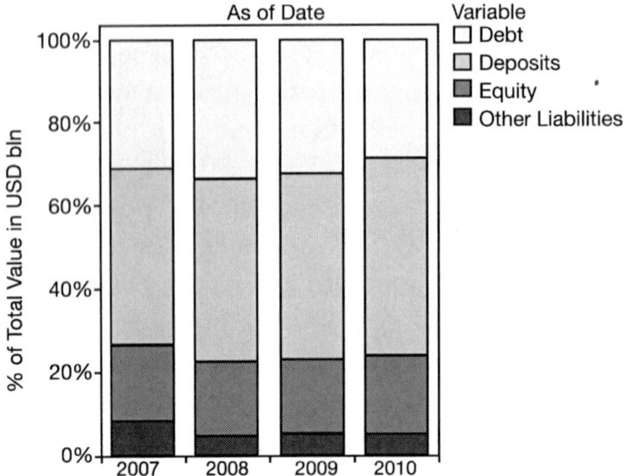


*Source*: MIX Market, 2007-2010. See data in Cross-Market Analysis.

**Fig. 2:** Funding Structure Evolution, 2007-10

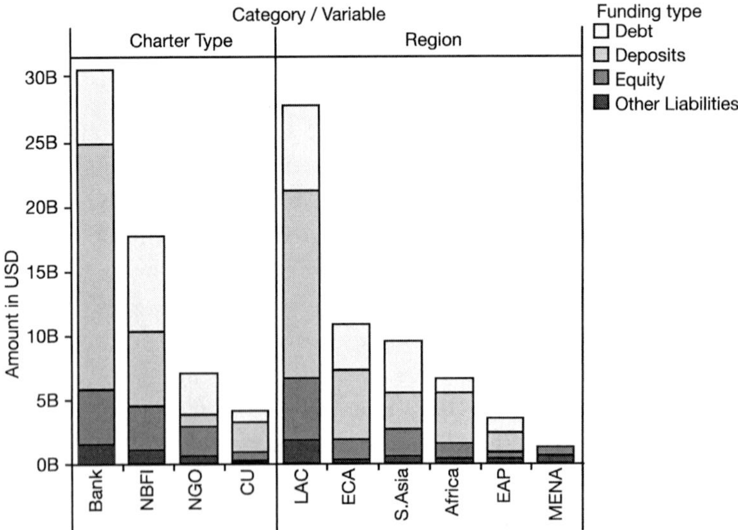


*Source*: MIX Market, 2010. EAP = East Asia and the Pacific, ECA = Eastern Europe and Central Asia, LAC = Latin America and the Caribbean, MENA = Middle East and North Africa, S. Asia = South Asia.

**Fig. 3:** Funding Structure of MFIs by Region, 2010

Table 13 shows the top 20 countries by the amount of their outstanding debt as of 2010 (in USD). MFIs operating in these markets reached 84 percent of all borrowers reporting to MIX Market in 2010. India and Bangladesh alone accounted for 59 percent of the global borrower base. While in some countries, like Bangladesh and Peru, much of this outreach as enabled by deposit mobilization, for MFIs operating in countries with low deposit volumes (such as India, Mexico, Morocco) debt financing played a key role in expanding access to credit for the poor.

**Table 13:** Top 20 Markets by Amount of Outstanding Debt as per the MIX Market data 2010

| Country | Debt (min. USD) | Deposits (min. USD) | Equity (min. USD) | Total Borrowers (thous.) |
|---|---|---|---|---|
| India | 4,044 | 247 | 1,196 | 30,318 |
| Peru | 2,158 | 5,330 | 1,234 | 3,325 |
| Mexico | 1,514 | 139 | 960 | 5,385 |
| Colombia | 1,135 | 3,991 | 1,080 | 1,491 |
| Brazil | 986 | 322 | 353 | 954 |
| Ecuador | 789 | 994 | 265 | 729 |
| Chile | 701 | 642 | 145 | 241 |
| Bangladesh | 681 | 2,028 | 885 | 19,662 |
| Bolivia | 568 | 2,019 | 363 | 918 |
| Azerbaijan | 585 | 440 | 228 | 354 |
| South Africa | 548 | 1,031 | 502 | 4 |
| Morocco | 512 | – | 128 | 706 |
| Bosnia and Herzegovina | 463 | 150 | 151 | 273 |
| Cambodia | 461 | 952 | 238 | 1,239 |
| Armenia | 384 | 197 | 201 | 247 |
| Serbia | 363 | 489 | 134 | 113 |
| Malaysia | 329 | 57 | 74 | 242 |
| Kenya | 318 | 1,528 | 402 | 1,146 |
| Mongolia | 291 | 1,232 | 131 | 390 |
| Philippines | 289 | 439 | 158 | 2,901 |
| Total | 17,150 | 22,228 | 8,826 | 70,638 |
| Total on MIX Market | 21,342 | 30,072 | 11,504 | 83,433 |

*Source*: MIX Market Database, 2010.

*4.1.5.1. Types of actors provide Debt financing to Retail Microfinance Institutions*: The importance of debt financing for MFIs raises a number of questions about how MFIs fund their operations. What types of actors lend money to MFIs? What instruments are used to finance them? How prevalent is cross-border funding? In which countries can MFIs access local market debt and why? How much do MFIs pay to borrow and what are the terms of their loans? How have funding flows, terms and costs changed now that investors have adjusted to higher risk in the aftermath of the global financial crisis and some leading markets' internal crises (e.g. Bosnia and Herzegovina, India, and Morocco)?

To answer these questions, MIX began collecting data from individual MFIs on the lender, origin, pricing, maturity and outstanding amount of each of their non-deposit liabilities with external parties, in 2007. MFIs have been reporting these data for four years (2007-2010), which gives us a unique opportunity to gauge how investors have adjusted to the changing nature of the microfinance industry. The data collected comprises a representative sample from all MFIs that report financial indicators to MIX (Table 14).

This data is publicly accessible via the Funding Structure Reports that can be found in the Profile and Reports section on MIX Market. The Funding Structure Reporting tools allow users to filter and group the data in a variety of combinations in order to answer questions about the funding landscape in a given region, for a type of lender or a microfinance institution or about the price and terms of debt. Furthermore, users can print, share and download the results of their queries.

Having a lens through which to analyze the hundreds of counterparties that lend to retail MFIs, we can now see which are the most active in the industry. Using the Funding Structure Reports, we see that in 2010 financial institutions provided the bulk of funding at 5.7 billion US$ and comprised 38 percent of total debt financing, followed by *DFIs* and *funds* at 2.8 and 3.3 billion US$ or 19 and 22 percent of the total, respectively. *Government* and *other* sources (including NGOs, foundations

**Table 14:** MIX Funders Typology

| Name | Subtype | Definition | Examples |
|---|---|---|---|
| Development Finance Institution (DFI) | None | Financial institutions owned by a government or governments and that raise private captital to finance projects with development objectives | IFC, SIDBI |
| Government | Multi- and Bilateral Development Agency | Bilateral or multilateral aid agencies, owned by government | JICA, UNCDF |
| Government | Development Programme | Government or other public programme with development objectives. | USAID-Tijara, IDESI Nacional, CAMFA |
| Government | Government Agency/ Programme | The administration, departments, or agencies of any sovereign entity | Ministry of Finance Luxembourg, BmZ Deutsch-GEO |
| Government | Regulator | A domestic central bank | Central Bank of BiH, IAS |
| Financial Institution | Commercial Bank | Bank or other regulated financial institution where private entities are majority shareholders | Citibank Nicaragua, Banplus |
| Financial Institution | Cooperative Society | Financial Institution owned by its members, not external shareholders | ALTERFIN, Consorzio Etimos |
| Financial Institution | Public Bank | Bank or other regulated financial institution where the government is a majority shareholder | United Bank of India, Republic of Srpska Investment-Development Bank |
| Fund | None | Professionally managed type of collective investment scheme that pools money from many investors | Dexia Microcredit Fund, Minlam Microfinance Fund, Oikocredit |
| Other | Private Corporation | Registered legal entities. The category does not include governments, non-profits, funds or financial institutions | Genesis Steel |
| Other | Individuals | A person or persons | |
| Other | NGO | Non-governmental organization | CORDAID, CARE |
| Other | Foundation | A non-profit corporation or other non-profit entity | ECLOF, FWWB, Hivos |

*Source*: MIX Market Database, 2010.

and individuals) funded MFIs with 1.7 billion US$ and 1.2 billion US$. It is important, however, to take the regional context into consideration when analyzing the funding landscape of the microfinance industry. For example, 47 percent of funding provided by financial institutions was concentrated in South Asia, driven primarily by the Indian market (Funding from financial institutions in India was 2.36 billion US$ in 2010, where legislation prohibits foreign investment and requires Indian banks to invest in "priority sectors" for development, with microfinance serving as one such sector. In contrast, cross-border funding from DFIs and funds is concentrated primarily in ECA and LAC.

*4.1.5.1 Cross-border versus Local Financing*: The source of funds—*cross-border* or *local*—has its own implications for the structure, pricing and terms of loans. Local funding may come from government agencies, which have a development goal and thus provide subsidized loans, or it can be supplied by local banks, which require commercial returns. In some countries (India, Uzbekistan, Ethiopia) local funding may be the main option for direct financing of MFIs if restrictions exist for foreign investment (though local apex bodies may be receiving their funding from cross-border funds). In other markets, local funding may not be available—for example where banks are competing with MFIs for clients and thus unwilling to finance MFIs (such as for NBFIs in Azerbaijan), or where local funding costs may be prohibitively high for many MFIs (various countries in ECA).

Cross-border funding, in turn, may be offered at lower rates than local funding but is mainly disbursed in US$ or EUR, which may lead to foreign exchange losses for MFIs (or their clients). In order to assess the funding situation in different markets, first we need to understand who the providers are. What are their primary objectives for lending (commercial, social, mixed, etc.), who are their constituents (taxpayers, institutional or individual investors, etc.), and are they cross-border or local providers of funds? In 2010 alone, MFIs had debt outstanding from close to a thousand different individual counterparties. These lenders ranged from small local NGOs to large international funds, from government programmes to local banks. MIX classified each counterparty with the goal of understanding the major sources of debt financing for MFIs, and establishing a baseline for analyzing trends in future years. The categories allow for analysis of integration into local financial markets, the role of specialized funds, and the support of government and development financing in funding MFI portfolios opportunities and constraints that MFIs face in terms of the cost, terms and structure of their loans, we need to assess the origin of their debt.

In 2010, 40 percent of debt financing was from cross-border investors, while local lenders provided the remaining 60 percent. Figure 4 shows a breakdown of cross-border versus local funding for different MFI charter types and regions. The majority of local funding was concentrated in two regions—South Asia and LAC. In South Asia, results are influenced by India as mentioned earlier. In Latin America, five markets—Peru, Mexico, Colombia, Brazil and Bolivia captured 87 percent of the total funding from sources headquartered in that continent. As the oldest and most mature region globally, LAC MFIs have much greater access to local commercial funding than peers in other regions. Of the local lenders in LAC, financial institutions are most active, followed by local DFIs. In Africa, financial institutions comprised the bulk of local lending, while funds were the most active among cross-border lenders. In MENA local lenders captured 77 percent of all funding going to MFIs, but this was mostly due to one large market—Morocco—where local commercial banks and one public bank, captured 80 percent of all local lending in the region. Funding in ECA was primarily cross-border, with funds and DFIs providing 76 percent of all funding.

NGOs and NBFIs were primarily funded through local financing—a result driven again by NBFIs and NGOs in South Asia and LAC. In contrast banks had more cross-border funding as the results were mostly influenced by banks in ECA that access foreign capital.

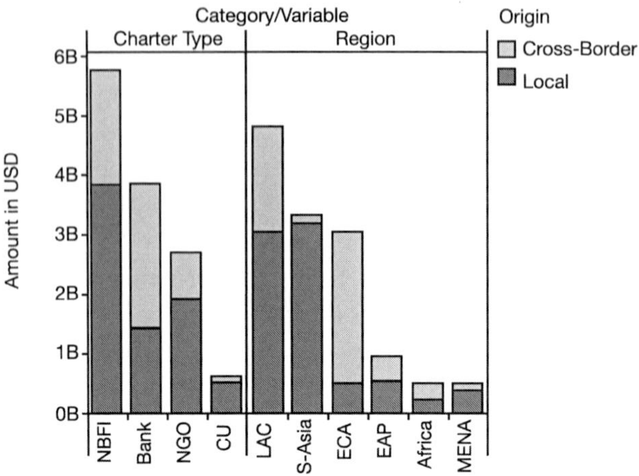


*Source*: MIX Funding Structure Data, 2010.

**Fig. 4:** Local and Cross-Border Funding by Charter Type and Region, 2010

The importance of local funding is also evidenced by its increasing role in the overall funding structure of MFIs. For a balanced data set of MFIs reporting in the period 2008-2010, local funding increased by 2.3 bn. US$, while cross-border funding decreased by 174 mn. US$. Figure 4 shows the trends in local and cross-border funding for the years 2008-10 by region. Most interestingly, in LAC cross-border and local funding were at the same level in 2008 but by 2010 funding from local sources almost doubled while foreign financing leveled off. The biggest drivers behind local funding growth in LAC were the markets in Peru, Mexico and Brazil, where commercial and public banks more than doubled their financing since 2008. In South Asia, local financing grew rapidly between 2008 and 2009, but there was a visible slowdown in 2010, due to the crisis in Andhra Pradesh in India and funders' retreat from the sector. In ECA, there was little change in funding observed in the past three years, consistent with the region's sluggish growth. The small decrease in cross-border funding was due to the significant shrinking of the ECA's biggest market—Bosnia and Herzegovina.

Initially, most of the MFIs were being sponsored by either donor agencies or National Bank for Agriculture and Rural

Development (NABARD), and they are often NGOs and not-for-profit organizations. As mentioned in section 3 that with the increase in the importance of this specialised financial service sector, NBFCs, Section 25 companies MACS and NGO turned MFIs entered as service providers in a big way, which made this sector more vibrant. The major source of funds for microfinance activities in India are the commercial banks but of late the VCs and PE investors are also investing in a big way to this sector. The outstanding loan to MFIs by the Commercial Banks in India was INR 1584.50 crore as on March 31, 2007, which increased by 73.5 percent to INR 2748.85 crore as on March 31, 2008 (NABARD, 2007-08). Flow of Venture Capital in this sector during 2007-08 gone up to 8 times as compared to 2004-05 and foreign capital investment in microfinance in the form of private equity (PE) has been constantly increased between 2004 and 2008 and during the last quarter of 2008-09, three big MFIs of India mobilized around INR 500 crores (Microfinance World, 2009). This is due to the fact that MF sector could prove their potential.

## 6. Constraints in Microfinance Implementation in India

### *6.1 Problems faced by Borrowers*

*1. Coercion*

One of the most important moral issues being raised in relation to microfinance is that of coercion. After 54 people killed themselves in the state of Andhra Pradesh in October 2010, Indian authorities placed microfinance institutions (MFI) under a microscope, and drafted new rules the MFI companies must follow. The farmers were reportedly deep in debt to microfinance institutions (MFIs). "Microfinance institutions charge exorbitant interest rates. The poor are driven to take their own lives because of their burden of debt and the brutal methods used to call in the loans", the former Chief Minister of Andhra Pradesh, India once said.

*2. Brutal and Aggressive Debt-Collection Tactics*

"The people calling in the loans are often not aware of the code of conduct of the MFIs". Many of the MFIs have been resort to brutal methods for collection of debt from these borrowers. News items like the one below are quite common in India.

*3. Joint Microfinance*

Joint micro-loans are granted to a group of people who are jointly responsible for repaying the loan. Individual failures to pay (due to illness or a "bad week") are avoided and group pressure serves as a strong incentive in ensuring responsible behaviour by making loans to individuals within a lending circle. The individuals meet regularly, ostensibly creating a self-help group. In reality, all the borrowers in the group are responsible for making the loan repayment if a member defaults, so peer pressure is a very strong factor. However, in case of default either due to business failures, unproductive expenditure or greed to consume more, all members are troubled.

*4. High Interest Rates*

Many in the urban centres would commit suicide if the banks start charging us 24 percent rate of interest. Even at 8.5 percent rate of interest, those who have drawn housing loans, find it difficult to make monthly EMI payments. Imagine the stress and threat under which the poor in the rural areas are being made to borrow at 24 percent rate of interest. Whatever the justification for charging 24 percent rate of interest, how can human beings exploit a hungry stomach in the name of a successful business model?

*5. Programme not aimed at lifting people out of poverty*

Microfinance serves not to lift people out of poverty but, assist those near or slightly above the poverty line. Money is given to those people who have a possibility of returning the principle amount. This leads to the fact that lending money to these people is feasible and sustainable, while lending to the poorest of the poor is not.

## 6.2 Problems faced by Lenders

*1. Sustainability*

The first challenge relates to sustainability. MFI model is comparatively costlier in terms of delivery of financial services.

An analysis of 36 leading MFIs by Jindal and Sharma shows that 89 percent MFIs sample were subsidy dependent and only 9 were able to cover more than 80 percent of their costs. This is partly explained by the fact that while the cost of supervision of credit is high, the loan volumes and loan size is low. It has also been commented that MFIs pass on the higher cost of credit to their clients who are 'interest insensitive' for small loans but may not be so as loan sizes increase. It is, therefore, necessary for MFIs to develop strategies for increasing the range and volume of their financial services.

*2. Lack of Capital*

The second area of concern for MFIs, which are on the growth path, is that they face a paucity of owned funds. This is a critical constraint in their being able to scale up. Many of the MFIs are socially oriented institutions and do not have adequate access to financial capital. As a result they have high debt equity ratios. Presently, there is no reliable mechanism in the country for meeting the equity requirements of MFIs. The IPO issue by Mexico based 'Compartamos' was not accepted by purists as they thought it defied the mission of an MFI. The IPO also brought forth the issue of valuation of an MFI.

*3. Financial Service Delivery*

Another challenge faced by MFIs is the inability to access supply chain. This challenge can be overcome by exploring synergies between microfinance institutions with expertise in credit delivery and community mobilization and businesses operating with production supply chains such as agriculture. The latter players who bring with them an understanding of similar client segments, ability to create micro-enterprise opportunities and willingness to nurture them, would be keen on directing microfinance to such opportunities. This enables MFIs to increase their client base at no additional costs. Those businesses that procure from rural India such as agriculture and dairy often identify finance as a constraint to value creation. Such businesses may find complementarities between an MFI's skills in management of credit processes and their own strengths in supply chain management.

ITC Limited, with its strong supply chain logistics, rural presence and an innovative transaction platform, the e-choupal, has started exploring synergies with financial service providers including MFIs through pilots with vegetable vendors and farmers. Similarly, large FIs such as Spandana foresee a larger role for themselves in the rural economy ably supported by value creating partnerships with players such as Mahindra and Western Union Money Transfer. The ITC has initiated a pilot project called 'pushcarts scheme' along with BASIX (a microfinance organization in Hyderabad). Under this pilot, it works with twenty women head load vendors selling vegetables of around 10-15 kgs per day. BASIX extends working capital loans of ₹ 10,000, capacity building and business development support to the women. ITC provides support through supply chain innovations by:

1. Making the Choupal Fresh stores available to the vendors, this avoids the hassle of bargaining and unreliability at the traditional mandis (local vegetable markets).
2. Continuously experimenting to increase efficiency, augmenting incomes and reducing energy usage across the value chain. For instance, it has forged a partnership with National Institute of Design (NID), a pioneer in the field of design education and research, to design user-friendly pushcarts that can reduce the physical burden.
3. Taking lessons from the pharmaceutical and telecom sector to identify technologies that can save energy and ensure temperature control in push carts in order to maintain quality of the vegetables throughout the day. The model augments the incomes of the vendors from around ₹ 30-40 per day to an average of ₹ 150 per day. From an environmental point of view, push carts are much more energy efficient as opposed to fixed format retail outlets.

## 7. Financial Inclusions Effected through Microfinance Services

The responsibility of meeting the credit needs in the rural areas of India was entrusted primarily with the cooperative sector and later to the commercial banks. One of the major objectives of the nationalization of major commercial banks in 1969/1980 was to improve the flow of formal institutional credit to rural households. Although these measures were ambitious and laudable, bank credit did not reach the poor people in adequate quantum. The financial sector reforms begun in 1992 have been systematically moving away from the social objective of the banking sector. The formal financial sector in India is shifting its focus from "mass banking" to "super-class banking". Though banking sector has witnessed tremendous changes in recent periods in terms of technological advancements, internet banking, online money transfers, etc., "financial exclusion" is a reality. It is in this context that the term "financial inclusion" gains importance and it is defined as the process of ensuring access to financial services and timely and adequate credit needed by vulnerable groups such as weaker sections and low income groups at an affordable cost. In countries with a large rural population like India, financial exclusion has a geographic and social dimension. Geographic exclusion is exposed through inaccessibility; distances and lack of proper infrastructure.

Building an inclusive financial sector has gained growing global recognition bringing to the fore the need for development strategies that touch all lives, instead of a select few. The overall strategy for financial inclusion, especially amongst the poor and disadvantaged segments of the population should comprise ways and means to effect improvements within the existing formal credit delivery mechanism, as well as an evolution of new models for extending outreach, and a leverage on technology solutions to facilitate large scale inclusion. Only two to five percent of the 500 million poorest households in the world have access to institutional credit. Of which, women receive a disproportionately small share of credit from formal banking institutions. The Women's Self-Help Group movement is bringing about a profound transformation in rural areas of India. Microfinance Institutions (MFIs) play a significant role in facilitating inclusion, as they are uniquely positioned in reaching out to the rural poor. Many of them operate in a limited geographical area, have a greater understanding of the issues specific to the rural poor, enjoy greater acceptability amongst the rural poor and have flexibility in operations providing a level of comfort to their clientele.

In recent periods, banking sector witnessed tremendous changes in terms of technological advancements, internet banking, online money transfers, etc. But it is a reality that access to such technology is restricted only to certain segments of the society. Indeed, some trends, such as increasingly sophisticated customer segmentation technology have led to restricted access to financial services for some groups. There is a growing divide, with an increased range of personal finance options for a segment of high and upper middle income population and a significantly large section of the population who lack access to even the most basic banking services. This is termed "financial exclusion". These people, particularly, those living on low incomes, cannot access mainstream financial products such as bank accounts, credit, remittances and payment services, financial advisory services, insurance facilities, etc.

Since formal credit institutions rarely lend to the poor, special institutional arrangements become necessary to extend credit to those who have no collateral to offer. Microfinance, by providing small loans and savings facilities to those who have been excluded from commercial financial services, has been promoted as a key strategy for reducing poverty in all its forms by agencies all over the world. Microcredit has been defined as "programmes that provide credit for self-employment and other financial and business services (including savings and technical assistance) to very poor persons" (Micro Credit Summit, 1997). Nowadays, microfinance represents something more than micro-credit—it also refers to savings, insurance, pawns and remittances, in sum to a much wider range of financial services (Tankha, 1999). In most cases, micro-credit programmes offer a combination of services and resources to their clients in addition to usual credit for self-employment. Also, this is an effort to provide a bridge between formal financial markets and the informal groups in the formal microfinance initiatives.

The basic idea of microfinance is that poor people are ready and are willing to pull themselves out of poverty if given access to economic inputs. The need for informality in credit delivery and easy access is demonstrated by the fact that Self-Help Groups (SHGs) and Microfinance Institutions (MFIs) constitute the fastest growing segment in recent years in reaching out to small borrowers. Microfinance is a new development in which Indian institutions have acquired considerable expertise and where up-scaling holds great promise both to expand the nature of financial services offered to micro-enterprises and to make these the springboard for entrepreneurial development (Planning Commission, 2006).

The SHG movement is bringing about a profound transformation in rural areas of India. MFIs play a significant role in facilitating inclusion, as they are uniquely positioned in reaching out to the rural poor. Many of them operate in a limited geographical area, have a greater understanding of the issues specific to the rural poor, enjoy greater acceptability amongst the rural poor and have flexibility in operations providing a level of comfort to their clientele. It is roughly estimated that there are about 1,000 NGO-MFIs and more than 20 Company facilitating the activities in all over India. There are today over 22 lakh such groups linked with banks.

The objective of the country is to enroll at least 50 percent of all rural women in India as members of SHGs over Microfinance has been recognized as an important tool in connecting the unbanked population to mainstream finance. The clearance of the draft document of the Microfinance Institutions (Development and Regulation) Bill by the Union Cabinet is an indication of the Government's faith in the sector. The RBI and NABARD have supported the propagation of microfinance considerably through the SHG-Bank Linkage Programme (SBLP) and have designed incentives to support microfinance institutions in forming Joint Liability Groups (JLGs). Commercial Banks are incentivised to lend to Microfinance institutions (MFIs) by placing MFIs under priority sector lending (PSL). PSL requirements mandate banks to ensure that 40 percent of their aggregate net banking credit goes to stipulated sectors that are considered important to foster financial inclusion.

## *7.1 Financial Inclusion: Government Promoted Initiatives*

Providing financial access to the poor by linking them with banks has always been an important priority of the Government of India (GoI). Financial inclusion, defined as the "process of ensuring access to appropriate financial products and services needed by vulnerable groups at an affordable cost in a fair and transparent manner by mainstream institutional players", is regarded as the most critical aspect of inclusive growth and development. The Government of India (GoI) and the Reserve Bank of India (RBI) have traditionally played a large role in establishing banks and other financial infrastructure in order to increase the poor's access to quality financial products. Banks and other apex financial institutions such as National Bank for Agriculture and Rural Development (NABARD) and Small Industries Development Bank of India (SIDBI) have supported and aided the government in a variety of ways towards this end. In spite of that, an estimated 40 percent of the population in India is still unbanked, implying that the existing financial system is yet to offer uncomplicated and affordable financial products that suit the requirements of poor and low-income clients and bring them into the formal financial sector.

This factsheet will highlight several financial inclusion measures taken by the Government of India and the RBI and outline their efforts and achievements as well as the obstacles faced by each initiative. Microfinance has been recognized as an important tool in connecting the unbanked population to mainstream finance. The clearance of the draft document of the Microfinance Institutions (Development and Regulation) Bill by the Union Cabinet is an indication of the Government's faith in the sector. The RBI and NABARD have supported the propagation of microfinance considerably through the SHG-Bank Linkage Programme (SBLP) and have designed incentives to support microfinance institutions in forming Joint Liability Groups (JLGs). Commercial Banks are incentivised to lend to Microfinance institutions (MFIs) by placing MFIs under priority sector lending (PSL). PSL requirements mandate banks to ensure that 40 percent of their aggregate net banking credit goes to stipulated sectors that are considered important to foster financial inclusion.

Self-Help Group Bank Linkage Programme (SBLP): Designed and developed by the NABARD to promote and link Self-Help Groups (SHGs) to banks in 1992, NABARD still supports this initiative by refinancing and promoting stakeholders such as banks, Non-Government Organizations (NGOs), and other government agencies and departments. As on March 2011, NABARD has provided ₹ 25.45 billions to banks covering their lending to SHGs. Around 4.82 million SHGs received loans from banks with an outstanding amount of ₹ 306.27 billion while 7.54 million SHGs have been linked to the banking system.

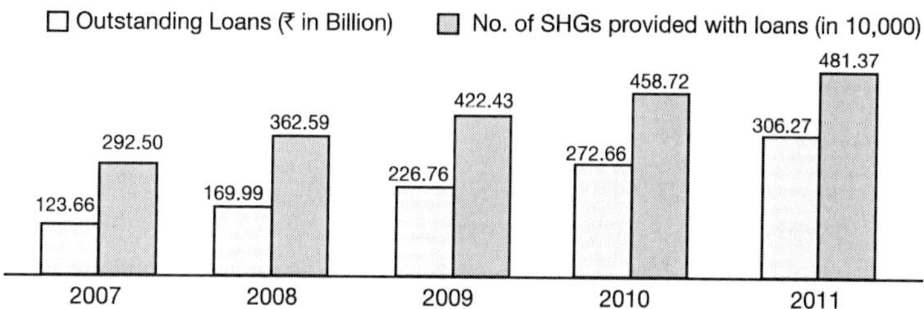


**Fig. 5:** Growth Trends in SBLP

*Source*: State of the Microfinance Sector, 2011.

Despite this growth in the number of SHGs being linked with banks (Fig. 5), it is reported that there is almost no growth in loans in real terms as the average disbursed loan per SHG has declined in real terms from ₹ 84,500 in 2010 to ₹ 81,000 in 20117. In addition, it is also reported that compared to the previous year, the SBLP had underperformed during the year 2011-12.

*Induction of SHG-2:* NABARD has recently acknowledged SHG's inadequate outreach in many regions in recent years, delays in opening of savings accounts and disbursement of loans, and non-approval of repeat loans even when first loans are repaid on time. This has motivated NABARD to prepare a strategy to revitalize the SHG movement leading with the induction of SHG-2 model. While the primary function of the SHG-2 model continues to be the promotion of savings-led credit product, some additional features have been added such as.

- Voluntary savings apart from compulsory savings,
- Allowing the sanction of a cash credit / overdraft system of lending for SHGs for a longer operational tenure, and
- Graduating selected members of the group that have entrepreneurship potential into a joint liability groups for borrowing larger amounts.

*Women SHGs Development Fund*: The Union Budget 2011-2012 has proposed to set up a "Women's SHG's Development Fund" with a corpus of ₹ 500 crore. The GoI created this fund to empower women and promote their SHGs and it is operated by NABARD through its two major microfinance funds- Financial Inclusion Fund (FIF) and the Financial Inclusion Technology Fund (FITF).

The FIF primarily supports capacity building inputs to service providers, resource centres, training institutes, financial institutions as well as promoting and nurturing SHGs. This fund will also support pilot projects for development of innovative products, processes and prototypes for financial inclusion. Likewise, FITF promotes technology innovation and solutions as well as research relating to technological interventions for financial inclusion.

### *7.2 RBI's Financial Inclusion Drive*

*No-Frills Accounts (NFAs)*: In the year 2005, the RBI, in its annual policy statement expressed the concerns of banking policies and practices that "tend to exclude rather than attract vast sections of the population". The RBI urged banks to review their existing practices to align with the objective of financial inclusion by providing all "unbanked" households in a district, with savings account by opening "no-frills" account (NFAs) with nil or very low minimum balance. While opening such bank accounts, banks are asked to relax their Know Your Customer (KYC) norms for individuals who do not foresee having more than ₹ 50,000 in all their combined accounts and whose annual total borrowing will not exceed more than ₹ 100,000. In addition, the RBI also announced a targeted drive for financial inclusion throughout the country, wherein each household would receive one 'no frills' bank account.

A study by CMF-IFMR found that in Cuddalore, Tamil Nadu, 25 percent of households remained excluded even after full inclusion was declared. The study also found that 72 percent of the accounts had zero or near zero balance even after a year. Likewise, another CMF-IFMR study reports that the 100 percent inclusion drive in Gulbarga district, Karnataka did not have any major impacts on excluded households as one-third of the households were without bank accounts even after the drive.

Nevertheless, the RBI has continued its efforts of financial inclusion. At the end of the year 2010-11, 74.4 million NFAs had been opened by the banking system with the outstanding savings balance in these accounts being ₹ 65.6 billion. It is also reported that banks opened 4.2 million overdraft accounts in select NFAs. However, there is still a big question on whether these accounts are actively used by account holders as the number of NFAs is taken to be an indicator of the extent of a bank's commitment to the inclusion plan, rather than usage of the accounts themselves. A study conducted by CMF-IFMR in Gulbarga found that, as observed in the Cuddalore study as well, 68 percent households had opened NFAs to receive MGNREGS wages. Likewise, in Andhra Pradesh, CMF-IFMR study found that 79 percent of accounts were opened either to receive government benefits (such as MGNREGS) or to increase the chances of receiving a loan. Another study conducted by CMF-IFMR found that the low usage of NFAs is due to narrow scope of NFAs such as caps on maximum balance, limited numbers of transactions in a month, etc. The study suggests that services offered under NFAs should be broadened to improve their usability.

*General Purpose Credit Cards (GCC) and Kisan Credit Cards (KCC)*: The RBI has advised all Scheduled Commercial Banks (SCBs), including Regional Rural banks (RRBs) to provide General purpose Credit Card (GCC) facility at their rural and semi-urban branches. The credit card is provided based on the assessment of income and cash flow of the household similar to that prevailing under normal credit cards. Likewise, the RBI has also introduced Kisan Credit Cards (KCC) scheme to provide "adequate and timely credit support from the banking system under a single window to the farmers for their cultivation and other needs. As on March 2011, almost 49 millions farmers are provided with Kisan Credit Cards and 950,000 clients are provided with General Purpose Credit Cards.

*Business Facilitators (BFs) and Business Correspondents (BCs)*: In order to ensure greater financial inclusion and increase the outreach of the banking sector, the RBI has proposed that banks use the services of NGOs/SHGs, MFIs and other civil societies (excluding NBFCs) as intermediaries in providing financial and banking services through the usage of Business Facilitators (BFs) and Business Correspondents (BCs). The BCs are permitted to carry out transactions on behalf of the banks as agents. The BFs can refer clients, pursue the clients' proposals and facilitate banks to carry out their transactions. The BCs can offer savings, credit, insurance and remittance services depending on the location and infrastructure. Today, a number of organizations such as Financial Information Network & Operations (FINO), EKO India Financial Services, and Zero Mass Foundation have begun working as BCs. By the year 2011, FINO and Zero Mass Foundation have reportedly linked 30 million and 8 million customers respectively with the banking system.

CMF-IFMR conducted a study to understand if the BC model is financially viable at the level of each stakeholder, and found that the agents are struggling to make their business profitable and financially sustainable as the current commission structure is not adequate to cover agents' costs. In addition, the study reports that agents are facing issues with cash management and liquidity due to unwillingness to share risks by both BCs and banks. The study concludes that the BC model has an immense potential in promoting financial inclusion in India, and thus more efforts have been made to promote the model among the agents and prospective clients.

### 7.3 Other Government Promoted Initiatives: Financial Inclusion being One of the Components

Swaranjayanti Gram Swarozgar Yojana (SGSY): It is a centrally sponsored scheme that follows the mechanism of forming SHGs of rural poor households, providing capacity building training and linking groups to banks. SGSY is primarily designed to promote self-employment oriented income generating activities for the Below Poverty Level (BPL) households in rural areas.

Since the inception of this programme in 1999, approximately 3.13 million groups have been formed. However, only 0.92 million groups are reported to be having outstanding loans from banks in March 2008. The loan size in the SGSY is reported to be higher than normal SHGs but SGSY groups have been faring poorly in repayment rates. It has been reported that non-performing assets (NPAs) in SGSY loans are at 5.72 percent compared to NPAs of all groups of SHGs of 2.9 percent. Even though some improvements were seen during the year 2010-11, banks are still reluctant to lend to SGSY groups due to issues with group quality and in certain cases, faulty selection of livelihood activities such as cottage industries set up without ensuring a market linkage to sell the products.

In the mid-term appraisal of the eleventh five-year plan, the Planning Commission has been critical of the performance of SGSY. The major problem identified in this report is that most members of SGSY are engaged in activities with low productivity and low returns due to lack of training and low usage of technology. While nearly two-thirds of the total funds were given out as subsidies, only 6 percent of the total SGSY funds were utilized for training and capacity building during the past decade. The Committee also criticized SGSY's low credit-subsidy ratio. Although the target for credit under SGSY increased moderately, the credit to subsidy ratio remained way below the target ratio of 3:1. The Committee explains that this is due to the failure to strengthen the demand side of credit by improving the capacity of the poor to absorb credit for income generating activities and due to supply side failures as well. The Committee has also criticized SGSY's uneven distribution of SHGs across regions, particularly mentioning that the performance of SGSY was unsatisfactory in states with high incidence of poverty due to functionaries of District Rural Development Agencies (DRDAs), Block Development Officers' (BDOs) inadequate knowledge of the programme, and banks' little interest in the initiatives.

Nevertheless, the SGSY programme has been successful in Southern states of Andhra Pradesh, Kerala and Tamil Nadu due to the existence of organizations that promote formation of SHGs and establish bank linkage. These organizations federate the SHGs into effective self-governing organizations with a hierarchy of appropriate functions. The robust network of SHGs and their federations have enabled the groups to act as financial intermediaries and involve institutional partnerships with the bankers. Based on the lessons of the implementation of the SGSY model in the last decade, the GoI has restructured SGSY as the National Rural Livelihood Mission, which was rolled out in 2010.

*National Rural Livelihood Mission (NRLM)*: Established in June 2010 by the Ministry of Rural Development (MoRD), GoI, it is modeled on the current poverty alleviation programme being implemented in Andhra Pradesh under the name Indira Kranti Patham (IKP).

The key strategies of NRLM are to:

- Implement the programme with greater emphasis on federations of SHGs,
- Provide flexibilities to states for designing specific action plans for poverty alleviation,
- Introduce interest subsidy for encouraging repayments of loans and provide multiple doses of credit,
- Improve training and capacity building efforts by setting up skill training institutes in each district,
- Facilitate market linkages, and
- Improve monitoring and evaluation process.

Even though NRLM indicates that there will be emphasis on creation of federations of SHGs, the clear role for the federations of SHGs as financial intermediaries has not been indicated.

*The Mahatma Gandhi National Rural Employment Guarantee Scheme (MGNREGS)*: This scheme aims to enhance the livelihood of the rural people by guaranteeing at least one hundred days of wage employment in a financial year to a rural household whose adult members volunteer to do unskilled manual work. As the payments are made through the bank/post office accounts, in 2010-11, nearly 10 crore bank/post office accounts have been opened.

A CMF-IFMR study reports that the state government of Andhra Pradesh has played a major role in increasing access to formal savings accounts due to its concrete effort to deliver all wages to participants in MGNREGS through formal saving accounts. This policy has a substantial impact on access to saving accounts because many MGNREGS participants lacked a formal savings account prior to the adoption of the policy. The study also found that vast majority of accounts (79%) were opened either to receive government benefits or to increase the chances of receiving a loan. This was prevalent in the case of post offices where accounts were used to receive government benefits. This has important implications, indicating that linking savings accounts to those who want to receive payments may be a good way to encourage financial inclusion and savings account usage.

*Aadhaar-Unique Identification Authority of India (UIDAI)*: The GoI has embarked an initiative to provide an individual identification number to every citizen of India and in 2009, it established the UIDAI to issue these cards on behalf of the GoI. This number provided by UIDAI will serve as a proof of identity and address, anywhere in India. The Aadhaar number will also enable people to have access to services such as banking, mobile phone connections and other government and non-government services in due course. In addition, the UIDAI has introduced a system in which the unbanked population will be able to open an account during enrollment with Aadhaar without going to a bank. The individual will be able to access such bank accounts through a micro-ATM network with large geographic reach. Currently, UIDAI is at an advanced stage of discussion with the RBI and Department of Revenue for updating the banks' KYC regulation to include Aadhaar authentication. If realized, this regulation can equal Aadhaar to become equal to KYC, which could possibly ease the account opening process without any need for physical documentation as online authentication from UIDAI can meet the requirements.

## 9. Key Issues and Challenges of Micro-Finance Programme Execution in India

### *9.1 Legal Issues*

The various Money Lending Acts enacted by the different states have not been successful in ensuring any discipline on the non-formal banking sector. Illegal (loan) contracts, though not judiciable, are enforced by the moneylenders through the muscle power tactics as well as the desire of the poor themselves not to lose credibility for taking loans in the next cycle. In a way, the moneylenders are themselves at risk, both legally and socially. They may, therefore, also need to be rehabilitated. This would require operating ethically and within the permissible limits. As per the Money Lender's Acts which are in force at present, registration and license for moneylending are mandatory. As an incentive, the professional moneylenders who are so registered may be allowed access to refinancing facility, same as the MFIs, if they allowed their accounts to be audited by the authorized regulator regularly. Under the Constitution of India (Seventh Schedule), moneylending is a State Subject. Any other law enacted in this context is, therefore is subservient to the law passed by the state legislature. The Seventh Schedule does not mention Private Money Lending. As such, all kinds of moneylending whether through institutional or non-institutional sources can get covered. A particular Money Lending Act (of a state) may thus come in conflict with another Act, enacted let us say, on behalf of RBI. One way to overcome this difficulty may be the Centre preparing a model "Money Lending Act" and passing it down to the states for enactment of a similar legislation.

### *9.2 Gender Issues*

Feminization of poverty has been associated with absence of economic opportunities and lack of access to economic resources such as credit for the women. The women face numerous problems like low level of assets ownership, illiteracy, inability to identify suitable activity, participation in low-return sectors, restricted business avenues, limited access to technology, lack of access to market, poor access to formal sector, poor capacity-building, etc. Therefore, direct involvement of women in the economic activities is imperative to achieve sustainable development and to alleviate poverty. An important component of the development strategy is empowering women economically and microfinance is emerging as an important measure in this development strategy.

### *9.3 Increasing Accessibility of the Poor*

The positive result of the growth of self-help groups is an increased availability of credit to poor household in rural areas. However, the poorest households are still not able to access credit and assistance provided by government programmes. They are not able to improve their income earning capacity by acquiring the right kind of assets or selecting the most suitable activity. Impact assessment studies of the schemes implemented by the Ministry of Rural Development confirm the benefits of self-employment programmes accrue to slightly better off rural households.

### *9.4 Rate of Interest*

The rate of interest charged in the microfinance sector depends on the cost of funds, cost of delivery of credit, cost of collection and payment, cost of providing for bad debts and profit margins. At present, the rate of interest charged is between 21 to 30 percent. The sustenance and economic viability of microfinance organizations depends on charging interest at the rate of 21-24 percent. Sa-Dhan (an association of MFIs) has laid down model mutual Code of Conduct for Microfinance Institutions. It advocates interest rate of 21-24 percent. The sector as a whole has been criticised for charging rates higher than the prevailing formal banking sector rates. To counter the criticism of high interest rates there is an urgent need for creating awareness about the need for charging cost-recovering interest rates. The microfinance organizations reach roughly one-fifth of the poor households and small percentage of non-poor households. Sustenance of these institutions and their continued support to the poor households depends on charging cost recovering rate of interest. The performance of the sector cannot be judged purely on the basis of rate of interest charged. The sector has numerous advantages like outreach, delivery and collection of loans, etc, which makes it more attractive than the formal sector. Loans are delivered and collected virtually at their doorstep and at intervals convenient to the borrower. It is therefore advisable not to put a cap on the interest rate and to encourage competition among service providers and leave it to the market to determine the interest rates within a range of 15-24 percent.

### *9.5 Unbalanced Geographical Growth*

The sector has witnessed an exponential growth during the last couple of years especially in southern part of the country. Some of the small scales NGOs have grown into large corporate institutions with some of them having more than one lakh membership. Some of them are offering technology based, demand based products and services to their members. However, eastern, northern, north-eastern and western states are lagging behind on account of absence of conducive socio-economic and political set-up required for such interventions. Absence of local institutions to start, manage and upscale credit programmes, lack of focus on the part of FIs/banks, lack of social services providers, etc. are some of the major problems. To overcome this unbalanced geographical growth, NABARD in 2005 identified 13 priority states accounting for 70 percent of India's poor for special efforts. As a result the share of the new loans of the four southern states came down from 49 to 46 percent in 2006. Number of new loans also came down sharply in A.P from 107,351 in 2005 to 48,589 in 2006 and repeat loans from 153,903 to 134,234. The number of new SHGs formed went up to 54 percent in north-east, 45 percent in west and 44% in the east when the national average was 25.4 percent. The growth in the central, northern and southern states ranged from 15 to 20 percent. Growth in these States, particularly in Uttaranchal and Assam was achieved basically by diversifying the use of partners. Partners like formal agencies, NGOs and banks were granted assistance for formation, training and nurturing of groups.

### *9.6 Choice of Productive Activities*

The poor households have limited choices while identifying productive activities. The SGSY programme unfortunately has not been a successful scheme. It emphasised on a cluster approach where ten key activities were identified per block and promoted. It does not take into consideration the market demands or capabilities of the beneficiaries. In some cases, the activities are selected just on the basis of what can be supplied by the poor households. Government departments and agencies, even NGOs have not succeeded in understanding the market demand and creating fresh demand for the products and services delivered by the Self-Help groups. Less importance is given to improve the quality, branding and packaging. The poor households adopt the activity recommended by the government functionaries without access to external expertise or guidance.

### 9.7 Assessment of Demand

Professional assessment of market demand must be made before hand. Suitable strategies should be evolved by involving trained persons before adopting the cluster approach. Guidance and counselling must be made available to the families to choose their skills and the activities they would like to undertake. Multiple activities should be offered, finances provided must also be flexible to meet their needs for consumption, production, housing, etc.

### 9.8 Subsidy

Subsidy is used to make self-employment programmes for poorer households viable. Sometimes this leads to promotion of unviable products which fail once the subsidy component is withdrawn. The policy of providing credit-linked subsidy to SHGs and individuals may be given up. A similar recommendation was made earlier in the Approach Paper to the Tenth Five-Year Plan. The budgetary support can be better used for providing infrastructure to the microfinance organizations.

### 9.9 Capacity building

The sector which is still in its infancy, faces shortage of experienced consultants/manpower/experts. There is a need to have good quality professionals, trained in best practices in governance for effective corporate governance. A need-based capacity building programme to meet the requirements of all categories of MFOs is essential to bring about sustainability in the sector. Some of the important areas where capacity building is needed are transformation, best practices, interest rate management, delivery management, managing growth, risk mitigation, product designing, market research, etc.

### *9.10 Records Maintenance*

Good quality group records help in transparency within the groups and also help the banks in loan appraisals and monitoring. In a recent study conducted across four states, it was found that only in 15 percent of the cases the quality of records maintained were found to be 'good', in 39 percent of cases, it was 'moderate' and it was 'weak' in 40 percent of the cases. The highest proportion of weak records, more than 50 percent, was found in groups promoted under the government agencies, whereas it was less than 50 percent in the case of groups promoted by NGOs or banks.

### *9.11 Auditing*

Absence of good auditing and maintenance mechanism of Self-Help Groups (SHGs) is a handicap. The initial enthusiasm in formation and bank linkage fades once government handouts for group formation and training are withdrawn. They tend to stop functioning after some time and the hard earned savings of group members fall into the hands of the last set of borrowers and are then not recovered. There is need to standardize and simplify accounting procedure and improve Book-Keeping procedures in such a way that all important information about the SHG are readily available. It would enable the banks to appraise and monitor loan portfolios. There is a need for more detailed, accurate and timely disclosure in financial statements and annual reports. Sa-Dhan, the association of MFIs, is reported to be finalizing with the Institute of Chartered Accountants of India, a standardized set of reporting formats compatible with both MFI requirements, and Indian accounting conventions and law.

### *9.12 Transparency*

In many cases there is absence of transparency regarding interest rate and other charges to the borrowers. As mentioned above, proper records are not maintained and there is no statutory requirement of audit. Some of the studies have shown that certain sections of the society are excluded. In some cases it is self-exclusion and in some, the existing members of the MFO exclude certain sections. Some are excluded because of the anticipated difficulties in meeting savings obligations, lack of understading and confidence in group processes, etc. These difficulties result in manipulation by a few and failure of organizations. Sa-Dhan, an association of MFIs, appears to be working on detailed code of conduct for transparency in dealings with borrowers and consumer protection issues.

### *9.13 Absence of Policy*

Absence of any explicit policy on Micro-Finance adversely affected its growth. However, the 'Micro-Financial Sector (Developments and Regulations)' Bill which is presently under consideration is expected to address the issue and the 'regulator' which has been proposed in the Bill is expected to put in place the required policy and regulatory framework.

### *9.14 Absence of Proper Database*

The microfinance sector as a whole is highly decentralized with no single agency responsible for its development. Information/ data on the sector is scattered and there are no firm estimates about the sector. Insufficient information impedes understanding and policy formulation. For a better understanding, monitoring and future planning there is a need for collection and compilation of information regarding the number of SHGs/MFIs, the loans disbursed, deposits, interest rates, etc. The scattered research carried out by various agencies also requires to be consolidated. Periodic surveys of microfinance organizations on all India bases may be considered so that all necessary information about the sector could be collected on a continuous basis. The survey can be done jointly by the NSSO and the state governments.

### *9.15 Low Outreach*

In India, MFI outreach is very low. It is a problem in growing the MFIs. There is about 28 percent client only 8 percent as compared to 65 percent in Bangladesh. Data show retention in the MFIs. This occurs because people are not the great potential of MFIs in increasing their outreach properly informed and educated about services and scale of operations. It has been observed that MF products provided by the institutions moreover the programmes focus a great deal of attention on women. Current client has higher default rate constitute evidence in support of the inclination of MFIs narrow margins and to bear a low effective interest rate so.

### 9.16 Loan Default and Poor Recovery Regime

Loan default is an issue that creates a problem in growth and expansion of the organization because around 73 percent loan default is identified in MFIs. Lack of understanding on the part of the clients, they also cannot correctly manage the loans given to them. As a result, they are not able to pay back the loan.

### 9.17 Low Education Level

The level of education of the clients is low. So it creates a problem in the growth and expansion of the organization because its percentage is around 70 percent in MFIs. Target population of MFIs is people of rural areas and they have no or less education level. As the percentage of people who have very less education.

### 9.18 Language Barrier

Language barrier makes communication with the clients (verbal and written) is an issue that creates a problem in growth and expansion of the organization because around 54 percent language barrier has been identified in MFIs. As the education level of clients is low so it is difficult to communicate with them. For this reason it is also difficult for the MFIs employees to make the clients to understand the policy and related details.

### 9.19 Late Payments

Late payments are an issue that creates a problem in growth and expansion of the organization because late payments are around 70 percent in MFIs. This usually occurs because clients are uneducated and they do not know how to manage their debt. They are unaware of the fact that late payment increases their loan payments.

### *9.20 Geographic Factors*

Around 60 percent of MFIs agrees that the Geographic factors make it difficult to communicate with clients of far-flung areas which create a problem in growth and expansion of the organization. MFIs are basically aimed to facilitate the BPL population of the country but due to lack of infrastructure in those areas it becomes difficult to reach them.

### *9.21 Poor Debt Management*

Clients are uneducated about debt management. 70 percent of the clients in MFIs are unaware of the fact that how to manage their debt. Because of the lack of education and understanding on the part of the clients, they also cannot correctly manage the loans given to them. So for this reason debt management creates a problem in growth and expansion of the organization.

## 10. Global Trends in Microfinance Development Initiatives

Microfinance as a part of financial sector is expected to be influenced directly or indirectly by the positive or negative changes that take place in the global economy or the regional financial markets. Understanding the trend and progress of global microfinance assumes greater importance in the present day context in view of its significant influence on the Indian microfinance sector. The Economist Intelligence Unit (EIU) has brought out a report entitled Global Microscope on the MFI sector for the year 2011. The study covered 55 countries. The countries had been ranked on the basis of various revised parameters, which include overall microfinance business environment, regulatory framework and practices, and supporting institutional framework and stability. The study concluded that, in the aftermath of the global financial crisis, microfinance has begun to enter a more mature and sustainable growth phase. After years of rapid expansion, the focus has turned to accelerating the improvements already underway in corporate governance, responsible finance practices and regulatory capacity and risk management. Further, risk management, which has become a post-crisis priority for all financial institutions, has improved considerably in the microfinance sector, which is essential, given that it is offering an increasingly diversified range of innovative financial services to the poor. The ranking of the top 10 countries in microfinance revealed that Peru continued to top the list with the highest score followed by Bolivia and Pakistan. India and Ghana, which were in the list of the top 10 countries during the year 2010 could not retain their positions in 2011 and hence got dropped from the list (Table 15). On the other hand, countries such as Uganda, Mexico and Panama have gained entry into the list of the top 10 countries. Uganda, which was displaced from the list last year, regained entry into the list in the ninth position, while its co-entrants, Mexico and Panama, have occupied the tenth position. On the whole, all the top-ranking countries, with the exception of Kenya, have declined in terms of their score as compared to their score in the preceding year. Under the overall business category, Bangladesh—the land of microfinance origin has been ranked 43rd, and Vietnam was in the last place.

Pakistan, Philippines and Uganda shared the first place in regulatory framework and practices, while Trinidad and Tobago have occupied the lowermost position in the list. Bolivia and Peru shared first rank in Supporting Institutional framework followed by Columbia and Armenia. Costa Rica has topped the list in terms of stability factor followed by South American countries, viz. Uruguay and Chile. As in the overall business category, Vietnam was in the bottommost position in terms of supporting institutional framework. Peru had an excellent record of legal framework, sophisticated regulators and government commitment, which purely focused on making the unbanked bankable. Bolivia had better price transparency and disclosure rules. Pakistan, placed in the third position, had a separate legal framework for microfinance banks and good networking. The Kyrgyz Republic has stepped down from the 12th position to the 21st rank globally. This is due to a change in the political regime, which halted regulatory overhaul. Latin America and the Caribbean have the largest number of top performing countries in the Global Microscope. The region has eight countries in the top 12 global positions. In addition, the first two places are occupied by Peru and Bolivia respectively. This had been possible mainly because of their very strong position in supporting institutional framework, even though these countries are not very strong in regulatory framework and practices. The Middle-East and North African countries have faced political unrest earlier this year, which seriously handicapped the functioning of the microfinance industry. Yemen is one of the most affected countries, which slid from the 27th to the 44th place.

**Table 15:** Ranking of the top 10 Countries in Microfinance in 2011

| Rank | Country | Score in 2011 | Change from 2010 |
|---|---|---|---|
| 1 | Peru | 67.8 | –6.5 |
| 2 | Bolivia | 64.7 | –4.9 |
| 3 | Pakistan | 62.8 | –2 |
| 4 | Kenya | 60.3 | 5.3 |
| 5 | El Salvador | 58.8 | –2.5 |
| 6 | Philippines | 58.5 | –13.3 |
| 7 | Colombia | 56.0 | –0.8 |
| 8 | Ecuador | 55.1 | –6.2 |
| 9 | Uganda | 53.7 | New entrant |
| 10 | Mexico and Panama | 53.6 | New entrant |

*Sources*: Global Microscope on the Microfinance.
Business Environment, 2009–11,
Economic Intelligence Unit Ltd. (www.eiu.com).

This instability has caused many MFIs to reduce their scale of operations, ending up with closure of banks too. Kenya is one of the strongest and most stable countries in this region. Kenya is placed in the fourth place and Uganda in the ninth place in the global list. But Uganda finds itself in the first place globally in terms of regulatory framework and practices. Clients are benefited with active microfinance markets. India has been pushed to the 27th rank with a score of 43.1 in the overall microfinance business environment. It occupied the 22nd rank in regulatory framework and practices, the 20th place in supporting institutional framework and the 40th rank in terms of stability. The Government of India had strongly promoted the Self-Help

Group model through the National Rural Livelihood Mission by offering cheap funding and also restricted market-based lending. In a study carried out by Microrate MIV survey 2011.

Latin American and the Caribbean (LAC) countries and Europe and Central Asia continue to account for the majority of microfinance investments receiving a combined total of 73 percent of all microfinance investments in 2010. J.P. Morgan's CGAP Global Equity Valuation Survey 2012 has reported that the LAC region had more than half of the investment followed by Asia. India is the major contributor with more than 92 percent of Asia's investment levels.

### *10.1 Region-wise Performance of MFIs in the World*

The growth and performance of microfinance sector at global level during the recent years has shown significant differences across regions. With a view to capture the direction of movement of the sector among the regions, a comparative analysis of the performance of the sector in regions like Africa, East Asia and Pacific, Eastern Europe, Central Asia, Latin America, Caribbean, Middle East and North Africa and South Asia is attempted in this section. The data from Mix Market for the period 2003–10 has been the basis for this analysis. The number of MFIs had, by and large, shown an upward trend in almost all the regions up to the year 2007 and 2008, after which the numbers have started dwindling in all the regions. In all the regions of the world, the number of MFIs has decreased during the year 2011 as compared to the previous year, except in East Asia and the Pacific, where the number remained unchanged (Fig. 6). The decrease in the number of MFIs has ranged from about 10 percent in LAC countries to close to 75 percent in the Middle East and the North African region. In South Asian countries the decline in the MFI count was about 50 percent. This is probably due to the overall economic situation as the world was experiencing severe economic recession during this period. The number of active borrowers during the year 2011 has declined in most regions of the world as compared to the preceding year, with the exception of LAC countries where there was a marginal increase in the number (Fig. 7). The decline in the number of active borrowers was the highest in MENA countries where the decline was about 70 percent between the years 2010 and 2011, while it was more than 40 percent in South Asian countries. The decline in active borrowers has reflected in reduction of deposits too.

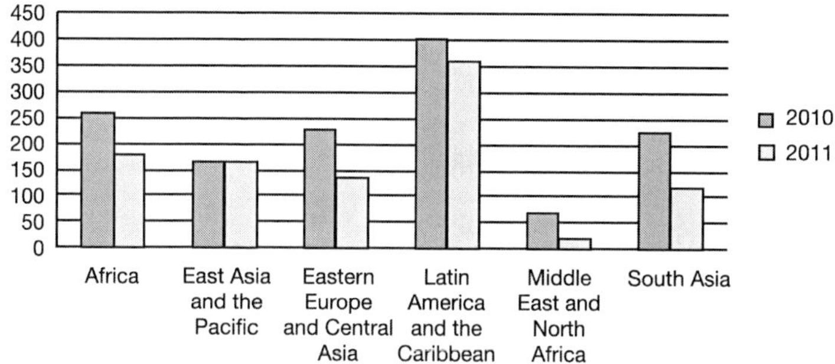


**Fig. 6:** Number of MFIs in different Regions

*Source*: http://www.microrate.com/media/downloads/2012/04/The-State-of-Microfinance-Investment-2011-MicroRate.pdf accessed in June 2012.

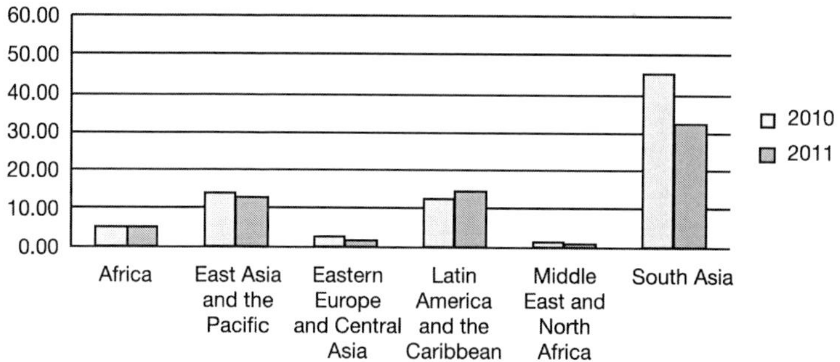


**Fig. 7:** Number of active borrowers (in millions)

*Source*: http://www.microrate.com/media/downloads/2012/04/The-State-of-Microfinance-Investment-2011-MicroRate.pdf accessed in June 2012.

The trend in the number of depositors shows a disheartening trend in most parts of the world with a decline in their numbers in recent years (Fig. 7). By the year 2010, the South Asia region had the highest number of depositors (23.73 million), though it declined by about 50 percent to about 12 million in the year 2011. Consequently, the African countries accounted for the highest number of depositors in the year 2011, with 16.25 million depositors though with a marginal decline from about 17 million in the preceding year. Middle and North African countries had the lowest number of depositors (0.1 million) in 2010, and this too had declined by 63 percent in 2011, thus making it negligible as compared to the other regions of the world. East Asian countries have recorded the highest year-on-year growth in the number of depositors, from about 6 million in 2010 to 7.73 million.

Due to the decline or stagnation in the number of deposits in most of the regions, there has been a marginal to steep decline in the deposit amounts between the years 2010 and 2011 in all the regions except in Latin American and Caribbean countries and the African region where there was an increase in the deposit amount (Fig. 7). The decline in the deposit amount was the steepest in East Asia and the Pacific region where the deposits registered a fall of 80 percent from about US$ 31 billion to 6 billion. In South Asia, a 50 percent decline in number of depositors has resulted in more than 80 percent decline in the deposit amount.

The MENA region has recorded the highest fall of about 95 percent in the deposit amount as a consequence of more than 60 percent decline in the number of depositors. Due to the moderate to steep decline in deposit amounts in most of the regions, the deposit amount at a global level has recorded a 40 percent decline from US$ 63 billion to US$ 37.5 billion. The gross loan portfolio has shown an increasing trend in all the regions of the world during the period 2009-10 (Fig. 8). In Eastern Europe and Central Asia, the increase was more pronounced with an increase of 60 percent, while it was around 20 percent in Africa, and East Asia and the Pacific, while the increase in other regions falling in between these two extremes. Though the sector seems to have achieved a positive growth in gross loan portfolio/total assets for almost all the countries during 2011 over the year 2010, it has shown a mixed trend during the period 2003–11 in most of the regions (Fig. 8). The ratio of gross loan portfolio to total assets was the lowest in East Asia

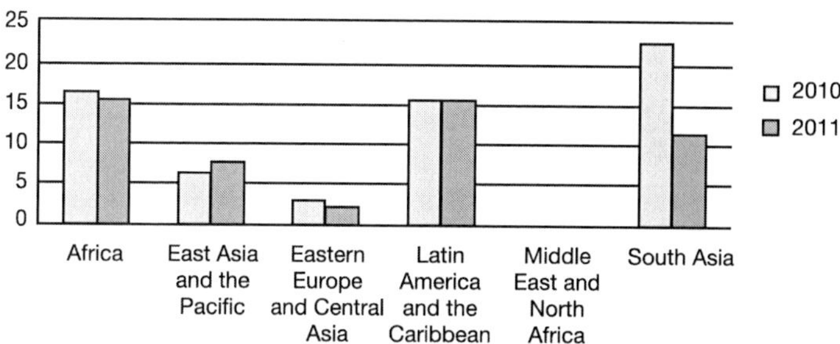


**Fig. 8:** Number of depositors (in millions)

*Source*: http://www.microrate.com/media/downloads/2012/04/The-State-of-Microfinance-Investment-2011-MicroRate.pdf accessed in June 2012.

and the Pacific countries, among all the regions of the world though this region has increased it from 54 percent to 62 percent between the years 2010 and 2011. African countries have also recorded a similar increase in their gross loan portfolio to total assets ratio. The Middle East and the North Africa region closely follow the South Asian countries in terms of their gross loan portfolio/total assets during the year 2011.

A country-wise analysis for South Asia reveals that the total assets in 2011 have declined for most of the countries as compared to the corresponding figures in the previous year. Attrition in total assets is found to be the highest in Bangladesh and Sri Lanka where the assets declined by about 97 in 2011 as compared to the previous year. Though India's assets declined by 50 percent between the years 2010 and 2011, India continued to top the list of South Asian countries in terms of total assets, with a total asset value of about US$2.90 billion. In terms of the median asset value, Bhutan topped the list of South Asian countries during the year 2010, with a median asset value of about US$95 million, though the figures of Bhutan are not available for the year 2011. The median asset values have increased for all the countries in South Asia during the year 2011 as compared to the previous year, though with wide differences across nations. Bangladesh topped the list of South Asian countries in terms of median asset value in 2011 (US$506 million), followed by Pakistan (US$56 million).

### 10.2 Challenges Facing the Indian Microfinance Sector

The Indian microfinance sector has seen unprecedented growth in this decade. Increased outreach, large investments and the growing role of private equity coupled with greater demand are some of the characteristics that could be marked with the recent development of the sector. The growing scale has brought with it its own set of challenges. Some of the key challenges discussed in the report are:

*Requirement of deposit services*—There are limited deposit services available for the poor in India. Under the SBLP, group savings accounts are opened in local banks, but these are used primarily for internal group lending, though with access to savings on exit. MFIs find it difficult to offer this service due to regulatory restraints. NBFCs hold a major chunk of the outreach and portfolio but are not permitted to accept member savings as deposits thereby leaving a large proportion of their clients (virtually all low income families around or below the poverty threshold) without access to this service.

*Deepening of outreach*—Unless SHPAs and MFIs know the depth of their outreach to clients below the poverty line (and different poverty lines) it will be difficult for them to address any issues related to the poor. In the fast paced growth of the sector it is particularly important to analyse if microfinance services providers are reaching down to those most in need and those not serviced by formal financial institutions. This is the common mandate (by and large) of most microfinance service providers and as tools have become available to measure poverty levels, the challenge is for institutions to define their target outreach more clearly, effectively segment their market and respond with appropriate products.

*Social performance management and reporting*—Whilst financial performance management and reporting has developed across the sector, with consensus on key indicators and ratios, the development of social performance management is just beginning. This is seen at the international level to be increasingly important, to ensure that microfinance meets its social goals as a double (or triple) bottom line sector. It will require some reorientation and skill building, to encourage SHPAs and

MFIs to go beyond the numbers to ensure quality services with consistent management and reporting.

*Sector slow down due to global economic crisis*—The global economic crisis has affected all sectors across countries and continents. Smaller MFIs face problems in obtaining debt funds from banks and find it difficult to maintain liquidity. The liquidity risk has the potential to hamper refinancing of existing clients, leading to the risk of a rise in the current default rate.

*Capacity building*—Capacity building and improving understanding of techniques for improving microfinance management is the key to effective microfinance operations and eventually for achieving the objective of financial inclusion with social value. The effective bridging of capacity building gaps requires regular intervention in a number of areas like keeping pace with the fast growth of the sector, geographical spread and diversity and local language constraints. The high attrition rate of MFI staff is also a challenge often inhibiting MFI managements from investing in staff capacity.

*Micro-credit plus*—Building capacities and skill level of borrowers for better utilisation of credit are considered as some of the biggest challenges. There is a need to combine micro-credit with appropriate improvements in infrastructure, technology transfers, skill development and strengthening of market linkages to enable BPL producers to earn a higher return on their efforts. This is the best way of facilitating and enabling poverty reduction.

*The problem of multiple lending*—With an increasing number of MFIs and expansion of operations, the issue of overlapping membership and potential over-indebtedness is beginning to emerge, particularly in certain areas of the country. This is an area that needs more research, and clearer guidelines for the sector on appropriate practice.

*Regulation*—Regulatory movement with regard to microfinance has been slow and debates are still underway—as to which institution should be entrusted with regulatory supervision of the sector, and how to regulate the new NBFCs which serve a substantial majority of MFI clients.

## REFERENCES


Akula, Bikram (2008), A fistful of rice, Harvard Business Review Press, Boston, USA.

Asian Development Bank (2000), Finance for the Poor: Microfinance Development Strategy, Manila: Asian Development Bank, Manila.

Awasthi, Dinesh N. (1994), Promoting Group Entrepreneurship, in Gautam Raj Jain and Debmuni Gupta (ed.) *New Initiatives in Entrepreneurship Education and Training*, Ahmedabad: Entrepreneurship Development Institute of India.

Awasthi, Dinesh N. (1996), Rural Entrepreneurship Development: Relevance, Approach and Issues". Working Paper, Ahmedabad: Entrepreneurship Development Institute of India.

Baland, J.M., Demont, T., Somanathan, R. (2011), Microfinance mechanisms: Evidence from observational panel data: mimeo.

Basix (2000, Equity for Equity—Available at http://www.basixindia.com/micro_finance_in_inda.asp

Besley, T., Coate, S. (1995), Group lending, repayment incentives and social collateral, *Journal of Development Economics*, 46(1), 1-18.

Bhole, B., Ogden, S. (2010), Group lending and individual lending with strategic default, *Journal of Development Economics*, 91 (2010): 348-36.

Campbell, J.Y., Jackson, H.E., Madrian, B.C., Tufano, P. (2011), Consumer Financial Protection, *Journal of Economic Perspectives*, 25(1), 91-114. URL http://www.aeaweb.org/articles.php?doi=10.1257/jep.25.1.91.

Chauhan, Brij Raj (1990). *Rural-Urban Articulations*, Etawah: A.C. Brothers.

Conroy, J.D. (2002), Microfinance in Malaysia: Time to rebuild, The Foundation for Development Corporation Brisbane. Australia.

Gabaix, X., Laibson, D. (2006), Shrouded Attributes, Consumer Myopia and Information Suppression in Competitive Markets, *Quarterly Journal of Economics*, 121, 505-40.

Gangopadhyay, S., Ghatak, M., Lensink, R. (2005), Joint Liability Lending and the Peer Selection E ect., *Economic Journal*, 115(506), 1005-15.

Ghatak, M. (1999), Group lending, local information and peer selection, *Journal of Development Economics*, 60(1): 27-50.

Government of India (1992), Eighth Five-year Plan (Vol. I), Objectives, Perspective, Macro-Dimensions, Policy Framework and Resources, Planning Commission, New Delhi.

Government of India (2011), Faster, Sustainable and more Inclusive Growth, Approach Paper to the 12th Five-Year Plan, October, 2011, Planning Commission, Government of India, New Delhi.

Harper, M. (2002), Promotion of Self-Help Groups under the SHG Bank Linkage Programme in India, paper presented at the Seminar on SHG Bank Linkage Programme, NABARD, New Delhi.

Hashemi, M. Syed., Sidney, R. Schuler and Ann P. Riley (1996), Rural Credit Programs and Women's Empowerment in Bangladesh, *World Development*, 24(4): 635-54.

Khandker, S. (1998), Fighting Poverty with Microcredit: Experience in Bangladesh. New York: Oxford University Press.

Ledgerwood, J. (1999), *Microfinance Handbook: An Institutional and Financial Perspective*, Washington, DC: World Bank.

Mallegaon Committee Report (2011), Report of the Sub-Committee of the Central Board of Directors of Reserve Bank of India to Study Issues and Concerns in the MFI Sector, RBI, January, 2011.

Maria, U. (2004), Essay on the Dynamics of Microfinance. Unpublished Master Dissertation, University of Maryland College Park, The United States.

Mehta, Aasha Kapur (1996a), Liberalisation and the Poor: Some Economic Issues, *Indian Journal of Public Administration*, Vol. XLII, July-September, No. 3: 407-20.

Mehta, Aasha Kapur (1996b), Recasting Indices for Developing Countries: A Gender Empowerment Measure, *Economic and Political Weekly*, Vol. 31, No. 43, October 26.

Mehta, Aasha Kapur (1998), Evaluation of DFID's Support to Poverty Reduction; India, Country Study: Poverty Analysis, Draft Working Paper, University of Birmingham.

Microfinance World (2009), Change can happen; *Financial Express*, India-Jan–March issue: pp 24-27.

Microcredit Summit Report (1997): http://www.microcreditsummit.org/resource/59/1997-microcredit-summit-report.html

Microfinance India—State of the Sector (2011), Chapter 2: Self-help group bank linkage programme—early signs of a new thrust.

Micro-Financial Sector (Development and Regulation) Bill, (2011), Planning Commission, Government of India, New Delhi.

National Bank for Agriculture & Rural Development (1999a), Task Force on Supportive Policy and Regulatory Framework on Micro-Finance: Summary and Recommendations, NABARD, Mumbai.

National Bank for Agriculture & Rural Development (1999b), *Handbook on Self-Help Groups Linkage Programme*, July, NABARD, Ahmedabad.

National Bank for Agriculture & Rural Development (1999), Micro-Finance and NABARD, Role and Perspectives, May, NABARD, Mumbai.

NABARD (2008), Report on Status of Microfinance in India 2007-08. (http://www.nabard.org/)

NABARD (2011), Status of microfinance in India 2010-2011, Retrieved April 20, 2012, Annual Report of National Bank for Agriculture and Rural Development.

Pankaj Kumar and Ramesh Golait (2009), Bank Penetration and SHG-Bank Linkage Programme: A Critique, *Reserve Bank of India Occasional Paper*, Vol. 29, No. 3, 2009

Planning Commission (2006), Towards Faster and More Inclusive Growth: An Approach to the 11th Five-Year Plan, Government of India, New Delhi, 2006.

Puhazhendhi, V. (2012), Microfinance India State of the Sector Report 2012, SAGE.

Puhazhendhi, V., and K.C. Badatya (2002), Self-help Group Bank Linkage Program for Rural Poor in India: An Impact Assessment, Bombay: NABARD.

Rajashekar, D. (2000a), Impact of Micro-Finance Programme on Poverty Programs and Gender Equality, Some Evidence from Indian NGOs, In Shahra Razvi (ed). *Shifting Burdens: Gender and Agrarina Change under Neoliberalism*, Broomfield: Kumarian Press Inc.

Rajasekhar, D. (2000b), Non-Governmental Organizations (NGOs) in India: Opportunities and Challenges, Working paper, 66, Bangalore: Institute for Social and Economic Change.

RBI (2009), Spread of Poverty and SHGs in Different Regions, *RBI Bulletin*, 2009.

Robinson, M. (2001), The Microfinance Revolution: Sustainable Finance for the Poor. Washington DC: World Bank.

Roy, S., R. Sane and S. Thomas (2011), An Economic, Policy and Legal Analysis of the Micro-Finance Institutions (Development & Regulation) Bill, 2011, Working Paper WP-2011-025, IGIDR.

Rosenberg, Richard, Adrian Gonzalez and Sushma Narain (2009), Are Microcredit Interest Rates Excessive?, CGAP Brief, Washington, 2009.

Rural bazar: http:// ruralbazar.nic.in

Rutherford, Stuart (1999), *The Poor and Their Money*. Oxford: Oxford University Press.

Sam-Daley-Harris (2009), State of the Microcredit Summit Campaign Report, Washington, USA, 2009.

Sa-Dhan (2008), Bharat Microfinance Report—Side by Side, December, 2008 (http://www.sa-dhan.net).

Simanowitz, Anton and Alice Walker (2002), Ensuring impact: Reaching the poorest while building financially self-sufficient institutions, and showing improvement in the lives of the poorest women and their families, unpublished background paper for the Microcredit Summit + 5, New York, 10-13 November, available at <http:// www.microcreditsummit.org/papers/papers.htm>.

Sinha, Sanjay. (2000), In: *The Role of Central Banks in Microfinance in Asia and the Pacific: Country Studies*, edited by A.D. Bank. Manila: Asian Development Bank: 61-89.

Sinha, Sanjay (2003), Financial services for low income families: An Appraisal, *IIMB Management Review*, 15, 2.

Small Industries Development Bank of India (SIDBI), Foundation for Micro Credit: A Profile, Lucknow: SIDBI.

Srinivasan, N. (2010), Microfinance State of the Sector Report, 2010, New Delhi; Sage Publications.

Tankha, A. (2002), Self-help Groups as Financial Intermediaries in India: Cost of Promotion, Sustainability and Impact, A Study by Sa-Dhan, New Delhi, 70-71. Available at: http://www.sa-dhan.net/Adls/Microfinance/PerspectiveMicrofinance/Self-help Groupsas Financial. pdf: Accessed on 30.06.2008.

The Microfinance Gateway, 'What is Microfinance?': Available at http://www.microfinancegateway.org/section/faq

*The New York Times* (1997), "Micro loans for the very poor" (editorial) February 16, 1997.

Thorat, U. (2007), Urban Cooperative Banks: Evolution of the Banks, Current Issues in Corporate Governance and Challenges in their Regulation and Supervision, *Monthly Bulletin*, Reserve Bank of India.

Varman, Mahendra P. (2005), Impact of Self-Help Groups on Formal Banking Habits, *Economic & Political Weekly*, Vol. XL, No. 17, 23 April, 2005.

Yunus, M. (1989), Grameen Bank: Organization and operation, in J. Levitsky (ed.), *Microenterprises in Developing Countries*. London: Intermediate Technology Publications.

Zaman, H. (2000), Assessing the Poverty and Vulnerability Impact of Micro-Credit in Bangladesh; A Case Study of BRAC; Retrieved from http://wwwwds. worldbank.org/external/default/WDSContentServer/IW3P/IB/1999/09/10/000094946_99082405303974/Rendered/PDF/multi_page.pdf

Zingales, L. (2009), The future of securities regulation. *Journal of Accounting Research* 47(2): 391-425.

# 2

# Microfinance Delivery Models

The concept of microfinance involves informal and flexible approach to the credit needs of the poor. There is no single approach or model that fits in all the circumstances. Therefore, a number of microfinance models emerged in different countries/ states according to the suitability to their local conditions. Broadly, the microfinance delivery methods can be classified into six groups as follows: Grameen Bank Model, Joint Liability Group Model, Individual Lending Model, the Group Approach Model, Village Banking Model, Credit Unions and Co-operative Model.

In India, and elsewhere, there is a wide variety of institutions in public as well as private sector which provide microfinance to the poor. These institutions can be broadly divided into two types. First type is the traditional formal financial institutions, while the second type is Microfinance Institutions (MFIs). The traditional financial institutions comprise of commercial banks, regional rural banks and co-operative banks. They provide microfinance services in addition to their general banking activities and are referred to as microfinance service providers. On the other hand MFIs are different types of financial institutions whose main financial activity is providing microfinance only. Many of these institutions are NGOs, Mutually Aided Co-operative Societies (MACS) and Non-Banking Financial Companies (NBFCs). In case of traditional financial institutions both private and public ownership are found but the MFIs are mainly in the private sector.

This chapter is dedicated to help understand and have clarity on the background and the basis of evolving various innovative forms of Microfinance models in different parts of the world, especially in India. An attempt has also been made to have a comparative analysis of various forms of model, highlighting therein the positional, the relative strengths, weaknesses and limitations in these models. The future challenges and sustainability aspects of these models are also discussed at some length.

## 1. Key Elements in Developing Microfinance Models

Microfinance is defined by the Canadian International Development Agency (CIDA) as pertaining to: "the provision of a broad range of financial services to poor, low income households and micro-enterprises usually lacking access to formal financial institutions" (Zeller, 2001). There is no one specific microfinance model and the term itself can refer to a wide range of financial services including credit for microenterprises, agriculture, housing, education and consumer purchases, savings programmes, insurance, related training and other financial based transactions (CIDA, 1999). Moreover, there exists significant variation among microfinance institutions in terms of organizational and ownership structure, lending methodologies, funding sources, and financial products offered. Some institutions are extensions of larger banks or governments or NGOs and others are client owned and governed by community members.

Microfinance Information eXchange (MIX) defines an MFI as "an organization that offers financial services to the very poor" (MIX, 2005). According to the UNCDF (2004) there are approximately 10,000 MFIs in the world but they only reach four percent of potential clients, about 30 million people. On the other hand, according to the Microcredit Summit Campaign Report (Microcredit Summit, 2005; Sam-Daley-Harris, 2009) as of December 31st, 2003, the 2,931 microcredit institutions that they have data on, have reported reaching "80,868,343 clients, 54,785,433 of whom were the poorest when they took their first loan". Even though they refer to microcredit institutions, they explain that they include "programs that provide credit for self-employment and other financial and business services to very poor persons" (Microcredit Summit Report, 1997; Sam-Daley-Harris, 2009). According to MIX perceptions, initially there were only three recognizable Microfinance Model patterns as briefly discussed below:

### *1.1 Rotating Savings and Credit Associations*

These are formed when a group of people come together to make regular cyclical contributions to a common fund, which is then given as a lump sum to one member of the group in each cycle (Grameen Bank, 2000). According to Harper (2002a and b), this model is a very common form of savings and credit. He states that the members of the group are usually neighbours and friends, and the group provides an opportunity for social interaction and is very popular with women. They are also called merry-go-rounds or Self-Help Groups (Fisher and Sriram, 2002; Fischer and Ghatak, 2010).

### *1.2 The 'Grameen' Solidarity Group Model*

This model is based on group peer pressure whereby loans are made to individuals in groups of four to seven (Berenbach and Guzman, 1994). Group members collectively guarantee loan repayment, and access to subsequent loans is dependent on successful repayment by all group members. Payments are usually made weekly (Ledgerwood, 1998, 1999). According to Berenbach and Guzman (1994), solidarity groups have proved effective in deterring defaults as evidenced by loan repayment rates attained by organizations such as the Grameen Bank, who use this type of microfinance model. The later variant of this model was the Self-Help Group (SHG) Model. This model is highly influenced by the success of Grameen Bank in Bangladesh. This model is commonly practiced with PSU banks and SHG linkage. PSU banks had ₹ 1000 crore exposure to SHG based loans, lent another 60 crore to MFIs (Grameen Bank, 2002 a and b). The SHG concept involves forming groups of 15-20 women who meets regularly, understand each other's problems and bond for a while. They are expected to save a small amount, keep the money in bank and earn interest. A member could borrow if she falls ill and could not go for work. She would return the money with 18-24 percent interest to the group. The recovery is almost certain due to the pressure and bonding with the group. Such groups formation and bonding takes a minimum of six to nine months.

The basic problem with this model is long operational time and lending for non-income generating activities. The pressure of repayment creates coercions which lead to multiple borrowing or illegal practices by the group member. The problem arises from the regulation point of view when it was first conceived.

### *1.3 Village Banking Model*

Village banks are community-managed credit and savings associations established by NGOs to provide access to financial services, build community self-help groups, and help members accumulate savings (Holt, 1994). They have been in existence since the mid-1980s. They usually have 25 to 50 members who are low-income individuals seeking to improve their lives through self-employment activities. These members run the bank, elect their own officers, establish their own by-laws, distribute loans to individuals and collect payments and services (Grameen Bank, 2000). The loans are backed by moral collateral; the promise that the group stands behind each loan (Global Development Research Centre, 2005). The basic methodology being used in commercial microfinance in India was innovated by Grameen Bank and later improvised by several players. This methodology involved the following elements:

1. Identify the potential customer.
2. Organize the potential customers into groups, so that they could address the issue of information asymmetry and lack of collaterals by transferring what could be an individual liability into a group liability and hold the group morally responsible for repayment—through a process of public oath.
3. Have standardized products, standardized operating systems and enforce discipline; ensure that the exceptions were dealt with severely.

Nevertheless, the four most important Micro-Finance models that are prevalent in India are:

**Model I**—individuals or group borrowers are financed directly by banks without the intervention/facilitation of any Non-Government Organization (NGO).

**Model II**—borrowers are financed directly with the facilitation extended by formal or informal agencies like Government, Commercial Banks and Micro-Finance Institutions (MFIs) like NGOs, Non Bank Financial Intermediaries and Co-operative Societies.

**Model III**—financing takes place through NGOs and MFIs as facilitators and financing agencies.

**Model IV**—is the Grameen Bank Model, similar to the model followed in Bangladesh.

In India, Model II of MF constitutes three-fourths of total microfinancing where activity/joint liability/Self-Help Groups are formed and nurtured by facilitating agencies and are linked directly with banks for the purpose of receiving credit.

In India, there is a diversity of approaches to microfinance, involving banks, government agencies and NGOs. Among other things, MFIs provide financial services whilst building their own financial sustainability. Most MFIs use groups as intermediaries for financial transactions, but there are different ways of working with groups. These may be broadly classified as the Self-Help Group model (SHGs) and the Grameen replicators (Grameen). In both models, the group is expected to assume joint liability for loans taken by its clients, but there are significant differences in service delivery. A small number of MFIs have an individual banking approach (IB) whilst some SFMC partners are Cooperatives usually catering to a specific economic sector—such as fishing, handlooms, dairying—rather than a microfinance model. The 45 MFIs (including one Apex MFI) associated with SIDBI represent the more established microfinance institutions in the country. Most of these MFIs follow the SHG model. They have been functioning as MFIs for at least 4 years, with experience of up to 10 years. In terms of scale, the range is from 1,500 to over 120,000 clients. The MFIs in this study represent the three main models of microfinance. Based on data for the sample MFIs, some key features that are fairly typical of each model are presented in Table 1.

**Table 1:** Operational Features of different Microfinance Models in India

| Operational features | SHG | Grameen | IB |
|---|---|---|---|
| Clients | Primarily women | Primarily women | Primarily men |
| Groups | 15 to 20 clients per group | usually 5 clients per group (organized into 'centres' of 4-6 groups) | Individual clients |
| Service focus | Savings and credit | Credit-regular cycle | Credit |
| Role of MFI staff | Guide and facilitate (groups may develop autonomy) | Organize (groups dependent on staff) | Organize |
| Meetings | Monthly | Weekly | Individual transactions—often daily |
| Savings deposits | ₹ 20-100/month | ₹ 5-25/week | Flexible |
| Interest on savings | Bank rate (4.25%) + profit share | 6-9% | 6% + |
| Initial Loan Size | ₹ 5-10,000 | ₹ 2-5,000 | ₹ 5-15,000 ₹ 35,000[a] |
| Effective interest rate (usual range) | 24-28% | 32-38% | 23-38% |
| Insurance | At a very preliminary stage: usually loan linked, some Life and Health, Sometimes links to national companies | | |
| Development services | Some associated programmes | A few small social projects | Enterprise support |

*Source*: Data for sample MFI.

Group based MFIs target women as clients. In the SHG model, groups can mature to be relatively autonomous: clients organize their own meetings (usually monthly), take decisions on financial transactions, circulate their savings as internal loans (group loans, at 18-36 percent interest), and group leaders/ office bearers play a significant role, guided by MFI staff. In the Grameen model, in contrast, MFI staff plays the main role in weekly meetings and transactions, focusing on a regular annual cycle of credit.

## 2. Microfinance Delivery Models in India

Almost 30 years after the first microfinance institutions were founded, the microfinance market is still in evolution. When microfinance started to expand during the 1980s, it was about lending to the rural poor for income-generating purposes —mainly through solidarity group loans of small and smallest amounts. Since then, microfinance has evolved into a more comprehensive development tool, with the aim to supply access to financial services for all unbanked people in emerging and developing markets. Besides the traditional microcredit, i.e. the financing of small entrepreneurs and start-ups, microfinance today refers to payment services, savings accounts, insurance and other financial services that can be offered on a small scale. Along with a widening of the product range, the base of microfinance customers and the ways of serving them have changed, too. Group lending has been increasingly replaced by individual contracting, and MFIs have expanded into urban areas and started to target wealthier clients.

Microfinance has its root in Bangladesh, where experimenting with micro-loans for the rural poor started in the 1970s. From there, the concept spread rapidly across the globe. Today, most borrowers still live in rural South Asia and the East Asia and Pacific (EAP) region. Over a period of about a couple of decades, microfinance has expanded also in Latin America and the Caribbean (LAC), in Eastern Europe and Central Asia (EECA), and in Sub-Saharan Africa (Sub-S. Africa).

The expansion of microfinance was also accompanied by a shift from group to individual lending. Because group lending is more difficult to apply in urban areas, and wealthier borrowers prefer individual contracts, individual lending is predominantly used in these cases. A shift towards individual contracts can also be observed in rural areas and in lending to low-income clients. Today, more than 90 percent of micro-credit to higher-income and more than 50 percent to low-income clients is provided on an individual basis. The concept of microfinance involves informal and flexible approach to the credit needs of the poor. There is no single approach or model that fits in all the circumstances. Therefore, a number of microfinance models emerged in different countries/states according to the suitability to their local conditions. Broadly, the microfinance delivery methods can be classified into six groups, with special reference to India, as follows:

### *2.1 Grameen Bank Model*

Grameen Bank model is one of the oldest and most successful models of microfinance. This model was developed in Bangladesh. In this model microfinance programme participants are organized into groups of five members. They make mandatory contribution to group savings and insurance fund. Each member maintains her individual saving and loan account with the bank and after contributing to the savings fund for a fixed time the group members receive individual loans from the bank. But the group is not required to give any guarantee for the loan repayment by its member. Repayment responsibility solely rests on the individual borrower and there is no form of joint liability, i.e. group members are not responsible to pay on behalf of a defaulting member. Loans are provided for six months to one year duration but repayments are made weekly. Bank staff makes periodic visits to the groups, maintain individual records of group members and facilitate all the financial transactions. This creates ease in working but hindrance in the empowerment of members. The members remain dependent on field officers regarding their all group related activities. Grameen model has been replicated in more than 40 countries in Asia, Africa, and Latin America with modifications to suit local conditions and cultures. The programme of BancoSol in Bolivia and most of the solidarity groups in Latin America follow this methodology. Many MFIs in India have also replicated this model (Microfinance Trends, Problems and Prospects: http://shodhganga.inflibnet.ac.in/bitstream/10603/3031/11/11_chapter%203.pdf).

### *2.2 Joint Liability Group (JLG) Model*

In this model, 4 to 10 individuals are organized in a group known as a Joint Liability Group (JLG). The group members can avail bank loans against mutual guarantee and there is no condition of their own saving fund. All members sign a joint liability contract, making each one jointly liable for repayment of all loans taken by all individuals in the group. Thus, only social collateral is provided to the lending institution. The JLGs are intended primarily to be credit groups and regular savings by the JLG members are not mandatory. The group exists only because its individual members are legally bound to one another. In this model, the progress of empowerment of group members remains very limited. In India these type of groups are generally made by most of the MFIs because such groups are easy to make as there are very less restrictions regarding the utilization of loan. NABARD is using this model for providing credit to the tenant farmers, cultivating land either as oral lessees or share-croppers, and small farmers who do not have proper title of their landholding. Many other countries are also using this model. There were segments within the poor, such as sharecroppers/oral lessees/tenant farmers, who were left out and whose loan requirements were much larger but who had no collaterals to fit into the traditional financing approaches of the banking system. To service such clients, Joint Liability Groups (JLGs), an upgradation of SHG model could be an effective way.

### *2.3 Individual Lending Model*

In this method, individuals can get loans without any membership of a group. This is a straightforward credit lending model in which micro-loans are given directly to the borrowers. In this model, the financial institutions have to make frequent and close contact with individual clients to provide credit products customized to the specific needs of the individual. It is most successful for larger, urban-based, production-oriented businesses. The model is followed by many financial institutions like the Association for the Development of Micro-Enterprises (ADEMI) in Dominican Republic, Bank Rakyat Indonesia, Senegal Egypt, Self-Employment Women's Association in India, etc.

### *2.4 The Group Approach Model*

The group approach delegates the entire financial process to the group rather than to the financial institutions. All financial activities like savings, getting loans, repayment of loans and record keeping are managed at the group level. In this method, 10-20 members are organised to form a group. These group members make regular savings of fixed amount in a common fund. The amount and frequency of savings is mutually decided by the group members. After the successful working of such a group for some months the group is linked to a financial institution for getting credit. The financial institutions issue loan in the name of group and whole group is considered responsible for repayment. The amount of loan depends upon the total accumulated amount of saving of the group. Group members themselves decide about the criteria of dividing the loan among the group members. With this loan the whole group may jointly start a micro-enterprise or the members may start their individual businesses. An individual may also use his loan for consumptive purpose or meeting other priority needs. The peer pressure in the group helps the timely repayment of loan. These type of group based credit delivery methods help to empower the group members because they remain involved in various group activities. They visit the bank, market and hold group meetings which help them to increase self-confidence. In India, the group based credit delivery method known as SHG-BLP is a predominant method of providing microfinance. Programme Hubungan Bank Danksm (PHBK) project in Indonesia and the Chikola groups of K-REP in Kenya are also using such group based credit delivery models (Microfinance Trends, Problems and Prospects: http://shodhganga.inflibnet.ac.in/bitstream/10603/3031/11/11_chapter%203.pdf).

### 2.5 Village Banking Model

This village banking model is an expansion of the group approach. This model was developed in Bolivia during the mid 1980s by the Foundation for International Community Assistance (FINCA), a non-profit microfinance organization. In this model, a Village Bank is developed by grouping 30 to 100 low-income individuals who seek to improve their lives through self-employment activities. The bank is financed by internal mobilization of members' saving fund as well as loans provided by the sponsoring MFIs. The MFIs lend capital to the bank, which then lends the money to its members. Members themselves run the village bank; they choose their members, elect their own officers, establish their own by-laws, distribute loans to individuals and collect savings and payments. Loan amounts are linked to the aggregate amount saved by individual bank members. Loans are repaid weekly in small installments. Thus, village banks have a high degree of democratic control and independence. The model is used by various MFIs like Co-operative for Assistance and Relief Everywhere (CARE) in Guatemala; Save the Children in El Salvador; Burkina Faso in Bolivia, Mali, and Ghana; Freedom from Hunger and Catholic Relief Services in Thailand and Benin, Opportunity International, Consultative Group for Assisting the Poor (CGAP), etc.

### *2.6 Credit Unions and Credit Co-operatives Model*

A credit union is a democratic, not-for-profit financial co-operative. It is owned and governed by its members, who are at the same time the owners and the customers of their co-operative society. Co-operatives are often created by persons belonging to the same local or professional community or sharing a common interest. Co-operatives generally provide their members with a wide range of banking and financial services. Members participate in all the major decisions and democratically elect officers from among themselves to monitor the administration of the co-operative. Loans are granted only to the members. SANASA Development Bank of Sri Lanka is an example of rural credit co-operative which is successfully working as a microfinance service provider.

#### *2.6.1 Linkage between Micro-Finance and PACS*

The share of primary agricultural credit societies (PACS) in rural credit stood at 18.6 percent in 1991. A good deal of this amount went to people who were relatively better-off, that is, to those who do not belong to the BPL households. Notwithstanding this, a certain percentage of the credit flow has benefited the poor. According to the World Bank NCAER study (2004) the share of PACS in micro-credit is as high as 30 percent or one-third. PACS are, as such, yet another important channel of microfinance.

In terms of retail outlets, the PACS are ahead of the banks and the MFIs at the all-India level, although they are observed to have greater concentration in Maharashtra and Kerala and very low in North Eastern states. The total membership of PACS is reported to be 120 million. The Scheduled Castes and Scheduled Tribes who generally comprise the weaker sections of the society constitute as high as 36-37 percent or approximately 45 million PACS members. This is much higher membership than under the SHG-Bank linkage programme, (currently around 30 million BPL households) and under the MFIs/LABs/NBFCs (around 1 million clients).

The co-operative structure is ideally based on the norm of "one man, one vote". The concept of 'social collateral' or 'group guarantee' holds good for the co-operatives as well. Group guarantee is supposed to be stronger in the cooperatives (of the poor) and the guiding principle is "one for all and all for one". What appears to work best under this model is greater proximity of PACS to its members and the credit history that determines the credit worthiness of the clients.

A large number of PACS in rural India have been, however, dominated by the powerful. The prudential norms of banking have also been ignored and loans have been extended to defaulting members. Besides, records are not maintained properly and accounting and book-keeping of most PACS are very weak. Political interference of one kind or the other, instead of improving the situation, has only contributed to the decline of PACS. Refinancing facility from apex organizations has consequently declined/stopped and in the absence of emphasis on thrift, the PACS have hardly sufficient funds for credit activity. Successive Committees constituted to suggest measures for revitalization of PACS have recommended for enactment of the Model Law of Cooperatives. It is an enabling Law that would make the credit cooperatives free from the State's prerogative to override the management (the control of the Registrar of Cooperatives). The recommendations also include diversification of credit portfolio by PACS/Cooperative Banks beyond crop loans. The credit cooperatives may thus also give consumer loan, housing loan and provide finance for services sector as well as distribute insurance products. This would call for capacity and infrastructure building of PACS and observance of prudential banking norms by PACS. The revitalization package proposed is, moreover, restricted only to viable PACS and any new infusion of funds by the apex banks will be linked to signing of a MOU.

### 2.7 Mixed Model

Some MFIs started with the Grameen model but converted to the SHG model at a later stage. However they did not completely do away with Grameen type lending and smaller groups. They are a mix of SHG and Grameen model. The main difference between these programmes is rather marginal. Grameen programmes have traditionally not given much importance to savings as a source of funds whereas SHGs place considerable emphasis on the source of funds. The SHG programmes have compulsory deposit schemes in which the members themselves determine the amount. The SHGs model is widely used in India. According to Mahajan (2005), Managing Director of BASIX, the SHGs and Grameen models offer economies of transaction cost to MFIs, but at the cost of members time because the unit of dealing is "group" rather than individual. In contrast, MFIs offering individual loans incur higher transaction costs for serving their borrowers. In summary, Fig. 1 capture the appropriateness of each of the models described and discussed above.

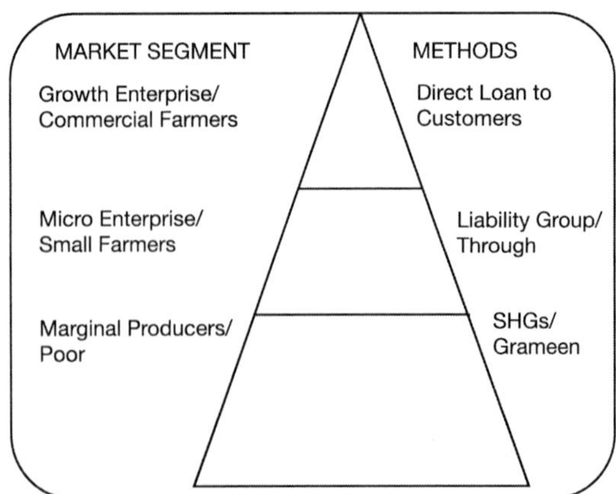


**Fig. 1:** Market Segment and Methodology Applied

*Source*: Mahanta et al. (2012).

### *2.8 Business Correspondent Model (BCM)*

Since 2006, the Reserve Bank of India (RBI) has permitted banks to use the services of third parties as business correspondents (BCs) to help increase the outreach of banking services. BCs are a mechanism that allows banks to offer its clients micro-loans, micro-savings, micro-insurance and micro-remittances services beyond its brick and mortar branches. The BC model is increasingly being recognized as the most suitable approach for achieving financial inclusion in the long run as it allows banks to service customers and extend their geographic reach at a much lower cost. There are five logically distinct players in the BC model:

1. *Banks* are the principals, as far as they have the legal relationship with end-customers as account issuers and must have lead branding in the service.
2. *Business Correspondents* (BCs) are entities appointed by the bank to offer banking services to bank clients beyond the brick-and-mortar branches of the bank. Their role is to oversee the orderly development and proper functioning of the bank's indirect channel. They must be have a direct contract with the bank, and are subjected to specific regulations issued by the RBI.
3. *Agent Network Managers* (ANMs). Mostly BCs also assume the role of Agent Network Managers but in very few models, BC contracts a separate entity to function as ANM. The ANMs' role includes: identifying, screening and training of new CSPs; supervising and offering ongoing business improvement advice to existing CSPs; or putting in place liquidity rebalancing mechanisms for CSPs (e.g. hiring 'runners' to collect or distribute cash to CSPs, or managing a set of bank accounts through which CSPs can deposit and withdraw money effectively). ANMs typically act as outsourced partners of BCs, though the degree of reliance on ANMs varies from one BC to the next.
4. *Customer Service Points* (CSPs) or agents are specific individuals or retail outlets that maintain the direct contact with customers. Their role is to collect account

opening documentation, offer cash-in and cash-out services, receive payments, and in some cases conduct certain credit processing and evaluation functions—all on behalf of the bank. The CSPs may be staff of or retail outlets directly owned by the BC, or they may be contracted by the BC to perform these functions.

5. *Technology Service Providers* (TSPs) provide an electronic solution that allows customers and CSPs to transact remotely, and provides BCs with management tools to oversee the entire branchless channel. The solution needs to be sufficiently low-cost, secure, scalable, robust and user-friendly to be adopted by a large number of users with a low support requirement. TSPs are typically contracted by banks, though in many cases the BC and TSP may be the same or related companies.

The BC model is highly dependent on technology, as the technology platform is what allows trust to be extended from the bank through the BC to individual CSPs. The platform must ensure that transacting parties are properly identified, that the necessary transaction request and confirmation information is collected and transmitted in real time, and that transactions are authorized, recorded and reconciled correctly. The technology solution may be defined by a set of key choices:

- *Device used to capture transaction requests*: using clients' mobile phone or a point-of-sale terminal operated by the CSP.
- *Client authentication mechanism*: using two-factor authentication (typically phone or card in the customers' possession + personal identification number [PIN]), or single-factor (fingerprint).
- *Communication environment*: online only (mobile or internet), or online + offline (involving local storage of transactions in smartcards and intelligent devices).

### 2.8.1 Business value of BC Model

The BC model offers banks a vision for tackling un-served customer segments in a way that is profitable and sustainable.

It is based on serving poor or remote communities at a much lower incremental cost per new customer acquired or per new village covered than traditional branch-based banking. However, this remains a speculative view for most banks, as they struggle to deploy BC networks in a scalable manner and to trigger sufficient usage by customers to produce significant revenue. While banks do not doubt that branchless banking is the key to financial inclusion, they are seeking answers to some fundamental questions:

- What is the customer value proposition that can drive client demand and recurring usage?
- What is the business model that aligns the incentives of the various players involved (banks, BCs, CSPs, ANMs, TSPs), consistent with the revenue that can be expected to be generated from low-value customers?
- How can they scale up the BC network, while limiting the upfront investment required and financial risks involved?

Noting the lukewarm response of banks to the BC model, in March 2010, the Reserve Bank of India asked all nationalized banks to submit detailed financial inclusion plans, which, collectively, would ensure full financial inclusion by March 2013. Subsequently, the Ministry of Finance (MoF) mandated all nationalized banks to financially include 73,000 out of 600,000 villages in India with a population of more than 2,000 people by March, 2012. The current focus of most commercial banks is to achieve the outreach target stipulated by the MoF by engaging a number of BC partners, and riding on the government's need to register masses of people in order to collect cash benefits from programmes such as the Mahatma Gandhi National Rural Employment Guarantee Act (MGNREGA) programme. Even as banks press ahead to meet their stated targets, they remain unsure of the commercial viability of the BC model. As a result, the BC model feels like it is being driven by a supply push, with insufficient evidence of client demand. Clear notions of customer value must drive the business case for banks and their BCs. Recurrent usage generates a willingness to pay by customers.

The customer value question can then lead to the business model question: how to tap into the customer willingness to pay through an appropriate pricing model, and how that revenue ought to be split across the various partners in the delivery chain. This process is illustrated in Fig. 2 below.

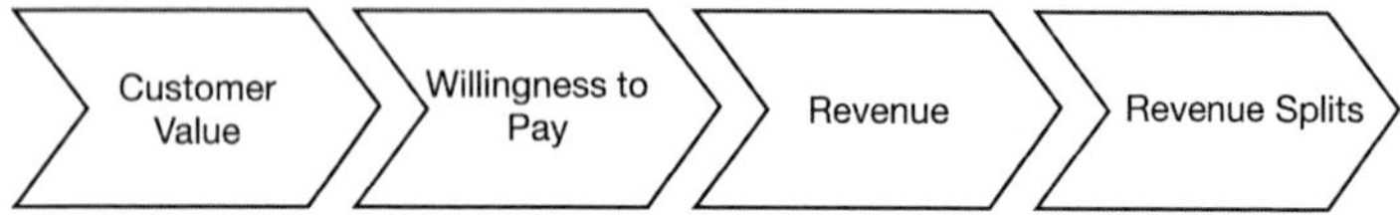


**Fig. 2:** The business case continuum

Customer value is generated by a combination of functionality (what I can do) and convenience (how I can do it). The functionality available through BC channels is extremely limited, as BC deployments still offer mainly a plain vanilla savings account with few features and often no payment options. In its current form, the BC model in India also offers little convenience to customers. Most BC deployments suffer from server downtime, spotty CSP coverage, insufficient float or opening hours at existing CSPs, and lack of CSP interoperability across banks and BCs. Trust in CSPs is also a problem, and that can be attributed to low usage for two reasons. On the demand side, customers fail to gain familiarity and get comfortable with banking services being available at locations that are not bank-owned. On the supply side, insufficient recurring revenue induces some agents to overcharge for the few transactions they do, which further undermines trust in the BC model.

#### *2.8.2 Current Products Offered under BC Model*

##### *2.8.2.1 Savings products*:

- No Frills Account (NFA) is a single, liquid account, and is not consistent with the fragmentation or mental model of savings of low-income households. A potential solution for this is to design the product in line with the planning of finances by these households, which leads to savings such as Pay Plan products.
- Recurring Deposits (RD)/Fixed Deposits (FD) are still mostly non-existent in the BC networks. Some products are simplistic and require committed savings from

clients who have unpredictable cash flows. There are no documented success cases of RD/FD products.

*2.8.2.2 Payments and receipts products*: MicroSave research suggests that customers primarily look for trust and time taken for delivery in a remittance channel/product. Further, remittance products thrive on network effects (Ignacio Mas et al. 2012). The current product offerings are only along select corridors and are not interoperable, which undermines network effects. At present, none of the existing remittance products offers the convenience provided by informal mechanisms (like couriers), which typically offer delivery of the cash at the recipient's doorstep. However, banks are rapidly becoming the cheapest, quickest, most secure and thus most trusted way to send money, and remitters and recipients alike seem to prefer this channel to the other options available. Electronic Benefit Transfers (EBT) payments are even more complicated as multiple benefits are paid in multiple accounts. Operational issues with the EBT processes also undermine the credibility of payment systems. With respect to bill payments, there are only few billers at present, while aggregators are mostly missing from the scene. In addition, the target clients of BCs, which are hitherto unbanked, do not use most the billers present. There are limited options to use payments and receipts for other financial services. Overdraft and linked credit scoring is not yet in the product line of services offered by most banks. Yet, the opportunity for mobilizing savings at the base of the pyramid may be larger than banks anticipate. Imagine the targeted was to induce a savings balance per account equivalent to a month's worth of household income—that seems like a reasonable threshold of impact. For a family living at the $2 per day poverty threshold, that translates into a savings balance of around $100. (That is $2 per day per person at purchasing power parity [PPP] exchange rate × 5 people per household × 0.3 PPP/market exchange conversion rate × 30 days per month.) Median savings balances of $100 can much more easily be profitable for banks to offer.

Once customers see value in the service offered, they will be willing to pay for the service. A recent MicroSave research indicates that customers are willing to pay for BC services if it offers convenience and functionality to them. With customers paying for the service, the revenue from the business will improve which will result in higher revenue splits for the stakeholders (Ignacio Mas et al. 2012). In areas where banks have an established presence and branches are heavily crowded (especially in urban areas), banks have a more specific incentive to offer e/m-banking services so as to decongest their branches. This allows them to move lower-value customers away from costly bank branches to cheaper agency banking alternatives. Here the business case is easier, as it depends strictly on cost reduction and not necessarily on additional clients or additional usage per client.

### *2.9 MFI Models*

The specialized MFIs or micro-finance movement since the 1990's is a new avenue of reaching the poor for their micro-credit needs. Some of the MFIs are based on the Grameen Model, which entails formation of a Centre comprising eight solidarity groups of five borrowers. Members of each solidarity group mutually guarantee each other loan. Ten Centres form a cluster and seven clusters form a (bank) branch and several branches together presumably form the Bank. This is typically based on the model of Grameen Bank of Bangladesh (Grameen Bank, 2010). All members save regularly and loan proposals are approved by the Centre; all loans are, moreover, repayable in 50 weekly installments. MFIs in India register themselves either as societies (under the Societies Registration Act, 1960), as trusts under the Trust Acts, as Non-Banking Financial Companies (NBFCs), or as Local Area Banks (LABs). All NBFCs requiring registration with the Reserve Bank of India should have a minimum capital of ₹ 2 crore. NBFCs intending to accept public deposits have to satisfy stipulated criteria and have to obtain specific authorization from the RBI. The issue of covering of NBFCs' deposits by Deposit Insurance and Credit Guarantee Corporation (DICGC) was examined several times, and it was found neither desirable nor feasible to extend such coverage. Sa-Dhan, an association of MFIs has argued for a new category of NBFCs, namely, Micro-Finance Company with a minimum equity capital requirement (capitalization) of ₹ 25 lakh. Such MFIs are designed to provide credit only; mobilization of savings is restricted to members and borrowers. The ratio of savings to net owned funds is recommended to be 1 : 1 initially, which may go up to 5 : 1 subsequently. This may, however, pose a problem of supervision by the regulator (RBI) if there are a large number of MFIs. A Micro-Finance Development Council was therefore proposed for performing the task of regulating such MFIs. The Government has, however, not favoured this idea (Sa-Dhan, 2008).

### *2.9.1 Agency Model of MFI*

The Internal Group on Rural Credit and Micro-Finance of RBI (July, 2005), came to the conclusion that parking of funds with MFIs is faced with two sets of exposures, namely, once at the MFI/NGO level and thereafter at the level of SHGs/ individual borrower level. The RBI has, nevertheless, favoured the Agency model of MFIs. Under this model, in addition to the MFIs, CSOs, etc., only those NBFCs which are incorporated under Section 25 of the Companies Act, 1956 are permitted to be appointed as 'Business Facilitators' (BFs) or as 'Business correspondents' (BCs). In the former case, the MFIs provide the non-financial services, such as, identification of borrower, processing and submission of applications to banks, etc. In the latter case, the MFI provide financial services as "pass through" agents for disbursal of small value credit, recovery of principal/ collection of interest or sale of micro-insurance/mutual fund products, etc. The loan amount, however, remains in the books of the bank. The banks need not obtain prior permission from RBI for appointing BCs and BFs. They are required to conduct thorough due diligence before appointing BFs/BCs, and as principals, are responsible for customer service and control operations. The banks also need to have operational guidelines for the purpose. The MFIs, moreover, provide First Loan Default Guarantee (FLDG) equal to 8-15 percent of the limit sanctioned in the form of security deposit with the bank so as to maintain its stake in the loan portfolio. The banks appear to have positive experience under this model as the MFIs have helped them overcome the problem of outreach in rural areas and have also reduced their transaction cost. In brief, the agency model of MFI is bank-driven.

### *2.9.2 MFI Bulk Lending Model*

While the Agency model may appear more appropriate in the case of small MFIs, the larger MFIs may like to operate independently of banks (e.g. as LABs). This category of MFIs belong to MFI Bulk Lending (Equity Participation) model whereby they can access funds in the form of cheaper loans, subordinated debts, equity or quasi-equity from agencies, such as, the Rashtriya Mahila Kosh, the SIDBI Foundation for Micro-Credit (SFMC), the Micro-Finance Development and Equity Fund (under the chairmanship of NABARD) as well as the FWWB (http://www.scribd.com/doc/51961407/REPORT-ON-MICROFINANCE).

## *2.10 Post Office Network and Banking Services*

The existing extensive formal banking structure is still not sufficient to meet the growing demand of rural credit. Lack of sufficient number of retail outlets of formal banking sector has been a big handicap in reaching the poor. There are approximately 1,55,000 post-offices in India, which is more in number than the combined outlets of all the banks and the (functional) PACS put together. Post-offices have been already into the business of collecting small deposits from people and have been providing services of transferring money. Post-office network could very well be considered for increasing the outreach of banking services, especially in remote and rural areas. One of the important principles of microfinance is to provide doorstep and timely delivery of financial service. The scheme of pigmy deposits pioneered by some banks in the past met these criteria. This experiment, however, failed because of unscrupulous agents who indulged in fraud. The post-offices are also known to have experimented with similar schemes and had a greater measure of success. They have a regular and paid staff and with little training and incentives, their services could be utilized very usefully.

## 3. A Critical Comparative Analysis of Microfinance Models

### *3.1 Grameen Bank Model of Bangladesh*

The Grameen Bank (GB) is based on the voluntary formation of small groups of five people to provide mutual, morally binding group guarantees in lieu of the collateral required by conventional banks. Women were initially given equal access to the schemes, and proved to be not only reliable borrowers but also astute entrepreneurs as well. GB has successfully reversed conventional banking practices by removing collateral requirements and has developed a banking system based on mutual trust, accountability, participation and creativity.

According to Professor Yunus the founder of the Grameen Bank, credit is seen as a cutting edge tool for affecting those inequalities that confine the poor to a poverty cycle and for releasing the inherent capacities in people. Thus, it restores some sort of social power which has been denied to the poor because they lack collateral. Professor Muhammad Yunus argued that the conventional banking system is anti-poor, anti-women and anti-illiterate and thus, has contributed to maintaining the status quo between the rich and poor (Yunus, 1989). Thus microcredit issued to small groups, is purported to enable them the opportunity to purchase equipment and other inputs and engage in micro-enterprises of their choice.

#### *3.1.1 Methodologies of the Grameen Bank Model*

As mentioned earlier, the GB is based on the voluntary formation of small groups of five people to provide mutual, morally binding group guarantees in lieu of the collateral required by conventional banks. Women were initially given equal access to the schemes and contrary to what was thought of, they proved to be not only reliable borrowers but also astute entrepreneurs. Intensive discipline, supervision and servicing, characterize the operations of the GB, which are carried out by bicycle bankers in branch units with considerable delegated authority. Group based lending is one of the most novel approaches of lending small amounts of Money to a large number of clients who cannot offer collateral. The size of the group can vary, but most groups have between four to eight members. The group self-selects its Members before acquiring a loan. Loans are granted to selected member(s) of the group first and then to the rest of the members. A percentage of the loan is required to be saved in advance, which points out the ability to make regular payments and serve as collateral. Group members are jointly accountable for the repayment of each other's loans and usually meet weekly to collect repayments. To ensure repayment, peer pressure and joint liability works very well. The entire group will be disqualified and will not be eligible for further loans, even if one member of the group becomes a defaulter.

### *3.1.2 Weaknesses of the Grameen Bank Model*

One of the most successful models replicated and discussed around the world is the Grameen model. The bank has successfully served the rural poor in Bangladesh with no physical collateral relying on group responsibility to replace the collateral requirements. However, I think the model has the following limitations:

- Setting up a Grameen bank requires putting up a huge mega structure that involves huge costs. Most of the funds obtained from external sources to finance micro projects end up being used to pay operational costs and salaries of personnel working in the mega structure.
- The Grameen Bank Model has degerated into a level where, the poor are being pushed into a cycle of multiple borrowings through the rolling of cash. That is, the poor keep on borrowing to pay previous engagement that is robbing Peter to pay Paul. This in addition to its usurious lending rates and high-handed collection mechanisms pushes the poor further below the poverty line. What ought to be a bank-aided socially purposive activity is now a private equity driven business with profits and valuations as the goal.
- It involves too much of external subsidy which is not replicable as the bank has not oriented itself towards mobilizing peoples' resources. Thus, in the absence of donors funded programmes and mezzanine assets financial self-sufficiency becomes questionable.

- The repayment system of 50 weekly equal installments is not practical because the poor do not have a stable job. In addition, in a typical agrarian community, during lean seasons it will become practically impossible for them to repay the loan.
- Pressure for high repayment drives members to money-lenders. Credit alone cannot alleviate poverty and the Grameen model is based only on credit. Consequently, haste can lead to wrong selection of activities and beneficiaries.
- The interest rate charged by the Grameen bank is by far higher than those charged by conventional banks. They charge more than 7 percent monthly, with the credit terms remaining inflexible and ill adapted to the activities of the poor clients. Grameen Bank defends it high interest rates in relation to moneylenders rather than low cost bank finance providers.
- Again, agriculture which in most developing countries is the principal activity of the poor is neglected. The Grameen model calls for the dynamics of joint liability. This mean that groups screen and self select their members to form a relatively homogeneous groups and consequently members typically share similar probability of defaulting on a loan. Again, the poor are again left out due to negative perception of poor people in a community, with no social groups willing to accept the poor.

### 3.2 The MC2 Model

MC2 are rural development micro-banks created and managed by a community in keeping to their local values and customs. The principal promoter of this concept, Dr. Paul K. Fokam drew inspiration from the Einstein's famous formula: Victory over Poverty (VP) is possible if the Means (M) and the Competences (C) of the Community (C) are combined. Hence the formula VP = M × C × C = MC2. In other words, MC2 is a community based micro banking approach whereby people and mostly the underprivileged endeavour to be self-reliant, create wealth with a view to improving their living conditions in a sustainable manner (Fotabong and Akanga, 2005). The model has two versions: a rural version, MC2 and an urban version dubbed MUFFA. The second version of the model is exclusively for women because studies and personal research of the founder show that women in urban areas are those most hit by poverty. Through MUFFA, these women have easy access to financial services which help them to start job creation and wealth generating small business activities. Consequently, the model is built and supported by four main pillars. These are the local populations, the non-governmental organization (NGO) Appropriate Development for Africa (ADAF), AfrilandFirst bank Group and some national and foreign partners (Fotabong and Akanga, 2005).

The objectives of the MC2 Micro-bank are simple.

- The first objective of the MC2 micro-bank is economic and financial sustainability from the perspective of the micro-bank, the individuals and group members.
- The second objective of MC2 is the social dimension. This involves targeting the poor, micro and small scale activities and consequently restoring dignity to target beneficiaries to see the importance of being masters of their destiny.

### *3.2.1 Methodologies of the MC2 Model*

The micro-bank is more developed and corrects the imperfections of micro-credit and micro-finance. It rest on the premise that, savings is the engine of progress and awareness is fuel to keep the engine rolling, while loans serve as a lubricants and finally appended and related service solution to the problem of poverty. MC2 model is not a packaged readymade one size fit all, although the core principles remain the same from one community to the other. Setting up a MC2 micro-bank involves five stages (Comparing MC2 Model versus other Microfinance Models:http://www.fgda.org/dati/ContentManager/files/Documenti_microfinanza/Comparing%20Microfinance%20Models.pdf).

*Stage One-Sensitizing the Poor and Raising their Awareness*

In the first stage of the MC2 micro-bank development, the target community population particularly the poor are sensitized and their awareness rose on:

- The importance of savings in their struggle for self-reliance. This is done through community gatherings, association gatherings and empowerment forums.
- The need to firstly rely on oneself before expecting any external assistance.
- The pride in remaining the sole masters of their own destiny.

Thus, in the first stage awareness is created. This is the fuel to keep the engine (savings) is rolling in the second stage.

*Stage Two: Mobilizing Resources*

At the second stage of the micro-bank development the engine (savings and resources) is mobilized. This involves getting stakeholders committed, raising the startup capital, paying individual shares subscription and fees, registering the micro-bank, and opening of individual accounts. These resources mobilized in stage two will enable the micro-bank commence the lending functions in the third stage of the micro-bank development.

*Stage Three: Three-Financing Individual Income Generating Activities*

In stage three, the micro-bank start granting credits to individual's income generating activities using the resources mobilized in stage two. At this level the micro-bank now completes it intermediary function of facilitating resources from areas of excesses to areas of deficits.

*Stage Four: Financing Common Interest Economic Projects*

In the fourth stage of micro-bank development, the micro-bank institution becomes involved in community development economic activities such as the construction of hospitals, health centres, community halls, schools, and public taps, etc. However, communities are caution that the best moment to engage in the fourth stage of MC2 development is some two to three years after it has achieved administrative and financial autonomy. That is when the MC2 can meet its various expenses (salaries, electricity, telephone bills and other consumables). At this level, any MC2 should be able of raising enough money from loans and other facilities offered to pay off fixed charges and even show a surplus that can be considered a profit. These surpluses should be built for a minimum of two years. It is at this stage that the impact of the MC2 micro-banking approach is deeply felt. For example, imagine a community capable of raising its own financial resources for the construction of a small hydro project (Fotabong and Akanga, 2005).

*Stage Five: Carrying Out Social Development Projects*

At the final stage of MC2, community social projects are being financed and carried out with the resources generated in stage three and four. That is the results are performance registered under stage three and four are primary for this phase to be carried out.

### *3.2.2 Weaknesses of the MC2 Model*

- Base on the stages of development outlined, it will take about four years for an MC2 to become financially sustainable and another four to five years to accumulate resources. This means, the second objective of the model which is that of social dimension will have to be put aside for at least 10-15 years. This limits the activities of the model within these periods to the economically viable members.
- Its low interest rate on savings 2.5 percent might limit resource mobilization only to true supporters of community development, and those intending to benefit credit in the future. This might cause an upward pressure on loan demand.
- Again, the model is increasingly appearing to be more of a distribution channel for the link bank. MC2 is a brand of the link bank with most of the services on offer being products and services of the link bank.
- It is clear and eminent in the model the collapse of MC2 or an MC2 unit wouldn't affect the link bank but a

problem at the level of the link bank might create panic and result to the suspension of some products such as I-Cards, Flash Cash, and Money First; since these products function on a platform provided by the link bank.

### *3.3 Village Banking Model of FINCA*

The village banking institution, Foundation for International Community Assistance (FINCA) implements a village banking model in its effort to create financially-sustainable solidarity groups. FINCA trains small community groups in a 22-module programme to form Community Credit Enterprises (CCE). These small enterprises, or companies, permit members to buy shares as shareholders and generate capital to offer sustainable credit and business models. The village banking model was first developed during the 1980s in Bolivia by John Hatch.

#### *3.3.1 Methodologies of the Village Banking Model*

According to the original model, village banking-FINCA works with groups of 30-60 members, usually all women. As soon as the village bank is inaugurated, it receives its first loan from the implementing agency (the local headquarters of FINCA or its affiliate) for on-lending to the individual members of the village bank. The sponsoring agency spends one to three months in setting up each bank, organizing the election of a management committee and training its members, as well as developing the rules and regulations to govern the village bank. The first individual loan (usually US$ 50) is repaid on a weekly basis in equal installments of principal and interest over a four-month period. The village bank collects these payments at regular meetings and, at the end of the 16th week; it repays the entire loan principal plus interest to the implementing agency. The funds circulating back and forth between the implementing agency and the village bank for loans to members constitute the external account. If the village bank repays in full, it is eligible for a second loan. If the village bank is unable to pay the amount due, the implementing agency stops further credit until reimbursement is made.

### *3.3.2 Weaknesses of the Village Banking Model*

- The village banking model of FINCA is over dependent on external funding. This puts the model at risk in a situation where funds are no longer being channeled into the village bank.
- Because funds are being channeled into the village bank at 10 percent interest rate, the villagers or credit beneficiaries end up paying interest rates of more than 2 percent on weekly basis. This high interest rate is not sensible considering the meager resources of the poor and the purpose put forth to defend this initiative.
- Again, the model requires compulsory 20 percent savings of the loan amount granted with beneficiaries compelled to repay the loan-principal, interest and savings within 16-24 equal weekly installments. This most often is ill adapted to the cycle of activities of the community particularly with agricultural financing most of which have but seasonal cash flow.
- Loans are exclusively granted for trading and micro-enterprise activities with a maximum amount granted to an individual being limited to $300 due to the lack of the village bank own resources.
- Most village banks are not registered and consequently are not covered by the law and again without an ongoing recruitment and mobilization drive for depositors the village bank can run into problems. Savings are the life-blood of an institution and it enables lending. Therefore concerted attempts to broaden the membership base and ultimately savings volumes are imperative. Most of the village banks have little or no government support.

## 3.4 The SKS and Non-Banking Finance Company (NBFC) Model

In India, NBFCs has emerged as a nearest substitute for those MFIs who want to go the for-profit route. The NBFC route is increasingly being chosen by profit driven MFIs. These institutions get their capital most often from the capital market and believe that, since the poor are bankable and lending to them can be commercially viable it is not necessary to depend on low cost funds to lend to them. Secondly, pioneers of this model believe that, since the amounts required are huge, the financial markets are the only way to mobilize resources. This would mean mobilizing debt at market rates of interest. These institutions make use of debts and mezzanine assets. They accept investment from the capital markets, complimented by borrowings from commercial banks and in turn the money is used for the financing of micro projects and activities of the poor that ends up pushing the poor further below the poverty line.

### *3.4.1 Methodologies of SKS and NBFC Model*

The model uses equity investors and lenders for resources mobilization. The coordinating microfinance set up a mega structure coordinating units where factory style recruitment and training are made for loan officers. Field offices are then set up through which credits are disbursed to beneficiaries through the loan officers at exorbitant interest rates. The objective of this model since it is investor driven is maximization of profit. The SKS microfinance model finances groups and individuals with contract requiring beneficiaries to do weekly repayments.

### *3.4.2 Weaknesses of the SKS Model*

- The objective of the SKS microfinance model is profit maximization, thus all efforts are made to put the interest rate above 35 percent.
- The model is heavily dependent on investors' and lender's funds as the SKS model do not accept deposit of any kind on their own.
- Over pressure on loans beneficiaries push customers to commit suicides as the loans are inflexible and ill adapted to the cycle of activities of the beneficiaries. In addition because of huge mega structure being set up by this model operational cost turn to be very high and this is transferred to the poor in the form of higher interest rate.
- The SKS starts it activities in urban areas before venturing into rural areas.

### *3.5 Self-Help Group (SHG) Bank Linkage Model*

The microfinance movement started in India with the introduction of the SHG-Bank Linkage Programme in the 1980s by NGOs that was later formalized by the Government of India in the early 1990s. Pursuant to the programme, banks, which are primarily public sector regional rural banks, are encouraged to partner with SHGs to provide them with funding support, which is often subsidized. A self-help group, or SHG, is a group of 10 to 20 poor women in a village who come together to contribute regular savings to a common fund to deposit with a bank as collateral for future loans. The group has collective decision-making power and obtains loans from the partner bank. The SHG then loans these funds to its members at terms decided by the group. Members of the group meet on a monthly basis to conduct transactions and group leaders are responsible for maintaining their own records, often with the help of NGOs or government agency staff. NABARD is presently operating three models of linkage of banks with SHGs and NGOs (NABARD, 2002):

**Model–1:** In this model, the bank itself acts as a Self-Help Group Promoting Institution (SHPI). It takes initiatives in forming the groups, nurtures them over a period of time and then provides credit to them after satisfying itself about their maturity to absorb credit. About 16 percent of SHGs and 13 percent of loan amounts are using this model (as of March 2002).

**Model–2:** In this model, groups are formed by NGOs (in most of the cases) or by government agencies. The groups are nurtured and trained by these agencies. The bank then provides credit directly to the SHGs, after observing their operations and maturity to absorb credit. While the bank provides loans to the groups directly, the facilitating agencies continue their interactions with the SHGs. Most linkage experiences begin with this model with NGOs playing a major role. This model has also been popular and more acceptable to banks, as some of the difficult functions of Social dynamics are externalized.

About 75 percent of SHGs and 78 percent of loan amounts are using this model.

**Model–3:** Due to various reasons, banks in some areas are not in a position to even finance SHGs promoted and nurtured by other agencies. In such cases, the NGOs act as both facilitators and microfinance intermediaries. First, they promote the groups, nurture and train them and then approach banks for bulk loans for on-lending to the SHGs. About 9 percent of SHGs and 13 percent of loan amounts are using this model.

### *3.6 Micro-Finance Institution (MFI) Model*

The MFI model has gained significant momentum in India in recent years and continues to grow as the viable alternative to SHGs. In contrast to an SHG, an MFI is a separate legal organization that provides financial services directly to borrowers. MFIs have their own employees, record keeping and accounting systems and are often subject to regulatory oversight. MFIs require borrowers from a village to organize themselves in small groups, typically of five women, that have joint decision-making responsibility for the approval of member loans. The groups meet weekly to conduct transactions. MFI staff travel to the villages to attend the weekly group meetings to disburse loans and collect repayments. Unlike SHGs, loans are issued by MFIs without collateral or prior savings. MFIs now exist in a variety of legal forms, including trusts, societies, cooperatives, non-profit NBFCs registered under Section 25 of the Companies Act, 1956, or Section 25 Companies, and NBFCs registered with the RBI. Trusts, cooperatives and Section 25 companies are regulated by the specific act under which they are registered and not by the RBI.

Attempts have been made by some of the associations of MFIs like Sa-Dhan to capture the business volume of the MFI sector. As per the Bharat Micro-Finance Report of Sa-Dhan, in March 2009, the 233 member MFIs of Sa-Dhan had an outreach of 22.6 million clients with an outstanding microfinance portfolio of INR 117 billion (US$ 2.5 billion) (Sa-Dhan, 2008).

### *3.6.1 Legal Forms of MFIs in India*

A MFI in India acquires permission to lend through registration. MFIs are registered as one of the following five types of entities (NABARD, 2009-2010):

- NGOs engaged in microfinance (NGO MFIs), comprising of Societies and Trusts;
- Cooperatives registered under the conventional state-level cooperative acts, the national level Multi-State Cooperative Societies Act (MSCA, 2002), or under the new State-level Mutually Aided Cooperative Societies Act (MACS Act);
- Section 25 Companies (not-for profit);
- For-Profit NBFCs; and
- NBFC-MFIs.

*NGO MFIs*: There are around 500 NGOs that provide microfinance services and operate as non-profits, although many of these NGO MFIs perform non-financial operations as well. NGO MFIs can be registered as a Society under the Societies Registration Act of 1860 or as a Trust under the Indian Trust Act of 1882.

*Cooperative Societies*: Approximately 100 MFIs in India operate as Cooperatives, registered under the Cooperative Societies Act of the respective state, the Central Multi-State Cooperative Act, 1984, or the new state-level MACS Act. The MACS Act was pioneered by Andhra Pradesh, which sought to prevent political interference in cooperative societies' operations. Some large cooperatives have acquired a banking licence from the RBI to operate as cooperative banks.

*Section 25 Companies*: Many NGO MFIs achieve a more formal corporate structure by registering under the Companies Act, 1956, as a Section 25 Company. These companies offer a structure that can more easily transform into an NBFC. They can accept equity investments, though they cannot offer dividends, and equity investments cannot be withdrawn at the closing of the company. Thus, these institutions often have difficulty attracting equity investments.

*NBFCs*: The mainstream financial sector in India is divided primarily into two categories, banks and NBFCs. Banks adhere to much more stringent regulation than NBFCs because they are all permitted to accept public deposits, and are considered to have consequent systemic risk. The NBFC encompasses many different types of financial companies, which are all subject to the same regulation requirements. Many MFIs have recently registered as NBFCs to take advantage of access to capital markets. NBFCs account for the great majority of the microfinance market in India, with about 50 NBFCs responsible for 80 percent of all microfinance portfolios.

NBFC-MFIs: For-profit institutions that qualify for priority sector lending funds are registered as NBFC-MFIs. This NBFC sub-category was created by RBI in May 2011 to classify NBFCs operating as MFIs which meet certain requirements. Currently, it is unclear how many NBFCs will elect to register as NBFC-MFIs, and how many will continue to operate as NBFCs. At this point, only priority sector funding requirements have been made applicable for NBFC-MFIs, though it seems that all existing NBFC regulations also apply to NBFC-MFIs.

### *3.6.2 The Formal Sector Institutions*

Traditionally, the formal sector Banking Institutions in India have been serving only the needs of the commercial sector and providing loans for middle and upper income groups. Similarly, for housing the HFIs have generally not evolved a lending product to serve the needs of the Very LIG primarily because of the perceived risks of lending to this sector. Following risks are generally perceived by the formal sector financial institutions:

- Credit Risk
- High transaction and service cost
- Absence of land tenure for financing housing
- Irregular flow of income due to seasonality
- Lack of tangible proof for assessment of income
- Unacceptable collaterals such as crops, utensils and jewellery.

As far as the formal financial institutions are concerned, there are Commercial Banks, Housing Finance Institutions (HFIs), NABARD, Rural Development Banks (RDBs), Land Development Banks, Land Development Banks, and Co-operative Banks (CBs). As regards the Co-operative Structures, the Urban Co-op Banks (UCB) or Urban Credit Co-op Societies (UCCS) are the two primary co-operative financial institutions operating in the urban areas. There are about 1,400 UCBs with over 3,400 branches in India having 14 million members. Their total lending outstanding in 1990-91 has been reported at over ₹ 80 billion with deposits worth ₹ 101 billion. Similarly there exist about 32,000 credit co.op societies with over 15 million members with their total outstanding lending in 1990-91 being ₹ 20 billion with deposits of ₹ 12 billion. Few of the UCCS also have external borrowings from the District Central Co-op Banks (DCCBs) at 18-19 percent. The loans given by the UCBs or the UCCS are for short term and unsecured except for few which are secured by personal guarantees. The most effective security is the group or the peer pressure.

The Government has taken several initiatives to strengthen the institutional rural credit system. The rural branch network of commercial banks have been expanded and certain policy prescriptions imposed in order to ensure greater flow of credit to agriculture and other preferred sectors. The commercial banks are required to ensure that 40 percent of total credit is provided to the priority sectors out of which 18 percent in the form of direct finance to agriculture and 25 percent to priority sector in favour of weaker sections besides maintaining a credit deposit ratio of 60 percent in rural and semi-urban branches. Further the IRDP introduced in 1979 ensures supply of credit and subsidies to weaker section beneficiaries. Although these measures have helped in widening the access of rural households to institutional credit, vast majority of the rural poor have still not been covered. Also, such lending done under the poverty alleviation schemes suffered high repayment defaults and left little sustainable impact on the economic condition of the beneficiaries.

### *3.6.3 Existing Informal Financial Sources*

The informal financial sources generally include funds available from family sources or local moneylenders. The local moneylenders charge exorbitant rates, generally ranging from 36 percent to 60 percent interest due to their monopoly in the absence of any other source of credit for non-conventional needs. Chit Funds and Bishis are other forms of credit system operated by groups of people for their mutual benefit which however their own limitations have. Lately, few of the NGOs engaged in activities related to community mobilization for their socio-economic development have initiated savings and credit programmes for their target groups. These Community based financial systems (CBFS) can broadly be categorised into two models: Group Based Financial Intermediary and the NGO Linked Financial Intermediary. Most of the NGOs like Sharan in Delhi, Federation of Thrift and Credit Association (FTCA) in Hyderabad or SPARC in Mumbai have adopted the first model where they initiate the groups and provide the necessary management support. Others like SEWA in Ahmedabad or Baroda Citizen's Council in Baroda pertain to the second model.

The experience of these informal intermediaries shows that although the savings of group members, small in nature do not attract high returns, it is still practised due to security reasons and for getting loans at lower rates compared to that available from moneylenders. These are short-term loans meant for crisis, consumption and income generation needs of the members. The interest rates on such credit are not subsidised and generally range between 12 to 36 percent. Most of the loans are unsecured. In few cases personal or group guarantees or other collaterals like jewellery is offered as security. While a census of NGOs in micro-finance is yet to be carried out, there are perhaps 250-300 NGOs, each with 50-100 Self-Help Groups (SHG). Few of them, not more than 20-30 NGOs have started forming SHG Federations. There are also agencies which provide bulk funds to the system through NGOs. Thus organizations engaged in microfinance activities in India may be categorised as Wholesalers, NGOs supporting SHG Federations and NGOs directly retailing credit borrowers or groups of borrower. The Wholesalers will include agencies like NABARD, Rashtriya Mahila Kosh, New Delhi and the Friends of Women's World Banking in Ahmedabad. Few of the NGOs supporting SHG Federations include MYRADA in Bengaluru, SEWA in Ahmedabad, PRADAN in Tamil Nadu and Bihar, ADITHI in Patna, SPARC in Mumbai, and ASSEFA in Chennai, etc. While few of the NGOs directly retailing credit to Borrowers are SHARE in Hyderabad, ASA in Trichy, RDO Loyalam Bank in Manipur.

### *3.6.4 Supply of Microfinance Services*

Over the years different attempts have been made by variety of institutions to offer financial services to the unserved and it is critical to learn from them. The original initiative takers were the co-operative banks and subsequently the Regional Rural Banks. In terms of sheer numbers they are large and number of branches run into tens of thousands. However the quality of execution has been diluted over the years and in many cases these institutions themselves have gone through very challenging times and some of them had to be recapitalized or amalgamated. Recently, there has been improvement in performance of these institutions and the same needs to continue. The universal banks themselves have tried a lot of things like Service area approach, Kissan Credit Cards, Bank-SHG linkage programme and other forms of priority sector lending.

In addition to the banking foray in this space, there has been lot of work done by NBFCs, MFIs, post offices. The post offices have provided reach through over one lakh outlets spread across the country which have been used by people for savings and even more often for remittances through money order. An important recent regulatory change has been the opening of the Business Correspondent (BC) channel to compliment the classical approach of bank branch led distribution. While initially restrictive in the kind of players who can be BCs, there has been significant relaxation in that norm and recently this has been opened up to profit making entities. Innovative cost reductions have been attempted more recently with the launch of the BC model. The initial rollout has seen some success stories and many failures. NBFCs constrained by opportunities to participate in the traditional financial services space have tried innovative solutions for different product lines such as tractor finance, second hand truck finance, gold loans, etc. They have tried creative approaches for reaching the customers and have complimented them with usage of technology as well as low cost manpower and local talent.

MFIs successfully built on what originally started as a NGO movement for organizing Self-Help Groups (SHGs). They did a very good job in terms of reach, customer coverage and loan ticket size (managing loans as small as ₹ 5,000). The total MFI outstanding grew extremely rapidly till 2010 and they brought a lot of innovation to the table. This was before they ran into difficult times due to a desire for faster growth and profitability which combined with indiscretion in some areas by a few participants resulted in a recent backlash on the model. The gross loan portfolio growth rates for MFI's dropped sharply from the almost 80 percent year on year growth experienced during the period 2007-10. In fact, the outstanding loan portfolio of several leading players shrunk from 2010 to 2011. Profitability has also dropped on account of rising loan losses. This change in business trajectory was partly precipitated by the sharp drop in repayments in Andhra Pradesh.

### 3.7 The 'Grameen Model'

The Grameen Model which was pioneered by Prof. Muhammed Yunus of Grameen Bank is perhaps the most well known, admired and practised model in the world. The model involves the following elements:

- Homogeneous affinity group of five
- Eight groups form a Centre
- Centre meets every week
- Regular savings by all members
- Loan proposals approved at Centre meeting
- Loan disbursed directly to individuals
- All loans repaid in 50 instalments.

The Grameen model follows a fairly regimented routine. It is very cost intensive as it involves building capacity of the groups and the customers passing a test before the lending could start. The group members tend to be selected or at least strongly vetted by the bank. One of the reasons for the high cost is that staff members can conduct only two meetings a day and thus are occupied for only a few hours, usually early morning or late in the evening. They were used additionally for accounting work, but that can now be done more cost effectively using computers. The model is also rather meeting intensive which is fine as long as the members have no alternative use for their time but can be a problem as members go up the income ladder. The greatness of the Grameen model is in the simplicity of design of products and delivery. The process of delivery is scalable and the model could be replicated widely. The focus on the poorest, which is a value attribute of Grameen, has also made the model a favourite among the donor community.

However, the Grameen model works only under certain assumptions. As all the loans are only for enterprise promotion, it assumes that all the poor want to be self-employed. The repayment of loans starts the week after the loan is disbursed —the inherent assumption being that the borrowers can service their loan from the ex-ante income. Both these assumptions could be questioned. There is enough literature to question whether it is the best model for the poorest—particularly when their ability to take risks with new enterprise might not be up to the mark. There are also questions raised on the fact that the Grameen model excludes many. One of the necessary conditions for this model to work is discipline and growth of the number of clients. By design this model might not be appropriate for sparsely populated areas like Kutch in Gujarat, or areas where there is a widespread migration of the labour class such as in parts of Rajasthan, Mahaboobnagar District of Andhra Pradesh and Bharuch District of Gujarat.

### *3.8 The Self-help Group (SHG) Model*

The SHG model is a model that is homegrown. Unlike other models of micro-credit, the SHG model starts off with savings as a base. The model is like the Grameen model, but not as regimented. Mainstream banking has accepted this model for a nationwide bank linkage programme and it is quite popular with bankers who see potential in microfinance. The essential design elements of the SHG model are as follows:

- Homogenous affinity group of 15-20 members
- Regular meetings
- Regular savings
- Lending decisions are of the group
- Group selects their leaders
- Group accesses external funds.

Groups federate at Cluster/Block level. Most of the groups in India have been promoted by NGOs. The groups tend to be dependent on the intervening agency for a long time to help them not only maintain accounts and conduct meetings, but also to manage the external interface with the bankers and others. The rate of growth of SHGs is not as fast as the Grameen groups, because of the heterogeneity of group formation. Since the design allows for flexibility and focuses on internal capability development, it may take a long time for penetration. Moreover not all promoters of SHGs have the same focus towards the poorest of the poor. Since there is no single external agency channeling credit, there is every danger that the groups might wither away after a while. However, some of the agencies of the state have seen these as effective channels for delivering the programme funds of various line departments. Since there is no single apex body, and most of the groups are independent, there is every danger that they would get misused as the co-operatives got misused in the past. SHGs tend to work better in areas where the credit culture is not severely damaged—particularly in the southern part of India. The Grameen model—which is more disciplined—seems to work in areas where the credit culture is severely impaired—particularly in the north and eastern parts. One of the benefits of the SHG model is that it begins with, and continues to promote member savings. Though SHGs rarely act as the main mode of saving for their members, they at least promote this fundamental financial habit. Further, the SHG model builds on the fact that India already has a large number of bank branches and this channel builds the 'last mile' linkage with the lower-income customers.

### 3.9 Individual Banking Model

Under the individual banking model, there are two sub models: one where joint liability groups are formed—thereby providing social collateral to the lending institution, the other being direct lending to individual clients. BASIX offers both the products, in addition to offering loans to intermediaries for on-lending. Both the models seem to be appropriate for larger clients—who either carry out enterprise on their own, or carry out enterprises that hire the other poor who want to be self-employed. The reason why this works with larger clients is because the transaction size is large enough to justify the transaction costs.

### 3.10 Business Facilitator and Correspondent Models

The Reserve Bank of India, in January 2006 issued an order to ensure greater financial inclusion and increase the outreach of the banking sector, through Business Facilitator Model and Business Correspondent Model. This enabled the commercial banks, including the RRB to use the services of NGOs, SHGs, MFIs and Civil Society Organization as intermediaries to provide financial and banking services through Business Facilitator and Correspondent Model. Under the Business Facilitator Model the Post Offices can also be used as intermediaries for providing services like (i) identification of borrowers and fitment of activities; (ii) collection and preliminary processing of loan applications including verification of primary information/data; (iii) creating awareness about savings and other products and education and advice on managing money and debt counselling; (iv) processing and submission of applications to banks; (v) promotion and nurturing Self-Help Groups/Joint Liability Groups; (vi) post-sanction monitoring ; (vii) monitoring and handholding of Self-Help Groups/Joint Liability Groups/Credit Groups/others; and (viii) follow-up for recovery.

Under the Business Correspondents Model NGOs/MFIs, Cooperative Societies, section 25 companies, registered NBFCs, not accepting Public Deposit and Post Offices may act as Business/ correspondent. In addition to the activities listed under the Business Facilitators Model the scope of activities of the Business

Correspondent included (i) disbursal of small value credit, (ii) recovery of principal/collection interes, (iii) collection of small value deposits, (iv) sale of micro insurance/mutual fund products/ pension products/other third party products, and (v) receipt and delivery of small value remittances/other payment instruments. The banks are expected to act diligently in employing the Business Facilitators and Correspondents. Both the Business Facilitators and Correspondents may be paid reasonable commission/fee by the banks. No fees can be directly charged by them for the services rendered to the customers. The banks are to specify clearly the role of the Business Facilitators and Correspondents and also give wide publicity both in electronic and print media. The banks are also to constitute Grievance Redressal Machinery within the banks for addressing the complaints about services rendered by the Business Correspondents and Facilitators. However, no major headway has been made in this direction. It was found that the banks have not employed both the Business Facilitators and Correspondents to meet the increasing rural credit requirements.

Some illustrative Examples are cited below highlighting some recent Innovations in Financial Services for the Poor in the context of Microfinance delivery mechanisms (CGAP. Prepared the paper for CGAP UNCDF Donor Training, "The New Vision of Microfinance: Financial Services for the Poor". Accessed from: http://www.globalenvision.org/library/4/1051 on 14 April, 2006):

1. CCACN (Central de Cooperativas de Ahorro y Crédito Financieras de Nicaragua) is marketing its "Agriculture Salary" savings product to farmers. The goal of the product is to smooth the flow of income from the proceeds of an annual or semi-annual harvest. Each credit union works with its farmers to identify their individual expenses and determine a monthly "salary" (portion of harvest proceeds on deposit combined with an above-market interest rate) to be withdrawn from the credit union. In its infancy stage, the credit unions have noted an interest from agriculture-based clients in such a savings management programme.

*Source*: WOCCU: A Technical Guide to Rural-Finance Exploring Products. WOCCU Technical Guide # 3, December 2003.

2. Caja los Andes in Bolivia offers four loan repayment options that fit the cash flow of various agricultural activities, including an end-of-term payment for both principal and interest that fits single crop activities, and unequal payments at irregular intervals for farmers that have planted several crops with different harvesting periods. Flexibility is also provided in loan disbursements, and farmers can receive the sanctioned loan amount in as many as three installments.
3. Prodem in Bolivia has introduced a combination of biometric fingerprint and Smart Cards to deliver financial services to its clients. Biometric technology measures an individual's unique physical or behavioural characteristics, such as fingerprints, facial characteristics, voice pattern, and gait, to recognize and confirm identity. Although the technology is still new, growing awareness of the importance of data security is increasing adoption steadily. Prodem's fingerprint verification has reduced fraud, error, and repudiation of transactions. Staff had not had to deal with forgotten PIN numbers or unauthorized use of cards and accounts so they have more time to provide personal service and advice to clients.
4. International Remittance Network (IRnet): In late 1999, WOCCU, in partnership with Vigo, a money transfer firm, launched IRnet. As of June 2003, 173 credit unions in Central America offer IRnet, expanding the possibilities for sending remittances through 800 US credit union points of service. The Central American credit unions distribute remittances primarily to rural clients. The distributing credit unions help to integrate remittance recipients into the formal financial sector through trained staff who cross-sell services. When a non-member enters a credit union to pick up a remittance, a staff person encourages this person to

become a credit union member and save a portion of the remittance in an interest-bearing voluntary savings account. *Source*: WOCCU: A Technical Guide to Rural-Finance Exploring Products. WOCCU Technical Guide December, 2003.

5. Unibanka (Latvia): Prior to introducing credit scoring, Unibanka, a commercial bank, viewed microfinance loans as too costly to deliver. With the assistance of Bannock Consulting, Unibanka instituted a credit-scoring system based on qualitative client data because sufficient quantitative data was not available to develop a statistical model. Branch staff now uses scorecards to evaluate microfinance loan applications quickly, which has reduced the cost of review and made microfinance lending profitable for Unibanka. *Source*: CGAP I.T. Innovation Series: Credit Scoring.
6. Managed ASCAs: A number of local organizations in the Nyeri District of Kenya provide management services to group-based loan funds. The groups operate as Accumulating Savings and Credit Associations (ASCAs) and receive management services provided by ASCA Management Agencies (AMAs). The AMA model serves a wider client base than the mainstream donor funded MFIs who tend to focus their attention on micro and small entrepreneurs. The clientele of AMAs are also drawn from other socio-economic strata, including salaried workers such as nurses, teachers and civil servants as well as subsistence and semi-commercial farmers. Hence their reach into the rural areas is much greater than the MFIs. *Source*: Nthenya Mule, Susan Johnson, Robert Hickson. Wambui Mwangi. The Managed ASCA Model: Innovation in Kenya's Microfinance Industry; Micro-Save Africa, 2001.
7. ICICI Bank (India): Two state banks in India (Corporation and Canara) partnered with an NGO to provide salaried low-income workers with access to savings. The project uses the already established

automatic teller machines (ATMs) in the factories to offer a recurring savings product, along with education on personal finance. *Source*: CGAP.

8. Microenterprise Access to Banking Services (MABS) in the Philippines nurtures the expanded use of the credit bureau by rural banks, which was started in 2001 to minimize client over indebtedness and defaults. MABS has helped to integrate the rural banks' microenterprise loan clients into an existing national credit bureau, by creating an e-mail encryption programme that allows rural banks to share information electronically at a low cost. *Source*: Anita Campion and John Owens, MABS: A Sustainable Approach to Rural Microfinance, Microbanking Bulletin, July 2003.
9. BASIX in India reduced transportation and transaction costs for its clients and decreased staff expenses by establishing tellers in manned phone booths operating in India. The company operating the phone booths receives a service fee and phone booth operators are being trained in basic collection operations and accounting. BASIX is currently redesigning the project after the pilot and preparing it for re-launching. Source: CGAP.
10. Credit, life, and funeral insurance: A WOCCU study on savings and credit cooperatives (SACCOs) in Kenya indicates that HIV/AIDS poses high levels of risk to rural finance institution soundness. The Cooperative Insurance Company (CIC), a professional insurance provider, insures over half of Kenya's more than one million credit union members who subscribe to policies through their credit unions. *Source*: WOCCU: A Technical Guide to Rural-Finance Exploring Products. WOCCU Technical Guide # 3, December 2003.
11. The National Microfinance Bank in Tanzania (NMB) was created to retain the extensive rural branch network of the National Bank of Commerce (NBC) when it was privatized in 1997. The key to making it commercially viable has been rigorous control of costs

through drastic simplification of the business model and tight managerial oversight. Key initiatives have been correct pricing of products, particularly payments and remittance services, which had traditionally been cross-subsidized by other product lines, and the development of microfinance products, mainly small (average US $400) individual loans. *Source*: Rural financial services: Implementing the bank's strategy to reach the rural poor (Work in Progress). Rural Private Sector, Markets, Finance and Infrastructure Thematic Group, Rural Sector Board, The World Bank. Washington, D.C. March 2003.

12. ADOPEM (Dominican Republic) thoroughly evaluated its PDA (Personal Digital Assistants) programme and recorded dramatic improvements. Client retention improved significantly, and the number of days between application and disbursement dropped from five days to two days. Expenses for paperwork dropped by 60 percent and data entry expenses dropped by 50 percent. Loan officer caseloads and other productivity measures increased by about 35 percent. *Source*: Charles Waterfield, with CGAP and echange LLC Staff, "Personal Digital Assistants, (PDAs)," CGAP IT Innovation Series. Washington, D.C.: CGAP, October 2003.

13. The international NGO Technoserve has developed an inventory credit scheme in Ghana that enables farmers' groups to obtain higher value for their crops by providing post-harvest credit through linkage with a rural financial institution. Instead of selling all of their crop at harvest—when prices are lowest—in order to meet cash needs, small-scale farmers in the scheme store their crop in a cooperatively-managed warehouse and receive a loan of about 75-80 percent of the value of the stored crop, which serves as collateral. This loan permits them to clear their accumulated debts and satisfy immediate cash requirements. Then, when prices have risen in the off-season, the farmers either

sell the stored crop or redeem it for home consumption. *Source*: Rural financial services: Implementing the bank's strategy to reach the rural poor (Work-in-Progress). Rural Private Sector, Markets, Finance and Infrastructure Thematic Group, Rural Sector Board, The World Bank. Washington, D.C. March 2003.

14. Savings-based, Agriculture-oriented Rural Credit Unions—SICREDI—Brazil specializes in agricultural lending, primarily for the production of rice, wheat, beef, fodder, fish, vegetables and for agricultural equipment. Loan approvals are based upon the members' savings history and credit record, with the size limited to 50 percent of production costs and dependent upon the potential return of crop sale at harvest as well as household income and debt obligations. The borrower makes monthly interest payments and then a balloon payment of the principal at harvest time. In addition, SICREDI participates in the PROAGRO national crop insurance, for which a premium is added on the loan rate. PROAGRO pays 100 percent of the loan loss if the crop fails. *Source*: WOCCU: A Technical Guide to Rural- Finance Exploring Products. WOCCU Technical Guide # 3, December 2003.
15. Producer Associations as Clients of a Financial Institution: GAPI and CLUSA in Mozambique: GAPI offers investment and working capital loans to fora (federations of associations) of small farmers and small and micro-enterprises. GAPI collaborates with CLUSA to set-up and register these fora. Loans are secured through a solidarity group-like guarantee between the participating fora. Each forum on-lends to its member associations, who collect the produce from their individual members and other area farmers and deliver it to the forum in return for the loan. About 80 percent of the profits from the sale of produce are handed back to the associations—the remaining 20 percent of the profits are kept by the forum as interest payments.

*Source*: Pearce, Douglas. "Buyer and Supplier Credit to Farmers: Do Donors Have a Role to Play?" prepared for paving the 'Way Forward for Rural Finance: An International Conference on Best Practices', held on June 2-4, 2003.

16. In South Africa, a network of 8,000 armored trucks equipped with thumbprint recognition and smart-card technology deliver pension payments of about $60 each month to 4.5 million South Africans. The potential of this vast infrastructure to offer pensioners other kinds of financial services is tremendous. *Source*: CGAP Donor Brief No. 17: How Donors Can Help Build Pro-poor Financial Systems, by Brigit Helms and Ruth Goodwin-Groen, with input from CGAP staff, February 2004.
17. Banco Postal in Brazil, a joint venture between the Post Office and the largest private bank (Bradesco) has offered banking (and payment) services through its network of postal branches in remote and poor areas of the country since March 2002. *Source*: The World Bank.
18. Tanzania Posts Corporation mini-buses offer passenger service along domestic regional routes. Postal outlets have become one-stop service centers that provide photocopying, telephone and money transfer services. They also sell stationery and newspaper and act as agents for others by accepting newspaper advertisements, selling lottery tickets, revenue stamps for radio stations, and tickets for boats between Dares Salaam and Zanzibar. *Source*: International Trade Forum, Issue 4/2002, Page 30.
19. Equity Building Society (EBS) in Kenya has emerged as one of Kenya's leading microfinance institutions, with over 155,000 savings clients and 41,000 borrowers. Once insolvent, EBS transformed itself into a profitable financial-service provider by rigorously focusing on the needs of its clients—in particular, by developing a wide range of market-based financial products and services,

including a mobile banking service. *Source*: CGAP Case Studies In Donor Good Practices No. 8. Donors as Silent Partners in MFI Product Development: MicroSave-Africa and Equity Building Society in Kenya. July 2003.

## 4. Challenges and Issues of the Microfinance Models

*High Rate of Interest Rate*: this is one of the basic problems with the existing model. The MFIs are justifying it with high operational cost. The borrowers are only facing the uncertainties of the failure of their business. The studies reveal that maximum borrowing is for agricultural needs, which is highly risky engagement. If the yield is low so the farmers are caught in one hand debt trap and on other hand starvation. It is difficult to pay weekly payments with such a high interest. The condition becomes miserable if borrowers borrow for non income generating activities.

*Multiple Lending Channels*: The Malegam Committee Report (2011) noted that repayment of old debt accounts for about 25 percent of new loans taken by JLG/SHG in Andhra Pradesh, while another 25 percent goes to income generating activities (Table 3). The borrowers borrow more than one MFI. They borrow from one MFI to repay loans to another MFI rather focusing on the pace of income generation activities. This causes debt trap and the conditions become same as Sahukar's lending.

**Table 2:** Multiple Lending Channels for funding JLG/SHGs in Andhra Pradesh

| Sl. No. | Range (Loan size) | Number of loan accounts | Amount of loan ₹ | Average loan amount ₹ |
|---|---|---|---|---|
| 1 | ₹ 0 to ₹ 500 | 46,687 (37,3%) | 1,72,52,074 (9.7%) | 370 |
| 2 | ₹ 500-₹ 1,000 | 37,125 (29.7%) | 3,48,79,579 (19.5%) | 940 |
| 3 | ₹ 1,000 to ₹ 3,000 | 3,0382 (24.3%) | 6,16,59,704 (34.5%) | 2,029 |
| 4 | ₹ 3,000 to ₹ 5,000 | 7591 (6.1%) | 3,39,40,225 (19.0%) | 4,471 |
| 5 | ₹ 5,000 to ₹ 7,000 | 1326 (1.1%) | 82,59,600 (4.6%) | 6,229 |
| 6 | ₹ 7,000 to ₹ 10,000 | 1329 (1.1 5) | 1,23,93,264 (6.9%) | 9,325 |
| 7 | ₹ 10,000 to ₹ 15,000 | 366 (0.3%) | 48,61,456 (2.7%) | 13,283 |
| 8 | ₹ 15,000 and above | 229 (0.2 %) | 54,74,722 (3.1%) | 23,907 |
| | Total | 1,25,035 (100%) | 17,87,20,624 (100%) | 1,429 |

*Source*: MRCP database (2002).

Coercive methods adopted for the repayment of loans (Table 3). The villagers are generally illiterate and weak so they could not resist. The pressure of the group members of JLGs/ SHGs is coercion.

**Table 3:** Coercive Methods are applied for repayment of loans of microfinance

| Purpose | % share m number of loan accounts | % Share w loan amount |
|---|---|---|
| Consumption | 35.27 | 28.99 |
| Agricultural loans | 53.37 | 57.41 |
| Off-fann enterprises | 7.98 | 10.95 |
| Loans for education | 3.38 | 2.65 |
| | 100 | 100 |

*Source*: MRCP database (2002).

Low penetration and bureaucratic hurdles in regulations: there is low penetration in the Northern India. There are lots of bureaucratic hurdles in the regulation (such as corruption, commission with groups, etc.). The local leader declares "no repayment" to gain the political mileage, but this causes serious problem for MFIs. The illiteracy and unawareness is another challenge for the penetration.

The major challenges faced by the various implementing agencies for successful demonstration of microfinance models include:

- While microfinance has no doubt added to the economic, social and financial empowerment of the poor, it has not managed to free them entirely from the clutches of informal moneylenders.
- There is skewed distribution of MFIs, with about 60 percent being located in the Southern states. The reasons for this include state government support, NGO concentration, and public awareness.
- *Self-Help Groups* which play a pivotal role in microfinance are beset by problems, such as poor accounting. NGO employees earn low salaries and are not given any incentives or recognition.

- *Government programmes* such as SGSY (Swarnajayanti Gram Swarojgar Yojana), which care of all the relationships with the bank and the borrowers, from end to end. This model enables them to operate with a relatively small equity base and increase the disbursement of loans significantly.
- *Banking Correspondent Model*: This model evolved to increase the savings in MFIs. The agents collect the savings from the poor on behalf of the banks; however, one drawback is that they are not allowed to collect money for Term Deposits.
- *Service Company Model*: This model, developed by ACCION, was used in some Latin American Countries. In it, banks form their own MFIs and work together to provide loans and other services are linked to specific states, have led to the migration of people to those regions in order to avail of subsidies, and diverted interest from self-help schemes.
- The current policies of SHGs are outdated and in need to have overhaul.
- The cost of delivery of financial services requires a relook. An analysis of 36 leading MFIs showed that 89 percent were subsidy dependent and only 9 percent were able to cover more than 80 percent of their costs, thanks to the high cost of supervision and small ticket size of loans.
- MFIs do not have adequate access to financial capital unlike the rest of the financial sector, and as a result are burdened by high debt equity ratios and equity shortfall.

## REFERENCES

Berenbach, S. and Guzman, D. (1994), "The Solidarity Group Experience Worldwide" in Otero, M. and Rhyne, E. (Eds), *The New World of Microenterprise Finance: Building Healthy Institutions for the Poor*, West Hartford, CT; Kumarian Press. 119-39.

CIDA (1999), Reference Guide for the Microfinance Sector, August 1999.

Fischer, G. and M. Ghatak (2010), Repayment Frequency in Microfinance Contracts with Present-Biased Borrowers, Economic Organisation and Public Policy Discussion Papers Series 021, London School of Economics.

Fisher, T. and Srinam, M.S. (ed.) (2002), Beyond Micro-Credit, Putting Development Back into Micro-Finance, New Delhi, Vistaar Publications.

Fotabong, LA., and Akanga, K. (2005), Microfinance and Poverty Reduction. The effect of microfinance institution on poverty alleviation in the South West Province of Cameroon, *USBE Zoom Microfinance*, Vol. 6, SOS FAIM, November, 2001.

Global Development Research Centre (2005), Accessed from http://lta.civicus.org/organisations/15-global-development-research-centre-gdrc

Grameen Bank (2000), Annual Report of the Grameen Bank, Dhaka, Bangladesh.

Grameen Info. (2002a), Homepage of the Grameen Info; September 2002; Online Document; Available: http://www.grameen-info.org/

Grameen Info. (2002b), Homepage of the Grameen Info; August 2002. Online Document; Available: http://www.grameen-info.org

Grameen Bank, Annual Report (2010), Bangladesh, Dhaka.

Harper, M. (2002), Promotion of Self-Help Groups under the SHG Bank Linkage Programme in India, paper presented at the Seminar on SHG Bank Linkage Programme, NABARD, New Delhi.

Holt, S. (1994), The village bank methodology: Performance and prospects. In O. Maria, and E. Rhyne, (Ed.), *The new world of microenterprise finance: Building healthy financial institutions for the poor*. Connecticut, CA: Kumarian Press.

Ignacio, Mas, Akhand J. Tiwari, Alphina Jos, Denny George, Krishna, U.M. Thacker, Nitin Garg, Raunak Kapoor,

Shivshankar V., Swati Mehta, Vartika Shukla (2012), Are Banks and Microfinance Institutions Natural Partners in Financial Inclusion?, MicroSave–Market-led solutions for financial services, May, 2012.

Ledgerwood, J. (1998), *Manuel de Microfinance-Une perspective institutionnelle et financière. Banque Mondiale*, Washington DC.

Ledgerwood, J. (1999). Microfinance Handbook: Sustainable Banking with the Poor, The World Bank, Washington DC.

Mahajan, Vijay (2005), From Microcredit to Livelihood Finance. *Economic and Political Weekly*, October 8, 2005.

Mahanta, Padmalochan, Gitanjali Panda and Shreekumar (2012), Status of microfinance in India, *International Journal of Marketing, Financial Services & Management Research*, Vol. 1 Issue 11, November, 2012, Online available at www.indianresearchjournals.com

Mallegaon Committee Report (2011), Report of the Sub-Committee of the Central Board of Directors of Reserve Bank of India to Study Issues and Concerns in the MFI Sector, RBI, January, 2011.

Microcredit Summit (2005), Campaign Update, June 2, 2005, (Online); Available from <www.microcreditsumit.org> (10th June 2005).

Microfinance Information eXchange (MIX, 2005), Ten frequently asked questions about microfinance, (Online); Available from <www.mixmarket: org/en/overview.asp> (2nd June 2005).

Microcredit Summit Report, 1997: http://www.microcreditsummit.org/resource/59/1997-microcredit-summit-report.html

Multi-State Cooperative Societies Act, 2002: http://agricoop.nic.in/imagedefault/cooperation/MSCSAct2002.pdf

MIX/CGAP: 2009 Sub-Sahara African Microfinance Analysis and Benchmarking Report, CGAP, Washington, April 2010.

MIX or Microfinance Information Exchange (2012) Asia Regional Snapshot.

NABARD (2002), SHG-Bank Linkage Programme for Rural Poor—An Impact Assessment NABARD, Mumbai, 2002.

Sam-Daley-Harris (2009), State of the Microcredit Summit Campaign Report, Washington, USA, 2009.

Sa-Dhan (2008), Bharat Microfinance Report—Side by Side, December, 2008 (http://www.sa-dhan.net).

Small Industries Development Bank of India (SIDBI), Foundation for Micro-Credit: A Profile, Lucknow: SIDBI.

Yunus, M. (1989), 'Grameen Bank: Organization and operation', in J. Levitsky (ed.), *Microenterprises in Developing Countries*. London: Intermediate Technology Publications.

UNCDF (2004), Basic Facts about Microfinance (Online), Available from <www.uncdf.org/english/microinance/facts.php> [23rd August 2004].

Zeller, Lapenu (2001), Distribution, Growth, and Performance of Microfinance Institutions in Africa, Asia, and Latin America, 2001, www.microfinancegateway.org/dbtw-wpd/exec

# 3

# Role of Microfinance Institutions in Mobilization of Financial Resources for Funding Micro-enterprise

Microfinance Institution is thematically a financial institution specializing in banking services for low-income groups or individuals. A microfinance institution provides account services to small-balance accounts that would not normally be accepted by traditional banks, and offers transaction services for amounts that may be smaller than the average transaction fees charged by mainstream financial institutions. The industry is in the need of an objective set of criteria that acts as a proxy for the maturity of microfinance institutions (MFIs). Access to credit can play a pivotal role in economic growth. Banks and lending institutions provide the services that allow people to save and invest available assets and resources, which further support and strengthens to take up economic activity. Within underdeveloped communities, the role of microfinance institutions provides the credit access and financial services needed to develop income-generating businesses along with self-employment opportunities.

Microfinance institutions provide small-scale financial services to poor people who are otherwise "excluded from the formal banking sector" (Morduch, 1999, 2000) and standard financial systems. Operating merely in developing and emerging countries, they have specialized in offering loans of minor scale to enable individuals to start small productive businesses and enhance entrepreneurship. Especially in rural areas of developing countries, the development of financial systems is often poor;

sometimes they have not fully emerged at all. In this case, microfinance institutions often represent a first opportunity for the local population to participate in financial systems and to benefit from access to business and capital.

Microfinance institutions fill a needed gap within the financial services industry by offering small loans, or micro-loans, to people unable to access conventional loan services. Microfinance institutions vary in size and function with some organizations focusing entirely on microfinancing, while others work as extensions of large investment banks. People living in underdeveloped areas such as Asia, Latin America, Kosovo and countries within the Sub-Saharan region can access needed financial resources through the services provided by microfinance institutions. Within any society, financial services provide a means for people and businesses to obtain credit and manage available assets on a continuous basis. Access to financial services enables existing businesses to grow and in the process provides the starting capital for starter businesses. Microfinance institutions provide these services within communities that have limited resources and few avenues for economic development. People within these communities can use micro-loans to develop small businesses based on their existing knowledge base and skill sets. In all such cases, mobilization of diverse sources of finance for capitalizing the financial institutions—in one form or the other, is vital especially to support the sustainable growth of micro-enterprises.

Bearing in mind the nature of such a challenging scenario currently confronted by the MFIs this chapter touches upon some of the key and emerging issues concerning the future growth perspectives of MFIs with focus on the modalities of mobilizing the financial resources to capitalize the MFIs in a self-sustaining manner. The aspects covered in the chapter, *inter alia*, include: Modality for broad-basing the financial resources for MFIs, demand for microfinance services, supply of microfinance services and competition for MFIs, raising capital for microfinance using diversified sources of funding, innovative microfinancing mechanisms, International initiatives, financial Performance of MFIs in India, institutional providers of rural finance and microfinance services, Government rural finance, microfinance to support SME Finance Programmes or Agencies etc.

### 1. Microfinance Institutions: The Concept

The idea to establish microfinance institutions traces back to Muhammad Yunus, who developed it as a way to eradicate poverty in his home country Bangladesh. In 1983, he founded Grameen Bank, the first institution which realized this concept and started to operate in the microfinance business in the proper sense (The Norwegian Nobel Committee, 2006; Grameen Bank, 2009). Together, Yunus and Grameen Bank were laureates of the 2006 Nobel Peace Prize awarded "or their efforts through microcredit to create economic and social development from below" (Yunus, 2003, 2008). Although there have been organizations concentrating on offering loans and saving opportunities to needy people before (Counts, 2008), Grameen Bank is known for successfully implementing the system of group-lending. In particular, it has proposed a number of indicators to measure the impact of poverty elimination methods (Counts, 2008). These consider primarily basic needs similar to the definition of the International Labour Organization in 1976 (Schubert, 2007), and the financial situation of the poor. The latter refers to weekly loan repayment rates and average annual balance of saving deposits. Yunus (2007, 2008) argues that global poverty does not emerge from market failures, but from capitalism as a theoretical concept which does not fully model real economic structures in general and economic behaviour of each individual in particular. Access to capital is indeed crucial for development, and the concept of free markets has also the capacity to contribute to poverty reduction. But the idea still missing is to incorporate a social component into economic systems to meet observed behaviour. The idea of micro-finance institutions meets both requirements. They provide access to capital on smallest scales, and ideally act as social businesses realizing economic behaviour augmented by social preferences. They enable poor people to engage in productive economic activities and thus contribute to development in low income population strata. According to Masanjala (2002), their mechanisms constitute for a long time missing link between the "arbitrariness of informal lenders" and the problems related to standard banking institutions.

Microfinance institutions (MFIs) are increasingly addressing the traditional financial market to fund their continued growth and to better serve their clients. In its early days, the microfinance sector was essentially driven by non-profit organizations and official development agencies. Over the last few years, these institutions, together with a few new entrants in the sector, have set up an increasing number of investment structures to fund MFIs. Common usage in the microfinance industry is "microfinance investment fund" as the generic term to identify all corporate investment structures which have been set up to provide equity and/or debt financing to MFIs, with investors acting as shareholders or as lenders.

For more than 30 years microfinance has been portrayed as a key policy and programme intervention for poverty reduction and 'bottom-up' local economic and social development. Microfinance (more accurately micro-credit, but in practice the terms are interchangeable) is the provision of tiny loans to the poor to help them establish or expand an income-generating activity, and thereby escape from poverty.

The microfinance movement began with the work of Dr. Muhammad Yunus in Bangladesh in the late 1970s, spreading rapidly to other developing countries. Most early microfinance institutions (MFIs), including Yunus's own iconic Grameen Bank, relied on funding from government and international donors, justified by MFI claims that they were reducing poverty, unemployment and deprivation (Yunus, 2004). In the 1980s, however, the expanding microfinance model operated in a transformed political and ideological environment. Market principles were in the ascendant, with growing emphasis on financial sustainability and the need to wean microfinance programmes of long-term donor support. It was felt that the poor should pay the full cost of any support received, rather than impose an additional tax burden on others.

This led to a push for MFIs to cover their own costs through greater commercialization, private ownership and profit-driven incentives with market-based interest rates. It was thought that market forces and profits would ensure financial self-sustainability, generating a cost-free increase in the supply of microfinance to the poor. To some extent this proved correct, with some MFIs making profits without subsidies. By the early 2000s, a number of developing countries—such as Bangladesh—had achieved the microfinance movement's 'holy grail': virtually every poor person had easy access to a microloan if they wanted one. Table 1 ranks the most microfinance-friendly countries in terms of microfinance penetration. With so many of the poor now able to establish or expand simple income-generating projects, there were hopes that poor communities the world over would soon escape poverty on an unprecedented scale.

**Table 1:** International Microfinance Programme penetration by 2009

| Global ranking | Country | Borrower accounts/ population |
|---|---|---|
| 1 | Bangladesh | 25% |
| | (Andhra Pradesh State, India) | 17%* |
| 2 | Bosnia and Herzegovina | 15% |
| 3 | Mongolia | 15% |
| 4 | Cambodia | 13% |
| 5 | Nicaragua | 11% |
| 6 | Sri Lanka | 10% |
| 7 | Montenegro | 10% |
| 8 | Viet Nam | 10% |
| 9 | Peru | 10% |
| 10 | Armenia | 9% |
| 11 | Bolivia | 9% |
| 12 | Thailand | 8% |
| 13 | India | 7% |
| 14 | Paraguay | 6% |
| 15 | El Salvador | 6% |

*Source*: Gonzalez (2010).

Individual microfinance programmes have most often been judged on the basis of impact evaluations. Most of the early impact evaluations were positive, but very thin in terms of robust evidence. Very often, the 'evidence' consisted of anecdotes from successful MFI clients, while less successful clients were ignored. As microfinance became more popular in the 1990s, displacing other interventions from the policy agenda, notably small and medium business development, there was growing pressure for more meaningful evaluations.

A widely cited study by Khandker (1998) on three major MFIs in Bangladesh—BRAC, Grameen Bank and RD-12—found that up to 5 percent of participants were able to lift their families out of poverty every year by borrowing from one of these MFIs. Littlefield et al. (2003), summarizing the literature available at the time, cited evaluation findings of higher incomes among microfinance programme participants than among non-participants. Goldberg (2005) found that most early impact evaluation studies reported a positive impact on poverty and income.

Most of these evaluations were undertaken by MFIs, microfinance advocacy groups, or international development agencies promoting and funding microfinance. Naturally, this raised concerns about potential bias, especially under-research on the downsides. As a result, a growing number of impact evaluations were commissioned from independent researchers, mainly university-based academics. Many of these independent studies (Morduch, 1998) questioned the rigour and validity of earlier evaluations, highlighting data and methodological problems.

There was a shift to more rigorous forms of impact evaluation, such as the randomized control trial (RCT) methodology. This aims to avoid the selection bias in the choice of treatment and control groups that might occur if, for example, those receiving a micro-loan were already more entrepreneurial than those in the control group. Any impact here would have to be attributed to this characteristic, rather than to a micro-loan. RCT methodology ensures that both groups studied are as identical as possible, aside from the receipt of micro-credit. Microfinance institutions broadly operate under a wide range of legal structures. They could be registered as: NGO, Trusts, Sec. 25 Companies, Cooperative Societies, Cooperative Banks, Regional Rural Banks, Local Area Banks, Public and Private Sector banks, Business Correspondents and Non-Banking Finance Companies.

**2. Broad-basing of Financial Resources for Capitalizing MFIs**

Microfinance Institutions (MFIs) can play a significant role in facilitating inclusion, as they are uniquely positioned in reaching out to the rural poor. Many of them operate in a limited geographical area, have a greater understanding of the issues specific to the rural poor, enjoy greater acceptability amongst the rural poor and have flexibility in operations providing a level of comfort to their clientele. There are several legal forms of MFIs. However, firm data regarding the number of MFIs operating under different forms is not available. It is roughly estimated that there are about 1,000 NGO-MFIs and more than 20 Company MFIs. Further, in Andhra Pradesh, nearly 30,000 cooperative organizations are engaged in MF activities. However, the companies MFIs are major players accounting for over 80 percent of the microfinance loan portfolio.

Most poor people manage to mobilize resources to develop their enterprises and their dwellings slowly over time. Financial services could enable the poor to leverage their initiative, accelerating the process of building incomes, assets and economic security. However, conventional finance institutions seldom lend down-market to serve the needs of low-income families and women-headed households. They are very often denied access to credit for any purpose, making the discussion of the level of interest rate and other terms of finance irrelevant. Therefore the fundamental problem is not so much of unaffordable terms of loan as the lack of access to credit itself (Kim, 1995). The lack of access to credit for the poor is attributable to practical difficulties arising from the discrepancy between the mode of operation followed by financial institutions and the economic characteristics and financing needs of low-income households. For example, commercial lending institutions require that borrowers have a stable source of income out of which principal and interest can be paid back according to the agreed terms. However, the income of many self-employed households is not stable, regardless of its size. A large number of small loans are needed to serve the poor, but lenders prefer dealing with large loans in small numbers to minimize administration costs. They also look for collateral with a clear title—which many low-income households do not have. In addition bankers tend to consider low income households a bad risk imposing exceedingly high information monitoring costs on operation.

Over the last ten years, however, successful experiences in providing finance to small entrepreneur and producers demonstrate that poor people, when given access to responsive and timely financial services at market rates, repay their loans and use the proceeds to increase their income and assets. This is not surprising since the only realistic alternative for them is to borrow from informal market at an interest much higher than market rates. Community banks, NGOs and grass-root savings and credit groups around the world have shown that these micro-enterprise loans can be profitable for borrowers and for the lenders, making microfinance one of the most effective poverty reducing strategies. To the extent that microfinance institutions become financially viable, self-sustaining, and integral to the communities in which they operate, they have the potential to attract more resources and expand services to clients. Despite the success of microfinance institutions, only about 2 percent of world's roughly 500 million small entrepreneurs are estimated to have access to financial services (Barry et al., 1996).

Although there is demand for credit by poor and women at market interest rates, the volume of financial transaction of Microfinance institution must reach a certain level before their financial operation becomes self-sustaining. In other words, although microfinance offers a promising institutional structure to provide access to credit to the poor, the scale problem needs to be resolved so that it can reach the vast majority of potential customers who demand access to credit at market rates. To be successful, financial intermediaries that provide services and generate domestic resources must have the capacity to meet high performance standards. They must achieve excellent repayments and provide access to clients. And they must build toward operating and financial self-sufficiency and expanding client reach. In order to do so, microfinance institutions need to find ways to cut down on their administrative costs and also to broaden their resource base. Cost reductions can be achieved through simplified and decentralized loan application, approval and collection processes, for instance, through group loans which give borrowers responsibilities for much of the loan application process, allow the loan officers to handle many more clients and hence reduce costs (Otero and Rhyne, 1994).

Microfinance institutions can broaden their resource base by mobilizing savings, accessing capital markets, loan funds and effective institutional development support. A logical way to tap capital market is securitization through a corporation that purchases loans made by micro-enterprise institutions with the funds raised through the bonds issuance on the capital market. Savings facilities make large scale lending operations possible. On the other hand, studies also show that the poor operating in the informal sector do save, although not in financial assets, and hence value access to client-friendly savings service at least as much access to credit. Savings mobilization also makes financial institutions accountable to local shareholders. Therefore, adequate savings facilities both serve the demand for financial services by the customers and fulfil an important requirement of financial sustainability to the lenders. Microfinance institutions can either provide savings services directly through deposit taking or make arrangements with other financial institutions to provide savings facilities to tap small savings in a flexible manner (Barry et al. 1996).

One way of expanding the successful operation of microfinance institutions in the informal sector is through strengthened linkages with their formal sector counterparts. A mutually beneficial partnership should be based on comparative strengths of each sector. Informal sector microfinance institutions have comparative advantage in terms of small transaction costs achieved through adaptability and flexibility of operations (Ghate et al., 1992; Ghate, 2007, 2008). They are better equipped to deal with credit assessment of the urban poor and hence to absorb the transaction costs associated with loan processing. On the other hand, formal sector institutions have access to broader resource-base and high leverage through deposit mobilization (Christen et al. 1994). Therefore, formal sector finance institutions could form a joint venture with informal sector institutions in which the former provide funds in the form of equity and the later extends savings and loan facilities to the urban poor. Another form of partnership can involve the formal sector institutions refinancing loans made by the informal sector lenders. Under these settings, the informal sector institutions are able to tap additional resources as well as having an incentive to exercise greater financial discipline in their management. Microfinance institutions could also serve as intermediaries between borrowers and the formal financial sector and on-lend funds backed by a public sector guarantee. Business-like NGOs can offer commercial banks ways of funding micro-entrepreneurs at low cost and risk, for example, through leveraged bank-NGO-client credit lines. Under this arrangement, banks make one bulk loan to NGOs and the NGOs packages it into large number of small loans at market rates and recover them (Women's World Banking, 1994; 1995).

Recently, though, an increasing number of MFIFs are being set up to mobilize the traditional capital markets, clearly targeted to these commercial investors. It is interesting to note that the most commercially oriented investment funds invest almost exclusively in debt instruments of MFIs, whereas the funds promoted by development-oriented institutions have a greater mix of investments with equity as well as debt products. There could be a very wide diversity of investment structures targeting MFIs.

A. Key differentiating factor striking a balance between the social returns of these vehicles and their financial returns.

B. Various broad categories of microfinance investment funds that can be identified based on the following criteria:

- Targeted MFIs and the terms offered
- Products proposed to the MFIs
- Shareholder structure, targeted investors and the returns offered
- Structure and objectives of the vehicle
- Role of the investment fund in the governance of the invested MFIs
- Availability and form of technical assistance (TA).

The three categories identified are the following:

- Microfinance development funds
- Quasi-commercial microfinance investment funds
- Commercial microfinance investment funds.

### 3. Demand of MFIs for Microfinance Services

The proposed Microfinance Services Regulation Bill defines microfinance services as providing financial assistance to an individual or an eligible client, either directly or through a group mechanism for:

(i) an amount, not exceeding rupees fifty thousand in aggregate per individual, for small and tiny enterprise, agriculture, allied activities (including for consumption purposes of such individual) or

(ii) an amount not exceeding rupees one lakh fifty thousand in aggregate per individual for housing purposes, or

(iii) such other amounts, for any of the purposes mentioned at items (i) and (ii) above or other purposes, as may be prescribed.

The demand for microfinance services—savings, credit and insurance—is apparently insatiable in India. In that sense, India is perhaps the largest emerging market for microfinance services. The demand scene of the microfinance in India can be appreciated in view of the following position status.

*Credit*: With a population of 1000 million, India has nearly 400 million people below or just above an austerely defined poverty line. Thus, approximately 75 million households need microfinance. Of these, nearly 60 million households are in rural India and the remaining 15 million are urban slum dwellers. The current annual credit usage by these households was estimated in 1998 to be ₹ 4,65,000 million or US$ 11 billion. This is based on the following statistics:

- Annual credit usage by 60 million rural poor households at an average of ₹ 6,000 is ₹ 360,000 million per annum—about two-thirds for consumption and one-third for production needs (based on a 1994 study carried out for the World Bank. The number has been rounded off and adjusted for 1998 prices).
- Annual credit usage by 15 million urban poor households at an average of ₹ 9,000 is ₹ 105,000 million per annum—about 55 percent for consumption and 45 percent for production needs (based on a 1995 study carried out for the SEWA Bank. The number has been rounded off and adjusted for 1998 prices).

Even though the unmet demand is large, the emerging "competition" from mainstream banks can overwhelm MFIs, which are still in their nascent stage. This is so as banks are able to cross subsidize their micro-credit, and charge interest rates below cost and can out-price any MFI. This has major implications for the sustainability of MFIs.

*Savings and Insurance*: Apart from credit, there is an unfulfilled demand for savings and insurance services. In the case of savings services, while banks have provided access to a large number of small depositors, the demand is nowhere near being met, particularly for small, frequent "recurring" deposits.

The Reserve Bank of India (RBI, 2008) has tightened up deposit taking activity since 1997, but this has, perversely, also led to legitimate MFIs being not allowed to take deposits and thus provide savings services to the poor. Savings services by MFIs are essential as transaction costs of savings in formal institutions were as high as 10 percent for the rural poor, because of small average transaction size and distance of banks from villages. In addition, savings deposits make MFIs sustainable in terms of sources of funds. The supply of insurance services to the poor has increased substantially over the 1990s, and there are a large number of low premium schemes covering them against death, accidents, natural calamities, and loss of assets due to fire, theft, etc. Livestock and asset insurance was extended to the poor along with the IRDP subsidized loans, and thus remained scheme driven, with little awareness among the customers. Crop and livestock insurance, however, is quite expensive and their reach to the poor is negligible, except when linked to government schemes.

### 4. Supply of Microfinance Services for MFIs

The total outreach of the existing specialized microfinance service providers is quite limited. Starting with credit first, we see that there is no authoritative countrywide estimate of microcredit disbursed or clients served. The total barely crosses ₹ 1500 million, which is not even 0.3 percent of the existing credit usage by poor families. The banking system in India gives a very large number (56 million in 1994) of small loans, accounting for nearly 93.6 percent of all bank loans by number and 18.0 percent by amount. Further, of these, accounts with outstanding below ₹ 7500 comprised 80.5 percent of the number of accounts and 49.5 percent of amount outstanding. In terms of purpose, 45.8 percent of amount was for small agricultural loans, 20.2 percent for tiny manufacturing and 18.8 percent for trade. Thus banks have been engaged extensively in small credit. Nevertheless, Indian banks are increasingly becoming more conscious of the potential of micro-credit, and they have started to compete with MFIs. This is particularly so in the case of lending to Self-Help Groups or SHGs. SHG lending was initiated by NGOs in the mid-1980s. In 1992, NABARD and the RBI recognized this effort and launched a pilot project for linking 500 SHGs with banks. When those efforts began in 1992, there was not much response by the banks. The pilot project was reviewed by an RBI appointed Task Force in 1995 which issued guidelines to streamline this work and for the provision of refinance and promotional support by NABARD. Banks were encouraged by NABARD to lend to SHGs/NGOs. With enhanced training and exposure for bank staff, financing to SHGs/NGOs gained momentum in the last three years. By March 31, 1999, banks have cumulatively financed ₹ 570 million, comprising nearly 33,000 SHGs all over India. NABARD has established a goal to help promote 1 million SHGs by 2008 AD. One million SHGs will absorb at least ₹ 50,000 million worth of funds. To meet this goal, obviously, the banking system has to cooperate with NABARD in an unprecedented big way. Whether that will happen in an era of increasing commercial bank autonomy and bottom-line pressure, has to be seen. Banks may be attracted by the steady supply of below market price funds from NABARD (currently given at 6.5 percent), but whether that is a sustainable strategy for NABARD at the scale it is planning, again remains to be seen.

From the point of view of MFI sustainability, having a huge demand for credit, savings and insurance services is not enough. The users should be able to pay full cost for these services. Over the years, there has been a lot of subsidy/grant extended to the financial services sector through various government schemes. This included loans at subsidized interest rates, subsidy on principal and in some cases, loan waivers. This had a great impact on the minds of the borrowers and has spoiled the repayment culture. Similarly, in the case of insurance, most schemes offering insurance to the poor are highly subsidized and thus it is unlikely that an MFI can compete with mainstream insurance providers. In order to make MFIs sustainable, the characteristics of demand need to be modified to ensure that diffused demand gets consolidated (such as by organizing borrowers into SHGs) and users become willing to pay full costs of services (at efficiency levels).

## 5. Institutional Providers of Rural Finance and Microfinance Services

The distinction between microfinance and small and medium enterprise (SME) finance and the recognition of the different types of financial institutions catering to those segments are important to the assessment of the adequacy of access and the effect of regulation. While different categories of borrowers often face similar constraints, lenders commonly distinguish between microfinance, which refers to credit provided to poor households and to informal (i.e. unregistered) micro-enterprises, and SME finance, which refers to credit given to enterprises registered as large micro-enterprises, small businesses, and medium-size enterprises. There are several important differences between the two categories of borrowers. Microfinance is most often provided by non-bank institutions such as NGO MFIs that are often based on the group-lending approach (although numerous microfinance loans may consist of loans to individuals rather than to groups), as well as various membership based financial cooperatives and mutual-assistance associations. SME finance is provided mainly by banks, building societies, and non-bank financial institutions (NBFIs) and does not use a group-lending approach.

Another important difference is security: Microfinance is almost never formally secured, although informal security (i.e. not legally binding) in the form of collateral interest over household goods and tools is commonly used, while SME finance usually allows a firm's assets or personal guarantees to legally secure small business loans. Those differences create a natural separation between the institutions that specialize mainly in microfinance and the institutions that provide small business loans, although some institutions do provide both kinds of finance services. Institutional providers of financial services to low-income rural households, micro-enterprises, and small businesses fall into several categories according to the scope of regulation, type of ownership, and type of services offered. The institutions can be differentiated on (a) whether they are required to obtain a license to carry out financial intermediation activities, to be registered with some central agency (but not required to obtain a license) that will provide non-deposit credit-only services, or to be registered as a legal entity; (b) what type of organizational format, including ownership and governance aspects, they have; and (c) what types of financial services are permitted and provided. The principal categories are:

- Government programmes or agencies for rural finance, microfinance, or SME finance
- Non-bank, nonprofit NGO MFIs
- Membership-based cooperative financial institutions (CFIs)

- Postal savings banks (PSBs) or institutions
- Development finance institutions
- Specialized banking institutions (usually licensed for limited operations, activities, or services to differentiate them from full-service commercial banks) such as rural banks, microfinance banks, and non-bank finance companies
- Commercial banks.

Key differences in the organization and operation of those different institutions are highlighted in Table 2. The institutions differ in terms of what products and services they are allowed by law and regulation to offer; whether they are subject to rigorous prudential regulation, internal governance structure, and accountability; and how funds for administrative and business operations are sourced. The differences arise from the applicability of legal and regulatory requirements, and those differences have important implications for the outreach and sustainability of the institutions.

**Table 2:** Institutional Providers of Financial Services of Microfinance

| *Institutional provider* | *Organizational format* | *Ownership* | *Regulatory status and how regulated* | *Financial services permitted to be offered* |
|---|---|---|---|---|
| Government rural or micro or SME finance programmes or agencies | Trust fund or agency | Government | Not regulated by banking authority | Wholesale or on-lending funds to participating institutions |
| Non-bank/ nonprofit/NGO MFIs | Nonprofit foundation, trust, or association | Private sector entities or organizations | Not regulated by banking authority | Microfinance loans only; no voluntary deposits |
| Membership-based cooperative financial institutions (CFIs) | Savings and credit cooperative organization (SACCO) or credit union | Members | Not regulated by banking authority, but may be regulated by department in cooperative | Savings and time deposits and loans to members only |

*Contd...*

| *Institutional provider* | *Organizational format* | *Ownership* | *Regulatory status and how regulated* | *Financial services permitted to be offered* |
|---|---|---|---|---|
| Postal savings banks (PSBs) | State-chartered institution | Government | Not regulated by banking authority | Savings and time (fixedl deposits only and money transfers |
| Development finance institutions | State-chartered institutions | Government | May or may not be regulated by banking authority | Wholesale certificates of deposit, loans, and credits |
| Specialized banking institutions | | | | |
| Rural banks | Limited liability company | Private sector investors or shareholders | Licensed or supervised by banking authority | Savings and time deposits, loans, and money transfers |
| Microfinance banks | Limited liability company | Private sector investors or shareholders | Licensed or supervised by banking authority | Savings deposits, microfinance loans, and money transfers |
| Non-bank finance companies | Limited liability company | Private sector investors or shareholders | Licensed but not necessarily supervised by banking authority | Wholesale certificates of deposit, loans, and credits |
| Commercial banks | Limited liability company | Private sector investors or shareholders, or state-owned institution | Licensed or supervised by banking authority | Demand and savings and time deposits, loans, credits, money transfers, and foreign exchange; full banking services |

*Source*: Financial Sector Assessment: A Handbook, The World Bank/IMF.

Not all institutional providers of financial services listed in Table 3 may exist in a given country for a number of important reasons, including the stage of development of the rural finance and microfinance sector. In a number of countries, rural finance and microfinance services may be provided by several types of institutions.

### 6. Raising Capital for Microfinance Institutions using Diversified Sources of Funding

Microfinance has been spread around the world as a popular poverty reduction strategy. In 1997, the Microcredit Summit Campaign was launched with the goal of servicing 100 million of the world's poorest households. This is in line with the Millennium Development Goals, agreed to at the United Nations Millennium Summit, which set a challenging goal of halving the absolute poverty in the world by 2015. Microfinance has a high potential to contribute to these Millennium Development Goals. As of December 2000, about 1,600 microfinance institutions reported to the Microcredit Summit that more than 19 million of the poorest households around the world have access to financial services. However, this leaves 81 million of the world's poorest people to be reached before the Campaign target of 100 million is achieved. If only 10 percent of the 1,580 microfinance institutions (MFIs) that reported to the Microcredit Summit could be scaled up to serve an average of 500,000 very poor households each, then the shortfall of 81 million could be overcome. However, without capital to cover its operations, to finance its lending operations, and to leverage financial resources from commercial institutions, it is unlikely that microfinance institutions would be able to achieve this objective.

Many pioneering MFIs all over the world have proven that they can deliver financial services to individuals and businesses that otherwise would not have access to financial services. However for many of these MFI's, the dependence on donor funds increasingly constitutes an obstacle to growth, and thus they are now turning to other, commercial sources of funds. The shortage of capital creates two major, interrelated problems for MFIs: (1) slower than optimal rates of growth due to shortage of funds, and (2) large operational deficits prior to institutional financial breakeven, which itself tends to limit optimal growth rates. These operating deficits limit MFI access to capital, even at market rates. Diversified Sources of Funding may include, among others, some of the following categories:

*A. Donor and Government Grants and Soft Loans*

Microfinance has received significant attention from the donor community, based upon its potential as a powerful tool for poverty alleviation. As such, many millions of dollars have been spent on promoting microfinance programmes around the world. For most MFIs, the principal source of funding is from grants and highly subsidized loans, or so-called soft loans. Soft loans are obtained from multilateral banks (e.g. the World Bank, Inter-American Development Bank alike), government aid agencies e.g. United States Agency for International Development (USAID), UK Department for International Development (DFID), foundations (e.g., Ford Foundation) and apex organizations (e.g. Women's World Banking, ACCION, FINCA). Usually such grants and soft loans include conditions and requirements as to how the funds should be spent and are in limited dollar amounts.

*B. Savings*

Historically, deposits (demand deposits, passbook savings, time deposits, certificates of deposits and the like) have been a primary source of funds for financial institutions. Hempel and Simonson (1999) have reported that, for US commercial banks, 97 percent of their total liabilities are made up of demand deposits and time deposits. Clearly, these savings accounts fuel the lending operations of the banks. Furthermore, Wisniwski (1999) reports that this has been true irrespective of the regional or cultural context in which the banks or related non-bank financial institutions have developed. However, in most developing countries, especially in South, East and Central Asia, MFIs are not permitted to re-deploy depositor savings until they can meet certain minimum capital requirements mandated by regulatory authorities. Unfortunately, such capital adequacy requirements are typically not met until the MFI is a mature institution, thereby precluding if from taking advantage of the potential leverage provided by these deposits. This particular issue is analysed in more details below.

*C. Raising Private Sector Capital*

During the last decade, the microfinance community has recognized the limitations of donor and government subsidies in reaching a significant scale and scope of operations. As many microcredit programmes apply the so-called graduation principle in their lending operations, increasing the size of repeat loans according to their repayment record of previous loans, it is essential to raise/attract sufficient funds to sustain this process. Thus, many MFI's are moving away from donor funding into the more traditional sources of capital financing that typical corporations use. Debt capital is often a first choice, either in the form of borrowings from commercial and central banks, or when capital markets are well-developed, long-term debt instruments. Hannig and Wisniwski (1999) point out that these debt obligations are attractive to both sides of the transaction, as they not only provide a steady source of income for the owners, but it also provides a stable source of funds for the issuers. Equity is another potential source of capital. In fact, certain quasi-equity structures that are in current use may include *a priori*:

- Donations to the MFIs can be thought of as an equity investment, although the donor does not expect to receive a return on investment (ROI) or other monetary return
- Apex organizations or Non-Governmental Organizations (NGOs) typically provide capital when they take an ownership position
- Venture capital funds, enterprise equity funds or quasi-equity investment funds
- Equity-like subordinated debt
- Private placement funds
- Limited partnerships or limited liability company participation
- Institutional or individual investors interested in social returns.

Clearly, none of the above represents equity as typically characterized by the financial community. Classical equity investors would require some ROI in the form of future cash flow receipts. Furthermore, many of the participations taken by the funds, partnerships and social investors above have characteristics more closely resembling debt than equity, namely, contractually bound repayment programmes.

*D. Non-bank, Non-profit NGO MFIs*

Non-bank, non-profit NGO MFIs include (a) mixed-purpose NGOs that have credit provisions in their socially oriented activities and (b) specialized credit-only MFIs. Those MFIs are generally private sector-owned institutions and are typically organized as non-profit foundations, trusts, or associations. In a number of cases, the MFIs are organized as formally incorporated entities under a country's Companies Act. Some MFIs are stand-alone local entities, while others may be affiliated with or sponsored by international NGOs such as FINCA, CARE, Catholic Relief Services, World Vision, ACCION International, and Women's World Banking. The geographical reach of their operations vary depending on their organizational and legal status and on the type of NGO sponsor, with some MFIs operating only at the district or county level others on a province-wide or region-wide basis, and a few on a nationwide scale.

*E. Membership-Based CFIs*

CFIs are (a) multipurpose cooperative associations (e.g. producers, services, marketing, and rural cooperatives) that include savings and credit functions; and (b) single-purpose, membership-based, financial cooperative organizations (e.g. credit unions and savings and credit cooperative organizations (SACCOs). CFIs, which have been in existence in many countries much longer than non-bank, non-profit NGO MFIs, are clearly distinguishable from the NGO MFIs in that their financial transactions (deposit taking and credit giving) are generally limited to registered members under a closed- or open-common bond, typically defined by geography (residence), occupation, or place of employment. The rights and privileges of ownership in CFIs are based on the one person–one vote principle, and management is exercised by members–owners. In general, CFIs will outnumber NGO MFIs in many countries, and their combined outreach will tend to be larger as well.

*F. Postal Savings Banks*

A Postal Savings Bank (PSB) has the ability to reach a very large number of depositors for savings and time deposits in generally small amounts, and to provide payments and transfer or remittance services, particularly in the rural areas in a number of countries, including Azerbaijan, Kenya, Pakistan, and Tanzania. However, PSBs are limited to deposit-taking and payment services and do not extend credit. PSBs are intended primarily to provide a safe and secure facility for the small savings of poor and low-income households, especially in rural areas, even though the management and boards of PSBs may be tempted to expand into rural finance and microfinance lending services to improve earnings. In practice, the priority should be on improving efficiency, cost-effectiveness, and governance before broadening the asset portfolio beyond safe assets such as bank deposits and government issues.

*G. Development Finance Institutions*

In many countries, development finance institutions (DFIs) has been established and funded by the government to develop and promote certain strategic sectors of the economy (e.g. highly capital intensive investments, the agricultural sector, etc.) to achieve social goals. DFIs are expected primarily to fill in the gaps in the supply of financial services that are not normally provided by the banking institutions. The DFIs also play a crucial role in the development of SMEs, the housing sector, and in some countries micro-credit. The key issue to monitor is the extent to which DFIs are accorded special benefits in the form of funding at lower rates, implicit government guarantees to the institutions' debts, favourable tax treatment, etc.

*H. Specialized Banking Institutions*

The regulatory framework for banking and finance in a number of countries also covers lower-tier licensed banks that have the legal capability for deposit-taking activities (generally limited to savings and fixed deposits) and for providing loans, but the capability excludes trust and investment services and foreign exchange or trading facilities. In some countries, banking activities may be limited to the geographical market area that is serviced (county or district, province, or region). The limited-service banking institutions, (e.g. rural banks and microfinance banks) are subject to prudential supervision by a country's central supervisory authority, and they are required to comply with reporting requirements and with applicable prudential standards. Non-bank finance companies involved in rural finance, microfinance, and SME finance—which do not take retail public deposits but are permitted to fund their operations and loan portfolios through commercial borrowings and wholesale, large-value, institutional deposits—are generally required to register and to obtain a license. However, those companies may not be prudentially supervised by a country's central supervisory authority.

*I. Commercial Banks*

Commercial banks may have direct participation in low-income markets as a result of their complying with directed or credit quota policies of government for targeted sectors. Sometimes, banks have indirect involvement in rural and microfinance as depositories of the operating funds of MFIs and CFIs, or they have involvement through commercially priced wholesale loans and credit facilities to MFIs and CFIs as bank clients. An important area to focus on is the existence of vertical and horizontal business relationships between commercial banks, on the one hand, and MFIs and CFIs, on the other. The importance of this point stems from the synergistic relationships that the smaller MFIs and CFIs can form with the larger commercial institutions from the formal sector, whereby the combination can reach a larger number of clients with resources than may be obtained from the latter large institution at commercial—not subsidized—rates and terms.

## 7. Mechanisms Adopted by some South Asian Nations in Microfinance Programmes

### *7.1 The Grameen Bank in Bangladesh*

The concept is the brainchild of Dr Muhammad Yunus of Chittagong University who felt concern at the pittance earned by landless women after a long arduous day's work labouring for other people. He reasoned that if these women could work for themselves instead of working for others they could retain much of the surplus generated by their labours, currently enjoyed by others. Established in 1976, the Grameen Bank (GB) has over 1000 branches (a branch covers 25-30 villages, around 240 groups and 1200 borrowers) in every province of Bangladesh, borrowing groups in 28,000 villages, 12 lakh borrowers with over 90 percent being women. It has an annual growth rate of 20 percent in terms of its borrowers. The most important feature is the recovery rate of loans, which is as high as 98 percent. A still more interesting feature is the ingenious manner of advancing credit without any "collateral security".

The Grameen Bank lending system is simple but effective. To obtain loans, potential borrowers must form a group of five, gather once a week for loan repayment meetings, and to start with, learn the bond rules and "16 Decisions" which they chant at the start of their weekly session. These decisions incorporate a code of conduct that members are encouraged to follow in their daily life, e.g. production of fruits and vegetables in kitchen gardens, investment for improvement of housing and education for children, use of latrines and safe drinking water for better health, rejection of dowry in marriages, etc. Physical training and parades are held at weekly meetings for both men and women and the "16 Decisions" are chanted as slogans. Though according to the Grameen Bank management, observance of these decisions is not mandatory, in actual practice it has become a requirement for receiving a loan.

Number of groups in the same village is federated into a Centre. The organization of members in groups and centres serves a number of purposes. It gives individuals a measure of personal security and confidence to take risks and launch new initiatives. The formation of the groups—the key unit in the credit programme—is the first necessary step to receive credit. Loans are initially made to two individuals in the group, who are then under pressure from the rest of the members to repay in good time. If the borrowers default, the other members of the group may forfeit their chance of a loan. The loan repayment is in weekly instalments spread over a year and simple interest of 20 percent is charged once at the year end.

The groups perform as an institution to ensure mutual accountability. The individual borrowing member is kept in line by considerable pressure from other group members. Credibility of the entire group and future benefits in terms of new loans are in jeopardy if any one of the group members defaults on repayment. There have been occasions when the group has decided to fine or expel a member who has failed to attend weekly meetings or willfully defaulted on repayment of a loan. The members are free to leave the group before the loan is fully repaid; however, the responsibility to pay the balance falls on the remaining group members. In the event of default by the entire group, the responsibility for repayment falls on the centre.

The Grameen Bank has provided an inbuilt incentive for prompt and timely repayment by the borrower, i.e. gradual increase in the borrowing eligibility of subsequent loans. A survey has shown that about 42 percent of the members had no income earning occupation (though some may have been unpaid family workers in household enterprises) at the time of application of the first loan. Thus, the Grameen Bank has helped to generate new jobs for a large proportion of the members. Only insignificant portion of the loans (6%) was diverted for consumption and other household needs. About 50 percent of the loans taken by male members were for the purpose of trading and shopkeeping. 75 percent of loans given to female members were utilized for livestock, poultry raising, processing and manufacturing activity.

### *7.1.1 Savings Programme*

It is compulsory for every member to save one Taka per week which is accumulated in the Group Fund. This account is managed by the group on a consensual basis, thus providing the members with an essential experience in the collective management of finances. Amounts collected from fines imposed on members for breach of discipline is also put into this account. The amount in the Fund is deposited with Grameen Bank and earns interest. A member can borrow from this fund for consumption, sickness, social ceremony or even for investment. Terms and conditions of such loans, which are normally granted interest free, are decided by the group. Factors behind success of the Grameen Bank are: participatory process in every aspect of lending mechanism, peer pressure of group members on each other, lending for activities which generate regular income, weekly collection of loans in small amount, intense interaction with borrowers through weekly meetings, strong central management, dedicated field staff, extensive staff training willingness to innovate, committed pragmatic leadership and decentralized as well as participatory style of working.

The Grameen Bank experience indicates the vital importance of credit as an entry point for upliftment programme for rural poor. If a programme is to have an appeal for people living in abject poverty, it must offer them clear and immediate prospects for economic improvement. Thereafter, it is easier to sell other interventions of social development, however unconventional they may appear, once improvements in standard of living are demonstrated. The Grameen Bank clearly shows that lack of collateral security should not stand in the way of providing credit to the poor. The poor can utilize loans and pay them if effective procedures for bank transactions with them can be established. In case of the Grameen Bank, formation of groups with a small group of like-minded rural poor has worked well, and group solidarity and peer pressure have substituted for collateral security.

### 7.2 Linking Banks with Self-Help Groups: A Pilot Project from Indonesia

In Indonesia, financial liberalization since 1988, disenchantment with traditional subsidized credit programmes and an openness to innovative approaches led the Central Bank to support a pilot project in which 13 participating banks, with the assistance of 12 NGOs, have lent to about 420 self-help groups (SHGs) in the first phase, to be on lent to their members. Some of the principles underlying the project and the guidelines that were issued to the implementing groups are listed below:

- The SHGs are to use part of their funds (almost 60%) for lending to their members and the rest for depositing in a bank to serve as the basis for refinancing from the bank.
- Savings are to come first: no credit will be granted by the SHG without savings by the individual members of the SHG. These savings are to serve as partial collateral for their loans.
- The joint and several liabilities of the members are to serve as a substitute for physical collateral for that part of loans to members in excess of their savings deposits.
- Credit decisions for on-lending to members are to be taken by the group collectively.
- Central Bank refinance is to be at an interest rate equal to the interest rate at which the savings are mobilized.
- All the intermediaries (the Central Bank, banks, NGOs and SHGs) will charge an interest margin to cover their costs.
- Interest rates on savings and credit for members are to be market rates to be determined locally by the participating institutions.
- Instead of penalties for arrears, the banks may impose an extra incentive charge to be refunded in the case of timely repayments.
- The ratio of credit to savings will be contingent upon the creditworthiness of the group and the viability of the projects to be implemented, and is to increase over time with repayment performance.
- SHGs may levy an extra charge on the interest rate for internal fund generation (which would be self-imposed forced savings).

Within the first ten months of the implementation period, by March 1990, 7 private banks and 11 branches of government banks had made 229 group loans to SHGs, which had retailed them to about 3500 members. Loans totalling about $0.4 million had been disbursed, on an average of about $2,000 per group and $118 per member. SHG savings deposits with the bank amounted to about $400 per group, giving a credit to savings ratio of about 5. NGOs have received loans from the banks at 22 to 24 percent which is only slightly higher than the refinancing rate of large to small banks. Rates to end users have been between 30 to 44 percent after the NGOs and SHGs have added their margins to cover costs and build funds to cover joint and several liability. Only one of the participating banks had sought a guarantee under the scheme from the Central Bank.

### *7.3 Pag IBIG Fund—Philippines*

Pag IBIG Fund is one of the most financially stable Government owned-and-controlled Corporations in Philippines today. Pag-IBIG is an acronym for Pagtulungan sa Kinabukasan (Partnership for the Future), Ikaw (You), Banko (Bank) Industriya (Industry) Gobyerno (Government). To date, it has a total of 1.2 million members with a fund base of US $ 800 million. The fund is a provident savings fund and a housing credit system for the wage earners. To make the fund a better instrument for the National Shelter Programme (NSP) a Presidential Decree was signed in December 1980 establishing the Home Development Mutual Fund (HDMF) as a separate entity to administer the provident fund for housing.

The main objectives of the HDMF are:

- To promote self-reliance and self-determination among workers through membership in an integrated nationwide savings system.
- To invest the provident savings of its members taking into consideration the profitability and safety of the funds as a means of providing them provident benefits upon termination of their membership in the Fund.

- To promote home ownership through the establishment of an affordable and adequate housing credit system for its members.
- To provide small and short loans and other benefits to its members.

For the effective working and success of the Fund it was decided to make membership to the Fund mandatory and it was also based on the conviction that people deserve higher incomes and in the process they themselves must be savers and as savers they themselves be the capital base of the nation. Waivers were granted to employers who prior to the creation of the Fund already had superior retirement and provident plans for their employees or employers whose plans are similar to those of the fund or who are incapable of paying counterpart contribution due to financial losses.

Savings and Housing are closely intertwined and the first step was to take care of the members' basic need for housing. The Fund instituted a systematic, regular and easy savings system and tapped new groups of savers who could not be reached by commercial banks and became a major source of funds for developing the economy. Membership to the fund was made voluntary in 1987. A member could withdraw his accumulated savings upon maturity of his membership after 20 years, permanent departure from the country, total disability, retirement or separation from service due to health. Housing loans were the Fund's greatest attraction, for which reason, a Trust Fund Agreement with the National Housing Mortgage and Finance Corporation (NHMFC) was entered into. The agreement allows the Fund to direct its lending through the NHMFC Secondary Mortgage Market System, where mortgage instruments are traded by NHMFC. The Fund was guaranteed a fixed return making it possible for the Fund to lend to its members at 9 percent p.a. and declare dividends.

The Government also established the Housing and Urban Development Coordinating Council (HUDCC) as the sole authority and policy-making body on housing, to take charge of identifying and redefining the mandates of housing agencies.

The HUDCC was to act as the lead funding agency and extend funding commitments to financial institutions who could act as loan originators for the home buyers'. To meet its major objective of assisting low and middle income families in meeting their housing requirements through the provision of appropriate and affordable housing loan packages, the HUDCC offers loan packages with interest rates ranging from 9 percent to 16 percent per annum depending upon the loan amount. Maximum loan amount per borrower is 46 times his monthly income, consisting of his monthly basic salary plus cost of living allowance plus the monthly equivalent of the weighted average of other income during the last three years. Maximum loan repayment period is 25 years but shall not go beyond the age of 70 for the principal borrower.

There was also an Appliance and Furniture Loan Programme (AFLP) that granted short-term loans. The loan amount was computed based on the length of the membership and the applicant's salary. The 2-year loan carries an interest of 10.75 percent p.a. Later the AFLP was expanded into the Multi-Purpose Loan Programme (MPL) which covers various needs: educational, medical and hospitalization, livelihood, minor home improvement, purchase of appliances and furniture etc. To qualify for a Multi Purpose Loan, a member must have made atleast 24-monthly contributions, must be an active Fund member and there must be a commitment from both employer and employee to continuously remit contributions at least for the term of the loan. The loan bears an interest of 10.75 percent p.a., paid in advance for the first year of the loan period. The second year interest is spread and paid equally over the 24-month term of the loan. The MPL continues to lend to members on a regular basis, it enables a member to borrow again after 50 percent of the outstanding loan has been repaid.

Thus, Pag-IBIG helps every Filipino to have his own house by pooling the savings of its members and channeling them for the long-term financing requirement of housing. Urban Community Development Office of Thailand: The People's Bank Urban Community Development Office (UCDO) was established in 1992 as a government sponsored organization with the mandate of enhancing the capacity of slum dwellers and urban poor, through credit provision process, to generate income on a stable basis and to obtain adequate housing with secure rights and improved living environment. UCDO facilitates the formation and strengthening of savings and credit organizations in urban poor communities through technical assistance and training on organization and management of the savings groups. The office provides wholesale loans to these member organizations to on-lend to individuals to support community development. Therefore, it serves as a bank for urban poor. To be eligible for UCDO loan, the saving group must have been engaged in savings activities for at least three months and demonstrate a clear management structure. Credit is provided as a tool to unleash communities' potential for self-improvement.

The credit from 'UCDO' consists of general purpose revolving loans to meet immediate household or community needs with a maximum three-year, income enhancement loans for up to five years to support equipment purchase and working capital, and housing loans of a maximum 15-year maturity to finance group housing projects including land purchase and non-project housing loans for up to 5 years. As of March 1996, $17.8 million of credit was disbursed to the benefit of about 3,000 families in 62 communities. Housing loans accounted for $12.6 million, followed by income enhancement loans ($3.8 million) and general purpose loans ($1.4 million). All committee members of a community group must sign their names as guarantors for a loan. In the case of housing projects, land titles or the housing may have to be put as collateral as well. The lending rate is set based on cost of funds and provision for bad debts and a markup for community organizations. Current rates are kept below commercial rates thanks to UCDO's access to low cost funds. The community can decide upon the loan amount and the repayment period within the prescribed maximum terms. The community or savings group may repay daily, weekly, fortnightly or monthly. The method of repayment is flexible and arranged according to the needs and process decided by the community.

### *7.4 Credit Mechanisms Adopted by HDFC (India) for Funding the Low Income Group Beneficiaries*

HDFC has been making continuous and sustained efforts to reach the lower income groups of society, especially the economically weaker sections, thus enabling them to realize their dreams of possessing a house of their own. HDFC's response to the need for better housing and living environment for the poor, both, in the urban and rural sectors materialized in its collaboration with Kreditanstalt fur Wiederaufbau (KfW), a German Development bank. KfW sanctioned DM 55 million to HDFC for low cost housing projects in India. HDFC's approach to low-income lending has been extremely professional and developmental in nature. Negating the concept of dependence, HDFC's low cost housing schemes are marked by the emphasis on people's participation and usage of self-help approach wherein the beneficiaries contribute both in terms of cash and labour for construction of their houses. HDFC also ensures that the newly constructed houses are within the affordability of the beneficiaries, and thus promotes the usage of innovative low cost technologies and locally available materials for construction of the houses. For the purpose of actual implementation of the low cost housing projects, HDFC collaborates with organizations—both, Governmental and Non-Governmental. Such organizations act as coordinating agencies for the projects involving a collective of individuals belonging to the Economically Weaker Sections. The projects could be either in urban or rural areas. The security for the loan is generally the mortgage of the property being financed. The construction work is regularly monitored by the coordinating agencies and HDFC. The loans from HDFC are disbursed depending upon the stages of construction. To date, HDFC has experienced 100 percent recovery for the loans disbursed to various projects.

Microfinance institutions in India have made significant progress during the last two decades in terms of outreach and penetration in unbanked areas through several innovations in credit delivery and terms of lending, thereby emerging as a structural addition to the financial system. However, high growth MFIs has encountered serious setbacks in their development due to adverse consequences of the Andhra Pradesh crisis and its dark shadow over the entire sector across the country. The negative growth in terms of outreach and loan portfolio from the second half of the crisis year 2010-11 continued into 2011-12. Despite the stagnating top line, the sector has been cautiously optimistic on account of strong regulatory initiatives, greater emphasis on client protection and improving governance with a social focus. There are several issues of concern over the sustainability of smaller MFIs in the new environment, which should be addressed seriously. The issues concerning performance of larger MFIs with specific reference to shrinking client outreach, liquidity constraints, etc., also need to be tackled effectively. The Indian MFIs that began the journey essentially as a single credit product programme have now moved onto a different realm with MFIs trying to understand their clients' financial needs in a more meaningful way and designing products to suit these needs within the scope of regulatory restrictions. While the initial phase consisted of a standard, one-year joint liability loan, during the course of time many institutions broadened the service range with innovative products, offered directly or through their sister organizations. Microfinance was supposed to move the product paradigm from single products to a basket of customized products based on client needs. The journey on this front has however not been without bumps. The period 2005–10 witnessed intense growth at the cost of innovation as it was easier to increase outreach with a standard product. Further, the regulatory framework did not permit broadening the range to savings and other services like remittances. The relative position of the Indian microfinance sector in the global context (Table 3) has shown a significant downfall during the last three years, which needs to be taken note of.

### 7.5. Progress and Performance of MFIs: A Case Study

The progress and performance of the MFIs have been analyzed using data from multiple sources. The overall industry outreach was analyzed using the data collected from 'The Bharat Microfinance Quick Report, 2012' published by Sa-Dhan comprising information from 167 MFIs. The individual

MFI data were sourced from the MIX Market that included a data set of 61 MFIs (Table 4).

**Table 3:** Relative position of Indian Microfinance Sector

| Particulars | 2009 | | 2010 | | 2011 | |
|---|---|---|---|---|---|---|
| | Score | Rank | Score | Rank | Score | Rank |
| Overall MF Business Environment | 62.1 | 4 | 59.1 | 8 | 43.1 | 27 |
| Regulatory Framework and Practices | 62.5 | 13 | 62.5 | 14 | 50.0 | 22 |
| Institutional Development/ Supporting framework | 66.7 | 3 | 58.3 | 7 | 40.0 | 20 |
| Investment Climate | 51.9 | 14 | 53.9 | 14 | – | – |
| Stability | – | – | – | – | 62.5 | 40 |

*Source*: Global Microscope on the Microfinance Business Environment, Economic Intelligence Unit Ltd., 2012 (www.eiu.com).

**Table 4:** Progress of MFIs

| | 2010 | 2011 | Growth rate (%) | 2012 | Growth rate (%) |
|---|---|---|---|---|---|
| No. of MFIs Reporting | 264 | 170 | | 167 | |
| Customer Outreach (Million) | 26.7 | 31.8 | 19.1 | 26.8 | –15.7 |
| Outstanding Loans (₹ Billion) | 183.44 | 215.56 | 17.5 | 209.13 | –3.0 |

*Source*: Data from Sa-Dhan's 'The Bharat Microfinance Quick Report, 2012.

It could be observed from Table 4 the that, while the year 2011-12 was the year when a number of developments took place to pull the MFI sector out of the crisis, it tested the MFIs' ability to survive in the worst times. The impact of the crisis on MFIs' performance was more prominent in the year 2011-12 as compared to the previous year. As against 264

MFIs that reported information during the year 2010, only 167 MFIs (two-thirds of the 264 that reported in 2010) shared information with Sa-Dhan, which at best indicated the lack of motivation among MFIs and at worst the closure/dormancy of the rest. Though the regulatory environment is becoming clear, the lack of funding to the MFIs has resulted in a negative growth of the MFIs. As per the data made available by Sa-Dhan (2008), the total client outreach of MFIs was recorded at 26.8 million with a gross loan portfolio of ₹ 209.13 billion (Table 4). Both the client outreach and loan portfolio registered negative growth in this year. There was negative growth in client outreach; the number of clients declining by 15.7 percent in the year 2011-12. However, the gross loan portfolio fared marginally better with a smaller decline of 3 percent. Customer outreach has recorded a relatively higher deceleration in growth rate as compared to the loan outstanding. The MFIs have been unable to retain their customers on account of the liquidity crisis, which affected the MFIs during the second half of the year 2010-11, but remained almost unchanged for the entire year 2011-12. A further problem is the loss of clients in AP who cannot be substituted easily by the MFIs. This can also be an indication that MFIs are adhering to 'the maximum two loans per borrower guideline'. This might have resulted in a lesser number of loans per borrower and thus a steeper decline in the industry outreach since the consolidation of clients reduces the overlap of clients, i.e. since the client being counted as an active borrower from multiple MFIs. This could also be considered a healthy sign in the direction of reducing multiple lending within the sector.

Among the MFIs operating in India, the list of top ten MFIs according to client outreach is provided in Table 5. The MFIs in the 10 ranking remained unchanged but for the new entrant CASHPOR into the list (Table 5) SKS retained first place in terms of client outreach, and Bandhan moved up to second place. However, in terms of gross loan portfolio Bandhan has emerged as the largest MFI in India. BASIX that occupied fifth place last year has dropped down to ninth place in the list. Both Equitas and Ujjivan have moved up by three places and stood at fifth and seventh place respectively. The outreach and portfolio

**Table 5:** Top 10 MFIs by Outreach

| Year | Outreach (million) | | Outreach growth % | Loan o/s (₹ billion) | | Outreach growth % |
|---|---|---|---|---|---|---|
| | 2011 | 2012 | | 2011 | 2012 | |
| SKS | 6.24 | 4.26 | –32 | 41.11 | 16.69 | –59 |
| Bandhan | 3.25 | 3.62 | 11 | 25.07 | 37.30 | 49 |
| Spandana | 4.19 | 3.44 | –18 | 34.58 | 27.15 | –21 |
| SHARE | 2.84 | 2.16 | –24 | 20.65 | 21.10 | 2 |
| Equitas | 1.53 | 1.19 | –22 | 7.94 | 7.24 | –9 |
| SKDRDP | 1.38 | 1.02 | –26 | 9.58 | 6.01 | –37 |
| Ujjivan | 0.84 | 0.82 | –2 | 6.25 | 7.03 | 13 |
| Grama Vidiyal | 0.93 | 0.82 | –12 | 5.2 | 5.20 | 0 |
| BASIX | 1.53 | 0.57 | –63 | 12.49 | 2.92 | –77 |
| CASHPOR | 0.43 | 0.46 | 7 | 2.38 | 3.23 | 36 |

*Source*: Data from MIX.org (MIX/CGAP: 2009-10, Mix, 2012).

data reported by AP based MFIs have to be adjusted with the default numbers so as to arrive at a truly comparable national position of MFIs.

Amongst the top 10 MFIs, only Bandhan and CASHPOR could achieve a positive growth in outreach (Fig. 1). All the other MFIs have shown a negative growth in outreach. BASIX recorded the steepest decline of 63 percent in clients outreach followed by SKS with 32 percent. BASIX and SKS have also recorded the steepest decline in gross loan portfolio with negative growth figures of 77 percent and 59 percent respectively. Only four amongst the top ten MFIs could achieve an increase in their portfolio.

Bandhan achieved the largest growth in loan portfolio with an increase of 49 percent followed by CASHPOR with an increase of 36 percent. Ujjivan, though had a slight decline in outreach, increased its loan portfolio by 13 percent. However, while Bandhan, CASHPOR and Ujjivan did not have any portfolio exposure in Andhra Pradesh, the rest of the MFIs had a significant portfolio exposure in Andhra Pradesh, India.

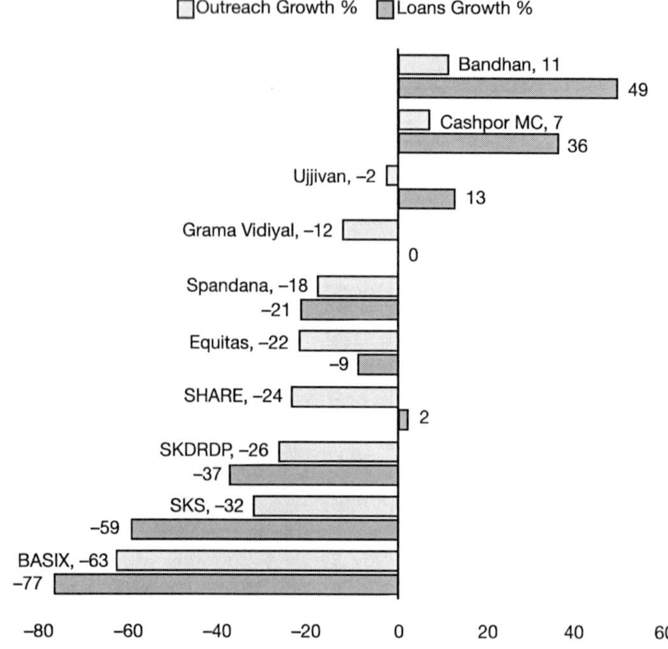


**Fig. 1:** Comparative Performance of Top 10 MFIs

*Source*: MIX market.

The outreach scenario for a larger number of MFIs is very much contrary to that of the last year. During the previous year, a greater number of MFIs recorded growth in outreach; however, during the year 2011-12 a majority of MFIs has shown decrease in the outreach. Figure 1 presents a frequency distribution of growth in client outreach for 61 MFIs that reported to MIX. While in the previous year 75 percent of the MFIs reported an increase in their outreach, only 35 percent of MFIs in the data set have reported an increase in the client outreach during the year 2011-12. The client outreach for 21 MFIs has declined by zero to 25 percent. Another 14 MFIs' outreach has declined by 26 to 50 percent (Fig. 1). Such reduction in outreach by MFIs during this year may be due to voluntarily reduced exposure by some MFIs as they were not clear about the risks. Some other

MFIs had to appraise clients rigorously for debt level and drop a number of clients who had other loans elsewhere. Small and medium MFIs had to reduce their staff and branches as they did not get bank loans. The AP crisis has taken many clients out of the system.

## 8. Innovative Micro-Financing Mechanisms: Some International Initiatives

In the past three years, international capital markets have awoken to the attractiveness of investing in microfinance. Approximately, $500 million has been raised in one-off transactions—collateralized debt obligations, private placements and direct securitizations of micro-loans. In addition, private sector debt and equity micro-finance funds have sprung up—for investors who prefer to give discretion to professional managers—and are now thought to control more than $2 billion. While traditional microfinance funders—non-profit organizations, governmental development agencies and individuals—are behind much of this surge of investment, the big change since 2004 is the introduction of private sector institutional investors seeking full market returns. These mainstream commercial investors, most located in Western Europe and the USA, are driving the opening of capital markets to microfinance.

When properly conducted, microfinance is a profitable, low risk and expanding financial activity. For example, the 26 widely dispersed microfinance institutions (MFIs) in Microfinance Securities XXEB, a $60 million collateralized debt obligation sponsored by Developing World Markets in 2006, have an average return on equity of more than 20 percent, a portfolio at risk (payment delays beyond 30 days) of only 2.5 percent, and are growing their loan portfolios by more than 30 percent per annum. Already, the number of borrowers served by MFIs is estimated at 100 million. With an average loan size of $170, the total market size is estimated at $17 billion. Yet the potential demand is 15 times the current market—estimated at 1.5 billion, or half the 3 billion global working poor. Thus microfinance represents a total commercial market of more than $250 billion. (Market size data in this case is derived from: "Optimizing

Capital Supply in Support of Microfinance Industry Growth", a presentation by McKinsey & Company to the Microfinance Investor Roundtable in Washington DC on 24 October, 2006.)

Currently more than 3/4 of the $17 billion funding total is raised from domestic markets. However, this number is skewed by the amount—almost $6 billion—coming from deposits in the few countries where MFIs are allowed to take deposits. Most of the estimated 10,000 existing MFIs are not deposit-taking institutions, and are unlikely to become so, given the cost and complexity of complying with regulations typically applied to institutions taking deposits from the public. Future funding for MFIs is thus unlikely to be sourced mainly from deposits. Domestic emerging country commercial banks, which should be major funding sources for MFIs, are typically averse to lending to them. Moreover, capital markets in most developing countries are thin and the major institutional players are averse to or legally constrained from significant investment in microfinance. For these reasons, it is unlikely that domestic sources in emerging countries will generate more than a fraction of the more than $200 billion that will need to be raised to satisfy potential demand. As Private Sector Involvement Working Group of Consultative Group to Assist the Poorest (CGAP, 1999) stated in 1997: There is a long way to go before MFIs can attract serious financial support from capital markets. We are on the very beginning of the learning curve. Creative efforts are now required to further develop financial instruments to facilitate the mobilization of funds for microfinance. Financial instruments that have become more widely used in practice since that 1996 pronouncement include the following prospective Microfinance sourcing options:

### *8.1 Credit Guarantees*

A credit guarantee is a financial instrument that encourages financial institutions to lend to retail microfinance institutions and/or directly to micro-enterprises that have good prospects of success, but are unable to provide sufficient collateral or do not have a suitable record of financial transactions (Bass, 2000). The guarantee functions as a promise by a guarantor to the lender that, in the event that the borrower defaults, the guarantor will repay the lender. An ancillary benefit to this guarantee activity is to familiarize banks with the client and, in this process, induce banks to lend to clients that otherwise would not eligible for bank credit. There are a growing number of guarantee schemes funded by multilateral donor agencies and financial institutions. For example, USAID set up a loan portfolio guarantee (LPG) programme for the Compagnie Bancaire de l'Afrique Occidentale (CBAO) in Senegal, and the International Finance Corporation (IFC) launched a Global Credit Enhancement Facility (GCEF) in Fall, 2001. Also, under the Micro and Small Enterprise Development Programme, USAID has used innovative financial instruments including guarantees to facilitate lending to buyers of MFIs. In setting a credit guarantee programme, the guarantor will want to set the fee structure based on the costs of monitoring and information gathering as well as the cost of the risk transfer service provided. It can often be difficult to establish a viable fee structure that fully compensates the guarantor for the services provided (Dayson et al. 1997, Doran and Levitsky, 1997; Levitsky, 1993).

Guarantee facilities help start a learning-by-doing process in which banks, donors, non-bank intermediaries, and micro-entrepreneurs learn to work together. The performance of guarantee schemes is dependent on the model chosen. To date, three types of guarantee models have been used to enhance the flow of finance to the micro-enterprise sector:

(i) *Individual Guarantee Model*

Under this model, the borrower and the bank are directly linked. The guarantor and the bank establish a cooperative agreement on the degree of risk sharing. The guarantor issues a guarantee agreement or standby letter of credit to the bank (Fig. 2). The bank appraises the loan application and, if borrowers fulfill their lending criteria, approves the loan. The guarantee entity, either public or private, is paid a fee for the guarantee by the borrowers, although the bank may collect this fee and pay the guarantor.

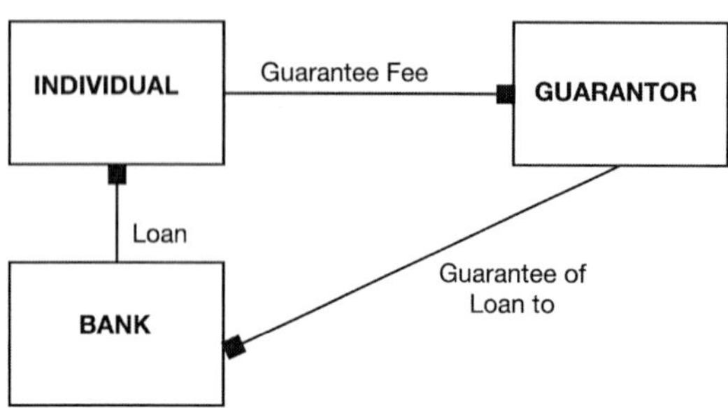


**Fig. 2:** Individual Guarantee Model

(ii) *Portfolio Guarantee Model*

This model reduces the guarantee entity's involvement with each borrower. Although the individual model requires the approval of guarantees for each loan, under the portfolio model, the guarantor negotiates portfolio criteria with the bank. If the programme is for micro-enterprise borrowers, criteria might include a maximum loan size, number of employees, and other limitations that ensure the borrower is part of the targeted sector. Loans that meet the required criteria are automatically guaranteed and disbursed (Fig. 3).

Experience shows that individual and portfolio guarantees have not been successful in increasing lending to the micro-enterprise sector because, while the guarantees reduce the risks of lending, they do not address the issue of transaction costs associated with lending to the micro-enterprise sector. For guarantees to encourage banks and other financial institutions to lend to the micro-enterprise sector, programmes will need to reduce the transaction costs to the bank by providing a significant portion of pre- and post-loan business support to entrepreneurs. Because the individual and portfolio models have failed to increase the flow of capital to the micro-enterprise sector, the intermediary model has emerged as a guarantee model for service provision to support emerging micro-entrepreneurs and smaller businesses.

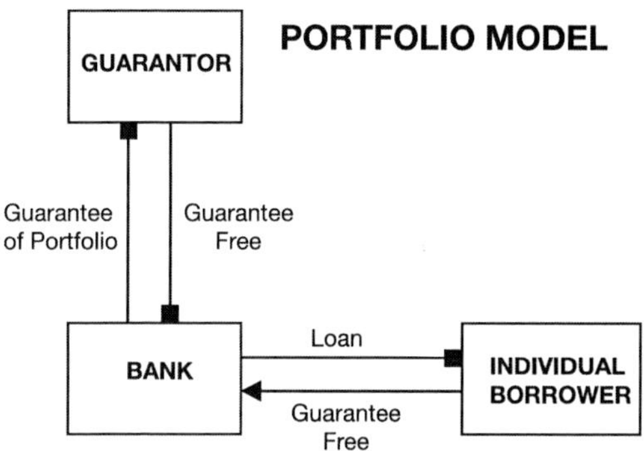


**Fig. 3:** Portfolio Guarantee Model

(iii) *Intermediary or "Wholesale" Guarantee Model*

This model has been adapted especially for the micro-enterprise sector. Under this model, micro-entrepreneurs are separated from the bank's normal risk/transaction costs, which are handled by a specialized lending organization that acts as an intermediary between the bank and the borrower (Fig. 4). The intermediary organization undertakes the appraisal, approval, monitoring, and supervising roles. The bank guarantees the loan to the intermediary institution. A number of microfinance networks have been experimenting with this model, including ACCION International, Women's World Banking, and Dévelopement International Desjardins.

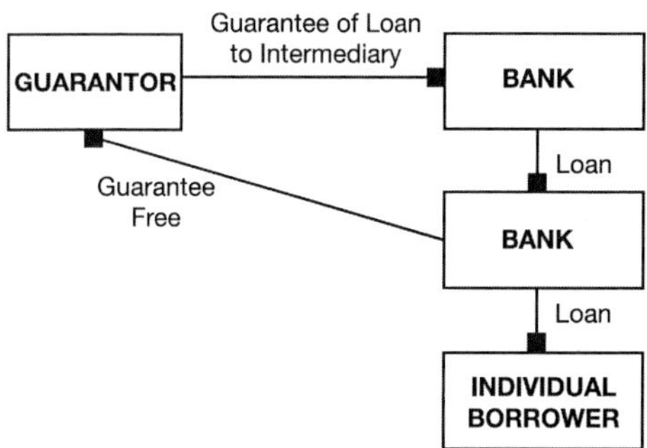


**Fig. 4:** Intermediary or "Wholesale" Guarantee Model

### 8.2 Securitization

Securitization is another innovative attempt to link microenterprises with capital markets. Typically, this structure requires the creation of a single purpose corporation (SPC) that buys the micro-enterprise portfolio and capitalizes itself by issuing debentures for the capital market. Mr. Michael Chu, former President and CEO of ACCION International once said: With the right partner; securitization can create an alternative micro-enterprise finance system that deals with the capital markets, in the language of the capital markets, in a market for which the capital markets are not suited. For example, ACCION International and its affiliate, Fundacion Ecuatoriana de Desarrollo (FED) piloted credit securitization in Ecuador. He explained: SPC's equity of approximately $2 million will come from FED, a local financial partner, ACCION International (through the Gateway Fund), and others. The SPC uses its cash to purchase $105 of portfolio from FED; but it pays FED $100 and puts the remaining $5 in a reserve which it pays on collection of the loan.

### 8.3 Debt Instruments

There are a few initiatives to issue debt instruments in microfinance. Bancosol, a microfinance institution in Bolivia, has issued certificates of deposit, which trade on the Bolivian stock exchange. Bancosol has also issued long-term debt instrument partially guaranteed by the USAID fund. Senior management of Bancosol has stated that the institution will continue to reduce its reliance on expensive interbank loans through the issuance of bonds and certificates of deposit. Over time, the hope is that savings mobilization will assume an ever larger proportion of funding. In Paraguay, ACCION's affiliate Fundacion Paraguaya, as an NGO, issued a debt instrument through the securities exchange of Paraguaya. Before issuing the paper, ACCION conducted a formal analysis employing a variant of an assessment tool used by bank examiners in the United States.

### *8.4 Specialized Equity Funds*

Specialized equity funds such as Profund, DEVCAP and AfriCap, created with donor support, take equity stakes in MFIs (Silva, 1998). Each of these vehicles has a unique structure, size and geographical focus—Profund focuses on Latin America and Caribbean, AfriCap focuses on Africa, while DEVCAP was established to support micro-enterprise lending by four U.S. development agencies (Save the Children, Catholic Relief Services, Appropriate Technology International and SEED Capital Development Fund) that support MFIs in 54 countries. These commercial investment funds focus on social returns, understanding that the financial returns will likely be below the appropriate risk adjusted market rate. These donor-supported funds are complemented by similar equity investments made by international investment companies. For example, The Triodos-Doen Foundation, founded in 1994, provides equity capital to MFIs all over the world in addition to loans and loan guarantees. The Calvert Targeted Community Investments and the Internationale Micro Investitionen Aktiengesellschaft (IMI) have similar equity investment programmes. In conjunction with MFI forays in the commercial capital markets, rating agencies that analyze MFIs for commercial investors have come into being and have also attracted donor interest. For example, the Inter-American Development Bank (IDB) and the Consultative Group to Assist the Poorest (CGAP, 1996, 2001) are launching the pilot phase of a joint initiative called the Microfinance Rating and Assessment Fund (MRAF). An objective of the Pilot Rating and Assessment Fund is to build a supply of competent ratings and appraisal services by supporting organizations that perform high-quality assessments, particularly agencies in developing countries.

### *8.5 Equity-Linked Microfinance*

As MFIs mature and transform from non-profit organizations into companies, including in some cases regulated institutions, their need for equity grows. With the high ROEs and fast growth of the industry, the IRR of MFI equity investment looks compelling on paper. Yet there have been only a handful of private equity funds set up to address this need. The major factor slowing the growth of commercial equity investment in MFIs is the small number of exits to-date. Most private equity investors look more to capital gains upon sale of their stakes and less to dividends as the principal component of their return.

This is appropriate in microfinance as MFIs need to retain earnings in the business to finance further growth if they are to escape an endless cycle of sourcing fresh equity. The only private equity fund that has gone through a complete cycle of investment and liquidation is ProFund International SA, which from 1995-2005 invested approximately $20 million total in 10 Latin American MFIs for an annual average return of 6 percent. ProFund is of interest here not for its financial returns—it was sponsored by socially motivated investors and did not set out to maximize profits—but for its success in realizing all 10 exits within its allotted 10-year life.

The fundamentals of micro-lending are roughly similar in most countries, as shown by the success of networks that apply a common methodology across the developing world. Strategic investors such as commercial banks, leasing companies and insurance companies will see the value in MFIs not just as lenders but as delivery vehicles for other financial services to a proprietary and loyal customer base. Already some Western European banks have purchased Eastern European banks that specialize in small and micro-enterprise lending in order to extend their footprint into the European Union hinterland. In addition, a Venezuelan bank recently purchased a large block of shares in a major Bolivian MFI, although political considerations may have counted as much as financial ones in the decision. Once an MFI is registered under the Companies Act, for it to undertake micro-credit activities, it needs to be further registered as either a NBFC under the RBI Act, 1934 or licensed as a local area bank (LAB) under the Banking Regulation Act, 1949. The RBI requires that a new NBFC must have a minimum start-up capital of ₹ 20 million, while a new LAB must have a minimum start-up capital of ₹ 50 million. As most MFIs are not in a position to raise this level of start-up equity because the people's equity can be only Rupees one or two million, it becomes essential to raise the balance equity from development finance institutions.

Start-up equity capital is difficult for most promoters of MFIs because most of them come from a developmental background. Yet, it is prudent to have reasonably high start-up capital requirements to ensure that MFIs are established as serious institutions. Thus, SIDBI, NABARD, and HUDCO should also consider making an equity investment in MFIs so as to strengthen their capital structure as well as give greater supervision. While development finance institutions in India are getting interested in micro-credit, for various reasons they are not yet in a position to provide equity funding to MFIs. For example, NABARD is not allowed to invest in equity under the NABARD Act, 1982. SIDBI though allowed to invest in equity, it has recently established a special foundation for micro-finance but it is mainly for providing loans and capacity building funds. HUDCO also has similar limitations. Thus, foreign development finance institutions can become an important source of equity finance for MFIs in the following manner:

- FIPB guidelines for foreign investment in financial services may be modified to include micro-finance activities. No additional restrictions should be put beyond what RBI as the regulator already prescribes.
- Further, the minimum level of foreign equity should be reduced from the level of US $ 500,000 to US $ 50,000, to enable smaller developmental investors to subscribe to the equity capital of an MFI.

Many foreign donors have taken a policy decision to experiment with funding mechanisms other than grants—soft loans, commercial loans, guarantees and equity. One of the issues related to loans from foreign donors is that of exchange rate risk. Most MFIs cannot bear or even get cover for long-term exchange rate fluctuations. Thus, many donors are willing to give loans which are denominated and repayable in Rupees. In this context, Donors, who are accustomed to give grants, should develop alternative mechanisms to provide equity support. This should be encouraged by the Government of India. The Department of Economic Affairs, Ministry of Finance, which deals both with donors and foreign investment, should take a view on this matter. Also, considering the lower cost funds that are available internationally, it is necessary that appropriate legislation be introduced to facilitate their flow. A new scheme, possibly called "External Developmental Borrowings (EDB)" may be established on the lines of the External Commercial Borrowings (ECB) scheme and powers given to RBI to administer it under the Foreign Exchange Regulation Act (FERA).

A study by CGAP (Chen, Rasmussen and Reille, 2010) examined microfinance crises in four countries: Morocco, Pakistan, Nicaragua and Bosnia-Herzegovina. It found that while there were some differences in the credit approaches in different countries, all of them were similar in terms of low emphasis on savings as a service or as a means of mobilizing resources—savings remained under 10 percent of outstanding loans in this sector, in contrast to the global average of 46 percent. Problems had emerged in all of these countries before 2007, but they were greatly accentuated by 2008-09, as microfinance borrowers were severely affected by the economic downturn, job losses, and declining flow of remittances. But this was really an aggravating factor rather than a basic cause of the problems of microfinance in these countries. Rather, three factors were the most important, and all of them reflect systemic features of the recent expansion of microfinance: extreme market competition and multiple borrowing; overstretched management systems and controls; and erosion of lending discipline. Thus the leading MFIs did not spread their lending out but rather tended to concentrate in certain geographical areas, thereby generating saturation and excess competition in the local market.

Partly this was because the micro-loans that were used by borrowers to engage in small productive activities resulted in too many competing producers for relatively limited markets for local goods and services. But in addition, multiple lending sources increased the likelihood that clients would borrow from more than one MFI, thereby reducing dependence on any single lender and increasing the probability of default. This geographical concentration is not just an accident: it is also because MFIs focus on low-hanging fruit by prioritizing localities with higher population density and more economic activity. Incidentally, this also makes them less likely to reach finance to the really poor and marginalized. Rapid expansion of MFIs, which was once again driven by incentives at the heart of the system, created overstretches in a number of ways. Staff were employed without adequate training, monitoring became more difficult and the internal controls that could control fraud were relaxed. Competition also eroded the credit discipline of MFIs themselves, as the incentives of middle managers downwards were increasingly oriented to maximizing the number of loans and clients. The similarity with the behavioural tendencies and incentives of other financial institutions in relatively under-regulated financial markets is obvious.

Incidentally, the very context of increased competition among MFIs in these markets also reduces the incentives for and likelihood of information sharing about clients across MFIs, a feature that has been noted in a study of Uganda (McIntosh, de Janvry and Sadoulet, 2005). This was found to lead to "a gradual deterioration in repayment performance and to a drop in savings, both of which are consistent with clients responding to rising competition by engaging in double-dipping". An extension of this argument (McIntosh and Wydick, 2005) is that as competition results in reduced returns from more profitable borrowers, it leads to the exclusion of poor borrowers, thereby undermining the supposed focus of microfinance in serving the underserved poor. As competition in turn aggravates the asymmetric information problems associated with borrower over indebtedness, the most impatient borrowers seek multiple loans, thereby creating outcomes that are less favourable for all borrowers (and lenders). Viada and Gaul (2011) point to the growing links between MFIs and the rest of the financial sector, which can in turn generate or accentuate some of these problems described above. They note that (when compared to the old aid donor-driven situation) competition for funding sources for the MFIs themselves encouraged MFIs to push the limits of their underwriting and risk management processes. The business success of microfinance attracted new and relatively large sources of both local and international funding, including private equity funds and other financial investors. As a result, MFIs were encouraged to increase loan portfolios to meet ambitious outreach goals or shareholder demands for increasing revenue growth. This in turn meant new pressures on management, as the boards of profit-making MFIs desired the managers to increase or at least maintain market share when facing increased competition. Such competitive pressures can easily foster aggressive loan origination policies and staff incentives based on loan volume. It is easy to see how this would contribute to declining portfolio quality and more rapid market saturation.

## 9. Institutional Arrangements for Delivery of Microfinance in India

In India, there is a wide variety of institutions in public as well as private sector which provide microfinance to the poor. These institutions can be broadly divided into two types. First type is the traditional formal financial institutions, while the second type is Microfinance Institutions (MFIs). The traditional financial institutions comprise of commercial banks, regional rural banks and co-operative banks. They provide microfinance services in addition to their general banking activities and are referred to as microfinance service providers. On the other hand MFIs are different types of financial institutions whose main financial activity is providing microfinance only. Many of these institutions are NGOs, Mutually Aided Co-operative Societies (MACS) and Non-Banking Financial Companies (NBFCs). In case of traditional financial institutions both private and public ownership are found but the MFIs are mainly in the private sector. These financial institutions use a hierarchical network starting from the apex wholesale level to the retail level financial institutes. The retail level banks and MFIs borrow funds from apex financial institutions and use their branch network to provide microfinance at the doorstep of poor people. Some of these apex and retail level financial institutions have been discussed below:

### *9.1. Apex Level Financial Institutions*

The formal microfinance service providers include a number of apex financial institutions. Some of them are like National Bank for Agriculture and Rural Development (NABARD), Small Industries Development Bank of India (SIDBI), Rashtriya Mahila Kosh (RMK), Friends of Women World Banking (FWWB), Housing Development Finance Corporation (HDFC), Housing and Urban Development Corporation Limited (HUDCO), and Rashtriya Gramin Vikas Nidhi (RGVN). They provide bulk amount of funds to retail level banks and MFIs for on-lending to the poor. There are different terms and conditions associated with each apex financial institute. The features of some of these institutions have been highlighted in Table 6. In addition to these apex financial institutions, many MFIs get funds from investors, lenders and donors also.

**Table 6:** Apex and Wholesale Financial Institutions in India

| S. No. | Organisation | SIDBI Lucknow | NABARD Bombay | RMK New Delhi | HUDCO New Delhi | HDFC Bombay | FWWB Ahmedabad | RGVN Guwahati |
|---|---|---|---|---|---|---|---|---|
| 1. | Background | Micro-credit scheme stalled in 1994. New SIDBI Foundation for micro-credit set up m Nov. 1998 | A Refinance institution set up in 1982. Promoting linkages of SHGs with banks since 1992 by Revolving Fund Assistance | Set up as an independent regd. society by Govt in 1993 to provide micro¬credit to poor women | Set up in 1970. Provide loan assistance for construction of house for economically weaker sections | Provide housing finance including - to low income groups through NGOs since 1992. Started supporting MFIs in 1997 | A non-profit organization set up in1982 as an affiliate of Women's World Banking started revolving loan fund m 1989 | A non-profit organization started in 1990. It has started NGO Support and credit and saving programme |
| 2. | Borrowers of these Organisations | 1. NGOs<br>2. SHG Federations<br>3. Co-operatives<br>4. Companies | 1. NGOs<br>2. SHG Federations<br>3. Co-operative Societies | 1. NGOs<br>2. SHG Federations<br>3. Women Development Corporations | 1. NGOs<br>2. SHG Federations<br>3. Co-operatives | 1. NGOs<br>2. Co-operatives<br>3. Companies | 1. NGOs<br>2. SHG Federations<br>3. Co-operatives<br>4. NBFCs<br>5. SHGs | 1. NGOs<br>2. SHG Federations<br>3. Associations of Entrepreneurs |
| 3. | Eligibility for Borrowing | 1. Organizations in existence for 3 years<br>2. Proven track record as per own criteria<br>3. Credit rating | 1. Registered Societies/Trusts involved in microfinance<br>2. Proven track record as per own criteria | Organization working with women and in existence for 3 years with proven track record as per own criteria | Organizationm existence for 3 years and has proven track record in microfinance as per own criteria | Proven track record as per own criteria | 1. Should be working with women and with minimum one year experience in MF<br>2. Membership of at least 800 women with at least 2 lakh of member savings | 1. Registered Societies/Trusts involved in microfinance<br>2. Proven track record as per own criteria |

*Contd...*

| S. No. | Organisation | SIDBI Lucknow | NABARD Bombay | RMK New Delhi | HUDCO New Delhi | HDFC Bombay | FWWB Ahmedabad | RGVN Guwahati |
|---|---|---|---|---|---|---|---|---|
| 4. | Interest rate (per annum) to recipient | 11-12.5% | (i)7.5% for 1st tier institutions<br>(ii) 9% for 2nd tier institutions | 8% | 9% | (i) 9% for housing<br>(ii) 12% for micro-enterprise | (i) 12% to SHGs<br>(ii) 13.5% to NGOs and other forms of MFIs<br>(iii) 14% to NBFCs | 9% |
| 5. | Maximum interest rates for on-lending to members | No ceiling | No ceiling | Not greater than 18% | 12% | (i) 15% for housing<br>(ii) 24% for (micro-enterprise) | As decided by Groups | As decided by Groups |
| 6. | Repayment Period | 3-5 years with or without moratorium | 3 to 5 yeas with one year moratorium | Short-term. 6-15 months<br>Long-term: 2-5 years with moratorium, if needed | 15 Year | 1. 15 Years for housing loans<br>2. 3 years for micro-enterprise loans | Varies between one and five years with moratorium of 6 months on principal repayment only. | Negotiable |

*Source*: Tankha (2002).

## 9.2 Retail Level Banks

At the retail level Commercial Banks, Regional Rural Banks, Co-operative Banks, and different types of MFIs provide microfinance services. In India, there are about 60,000 retail credit outlets of the formal banking sector in the rural areas comprising 20,571 rural and 12,283 semi-urban branches of commercial banks, 14,142 branches of the Regional Rural Banks and 12,128 branches of district level co-operative banks. Besides this, there are almost 92,000 co-operative credit societies at the village level. On an average, there is at least one retail credit outlet for about 4,700 rural people. These banks used to provide loans directly to SHGs. The commercial banks and regional rural banks also provide their credit facilities to MFIs for its on-lending to groups. This is helpful in widening the range of lending institutions.

## 9.3. Institutional Arrangement for Microfinance Institutions

Microfinance institutions (MFIs) are the organisations or associations of individuals that provide financial services to the poor. In India, there is a wide range of such organizations with diverse legal forms, varying significantly in size, outreach, mission and credit delivery methodologies. Figure 5 represents the hierarchy of financial institutions for the microfinance disbursement.

Following the guidelines of RBI all scheduled commercial banks including RRBs give bulk loans (classified as a priority sector) to MFIs for on-lending to groups and other small borrowers. At present, both public and private banks are extending considerable loans to MFIs at interest rate ranging from 8 to 11 percent per annum.

### *9.3.1 Legal Forms of MFIs*

The MFIs are an extremely heterogeneous group registered as Non-Banking Financial Companies (NBFCs), societies, trusts and co-operatives. On the basis of their legal forms, the MFIs in India can be broadly subdivided into three categories: Non-Profit making, mutual benefit making and profit making MFIs (Satish, 2005).

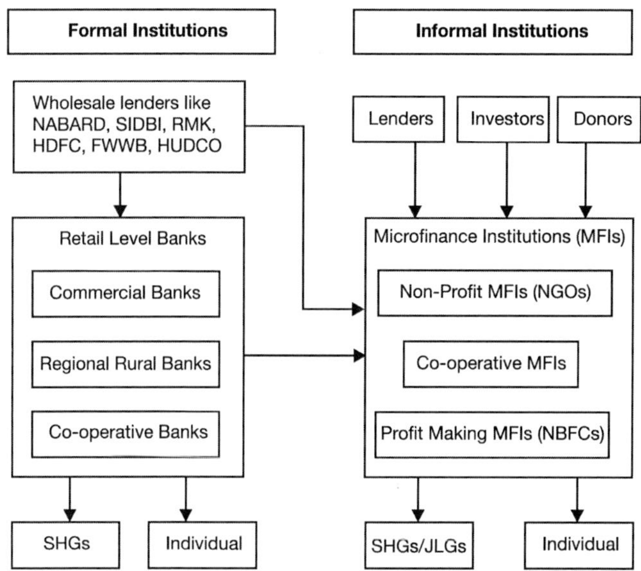


**Fig. 5:** Institutional Arrangement for Microfinance Disbursement in India

*Source*: Tankha (2002); Satish (2005).

Majority of the MFIs are operating on small-scale with clients ranging between 500 to 1500 per MFI and not more than 10 MFIs have an outreach of 1 lakh microfinance clients.

**(i) Non-profit Making MFIs**—The non-profit making MFIs include NGOs and non-profit making companies. The table provides that a large number of NGOs have undertaken the task of financial intermediation without any profit. Majority of these are registered as trusts or societies. These NGOs are not formally regulated and they are prohibited by RBI from taking collected savings of their clients or deposits from the public. The bye-laws of these institutions are generally restrictive in allowing any commercial operations. The companies registered under Section 25 of the Companies Act are also non-profit companies. The activities of these companies are restricted to charity or other social purposes. Section 25 companies are formally recognized and regulated by the RBI. These companies, being non-profit in character, cannot take group savings of their clients.

(ii) **Mutual Benefit MFIs**—The mutual benefit MFIs are the Mutually Aided Co-operative Societies (MACS). These are registered under the State Co-operative Societies Act and are not regulated by RBI (2008).

(iii) **For Profit MFIs**—For profit MFIs include Non-Banking Financial Companies (NBFCs). The MFIs in India which are larger in size belong to this category. These companies are registered under the Companies Act, 1956; and are regulated by RBI. These companies can deposit the savings of their clients with them. NBFCs, along with Section-25 companies, account for about 80 percent of microfinance outreach in India, both in terms of clients served as well as loan portfolios. Some of the large NBFCs in the field of microfinance are: Sanghamitra, BASIX, SHARE Microfinance Ltd., Indian Association for Savings and Credit (IASC), Cashpor, etc.

## *9.4 Microfinance Delivery Models in India*

In India, microfinance is provided through the SHG-Bank Linkage Model (SHGBLM) and Microfinance Institution (MFI) Model. The SHG-BLM developed by NABARD is widely prevalent throughout the country. In this model, the informal SHGs are credit linked with the formal banking system. On the other hand, MFI model is used by the various MFIs which emerge to reach the rural poor people in the areas not served by the formal banking sector. These MFIs provide financial services to the individuals or to the groups like SHGs, JLGs and Grameen groups.

### *9.4.1 Self-Help Groups (SHGs) and their Functioning*

SHGs are small, informal and homogeneous groups of 10 to 20 members each. These groups are formed by the bank officials, NGOs and various other institutions at the village level. Members of almost equal economic and social status are chosen to minimise any mutual conflict. Each such group is given a name and each group has a head, cashier and secretary, democratically elected by the group members to manage the group affairs. The members are encouraged to make a voluntary thrift on regular basis. The group members mutually decide about the amount and frequency for individual savings to be deposited in the group account. They use this pooled resource to make small interest bearing loans to their members within the group. This process, known as inter-loaning, gradually builds financial discipline among the group members and they learn to handle resources of a size that is much beyond their individual capacities. The SHG members begin to understand that resources are limited and have a cost.

Once the groups show this mature financial behaviour (generally after six months of group formation), banks are encouraged to provide loan to the SHG in certain multiples (three to four times) of their accumulated savings. The bank loans are given without any collateral and at specified interest rates. Banks find it easier to lend money to the groups rather than providing small funds to individual members. The peer pressure ensures timely repayments and replaces the collateral for the bank loans. Generally, the banks charge between 9-10 percent rates of interest per annum from the SHGs. The group members themselves decide the terms of loans and the criteria of dividing the loan among the group members. If only some of the group members use the whole loan then they have to pay interest to the group account also. The rate of interest is mutually decided by the group members. The group gets the second loan from the bank only after repaying the first loan successfully and so on. The conceptual thinking behind SHG initiative is that the mutual help within the participants of the programme can be a powerful vehicle in the upward socio-economic transition of the poor.

### *9.4.2 SHG-Bank Linkage Model*

SHG-Bank Linkage Model (SHG-BLM) is developed in India to provide microfinance with the help of vast rural network of the formal financial sector. In this model, the informal SHGs are credit linked with the formal financial institutions. The SHG-BLM has emerged as a dominant model in terms of number of borrowers and loans outstanding. This model is flexible, independence creating, and imparts freedom of saving and borrowing according to the requirements of group members.

Due to widespread rural bank branch network, the SHG-BLM is very suitable to the Indian context. Microfinance movement started in India with the introduction of SHG-Bank Linkage Programme (SHG-BLP). The programme uses SHGs as an intermediation between the banks and the rural poor to help in reducing transaction costs for both the banks and the rural clients. Banks provide the resources and bank officials/NGOs/ government agencies organize the poor in the form of SHGs. Under this programme, loans are provided to the SHGs with three different methodologies:

**Model I:** SHGs Formed and Financed by Banks: In this model, banks themselves take up the work of forming and nurturing the groups, opening their savings accounts and providing them bank loans.

**Model II:** SHGs Formed by Agencies Other than Banks, but Directly Financed by Banks: In this model, NGOs and other formal agencies in the field of microfinance facilitate organizing, forming and nurturing of SHGs and train them in thrift and credit management. The banks directly give loans to these SHGs.

**Model III:** SHGs Financed by Banks Using Other Agencies as Financial Intermediaries: This is the model where the NGOs take on the additional role of financial intermediation along with the formation of group. In areas where the formal banking system faces constraints, the NGOs are encouraged to form groups and to approach a suitable bank for bulk loan assistance. This method is generally used by most of the NGOs having small financial base. Table 7 shows the SHGs linked to banks and the amount of loans disbursed under the three models. It shows that the microfinance programme in India is dominated by Model II. It is found that up to March 2006, 20.1 percent of the total credit linked SHGs are formed under Model I; and these groups are provided 14.4 percent of the total bank loans disbursed under the programme. Approximately seventy-four percent of the total SHGs are formed under Model II. These groups are provided 80.7 percent of the total loans. The share of Model III is relatively small. Approximately six percent of the total SHGs financed with 4.9 percent of the total loan fall under this category.

**Table 7:** Model-wise Bank Linkage of SHGs in India (up to March 2006)

| Model Type | 2004 | | 2005 | | 2006 | |
|---|---|---|---|---|---|---|
| | Number of SHGs ('000) | Bank Loans (in ₹ Crore) | Number of SHGs ('000) | Bank Loans (in ₹ Crore) | Number of SHGs ('000) | Bank Loans (in ₹ Crore) |
| Model I | 218 (20.0) | 550 (14.0) | 343 (21.2) | 1,013 (14.7) | 449 (20.1) | 1,637 (14.4) |
| Model II | 777 (72.0) | 3,165 (81.0) | 1,158 (71.6) | 5,529 (80.1) | 1,646 (73.5) | 1,200 (80.7) |
| Model III | 84 (8.0) | 189 (5.0) | 117 (7.2) | 356 (5.2) | 143 (6.4) | 561 (4.9) |
| Total | 1,079 (100) | 3,904 (100) | 1,618 (100) | 6,898 (100) | 2,238 (100) | 11,398 (100) |

*Source*: NABARD Data.

*Note*: The figures given in parentheses indicate percentages of SHGs and bank loans.

*MFI Model*

The MFI model has also gained momentum in India in the recent past. MFI model is found worldwide whereas the SHG-BLM model is an Indian model. In MFI model MFIs borrow large amount of funds from the apex financial institutions, donors and banks for on-lending to the individuals or groups. These MFIs provide financial services to the individuals or to the groups like SHGs, JLGs and Grameen groups.

***SHG vs. MFI Model***

Some features of both the models have been compared on the basis of type of group in Table 8. An important difference between SHG-BLM and the other groups (Grameen and Joint liability groups) is that in the former the loan is a single loan to the group as a whole, which is then divided by the group member, whereas in Grameen and Joint liability groups the MFIs provide loans to individual members, although disbursement and collection are facilitated by the group mechanism. In this way, there is limited participation of group members in Grameen and JLGs. Therefore, individual lending results in less empowerment of its clients as compared to the SHG-BLM.

**Table 8:** Features of Microfinance Delivery Approaches

| Feature | SHG Model | MFI Model | |
|---|---|---|---|
| | | Grameen | Individual Banking |
| Type of Clients | Primarily women | Primarily women | Women/Men |
| Group Size | 10-20 members per group | Usually 5 members per group | Individual Clients |
| Services | Services and credit | Services and credit | Credit |
| Credit Delivery | In the name of group | Individual | Individual |
| Role of field staff | Organize, Guide and Facilitate | Organize (group dependent on staff) | Organize |
| Record keeping | By group | By field staff | By field staff |
| Group Meetings | Monthly | Weekly | No meetings |
| Meetings with officials | Monthly | Weekly | Unscheduled |
| Amount of Saving | ₹ 20-100 per month | ₹ 5-25 per week | Flexible |
| Initial loan amount | 3-4 times of group saving | ₹ 2,000-5,000 | ₹ 5,000-150,000 |
| Interest rate | 9-11 percent | Varies largely between MFIs (12-30 percent) | Generally, more than Grameen model |
| Effect on Empowerment of members | High | Low | Very low |

*Source*: Puhazhendhi, V. (2012): *Microfinance India State of the Sector Report*, 2012, SAGE.

Table 9 shows the number of individuals who are provided microfinance loans under the SHG-BLM as well as the MFI model. It is important to note that in some of the southern states the microfinance programme has reached the saturation point; and the MFIs are competing to find the new eligible clients. In this situation, same individuals are getting loans under both the models from different MFIs. So, the table also shows the data adjusted for this overlap. The table reveals that up to

March 2007, 48.06 million individuals are covered under the microfinance programme out of which 79.11 percent are formed under SHG-BLM and 20.89 percent under the MFI model. The programme outreach increases to 59.21 million by March 2008. But the data adjusted for the overlap shows that 54.87 million individuals are covered under the microfinance programme by March 2008.

**Table 9:** Microfinance Outreach in India (in millions)

| Type of Model | Number of People Covered | | Growth in Outreach |
|---|---|---|---|
| | Up to March 2007 | Up to March 2008 | |
| SHG-BLM | 38.02 (79.11) | 45.20 (76.34) | 7.18 |
| MFI Model | 10.04 (20.89) | 14.01 (23.66) | 3.97 |
| Total | 48.06 (100) | 59.21 (100) | 11.15 |
| Total Adjusted for Overlap | 44.97 | 54.87 | 9.90 |

*Source*: Srinivasan (2009); Srinivan and Sriram, 2006.

*Note*: The figures given in parentheses indicate percentages of people covered under Microfinance programme.

Table 10 shows the region-wide spread of microfinance programme under SHG-BLM and MFI models. Table 10 shows that up to March 2008 approximately 45 million people are provided with microfinance under SHG-BLM and 14 million under the MFI model. Perusal of table shows that the programme is mainly concentrated in the southern region. Approximately 48 percent and 55 percent of the people who are provided microfinance under these two models belong to the southern region of India. However the spread of the programme is limited in the north and north-eastern region. Out of the total microfinance outreach in India approximately 5 percent and 3 percent of the clients belong to north and north-eastern region, respectively. The spread of the microfinance programme is shown separately for the Punjab state. Table 10 shows that the programme outreach is very limited in Punjab and there are just 0.2 percent of the total microfinance clients of India. The table also shows that in Punjab the microfinance programme is expanded only through the SHG-BLM and there are no MFI clients.

**Table 10:** Region-wise Spread of Microfinance Programme (up to 2008)

| S. No. | Region | Cumulative Number of SHGs | Number of SHG Members | Number of MFI Clients | Total Microflnance Clients |
|---|---|---|---|---|---|
| 1 | Northern Region | 2,30,740 (6.63) | 29,99,620 (6.63) | 1,13,102 (0.80) | 31,12,722 (5.25) |
| | Punjab | 8,965 (0.26) | 116,545 (0.26) | Nil | 116,545 (0.20) |
| 2 | North Eastern Region | 1,19,857 (3.45) | 15,58,141 (3.45) | 1,75,589 (1.25) | 17,33,730 (2.92) |
| 3 | Eastern Region | 6,72,201 (19.33) | 87,38,613 (19.33) | 34,75,622 (24.70) | 1,22,14,235 (20.60) |
| 4 | Central Region | 4,05,707 (11.67) | 52,74,191 (11.67) | 10,14,202 (7.21) | 62,88,393 (10.61) |
| 5 | Western Region | 3,74,561 (10.77) | 48,69,293 (10.77) | 15,85,681 (11.27) | 64,54,974 (10.89) |
| 6 | Southern Region | 16,74,811 (48.15) | 2,17,72,543 (48.15) | 77,04,449 (54.77) | 2,94,76,992 (49.73) |
| Total | | 34,77,965 000) | 4,52,13,545 (100) | 1,40,68,645 (100) | 5,92,82,190 (100) |

*Source*: Srinivasan (2009).

*Note*: The figures given in parentheses indicate percentages of SHGs and Microfinance members.

### *9.4.3 Progress of SHG-Bank Linkage Programme in India*

Initially, there was a slow progress in the programme up to 1999 as only 32,995 groups were credit linked during the period 1992 to 1999. Since then the programme is growing rapidly. Table 11 shows the total number of SHGs credit linked with banks and the bank loan disbursed to these groups from 1992-93 to 2007-08. The table shows that 255 SHGs were given ₹ 2.9 million of bank loans during the period 1992-93. In 1999-2000 the number increased to 1,14,775 with bank loans of ₹ 1,929.8 million. This cumulative number of credit linked SHGs has increased to about 34.78 lakh and the amount of bank loan given to these groups increased to ₹ 2,22,680 million up to March 2008. Microfinance through SHGs has reached to such a position in India that it is acknowledged as the biggest microfinance programme in the world. The data reveals that though the cumulative number of SHGs provided with bank loans increases but the rate of growth is relatively slow as compared to the previous years. Table 11 shows that the rate of growth of SHGs and bank loans disbursed to them is negative during the year 2007-08. One of the reasons may be that the programme has rapidly expanded in the southern states of India and has reached a saturation point in some of these states.

**Table 11:** Number of SHGs linked to Banks in India (1992-93 to 2007-08)

| Year | New SHGs Financed by Banks | | | Bank loans (in ₹ Miillion) | | |
|---|---|---|---|---|---|---|
| | Number | Growth % | Cumulative Number | Amount | Growth % | Cumulative Amount |
| 1992-93 | 255 | – | 255 | 2,090 | – | 2.9 |
| 1993-94 | 365 | 43 | 620 | 3.60 | 24 | 6.5 |
| 1994-95 | 1,502 | 312 | 2,122 | 18.00 | 400 | 24.5 |
| 1995-96 | 2,635 | 75 | 4,757 | 36.10 | 101 | 60.6 |
| 1996-97 | 3,841 | 46 | 8,598 | 57.80 | 60 | 118.4 |
| 1997-98 | 5,719 | 49 | 14,317 | 119.20 | 106 | 237.6 |
| 1998-99 | 18,678 | 332 | 32,995 | 32,995 | 179 | 570.7 |
| 1999-2000 | 81,780 | 231 | 1,14,775 | 1,359.10 | 308 | 1,929.8 |
| 2000-01 | 1,49,050 | 82 | 2,63,825 | 2,879.20 | 113 | 4,809.0 |
| 2001-02 | 1,97,653 | 33 | 4,61,478 | 5,454.00 | 89 | 10,263.0 |
| 2002-03 | 2,55,882 | 29 | 7,17,360 | 10,224.00 | 87 | 20,487.0 |
| 2003-04 | 3,61,731 | 41 | 10,79,091 | 18,555.00 | 81 | 39,042.0 |
| 2004-05 | 5,39,385 | 49 | 16,18,476 | 29,938.00 | 61 | 68,980.0 |
| 2005-06 | 6,20,089 | 15 | 22,38,565 | 44,990.00 | 50 | 1,13,970.0 |
| 2006-07 | 6,86,408 | 11 | 29,24,973 | 66,437.00 | 48 | 1,80,407.0 |
| 2007-08 | 5,52,992 | –19 | 34,77,965 | 42,273.00 | –36 | 2,22,680.0 |

*Source*: NABARD Annual Reports (2007 and 2008).

### *9.4.4 Regional spread of SHG-BLP*

Table 12 shows the spread of SHG bank linkage programme in different six regions of India, i.e. northern region, north-eastern, eastern, central, western and southern region. Northern region includes the states of Punjab, Haryana, Himachal Pradesh, Jammu & Kashmir and Rajasthan. North-eastern region covers Assam, Sikkim, Tripura, Meghalaya, Arunachal Pradesh, Mizoram and Nagaland states. Eastern region covers Bihar, West Bengal, Jharkhand, Odisha, and Andaman & Nicobar Islands. Central region includes Madhya Pradesh, Chhattisgarh, Uttarakhand and Uttar Pradesh. Western region includes Goa, Gujarat and Maharashtra states. Southern region includes Andhra Pradesh, Karnataka, Kerala, Tamil Nadu and

Puducherry. Table 12 clearly reveals that the SHGs are mainly concentrated in southern region. The main reason of this is the prevalence of voluntary organizations in the spread of linkage banking programme. The largest MFIs of India, such as SHARE, Spandana, CDF, MYRADA, SKS and PREM are also concentrated in southern region. The spread of microfinance programme is almost negligible in the north-eastern states. But the table shows that the microfinance programme is gradually developing in all the regions. The share of southern states in the number of groups linked to the banks is declining, while the share of other regions is improving. The table further provides that over the time period from 2001-08 there is a positive growth of the SHG-BLP in all the regions, except the southern part. The share of southern states in the total credit linked SHGs is 48.2 percent in 2008 as compared to 71.2 percent in 2001. In the year 2008, the share of northern region in the total credit linked SHGs was 6.6 percent, share of north-eastern region was 3.4 percent and the share of eastern, central and western regions was 19.3, 11.7 and 10.8 percent respectively.

**Table 12:** Region-wise Cumulative Growth in SHGs Linked to Banks

| Region | Cumulative Number of SHGs Linked to Banks | | | | | | | |
|---|---|---|---|---|---|---|---|---|
| | March 2001 | March 2002 | March 2003 | March 2004 | March 2005 | March 2006 | March 2007 | March 2008 |
| Northern Region | 9,012<br>(3.4) | 19,321<br>(4.2) | 34.923<br>(4.9) | 52,396<br>(4.9) | 86,018<br>(5.3) | 1.33,097<br>(5.9) | 1.82.018<br>(6.2) | 2,30,740<br>(6.6) |
| North-eastern Region | 477<br>(0.2) | 1.490<br>(0.3) | 4,069<br>(0.6) | 12.278<br>(1.1) | 34,238<br>(2.1) | 62.517<br>(2.8) | 91.754<br>(3.1) | 1,19,857<br>(3.4) |
| Eastern Region | 22 252<br>(8.4) | 45.892<br>(9.9) | 90.893<br>(12.7) | 1,58,237<br>(14.7) | 2.65.628<br>(16.4) | 3.94.351<br>(17.6) | 5,25,881<br>(18.0) | 6.72,289<br>(19.3) |
| Central Region | 28,851<br>(10.9) | 48.181<br>(10.4) | 81.583<br>(11.4) | 1,27,009<br>(11.8) | 1,97.365<br>(12.2) | 2.67.915<br>(12.0) | 3,32,729<br>(11.4) | 4,05,707<br>(11.7) |
| Western Region | 15.543<br>(5.9) | 29,318<br>(6.4) | 42.180<br>(5.9) | 54,815<br>(5.1) | 96.266<br>(6.0) | 1,66,254<br>(7.4) | 2.70.447<br>(92) | 3,74,561<br>(10.8) |
| Southern Region | 1.87.690<br>(71.2) | 3.17,276<br>(68.8) | 4.63.712<br>(64.5) | 6,74,356<br>(62.4) | 9.38.941<br>(58.0) | 12,14,431<br>(54.3) | 15,22.144<br>(52.1) | 16,74.811<br>(48.2) |
| All India | 2.63.825<br>(100) | 4,61.478<br>(100) | 7,17.360<br>(100) | 10.79,061<br>(100) | 16.18,456<br>(100) | 22.38,565<br>(100) | 29,24,973<br>(100) | 34,77.965<br>(100) |

*Source*: NABARD Annual Reports.

*Note*: The figures given in parentheses indicate percentages of credit linked SHGs.

### 9.4.5 Percentage Share of SHGs

Table 13 exhibits the percentage of credit linked SHGs for different regions over three time periods, i.e. 2002, 2005 and 2008. The figure highlights that the percentage share of SHGs in all the regions is almost increasing, while the percentage share of the southern part is decreasing.

**Table 13:** Region-wise Spread of SHG-Bank Linkage Programme

| Region | Cumulative Number of SHGs Linked to Banks | | | | | | | |
|---|---|---|---|---|---|---|---|---|
| | March 2001 | March 2002 | March 2003 | March 2004 | March 2005 | March 2006 | March 2007 | March 2008 |
| Northern Region | 9,012 (3.4) | 19,321 (4.2) | 34.923 (4.9) | 52,396 (4.9) | 86,018 (5.3) | 1.33,097 (5.9) | 1.82.018 (6.2) | 2,30,740 (6.6) |
| North-eastern Region | 477 (0.2) | 1.490 (0.3) | 4,069 (0.6) | 12.278 (1.1) | 34,238 (2.1) | 62.517 (2.8) | 91.754 (3.1) | 1,19,857 (3.4) |
| Eastern Region | 22 252 (8.4) | 45.892 (9.9) | 90.893 (12.7) | 1,58,237 (14.7) | 2.65.628 (16.4) | 3.94.351 (17.6) | 5,25,881 (18.0) | 6.72,289 (19.3) |
| Central Region | 28,851 (10.9) | 48.181 (10.4) | 81.583 (11.4) | 1,27,009 (11.8) | 1,97.365 (12.2) | 2.67.915 (12.0) | 3,32,729 (11.4) | 4,05,707 (11.7) |
| Western Region | 15.543 (5.9) | 29,318 (6.4) | 42.180 (5.9) | 54,815 (5.1) | 96.266 (6.0) | 1,66,254 (7.4) | 2.70.447 (9.2) | 3,74,561 (10.8) |
| Southern Region | 1.87.690 (71.2) | 3.17,276 (68.8) | 4.63.712 (64.5) | 6,74,356 (62.4) | 9.38.941 (58.0) | 12,14,431 (54.3) | 15,22.144 (52.1) | 16,74.811 (48.2) |
| All India | 2.63.825 (100) | 4,61.478 (100) | 7,17.360 (100) | 10.79,061 (100) | 16.18,456 (100) | 22.38,565 (100) | 29,24,973 (100) | 34,77.965 (100) |

*Source*: Puhazhendhi, V. (2012).

### 9.4.6 Role of Microfinancing Banks

Various public and private sector banks such as commercial banks, RRBs and cooperative banks are involved in providing microfinance to the SHGs. Table 14 shows the share of these agencies in the total credit linked SHGs and in the total loans disbursed.

Table 14 reveals that 55 percent of the total credit linked SHGs received loans from commercial banks, 31 percent from RRBs and the remaining 14 percent from the co-operative banks up to March 2007. Commercial banks contributed 63 percent of the total amount of loans disbursed to the SHGs, while RRBs and co-operative banks shared approximately 28 percent and 9 percent of the total loans amount. The SHG bank linkage has become a part of business for all the 27 public sector and 20 private sector commercial banks. NABARD data

**Table 14:** Agency-wise Number of SHGs Financed

| Agency | Up to March 2006 | | Up to March 2007 | |
|---|---|---|---|---|
| | No. of SHGs Financed | Bank Loan (in ₹ Million) | No. of SHGs Financed | Bank Loan (in ₹ Million) |
| 1. Commercial Banks | 11,88,040 (53) | 69,874.5 (61) | 15,94,787 (55) | 1,13,975.6 (63) |
| 2. RRBs | 7,40,024 (33) | 33,221.5 (29) | 9,10,807 (31) | 50,310.1 (28) |
| 3. Co-operative Banks | 3,10,501 (14) | 10,879.5 (10) | 4,19,379 (14) | 16,121.7 (09) |
| Total | 22,38,565 (100) | 1,13,975.5 (100) | 29,24,973 (100) | 1,80,407.4 (100) |

*Source*: NABARD Annual Reports.

*Note*: The figures given in parentheses indicate percentages of SHGs and bank loans.

of SHG-BLP up to March 2006 shows that State Bank of India credit linked the highest number of SHGs (3,92,494), followed by Andhra Bank (1,13,466) and Indian Bank (96,460), (not shown in the table).

The regional rural banks also finance SHGs in a significant way. All the 159 RRBs in the country are participating in the SHG-BLP. Maximum number of SHGs has been linked by Pandiyan Grameen Bank in Tamil Nadu and Puducherry (45,672) followed by Srivishakha Grameen Bank (35,875) and Nagarjuna Grameen Bank (27,879) both in Andhra Pradesh. Up to March 2006, as many as 337 central co-operative banks were involved in SHG-BLP. Maximum number of SHGs have been linked by Hooghly Cooperative Bank (18,015) in West Bengal followed by South Canara Co-operative Bank (10,851) and Hassan Co-operative Bank (10,389) both in Karnataka.

### *9.4.7 Reviewing recovery status of bank loans*

The success of any scheme is gauged from the criteria of the recovery status of bank loans. If the members of the scheme are net gainers then they will like to return loans at regular intervals in order to gain more funds. Table 16 shows the recovery status of the bank's loans given to the SHGs as reported by 290 and 329 commercial banks, RRBs and co-operative banks by the end of March 2007 and 2008 respectively. The data up to March 2008 clearly shows that 46.5 percent of the banks reported above 95 percent loan recovery rate. Approximately, twenty-one per cent of the banks showed the loan recovery rate between 80 to 94 percent. About twenty-three percent of the banks recovered 50 to 79 percent of the loans given to SHGs under the microfinance programme and just 8.8 percent of the banks reported that the loan recovery rate is less than 50 percent (Table 15). Therefore, it can be said that recovery of loans given under microfinance programme is very good, which is quite essential for programme sustainability. It may also be interpreted that the microfinance scheme is working well for both SHG members as well as the funding institutions.

**Table 15:** Recovery Status of Bank Loans Given to SHGs

(For the Years 2007 and 2008)

| Agency | Year | No. of Banks Reported Recovery Data | Recovery Status of Bank Loans Given to SHGs | | | |
|---|---|---|---|---|---|---|
| | | | 95% and Above | 80-94% | 50-79% | Less than 50% |
| Commercial Banks | 2007 | 36 (100) | 11 (30.6) | 15 (41.7) | 10 (27.7) | – |
| | 2008 | 33 (100) | 18 (54.5) | 06 (18.2) | 09 (27.3) | – |
| Regional Rural Banks | 2007 | 73 (100) | 20 (27.4) | 35 (47.9) | 13 (17.9) | 05 (6.8) |
| | 2008 | 70 (100) | 22 (31.4) | 25 (35.7) | 17 (24.3) | 06 (8.6) |
| Co-operative Banks | 2007 | 181 (100) | 76 (42.0) | 55 (30.4) | 35 (19.3) | 15 (8.3) |
| | 2008 | 226 (100) | 113 (30.0) | 39 (17.3) | 51 (22.6) | 23 (10.2) |
| Total | 2007 | 290 (100) | 107 (36.9) | 105 (36.2) | 58 (20.0) | 20 (6.9) |
| | 2008 | 329 (100) | 153 (46.5) | 70 (21.3) | 77 (23.4) | 29 (8.8) |

*Source*: Puhazhendhi, V. (2012): *Microfinance India State of the Sector Report*, 2012, SAGE.

## 10. Financial Performance Assessment of MFIs in India

The recent emerging trend in the Microfinance industry in India has led to a greater emphasis on transparency and financial viability of Microfinance Institutions (MFIs). This trend is not uncommon for any nascent and growing industry. An important aspect of this trend has been greater focus on financial and institutional indicators to measure the impact and performance of MFIs. However, it is hard to achieve transparency and viability sans standard (uniform) measures to assess financial condition, impact and performance. It is also recognized that the development of standards also contributes in building ground to take the sector towards self-regulation. A variety of measurements have been used globally to measure MFIs' performance, many of which have been recognized as standard indicators. A closer look at these measures reveals that these indicators are being calculated and applied in many different ways. To overcome this issue, Sa-Dhan—The Association of Community Development Finance Institutions (ACDFI) initiated the process of development of minimum sectoral standards for the Indian Microfinance industry, ever since its inception (1998). Sa-Dhan, through its sub-group on standards has finally arrived at financial performance standards for Indian MFIs, through a series of consultative meetings (Sa-Dhan, 2008).

Microfinance Institutions have been expected to reduce poverty, which is considered as the most important development objective (World Bank, 2000). Robinson defines Microfinance as small-scale financial services for both credits and deposits that are provided to people who farm or fish or herd; operate small or micro-enterprises where goods are produced, recycled, repaired or traded; provide services; work for wages or commissions; gain income from renting out small amounts of land, vehicles, draft animals, or machinery and tools; and to other individuals and local groups in developing countries, in both rural and urban areas (Robinson, 2001). Subsidized credit has long been believed to be the panacea for the eradication of poverty for decades now. But perhaps the only thing subsidized credit could create was Non-Performing Assets (NPAs).

The realization that the core issue for the poor was access to credit rather than the cost of credit came very late. Microfinance is often credited with putting an end to the interest rate debate for the poor. A host of players have entered microfinance space, each having a reason of its own. It is believed that, Microfinance, unlike other developmental efforts, gives quick and tangible results (Srinivasan and Sriram, 2006). Many NGOs that were early entrants gradually metamorphosed into full-fledged lenders, developmental professionals left their cushy careers to set up microfinance firms. Even many banks have experimented with working exclusively with self-help groups and therefore have microfinance branches.

The players range from not-for profits organizations trying to achieve developmental objective through microfinance to commercial banks that view microfinance as good, sound banking, a good source of deposits, and low-risk mass lending. In fact, the success of self-help groups in microfinance led many to use them to achieve many other objectives as well. Many governmental schemes are being routed through microfinance, including a very large project funded by the World Bank and being implemented in a southern state of India. Similarly, organizations like Hindustan Lever has looked at the potential of these groups as a channel for retailing and has launched a programme called Project 'Shakti' to tap the smaller villages through the micro-credit. They are also being harnessed as an alternative distribution channel. This amount is almost too free riding since these channels have been developed by the MFIs after a lot of persistent hard work and investment. The companies that initiated this are reputed ones like HLL, EID Parry and Philips, etc. (Srinivasan and Sriram, 2006).

As microfinance firms are viewed predominantly as instruments of social change, their performance has been often measured by non-financial parameters. The concept of social performance has seemed to overshadow the state of financial health of these enterprises. However, the accepted criteria in a number of studies to study the performance of any MFI have been the twain of Financial Performance and Outreach (Chaves and Gonzales-Vega, 1996, Ledgerwood, 1999, Yaron, 1992 and 1994, Yaron et al. 1997 and 1998). However, there exist various social performance assessment tools and institutionalized rating processes but assessment of financial performance has yet to gain ground. Some of the more popular tools include MFC

Social Audit, ACCION SOCIAL, USAID SPA Audit, MCRIL, Micro-finanza Rating, Micro Rate (SPA), CGAP-Grameen-Ford Progress out of Poverty Index (PPI), etc. (Sen, 2008). These tools often focus on outreach indicators. Outreach indicators are considered as proxies for impact of MFI on development (Yaron et al., 1997).

The financial performance assessment is devoid of such a multitude of options and methodologies despite critical importance of financial sustainability. Though an ambition for sustainable institutions has been often articulated, there was also an opinion that most microfinance institutions working in this field have been unsustainable (Dayson and Quach, 2006). Research studies have shown that this is predominantly connected to the perception of micro-borrowers, risk and creditworthiness, and the diseconomies of scale in making small loans (Dayson et al., 2006). Microfinance has been attractive to lending agencies because of demonstrated sustainability and low cost of operations. In India, the engagement of NABARD and SIDBI shows that they see long-term prospect for this sector (Srinivasan and Sriram, 2006). However, the methodologies to study financial sustainability are fewer. Review of studies reveals that amongst those available, most of the tools available cover social as well as financial performance. Principal among them are CAMEL model by ACCION, PEARLS model by WOCCU, GIRAFE Rating by PlaNet and MicroRate (CGAP, 2001). Amongst these, except the PEARLS methodology by World Council of Credit Unions (WOCCU), all others are hybrid models using both qualitative and quantitative data (Arsyad, 2005). These methodologies are proprietary and not available for use in public domain. It can be seen that without sound financial performance the sustainability of these microfinance institutions is not possible. Increasingly questions are being raised over the cost of funds for these enterprises and their ability to earn margins sufficient to cover their operational costs and still leave some profit (Arsyad, 2005). It has been pointed out repeatedly that MFIs need to be economically viable and sustainable in the long run (Srinivasan and Sriram, 2006). In fact studies have found strong linkage between the financial sustainability of microfinance institutions and achievement of their social objectives. Low income customers are more likely to borrow from institutions they see as financially viable (Zeller et al., 2003).

The direct provision of rural finance, microfinance, and SME finance loans and credit facilities by government agencies or programmes should be noted and examined in the assessment of adequacy of access. Those government programmes usually have an unfair competitive advantage over and tend to crowd out the private sector-based providers of similar financial services to households, microenterprises, and small businesses. In a number of countries, state-owned development finance institutions or specialized banks are the institutional vehicles used. The key issues to address in the assessment, aside from whether the institutional vehicles are reaching their target sector or client base and have, in fact, contributed to the development and expansion of the target sector, are (a) efficiency of loan collection, (b) incidence of loan defaults and adequacy of loan-loss provisions, (c) claims on budgetary or fiscal resources for loan guarantees and additional capital to cover operating losses, and (d) level of solvency or insolvency.

After more than a decade of experimentation, the Microfinance sector in India has graduated to take-off stage and has begun to scale up rapidly, attracting substantial attention and resources. In the context of sustained growth of Microfinance in India and given the twin imperatives of enhanced sustainability and expanded outreach, there is growing emphasis on professional growth of the sector. 'Standards setting' is one of the tested means to achieve professionalism. Several global initiatives have been undertaken to promote development of reliable financial standards (including performance, accounting and governance standards) to compare Microfinance Institutions (MFIs) operating in different environments and across the world. In addition, MFIs themselves have together attempted (especially, on a regional and/or national basis) to define a conceptual framework for assessment—using commonly agreed indicators and standards.

As an overview it may be summed-up that a new paradigm that emerges is that it is very critical to link poor to formal financial system, whatever the mechanism may be, if the goal of poverty alleviation has to be achieved. NGOs and CBOs have been involved in community development for long and the experience shows that they have been able to improve the quality of life of poor, if this is an indicator of development. The strengths and weaknesses of existing NGOs/CBOs and microfinance institutions in India indicate that despite their best of efforts they have not been able to link themselves with formal systems. It is desired that an intermediary institution is required between formal financial markets and grass-root. The intermediary should encompass the strengths of both formal financial systems and NGOs and CBOs and should be flexible to the needs of end users. There are, however, certain unresolved dilemmas regarding the nature of the intermediary institutions. There are arguments both for and against each structure.

## 11. Major Risks to Microfinance Institutions

Many risks are common to all financial institutions. From banks to unregulated MFIs, these include credit risk, liquidity risk, market or pricing risk, operational risk, compliance and legal risk, and strategic risk. Most risks can be grouped into three general categories: financial risks, operational risks and strategic risks, as in Table 16 below.

**Table 16:** Major Risk Categories of Microfinance

| Financial Risks | Operational Risks | Strategic Risks |
|---|---|---|
| Credit Risk | Transaction Risk | Governance Risk |
| Transaction Risk | Human Resources Risk | Ineffective oversight |
| Portfolio Risk | Information and | Poor governance |
| Liquidity Risk | Technology Risk | structure |
| Market Risk | Fraud (Integrity) Risk | Reputation Risk |
| Interest Rate Risk | Legal and | External Business Risks |
| Foreign Exchange Risk | Compliance Risk | Event Risk |
| Investment Portfolio Risk | | |

*Source*: GTZ (2000a).

Financial institution managers (and regulators) review these risks in light of (i) the institution's potential exposure to loss, (ii) the quality of internal risk management and information systems, and (iii) the adequacy of capital and cash to absorb both identified and unidentified potential losses.

## *11.1 Financial Risks*

The business of a financial institution is to manage financial risks, which include credit risks, liquidity risks, interest rate risks, foreign exchange risks and investment portfolio risks. Most microfinance institutions have put most of their resources into developing a methodology that reduces individual credit risks and maintaining quality portfolios. Microfinance institutions that use savings deposits as a source of loan funds must have sufficient cash to fund loans and withdrawals from savings. Those MFIs that rely on depositors and other borrowed sources of funds are also vulnerable to changes in interest rates. Financial risk management requires a sophisticated treasury function, usually centralized at the head office, which manages liquidity risk, interest rate risk, and investment portfolio risk. As MFIs face more choices in funding sources and more product differentiation among loan assets, it becomes increasingly important to manage these risks well.

### *11.1.1 Credit risk*

Credit risk, the most frequently addressed risk for MFIs, is the risk to earnings or capital due to borrowers' late and non-payment of loan obligations. Credit risk encompasses both the loss of income resulting from the MFI's inability to collect anticipated interest earnings as well as the loss of principle resulting from loan defaults. Credit risk includes both transaction risk and portfolio risk (GTZ, 2000a).

### *11.1.2 Transaction risk*

Transaction risk refers to the risk within individual loans. MFIs mitigate transaction risk through borrower screening techniques, underwriting criteria, and quality procedures for loan disbursement, monitoring, and collection.

*11.1.3 Portfolio risk*

Portfolio risk refers to the risk inherent in the composition of the overall loan portfolio. Policies on diversification (avoiding concentration in a particular sector or area), maximum loan size, types of loans, and loan structures lessen portfolio risk.

Management must continuously review the entire portfolio to assess the nature of the portfolio's delinquency, looking for geographic trends and concentrations by sector, product and branch. By monitoring the overall delinquency in the portfolio, management can assure that the MFI has adequate reserves to cover potential loan losses.

MFIs have developed very effective lending methodologies that reduce the credit risk associated with lending to micro-enterprises, including group lending, cross guarantees, stepped lending, and peer monitoring. Other key issues that affect MFIs' credit risk include portfolio diversification, issuing larger individual loans, and limiting exposure to certain sectors (e.g. agricultural or seasonal loans). Each type of lending has a different risk profile and requires unique loan structures and underwriting guidelines. Effective approaches to managing credit risk in MFIs include:

- Well-designed borrower screening, careful loan structuring, close monitoring, clear collection procedures, and active oversight by senior management. Delinquency is understood and addressed promptly to avoid its rapid spread and potential for significant loss.
- Good portfolio reporting that accurately reflects the status and monthly trends in delinquency, including a portfolio-at-risk aging schedule and separate reports by loan product.
- A routine process for comparing concentration of credit-risks with the adequacy of loan loss reserves and detecting patterns (e.g. by loan product, by branch, etc.).

The importance of a "credit culture" in minimizing problems and increasing operational efficiencies cannot be overstated. MFI senior managers need to set up systems that compel and offer incentives to loan officers to prevent, disclose, and respond to problem loans quickly, so as to limit potential credit-related losses. ASA, a microfinance organization in Bangladesh, has instituted impressive credit systems to minimize credit risk.

### *11.2 Liquidity Risk*

Liquidity risk is the possibility of negative effects on the interests of owners, customers and other stakeholders of the financial institution resulting from the inability to meet current cash obligations in a timely and cost-efficient manner. Liquidity risk usually arises from management's inability to adequately anticipate and plan for changes in funding sources and cash needs. Efficient liquidity management requires maintaining sufficient cash reserves on hand (to meet client withdrawals, disburse loans and fund unexpected cash shortages) while also investing as many funds as possible to maximize earnings (putting cash to work in loans or market investments). For guidelines on how to improve liquidity management, MFIs should refer to *Liquidity Management: A Tool Kit for Microfinance Institutions*, published by GTZ in January 2000 (GTZ, 2000b). A lender must be able to honor all cash payment commitments as they fall due and meet customer requests for new loans and savings withdrawals. These commitments can be met by drawing on cash holdings, by using current cash flows, by borrowing cash, or by converting liquid assets into cash.

Liquidity management is not a one-time activity in which the MFI determines the optimal level of cash it should hold. Liquidity management is an ongoing effort to strike a balance between having too much cash and too little cash. If the MFI holds too much cash, it may not be able to make sufficient returns to cover the costs of its operations, resulting in the need to increase interest rates above competitive levels. If the MFI holds too little cash, it could face a crisis of confidence and lose clients who no longer trust the institution to have funds available when needed. Effective liquidity management protects the MFI from cash shortages while also ensuring a sufficient return on investments. Cash management refers to the mechanics of consolidating cash at the head office and investing it at the local bank in interest bearing accounts.

Effective liquidity risk management requires a good understanding of the impact of changing market conditions and the ability to quickly liquidate assets to meet increased demand for loans or withdrawals from savings. Some principles of liquidity management that MFIs use include:

- Maintaining detailed estimates of projected cash inflows and outflows for the next few weeks or months so that net cash requirements can be identified.
- Using branch procedures to limit unexpected increases in cash needs. For example, some MFIs, such as ASA, have put limits on the amount of withdrawals that customers can make from savings in an effort to increase the MFI's ability to better manage its liquidity.
- Maintaining investment accounts that can be easily liquidated into cash, or lines of credit with local banks to meet unexpected needs.
- Anticipating the potential cash requirements of new product introductions or seasonal variations in deposits or withdrawals.

Liquidity management has a short-term focus (the section on investment portfolio risk below discusses longer-term cash management issues). Often, liquidity projections are extended up to a year with diminishing detail on the far end of the timeline.

### *11.2.1 Liquidity risk and credit risk interact*

This implies that a loan that is not repaid when due represents a credit risk and a loss of liquidity. A significant increase in delinquency (e.g. in the event of natural disaster) suddenly reduces the cash inflow from loan repayments and may increase cash outflows for new loans. This squeezes cash reserves and increases liquidity risk. Conversely, liquidity management can be especially important in MFIs where a client's propensity to repay is influenced by her future access to loans. Rumors that an MFI might not be able to extend credit immediately upon repayment because it has run out of cash could cause borrowers to default in an effort to protect against their own impending cash shortage (Campion and White, 1999).

### 11.3 Market Risk

Market risk includes interest rate risk, foreign currency risk, and investment portfolio risk.

### 11.4 Interest Rate Risk

Interest rate risk arises from the possibility of a change in the value of assets and liabilities in response to changes in market interest rates. Also known as asset and liability management risk, interest rate risk is a critical treasury function, in which financial institutions match the maturity schedules and risk profiles of their funding sources (liabilities) to the terms of the loans they are funding (assets). The savings and loan crisis in the 1980s in the United States resulted largely from the mismatching of assets and liabilities. The savings and loan institutions (S&Ls) had financed themselves primarily with short-term deposits while investing in long-term, fixed interest rate mortgages. When the cost of short-term funding rose quickly, the S&Ls were not able to restructure their asset base fast enough to avoid significant losses (Greenbaum, Stuart and Anjan Thakor, 1998).

In MFIs, the greatest interest rate risk occurs when the cost of funds goes up faster than the institution can or is willing to adjust its lending rates. The cost of funds can sometimes exceed the interest earned on loans and investments, resulting in a loss to the MFI. Interest rate changes can also affect fee income, since most fee income is associated with loan products that are interest rate sensitive. Interest rate risk management is most important to MFIs that make longer-term loans and rely on capital markets for a large percentage of their funds. In most environments, the interest rates paid to savers tend to move more slowly. MFIs operating in inflationary economies face additional asset and liability management issues.

Below are two common approaches to interest rate risk management among financial institutions.

- To reduce the mismatch between short-term variable rate liabilities (e.g. savings deposits) and long-term fixed rate loans, managers may refinance some of the short-term borrowings with long-term fixed rate borrowings. This might include offering one and two-year term deposits as a product and borrowing five to ten-year funds from other sources. Such a step reduces interest rate risk and liquidity risk, even if the MFI pays a slightly higher rate on those funding sources.

- To boost profitability, MFIs may purposely "mismatch" assets and liabilities in anticipation of changes in interest rates. If the asset liability managers think interest rates will fall in the near future, they may decide to make more long-term loans at existing fixed rates, and shorten the term of the MFI's liabilities.

### *11.4.1 Managing interest rate risk*

Interest rate risk is the risk of financial loss from changes in market interest rates. The greatest interest rate risk occurs when the cost of funds goes up faster than the financial institution can or is willing to adjust its lending rates.

By lending long and borrowing short, the MFI can take advantage of the cheaper funding in the future, while locking in the higher interest rates on the asset side. In this case, the MFI has increased the interest rate risk in the hope of improving the profitability of the bank. Many banks maintain a financial model that reflects the investment portfolio and the loan portfolio so they can test the institution's sensitivity to an increase or decrease in interest rates. MFIs could begin using similar tests as they try to maximize profitability by taking "reasonable" risks in asset and liability management. An MFI's sensitivity to changes in interest rates (increases or decreases) affects short- and long-term profitability.

Most financial institutions and some regulated MFIs have a separate fund management or treasury department whose main function is to manage risks associated with interest rate changes. Asset and liability management functions are usually centralized in the head office to cost-effectively manage borrowed funds and the investment portfolio (idle funds not lent). Branch offices may have some discretion over how much is funded from deposits and how much comes from loans. A branch manager may choose to borrow from headquarters at a certain interest rate, or increase deposits if those have a lower cost of funds.

*11.4.2 Interest rate risk interacting with liquidity rate risk*

Liquidity and interest rate risk occur simultaneously when the maturities of assets and liabilities are mismatched. This can magnify the impact on the cash flow and profitability for the MFI. Managing financial assets and liabilities is thus an extremely important part of liquidity management, as well as interest rate risk management.

## 11.5 Foreign Exchange Risk

Foreign exchange risk is the potential for loss of earnings or capital resulting from fluctuations in currency values. Microfinance institutions most often experience foreign exchange risk when they borrow or mobilize savings in one currency and lend in another. For example, MFIs that offer dollar savings accounts and lend in the local currency risk financial loss if the value of the local currency weakens against the dollar. Alternatively, if the local currency strengthens against the dollar, the MFI experiences a financial gain.

Principles in practice by MFIs to reduce foreign exchange risk include:

- Due to the potential severity of the downside risk, an MFI should avoid funding the loan portfolio with foreign currency unless it can match its foreign liabilities with foreign assets of equivalent duration and maturity. In Ghana, the appreciation of the dollar actually caused many MFIs that were dependent on dollar denominated loans to begin mobilizing local savings in 1999 to reduce the currency mismatch of assets and liabilities.
- Some MFIs have used interest rates swaps or futures contracts to "lock-in" a certain exchange rate, which protects the MFI from uncertainty.

## 11.6 Investment Portfolio Risk

For some MFIs, such as Mibanco in Peru, a significant percentage of the institution's assets are in cash and investments rather than in loans. The investment portfolio represents the source of funds for reserves, for operating expenses, for future loans or for other productive investments. Investment portfolio risk refers mainly to longer-term investment decisions rather than short-term liquidity or cash management decisions. The investment portfolio must balance credit risks (for investments), income goals and timing to meet medium- to long-term liquidity needs. An aggressive approach to portfolio management maximizes investment income by investing in higher risk securities. A more conservative approach emphasizes safer investments and lower returns.

Principles used to minimize investment portfolio risks by MFIs include:

- To reduce investment portfolio risk, treasury managers stagger investment maturities to ensure that the MFI has the long-term funds needed for growth and expansion. In addition, they consider the credit, inflation, and currency risks that might threaten the value of the principal investment. Short-term investments, for example, carry less risk of losing value due to inflation.
- Most financial institutions have policies establishing parameters for acceptable investments within the investment portfolio, and they range from very conservative to more aggressive for a portion of the investment portfolio. These policies set limits on the range of permitted investments as well as on the degree of acceptable concentration for each type of investment.

### *11.7 Operational Risks*

Operational risk arises from human or computer error within daily product delivery and services. It transcends all divisions and products of a financial institution. This risk includes the potential that inadequate technology and information systems, operational problems, insufficient human resources, or breaches of integrity (i.e. fraud) will result in unexpected losses. This risk is a function of internal controls, information systems, employee integrity, and operating processes. For simplicity, this section focuses on just two types of operational risk: transaction risk and fraud risk.

### *11.7.1 Transaction risk*

Transaction risk exists in all products and services. It is a risk that arises on a daily basis in the MFI as transactions are processed. Transaction risk is particularly high for MFIs that handle a high volume of small transactions daily. When traditional banks make loans, the staff person responsible is usually a highly trained professional and there is a very high level of cross-checking. Since MFIs make many small, short-term loans, this same degree of cross-checking is not cost-effective, so there are more opportunities for error and fraud. The loan portfolio usually accounts for the bulk of the MFI's assets and is thus the main source of operational risk. As more MFIs offer additional financial products, including savings and insurance, the operational risks multiply and should be carefully analyzed as MFIs expand those activities. Table 17 below presents common operational risks in the management of a microfinance loan portfolio.

**Table 17:** Operational Risks in Loan Portfolio Management

| Common Operational Risks in MFIs: |
|---|
| The MIS does not correctly reflect loan tracking, e.g. information disbursed, payments received, current status of outstanding balances. |
| Lack of effectiveness and insecurity of the portfolio management system, e.g. external environment Is not safe, software does not have internal safety features (i.e. no backups), inaccurate MIS and untimely reports. |
| Inconsistencies between the loan management system data and the accounting system data. |
| Misrepresentation of loan payoffs, e.g. through refinancing, payoffs with inadequate collateral or post dated cheques. |
| Rescheduling disguises loan quality problems, e.g. rescheduled loans treated as on-time. |
| Inconsistent implementation of the loan administration. |
| Lack of portfolio related fraud controls, e.g. no client visits to verify loan balances. |
| Loan tracking information is not adequate, e.g. no aging of portfolio outstanding, inadequate credit histories. |

### *11.8 Common Operational Risks in MFIs*

- The MIS does not correctly reflect loan tracking, e.g. information disbursed, payments received, current status of outstanding balances
- Lack of effectiveness and insecurity of the portfolio management system, e.g. external environment is not safe, software does not have internal safety features (i.e. no backups), inaccurate MIS and untimely reports.
- Inconsistencies between the loan management system data and the accounting system data. Misrepresentation of loan payoffs, e.g. through refinancing, payoffs with inadequate collateral or post dated cheques. Rescheduling disguises loan quality problems, e.g. rescheduled loans treated as on-time.

Inconsistent implementation of the loan administration can also lead to the following risks:

Lack of portfolio related fraud controls, e.g. no client visits to verify loan balances Loan tracking information is not adequate, e.g. no aging of portfolio outstanding, inadequate credit histories. For MFIs, key steps to reduce transaction risk include:

- Simple, standardized and consistent procedures for cash transactions throughout the MFIs.
- Effective ex-ante internal controls that are incorporated into daily procedures to reduce the chance of human error and fraud at the branch level (e.g. require dual signatures, separate lines of reporting for cash and programme transactions).
- Strong ex-post internal controls (i.e. internal audit) to test and verify the accuracy of information and adherence to policies and procedures. These internal controls help ensure that management reporting information is providing the most accurate information, and reduce the occurrence of problems. The GTZ/Micro-Finance Network's technical guide, Improving Internal Control, describes in detail the process for developing an internal control system linked to risk management.

- Using computer systems and minimizing the number of times data has to be manually entered reduces the chance and frequency of human error.

### 11.9 Liability Structure of Microfinance Loans to Minimize Risks

There are three basic models of liability employed by MFIs. Each poses differences in potential impacts (e.g. group-liability programmes may generate positive or negative impacts on risk-sharing and social capital) as well as targeting (traditionally, individual-lending programmes reach a wealthier clientele).

1. *Solidarity Groups*: The classic microfinance model, often referred to as the "Grameen model" after the pioneering Grameen Bank in Bangladesh, involves 5-person solidarity groups, in which each group member guarantees the other members' repayment. If any of the group members fail to repay their loans the other group members must repay for them or they face losing access to future credit.
2. *Village Banking*: Village banking expands the solidarity group concept to a larger group of 15-30 women or men who are responsible for managing the loan provided by the MFI (the "external account"), as well as making and collecting loans to and from each other (the "internal account"). In India, Self-Help Groups (SHGs) operate according to a similar format.
3. *Individual Lending*: Individual lending is simply the provision of microfinance services to individuals instead of groups. Individual lending can be hard to distinguish from traditional banking since they have similar forms. This is especially true where MFIs require collateral (or collateral substitutes such as household items with low market value but high personal value to the borrower) from borrowers, as collateral free lending has traditionally been one of the hallmarks of microfinance.

### 11.10 "Other" Microfinance Services

Many microfinance programmes offer services beyond credit. The most basic such service is savings (credit unions and cooperatives, for instance, rely heavily on savings), although only a few programmes focus solely on savings (on the premise that what the poor need most is a safe place to store their money). Some MFIs require mandatory savings each week from each borrower as well as each group, although, depending on the individual MFIs' policies of collection of mandatory savings in case of default, this is often more appropriately called "cash collateral", rather than "savings". Some of these programmes also collect voluntary savings, allowing clients to deposit as much as they like each week. Recently MFIs have begun to offer (either independently or bundled with credit) a wide variety of services, including insurance (life insurance and/ or health insurance), business development skills training, and remittances. A popular form of training is credit with education, developed by Freedom from Hunger, which includes modules on both business and health training. While MFIs offering credit with education have demonstrated that the modules can be provided at low cost, some MFIs retain their focus on credit and savings, arguing that the poor already have all the business skills they need—what they need most is the cheapest possible source of credit.

## 11.11 Categorization of Savings Options

Regulatory requirements mandate that NBFCs have to depend largely on vending of third party products so as to provide savings options to their clients. The other option is to provide quasi-savings products like gold acquisition loans, which could be delivered by the NBFC itself as its own proprietary product. In both these cases, the opportunity for the organization to mobilize funds would be non-existent and the financial incentive to the organization would be in terms of revenue from fee income or interest spread.

### *11.11.1 Saving options*

1. *Bank Led Savings Options*

Business Correspondent (BC) model has been used by commercial banks to provide savings as well as term deposits to end-clients where branch infrastructure is limited or absent. The RBI has been encouraging the model which depends on third party agents to provide the service. There have been many initiatives involving the electronic and mobile banking solutions within the BC model so as to enable efficient delivery of customer solutions. The model typically focused on providing no-frills accounts; but lately some banks have also started delivering normal savings accounts, recurring deposits and term deposits also using the BC channel.

2. *Proprietary Options*

The most prominent proprietary savings option seen in India has been the Gold Acquisition Loan which is a quasi-savings instrument working on the principle of reverse savings. Some prominent MFIs as well as NBFCs primarily working in South India have been offering gold acquisition loans to their clients so as to enable a build-up of savings balances in the form of gold.

3. *Mutual Fund Products Option*

Money market mutual funds are in general considered to be relatively stable, highly liquid instruments since they focus on investing in debt (largely government debt of short duration like T Bills) and since they have historically shown very little day-to-day fluctuation in their Net Asset Values (NAV). Some organizations have adapted money market instruments to provide a savings bank account proxy for their clients.

4. *Pension Products Option*

Pension products which provide a regular income post retirement have been in vogue for a long time in India. But most of the pension schemes have been directed at the organized sector and generally directed at middle-higher income groups. Recently, there have been several voluntary pension products oriented at the bottom-of-the-pyramid customers and delivered through channel partners including MFIs. Government of India's New Pension Scheme (NPS) which also has a voluntary nature as well as a provision for periodical withdrawals is an interesting option, which can combine the attributes of a voluntary savings product into a pension product. The government is also considering the introduction of an option for unorganized workers under the NPS.

5. *Insurance Products Option*

Insurance products combining the features of life insurance as well as term savings are another option available to MFIs for exploration. ULIPs are one option available for further exploration. Another route to take would be to offer endowment policies in partnership with life insurance companies.

## REFERENCES

Arsyad, Lincolin (2005), An Assessment of Microfinance Institution Performance: The Importance of Institutional Environment, *Gadjah Mada International Journal of Business*, September-December 2005, Vol. 7, No. 3, pp. 391-427.

Barry, Nancy, Armacost, Nicola and Kawas Celina (1996), Putting Poor People's Economics at the Center of Urban Strategies, Women's World Banking, New York.

Bass, J. (2000), Innovations in Microfinance?, Technical note No. 7, Bamako: Mali.

CGAP (1996), Private Sector Involvement Working Group Discussion Paper for the September 1996 Meeting 13.

CGAP (1999), External Audits of Microfinance Institutions: A Handbook.Technical Tools Series, no. 3. Washington, D.C.: CGAP, March. http://www.cgap.org/html/p_technical_guides.html

CGAP (2001), Micro Rating and Assessment Fund, www.cgap.org

Chaves, R.A., and C. Gonzales-Vega (1996), The Design of Successful Rural Financial Intermediaries: Evidence from Indonesia, *World Development*, Vol. 24, No. 1, pp. 65-78.

Chen, Greg, Stephen Rasmussen and Xavier Reille (2010), Growth and vulnerabilities in microfinance, CGAP Focus Note No. 61.

Chriseten, R. Peck Rhyne, Elisabeth and Vogel, Robert C. (1994), Maximizing the Outreach of Microenterprise Finance: The Emerging Lessons of Successful Programmes, September IMCC, Arlington, Virginia, USA.

Counts, A. (2008), *Small Loans, Big Dreams, How Nobel Prize Winner Muhammad Yunus and Microfinnance are Changing the World?* (2008), Hoboken (NJ): Wiley.

Dayson, Karl and Quach, Hao (2006), Toward a Performance Assessment of Microfinance Institutions in Europe, Finance and the Common Good, No. 25, Autumn 2006.

Doran, A. and J. Levitsky (1997), Credit Guarantee Schemes for Small Business Lending—A Global Perspective, London, 1997.

Financial Sector Assessment: A Handbook (2011), The World Bank, IMF: http://www-wds.worldbank.org/external/default/WDSContentServer/WDSP/IB/2005/10/12/000012009_20051012134613/Rendered/PDF/337970rev0Fina10Assessment01PUBLIC1.pdf

Ghate, P. (2007), Microfinance in India: A State of the Sector Report, 2006, Microfinance India Publications, New Delhi.

Ghate, P. (2008), Microfinance in India: A State of the Sector Report, 2007, Microfinance India Publications, New Delhi.

Goldberg, Nathanael (2005), Measuring the Impact of Microfinance: Taking Stock of What We Know, Grameen Foundation, December 2005.

Ghate, P. et al. (1992), *Informal Finance: Some Findings from Asia*, Oxford University Press, Hong Kong.

Gonzalez, A. (2010), Is Microfinance Growing Too Fast? Washington, DC: Microfinance Information Exchange (MIX).

Grameen Bank (2009), 10 Indicators. www.grameen-info.org/index.php?option =com content&task=view&id=23&Itemid=126, retrieved on July 14, 2009.

Greenbaum, Stuart I. and Anjan Thakor (1998), *Contemporary Financial Intermediation*, Harcourt Brace College Publishers, April 1998, p. 169.

GTZ (2000a), *A Risk Management Framework for Microfinance Institutions*, published by GTZ, July 2000.

GTZ (2000b), *Liquidity Management: A Tool Kit for Microfinance Institutions*, published by GTZ, January 2000.

Hannig, A. and S. Wisniwski (eds) (1999), Challenges of Micro-savings Mobilization—Concepts and Views from the Field, Eschborn: Deutsche Gesellschaft fur Technische Zasummenarbeit (GTZ) GmbH.

Hempel, G.H. and D.G. Simonson (1999), Bank Management-Text and Cases 5th edition, New York: John Wiley & Sons.

Khandker, Shahidur R. (1998), Fighting Poverty with Microcredit: Experience in Bangladesh, Oxford, University: New York, NY, 1998.

Kim Kyung-Hwan (1995), Access to Credit, Term of Housing Finance and Affordability of Housing, *Housing Finance International*, 9(4), June 22-27.

Ledgerwood, J. (1999), *Microfinance Handbook: An Institutional and Financial Perspective*, Washington, DC: World Bank.

Levitsky, J. (1993), Credit Guarantee Funds and Mutual Guarantee Systems, *Small Enterprise Development*, Volume 4, Number 2, 1993.

McIntosh, Craig, Alain de Janvry and Elisabeth Sadoulet (2005), How rising competition among microfinance institutions affects incumbent lenders, *Economic Journal*, October, Vol. 115: 987-1004.

McIntosh, Craig and Bruce Wydick (2005), Competition and microfinance, *Journal of Development Economics*, Vol. 78: 271-98.

Masanjala, W. H. (2002), Can the Grameen Bank be Replicated in Africa? Evidence from Malawi, *Canadian Journal of Development Studies*, 23(1): 87-103.

MIX/CGAP (2009), Sub-Sahara African Microfinance Analysis and Benchmarking Report, CGAP, Washington, April 2010.

MIX or Microfinance Information Exchange (2012), Asia Regional Snapshot: Accessed from: http://www.themix.org/publications/mix-microfinance-world/2013/01/2012-eastern-europe-and-central-asia-regional-snapshot

Morduch, J. (1998), 'Does Microfinance Really Help the Poor? New Evidence on Flagship Programs in Bangladesh', presented at Stanford, UC-Berkeley, University of Washington, RAND, University of Toronto, Princeton, and Yale.

Morduch, J. (1999), The Microfinance Promise. *Journal of Economic Literature*, 37 (4): 1569-1614.

Morduch, J. (2000). The microfinance Schism, *World Development*, 28(4): 617-29.

NABARD (2007), Report on Status of Microfinance in India 2006-07 (http://www.nabard.org/).

NABARD (2008), Report on Status of Microfinance in India 2007-08 (http://www.nabard.org/).

Otero, M. and Rhyne, E. (1994), The New World of Micro-enterprise Finance—Building Healthy Financial Institutions for the Poor, Kumarian Press, West Harford, Connecticut, USA.

Puhazhendhi, V. (2012), Microfinance India State of the Sector Report 2012, SAGE.

Reserve Bank of India (2008), Report on Trend and Progress of Banking in India 2007-08, Reserve Bank of India Publications, Mumbai, India.

Robinson, M.S. (2001), The Microfinance Revolution: Sustainable Finance for the Poor, Washington, D.C.: The World Bank.

Satish, P. (2005), Mainstreaming of Indian Microfinance, *Economic and Political Weekly*, Vol. 40, No. 17, p. 1733.

Sa-Dhan (2008), Bharat Microfinance Report, December, 2008 (http://www.sa-dhan.net).

Schubert, R. (2007), Kapitel I: Grundlagen, Scriptum for the lecture "Entwick-lungslander in der Weltwirtschaft", autumn term, 2007 (Available at the Chair of Economics, Swiss Federal Institute of Technology, Weinbergstrasse 35, CH (8092 Zurich).

Sen, Mitali (2008), Assessing Social Performance of Microfinance Institutions in India. *The ICFAI Journal of Applied Finance*, Vol. 14, No. 86, pp. 77-86.

Silva, A. (1998), Taking Equity in Microfinance—The PROFUND Experience?; Second Annual Seminar on New Development Finance at the Goethe University of Frankfurt, Germany.

Srinivasan, R. and Sriram, M.S. (2006), Microfinance in India: Discussion, *IIMB Management Review*, pp. 66-86.

Srinivasan, N. (2009), Microfinance India State of the Sector Report 2008, Sage Publications, New Delhi.

Tankha, A. (2002), Self-help Groups as Financial Intermediaries in India: Cost of Promotion, Sustainability and Impact, A Study by Sa-Dhan, New Delhi, pp. 70-71. Available at: http://www.sa-dhan.net/Adls/Microfinance/PerspectiveMicrofinance/Self-help Groups as Financial. pdf (Accessed on 30.06.2008).

The Norwegian Nobel Committee (2006), Nobel Peace Prize 2006; Nobel peaceprize.org/enGB/laureates/laureates-2006, retrieved on July 4, 2009.

Viada, Luis and Scott Gaul (2011), The tipping point: Over indebtedness and investment in microfinance, *Microbanking Bulletin*.

Wisniwski, S. (1999), Microsavings Compared to Other Sources of Funds in Hannig, A. and S. Wisniwski (eds) (1999), Challenges of Microsavings Mobilization—Concepts and Views from the Field, Eschborn: Deutsche Gesellschaft fur Technische Zasummenarbeit (GTZ) GmbH.

Women's World Banking (1994), United Nations Expert-Group on Women and Finance, New York.

Women's World Banking (1995), The Missing Links: Financial Systems that Work for the Majority, Women's World Banking, New York.

World Bank (2000), World Development Report: 2000/2001, Washington DC. The World Bank, www.mixmarket.org

Yaron, Y. (1992), Successful Rural Finance Institutions, World Bank Discussion Papers, Washington, D.C.: The World Bank.

Yaron, Y. (1994), What Makes Rural Finance Institutions Successful?, *The World Bank Research Observer*, Vol. 9, No. 1, pp. 49-70.

Yaron, Y., Mc. D. Benjamin, and G. Piprek (1997), Rural Finance: Issues, Design, and Best Practice, Environmentally and Socially Sustainable Development Studies and Monograph Series 14, Washington, D.C.: The World Bank.

Yaron, Y., Mc D. Benjamin, and S. Charitonenko (1998), Promoting Efficient Rural Financial Intermediation, *The World Bank Research Observer*, Vol. 13, No. 2, pp. 147-70.

Yunus, M. (2003), Banker to the Poor: Micro-Lending and the Battle against World Poverty. London: Aurum Press Limited.

Yunus, Muhammad (2004), Grameen Bank, www.grameen-info.org (accessed 5/9/04).

Yunus, M. (2007), Creating a World without Poverty, Social Business and the Future of Capitalism.

Yunus, M. (2008). A poverty-free world: When? How? Romanes Lecture, Sheldonian Theatre Oxford.

Zeller, Manfred and Meyers, Richard (2003), The Triangle of Microfinance: Financial Sustainability, Outreach and impact, John Hopkins University Press, Baltimore, USA.

# 4

# Impact of Microfinance on Socio-economic Development: Scanning the Global Scene

Micrfinance industry is one of the fastest growing set of financial driven initiatives aimed at alleviating poverty, aid economic growth and support future growth through financial inclusion. A growing number of microfinance institutions are attempting to build the human capital entrepreneurs in order to improve the livelihood of their clients and help further their mission of poverty reduction. Increased household income, access to health care and education and better living conditions are just a few ways in which microfinance and complimentary services is impacting the poor and underserved population around the world (http://www.global partnership.org).

Over the past 30 years, microfinance (MF) has grown to a $30 billion industry involving over 3,000 organizations. Half of these microfinance institutions, however, have nothing more than anecdotal stories about the impact of MF on poverty. The connection between MF and poverty eradication is far from resolved. Measuring mission impact is a crucial issue facing every Microfinance Institution (MFI). MFIs serve the dual goals of financial return and social mission achievement. The techniques for measuring financial return are well understood. A controversy persists, however, about what are the true impacts of microfinance on poverty—the level of social mission achievement. Over the past decade, several have declared the debate settled (Goldberg, 2005; Khandker, 2005; Mahjabeen,

2008; Quach et al. 2005), while others claim that the issue has not been addressed with adequate rigour (Dichter, 2007; Jamal, 2008; Karnani, 2007; Khan, 2008; Misra, 2006; Park and Ren, 2001). As of today, only 55 percent of MFIs use a formal quantitative measurement tool to assess the impact of their work to reduce poverty (Daley-Harris, 2009). Two reasons for the persistence of this controversy are (1) lack of rigorous theorizing as to what causes changes in poverty levels and how instrumental MF is in affecting those causes (Armendariz, de Aghion, and Morduch, 2007), and (2) inadequate measurement of the effects of MF on changes in poverty levels.

Millenium Development Goals are centred on the reduction of extreme poverty, promoting gender equality and empower women and the development and implementation of strategies for decent and productive work for the youth. It is hoped that microfinance institutions will assist in the achievement of these goals as they are a viable tool used in the eradication of poverty thus improving social and economic welfare of the people. The concept has become a top agenda item at the international fora and thus the United Nations has enlisted microfinance as one of the surest ways of meeting its millennium development goals if it is carefully implemented through sustainable institutions (Hulme and Moseley, 1996, 1998; Johnson and Rogalyn, 1999). It can be argued that the services provided by MFIs should promote livelihood by creating wealth or assets, increasing food security, reducing risk and variance in income and realize a reduction in rural to urban migration (Fisher et al. 2002).

In light of the above background this chapter seeks to establish as to what extent and the mode in which the increase in the number of microfinance institutions as well as the various microfinance development programmes/initiatives have impacted the socio-economic lives of people; especially in relation to creation of self-employment opportunities, entrepreneurship development, poverty alleviation and improving income levels, etc. as a result of enhanced level of microfinance services provided by microfinance and other institutions/organizations at large globally. Some illustrative cases of success stories of microfinance programmes in different parts of the world, especially in Asia, Africa, Latin America are highlighted with to view to share some global experiences.

## 1. Microfinance: A Gateway for an Integrated Approach to Development

Measuring mission impact is a crucial issue facing every Microfinance Institution (MFI). MFIs serve the dual goals of financial return and social mission achievement. The techniques for measuring financial return are well understood. A controversy persists, however, about what are the true impacts of microfinance on poverty—the level of social mission achievement. Over the past several years, microfinance has been under increased scrutiny as the global development community has gradually realized that microfinance is not the once acclaimed anti-poverty silver bullet. Three of the most significant criticisms of microfinance that the domains of popular news media, practitioners, and academia have put forward are the following: some MFIs are profiting greatly from lending to impoverished clients, the unjust profiting of MFIs can lead borrowers to stop repaying their loans, and it is unclear whether microfinance truly succeeds in lifting people out of poverty. The titles of these recent news articles encapsulate these major microfinance problems that have been identified: Banks making big profits from tiny loans (MacFarquhar, 2010). India microcredit sector faces collapse from defaults (Bajaj and Polgreen, 2010), and Microcredit not the silver bullet for poverty (Morris Madeline, 2011). There is still little to no consensus among academics regarding the impact of microfinance, although there are a slowly growing number of studies that attempt to scientifically estimate the effects on clients' lives. Dean Karlan, a Yale professor of Economics and one of the most prominent microfinance researchers, summarizes microfinance's impacts: The lesson is simply that it didn't save the world. It is not the single transformative tool that proponents have been selling it as, but there are positive benefits.

In 2005, the MIT Poverty Action Lab carried out the first study to conduct a randomized evaluation of the impact of introducing microcredit in a new market (Banerjee et al. 2010). The researchers selected MFI branches to open in half of the slums in one Indian region, while the other half did not receive the intervention. The product that was offered was the standard group banking loan (but not integrated with social services) in which groups comprised of ten women each received loans and were jointly responsible for the loans of their group at large. The results revealed that the introduction of microcredit has both varied and noteworthy effects on the creation and expansion of businesses, and on the character of household expenditures. While the study showed that microcredit can enable households to borrow money and invest in businesses, it showed no impact on the client's social situation in terms of characteristics such as health, education, or women's decision-making in the short-term (i.e. after fifteen to eighteen months served by an MFI).

A small body of literature has pursued the question of whether microfinance has the potential to serve as an effective strategy to achieve the Millennium Development Goals (MDGs). In a 2003 paper, researchers from the Consultative Group to Assist the Poor (CGAP) argued that microfinance plays an important role in meeting the MDGs, principally by: eradicating poverty, promoting children's education, improving health outcomes for women and children, and empowering women in society. The authors argued that determinants of an individual's standard of living such as employment, education, and healthcare actually depend on a population's access to financial services; these determinants can only be improved when households have increased control over financial resources. While this study revealed that the delivery of financial services can be relied upon as a tool to fight poverty while at the same time remaining sustainable and scalable for organizations, evidence from my study also suggests that it is possible for the MFIs to make even more progress towards the MDGs by providing their clients with non-financial services in addition to financial services.

Since first coming to prominence in the 1970s microfinance has come to play a very important role in the field of development, as illustrated by the launch of the Microcredit Summit in 1997. The Summit aims to reach 175 million of the world's poorest families, especially the women of those families, with credit for the self-employed and other financial and business services, by the end of 2015 (Microcredit Summit, 2005). More recently, 2005 was the UN's International Year of Microcredit. Microfinance has a very important role to play in development according to its proponents. According to UNCDF (2004) microfinance plays three key roles in the development process such as:

- helps poor households meet basic needs and protects against risks,
- is associated with improvements in household economic welfare,
- helps to empower women by supporting women's economic participation and so promotes gender equity.

Otero (1999) states that microfinance creates access to productive capital for the poor, which together with human capital, addressed through education and training, and social capital, achieved through local organization building, enables people to move out of poverty. By providing material capital to a poor person, their sense of dignity is strengthened and this can help to empower the person to participate in the economy and society (Otero, 1999). Otero also states that microfinance has a role at an institutional level in that it seeks to create institutions that deliver financial services to the poor, who are continuously ignored by the formal banking sector. By addressing this gap in the market in a financially sustainable manner, an MFI can become part of the formal financial system of a country (Otero, 1999). More recently, commentators such as Littleield, Murduch and Hashemi (2003), Simanowitz and Brody (2004) and the IMF (2005) have commented on the critical role of microfinance in achieving the MDGs. Simanowitz and Brody (2004) state, "Microfinance is a key strategy in reaching the MDGs." Littlefield, Murduch and Hashemi (2003) state that microfinance can have a strong impact on the achievements of the MDGs as it can deliver social benefits on an ongoing, permanent basis and on a large scale. Referring to various case studies, they show how microfinance has played a role in eradicating poverty, promoting education, improving health and empowering women.

Wright (2000) states that much of the skepticism of MFIs stems from the argument that microfinance projects fail to reach the poorest, generally have a limited effect on income, can drive women into greater dependence on their husbands and they fail to provide additional services desperately needed by the poor. There is also a danger that microfinance may siphon funds from other projects that might help the poor more (Navajas et al. 2000). Another criticism of microfinance is that very few MFIs are financially sustainable. According to the IMF (2005), the MFIs that have become self-sustainable tend to be larger and more efficient, and so tend not to target the very poor, as targeting the less poor leads to increases in loan size and improved efficiency indicators, whereas MFIs focusing on the poorest tend to remain dependent on donor funds (IMF, 2005). This is where a compromise exists between the social mission and commercial mission of an MFI.

**2. Macroeconomic Dimension of Microfinance**

Over the past several decades, microfinance—i.e. credit targeted toward small-scale entrepreneurial activities of the poor who may otherwise lack access to financing—has become a pillar of economic development policies. In recent years, there has been a concerted effort to expand such programmes with the goal of alleviating poverty and promoting development. Between 1997 and 2006, access to microfinance grew by up to 29 percent a year, reaching a scale at which macroeconomic considerations become relevant. The Microcredit Summit Campaign as of 2010 reports 3,552 institutions serving 155 million borrowers, which including borrowers and their households affect 533 million people, roughly the size of Latin America. For various countries, microfinance loans represent a significant fraction of their GDP. Despite the growth and prevalence of microfinance and its importance in academic and policy circles, quantitative analyses of these programmes are almost exclusively limited to micro evaluations. The macroeconomic effects of economy-wide microfinance have been largely unexplored.

In partial equilibrium (PE), microfinance induces a high rate of entry among marginally productive entrepreneurs, increasing the capital/labour demand and output, but lowering the aggregate total factor productivity (TFP). In GE, however, the increase in wage that results from marginal entrepreneurs selecting out of the labour supply—and demanding labor instead—has strikingly different impacts on output, capital, and TFP. In redistributing income away from individuals with high saving rates (high-ability entrepreneurs) to those with low saving rates (marginal entrepreneurs and workers), microfinance leads to lower aggregate saving and capital accumulation. Higher wages and interest rates also lead low-productivity entrepreneurs to exit, and TFP actually increases with microfinance in contrast to the PE result. In net, the lower capital accumulation and higher TFP lead to positive overall impacts on consumption and output, but the magnitudes are substantially smaller than in PE. More importantly, the GE results affirm that microfinance is a pro-poor redistributive policy, benefiting the poor—marginal entrepreneurs directly and workers indirectly through higher wages—and potentially hurting the most able and rich entrepreneurs through the higher factor prices.

### 2.1 Microcredit Development Programmes and their Impacts

Microfinance programmes and other credit programmes targeted toward small-scale entrepreneurs are prevalent and still growing fast. The Microcredit Summit Campaign reports 3,552 institutions with loans to 155 million clients throughout the world as of 2010. For comparison, the numbers in 1997 were 618 institutions and 13 million clients. The six-fold increase in the number of institutions and the twelve-fold increase in the number of borrowers over this period certainly overstate the actual growth because of an increase in survey participation, but the growth is still real and dramatic. For example, a single programme, the National Bank for Agriculture and Rural Development (NABARD) in India grew from 146,000 to 49 million clients over this period. By the same token of incomplete survey participation and coverage, these numbers certainly understate the actual number of institutions and borrowers. Micro-loans are, almost by definition, small, and typically relatively short-term (i.e. one year or shorter), and have high repayment rates. A broad vision of the structure of micro-credit can be gleaned from the Microfinance Information Exchange (MIX) dataset, which provides comparable data over 1,127 microfinance institutions (MFIs) in 102 countries, totalling 65 billion dollars in outstanding loans and 90 million borrowers in 2009. The average loan balance per borrower is 655 dollars in 2009, but because loans are typically in poor countries, they are equivalent on average to one-fifth of per capita gross national income. Moreover, since microfinance is often targeted toward the poorer segments of the economy, the average loan amounts to a substantially larger fraction of the income of actual borrowers. An important achievement of microfinance is its success in providing uncollateralized loans with relatively low default rates. In 2009, only 5 percent of loans were more than 90 days delinquent.

**Table 1:** Microfinance Facts from the MIX Data

| Country | Fraction of Borrowers | MF Loans to GDP | Average Loan Size | Per Capita Income | Total Credit to GDP |
|---|---|---|---|---|---|
| Bangladesh | 0.13 | 0.028 | 112 | 547 | 0.37 |
| Mongolia | 0.13 | 0.129 | 1,393 | 1,410 | 0.62 |
| Peru | 0.11 | 0.041 | 1,590 | 4,658 | 0.21 |
| Bolivia | 0.09 | 0.107 | 1,926 | 1,776 | 0.31 |
| Vietnam | 0.09 | 0.044 | 510 | 1,024 | 1.06 |
| Kenya | 0.04 | 0.036 | 744 | 803 | 0.20 |
| India | 0.02 | 0.003 | 146 | 1,154 | 0.53 |
| Mean<br>Std. Dev. | 0.02<br>0.03 | 0.004<br>0.020 | 655<br>3,192 | 3,192<br>3,071 | 0.50<br>0.30 |

*Source*: The MIX Database.

Table 1 reports on various compiled statistics on micro-credit for the top five countries in terms of the number of borrowers as a fraction of the population (first column), as well as Kenya, which has the most penetration in Africa, and India, which has the largest absolute number of microfinance clients. This number overstates historical default rates, as it partly reflects the impact of the global recession. For instance, the figure for 2008 is 3 percent. There is also significant heterogeneity in delinquency rates across countries. In the MIX data, 10 percent of the countries report less than 1 percent of loans as delinquent, while slightly over 10 percent of the countries report more than 10 percent of loans in this category, with the Central African Republic showing the highest delinquency rate at 24 percent significant levels, with up to 13 percent of the population being active borrowers, and the value of total outstanding microfinance loans can be as large as 13 percent of GDP (second column). In Table 1 we also see that the expansion of microfinance is particularly important among the poorest countries (fourth column), where credit markets are very underdeveloped, as measured by the ratio of total credit to GDP (last column). Non-governmental organizations (NGOs) and private for-profit institutions play a large role in global microfinance. In the MIX data, NGOs constitute 37 percent of the institutions and reach 30 percent of the borrowers. Private banks make up only 7 percent of the institutions, but, because they are larger, they account for 27 percent of the borrowers and 63 percent of the total value of loans in the data. Government initiatives in microfinance and other credit programmes targeted toward small-scale entrepreneurs are also important, and many of these are not included in the MIX data. With the help of this database public programmes on microfinance services in India and Thailand have also been reviewed. There have been recent micro-evaluations in these two countries, one evaluating a public intervention (Thailand) and the other private (India).

In India, the banking and credit sector is dominated by state-owned banks. NABARD is the government's rural development bank, which operates through state co-operative banks, state agricultural and rural development banks, regional rural banks, and even commercial banks. A major programme of NABARD is the promotion of small-scale Self-Help Groups (SHGs) for saving and internal lending. In 2009, 4.2 million credit-linked SHGs had roughly 5.1 billion dollars in outstanding loans, of which 2.7 billion was new loans. We calculate an average loan size of 1,200 dollars, or roughly 104 percent of the Indian per capita income. In addition, another 80 million dollars went to microfinance institutions. These loans were then distributed to members of the SHGs. Once we incorporate NABARD's numbers into the Indian data in Table 1, the number of borrowers as a fraction of the population in India increases to 6 percent, and the value of outstanding loans is close to 1 percent of GDP. In addition, Banerjee and Duflo (2008) describe regulations governing all (private and public) banks that stipulate that 40 percent of credit must go toward priority sectors—agriculture, agricultural processing, transportation, and small-scale industries. Large firms (plants and machinery in excess of 10 million rupees in 2000) were excluded from the priority sector. They show that these regulations are indeed binding and even mainstream banks target small borrowers.

Thailand is another country that has had a large, government-sponsored expansion of credit to village banks for microfinance. In 2001, the Thai Million Baht Village Fund programme was inaugurated, which offered one million baht (about 25,000 dollars at the time) to each of the nearly 80,000 villages in Thailand, as a seed grant for starting a village lending and saving fund. The 1.5 billion dollars was tantamount to about 1.5 percent of the Thai GDP at the time. Loans were typically made without collateral, up to 1,250 dollars, but most loans were annual loans of about 500 dollars, or 40 percent of the per capita income at the time. Kaboski and Townsend (2007) show that borrowing limits varied by village size, and they estimate that the programme allowed households to borrow up to 91 percent of annual household income in the smallest villages. The experience of the funds also varied, but typically showed high repayment rates (97 percent) over several years. These funds were evaluated, and successful funds were offered to leverage their capital through loans of up to an additional one million baht from the Government Savings Bank and the Bank of Agriculture and Agricultural Cooperatives, becoming true village banks. In addition, the Bank of Agriculture and Agricultural Cooperatives and the Government Savings Bank, a more urban bank, channel credit toward lower-income borrowers, and all financial institutions are required to hold a minimum amount of assets in these two public banks, providing an implicit subsidy. The former was an early pioneer in joint liability lending, while the latter claims to be one of the largest microfinance institutions in the world.

A theoretical literature has emphasized the aggregate and distributional impacts of financial intermediation in models of occupational choice and financial frictions (Banerjee and Newman, 1993; Banerjee et al., 2009, Aghion and Bolton, 1997; Lloyd-Ellis and Bernhardt, 2000; Erosa and Hidalgo Cabrillana, 2008). In these studies, improved financial intermediation leads to more entry into entrepreneurship, higher productivity and investment, and a general equilibrium effect that increases wage. It is shown that the distribution of wealth and often the joint distribution of wealth and productivity are critical. A related literature has found the impacts of better financial intermediation in these models on aggregate productivity and income to be sizable (Gine and Townsend, 2004; Gine and Karlan, 2010; Amaral and Quintin, 2010). Buera and Shin (2010) and Buera et al. (2011) show the importance of endogenous saving responses and general equilibrium effects through interest rates in quantitative assessment.

## 3. Microfinance and Poverty Alleviation Nexus

### *3.1 The Theoretical Insights*

Poverty alleviation has been one of the key development challenges over the decades. One of the identified key constraints facing by the poor is lack of access to formal sector credit. It will facilitate them to take advantage of economic opportunities to increase their level of output, hence move out of poverty. Credit is considered to be an essential input to increase productivity, mainly land and labour. It is believed that credit boots income levels, increases employment at the household level and thereby alleviates poverty. Credit facilitates poor people to triumph over their liquidity constraints and under take some income generating activities. Furthermore, credit helps poor people to smoothen their consumption patterns in times of lean periods of the year (Binswanger and Khandker, 1995). The improved consumption is an investment in the productivity of the labour force or human capital. Hence, credit will maintain the productive capacity of rural poor households (Heidhues, 1995; Hulme and Mosley, 1996; Mosley and Hulme, 1998; Hulme, 2000; Navajas et al., 2000). The proposed goal of microfinance sector is to improve the welfare of the poor as a result of better access to small loans. The lack of access to credit for the poor may have negative consequences for various household level outcomes including technology adoption, agricultural productivity, food security, nutrition, health and overall welfare. Access to credit therefore affects welfare outcomes by alleviating the capital constraints of poor households. Table 2 regroups the poverty factors identified in the literature as a first step toward a model of poverty in Malawi.

**Table 2:** Factors of Poverty in Malawi

| National (Exogenous) Drivers | Household (Exogenous) Drivers | Household Controllable Drivers | Monetization of work | Measures of Socioeconomic Status |
|---|---|---|---|---|
| • Transportation and Communication infrastructure<br>• Government and NGO safety net<br>• Good government, civil peace, safety<br>• Environmental and economic shocks<br>• Agricultural land availability and distribution<br>• Healthcare and educational infrastructure | • Head of Household education, gender and age<br>• Size of household especially number of working age<br>• Household location: urban/rural and region<br>• Historic malnutrition (Stunting)<br>• Land ownership<br>• Household shocks, such and death of Hof HH<br>• Religious background | • Crop diversification, especially to cash crops<br>• Fertilizer and irrigation<br>• Livestock ownership<br>• Cash income activity<br>• Self-employment and micro-enterprise | • Cash income<br>• Non-cash income including crops and poultry and consumed by the household<br>• Barter exchanges<br>Monetary Shifting<br>• Health and crop insurance<br>• Savings<br>• Use of (access to) credit: MF | • Educational access<br>• Healthcare access<br>• Dwelling<br>• Food consumption<br>• Non-food consumption<br>• Use of safety net programmes<br>• Hope: attitude about socioeconomic condition and future |

*Source*: William J. Oliver (2010), Impact of Microfinance on Socio-economic Status of the Poor: The case of Malawi, Western Reserve University.

Over the past 30 years, microfinance (MF) has grown to a $30 billion industry involving over 3,000 organizations. Half of these microfinance institutions, however, have nothing more than anecdotal stories about the impact of MF on poverty. The connection between MF and poverty eradication is far from resolved. This aspect in fact addresses an ongoing debate by drawing upon two bodies of literature: poverty eradication and microfinance measurement. It articulates a causal model of the effects of MF on poverty that is unique in three regards. First, it measures the effect on socioeconomic status (SES) using for the first time a reflective multi-dimensional construct in contrast to deploying a financial surrogate for SES such as purchasing power parity (PPP). Second, it applies variables in measuring SES that are viewed as reflections of their origin—the level of poverty. This draws upon factor analytic techniques in contrast to earlier stepwise approaches. Third, on the cause side, in contrast to positing a direct effect the model evaluates MF for its moderating effects on the causal positive association between income and SES. The empirical setting for validating the proposed model is Malawi, a country of extreme poverty in central Africa. In this case the experiment was designed to transform an existing World Bank data set on household income and poverty in Malawi into a causal model using structural equation modeling (SEM). Our analysis shows that MF has a significant interaction with income in its impact on SES, thus demonstrating its instrumental value in reducing poverty. Contrary to earlier studies we find no differences across gender or income levels for the impacts of MF. Also contrary to previous literature, the effect is different between urban and rural households. The proposed approach offers a handy protocol to evaluate rigorously the impacts of MF or other poverty reducing efforts in other countries and contexts enabling cumulative empirical findings. On a practical level the study offers some guidelines how to target future microfinance operations.

Access to credit in addition increase the poor households' risk bearing ability, improves their risk—copying strategies and enables consumption smoothing over time. By so doing, microfinance is argued to improve the welfare of the poor (Navajas et al., 2000; Diagne and Zellar, 2001). Microfinance programmes have a potentially significant contribution to economic, social, political and psychological empowerment of the poor in general, women in particular. Regardless of their scale, outreach, location and the type of clients, all microfinance programme interventions target one thing in common—human development that is geared towards both the economic and social uplift of the people that they cater for. There are a couple of studies argue that microfinance very helpful in improving the economic and social welfare of the member households (Hossain, 1988; Remeny and Benjamin, 2000; Otero and Rhyne, 1994; Khandker, 1998; 2003). The study by Mosley (2001) reveals that the achievement of microfinance in reducing the poverty in Bolivia, Bangladesh and Indonesia is quite impressive and reached reasonably large number of poor (not the vulnerable poor or extreme poverty).

Zellar and Sharma (1998) argued that microfinance could help to establish or expand family enterprises, potentially making the difference between grinding poverty and economically secure life. The impact studies from Bangladesh shows that participation in microfinance programme can exert a large positive impact on self-employment profits (McKernan, 2002), while Pitt and Khandker (1996, 1998) find that has a significant impact on the well-being of poor households and that this impact is greater when credit is targeted to women. The programme participation has positive impacts on household income, production, and employment, particularly in the rural non-farm sector. Some of the studies find that microfinance programme participation exerts a statistically significant impact on one or more aspect of female empowerment, such as contraceptive use or intra-household decision-making (Hashemi et al., 1996; Goetz and Gupta, 1996; Schuler and Hashemi, 1994). Otero (1999) illustrates that microfinance creates access to productive capital for the poor, together with human capital, addressed through education and training and social capital achieved through local organization building, enables people to move out of poverty. By providing material capital to a poor person, their sense of dignity is strengthened and this can help to empower the person to participate in the economy and society (Otero, 1999).

More recently, Littlefield, Morduch and Hashemi (2003), Simanowitz and Brody (2004) have commented on the critical role of microfinance in achieving the Millennium Development Goals (MDGs). They state that microfinance is a key strategy in reaching the MDGs and in building global financial system that meet the needs of the poorest people. Microfinance is unique among development interventions; it can deliver social benefit on an ongoing, permanent basis and a large scale. In a comprehensive study by Hulme and Mosley (1996) argue that well-designed programmes can improve the incomes of the poor and can move them out of poverty. Microfinance programme target—both economic and social poverty through the credit and non-credit services. This referred in microfinance programme as "credit plus services" (Edgcomb and Barton, 1998) as they provide services (such as savings, insurance, health services, adult literacy) or training that go beyond financial services. However, impacts of these services have been little documented up to now (Zellar and Meyer, 2002; Godquin, 2004).

### 3.2 Impact on Vulnerable Poor of the Society

The World Development Report 2000/2001 (World Bank, 2000) lists the idiosyncratic risks faced by the poor, such as illness, injury, old age, violence, harvest failure, unemployment and food prices. Furthermore, the poor face an additional chronic risk induced by inequality, class relations, exploitation, concentrations of unaccountable power and social exclusion such as absence of "community" membership. In evaluating the evidence of the effect of microfinance on its widespread vulnerability, Pitt and Khandker (1996, 1998) and Morduch (1998, 1999) found a positive impact. They find signs of consumption-smoothing across seasons, a result that can be traced to increase smoothing of labour across seasons. According to the World Bank (2001), however, the evidence of the poverty-reducing impact of microfinance is inconclusive—targeting has not been universally successful, and studies have documented barriers to participation in programmes for the very poor. A large proportion of micro-credit loans are being used for consumption-smoothing, especially for extremely poor households. Although consumption-smoothing is used as a form of insurance and is crucial for the very poor households, credit used for non-investment purposes does not generate income. This suggests that, for the very poor households, consumption-smoothing occurs at the expense of long-term improvements in economic status. Moreover, microfinance turns out to be completely inadequate if a disaster strikes the whole community, as was the case with the floods in Bangladesh in 1998.

The trade-off between the long-term objectives of microfinance and its short-term use for consumption-smoothing suggests that providing alternative means for reducing risk in the form of insurance and saving schemes would enable microfinance to achieve its long-term poverty reduction objectives. In general, it is safe to say that microfinance helps smooth the seasonal characteristics of much of the rural economic activity. By combining loans with savings and insurance products, microfinance can further help to minimize the use of loans for consumption. Montgomery (1996) suggests that financial products such as saving facilities, insurance (against, for example, natural disasters) and small consumption loans with flexible repayment periods might be more suitable to the needs of the poorest. They would increase the short-term impact, in terms of the productivity of the asset which the loan finances. In addition, by gradually reducing the income vulnerability of the poor households, they would also encourage them to take riskier investments in working capital, hiring non-family labour and increasing fixed capital. Sharma (2000) emphasizes that access provides good returns to poor households only when complementary inputs such as seeds or irrigation water, or market access are present. Sharma further explains that this is also true for increases in food security of the household via increases in household productivity and income. However, unlike investment benefits, insurance benefit studies show a consistent positive impact.

In a recent study, Amin, Rai and Topa (2003) use a unique panel dataset from northern Bangladesh with monthly consumption and income data for 229 households before they received loans. They find that while micro-credit is successful in reaching the poor, it is less successful in reaching the vulnerable, especially the group most prone to destitution (the vulnerable poor). Coleman (1999, 2004) also finds little evidence of an impact on the programme participants. The results, Coleman further explains, are consistent with Adams and von Pischke's assertion that "debt is not an effective tool for helping most poor people enhance their economic condition" and that the poor are poor because of reasons other than lack of access to credit.

Despite the growth of microfinance, programmes specifically designed to target the poor are still not very widespread. It is still being debated whether reaching the poorest with these programmes is even desirable. An added concern is that funds are targeted to help the poor and/or landless, but there is generally little available to help small and medium-size farmers from falling deeper into poverty. The ability of micro-credit programmes to help the poorest is limited, because they lack the necessary skills, such as accounting ability and entrepreneurship, to create and sustain a business. To make the programmes effective for the poorest would require greater resources for literacy and basic training programmes. Therefore, credit-based programmes should be one component of a poverty reduction strategy. An argument could also be made that focusing on those near the poverty line would still help society as a whole and, at the same time, increase the programme's chances of becoming self-sufficient (Brahm, 2000). Zaman (2000) finds that the impact on poverty tends to be dependent on reaching a certain economic threshold and, to a lesser extent, on how poor the household is to start with. He further finds that households that join micro-lending programmes a few years after they have been established in a village tend to be less poor than the initial members. Matin and Hulme (2003), examine evidence from BRAC's (Bangladesh Rural Advancement Committee) IGVGD programme (Income Generation for Vulnerable Group Development Programme), that seeks to reach Bangladesh's "hardcore poor" by combining elements of livelihood protection (food aid) with livelihood promotion (skills training and microfinance). Although they do find evidence that the IGVGD can reach deeper than purely promotional schemes and can benefit the chronic poor, it cannot totally replace programmes of pure social protection. A small proportion of the population will always need more traditional "social welfare" support to avoid persistent deprivation.

### *3.3 Impact of Microfinance on Poverty Alleviation*

Microfinance was conceived as a sustainable tool for poverty alleviation. Since becoming popular in Bangladesh in the 1970s, it now reaches more than 100 million poor people all over the world through a combined portfolio of $15 billion. Microfinance helps dampen poverty by raising incomes and human capital stock. It also reduces the vulnerability of the poor to internal and external shocks. Livelihoods financed through microfinance boost income, which, in turn, is spent to increase food consumption, attain better education, maintain good health, improve housing conditions, and acquire durable goods and assets. The biggest impact of microfinance has been in helping the poor smooth their consumption. In the Philippines, government figures indicate that microfinance now reaches 7 million individuals through the services of 500 microfinance institutions (MFIs) with a combined portfolio of $12 billion.

The microfinance industry also employs directly about 35,000 people and an additional 1,400,000 indirectly through the micro-enterprises financed by the industry. A supportive regulatory and policy environment, including the phase-out of government directed credit programmes, helped spur the growth of microfinance in the country. Because of its effectiveness and profitability, microfinance has assumed a commercial character, which provides strong incentives for private funds to invest in it. Microfinance has penetrated the financial system as a viable investment vehicle. Its profitability is drawing investors from capital markets. This has enabled its proponents to increase rapidly their outreach toward the poor. These investments also facilitate the MFIs drive for scale, thereby enhancing competition, which then stimulates operational efficiency among competitors. Competition spurs an MFI to cut costs, provide products that are more responsive to the needs of its clients, and generate higher returns in the process. At the same time, the demand for higher return on investment is pushing MFIs to focus more on profitability, with poverty reduction taking a secondary role. There are also preliminary indications that the increasing competition among MFIs encourages multiple borrowing among microfinance clients, possibly leading to problems of over-indebtedness; this recent phenomenon, however, requires further research scrutiny. Microfinance is a sustainable tool for poverty reduction.

The unique character of microfinance is that it is not dependent on direct subsidy. It also facilitates the participation of the private sector in efforts to reduce poverty. A number of private companies are already implementing models of CSR-driven ventures with micro-entrepreneurs, in turn, can serve as strategic investment. The cost subsidy may eventually recede and the profitability of these ventures with micro-entrepreneurs may rise as the business achieves economies of scale. Private sector participation in poverty reduction, in turn, leaves the government with more resources to address the basic needs of the extreme poor, who have proven to be difficult to reach using the existing financial tools and capacity of the microfinance industry Recognizing the limits of the traditional mode of microfinance, many MFIs have recently diversified their services to include micro-insurance, micro-housing, and business development services (BDS). This trend reflects growing sensitivity to client needs as MFIs experience success in repayment rates. MFIs are also moving into the delivery of business development services or "microfinance plus", to promote the sustainability of clients' businesses. Thus, microfinance is evolving into micro-enterprise development, which combines financial and non-financial services in helping the poor integrate more fully into the formal economy. However, the question of whether MFIs should be moving away from their key areas of comparative advantage micro-credit and savings—remains a subject of debate. Facilitate access of micro-entrepreneurs to business development services and facilitate their registration to enable them to enter the formal economy micro-enterprises graduate into small-enterprise level. While BDS is becoming a popular intervention in microenterprise development, the provision of non-financial services needs to be scaled up to help the poor enter the formal market economy.

The key to promoting progress is in finding sustainable, commercial relationships that will support fledgling micro-entrepreneurs' integration into the mainstream market. Much of this effort will involve business development services, including documenting case studies of established businesses that can serve as templates for micro-entrepreneurs. These market opportunities need to be identified and made explicit to microfinance players to enable them to grow their businesses and integrate into the mainstream. The government should allocate more resources for business development services of such agencies as the Department of Trade and Industry, the Department of Agriculture, and the Department of Science and Technology and direct these agencies to extend their services to micro-enterprises, particularly those in rural areas. The policy environment for micro and small enterprises also needs to be improved in order to make the market work for the poor. In addition, government should make it easy for micro-enterprises to register as formal businesses so they can participate more fully in the formal market. The executive department must enact measures to encourage LGUs to facilitate the registration of MSMEs. The academe should also conduct case studies of registration systems and use the results of such studies to design suitable registration systems for micro-entrepreneurs.

Promotion of micro-entrepreneurship among underprivileged women is considered as a very powerful tool to combat poverty and empower them economically. Entrepreneurship development amongst the underprivileged women is a long process which usually goes through various stages such as targeting and tapping potential entrepreneurs, developing their confidence, capacities and aspiration levels to take up entrepreneurial challenges, providing access to financial as well as non-financial resources such as credit, business skills, marketing, brand building, etc. and finally linking the micro-enterprises to market for growth and expansion. Before emergence of microfinance the main emphasis of government policies was on provision of subsidized capital with minimal business training. Most of the efforts were found to be ineffective as either the funds were mis-utilized or the programmes were not supported by other non-financial services like business training, networking, confidence building, awareness building, etc. The main difference between government sponsored entrepreneurship development programmes and microfinance programmes is that unlike the former, microfinance programmes create social capital which is helpful in awareness building and capacity building.

Most poor people manage to mobilize resources to develop their enterprises and their dwellings slowly over time. Financial services could enable the poor to leverage their initiative, accelerating the process of building incomes, assets and economic security. However, conventional finance institutions seldom lend down-market to serve the needs of low-income families and women-headed households. They are very often denied access to credit for any purpose, making the discussion of the level of interest rate and other terms of finance irrelevant. Therefore the fundamental problem is not so much of unaffordable terms of loan as the lack of access to credit itself (Kim, 1995). The lack of access to credit for the poor is attributable to practical difficulties arising from the discrepancy between the mode of operation followed by financial institutions and the economic characteristics and financing needs of low-income households. For example, commercial lending institutions require that borrowers have a stable source of income out of which principal and interest can be paid back according to the agreed terms. However, the income of many self-employed households is not stable, regardless of its size. A large number of small loans are needed to serve the poor, but lenders prefer dealing with large loans in small numbers to minimize administration costs. They also look for collateral with a clear title—which many low-income households do not have. In addition bankers tend to consider low income households a bad risk imposing exceedingly high information monitoring costs on operation.

Over the last ten years, however, successful experiences in providing finance to small entrepreneur and producers demonstrate that poor people, when given access to responsive and timely financial services at market rates, repay their loans and use the proceeds to increase their income and assets. This is not surprising since the only realistic alternative for them is to borrow from informal market at an interest much higher than market rates. Community banks, NGOs and grass-root savings and credit groups around the world have shown that these microenterprise loans can be profitable for borrowers and for the lenders, making microfinance one of the most effective poverty reducing strategies. To the extent that microfinance institutions become financially viable, self-sustaining, and integral to the communities in which they operate, they have the potential to attract more resources and expand services to clients. Despite the success of microfinance institutions, only about 2 percent of world's roughly 500 million small entrepreneurs are estimated to have access to financial services (Barry et al., 1996).

Although there is demand for credit by poor and women at market interest rates, the volume of financial transaction of microfinance institution must reach a certain level before their financial operation becomes self-sustaining. In other words, although microfinance offers a promising institutional structure to provide access to credit to the poor, the scale problem needs to be resolved so that it can reach the vast majority of potential customers who demand access to credit at market rates. The question then is how micro-enterprise lending geared to providing short-term capital to small businesses in the informal sector can be sustained as an integral part of the financial sector and how their financial services can be further expanded using the principles, standards and modalities that have proven to be effective. To be successful, financial intermediaries that provide services and generate domestic resources must have the capacity to meet high performance standards. They must achieve excellent repayments and provide access to clients. And they must build toward operating and financial self-sufficiency and expanding client reach. In order to do so, microfinance institutions need to find ways to cut down on their administrative costs and also to broaden their resource base. Cost reductions can be achieved through simplified and decentralized loan application, approval and collection processes, for instance, through group loans which give borrowers responsibilities for much of the loan application process, allow the loan officers to handle many more clients and hence reduce costs (Otero et al., 1994).

Microfinance institutions can broaden their resource base by mobilizing savings, accessing capital markets, loan funds and effective institutional development support. A logical way to tap capital market is securitization through a corporation that purchases loans made by microenterprise institutions with the funds raised through the bonds issuance on the capital market. There is at least one pilot attempt to securitize microfinance portfolio along these lines in Ecuador. As an alternative, BancoSol of Bolivia issued a certificate of deposit which is traded in Bolivian stock exchange. In 1994, it also issued certificates of deposit in the U.S. (Churchill, 1996). The Foundation for Cooperation and Development of Paraguay issued bonds to raise capital for micro-enterprise lending (Grameen Trust, 1995).

Savings facilities make large scale lending operations possible. On the other hand, studies also show that the poor operating in the informal sector do save, although not in financial assets, and hence value access to client-friendly savings service at least as much access to credit. Savings mobilization also makes financial institutions accountable to local shareholders. Therefore, adequate savings facilities both serve the demand for financial services by the customers and fulfil an important requirement of financial sustainability to the lenders. Microfinance institutions can either provide savings services directly through deposit taking or make arrangements with other financial institutions to provide savings facilities to tap small savings in a flexible manner (Barry, 1995). Convenience of location, positive real rate of return, liquidity, and security of savings are essential ingredients of successful savings mobilization (Christen et al., 1994).

Once microfinance institutions are engaged in deposit taking in order to mobilize household savings, they become financial intermediaries. Consequently, prudential financial regulations become necessary to ensure the solvency and financial soundness of the institution and to protect the depositors. However, excessive regulations that do not consider the nature of microfinance institution and their operation can hamper their viability. In view of small loan size, microfinance institutions should be subjected to a minimum capital requirement which is lower than that applicable to commercial banks. On the other hand, a more stringent capital adequacy rate (the ratio between capital and risk assets) should be maintained because microfinance institutions provide uncollateralized loans.

Governments should provide an enabling legal and regulatory framework which encourages the development of a range of institutions and allows them to operate as recognized financial intermediaries subject to simple supervisory and reporting requirements. Usury laws should be repelled or relaxed and microfinance institutions should be given freedom of setting interest rates and fees in order to cover operating and finance costs from interest revenues within a reasonable amount of time. Government could also facilitate the process of transition to a sustainable level of operation by providing support to the lending institutions in their early stage of development through credit enhancement mechanisms or subsidies.

One way of expanding the successful operation of microfinance institutions in the informal sector is through strengthened linkages with their formal sector counterparts. A mutually beneficial partnership should be based on comparative strengths of each sector. Informal sector microfinance institutions have comparative advantage in terms of small transaction costs achieved through adaptability and flexibility of operations (Ghate et al., 1992). They are better equipped to deal with credit assessment of the urban poor and hence to absorb the transaction costs associated with loan processing. On the other hand, formal sector institutions have access to broader resource-base and high leverage through deposit mobilization (Christen et al., 1994). Therefore, formal sector finance institutions could form a joint venture with informal sector institutions in which the former provide funds in the form of equity and the later extends savings and loan facilities to the urban poor. Another form of partnership can involve the formal sector institutions refinancing loans made by the informal sector lenders. Under these settings, the informal sector institutions are able to tap additional resources as well as having an incentive to exercise greater financial discipline in their management.

Microfinance institutions could also serve as intermediaries between borrowers and the formal financial sector and on-lend funds backed by a public sector guarantee (Phelps, 1995). Business-like NGOs can offer commercial banks ways of funding micro-entrepreneurs at low cost and risk, for example, through leveraged bank-NGO-client credit lines. Under this arrangement, banks make one bulk loan to NGOs and the NGOs packages it into large number of small loans at market rates and recover them (Women's World Banking, 1994). There are many ongoing researches on this line but context specific research is needed to identify the most appropriate model.

Hulme and Mosley (1996) in a comprehensive study on the use of microfinance to combat poverty, argue that well-designed programmes can improve the incomes of the poor and can move them out of poverty. They state that "there is clear evidence that the impact of a loan on a borrower's income is related to the level of income" as those with higher incomes have a greater range of investment opportunities and so credit schemes are more likely to benefit the "middle and upper poor" (1996). However, they also show that when MFIs such as the Grameen Bank and BRAC provided credit to very poor households, those households were able to raise their incomes and their assets (1996).

Microfinance is about providing financial services to the poor who are not served by the conventional formal financial institutions—it is about extending the frontiers of financial service provision. The provision of such financial services requires innovative delivery channels and methodologies. The needs for financial services that allow people to both take advantage of opportunities and better management of their resources. Microfinance can be one effective tool amongst many for poverty alleviation. However, it should be used with caution—despite recent claims, the equation between microfinance and poverty alleviation is not straight-forward, because poverty is a complex phenomenon and many constraints that the poor in general have to cope with. We need to understand when and in what form microfinance is appropriate for the poorest; the delivery channel, methodology and products offered are all inter-linked and in turn affect the prospect and promise of poverty alleviation. Access to formal banking services is difficult for the poor. The main problem the poor have to take when trying to acquire loans from formal financial institutions is the demand for collateral asked by these institutions. In addition, the process of acquiring a loan entails many bureaucratic procedures, which lead to extra transaction costs for the poor. Formal financial institutions are not motivated to lend money to them. In general, formal financial institutions show a preference for urban over rural sectors, large-scale over small scale transactions, and non-agricultural over agricultural loans. Formal financial institutions have little incentives to lend to the rural poor for the following reasons.

- *Administrable difficulties*

  Small rural farmers often live geographically scattered, in areas with poor communication facilities, making loan administration difficult.

- *Systematic risks*

  Agricultural production is associated with some systemic risks, such as drought and floods, which is reflected in a high covariance of local incomes.

- *Lack of information*

  The absence of standardized information, Standard lending tools, such as financial statements or credit histories, does not exist in these areas.

*Repayment problems*: The repayment of working capital may be required only once a year for example during the harvest season. On the other hand, access to informal loans is relatively easy, convenient, and available locally to low income households for the following reasons:

- Informal moneylenders use interlinked credit contracts to reduce default risk such as development of business relationship with the clients.
- Informal moneylenders have local information which helps them to appraise credit needs and credit worthiness of the client.
- Informal moneylenders are considering the needs and requirements of clients even for small amount of loan.
- Informal moneylenders will profit from social sanctions such as those that may exist among members of a family. These sanctions may serve as a substitute for legal enforcement.
- Informal moneylenders use specific incentives to stimulate repayment, such as repeat lending to borrowers who repay promptly, with gradually increasing loan size.

Despite the fact that many rural poor acquire their loans from the informal financial sector in rural areas of developing countries; the sector has some basic limitations. A common feature of many rural communities is that much of the local information does not flow freely; it tends to be segmented and circulates only within specific groups. Usually the informal credit market is based on local economies and is thus limited by local wealth constraints and the covariant risks of the local environment. Since most of the world's poor do not have access to basic financial services that would help them manage their assets and generate income. To overcome poverty, they need to be able to borrow, save, and invest, and to protect their families against adversity. Another shortcoming of the two financial sectors in developing countries is their inability to satisfy the credit needs of the poor that has led to the new development of microfinance. Microfinance is believed to be able to reduce the above-mentioned inadequacies of formal and informal financial institutions and is emerging as an important credit partner to the poor in the developing world. The various types of microfinance services that can be extended to poor people to meet the general household financial goals may be seen in Table 3.

**Table 3:** Microfinance Services to Poor people to meet their general Household Financial goals

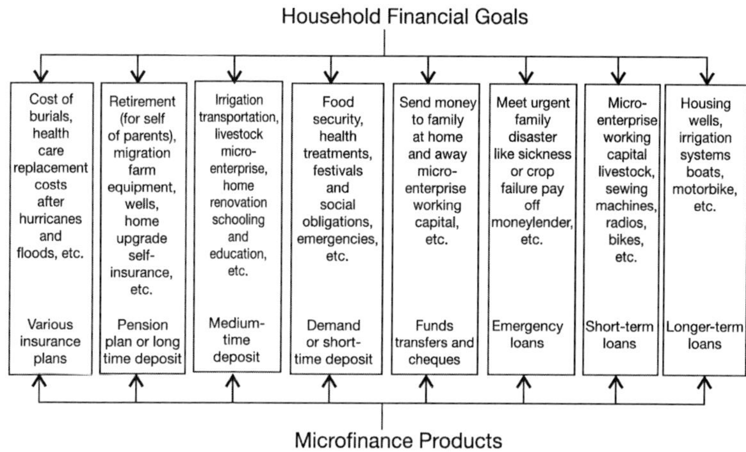


*Source*: Brett Matthews, Mathwood Consulting Company.

### 3.4 Schemes of the Government of India on Poverty Alleviation

There are so many schemes for the upliftment of poor In India. One of them Micro-credit programmes is run primarily by NABARD in the field of agriculture and SIDBI in the field of Industry, Service and Business (ISB). The success of Micro-credit programme lies in diversification of services. Microfinance Scheme of SIDBI is under operation since January, 1999 with a corpus of ₹ 100 crore and a network of about 190 capacity assessed rated MFIs/NGOs. Under the programme, total amount of ₹ 191 crore have been sanctioned upto 31st December, 2003, benefiting over 9 lakh beneficiaries. Under the programme, NGOs/MFIs are supposed to provide equity support in order to avail SIDBI finance. But they find it difficult to manage the needed equity support because of their poor financial condition. The problem has got aggravated due to declining interest rate on deposits. The office of the development commissioner (Small Scale Industries) under the Ministry of SSI is launching a new scheme of Micro-finance Programme to overcome the constraints in the existing scheme of SIDBI, whose reach is currently very low. It is felt that Government's role can be critical in expanding reach of the scheme, ensuring long-term sustainability of NGOs/ MFIs and development of Intermediaries for identification of viable projects.

Salient Features of some of the lead Microfinance Programmes of the Government of India are as follows:

(a) *Arranging Fixed Deposits for MFIs/NGOs*: Under this scheme government of India arrange money to MFI/ NGO like SIDBI for micro-credit to poor.

(b) *Training and Studies on Micro-Finance Programme*: Government of India would help SIDBI in meeting the training needs of NGOs, SHGs, intermediaries and entrepreneurs and also in enhancing awareness about the programme. Institution building for 'intermediaries' for identification of viable projects: The Government of India would help in institution building through identification and development of 'intermediary organization', which would help the NGOs/SHGs in identification of product, preparation of project report, working out forward and backward linkages and in fixing marketing/technology tie-ups. The SISIs would help in the identification of such intermediaries in different areas.

(c) *Budgetary Provision for the Scheme During 10th plan*: There was a budgetary provision in 10th Five-year Plan and hoping more funds in next plan.

(d) *Administrative Arrangement*: A committee has been formed to control and monitor the administrative arrangement of MFI/NGOs.

### *3.5 Impact on Livelihood Support Systems*

A livelihood security approach according to Concern (2003) aims for a holistic analysis and understanding of the root causes of poverty and how people cope with poverty. They identify livelihood shocks such as natural disasters and drought, the social, political and economic context, and people's livelihood resources such as education and local infrastructure as factors affecting people's livelihood security (Concern, 2003). Therefore, when analyzing the impact microfinance is having on livelihood security, as is the objective of this dissertation, a holistic analysis of people's livelihood security must be conducted, rather than just focusing on the material/economic impact microfinance is having on the livelihoods of the poor.

### *3.5.1 Socio-economic Impact analysis*

McGregor et al. (2000) states that wider social and economic impacts can occur through the labour market, the capital market, the market for goods consumed by poor people, through production linkages and through clients participation in social and political processes.

#### *A. Impact on a Household Level*

Robinson (2001) in a study of 16 different MFIs from all over the world shows that having access to microfinance services has led to an enhancement in the quality of life of clients, an increase in their self-confidence, and has helped them to diversify their livelihood security strategies and thereby increase their income

#### *B. Empowering Women*

Morduh and Hanley (2002) state that access to MFIs can empower women to become more confident, more assertive, more likely to take part in family and community decisions and better able to confront gender inequities. Hulme and Mosley (1996) state that microfinance projects can reduce the isolation of women as when they come together in groups they have an opportunity to share information and discuss ideas and develop a bond that was not there previously. In other words, Microfinance can have the impact both at the household as well as community levels (Fig. 1).

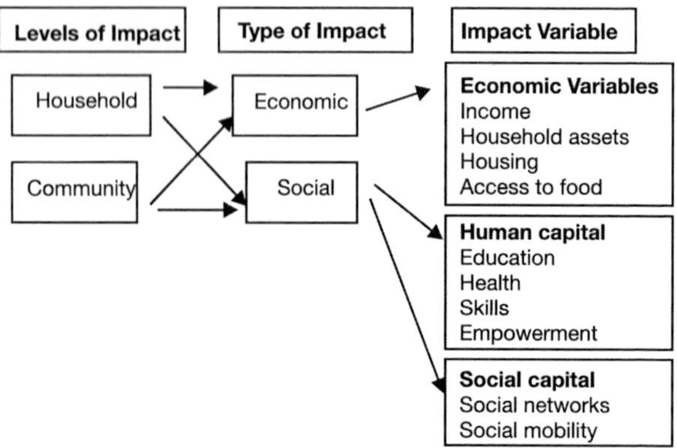


**Fig. 1:** Potential Impact of Microfinance at Household and Community Levels

*Source*: Trócaire, 2005a and b.

The field of microfinance institutions (MFIs) is still a fairly recent topic in economic research. Although the first MFIs have already been established in the 1980s such as the Grameen Bank (2009) founded by 2006 Nobel Peace Prize Laureate Muhammad Yunus (Yunus, 2004), the extent to which they have been profoundly analysed in economic research is still small.

In general, analyses of MFIs in qualitative impact studies and quantitative empirical, econometrics-based studies are distinguished. While the former covers qualitative case studies of an individual MFI, the latter aims at detecting general patterns to draw conclusions about common characteristics. Half-way between qualitative impact studies and quantitative econometric assessments, social performance measurements combine both mainstream analyses. Pilot studies are the most frequent embodiment thereof. Using impact studies to study one MFI in all detail may reveal useful results for this individual case, but conclusions cannot be generalized, and even transferring insights to similar institutions in the same geographic region is difficult. As control groups are completely missing, it may prove to be difficult to disentangle effects of microfinance itself. In fact, if the chosen MFI bears atypical characteristics that other MFIs do not have in common, this is clear sign of selection bias which leads to false conclusions if the findings are applied to make predictions about other MFIs. Purely qualitative assessments are not able to account for reverse causation or spurious correlations, which further stresses the arguments above. Though, impact studies have constituted the most frequent method to analyze MFIs so far. As, for example, emphasized by Morduch (1999), the scarcity of data was the main reason for significant underrepresentation of econometric-based empirical studies on any topic on MFIs. This field of study is not only worth to turn one's attention to due to the claim of scientific evaluation. But the results obtained from in-depth empirical analyses may reveal important insights into MFIs and their impact on economic development.

Many public policies in the recent times have been focused towards poverty reduction, finding ways to improve household productivity and thereby incomes. Since the 1960s and 1970s, there have been policies on the role of microfinance in the rural development process. These policies focused on the provision of agricultural credit as a necessary support to the introduction of new, more productive agricultural technologies that would ensure that farmers improve their incomes and feed the nation (Moll, 2005). Later, this approach broadened to include individuals involved in both small and micro-enterprises like handcrafts and home based business.

### *3.6 Rural Poverty and the Microfinance Promise in a Vicious Cycle*

Microfinance programmes have a potentially significant contribution to economic, social, political and psychological empowerment of the poor in general, women in particular. Through access to timely credit, savings, insurance and entrepreneurial training, etc. women have become successful entrepreneurs, increased their household income and well-being. Regardless of their scale, outreach, location and the type of clients, all microfinance programme interventions target one thing in common—human development that is geared towards both the economic and social uplift of the people that they cater for. However in real life situation, as experienced in implementation of various microfinance programmes that the poor households are mostly held up in a vicious cycle of poverty, where labour, their best resource is "locked up as unproductive" due to different constraints including a liquidity constraint. For example a poor household may have family members who are willing to work in the family garden to grow crops. However if they cannot afford improved crop varieties and farm inputs then the returns to their labour are not enough to ensure a good standard of living. In other words, the poor can be held up in a vicious cycle of poverty out of economic and family compulsions because of limited resources (Fig. 2).

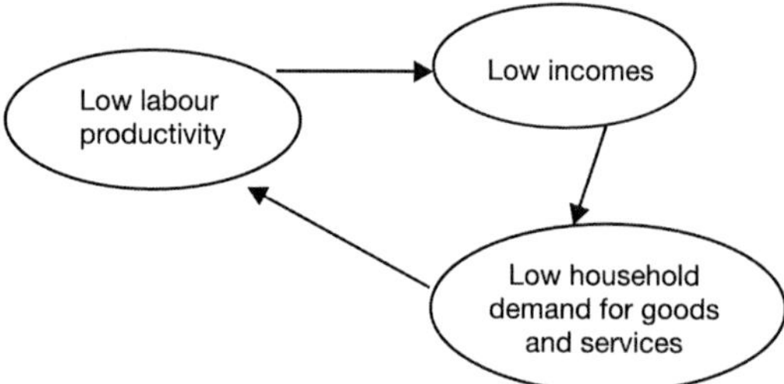


**Fig. 2:** The poor are held up in a Vicious Cycle of Poverty with low labour Productivity and income

*Source*: Joy M. Kiiru, Centre for Development Research (ZEF), Bonn University (http://african-women-economists.com/joy-kiiru microfinance-entrepreneurship-and-rural-development.pdf) Kiiru and Mburu (2006).

Many governments and donor communities believe that the liquidity constraint is the most important constraint impeding poor households and that if it is addressed it will be possible for households to escape poverty. Economists argue that to break the vicious cycle of poverty, there needs to be an outside force that will intervene at some point of the cycle to improve demand for goods and services. This could be done by for example injecting some liquidity, thereby unlocking the productivity of household labour. Microfinance promises not only to break the vicious chain of poverty but also it promises to initiate a whole new cycle of virtuous spirals of self-enforcing economic empowerment that lead to increased household well-being. Figure 3 illustrates the unique scenario unleashing the mode of unlocking of household labour that was apparently locked up due to the liquidity crunch.

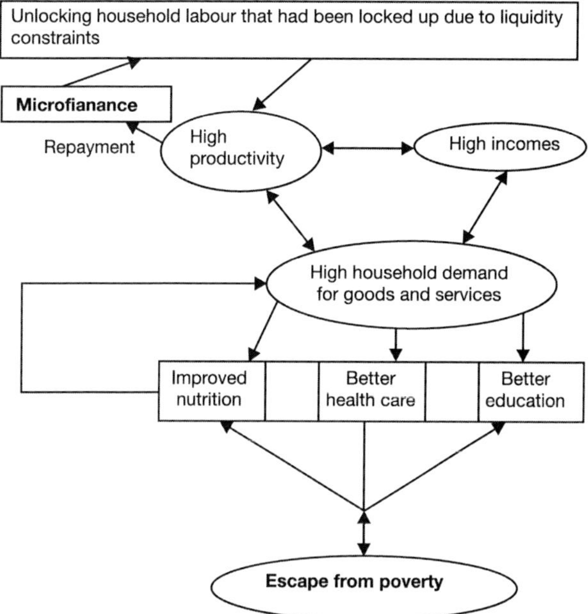


**Fig. 3:** Microfinance Promise for Poverty alleviation despite Liquidity crunch

*Source*: Joy M. Kiiru, Centre for Development Research (ZEF), Bonn University (http://african-women-economists.com/joy-kiiru/microfinance-entrepreneurship-and-rural-development.pdf) & Kiiru and Mburu (2006).

Such is the model that has promoted the microfinance institution and given it the "polite and respectable" image it currently enjoys. There are several assumptions that go with this model, first it is assumed that all poor people can become micro-entrepreneurs if only they were given a chance through credit; and even if this assumption were to be granted, the model further assumes that there is a vibrant market for goods and services and that it is possible for micro-entrepreneurs to get linked up to markets for their products: otherwise how else is microfinance supposed to improve incomes if there was no demand for goods and services. Lastly, some proponents of the model also assume that the fact that the poor can repay at market interest rates or slightly above market rates it is a good indication that they are improving their financial status and therefore it is a sign of good impact of microfinance; the irony being that even before the microfinance revolution many governments and non-governmental organisations believed that informal moneylenders were exploiting the poor and that is why it was justified to bring to the poor a cheaper alternative; yet the poor were still paying for the moneylender services!!

Regarding the argument that microfinance enables households to start income generating enterprises, development economists argue that if every informal self-employment is to be defined as entrepreneurship then lots of such entrepreneurship in a country does not necessarily mean economic growth or the reduction of poverty (Acs, 2006). Acs continues to say that, "If by entrepreneurship, one allows inclusion of any type of informal self-employment, then high levels of such entrepreneurships may actually mean either that there are substantial bureaucratic barriers to formally creating a new business, or simply that the economy is creating too few conventional wage-earning job opportunities. Under these circumstances, we might reasonably hypothesize that high level of sole-proprietorship informal entrepreneurship would correlate with slow economic growth and lagging development (Acs, 2006). Logically, it cannot be expected that microfinance is a "magic bullet" against poverty. In some contexts just like research has demonstrated microfinance could work well for the poor Khandker (2005), Morduch (1999) and in other contexts it may not work the same way Kiiru and Mburu (2006), Kiriti (2006). Once researchers and policymakers agree that microfinance cannot be a panacea against poverty then research would concentrate more on what works and the context in which it works.

### *3.7 Impact on Vulnerable Poor of the Society*

The World Development Report 2000/2001 (World Bank, 2000) lists the idiosyncratic risks faced by the poor, such as illness, injury, old age, violence, harvest failure, unemployment and food prices. Furthermore, the poor face an additional chronic risk induced by inequality, class relations, exploitation, concentrations of unaccountable power and social exclusion such as absence of "community" membership. In evaluating the evidence of the effect of microfinance on vulnerability, Pitt and Khandker (1998) and Morduch (1998) find a positive impact. They find signs of consumption-smoothing across seasons, a result that can be traced to increase smoothing of labour across seasons. According to the World Bank (2001), however, the evidence of the poverty-reducing impact of microfinance is inconclusive-targeting has not been universally successful, and studies have documented barriers to participation in programmes for the very poor. A large proportion of microcredit loans are being used for consumption-smoothing, especially for extremely poor households. Although consumption-smoothing is used as a form of insurance and is crucial for the very poor households, credit used for non-investment purposes does not generate income. This suggests that, for the very poor households, consumption-smoothing occurs at the expense of long-term improvements in economic status. Moreover, microfinance turns out to be completely inadequate if a disaster strikes the whole community, as was the case with the floods in Bangladesh in 1998.

The trade-off between the long-term objectives of microfinance and its short-term use for consumption-smoothing suggests that providing alternative means for reducing risk in the form of insurance and saving schemes would enable microfinance to achieve its long-term poverty reduction objectives. In general, it is safe to say that microfinance helps smooth the seasonal characteristics of much of the rural economic activity. By combining loans with savings and insurance products, microfinance can further help to minimize the use of loans for consumption. Montgomery (1996) suggests that financial products such as saving facilities, insurance (against, for example, natural disasters) and small consumption loans with flexible repayment periods might be more suitable to the needs of the poorest. They would increase the short-term impact, in terms of the productivity of the asset which the loan finances. In addition, by gradually reducing the income vulnerability of the poor households, they would also encourage them to take riskier investments in working capital, hiring non-family labour and increasing fixed capital. Sharma (2000) emphasizes that access provides good returns to poor households only when complementary inputs such as seeds or irrigation water, or market access are present. Sharma further explains that this is also true for increases in food security of the household via increases in household productivity and income. However, unlike investment benefits, insurance benefit studies show a consistent positive impact.

In a recent study, Amin, Rai and Topa (2003) use a unique panel dataset from northern Bangladesh with monthly consumption and income data for 229 households before they received loans. They find that while microcredit is successful in reaching the poor, it is less successful in reaching the vulnerable, especially the group most prone to destitution (the vulnerable poor). Coleman (1999) also finds little evidence of an impact on the programme participants. The results, Coleman further explains, are consistent with Adams and von Pischke's assertion that "debt is not an effective tool for helping most poor people enhance their economic condition" and that the poor are poor because of reasons other than lack of access to credit.

Despite the growth of microfinance, programmes specifically designed to target the poor are still not very widespread. It is still being debated whether reaching the poorest with these programmes is even desirable. An added concern is that funds are targeted to help the poor and/or landless, but there is generally little available to help small and medium-size farmers from falling deeper into poverty. The ability of micro-credit programmes to help the poorest is limited, because they lack the necessary skills, such as accounting ability and entrepreneurship, to create and sustain a business. To make the programmes effective for the poorest would require greater resources for literacy and basic training programmes. Therefore, credit-based programmes should be one component of a poverty reduction strategy. An argument could also be made that focusing on those near the poverty line would still help society as a whole and, at the same time, increase the programme's chances of becoming self-sufficient (Brahm, 2000). Zaman (2000) finds that the impact on poverty tends to be dependent on reaching a certain economic threshold and, to a lesser extent, on how poor the household is to start with. He further finds that households that join micro-lending programmes a few years after they have been established in a village tend to be less poor than the initial members. Matin and Hulme (2003), examine evidence from BRAC's (Bangladesh Rural Advancement Committee) IGVGD programme (Income Generation for Vulnerable Group Development Programme), that seeks to reach Bangladesh's "hardcore poor" by combining elements of livelihood protection (food aid) with livelihood promotion (skills training and microfinance). Although they do find evidence that the IGVGD can reach deeper than purely promotional schemes and can benefit the chronic poor, it cannot totally replace programmes of pure social protection. A small proportion of the population will always need more traditional "social welfare" support to avoid persistent deprivation.

### *3.8 Impact on Employment*

Many micro-enterprises are engaged in rudimentary activities such as food or craft production for sale at the market or establishing a service business. Such enterprises do not generate many jobs outside the family. Employment is a reflection of both the supply of and demand for labour. It can rise or fall depending on how much and in what ways programmes affect farm and non-farm production. If, for example, increased production is attained through improved technology of rural non-farm activities, then it is unlikely to have a positive and significant impact on village-level employment. However, if production technology does not change, an overall increase in production can lead to employment expansion. Pitt and Khandker (1998) attempted to rationalize that given the small loan size and the type of activities undertaken by micro-entrepreneurs, it is unlikely that capital intensity has increased. Given that the labour and the capital intensity of rural non-farm production is unchanged, increased microfinance implies that employment can be expected to rise. However, if increased income as a result of microfinance programmes results in a decrease in labour supply (income effect), it can negatively affect labour supply of particular type, for example male labour supply. As a result employment may decline, given the demand for labour. Therefore, the net impact cannot be determined *a priori*.

Microcredit programmes seem to reduce wage-employment and income, but raise self-employment and corresponding income for programme-participating households. One might expect that a reduction of employment in the wage market might increase wages, but this may not happen because the wage-employment gap may be filled by previously unemployed or underemployed wage workers. Khandker et al. (1998) find mixed results for the effect of microfinance on wage rates in the farm and non-farm sector. They find that growth in self-employment has been achieved at the expense of wage-employment, which implies an increase in rural wages. They emphasise that an upward shift in the labour demand curve is required for both improved productivity and wage gains on a sustainable basis, which can only be supported through structural transformation of the rural economy. Evidence from their study on three microfinance institutions in Bangladesh suggests that only the Grameen Bank made a positive and significant impact on rural male wages by inducing an increase of 13.5 per cent (Grameen Bank, 2009).

### 3.9 Impact on Women and Children

Several studies show that women are more reliable in repaying loans (Hulme and Mosley, 1997), so micro-lenders concerned about sustainability would improve their financial situation by targeting female borrowers. Some studies have shown that loans to women are actually under the control of men (Goetz and Gupta, 1996; Hulme and Mosley, 1996). It is also argued that microcredit programmes make the poor economically dependent on the programme itself (Bouman and Hospes, 1994). Furthermore, Pitt and Khandker (1998), using World Bank data, find that lending to women has little effect on labour supply, but it can increases leisure (i.e. time taken off from market work) for men. Moreover, non-land assets increase substantially when borrowing is done by women, but not by men. Schooling of boys is increased, irrespective of the gender of the borrower. However, the schooling of girls increases only when the women borrow from the Grameen Bank, suggesting that women borrowers in other programmes use their daughters for household and family chores while they engage in income-generating activities as a consequence of the loan.

Micro-credit programmes make it possible for participants (mostly women), who were unemployed before, or involved in household chores, to become self-employed in microcredit-financed small enterprises. Moreover, even if loans are given to women, many small enterprises require male labour for marketing and other purposes. It is also common that women take loans to finance their husbands' self-employed activities. As micro-enterprises grow, more and more family members become involved. Research also indicates that self-employment may lead to an increased incidence of child labour. On a community-wide basis, the presence of a microfinance programme had a broader impact on employment patterns with an increase in female labour force participation and an increase in the number of non-farm jobs.

The impact of microfinance programmes extends beyond the economic and employment situation of the households. There is increasing evidence of effects of microfinance on schooling, health, fertility, child labour and women's empowerment. Evidence from Khandker (1998) shows that programme participation had a significant impact on children's schooling, especially for boys. Credit given to women also increases the nutritional well-being of both male and female children. Schuler and Hashemi (1994) use contraceptive use and incidence of abuse as measures of women's empowerment and find that, although women are empowered by the micro-credit using the first indicator; it fails on the second measure. In contrast, Khandker (1998) finds a decline in the use of contraceptives among participants but suggests that participants were more likely to have higher levels of contraceptive use before entering the programme. Although evidence of empowerment of women is unclear, there is clear evidence that microcredit programmes do reduce the isolation of women through the group activities and networking that the programmes facilitate (Brahm, 2000). Women tend to have control when the loans are used for what are seen as traditional women's activities, which serves to reinforce traditional gender roles. Anderson, Locker and

Nugent (2002) suggest that microfinance creates opportunities for social capital to lower the costs of collective action and hence the costs of managing common pool resources. Results from their survey of Microcredit Summit members suggest that some of the microfinance institutions (MFIs) have intentionally linked their financial services to environmental resource goals and that many more MFIs may be having inadvertent effects upon the environment. However, on the authors' own admission, the evidence regarding the strength and direction of these relationships is still very thin and must be augmented before strong conclusions can be drawn. Several micro-credit institutions combine credit with health, education, or other programmes. Studying such programmes in Honduras and Ecuador, Smith (2002) finds evidence that, for both countries, health bank participation significantly raises subsequent healthcare over credit only participation, and at least reduces the tendency to switch from breast-feeding to bottle-feeding as income rises. Given these results, the author concludes that tie-ins cannot be dismissed as unproductive interference.

## 4. Global Experiences in Successful Microfinance Programmes: Some illustrations

Microcredit is the most well-known aspect of microfinance and has been able to spread rapidly around the globe because variable quality of institutions offers little financial downside for clients. However managing this expansion of credit services, and building upon it to offer other products like savings and insurance, has been approached very differently by countries around the world. If a microfinance institution is mismanaged, or goes bankrupt, the customer's situation is left unchanged. Products like savings, pensions, and insurance for the poor have been less welcomed by regulators and the traditional financial sector because of the added responsibilities of such products. Micro-Finance institutions who offer such products must be subject to prudential regulation to insure their solvency so that customer deposits or other obligations are not lost, damaging the financial situation of the client. In this section we will briefly view the development, structure, and result of four approaches from Bolivia, Cambodia, Bangladesh and the Philippines.

### 4.1 Bolivia

The development, implementation, and impact of Bolivia's microfinance regulatory reform in the 1990s have made it one of the most successful microfinance sectors in the world. Savings, money transfers, and insurance products were slower to develop due to the difficulty of modifying these products for the poor. An early failed foray by Bancosol into savings mobilization further reinforced the image of savings as a difficult product to offer and delayed its uptake by another few years. Bancosol expanded too aggressively its deposit service throughout its branches before its MIS was fully capable of handling substantial volume. The system collapsed, causing delays of days in savings withdrawals, which in turn led to long lines of upset clients attempting to pull their savings back out. Regulation followed the development of the industry, and very much responded to the need of leading institutions to become regulated to broaden their funding base. At the time of their approval, most of the non-profits were performing at a level where their financial results met or exceeded those in the commercial banking sector. The regulated MFIs have grown while the unregulated have been starved for lending funds. The regulation of a large segment of the microfinance industry has excluded those that have not chosen to transform from large sources of funding. As a result, the unregulated sector has not grown in its overall number of clients and has shrunk in it relative market share. The Bolivians believe that the substantial cost involved in the transformation process has been necessary to ensure that the transformed entities became solid participants in a revitalized financial sector.

### 4.2 Cambodia

The Government of Cambodia's primary policy instrument for enabling the development of inclusive financial service has been the regulatory and supervisory regime of the National Bank of Cambodia (NBC). The NBC engaged the emerging microfinance industry in its early stages and has continually adapted the regime to enable the development of the institutions and their integration into the formal financial system.

In 2000, the NBC issued regulation that created two ways for non-profit credit organizations to be formally associated with the NBC. Organizations that are structured legally as a limited liability company or a cooperative, and have US$ 60,000 in capital, are eligible for an MFI license, and then subject to regulation, reporting requirements, and off- and on-site supervision. Alternatively, organizations can register with the NBC, though with a more limited operating mandate. In 2007, the NBC issued regulations that created the Micro-Finance Deposit Taking Institution license. This allowed licensed MFIs with a minimum capital of US$ 2.4 million, and meeting other requirements, to collect savings and fixed deposits. These specialized microfinance licenses complement the existing tiers in the banking system, which are also accessible to microfinance organizations that grow to the point of qualifying for the requirements.

The Rural Credit Specialized Bank also has a minimum capital requirement of US$ 2.4 million. These "narrow bank" options are particularly important as the minimum capital for a full commercial banking license will be raised to US$ 36 million in 2010 to encourage a consolidation of the banking system.

In addition to the tiered licensing regime, the NBC has also issued regulation that aligns regulations and supervision with international best practice for related to microfinance operations (e.g. loan classification and loss provisioning). At the end of 2009, the Cambodian microfinance sector consisted of one commercial bank, two newly licensed Micro-Finance Deposit Taking Institutions, 16 licensed Micro-Finance Institutions, and 26 registered rural credit operators. The evolution of the sector has been well guided by the commitment of the National Bank of Cambodia to continually employ its regulations and supervision capacity to support a deepening of the financial market.

### 4.3 Bangladesh

The microfinance sector in Bangladesh is regulated by the MRA, which requires a microfinance institution to acquire a license in order to operate. MFIs with licenses are expected to have better access to all the stakeholders, especially the providers of funds including donors and financial institutions.

A report (MRA, 2010) prepared by the MRA found that MFIs can now run their operations from their own and locally borrowed financial resources. According to the latest available data about 70 percent of their fund comes from clients' savings (40%) and capital fund and reserves (27%). Dependence on donor funds has shrunk to only 5 percent. MFIs are now able to integrate themselves more with the formal sector. More than 25 percent of their resource requirement comes from borrowing from the commercial banks. Microcredit Regulatory Authority (MRA) has conducted a research on the impact of introduction of licensing system. The findings of that research (Nuruzzaman, 2010) show that licensing MFIs in Bangladesh has two-fold impacts, first on Beneficiaries of MFIs and second on MFI itself as explained below:

*Impact on Beneficiaries of MFIs*

- Licensing exerts positive influence on beneficiaries in building their confidence on MFIs.
- Savings of the beneficiaries of the licensed-MFIs increased at a higher rate than that of unlicensed ones.

*Impact on Micro-Finance Institutions*

- Licensed MFIs could increase their coverage at a higher pace.
- Annual income of the licensed-MFIs became significantly higher than that of unlicensed-MFIs.
- Small licensed-MFIs' capital growth rate are higher than that of small non-licensed MFIs during 2005-2009. The average capital of licensed MFIs became 5 to 10 times higher than the non-licensed MFIs.
- Positive profits during the period were received by licensed-MFIs. However, among the licensed-MFIs, operating profits of medium and small organizations recorded increases while the big organizations faced declines.

Another research (Khan et al., 2010) conducted by MRA found robust positive impact of licensing on both credit expansion and savings mobilization by the MFIs. In the pursuit of attaining coverage the very big and big MFIs were more successful, while small MFIs dwindled.

### 4.4 Philippines

The policies and regulatory framework for microfinance established in the Philippines have just begun to have an impact on the sector. A capitalized entity intended to act as an ally to MFIs called the PCFC was created since commercial banks were reluctant to lend directly to micro-enterprises due to perceived costs and risks of micro-credit. This lead to the development of a microfinance-focused regulatory framework which now permits NGO MFIs to mobilize savings deposits structure lending in a way that would allow MFIs to better attract funding. The new regulation also created licensing of new thrift banks, rural banks, and cooperative banks. The regulator opened the opportunity for NGO MFIs to transform into formal banking institutions and for existing banks to establish new thrift or rural banks. Although microfinance banks still comprise a small portion of the banking system, the entry into microfinance by rural banks, thrift banks, and coop banks is significant for constituting the start of microfinance mainstreaming and commercialization. To encourage the expansion of microfinance services and integration of the microfinance sector into the financial system, wholesale and sub-wholesale loans of regular commercial and thrift banks to microfinance institutions are eligible for compliance with priority-sector credit quotas. Moreover, the regulator has opened its rediscounting window for the refinancing of eligible microfinance loans. Two of the major end-results are (a) government has been able to keep its involvement in microfinance and priority-sector credits to a minimum and on an indirect basis, and (b) microfinance continues to develop and grow, while remaining a principally private-sector activity.

The timeline for development of regulated microfinance in the Philippines stretches over a period of some 8 years, from 1993 through 2001. Micro-Finance was integrated into the regulated formal financial system through existing laws, without having to enact a specialized microfinance regulatory framework. It is also important to point out that dialogue and consensus building included microfinance practitioners and institutions, umbrella organizations for the Rural Banks and Thrift Banks, as well as key officials from government financial policy agencies. Some of the key results in microfinance are the following:

- When the Rural Micro-enterprise Finance Project was completed at the end of 2002, 618,906 clients had been reached, of which 97 percent were women. In June 2006, when the survey design was being formulated, the records of the People's Credit and Finance Corporation showed that the programme had served 1.6 million borrowers.
- The average loan size of sample borrowers was $106 or about 7 percent of per capita gross domestic product (GDP). Microfinance borrowers from NGOs had lower average loan sizes ($68); those borrowing from cooperatives had a higher average loan size ($106). Borrowers from banks were in the middle range ($84). These figures suggest that NGOs tend to reach deeper in outreach than regulated institutions such as banks and cooperatives.
- The survey results show that existing respondent clients have, on average, been in the programme for 75 months (about 6 years and 3 months). They have, on average, cumulatively borrowed P70,000 in loans and are on their 7th loan cycle. Of the existing clients, 9 percent are problem clients while 2 percent are graduates.

In essence, the survey results indicated that the majority of the existing clients, new clients, and nonparticipating households deemed to be qualified for the programme were not poor according to the official definition of poverty. This is in contrast to the other studies, which found that most of the microfinance programme clients were poor. Khandker (2003), for instance, found that 90 percent of the microfinance program participants in Bangladesh in the 1991/1992 survey and 70 percent in the 1998/1999 survey were poor. Montgomery (2005) found that 70 percent of the microfinance clients of Khushhali Bank in Pakistan are poor. Given these findings, there may be a need to reexamine the targeting approach of the microfinance implementers in the Philippines.

### 4.5 Uzbekistan

Micro-credit programmes in Uzbekistan were initiated by the United Nations Development Programme (UNDP) in 1998 through the implementation of two pilot projects in Kashkadarya and Karakalpakistan. Those projects supported the establishment of three non-governmental microfinance institutions. The main goals of the projects were to expand access to financial resources for the low-income groups, and to assist them in trade, small-scale production and micro-businesses based on family assets. Those projects led to the adoption of national legislation "On Measures for the Development of Microfinance in the Republic of Uzbekistan" (Decree #309, August 2002).

Currently, commercial banks, savings and credit unions, non-government microfinance institutions, credit lines of off-budget funds (such as the Dehkan and Farming Entities Support Fund, the State Employment Fund) and international financial institutions (EBRD, ADB) provide microfinance services. Interest rates and amounts of credit vary considerably depending on the type of financial institutions dealing with micro-credits. Commercial banks offer micro-credit of about $2,500 to $3,000, whereas credit unions provide not much more than $1,000. Such advantages as low interest-rate, opportunity to obtain credits in cash, generous timeframes and a long grace period characterize micro-credits from off-budget funds. Activities of credit unions focus on the more affluent clients. The non-banking sector, represented by NGO-Microfinance institutions, mainly functions on donor financing. Although the prime cost of credit funds is zero or almost zero, NGO-Microfinance institutions' charge relatively high interest rates (4-6.5% per month). Generally, interest income and donor grants limit the volume of their loan capital and expanding microfinance activity. If they gain access to diversified financial sources, they can lower their interest rates.

Overall, microfinance in Uzbekistan consists mainly of micro-credits. Microfinance institutions across the country cover only 9 percent of the demand. Therefore, a huge market exists for new microfinance institutions in Uzbekistan. The NGO-Microfinance institution model increases the potential of microfinance in Uzbekistan—especially, in easing the access of poor groups to micro-credits. Unlike commercial banks and credit unions, NGO-Microfinance institutions influence the employment and incomes of the poorest people. In practice, NGO-Microfinance institution micro-credits remain accessible equally in cities and farming communities and thus can help reduce social divisions between rural and urban communities, as well as lower the pressures for migration toward urban areas or abroad.

## 5. Impact of Microfinance in South Asia, Latin America and the Caribbean

The microfinance movement has changed perceptions towards helping the poor in both, South Asia and Latin America. In many countries, microfinance has been used as a tool to increase financial depth in rural areas and it has typically targeted very low-income groups who would normally be excluded by conventional financial institutions (Weiss and Montgomery, 2004). There is extensive literature on the range of institutional arrangements employed by different countries, the types of services microfinance institutions (MFIs) provide and the extent of outreach. However, there is agreement amongst the academic development community about the fact that we still know very little about the impact of micro-credit (Weiss and Montgomery, 2004). The overall consensus concerning the extent of what we currently know about microfinance was bluntly expressed in the following statement: MFI field operations have far surpassed the research capacity to analyze them, so excitement about the use of microfinance for poverty alleviation is not backed up with sound facts derived from rigorous research. Given the current state of knowledge, it is difficult to allocate confidently the public resources to microfinance development programmes (Zeller and Meyer, 2002).

Microfinance used to be known as micro-credit. Micro-credit refers to the practice of issuing small loans without additional services. Today, since micro-credit is offered along with a range of other services, the term microcredit has been replaced with the term microfinance. Throughout this dissertation, the terms micro-credit and microfinance are used interchangeably to describe loans and services provided by MFIs.

The issue of micro-credit became prevalent in the 1980s, although an early experiment of this lending scheme dates back 30 years ago in Brazil, Bangladesh and a few other countries (*ibid.*). Micro-credit came about from the need to provide the very poor access to credit without the collateral requirements typically imposed by the formal banking sector. In this context, micro-credit has focused on clients whose alternative sources of credit have typically been in the informal sector where they are subject to violence and abuse by moneylenders. Micro-credit is loaned to a micro-entrepreneur by a bank or other institution and is often offered without requiring collateral from a group or an individual. Some of the main characteristics of the micro-credit lending model include the following:

*Group lending*: This type of lending scheme is also known as solidarity group lending or village banking and it is a self-monitoring mechanism that allows individuals to gain access to micro-credit by securing collateral through group savings or guaranteeing a loan through a group repayment pledge. In this lending model, the incentive to repay is based upon peer pressure. If a group member defaults, the other group members make up the payment amount.

*Individual lending*: This type of lending practice focuses on providing micro-credit to one client at a time and does not require collateral or a guarantee for the loan. Many micro-credit loans are working capital loans used by the borrower to purchase additional inventory for their business, such as flour for the food entrepreneur or to acquire equipment. Over time, the issue of micro-credit has expanded to the provision of other financial services not available to poor borrowers in the informal sector. Microfinance has attempted to meet the needs of poor borrowers by offering many services such as loans, savings, transfer services (remittances), insurance, education and skill training. Many financial institutions can provide these services, including non-governmental organizations (NGOs), cooperatives, credit unions, private commercial banks, non-bank financial institutions and some state-owned banks. In many countries, microfinance programmes lend predominately to poor women who are self-employed in the informal sector. In the Grameen Bank in Bangladesh, for instance, 97 percent of their seven million borrowers are women. One of the reasons for focusing on providing credit to women is that women are believed to be poorer and more credit constrained than men (Burjorjee et al., 2002). In this context, microfinance has been used as a tool to provide access to financial services to women as well as a way to help them become entrepreneurs, empower them, induce higher levels of mobility and increase political participation (Hashemi et al., 1996).

### *5.1 Impact of Microfinance in Latin America and the Caribbean*

Latin American MFIs have had tremendous success in expanding financial services to underserved groups. Since the late 1980s, microfinance clients have been growing to make Latin America one of the largest providers of microfinance in the world along with South East Asia. Through MFIs, financial services are currently available to nearly six million low income borrowing households in Latin America and the Caribbean (LAC) (Navajas and Tejerina, 2006). Microfinance lending in LAC ranges in design and structure. There are non-regulated MFIs that focus lending predominately in less urbanized areas. NGOs continue to be the most significant source of non-regulated microfinance. On the other side of the regulation spectrum, in countries like Peru, Bolivia and Honduras, we find MFIs that are specialized non-bank charters. Such non-bank institutions are regulated financial institutions that are required to comply with the regulations put in place by the designated financial authority. The main difference between these institutions and a full service bank is typically lower capital requirements and a limited scope of services provided (Navajas and Tejerina, 2006). In LAC, the provision of microfinance by commercial banks has become a common trend. For some banks like MiBanco in Peru and ProCredit in Ecuador, their primary line of business is microfinance. Other banks such as BanHcafe in Honduras, Banco Pichinca in Ecuador and Banco Santander in Chile are adopting microfinance as a new product (Westley, 2006). Table 4 shows some of the trends in microfinance and the extent of coverage over time.

Apparent in Table 4 is the increase in the number of clients served by MFIs. By the year 2005, MFIs in LAC had nearly six million clients and an outstanding portfolio of over US$5.4 billion. According to Navajas and Tejerina (2006), the estimates in their study do not include the number of clients with access to remittances, deposits, payment services and other financial services. The estimates are also not adjusted for borrowers with multiple loans at a given time.

**Table 4:** MFIs in Latin America and the Caribbean, 2005 and 2001

| Type of Institution | Number of Institution | Portfolio (US$ Million) | Borrowers | Average Loan (US$) |
|---|---|---|---|---|
| Data from 2005 (23 countries) | | | | |
| Regulated MFIs | 98 | 4,407 | 3,851 | 1,144 |
| Downscale (Banks and Financieras)[a] | 31 | 1,810 | 1,233,873 | 1,467 |
| Greenfields[b] | 30 | 1,005 | 738,671 | 1,361 |
| Upgrades[c] | 37 | 1,592 | 1,879,221 | 847 |
| Non-regulated MFIs | 238 | 1,030 | 2,100,951 | 490 |
| All MFIs-2005 | 336 | 5,437 | 5,952,713 | 913 |
| Data from 2001 (17 countries) | | | | |
| Regulated MFIs | 60 | 901 | 936.936 | 962 |
| Downscale (Bank and Financieras)[a] | 21 | 343 | 365,171 | 936 |
| Upgrades[c] | 39 | 558 | 571,765 | 976 |
| Non-regulated MFIs | 124 | 288 | 869,509 | 332 |
| All MFIs-2001 | 184 | 1,189 | 1,806,45 | 659 |

a Downscales: regulated financial institutions that added microcredit as a new line of business.

b Greefields: MFIs that started operating as regulated financial institutions since their inception.

c Upgrades: NGOs that have transformed themselves into regulated financial institutions.

*Source*: Navajas and Tejerina, 2006.

Another important trend is the fact that regulated MFIs have a significant market share in micro-lending. In 2001 52 percent of microfinance clients were served by regulated MFIs and this percent increased to 65 percent by 2005. According to Navajas and Tejerina (2006), the annual growth rate for the number of borrowers is 35 percent annually and 46 percent for the growth in portfolio.

Table 5 shows the magnitude of microfinance coverage in the LAC region. The countries are listed according to the number clients they have. Mexico ranks at the top and Peru, Columbia and Bolivia follow with well-established microfinance markets.

**Table 5:** Microfinance in Latin America and the Caribbean (circa 2005)

| Country | Number of MFIs | Portfolio (US$ Millions) | Borrowers | Average Loans (US$) |
|---|---|---|---|---|
| Mexico | 39 | 471 | 1,217,920 | 387 |
| Peru | 67 | 1,516 | 1,174,361 | 1,291 |
| Columbia | 22 | 315 | 608,282 | 518 |
| Bolivia | 21 | 635 | 548,242 | 1,158 |
| Nicaragua | 21 | 261 | 399,614 | 652 |
| Guatemala | 21 | 273 | 363,286 | 753 |
| Ecuador | 20 | 322 | 327,065 | 985 |
| Chile | 5 | 663 | 297,995 | 2,223 |
| Brazil | 16 | 91 | 289,697 | 313 |
| Dominican Republic | 13 | 158 | 145,332 | 1,087 |
| El Salvador | 11 | 138 | 143,461 | 964 |
| Honduras | 14 | 80 | 143,118 | 560 |
| Haiti | 9 | 24 | 81,222 | 374 |
| Paraguay | 5 | 71 | 59,936 | 1,193 |
| Costa Rice | 19 | 341 | 45,607 | 7,469 |
| Venezuela | 5 | 37 | 44,969 | 816 |
| Panama | 6 | 16 | 28,103 | 552 |
| Uruguay | 3 | 10 | 7,155 | 1,422 |
| Argentina | 10 | 4 | 10,649 | 402 |
| Jamaica | 3 | 4 | 10,401 | 376 |
| Guyana | 1 | 2 | 4,184 | 413 |
| Trinidad | 1 | 3 | 1,733 | 1,500 |
| Barbados | 1 | 4 | 384 | 9,446 |
| Total | 336 | 5,437 | 5,952,716 | 913 |

*Source*: Navajas and Tejerina, 2006.

An interesting aspect of the microfinance market in LAC is that the countries are different in the number of MFIs they have and the average loan size. Peru for instance, does not have as many borrowers as Mexico but it outranks Mexico in both the number of MFIs and the average size of the loans disbursed. Costa Rica does not rank at the top in the number of borrowers, but it does rank second to Barbados in the average size of the loans its MFIs provide.

### *5.2 Impact of Microfinance in South Asia*

The number of MFIs serving the South Asian region varies from country to country. There are many factors that contribute to the extent of coverage of MFIs in the South Asian microfinance sector. Such factors include the modes of delivery mechanism by which credit is disbursed, the extent of competition and institutional frameworks as well as the historical context of the country. Some countries have a very mature market and low barriers to entry and this has contributed to the significant growth of MFIs in these countries (Alamgir, 2009). As illustrated in Table 6, Bangladesh is a good example of a market where microfinance has penetrated to a significant extent. Currently, there are 518 NGO-MFIs registered with the recently established Microcredit Regulatory Authority (MRA) and there are a number of unregulated MFIs throughout the country.

**Table 6:** Number of MFI Branches by South Asian Countries

| Country | Number of Branches | Number of Branches per 100 Sq Km Land Area | Average Annual Growth between 2006 and 2008 |
|---|---|---|---|
| Afghanistan | 283 | 0.43 | 6% |
| Bangladesh | 14,441 | 110.94 | 5% |
| Nepal | 590 | 4.13 | 12% |
| Pakistan | 1,281 | 1.88 | 12% |
| Sri Lanka | 1,465 | 22.67 | 1% |

*Source*: Microfinance Institute, Overview Report 2010. See MRA at www.mra.gov.bd. Accessed on January 2011.

Although Bangladesh and Sri Lanka have a more mature microfinance sector in terms of coverage, all of the South Asian countries have experienced growth in their respective microfinance sector. According to the data presented in Table 6, Nepal and Pakistan have experienced the largest growth from 2006 to 2008. In Table 4 we can see the extent of microfinance coverage in South Asia in terms of the number of borrowers each country had as of 2007. Sri Lanka and Bangladesh are by far the largest hosts of microfinance schemes. An interesting number to look at is the growth rate in coverage from 2006-2007. Pakistan and Afghanistan display a tremendous growth in microfinance over this period. In the case of Pakistan a significant driver in the increase of microfinance has been the effort of the Pakistan Poverty Alleviation Fund (PPAF) to alleviate poverty. In addition, the government of Pakistan established the Khushali Bank to provide financial services to the underserved population. In Afghanistan, the country has adopted microfinance as a tool to alleviate poverty and to facilitate the process of democratization in the country (Alamgir, 2010).

## 6. Socio-economic Impact of Microfinance: A Review of Literature

Various aspects of microfinance and micro-enterprises have been discussed in the literature. Few empirical studies have quantified the impact of microfinance on poverty, some have focused on the relation between microfinance and socio-economic indicators, few concentrated on the sustainability and profitability, and few others estimated the return to capital invested in the micro-enterprises (Shirazi, 2008). Microfinance surely bring some changes, which could be positive or negative on individuals, households and institutions (Cheston et al., 1999 and Baker, 2000). Some studies have been focused on the growth of income and expenditures of the borrowers due to microfinance. Hulme and Mosley (1996), for instance, based on the counter factual combined approach, analyzed the impact of microfinance on poverty alleviation using sample data for Indonesia, India, Bangladesh and Sri Lanka and found that growth of income of borrowers always exceeds that of control group and the increase was larger for better-off borrowers.

Similarly, Nelly et al. (1996) found positive benefits for the borrowers. Khandker (1998), based on double difference comparison between eligible and ineligible households and between programme and control villages, focusing on Grameen, Bangladesh and Bangladesh Rural Advancement Committee (BRAC), found that micro-credit alleviated poverty up to 5 percent annually. Furthermore, it was found, that a loan of 100 Taka to a female borrower, after it is repaid, allows a net consumption increase of 18 Taka. For Thailand village banks, Coleman (1999), using the same approach as that of Khandker (1998), found no evidence of any impact of microfinance. Another study by Coleman (2004), found that programmes are not reaching the poor as much as they reach relatively wealthy people. Khandker (2003), found that microfinance helps to reduce extreme poverty much more than moderate poverty i.e. 18 percentage points as compared with 8.5 percentage points over seven years. Welfare impact is also positive for all households, including nonparticipants, as there were spillover effects.

Swain (2004) examines empirical evidence from literature to see the goodness of microfinance as a good poverty alleviation strategy. The evidence shows that microfinance influence is much felt by households at the brink of poverty line, instead of the core poor. Microfinance also reduces vulnerability and smoothing consumption of poor households. Navajas et al. (2000) examine the coverage of five MFIs in Bolivia and discover that majority of the borrowers were close to the poverty line. They also find that group lenders had more depth of outreach than individual lenders, urban poorest were more likely borrowers and rural borrowers were among the poorest of all clients. Also, Servon (1997) studies three MFIs in the US and finds that they served those at the margin of the mainstream economy, not the very poor. Barnes et al. (2001) examining MFI in Uganda found positive impact on enterprise level, increased in assets and net revenue, reduced financial vulnerability and increased value, skill and education. However, Schreiner (1999) finds that microfinance is not an effective tool for poverty reduction in US because of weak social cohesion, though it may move more people from welfare to self-employment. Mosley (2001), using data from Latin American countries, found a positive growth of income and assets of the borrowers than control group. The growth of income of the better-off borrowers was larger. However, he could not find any evidence of impact of microfinance on extreme poverty. Banegas et al. (2002), employing Logit model, found positive impact on the income of borrowers. Gallup Pakistan (2005), using counter factual, combined approach, found positive impact of PPAF microfinance on the consumption, income and assets of the borrowers. Shirazi and Khan (2009) employed Counter-factual "Combined approach" and found that Micro-credit has reduced the poverty about 3 percentage points on average in Pakistan during 2003/4-2004/5. Waqar et al. (2008), estimated the long-term effect of credit on growth and poverty in Pakistan, found out that agricultural credit has a positive impact on the Gross Domestic Product and its effect was more pronounced on the Agriculture GDP. Furthermore impact of agricultural credit in reducing poverty was significant both in the short run and long run Montgomery (2005) found a positive impact of Khushhali Bank of Pakistan microfinance lending on the income, empowerment, health and education of the poor. However, he did not find any impact on consumption expenditure of the very poor. His study, in general, shows that even poorest of the poor benefited from the Khushhali Bank's microfinance programme.

Saboor et al. (2009) estimated the impact of credit on the income and production level of small farmers using a randomly collected data from Rawalpindi District in Pakistan. The study reveals that for small farmers, credit was not a profiting activity. However, all respondents argued that their expenditures were increasing and they concluded that the credit system should further be improved so that the full benefits could be reaped both in the crop and livestock sectors and miss-utilization of credit by farmers could be minimized. Arif (2006) reviewed poverty reduction programmes in Pakistan. He found that various criterion have been used for targeting the poor by different organizations. His review portrays that microfinance organizations use a loose criterion to identify poor and non-poor households. He further pointed out that "evidence on the targeting efficiency of microfinance is slim". Shirazi (2008) estimated that micro-credit has increased the return to investment of the borrowers. In his study, using Pakistan Gallup data, 2005, he found that micro-credit has increased the returns to investment of 79 percent of the borrowers in the range of 15 to 89 percent per year. Furthermore, the average weighted rate of return to investment was 4.57 percent per month or uncompounded rate of 54.89 per year. He found that female borrowers were making more return than their male counterparts.

Few studies, which have been summarized in Rahman (2004), have focused on the impact of micro-credit on employment and increase in income and expenditure of the borrowers in Bangladesh. Results of these studies show that income of the recipients of micro-credit has increased in the range of 8-40 percent. Micro-credit has been successful in creating a positive impact on employment. Furthermore, Studies show that micro-credit has positively contributed to the social investment, school enrolment, social empowerment, girls schooling and women's non-land asset. Some studies (Choudhury and Bhuiya, 2001; Barnes et al., 2001; Chen and Snodgrass, 2001) have identified significant positive effects of microfinance on the human resource development among the participants in various countries. Chowdry and Alam (2007) found that the participation of a household in the micro-credit programme of the Grameen Bank increases consumption of that household significantly. However, there is non-linearity in the increasing trend in consumption of participating households. The consumption level goes up gradually with the increase in the membership duration up to five years of membership, but the growth rate starts declining after that period of membership. Similarly Naveed (1994), Amin et al. (1998) and Hashemi et al. (1996) found positive impact of microfinance on the women empowerment and welfare. Many impact studies have been made on Grameen bank from different perspectives, which conclude that Grameen Bank's members have been better off in terms of wide range of economic and social indicators including increased income, improved nutrition, better food intake, better consumption on clothing, better housing, lower child mortality, lower birth rate, higher adoption of family-planning practices, better health care, better access to education for the children, empowerment of women participation in social and political activities (Yunus, 2004).

Literature also highlight the beneficial role of microfinance for the poor by smoothing their consumption expenditure, increasing income and savings and diversify their income sources (Dichter, 1999; Panjaitan et al., 1999; Remenyi and Quinones Jr., 2000; Morduch, 1998, Khandker, 2003; McKerman, 2002 and Simonwitz, 2002). Wydick (1999) examining the effect of micro-enterprise lending on child schooling in Guatemala using logistic regression found that access to credit increases the schooling investment on child and reduces the likelihood of withdrawing children from school to provide family labour. Although the main objective of the microfinance is to make the funds available for investment in micro-enterprises and thus lift the poor people out from poverty and promoting growth, Dichter (2007) casts doubt and says that "recent experience and the economic history of rich countries, however, suggest that these expectations are unrealistic. Most people, poor or otherwise, are not entrepreneurs, so there is little reason to think that mass credit would in general lead to viable business start-ups." Also not all lending programmes have been successful. Fifty branches of two major MFIs in Krishna district were closed down by the authorities in Andhra Pradesh as a result of allegation of charging interest and forced loan recovery (Shylendra, 2006). Credit at certain time may be disempowering, leading to increase tension within the family (Goetz and Sen Gupta, 1996). Researchers have found borrowers starving themselves to meet repayments and sometimes experienced the disgrace of losing their asset as collateral and loss of self-pride and even sleep as a result of worry on finding money to meet next installment (Copestake, 2002, 2007). Researchers have also queried group lending. Group lending can be costly to implement, with high default rate, insufficient number of borrowers in a group and perpetual reliance on subsidies (Bhatt and Tang, 2001).

### *6.1 Impact of Microfinance on Social Performance*

Based on the comprehensive literature review, the suggested definition of social performance in the context of microfinance may be summarized at the outset as follows (Table 7):

**Table 7:** Economic and Social Performances and Impact for MFIs

| | | Core social issues | Economic/Financial issues |
|---|---|---|---|
| Global performance of the institution | Performance monitoring (intentions and actions of the MFI) | – Outreach to the poor and excluded: who are the clients?<br>– Adaptation of the services and products to the target clients<br>– Social and political capital of the clients/ Empowerment: participation in MFI decision making; "voice" for those being served to avoid "mission drift"<br>– Social responsibility of the MFI: relation with client and community | – Portfolio quality<br>– Efficacy and productivity<br>– Financial management<br>– Profitability<br>– Qualilty and diversity of the financial services offered |
| | Impact assessment (outcome) | – Employment creation for the excluded population<br>– Empowerment: position of individuals in their family and communities; social capital building<br>– Health improvement<br>– Child education, etc. | – Change in income and expenditure<br>– Change in assets and living standard<br>– Food security<br>– Employment creation at community level |

One can distinguish four major dimensions of social performance as follows:

1. *Outreach to the Poor and Excluded*: *Mission and Targeting Strategies*. MFI have generally been developed to reach a population excluded from the classical financial system. MFIs can have the objective of reaching socially excluded populations or the poor, or simply to offer financial services in a region where classical banking systems are absent. The depth of outreach of the MFI can be measured to evaluate its focus on the economically and socially excluded population.

2. *Adaptation of the services and products to the target clients.* It is not enough to decide to reach a target population. The MFI must learn about the target population and work on the design of its financial services so that they can fit with the needs and the constraints of the clients. "Pro-poor" services are too often standardized. Social performance indicators can analyse the process leading to service definition and the extent to which the MFI knows about its clients' needs.
3. *Improving social and political capital of clients and communities.* For the MFI, trust between the MFI and the clients can reduce the transaction costs and improve repayment rates. It thus can foster collective action and reduce free-riding, opportunistic behaviour, and reduce risks. For the clients, strengthening their social and political capital can enhance their social organization (collective action, information sharing, political lobbying, etc.). Social performance indicators should measure the degree of transparency, the effort of the MFI towards giving voice to its clients within the organization and beyond (community, local government, national government, etc.).
4. *Social responsibility of MFI.* Social awareness is a necessary pre-requisite for socially responsible corporate behaviour. Social responsibility requires an adaptation of the MFI corporate culture to their cultural and socio-economic context, an adequate human resource policy, credit guarantees adapted to the local conditions, and balanced relationships between staff and clients (in particular in MFIs where there are elected clients who participate in decision-making).

Social performances of an MFI rely on these four dimensions. Poverty outreach, shaded in Table 7, is one among the different dimensions of social performances. An MFI can choose to focus on one or several dimensions but for a global overview, social performance cannot be reduced to poverty outreach. Within these dimensions, several sub-dimensions can be distinguished, and a number of questions can be generated for each sub-dimension. Each question is measured by an operational indicator.

## 7. Evidence for a Microfinance Impacting Poverty Reduction: Some Snapshots

### *7.1 Khandker, Shahid (2001), Does Microfinance really benefit the Poor? Evidence from Bangladesh, Paper delivered at Asia and Pacific Forum on Poverty: Reforming Policies and Institutions for Poverty Reduction held by the Asian Development Bank, Manila*

A follow-up survey done in 1998/1999 included the households from the previous survey (1991/1992—on which the conclusions in the book Fighting Poverty with Microcredit: Experience in Bangladesh are based), new households from the same villages, new households from new villages in old thanas, and three more thanas are surveyed. The drop-out rate increased from 5 percent to 10 percent from 91/92 to 98/99.

"Microfinance participants do better than non-participants in both 91/92 and 98/99 in per capita income, per capita expenditure, and household net worth. The incidence of poverty among participating households is lower in 98/99 than in 91/92 and lower than among nonparticipating households in both periods." "The programmes have spillover effects on the local economy, but the impacts are very small."

### *7.2 Pitt, Mark M., Shahidur R. Khandker, Omar Haider Chowdhury and Daniel Millimet; Credit Programs for the Poor and the Health Status of Children in Rural Bangladesh. International Economic Review*

"...we find that women's credit has a large and statistically significant impact on two of three measures of the health of both boy and girl children. Credit provided (to) men has no statistically significant impact.... A 10 percent increase in (latent) credit provided to females' increases the arm circumference of their daughters by 6.3 percent, twice the increase that would be expected from a similar proportionate increase in credit provided to men. Female credit also has a significant, positive but somewhat smaller effect on the arm circumference of sons. Female credit is estimated to have large, positive and statistically significant effects on the height-forage of both boys and girls." No statistically significant effects were found for Body Mass Index (BMI).

### *7.3 McCulloch, Neil and Bob Baulch (2000), Simulating the Impact of Policy upon Chronic and Transitory Poverty in Rural Pakistan, Journal of Development Studies, 36 (6)*

Is poverty static? Anti-poverty programmes often assume so. Recent studies suggest, however, that poor households move in and out of poverty a great deal. Research from the UK Institute of Development Studies shows that poverty has two parts: a chronic part and a transitory part. The researchers therefore examined the impact of two different types of policy—those designed to smooth out incomes and those designed to promote income growth—on the extent of transitory and chronic poverty in rural Pakistan. The study suggests that policies which help households to smooth income can dramatically reduce transitory poverty. But in the long-term, only large and sustained growth in household incomes will reduce chronic poverty.

The results of applying different measures of transitory and chronic poverty to the income data suggest that 68 percent of total poverty is transitory, arising from variations in households' incomes. Implications for anti-poverty policy include:

- Enhancing the ability to smooth out income fluctuations could lead to large reductions in overall poverty in the short-term.
- Possible interventions could include provision of micro-credit, seasonal public works, crop insurance and food price stabilization schemes.
- Reduction in chronic poverty will still require improvements in the human and physical capital of the poor. Improving education, particularly of the household head, reduces poverty since it can help people formulate effective strategies for income generation.

### 7.4 Wright, Graham A.N. (2000), Microfinance Systems: Designing Quality Financial Services for the Poor. Zed Books Ltd. London & New York, and the University Press Limited, Dhaka

Wright provides a comprehensive review of the research to date looking at the case for providing appropriate, quality financial services for the poor, and outlining the principles and methods that could/should be followed to design quality Microfinance Systems. Economic impact of Micro-credit was recorded as:

- Hossain (1988) and Kamal (1996): "Grameen Bank members had incomes about 43 percent higher than the target group in the control villages, and about 28 percent higher than the target group nonparticipants in the project villages".
- World Bank in collaboration with the Bangladesh Institute of Development Studies, and cited by Hashemi Morshed (1997) showed that the Grameen Bank not only "reduced poverty and improved welfare of participating households but also enhanced the household's capacity to sustain their gains over time".
- Chowdhury et al. (1991) "asserted that women (and men) participating in BRAC sponsored activities have more income (both in terms of amount and source), own more assets and are more often gainfully-employed than non-participants".
- Mustafa and Ara et al. (1996) confirmed this (above for BRAC) and noted that "members have better coping capacities in lean seasons and that these increased with length of membership and amount of credit received".
- Mustafa Ara et al. (1996) also noted an increase in assets of 112 percent for those who had been members for 48 months or more and increase in household expenditure of 28 percent.

Schuler and Hashemi (1994) concluded that Grameen Bank members were statistically more likely to be using contraceptives (59 percent of Grameen members as opposed to 43 percent of a matched control group). Similarly, a recent Asian Development Bank report noted that, "Contraceptive use goes up among members because they are better able to overcome the barriers to obtaining access to contraceptive services (lack of mobility, cash, information, among others). Contraceptive use goes up among non-members because of the diffusion effect of changing fertility norms in the village as a whole." Nutritional indicators also seem to improve where Microfinance institutions have been working. Hashemi and Morshed (1997) cite a study conducted by the World Bank in collaboration with the Bangladesh Institute of Development Studies, which showed that the Grameen Bank not only 'reduced poverty and improved the welfare of participating households, but also enhanced the household's capacity to sustain their gains over time. This was accompanied by an increased caloric intake and better nutritional status of children in households of Grameen Bank participants.'"

"Todd (1996) worked with Grameen members who had been borrowing for a decade in Tangail. They concluded: 'Perhaps their most significant finding was that, compared with 18 percent of non-members, 58 percent of the Grameen borrowers had crossed over the extreme poverty line (defined by an annual income sufficient to provide each family member with a daily intake of 1,800 calories). Of the 42 percent of the Grameen borrowers who failed to cross the poverty line, fully 60 percent had experienced a serious illness in the family—most commonly tuberculosis, typhoid, jaundice, and gastric ulcer. Grameen loans prevented these families from becoming destitute, but they were insufficient to overcome their crises' (Bornstein, 1996)." "One important initiative should indeed begin to help us to understand these issues better. In the Comilla District in Bangladesh, BRAC and ICDDRB are working together to use ICDDRB's unique Matlab research infrastructure to examine the effects of different interventions on the population's well-being. Nonetheless, since BRAC's RDP programme includes several interventions not commonly associated with 'minimalist' Microfinance programmes—for example adult functional education...the research design is still lacking a pure Microfinance intervention. Chowdhury and Bhuiya (1998) suggest a significant decrease in severe malnutrition closely associated with the length of BRAC membership—though whether disentangling the contribution of the Microfinance services from the other BRAC interventions (particularly the functional education component) has not been attempted."

### *7.5 Barnes, Carolyn and Erica Keogh (1999), An Assessment of the Impact of Zambuko's Microenterprise Program in Zimbabwe: Baseline findings, Working Paper, Management Systems International (MSI), http://www.mip.org*

In a Zimbabwe study, there are major differences in income distribution. For example, nearly half of the new client and non-client households had a monthly income of less than Z$2,000, compared with about one-fifth of the repeat client households. In contrast, half of the repeat clients had an estimated monthly household income of Z$4,000 or more. Members of repeat borrower households have on average one year of education more than those of non-client households. The average number of income sources was 2.5 for clients households compared with 2.1 for non-clients. Similar numbers in the Uganda study were 3.23 compared with 2.53.

### *7.6 Chen, Martha Alter and Donald Snodgrass (1999), An Assessment of the Impact of SEWA Bank in India: Baseline Findings. Harvard Institute for International Development: http://www.mip.org*

In a SEWA BANK study, the proportion is about 40 percent compared with 50 percent and 62 percent of saver only and non-client households, respectively. The median income is 30 percent and 61 percent higher than for a saver-only and non-client household, respectively. Borrower and saver-only enrollment rates (both 58%) were both greater than the rate for non-client households (52%). Average daily expenditure on food is 21 percent higher than in non-client households. In contrast, saver only households enjoy only a small dietary margin over non-client households. Average daily expenditure on food is only 5 percent higher than in non-client households. The average number of income sources was 2.7 for client households compared with 2.5 for both saver-only and non-client households. It is interesting to note that the net impact of the widespread closure of large textile mills in Ahmedebad City appears to be that the borrower households suffered greater setbacks (more jobs lost and less compensation paid) but were able to recover more quickly (more laid-off workers are currently economically active) than saver-only and non-client households. Interestingly, fewer other household members in borrower households (60%) than saver-only (73%) or non-client (74%) households took on additional work.

### 7.7 Cohen, Monique. October (1999), Opening Up the Impact Assessment Agenda, AIMS. Paper prepared for the Latin American Microfinance Meeting

"Maintaining access to MFI programme credit, in itself, is a protection risk management strategy for many clients. They go to great lengths to ensure repayment, particularly when confronted with a crisis or shock. Informal sources of finance are mobilized to ensure repayment. Repayment means that one can gain access to a new loan, a new 'chunk' of money and then start on the road to recovery, restocking a microenterprise, rebuilding a house, or repaying school fees. (NP) Once a shock or stress even occurs, people use various strategies to cope: they modify consumption, raise additional income by mobilizing labour or selling assets, they draw on informal and formal savings, and draw down claims on informal group based insurance mechanisms. Microfinance clients seek to conserve productive assets and thus maintain their income earning potential if at all possible. Across the four countries there was a reluctance to withdraw children from school, cash in savings (particularly where savings are linked to loan size or earmarked for future investments), or sell productive assets. MFI services were only drawn upon when other options were exhausted or failed. Overall the study found that MFIs play more of a role in helping clients protect against risks ahead of time than cope with shocks after they occur."

### 7.8 Marcus, Rachel, Beth Porter and Caroline Harper (1999), Money Matters: Understanding Microfinance. Save the Children. London

The book draws on a wide range of experience and examines Save the Children's microfinance projects in light of current trends and research, and concludes: "Microfinance can clearly help reduce poverty and vulnerability. Improvements to livelihood security are usually more incremental than the dramatic success stories sometimes quoted. However, for the people concerned, small changes in livelihoods may be significant." And that "Microfinance clearly contributes to improvements in children's welfare through increased incomes and thus: improved nutrition, housing, health and school attendance, and reductions in harmful child labour." "The evidence of impact on children's well-being is particularly strong and should allay fears that microfinance has a negative impact on children."

"All programmes for which information is available, report improvements to participants incomes, assets and livelihood security.... These changes are most notable among long-term participants who have invested their loans more profitably as they have become more familiar with handling finance.

- Participants consistently report increased incomes. In Mali—women borrowers reported increases in income of 50 percent.
- Vietnam—participants state that they are now short of rice for less than one month per year compared to three previously; participants have also diversified their productive activities and have acquired more assets than non-borrowers.
- Honduras—availability of credit prevented some borrowers from having to sell their produce at below market rates to landowners and merchants to obtain an advance in the lean season, thus increasing their incomes.

"Improvements in school attendance or in provision of educational materials are also widely reported. Invariably this related to increased household income. In Honduras, participants stated that participation in the credit and savings programme had enabled them to send several children to school at a time, and had reduced drop-out in the higher primary school grades (Arcon and Colindres, 1997). ....Where taking credit was enabling people to develop agriculture or other enterprises close to home and reducing the need to migrate for seasonal work, children's chances of attending school were greatly increased." Microfinance is an increasingly popular component of programmes aiming to reduce the need for children to work."

### 7.9 Panjaitan-Drioadisuryo. D.M. Rosintan and Kathleen Cloud (1999), Gender, Self-Employment and Microcredit Programs: An Indonesian Case Study, Quarterly Review of Economics & Finance. 39

Conclusions are based on the results of a study that was conducted on the island of Lombok (Indonesia). Credit was given to women who were under the poverty line (then equivalent to $96 per capita per year) from BRI.

"On average, the income of sample members had increased by 112 percent (although a very few also became poorer), and the income of 90 percent of these families increased enough to move them above the poverty line."

"Overall the SFDP appears to have been very successful. The women who received the loans increased their income substantially, improved their families' nutrition and faithfully repaid their loans. They also had higher aspirations for their children's education and were more likely to reduce fertility."

### 7.10 Seibel, Hans Dieter and Dolores Torres (1999), Are Grameen Replications Sustainable, and Do They Reach the Poor? The Case of CARD Rural Bank in the Philippines, Journal of Microfinance, 1 (1)

The Grameen Bank in Bangladesh is known worldwide for its success in providing credit to the poor. However, subsequent replications of its methodology in other parts of the world have been less successful. A Grameen replicator in the Philippines, the Center for Agriculture and Rural Development (CARD), has recently set itself firmly on the path to sustainability by becoming a formal sector, rural bank—the first credit NGO in the country to do so. During the period, from 1993 to June 1999, CARD's all-female outreach soared from 1,711 to 26,369. Its operational self-sufficiency ratio increased from 0.46 to 1.09. At the end of

June 1999, CARD's loan portfolio stood at US$2.7 million, its repayment rate was 99.9 percent, and its financial self-sufficiency ratio was 0.85. The principal lesson to be learned from the CARD's success is that Grameen-type microfinance institutions (MFIs) can be sustainable and can substantially increase their outreach. CARD's social capital comprises (a) a core of good Grameen practices, such as high moral commitment on the part of the leaders, based on values instilled through training; peer control, to preclude adverse selection and moral hazard; and a strict credit discipline; (b) innovative adaptations to suit the Philippine context, such as the adoption of rural bank status under central bank supervision; vigorous mobilization of voluntary savings; the provision of differentiated, profit making loan and insurance products; and a broadening of the clientele to include poor and non-poor depositors, while adhering to its mission of lending to poor women only.

### *7.11 Barnes, Carolyn; Gayle Morris and Gary Gaile (1998), An Assessment of the Impact of Microfinance Services in Uganda: Baseline Findings. AIMS Paper; Management Systems International. Washington, D.C.*

In a Uganda study, although no findings were reported on the level of poverty between client and non-client households, total expenditures on education, business and household assets, remittances to rural households, and agricultural inputs were used a proxy indicator of the relative poverty or wealth level of client and non-client households. Client households on average spent 35 percent more than non-client households. Borrower households spend 38 percent more on education than non-client households and have an average an extra year of education. Clients in the FOCCAS microfinance programme in Mbale receive instruction in breastfeeding, disease prevention (including AIDS, diarrhea, and malaria), and family planning practices. Of those who had learned about improved health and nutrition practices, 95 percent of clients compared to 72 percent of non-clients had tried a practice related to improved health or nutrition of their children. 32 percent of clients compared to 18 percent of non-clients had tried an AIDS-prevention practice.

### *7.12 Khandker, Shahidur R. (1998), Fighting Poverty with Microcredit: Experience in Bangladesh. Oxford University Press, Inc. New York*

Measures the varying effects of three micro-credit programmes (Grameen, BRAC and RD-12) on participants (male and female), as well as the impact on the local economy. Effects consider cumulative borrowing, thus reflecting both the impact of credit and the duration of programme participation. Microfinance reduces poverty by increasing per capital consumption among programme participants and their families. Poverty reduction estimates based on consumption impacts of credit show that about 5 percent of programme participants can lift their families out of poverty each year by participating and borrowing from microfinance programmes.

Microcredit programmes also help smooth consumption, as well as the seasonality of labour supply. Targeted credit also improves the nutritional status of children. The nutritional impact of credit is especially large for girls, and the impact is larger for loans made to women. Micro-credit had a significant and positive impact on schooling, especially for boys.

At the participant level, borrowing had a positive impact on:

- Per capita expenditure for women (and for men in the RD-12 programme).
- Net worth with the impact much stronger for women.
- Children's schooling, especially for boys (for girls, the only statistically significant increase was found in the Grameen programme).
- Children's nutritional status—women's credit had large and statistically significant impact on height and arm circumference, and men's credit had a positive impact on girl's body mass index (but not on boy's).

At the village level, borrowing had a positive impact on:

- Production—value of annual production of programme villages was more than twice that of non-programme villages.

- Income—differences in income between programme and non-programme villages were due largely to differences in non-farm income (Grameen and BRAC increased average household income from different sources; RD-12 impact on aggregate income was not statistically significant, but it did increase farm income by 62 percent without a corresponding growth in rural non-farm income).
- Employment—increased for Grameen Bank villages (because of large increases in self-employment in non-farm activities).
- Wages—"Among the three micro-credit programmes, only Grameen Bank (GB) had a positive and significant impact on rural wages.... Given that GB operates in poorer villages, the wage increase is a clear sign that GB contributed to the growth of the village economy."
- School enrollment—BRAC increased village level school enrollment rates.
- Fertility—net impact of Grameen was to lower recent fertility by 13 percent.
- Contraceptive Use/Fertility—borrowing by men appears to reduce fertility, while participation by women appears to increase fertility.
- Men's Credit—only men's credit from Grameen Bank had a statistically significant effect in increasing contraceptive use among 14- to 50-year-old women in participating households.
- Women's Credit—from any of the three programmes reduced the use of contraceptives among participants. Further statistical analysis suggests that this is because women who join micro-credit programmes have already been using contraceptives more than observationally equivalent women.

### 7.13 *MkNelly, Barbara and Christopher Dunford (1998), Impact of Credit with Education on Mothers and Their*

***Young Children's Nutrition: Lower Pra Rural Bank Credit with Education Programme in Ghana. Ref: Freedom from Hunger Research Paper No. 4, Freedom from Hunger, Davis, CA***

The increase in net farm monthly income (revenue minus costs) was $36 for participants, $18 for non-participants (note: non-participants became participants after the initial 3-year study was complete thus negating the possibility of a self-selection bias as to the type of women who choose to participate in micro-credit programmes) and $17 for control group residents. Participants tended to be engaged in a greater diversity of income-generating activities than nonparticipants. 80 percent of the participant sample had secondary work as compared to only 50 percent of the non-participants and 60 percent of the control group. Despite involvement in their loan-financed activities, participants did not wean their children any earlier than did non-participants. Children of participants also experienced significantly greater improvement in feeding frequency as compared to the children of the two non-participant groups. The nutritional status of participants' one-year-old children—both in terms of weight-for-age and height-for-age—was also significantly improved between the years relative to the children of residents of control communities.

Relative to non-participants or control community residents, participants reported significantly greater positive change in a variety of the health/nutrition practices promoted by the education component of the programme; e.g. giving newborns colostrums; introducing liquids and first foods closer to the ideal age of about 6 months; rehydrating children who had diarrhea by giving them either ORS or home liquids, etc.

"Women frequently mentioned that what influenced them most as to what income-generating activities they might undertake was whether they had working capital or could get the necessary inputs on a credit basis."

Repayment rate: 98.7 percent. Cost recovery within 3-5 years of start up under the Impact study on 370 mother-one-year-old-child pairs for baseline in 1993. Follow-up 1996 for 300 mothers subdivided in 3 groups of 100:

- CWE for at least one year
- In CWE community but who hasn't joined
- In a non-CWE community.

Results:

- Diarrhea prevention: CWE mothers delayed very significantly in giving water to newborns, by almost 3 X.
- Women's income more than doubled.
- CWE mothers are 2, 5 X more confident about counseling other mothers about health care for the children. This extends benefits of CWE to non-participants.
- Positive and significant impact on Height for Age in favour of CWE children.
- No improvement of BWI (body/weight index) in the women.
- Number and duration of periods with less food more than halved in CWE 81 percent cost recovery in 6 months.

**Conclusion:** This combination of positive impact and financial sustainability make credit linkage with Education—a strategy with exciting potential for widespread and sustainable impact on child survival.

## REFERENCES

Acs, Z. (2006), How Is Entrepreneurship Good for Economic Growth? *Journal of Innovations Technology/Governance/ Globalization*, Vol. 01 (01): 97-107.

Aghion, P. and B. Armendariz de Aghion (2002), Poverty and Development: A New Growth Perspective, unpublished draft, Department of Economics, Harvard University, USA.

Aghion, P. and P. Bolton (1997), A Theory of Trickle-Down Growth and Development, *Review of Economic Studies*, 64: 151-72.

Alamgir, Dewan A.H. (2009), State of Microfinance in Bangladesh, Institute of Microfinance, Prepared as part of the project on State of Microfinance in SAARC Countries.

Amaral, P. and E. Quintin (2010), Financial Intermediation and Economic Development: A Quantitative Assessment, *International Economic Review*, 51, 785-811.

Amin, S., A.S. Rai, G. Ropa (2003), Does Microcredit Reach the Poor and Vulnerable?; Evidence from Northern Bangladesh. *Journal of Development Economics*, vol. 70, pp. 59-82.

Amin, Ruhul, Stan Becker, and Abdul Bayes (1998), NGO-promoted microcredit programs and women's empowerment in rural Bangladesh, Quantitative and qualitative evidence, *The Journal of Developing Areas,* 32: 221-36.

Anderson, C.L., L. Locker, and R. Nugent (2002), Microcredit, Social Capital and Common Pool Resources, *World Development*, Vol. 30 (1): 95-105.

Arif, G.M. (2006), Targeting Efficiency of Poverty Reduction Programs in Pakistan, Working paper No. 4, Asian Development Bank, Manila, Philippines.

Armendariz, B., B. de Aghion, and J. Morduch (2007), *The Economics of Microfinance*. The MIT Press.

Bajaj, Vikas, and Lydia Polgreen (2010), India microcredit faces collapse from defaults, *New York Times* 17 Nov. 2010.

Baker, J. L. (2000), *Evaluating the Impact of Development Projects on Poverty: A Handbook for Practitioners*, Washington D.C: The World Bank, USA.

Banegas, O., S. Jarrin, B. Rojas, H. Nuselder, and A. Sanders (2002), " HIVOS Outreach and Impact of Microcredit: Case Studies of Banco Solidario (Ecuador) and Caja los Andes (Bolivia)". Centro de Estudios para el Desarrollo Rural-Free University of Amsterdam, mimeo, San Jose.

Banerjee, A.V. and A.F. Newman (1993), Occupational Choice and the Process of Development, *Journal of Political Economy*, 101: 274-98.

Banerjee, A.V. and E. Duflo (2008), Do Firms Want to Borrow More? Testing Credit Constraints Using a Directed Lending Program, Manuscript, Massachusetts Institute of Technology, USA.

Banerjee, A., E. Duflo, R. Glennerster and C. Kinnan (2009), The Miracle of Microfinance? Evidence from a randomized evaluation, Cambridge, MA: MIT, May (mimeo).

Barry, N. (1995), The Missing Links: Financial System that Works for the Majority, Women's World Banking, New York.

Barry, Nancy, Armacost, Nicola and Kawas Celina (1996), "Putting Poor People's Economics at the Center of Urban Strategies", Women's World Banking, New York.

Bhatt, N. and S.Y. Tang, (2001), Delivering microfinance in developing countries: Controversy and policy perspectives, *Policy Studies Journal*, 29(2): 319-33.

Binswanger, H.P. and S. Khandker (1995), The Impact of Formal Finance on the Rural economy of India, *The Journal of Development Studies*, Vol. 32 (2): 234-62.

Bornstein, David (1996), "The Price of a Dream", Simon & Schuster, New York, 1996 and University Press Limited, Dhaka, 1996.

Bouman, F.J.A. and Otto Hospes (Eds.) (1994), *Financial Landscapes Reconstructed: The Fine Art of Mapping.* Boulder, Colorado, Westview Press.

Brahm, E. (2000), Can Microfinance Eliminate Poverty? A Literature Review, in *Continuities and Change in the Global Economy*, edited by Dr Ed, Greenberg.

Buera, F.J. and Y. Shin (2010), Financial Frictions and the Persistence of History: A Quantitative Exploration, Working Paper 16400, National Bureau of Economic Research.

Buera, F.J., J.P. Kaboski, and Y. Shin (2011), Finance and Development: A Tale of Two sectors, *American Economic Review*, 101: 1964-2002.

Burjorjee, M. Deena, Rani, Deshpande and C. Jean Weidemann (2002), Supporting Women's Livelihoods Microfinance that Works for the Majority. A Guide to Best Practices, United Nations Capital Development Fund, Special Unit for Microfinance. http://www.uncdf.org/english/microfinance/pubs/thematic_papers/gender/supporting/part_1.php

Cheston, S., L. Reed, V. Harper, L. Hill, N. Horn, S. Salib, and M. Walen (1999), Measuring Transformation: Assessing and Improving the Impact of Microcredit, Prepared for the Microcredit Summit Meeting of Councils in Abidjan, Cote d'Ivoire, 24-26 June 1999; Available from http://www.microcreditsummit.org/papers/impactpaper.pdf [August 30, 2008].

Chowdhury, A.M.R. and A. Bhuiya (2001), Do Poverty Alleviation Programmes Reduce Inequity in Health: Lessons from Bangladesh, in *Poverty Inequity and Health*, ed. D. Leon and G. Walt (Oxford: Oxford University Press).

Chowdhury, M. and Jahangir Alam (2007), Does the Participation in the Microcredit Programs Increase Consumption of Participating Households?, The Case of the Grameen Bank in Bangladesh, In: University of Dhaka, Center for Microfinance and Development/Working Papers, RePEc: ags: udcmdw: 46545.

Chriseten, R. Elisabeth Peck Rhyne, and C. Vogel Robert (1994), Maximizing the Outreach of Microenterprise Finance: The Emerging Lessons of Successful Programs, September IMCC, Arlington, Virginia, USA.

Churchill, C.F. (1996), An Introduction to Key Issues in Microfinance: Supervision and Regulation, Financing Sources, Expansion of Microfinance Institutions, Microfinance Network, Washington, D.C. February, 1996.

Coleman, B.E. (2004), Microfinance in Northeast Thailand: who benefits and how much?; *World Development.*

Coleman, B.E. (1999), The impact of group lending in Northeast Thailand, *Journal of Development Economics*, Vol. 60(1): 105-41.

Concern (2003), Concern's Worldwide Livelihood Security Policy, Community Development Programme, Dhaka, Bangladesh: https://www.concern.net/sites/default/files/resource/2011/02/livelihood_security_policy.pdf

Copestake, James (2007), Mainstreaming microfinance: Social performance management or mission drift?, *World Development*, 35(10): 1721-38.

Copestake, James (2002), Inequality and the Polarizing Impact of Microcredit: Evidence from Zambia's Copperbelt, *Journal of International Development* 14: 743-55.

Diagne, A. and M. Zellar (2001), Access to credit and its impact in Malawi, Research Report No. 116 Washington, D.C., USA: International Food Policy Research Institute (IFPRI), Washington DC.

Dichter, Thomas (2007), A Second Look at Microfinance: The Sequence of Growth and Credit in Economic History, Centre for Global Liberty & Prosperity, Development Policy Briefing paper, No. 1, 15 February, 2007.

Edgcomb, E. and Barton, L. (1998), Social intermediation and microfinance programs: A literature review, Microenterprise Best Practices, USAID.

Erosa, A. and A. Hidalgo Cabrillana (2008), On Finance as a Theory of TFP, Cross-Industry Productivity Differences, and Economic Rents, *International Economic Review*, 49: 437-73.

Fisher, T.; M.S. Sriram; M. Harper; A. Kanikar; F. Sinha; S. Sinha; M. Titus (2002), Beyond Micro Credit: Putting Development back into Microfinance, New Delhi Oxford, Oxfam/New Economics Foundations/Vista Publications.

Gallup Pakistan (2005), PPAF Micro Credit Financing: Assessment of Outcome, Pakistan Poverty Alleviation Fund, Pakistan. (Unpublished)

Ghate, P. et al. (1992), *Informal Finance: Some Findings from Asia*, Oxford University Press, Hong Kong.

Gine, X. and D. Karlan (2010), Group versus Individual Liability: Long Term Evidence from Philippine Microcredit Lending Groups, Manuscript, Yale University, New Haven.

Gine, X. and R.M. Townsend (2004), Evaluation of Financial Liberalization: A General Equilibrium Model with Constrained Occupation Choice, *Journal of Development Economics*, 74: 269-307.

Godquin, M. (2004), Microfinance repayment performance in Bangladesh: How to improve the allocation of loans by MFIs. *World Development*, 32(11), 1909-26.

Goetz, A.M. and R. Sen Gupta (1994), Who takes the credit? Gender, Power and control over loan use in rural credit programmes in Bangladesh, *World Development*, 24(1): 45-63.

Goldberg, N. (2005), Measuring the Impact of Microfinance: Taking Stock of What We Know. Washington, DC: Grameen Foundation USA.

Grameen Bank (2009), What is Microcredit? Retrieved November 13, 2009, from http://www.grameen-info.org/index.php?option=com_content&task=view&id=28&Itemid=108

Grameen Trust (1995), Grameen Dialogue No. 24, Dhaka, October, 1995.

Hashemi, Syed M. (1997), Building up Capacity for Banking with the Poor: The Grameen Bank in Bangladesh, Microfinance for the Poor? (Ed.) Hartmut Schneider. Development Centre for the OECD. 109-28.

Hashemi, S.S. Schuler and I. Riley(1996), Rural Credit programs and Women's Empowerment in Bangladesh, *World Development*, Vol. 24, No. 4: 635-53.

Hashemi, S.M. and L. Morshed (1997), Grameen Bank: A Case Study, In *Who Needs Credit? Poverty and Finance in Bangladesh* (eds) G.D. Wood and I. Sharif, University Press Limited, Dhaka and Zed Books, UK.

Heidhues, F. (1995), Rural Finance Markets—An Important tool to fight against poverty, *Quarterly Journal of International Agriculture*, 34(2): 105-08

Hossain, M. (1988), Credit for Alleviation of Rural Poverty: The Grameen Bank in Bangladesh, Washington DC: IFPRI, USA.

Hulme David (2000), Impact Assessment Methodologies for Microfinance: Theory, Experience and Better Practices, *World Development*, 28(1): 79-98.

Hulme, D. and Mosley, P. (1996), *Finance Against Poverty*, Volumes 1 and 2, Routledge: London.

Hulme, D. and P. Mosley (1998), Microenterprise Finance: Is There a Conflict Between Growth and Poverty Alleviation?, *World Development*, Vol. 26(5): 783-90.

IMF (2005), Microfinance: A View from the Fund, IMF, Washington DC.

Jamal, H. (2008), Exploring the impact of Microfinance in Pakistan, Unpublished Research Report, Social and Policy Development Centre.

Johnson, S. and Rogaly, B. (1999), *Microfinance and Poverty Reduction*, Oxfam.

Kamal, A. (1996), Poor and the NGO Process: Adjustments and Complicities, In *1987-1994: Dynamics of Rural Poverty in Bangladesh* (eds.) H.Z. Rahman, M. Hossain and B. Sen. Bangladesh Institute of Development Studies.

Karnani, A. (2007), Microfinance misses its mark. *Stanford Social Innovation Review*, 34-40.

Khandker, S.R., H.A. Samad and Z.H. Khan (1998), Income and Employment Effects of Micro-credit Programmes: Village-level evidence from Bangladesh, *The Journal of Development Studies*, Vol. 35 (2): 96-124.

Khandker, S. (2005), Microfinance and poverty: evidence using panel data from Bangladesh, *The World Bank Economic Review*, 19(2): 263.

Khandker, Shahidur R. (1998), Fighting Poverty with Micro-credit: Experience in Bangladesh, New York: Oxford University Press, U.K.

Khandker, Shahidur R. (2003), Microfinance and Poverty: Evidence Using Panel Data from Bangladesh, The World Bank, Policy Research Working Paper #2945.

Khan, F. (2008), The Limits of Success? NGOs, Microfinance and Economic Development in Pakistan's Northern Areas, Paper presented at the Third Annual Himalayan Policy Research Conference.

Khan, S.A., N. Islam and K. Khatun (2010), A Study on Resource Mobilization by the MFIs in Bangladesh, Microcredit Regulatory Authority, Dhaka, Bangladesh.

Kim Kyung-Hwan (1995), Access to Credit, Term of Housing Finance and Affordability of Housing, *Housing Finance International*, 9(4), June 22-27.

Kiriti-Nganga, T.W. (2007), Micro-Finance and Poverty Alleviation: How Effective is it in Alleviating Gender Based Poverty? In Clem Tisdell (ed.), *Poverty, Poverty Alleviation and Social Disadvantage: Analysis, Case Studies and Policies*, Serials Publications, New Delhi.

Kiiru, J. and Mburu, J. (2006), User Costs of Joint Liability Borrowing and their Effect on Livelihood Assets for Rural Poor Households: Forthcoming, *International Journal of Women, Social Justice and Human Rights.*

Kiiru, Joy, M. Empirical Evidence from Makueni District, Kenya, Centre for Development Research (ZEF), Bonn University (http://african-women-economists.com/joy-kiiru/microfinance-entrepreneurship-and-rural-development.pdf).

Littlefield, E., J. Morduch and S. Hashemi (2003), Is Microfinance an effective strategy to reach the Millennium Development Goals?, CGAP Focus Note No. 24, January, 2003.

Lloyd-Ellis, H. and D. Bernhardt (2000), Enterprise, Inequality and Economic Development, *Review of Economic Studies*, 67, 147-68.

MacFarquhar, Neil (2010), Banks making big profits from tiny loans, *New York Times*, 13 April 2010.

Mahjabeen, R. (2008), Micro-financing in Bangladesh: Impact on households, consumption and welfare, *Journal of Policy Modeling*, 30(6): 1083-92.

Matin, I. And D. Hulme (2003), Programs for the Poorest: Learning from the IGVGD Program in Bangladesh, *World Development*, Vol. 31(3): 647-65.

McKernan, Signe-Mary (2002), The Impact of Micro-Credit programs on Self-Employment Profits: DO Non-Credit Program Aspects Matter, *The Review of Economics and Statistics*, 84 (1): 93-115.

Mcregor J., A. Simanowitz, S. Johnson and P. Mosley (2000), How can impact assessment take into account wider social and economic impacts?: Available online at: http://www.microfinancegateway.org/content/article/detail/2650/.

Microfinance Institute, Overview Report 2010. See MRA at www.mra.gov.bd. Accessed on January, 2011.

Misra, A. (2006), Microfinance in Indian and Millennium Development Goal: Maximizing Impact on Poverty. Victoria: University of Wellington.

Moll, H. (2005), Microfinance and Rural Development: A long term perspective, *Journal of Microfinance*, Vol. 7 (2): 13-23.

Montgomery, H. and John Weiss (2005), Great expectations: Microfinance and poverty reduction in Asia and Latin America, ADB Institute Research Paper Series No. 63, February, 2005.

Morduch, J. (1998), 'Does Microfinance Really Help the Poor? New Evidence on Flagship Programs in Bangladesh', presented at Stanford, UC-Berkeley, University of Washington, RAND, University of Toronto, Princeton, and Yale.

Morduch, J. (1999), The Microfinance Promise, *Journal of Economic Literature*, 37(4): 1569-1614.

Morduch, J. and Haley, B. (2002), Analysis of the Effect of Microfinance on Poverty Reduction, NYU Wagner, Working Paper No. 1014, New York University, NY.

Morris, Madeline (2011), Microcredit not the 'silver bullet' for poverty. BBC News 24 Jan. 2011.

Mosley, Paul (2001), Microfinance and poverty in Bolivia, *The Journal of Development Studies* 37: 101-32.

Mosley, Paul and David Hulme (1998), Microenterprise finance: Is there a conflict between growth and poverty alleviation? *World Development*, 26: 783-90.

Mosley, P. (2001), Microfinance and Poverty in Bolivia, *Journal of Development Studies*, Vol. 37, No. 4: 101-32.

Mustafa, S.I. Ara et al. (1996), Beacon of Hope: An Impact Assessment of BRAC's Rural Development Programme, BRAC. Dhaka.

Navajas, S., M. Schreiner, R.L. Meyer, C. Gonzalez-Vega, and J. Rodrigez-Mesa (2000), Microcredit and the Poorest of the Poor: Theory and Evidence from Bolivia, *World Development*, 28: 333-46.

Navajas, Sergio and Tejerina Luis (2006), Microfinance in Latin America and the Caribbean: How Large is the Market?, Inter-American Development Bank, Sustainable Development Department Best Practice.

Navajas, Sergio et al. (2000), Microcredit and the Poorest of the poor: Theory and evidence from Bolivia, *World Development*, 28: 333-46.

Naved, R. (1994), "Empowerment of Women: Listening to the Voices of Women". In *The Bangladesh Development Studies —Special issue on Women, Development and Change*, Vol. xxii, Nos. 2&3: 121-179, ed. Amin, BIDS., Dhaka.

Nuruzzaman, Md. (2010), Impact of Introduction of Licensing System on Microfinance Sector in Bangladesh, Microcredit Regulatory Authority, Dhaka, Bangladesh.

Otero, M. (1999), Bringing developments back into microfinance, *Journal of Microfinance*, 1(1): 8-19.

Otero, Maria and Rhyne Elisabeth (Eds) (1994), The New World of Microenterprise Finance: Building Healthy Financial Institutions, Kumarian Press: West Hartford, Connecticut. USA.

Panjaitan-Drioadisuryo, D.M. Rositan, and Kathleen Cloud (1999), Gender, Self-Employment, and Microcredit Programs: An Indonesian Case Study, *Quarterly Review of Economics and Finance*, Vol. 39.

Park, A. and Ren, C. (2001), Microfinance with Chinese Characteristics. *World Development*, 29(1), 39-62.

Pitt, M. and S. Khandker (1996), Household and Intra-household impacts of the Grameen Bank and Similar Targeted Credit Programs in Bangladesh, World Bank Discussion Papers, No. 320, Washington, D.C.

Pitt, M. and S. Khandker (1998), The Impact of Group-Based Credit Programs on Poor Households in Bangladesh: Does the Gender of Participants Matter, *Journal of Political Economy*, 106(5): 958-96.

Quach, M., A. Mullineux, and V. Murinde (2005), Access to credit and household poverty reduction in rural Vietnam: A cross-sectional study, The Birmingham Business School, The University of Birmingham Edgbaston.

Rahman, R.I. (2004), "Future Challenges Facing the MFIs of Bangladesh: Choice of Target Groups, Loan. Rahman, Zillur and Hossain, eds. (1995), *Rethinking Poverty: Bangladesh as a Case Study*. New Delhi: Sage Publications.

Remenyi, Joe and Benjamin, Quinones Jr. (2000), Microfinance and Poverty Alleviation, case study from Asia and the Pacific, New York: Pinter Publishers Ltd.

Robinson, M. (2001), The Microfinance Revolution: Sustainable Finance for the Poor, Washington DC: World Bank, USA.

Saboor, A., M. Husain and M. Munir (2009), Impact of Micro Credit in Alleviating Poverty: An Insight from Rural Rawalpindi, Pakistan, *Pakistan Journal of Life and Social Science*. 7(1): 90-97.

Schuler, S.R. and S.M. Hashemi (1994), Credit Programmes, Women's Empowerment and Contraceptive Use in Rural Bangladesh, Studies in Family Planning, 25 (April): 65-76.

Schreiner, Mark (1999), Self-employment, microenterprise, and the poorest Americans, *The Social Service Review*, 73: 496-523.

Servon, Lisa J. (1997), Microenterprise programs in U.S. inner cities: Economic development or social welfare? *Economic Development Quarterly*, 11: 166-80.

Sharma, M. (2000), Impact of Microfinance on Poverty Alleviation: What Does Emerging Evidence Indicate? Rural Financial Policies for Food Security of the Poor, International Food Policy Research Institute, Policy Brief No. 2.

Shehabuddin, R. (1992), The impact of Grameen Bank in Bangladesh, Empowering rural women. Dhaka: Grameen Bank.

Shirazi, Nasim Shah and Aman Ullah Khan (2009), Role of Pakistan Poverty Alleviation Fund in Poverty Alleviation: A case of Pakistan, *Pakistan Economic and Social Review,* Vol. 47, No. 2: 215-28

Shirazi, Nasim Shah (2008), Return on Investment in Microenterprises: Experience of the Borrowers of Pakistan Poverty Alleviation Fund, *Forman Journal of Economic Studies*, Vol. 4, January-December, 2008.

Shylendra, H.S. (2006), "Microfinance Institutions in Andhra Pradesh: Crisis and Diagnosis". *Economic and Political Weekly*, pp. 1959-63.

Simanowitz, A. and Brody, A. (2004), Realizing the potential of microfinance, *Insights*, 51: 1-2.

Simonwitz, A. (2002), Apprising the Poverty Outreach of Microfinance: A Review of the CGAP Poverty Assessment Tool (PAT), Brighton, UK: Imp-Act, Institute of Development Studies, www.impact.org.

Smith, S.C. (2002), *Village Banking and Maternal and Child Health: Evidence from Ecuador and Honduras*, Vol. 30 (4): 707-23.

Todd, H. (1996), Woman at the Center: Grameen Bank after One Decade. University Press Limited, Dhaka.

Trócaire (2005a), Development Priorities, (Online): Available from <www.trocaire.org/international/developmentprioritiesintroduction.htm>.

Trócaire (2005b), About Us (Online): Available from <www.trocaire.org/aboutus/aboutusintroduction.htm> (20th September, 2005).

Waqar A., H. Zakir, M.S. Hazoor and H. Ijaz (2008), Impact of Agriculture Credit on Growth, Washington, D.C., USA.

Weiss, John and Montgomery Heather (2004), Great Expectations: Microfinance and Poverty Reduction in Asia and Latin America, ADB Institute Discussion Paper No. 15.

William, J. Oliver (2010), Impact of Microfinance on Socio-economic Status of the Poor: The case of Malawi, Western Reserve University, Malawi.

World Bank (2000), World Development Report "Attacking Poverty", World Bank, 2001. Risk Management in South Asia–A Poverty Focused Approach, Report No. 23509-SAS, World Bank, Washington D.C.

Women's World Banking (1994), United Nations Expert Group on Women and Finance, New York.

Wright, G.A.N. (2000), *Microfinance Systems: Designing Quality Financial Services for the Poor*, Zed Books Ltd., London and New York.

Wydick, W. Bruce (1999), The effect of microenterprise lending on child schooling in Guatemala, *Economic Development and Cultural Change* 47: 853-69.

Yunus Muhammad (2004), Expanding Microcredit Outreach to Reach the Millennium Development Goals: Some Issues for Attention, In *Attacking Poverty with Microcredit*, Ed. Salehuddin Ahmed and M.A. Hakim The University Press Ltd. Dhaka, Bangladesh.

Yunus, Muhammad (2006). Nobel lecture. Available at: <URL: http://nobelprize.org/nobel_prizes/peace/laureates/2006/yunus-lecture-en.html> Access Date: 16 April, 2007.

Zaman, Hassan (2000). Assessing the Poverty and Vulnerability Impact of Micro-Credit in Bangladesh: A Case Study of BRAC. Washington.

Zeller, Manfred and Meyer L. Richard (2002), The Triangle of Microfinance—Financial Sustainability, Outreach and Impact, IFPRI, Washington & The Johns Hopkins University Press.

Zeller, M., M. Sharma, A.U. Ahmed and S. Rashid (2001), Group-Based Financial Institutions for the Rural Poor in Bangladesh—An Institutional and Household-level Analysis, Research Report 120, IFPRI, Washington, D.C.

# 5

# Role of Microfinance on Enterpreneurship and Micro-enterprise Development

Micro-enterprise refers to any economic unit engaged in the production and distribution of goods and services at household level. It is primarily of self-employed nature, employing him/her in the enterprise and sometimes some family members. The enterprise runs on little amount of capital investment at a fixed market centre or mobile business locations. This sector is identified with features like reliance on indigenous resources, family ownership of enterprises, small scale of operation, labour-intensive, adapted technology, and minimum skill. Micro-enterprise, therefore, is particularly suitable for poor communities.

Microeconomic enterprises play a vital role in poverty reduction in both rural and urban areas, and reinforce urban-rural linkages for economic and social development in Nepal. The linkages are essential not only for utilization of local resources but also in acting as agents for the flow of goods and services between urban and rural areas. Their roles are important since they possess the features like self-employment generation, employment to poor and women, use of local resources, meeting basic needs of the poor, traditional enterprise/skill and craftsmanship, labour intensive, self-satisfaction on the job, entrepreneurship and innovative (skill learned through apprenticeship method), and fair income distribution among the poor.

In developing countries there are nearly 90 percent of the people which have lack of access to financial services from the institutions, either for credit or saving purpose. Especially for the poor who already have lack assets this situation become more critical for them. In micro-enterprises generally there is need for small capital but it is still difficult for the poor people to manage even that small quantity of capital. Resultantly, these lacks of capital hinder the growth of micro-enterprise (Robinson, 2002). Entrepreneurship is one of the commonly terms used in business, management, economics and other related fields. Entrepreneurship means innovation, creativity, leadership, profit maximization or start of a new business. Entrepreneurship helps in the process to increase economic growth, employment generation, increase national income and also creating innovation (Zahid and Ismailo, 2008). Two schools of thought mainly discuss about entrepreneurship as: Schumpeter's theory of entrepreneurship and Austrian theory of entrepreneurial discovery. The Schumpeter theory explains entrepreneurship as innovation with a combination of tool and forces and the different methods to produce new innovative products as for the Austrian theory of entrepreneurship, entrepreneur anticipating market and need of customers exactly and correctly and produce more cheaply than competitor and earn more money.

Microfinance hits the history in Bangladesh when Dr. Muhammad Yunus, Father of Microfinance, lend the first micro-loan from his own pocket. The purpose is to save these poor people from the local moneylenders who charge high interest rates and also to establish income generating activity for them. In 1976, Muhammad Yunus launch the research project to provide micro-credit and banking services to the poor people. In addition to that, micro-credit programme is based on unique mechanism such as group lending, social collateral and distinctive payment methods. It isn't based on checking credit history, income sources and bank balances but works on character based lending and thus managed to give loans to those who lacking credit histories. They are also denied of access to conventional finance. In 1983, Mohammad Yunus formally establishes a Grameen bank which is a milestone in the development of the microfinance industry. The objective of this bank is to give small loans at affordable rates to poor people, especially to women. The high number of clients and extremely high repayments rates is an impressive achievement for the bank. The micro-credit programme has not been restricted to Bangladesh as the similar activities are also under way in different parts of the world including Indonesia (1972), India (1990s) and, more importantly, in Latin America where micro-credit operations were rapidly developed. In the end, Dr. Muhammad Yunus is awarded a Nobel peace prize for his great achievement in 2006 (Bateman, 2010).

Microfinance institutions support two types of micro-entrepreneurs: one is potential micro-entrepreneur and the second is existing micro-entrepreneur. The micro-entrepreneurs mean the creation and the existing entrepreneurs mean the expansion of that entrepreneurship. Microfinance Institutions assist potential micro-entrepreneurs by providing financing and training to enable them to start a business activity. This help to potential micro-entrepreneurs is for pro-poor mostly. The objective of targeting the poor is to make them able to start their own business and enabling them to increase their revenues and to reduce their level of poverty. Microfinance institutions also provide services to existing micro-entrepreneurs. Other financial services available to the existing micro-entrepreneurs are money transfer using mobile banking to facilitate their transfers and other financial operations, micro-insurance to insure their business operations and the unexpected that affect the smooth functioning of the business like the sickness or the death of the micro-entrepreneur. The microfinance institutions also offer non-financial services to existing micro-entrepreneurs enabling them to expand and develop their activities, their skills and to empower them. The non-financial services supply to existing micro-entrepreneurs is managerial training, technical assistance, and analysis of the sector of activity (Ledgerwood, 1998, 1999).

The chapter is dedicated to highlight the significance and importance of microfinance in the development of entrepreneurship leading to sustained growth of micro-enterprise. The implicit need of providing greater institutional and organizational support for wider participation through empowerment is stressed. In this endeavour, the proactive role of Microfinance Institutions on the growth of women entrepreneurs is discussed with the help of some illustrative country and project experiences. Some aspects relating to the unique role of entrepreneurship in reducing poverty in the LDCs, with inherent scope for the future prospect of commercial ventures with institutional and collaborative support from all concerned, has also been discussed.

## 1. Microfinance and Development of Micro-Entrepreneurship

### *1.1 Microfinance and Small Businesses*

Accessing credit is considered to be an important factor in increasing the development of small businesses, it is thought that credit augment income levels, increases employment and thereby alleviate poverty it is believed that access to credit enables poor people to overcome their liquidity constraints and undertake some investments (Hiedhues, 1995). According to the encyclopedia free online dictionary, access can be defined as, the right to obtain or make use of or take advantage of something (as services or membership). Access to financial services by smallholders is normally seen as one of the constraints limiting their benefits from credit facilities; in most cases the access problem, especially among formal financial institutions, is one created by the institutions mainly through their lending policies; this is obvious in the form of prescribed minimum loan amounts, complicated application procedures and restrictions on credit for specific purposes therefore, small-scale enterprises reliable access to short-term and small amounts of credit is more valuable, and emphasizing it may be more appropriate in credit programmes aimed at such enterprises (Yehuala, 2008). According to Hossain (1988), the Grameen Bank experience shows that most of the conditions imposed by formal credit institutions like collateral requirements should not actually stand in the way of smallholders and the poor in obtaining credit the poor can use the loans and repay if effective procedures for disbursement, supervision and repayment have been established.

According to Diagne and Zeller (2001), argue that lack of access to credit by the poor just below or just above the poverty line may have negative consequences for Small businesses and overall welfare, access to micro-credit further increases small businesses and enables consumption smoothing overtime. With these arguments, microfinance is assumed to improve the welfare of the poor people. Across developing countries, small enterprises are turning to Microfinance Institutions (MFIs) for an array of financial services; this is because Microfinance is acknowledged as one of the prime strategies to achieve the Millennium Development Goals (MDGs) which are: poverty and hunger reduction, universal primary education, reduction of child mortality, combating diseases, malaria and environmental sustainability, because of access to sustainable financial services enables owners of small businesses to finance income, build assets, and reduce their vulnerability to external shocks (Mahjabeen, 2008). According to Wydick and Kevan (2001), the provision of credit to the poor serves two purposes. First, as borrowed capital is invested in small enterprises, it often results in significant short-term increase in household expenditure and welfare. Secondly, micro-enterprises credit encourages economic growth in the informal sector through promoting increase capitalization of business, employment creation, and long-term income growth.

Generally, the accessibility of a good financial service is considered as one of the engines of economic development, the establishment and expansion of financial service is also one of the instruments to break the vicious circle of poverty (Yehuala, 2008). The several literatures showed that the microfinance provides financial services to support small businesses, poor people and low income group; and also microfinance becomes a tool for fighting poverty, the main findings show that few numbers of small businesses and poor people access microfinance service. Therefore, the accessibility of microfinance for small businesses has not got adequate research attention in Mogadishu, Somalia. That means there is a gap in literature which needed to be covered by research. Therefore, this study attempts to fill this gap by investigating the situations exist in Mogadishu.

Entrepreneurship development amongst underprivileged women requires development of different skills. The various types of entrepreneurial skills can be categorized in following manner:

(a) *Personal entrepreneurial skills*: which include self-awareness, confidence building, responsibility taking, emotional stress coping and creative thinking.

(b) *Entrepreneurial skills*: which include identifying opportunities, scanning business opportunities, convincing abilities, marshalling resources, etc.

(c) *Technical abilities*: which include understanding of domain knowledge, operational skills, managing the operations such as buying and selling, procuring, manufacturing, etc.

(d) *Managerial abilities*: which include planning, organizing, supervising, managing finances, legalities and administration, etc.

One of the major hurdles in developing these skill sets in women belonging to weaker section of society is lack of motivation, aspirations and self-confidence to improve one's conditions. As most of the microfinance clients come from the class where they are continuously denied equal opportunities and access to basic resources and at the same time they are discouraged to think and take decisions independently due to socio-economic as well as cultural constraints, the development of self-confidence and self-reliance is a major milestone in the path of entrepreneurial development. Social capital created through network and team building in microfinance programmes can play a vital role in building these skill sets for women. Firstly, team building and networking facilitated by collective action helps in removing the inhibitions relating to exploring new ideas, coming forward and seeking information which mainly come from low self esteem and low awareness level. Secondly, it brings together people with entrepreneurship skills at various stages of development and allows free communication and exchange of ideas which helps learning and seeking reinforcement from each other.

The relationship between microfinance, creation of social capital and development of entrepreneurial abilities needs to be analysed critically. Main focus of most of the microfinance programmes is on empowerment of women belonging to underprivileged society. The central concept of the empowerment of women is to address the issues related to their subordination, inequality and inequity. It focuses on the shift from the position of powerlessness towards strategic and active participation in social, economic and political spheres. Rowlands (1997) stated that it is a process whereby women become able to organize themselves to increase their own self-reliance, to assert their independent rights to make choices and to control resources which will assist in challenging and eliminating their own subordination. Mayoux (2001) explained that microfinance programme is assumed to bring out virtuous spirals by assisting poor women in giving access to credit. It is assumed that women's access to credit and savings will help them to start small economic activities, enhance family incomes and take a bigger role in decision-making which further will help them to optimize their own and family level welfare. Along with this group formation leads to wider social and political movements and helps women to improve their status at home as well as in community. The underlying assumption is that group based microfinance provides significant benefits to women not only in terms of reducing poverty level but also brings out empowerment through a series of interlinked and mutually reinforcing virtuous spirals.

### *1.2 Relationship between Microfinance and Social Capital*

The relationship between microfinance and social capital is vital for promotion of micro-entrepreneurship. The broad meaning of social capital is facilitating collective action for mutual benefit. Social capital resides in relation between individuals and its impact can be seen on individual level as well as on community or group level. It refers to quality of human relationship existing within some well defined social groups which has impact on achieving mutual benefits. Coleman (1988) defines social capital as an asset embedded in relationships that facilitates instrumental action among people and the sharing of knowledge and resources from one person to another. Putnam (1993) describes social capital as those features of social organization such as trust, norms and networks that can improve efficiency of society by facilitating coordinated action. World Bank also defines social capital as the norms and network that enables collective action and shapes quality and quantity of society's social interactions. It considers social capital as one of the vital resource to bring out the desirable outcomes for any development programme. Bourdieu (1985) elaborates different forms of social capital such as bonding social capital which connects individual to groups and networks, bridging social capital which ties relationships between different socio-economic and ethnic class and linking social capital which ties poor people with the other members of positions such as organization, development officers, etc.

Social capital in any society can be seen in different dimensions such as groups and networks existing in the society which promote and protect relationships and improve welfare, trust and solidarity which foster greater cohesion and willingness to take initiative in social context based on the assumption that others will respond as expected, collective action and cooperation which foster the abilities of people to work together towards resolving community/social issues, social cohesion and inclusion which mitigates the risk of conflict and promotes equitable access to benefits of development by enhancing participation of the marginalized and lastly information and communication which provide improved access to information via network. More than any other development programme the link between microfinance and social capital is stronger and clear. Social capital cultivated through peer group development replaces conventional collateral requirements and improves credit worthiness of millions of clients especially women. Along with that it also contributes other benefits such as greater sense of community, trust, reliance on each other in times of crisis, sharing of information, skill upgradation, better decision-making and bargaining power within family and in community and creation of support system (Basargekar, Prema, 2012).

Microfinance programme by nature and by objectives depends on creating virtuous spiral the base of which is creation and utilization of social capital (Mayoux, 2001). Access to savings and credit contributes to economic empowerment of women through productive use of credit. It leads to better control over resources by women and better well-being of themselves as well as their families. It further enables them to renegotiate and bring out changes in gender relations in their families as well as in local or community level which leads to social and political empowerment. At all these levels social capital in terms of networking, higher access to information and skill upgradation and collective action to tackle gender and social issues enhances their abilities to bring out desirable change.

Ismawan (2002) explained the relationship between economic intermediation through microfinance programme on existing social capital. He stated that microfinance helps building social capital to enhance degree of information sharing, democratic participation, collective decision-making and sustainable development. Ronchi (2004) stated that social capital and microfinance reinforce each other. Any sustainable development requires combination of natural capital, physical capital and human capital. Microfinance programmes make use of existing social capital in the society and link that to physical capital to foster economic growth. The higher the social capital, higher the cost of defecting and missing of mutual benefits which enhances repayment performance. Similarly higher the social capital, higher the trust builds amongst members and higher will be the impact of microfinance programmes on other aspects besides access to credit. Ronchi (2004) studied the role of social capital in implementation of microfinance programmes in Ecuador and concluded that it has helped in bringing wider political participation, stronger interventions in decision-making process and more bargaining position for poor women. Oksan (2008) throws light on how microfinance programme can contribute to the political awareness and social activism of its clients through the process of development of self-efficacy and social capital.

Number of studies focused on role of social capital in encouraging and sustaining micro-entrepreneurship. Morris, Woodworth and Hiatt (2006) made a comparative analysis of financial performance of individual lending and cooperative micro-lending to self-employed entrepreneurs in Bulgaria and Philippines. They concluded that cooperative micro-lending leads to higher survival rates and better performance of self-employed entrepreneurs due to higher level of social capital created by organizations. The social capital created through social ties and network help self-employed women entrepreneurs in having flexibility in interest payment and repayment schedule, training and skill upgradation, networking with suppliers and customers as well as sharing responsibilities such as child care, etc. Woodworth (2008) has shown a strong connectivity in success of micro-entrepreneurship and development of social capital. In fact he gives more importance to access to social capital than to financial capital as it is this intangible asset which helps micro-entrepreneurs in various ways such as leveraging relationships in building customers and suppliers, expanding businesses, reducing stress in times of economic crisis and building commitments towards your enterprises. Gomez and Santor (2001) study the effect of social capital on the performance of small entrepreneurs in terms of net earnings by making comparison between performances of entrepreneurs taking loan from group based lending activity by microfinance institution and individual lending programmes. The positive relationship between social capital and better economic performance of the entrepreneurs comes through better 'instrumental support' such as provision of start-up capital, non-interest bearing loans, cheap or free labour, etc.; 'productive information' such as transfer of business knowledge, valuable referrals, etc., and 'psychological aid' in handling personal problems and helping in times of emotional stress.

### *1.3 Linkage between Microfinance Programmes and Promotion of Micro-Entrepreneurship*

The link between microfinance programmes and promotion of micro-entrepreneurship is clear and examined by many researchers. Ghate, Ballon and Manalo (1996) make a case for development of micro-entrepreneurship through microfinance by stating that many livelihood enterprises which are usually source of second income have potential to grow via access to credit. The study conducted by ADB in 1997 concludes that the role of micro-enterprises in the household economy in terms of reducing poverty, empowering women, generating employment is significant. The study also highlights the importance of nonfinancial services in efforts to help develop micro-enterprises and provides a framework for donors for the further development of policy and operations to support micro-enterprise development. The impact assessment study of development of micro-entrepreneurship through microfinance in Tanzania (Raftus, 1998) found that the micro-entrepreneurs used loans received from the programmes for buying new items, increasing inventory stock and improving quality of the product or service. Barnes and Keogh (1999) make a comparative study between repeat micro-entrepreneurs client, new clients and non client micro-entrepreneurs in Zimbabwe. Their study concludes that repeat clients of microfinance programmes are better off economically and have used their loan fund for the growth of the enterprises.

The overall results of the study establish that participation in micro-enterprise programmes has led to improvements in the economic welfare of households, enterprise growth and stability, increases in empowerment of women and strengthened social networks. The empirical study in Cameroon (Mayoux, 2001) shows that credit made available from microfinance programmes undoubtedly helped women to set up micro-enterprises. It was also seen that the social capital in the form of kinship, and network helped most of the economic activities in business development and survival in times of crisis. Dumas (2001) studied the impact of an entrepreneurship training and education programme designed to prepare low-income women to start their own businesses. Results showed that the training empowered participants to achieve economic self-sufficiency; helped them start to build strong business and life management skills; may have an influence on the growth of locally controlled businesses and has helped create new job in the inner-city neighbourhoods. In an another impact assessment study of the PULSE programme targeted at economically active poor to promote micro-enterprises in Zambia (Copestake, Bhalotra and Johnson, 2001) it was found that the borrowers who graduated from 1st loan to 2nd loan experienced significant growth in their profits mainly due to diversification of business. Business training, marital status, loan availability for increasing stocks had a positive impact on business performance, whereas rigid group enforcement of fixed loan repayment schedules without regard to fluctuating demand and income acted as hindrance for better growth.

Afrane (2002) conducted an impact assessment study of two microfinance projects for small and micro-enterprises in Ghana and South Africa. The author concluded that microfinance interventions have achieved a significant improvement in terms of increased incomes and better access to facilities and has an empowering effect particularly on women. Coyle (2003) emphasized on the importance of micro-entrepreneurship in creation of jobs and income, equitable distribution of income, building strong backward and forward linkages with other sectors and reduction of income linkages from communities microfinance plays a vital role in reaching micro-entrepreneurs and it needs to take challenges in identifying local leaderships, developing leadership, developing suitable products by bringing out continuous innovations.

The findings of EDA Rural System (2005) show that the programme has enabled households from all income brackets to invest in productive assets and diversify their livelihoods. The comparative analysis between clients and non clients show significant difference in income generation, acquisition of assets and diversification of sources Bates (2005) explored the role of government sponsored microfinance programme in development of micro-enterprises in New York. He concluded that the programme has helped in creating new job opportunities to low to moderate income persons. Tripathi (2005) makes a comparative analysis of empowerment level of three categories of microfinance clients such as micro-entrepreneurs, non-entrepreneurs and housewives. He concludes that the level of empowerment in terms of reduction in gender inequity, higher level of decision-making and asset ownership, equity in food consumption pattern is higher in case of micro-entrepreneurs than other categories. However in case of work load burden, micro-entrepreneurs have to share a higher load. In an comparative study of micro enterprise development of two different programmes in south Africa. Hietalahti and Linden (2006) found that the overall effect of micro-enterprise development in building confidence, increasing willingness to participate in community activities is found out to be positive.

In short, it can be stated that microfinance programmes help in creating entrepreneurial environment amongst women belonging to weaker section of society by the process of firstly by creating social capital to bring them on a common platform to exchange ideas and learn from each other, secondly, developing their personal entrepreneurial skills by motivating them to embark the path of self-reliance and self-development, and thirdly by allowing them to recognize opportunities and developing their capacity building required to set up micro-business. The advantage of promoting entrepreneurship development programme through microfinance programme is that the focus of entrepreneurship development gets shifted from implementation of programme and fulfilling the targets to development of individual entrepreneurial skills. Microfinance plays a vital role in reaching micro-entrepreneurs and it needs to take challenges in identifying local leaderships, developing leadership, developing suitable products by bringing out continuous innovations. The findings of EDA Rural System (2005) show that the programme has enabled households from all income brackets to invest in productive assets and diversify their livelihoods. The comparative analysis between clients and non-clients show significant difference in income generation, acquisition of assets and diversification of sources.

Bates (2005) explored the role of government sponsored microfinance programme in development of micro-enterprises in New York. He concluded that the programme has helped in creating new job opportunities to low to moderate income persons. Tripathi (2005) makes a comparative analysis of empowerment level of three categories of microfinance clients such as micro-entrepreneurs, non-entrepreneurs and housewives. He concludes that the level of empowerment in terms of reduction in gender inequity, higher level of decision-making and asset ownership, equity in food consumption pattern is higher in case of micro entrepreneurs than other categories. However in case of work load burden, micro-entrepreneurs have to share a higher load. In another comparative study of micro-enterprise development of two different programmes in South Africa. Hietalahti and Linden (2006) found that the overall effect of micro-enterprise development in building confidence, increasing willingness to participate in community activities is found out to be positive.

In short, it can be stated that microfinance programmes help in creating entrepreneurial environment amongst women belonging to weaker section of society by the process of firstly by creating social capital to bring them on a common platform to exchange ideas and learn from each other, secondly, developing their personal entrepreneurial skills by motivating them to embark the path of self-reliance and self-development, and thirdly by allowing them to recognize opportunities and developing their capacity building required to set up micro business. The advantage of promoting entrepreneurship development programme through microfinance programme is that the focus of entrepreneurship development gets shifted from implementation of programme and fulfilling the targets to development of individual entrepreneurial skills.

### *1.4 Entrepreneurial Microfinance in Bangladesh*

In countries like Bangladesh, where a majority of the population are poor, it is very difficult for the traditional financial institutions to ensure loans for most loan applicants. For the poor it is most desirable if they can get collateral-free working capital loans to initiate their small and medium size enterprises (SMEs). In low-income developing countries, entrepreneurship and SMEs have been recognized as important factors that contribute to the local employment creations and economic development. SMEs and entrepreneurial microfinance are closely intertwined. Without entrepreneurial microfinance it is difficult for the poor to initiate SMEs, and when they have both, the entrepreneurial microfinance and SMEs, they can work to increase their income and employability, accumulate assets, and contribute to their socioeconomic inclusion. All these factors together not only contribute to the lives of the beneficiaries, but also create multiplier impacts on the community. It creates local business and generates local consumer demand. In a typical rural community, SMEs also contribute to developing social relations or networks, civic engagement, community solidarity, and social capital (Ssewamala, Lombe, and Curley, 2006). Promotion of SMEs also work function as the 'safety net' for unemployed people, particularly in the societies where unemployment insurance is not available (Tokman, 1996).

In Bangladesh the entrepreneurial microfinance through different microfinance programmes has come to occupy a central place in poverty-oriented strategies. It has a number of features in common. It mostly aims to serve poor rural women; lend small amounts of money to individuals as members of groups, and rely on group liability for ensuring loan repayment. This can also subsidize the administrative costs rather than interest rates, and loans are repaid generally in weekly installments. Apart from these, poor credit recipients also receive different types of capacity and skill development trainings (Kabeer, 2001).

During the last two decades, hundreds of nongovernment organizations (NGOs) have emerged in Bangladesh with the motivations to support poor rural women by providing collateral free small loans. These NGOs also provide and organize various social services like social mobilization, health care, literacy and education, sanitation, water supply, agriculture, etc. Grameen Bank and BRAC (Bangladesh Rural Advancement Committee) are two of the most successful and the largest NGOs in Bangladesh that have created opportunities for the poor women to become small and medium entrepreneurs. In most of the cases SMEs made positive impacts on the women's socioeconomic lives. However, the mechanism is also not out of criticism. It is not very uncommon that microfinance generates dependency on credit for poor women, and so they are trapped on the credit cycle, creating a new form of dependency and poverty.

## 2. Role of Microfinance in Entrepreneurship Development: A Review

For any business development, credit is an important thing. Absence of credit is a wall for investment and also for the economic growth. Access to credit can increase the adoption of new and more advance technologies which allow the poor households to expand their enterprises and improve their income level and reduce poverty. Availability of credit increases the level of household's productive and physical assets and also improves the consumption of the poor. Entrepreneurship is one of the commonly terms used in business, management, economics and other related fields. Entrepreneurship means innovation, creativity, leadership, profit maximization or start of a new business. Entrepreneurship helps in the process to increase economic growth, employment generation, increase national income and also creating innovation (Zahid and Ismailov, 2008). Two schools of thought mainly discuss about entrepreneurship as: Schumpeter's theory of entrepreneurship and Austrian theory of entrepreneurial discovery. The Schumpeter theory explains entrepreneurship as innovation with a combination of tool and forces and the different methods to produce new innovative products as for the Austrian theory of entrepreneurship, entrepreneur anticipating market and need of customers exactly and correctly and produce more cheaply than competitor and earn profit (Swedberg, 2000). Microfinance hits the history in Bangladesh when Dr. Muhammad Yunus—Father of Microfinance, lend the first micro-loan from his own pocket. The purpose is to save these poor people from the local moneylenders who charge high interest rates and also to establish income generating activity for them. In 1976, Muhammad Yunus launch the research project to provide micro-credit and banking services to the poor people. In addition to that, micro-credit programme is based on unique mechanism such as group lending, social collateral and distinctive payment methods.

Microfinance institutions support two types of micro-entrepreneurs: one is potential micro-entrepreneur and the second is existing micro-entrepreneur. The micro-entrepreneurs mean the creation and the existing entrepreneurs mean the expansion of that entrepreneurship. Microfinance Institutions assist potential micro-entrepreneurs by providing financing and training to enable them to start a business activity. This help to potential micro-entrepreneurs is for pro-poor mostly. The objective of targeting the poor is to make them able to start their own business and enabling them to increase their revenues and to reduce their level of poverty. Microfinance institutions also provide services to existing micro-entrepreneurs. Other financial services available to the existing micro-entrepreneurs are money transfer using mobile banking to facilitate their transfers and other financial operations, micro-insurance to insure their business operations and the unexpected that affect the smooth functioning of the business like the sickness or the death of the micro-entrepreneur. The microfinance institutions also offer non-financial services to existing micro-entrepreneurs enabling them to expand and develop their activities, their skills and to empower them. The non-financial services supply to existing micro-entrepreneurs is managerial training, technical assistance, and analysis of the sector of activity (Ledgerwood, 1998, 1999).

Different studies have been conducted on different aspects of microfinance such as importance of microfinance, beginning of microfinance, performance of microfinance institutions, effectiveness of microfinance, etc. However this study is concerned with role of microfinance on entrepreneurship development. The review of different studies is presented below:

Olajide (1980) recognized two sources of credits for entrepreneurs named as internal and external. He found that when the internal funds increase from net flow due to entrepreneurial activities, the external funds also increase from loans extended by microfinance providers. Rural enterprise needs capital which is held by microfinance providers, as financing to micro-enterprise is universal not only in rural areas but even in urban areas. Credit for small and medium enterprises provides an important tool for the development of industrialization and improving the efficiency of the enterprise and increase productivity.

The clients of microfinance banks are mostly self-employed low income entrepreneurs in urban and rural areas and include traders, subsistence farmers, street vendors, service providers, etc.

Gobbi et al. (2005) and Sarbina (2005) have studied on "Nepal and Pakistan microfinance and micro-enterprise development: Their contribution to the economic empowerment of women" used primary data interviewed more than 100 women from the three different MFIs from each country. They found that micro-finance and micro-enterprise development may serve as a tool towards the positive social change and contribute in improving the political and social status of women. Bharti and Shylendra (2011) have made a study on the Microfinance and sustainable micro-entrepreneurship development. They found that Microfinance plays an important role in micro-enterprise development. Micro-enterprise needs not only credit but they also need a variety of other services for its growth and development. Credit alone is not sufficient for promoting micro-enterprise but in the presence of lack of access to credit it is also difficult for any non-financial support to work.

The role of various microfinance services such as savings, insurance and money transfer in promoting sustainable micro-entrepreneurship need to be explored and given attention. Government and non-government entities also need to work together for creation of enable environment. Then these micro-enterprises can grow and contribute efficiently towards the larger objective, which is to reduce poverty.

Zahid and Ismailov (2008) elaborate that entrepreneurship and microfinance tools for empowerment of poor case of Akhuwat Pakistan. The study uses qualitative approach for research. They found that Akhuwat is a non-profit organization which is providing interest free loans to the poorest people of Pakistan. And they have basic that everybody should think firstly about their local problems, if they look at problems locally, there would not be any global problems in the world. To achieve Sustainable development is a problem, that is now globally dispersed and consistently growing number of initiatives of Social Entrepreneurs trying to add their little value to social value creation.

Ojo Olu (2009) has tried to find out "Impact of microfinance on entrepreneurial Development: the case of Nigeria" used survey research design. He found that in Nigerian economy there is positive relationship between microfinance institution and extension of GDP in the economy but there is not significant impact of these institutions on interest rate. The results summarized from the study shows that the microfinance institutions and their activities need a long time in the determination of the pattern and level of economic activities and development in the Nigerian economy. Popoola et al. (2011) argued the impact of microfinance institutions on the development of small scale enterprises in Nigeria. The study used both primary and secondary data. Their results showed that positive and significant relationship exist between microfinance institutions loans and small-scale performance. There is positive contributions of microfinance institutions loans towards promoting small-scale enterprises market share, production effectiveness and competitiveness.

Tonelli (2011) studied on Entrepreneurial Becoming: an Educational Pathway out of Poverty. The finding of this paper is the process of entrepreneurial becoming that is not just about access to finance but especially learning and, when successful, this process supports the transformation of survival micro-enterprises into entrepreneurial micro-businesses. The concept of 'becoming' contains an implicit temporal dimension. Becoming suggests a transformation over time, a change from what one is already. In this study a significant change in understanding how a business needs to operate, in recognizing opportunities, thinking more creatively, and building self-confidence. These different studies show that various studies conduct on microfinance and entrepreneurship development. In this the investigator found the role of microfinance institutions in entrepreneurship development in district Gujrat Pakistan and also measured the level of satisfaction of microfinance institution clients toward their respective banks there is no study find out on the District Gujarat Pakistan.

Despite the crucial role of women entrepreneurs in the economic development of their families and countries; it is, however, discovered that women entrepreneurs have low business performance compared to their male counterparts (Akanji, 2006); and this is caused by factors which normally affect entrepreneurial performance. Such factors include lack of credit, saving, education or training, and social capital (Shane, 2003). Literature supports the fact that women entrepreneurs, mostly in developing countries, do not have easy access to credit for their entrepreneurial activity (Ibru, 2009; Iganiga, 2008; Iheduru, 2002; Kuzilwa, 2005; Lakwo, 2007; May, 2007; Okpukpara, 2009), whereas the rate of women participation in the informal sector of the economy is higher than males (Akanji, 2006; Akinyi, 2009). Lack of capital to start or run business led them to request for credits from microfinance institutions (Ibru, 2009; Kuzilwa, 2005). This is due to poverty, unemployment, low household and business income and inability to save (May, 2009; Otero, 1999; Porter & Nagarajan, 2005; Roomi & Parrot, 2008). Women entrepreneurs, mostly in developing countries, lack the ability to save (Akanji, 2006; Mkpado & Arene, 2007), yet savings are needed to protect income, act as a security for loan and could be re-invested in the business (Akanji, 2006).

Savings as a micro-finance factor enable people with few assets to save, since they could make weekly savings as well as contribute to group savings, and such savings are mobilized by the micro-finance institutions for further lending to other clients (Mkpado & Arene, 2007). Women entrepreneurs, especially in developing countries lack training (IFC, 2007) and entrepreneurial process is a vital source of developing human capital as well as plays a crucial role in providing learning opportunity for individuals to improve their skills, attitudes and abilities (Brana, 2008; Cheston & Kuhn, 2002; Shane, 2003). Again, the effect of training on women entrepreneurs' performance, especially in developing countries, has not been adequately addressed in the literature. Taking cognizance of the peculiar situations of most women in developing countries in terms of poverty, low educational levels and other societal discriminations (Porter & Nagarajan, 2005; Roomi & Parrot, 2008); training is a very important microfinance factor for women entrepreneurs as it would provide the skills and experience needed for business (Akanji, 2006, Cheston & Kuhn, 2002; Kuzilwa, 2005).

Literature supports the fact that majority of microfinance institutions' clients do not have specialized skills, and so cannot make good use of microfinance factors (Karnani, 2007), hence they need training. Paid employment provides prior business experience that is vital for enterprise success, yet women entrepreneurs mostly in developing countries lack this (Brana, 2008). This further strengthens the need for training as a microfinance factor for the women entrepreneurs. Again, there are suggestions from literature of the need to study credit jointly with training on entrepreneurship performance in developing countries because of low educational levels of women entrepreneurs in low-income countries (Harrison & Mason, 2007; Ibru, 2009; Kuzilwa, 2005; Tazul, 2007). Education is related to training, and women entrepreneurs in high-income countries are better educated than those in low income countries (Ibru, 2009). Literature confirms that skill training and tertiary education have positive effect on enterprise performance (Akanji, 2006; Cheston & Kuhn, 2002; Kuzilwa, 2005). Many women lack this, especially in developing countries (Ibru, 2009), whereas the exploitation of entrepreneurial opportunity depends on the entrepreneur's level of education, skills or knowledge acquired through work experience, social network and credit (Shane, 2003); hence the need for training as a microfinance factor especially in developing economies is highlighted. Social capital is vital for start-ups and growing firms and women entrepreneurs, especially in developing countries, lack social connections that are a source of information for access to microfinance factors (Olomola, 2002). Again, social capital has been widely measured and found to have positive impact on the performance of women enterprises in developing countries (Brata, 2004; Lawal et al., 2009; Mkpado & Arene, 2007; Olomola, 2002).

Many studies abound on the relationship between one or a combination of credit, savings, training and social capital, and women entrepreneurs' performance (Akanji, 2006; Cheston

& Kuhn, 2002; Kuzilwa, 2005; Lawal et al., 2009; Olomola, 2002; Reavley & Lituchy, 2008) but there is scarcity of research that jointly links credit, savings, training and social capital to women entrepreneurs' performance especially in developing countries, Nigeria inclusive. Also, limited studies are available on the mediating relationship between opportunity and women entrepreneurs' performance (Tata & Prasad, 2008; Shane, 2003) and the moderating relationship between attitude to risk and women entrepreneurs' performance (Crisp & Turner, 2007; Vob & Muller, 2009). Women entrepreneurs in this context lack credit, savings, training and social capital for entrepreneurial activity and subsequent business performance (Akanji, 2006; Cheston & Kuhn, 2002; Ibru, 2009; Kuzilwa, 2005; Olomola, 2002). Whereas the Entrepreneurship Theory (Shane, 2003) postulates that business environment provides opportunity for entrepreneurial activities to those entrepreneurs who could identify them, and their decision to exploit such opportunities leads to the demand for microfinance in terms of resource acquisition.

Acquisition of microfinance could also lead to opportunity for entrepreneurial activity. Appropriate use of acquired resources through good business strategy and organizational design could lead to business performance (Brana, 2008; Koontz & Weihrich, 2006; Salman, 2009; Shane, 2003). Again, microfinance factors could not lead to business performance without opportunity for entrepreneurial activity. Financial management theorists believe that funds could only be sourced to finance a predetermined project, business or contract (Van Horne, 1980). As such, microfinance could only lead to business performance when there is the tendency to engage in new business or business expansion (Antoncic, 2006; Shane, 2003). Limited studies are also available on attitude towards risk-taking moderating the relationship between microfinance factors, opportunity for entrepreneurial activity, and women entrepreneurs' performance (Crisp & Turner, 2007; Vob & Muller, 2009). Entrepreneurship theory (Shane, 2003) stated that entrepreneur's ability to discover and exploit opportunity for entrepreneurial activity differs between individuals and depends on individual's attitude towards risk taking. For instance, a risk-averse individual is less likely to exploit entrepreneurial opportunity (Shane, 2003). As such, a person may not search for or discover entrepreneurial opportunity if he/she has a negative attitude towards risk-taking. In the same vein, an individual may have an innovation business or service idea, and great likelihood to access microfinance but may not utilize the opportunity if he/she fears risk. Behavioural theories such as the Theory of Planned Behaviour, specifically the Intention Theory (Ajzen, 1991) concluded that attitude towards behaviour leads to intention which eventually leads to actual behaviour. Other supporting behavioural theorists (Crisp & Turner, 2007) found that attitude and behavioural intention are positively related.

Evidences from literature show that adequate credit aids entrepreneurship performance (Kuzilwa, 2005; Lakwo, 2007; Martin, 1999; Ojo, 2009). The result of such credit assistance to entrepreneurs, especially women, is often seen in improved income, output, investment, employment and welfare of the entrepreneurs (Kuzilwa, 2005; Lakwo, 2007; Martin, 1999). Credit had positive impact on business performance of entrepreneurs in Kenya (Green et al., 2002), income and well-being of women in Uganda (Lakwo, 2007). Credit and savings had positive impact on performance in Nigeria (Ojo, 2009). Credit and training had positive impact on women entrepreneur's performance in Tanzania (Kuzilwa, 2005). Savings acts as insurance for credit since women entrepreneurs lack physical collaterals (Akanji, 2006; Mkpado & Arene, 2007; Versluysen, 1999). Savings has been found to have positive effect on enterprise productivity in Nigeria (Ojo, 2009).

Credit, savings and training were found to have positive impact on women entrepreneurs' income and well-being in Haiti, Kenya, Malawi and Nigeria (UNCDF/UNDP, 2003). Savings and credit was also found to have positive effect on women entrepreneurs' well-being in Bangladesh, Indonesia, Ghana and Mexico (Vonderlack & Schreiner, 2001). Equally suggested by literature is the fact that credit and training should go together, however little the training may be (Ibru, 2009; Kuzilwa, 2005). Skill training is necessary to provide the needed entrepreneurial skill for small business start-up while business or management training provides the needed managerial competence for routine and corporate decisions (Cunha, 2007; Jill et al., 2007; Robinson & Malach, 2004; Ying, 2008).

As such, training had positive impact on women entrepreneurship performance in Nigeria, Ghana, USA, Tanzania and Canada respectively (Ibru, 2009; Cheston & Kuhn, 2002; Jill et al., 2007; Kuzilwa, 2005; Reavley & Lituchy, 2008). Women entrepreneurs, especially in developing countries, lacked social connections that are a source of credit and market information (Olomola, 2002), whereas social capital has been found to have positive impact on the performance of women entrepreneurs (Brata, 2004; Lawal et al., 2009; Mkpado & Arene, 2007; Olomola, 2002).

## 3. Role of Microfinance Institutions on the Growth of Women Entrepreneurs

As some microfinance institutions are scaling up, they are finding it beneficial to grow with their women clients, and in that way are assisting them in scaling up their businesses as well. This is the case of MiBanco Peru, which, as it becomes a commercial bank, includes as part of its strategy looking at ways to enhance the skills of women micro-entrepreneurs in Latin America to assist them in achieving scale. To achieve this goal, MiBanco has created the "Crecer mi Negocio" Programme, which enables women to access bigger loans for equipment rather than small individual loans. MiBanco is also bundling its loans with a minimum of 150 hours of training for the women businesses that have qualified for at least $10,000 credit. The training course is developed with Thunderbird University in the United States and a university in Peru. Similarly, Sero Lease in Tanzania, which from the onset provided micro-leases to its women entrepreneur clients, also couples its loans with training that covers not only business and financial management but ways to access markets as well. Most importantly though, Sero Lease has partnered with Exim Bank in Tanzania in order to offer a very early opportunity to its women clients to establish a relationship with a commercial bank by opening a "Tumaini" (savings) account. Through this mechanism, Sero Lease women clients are able to establish and grow their relationship with a commercial bank that, once they reach a certain level of growth, can provide the appropriate financial services for these women to sustain the expansion and development of their business.

### *3.1 Equity is Equally Important for the Growth of Women Entrepreneurs*

Although commercial banks and microfinance institutions are more often approached for financing, other sources such as equity funds or angel/investment funds may be more appropriate for women entrepreneurs, especially at the startup stage. Women-owned businesses attract less than 5 percent of venture capital funds worldwide. As do other businesses, women-owned enterprises need to be properly capitalized if they are to achieve sustainable growth. Investment funds such as equity and angel funds provide the solution not just for accessing seed funding, but also for obtaining hands on coaching very early on in the business, which may increase survival rates. Although not many of current existing funds are specifically targeting women-owned SMEs, a couple is starting to arise both in developed and developing countries. The stocktaking exercise identified four, two of which are already showing promising results. UK-based Trapezia Fund is the first equity fund dedicated to the venture capital requirements of women-centered business in the United Kingdom and in Europe.

Trapezia offer the opportunity to invest in women-focused businesses for 3 to 5 years. The fund, which uses tax rebates to incentivize investors, started with £4.5 million in November 2006. It has invested amounts of £240,000 to £550 in a diversified portfolio of 10 companies led by women. As the investments are relatively new, it is too early to discuss returns. A Trapezia II fund is currently in negotiation to meet the demand of women entrepreneurs in the United Kingdom. Similarly in South Africa, the Women Enterprise Development Initiative (WEDI) is a seven-year, $250 million closed-end, women-owned SME equity fund that combines high social impact investing and above average returns on investment by supplying up to 1 percent of funds under management in the proper assessment and ongoing support required for women entrepreneurs to be successful in the medium- and long-term. WEDI incorporates a multi-disciplinary and holistic approach to enterprise development, while providing additionality with capacity building to the services of the women-owned SMEs to build long-term growth. Operating out of South Africa, the fund covers the Southern African Development Community (SADC) region. WEDI is also fairly new, and it is thus too early to discuss returns.

### *3.2 Global Interest in Promoting Women Entrepreneurs*

The state of women in enterprise development—the starting and growing of individual enterprises—is a major concern among governments in most countries. However, much of this interest is relatively recent. One of the global impetuses in developing countries was the United Nations Decade for Women (1976-1985). In 1979, the General Assembly of the United Nations adopted the International Convention on the Elimination of All Forms of Discrimination against Women (CEDAW), and this paved the way for greater government attention everywhere on the role of women in development programmes and on strategies for eliminating discriminatory practices against women. During the Decade for Women, women's contributions to family income and their roles as producers of goods were documented, and evidence provided that economic development policies often failed to benefit women and, in many cases, even hurt them (Yudelman, 1987). During the 1980s, the question of how to integrate women effectively into development projects was more systematically researched, and the objective of development policies became more focused on how to increase women's access to education, skills training, credit, land and other productive resources to enable them to participate fully in economic activity. At the same time, there was a growing recognition that prevailing patriarchal structures and stereotypical attitudes towards women's roles in society impacted negatively on the ability of women to function as economic agents in society. Peterson and Weiermair (1988) argued that women had been wrongly perceived as a marginal economic group, rather than as a positive socio-economic force. As entrepreneurs they had significant untapped potential as wealth creators.

The Beijing Platform of Action, adopted in September 1995, was a key event in influencing governments to adopt National Gender Policies and to put into place further mechanisms to ensure that women and men had the same rights, obligations and opportunities in all areas of life, including economic activity. Nevertheless, women in developing countries are still too often subject to the persistent burden of poverty; unequal access to resources and participation in economic policy-making; inequality in access to education, skills development and training; unequal access to health and related services; and inequality with men in the sharing of power and decision-making.

In June 2003, the African Development Bank (AfDB) Group held its annual meetings in Addis Ababa, Ethiopia. This was the first occasion on which the Bank organized a special forum on the theme of African Women in Business. At this event, the Bank previewed its new documentary film on African Women Entrepreneurs, and shared preliminary findings from its research on African Women in Business. The film and the research report were formally launched in the Banks' annual meetings in Kampala, Uganda one year later. Therefore, since 2004 the AfDB has designated the mainstreaming of African Women In Business (AWIB) as a new priority.

The Addis Ababa forum in June 2003 made a strong statement about the Bank's vision on the role of women entrepreneurs in private sector development, poverty reduction, and sustainable growth and development. It also provided the first opportunity for the Bank to share its vision with other key development partners in Africa, such as the International Labour Organization (ILO). The ILO was invited to participate in this Forum, and shared its own experiences based on recent studies on issues relating to the growth of women-owned enterprises in Ethiopia, Tanzania and Zambia. The highly complementary roles of the AfDB and ILO became immediately obvious—the Bank specializing in financial support services; the ILO specializing in creating more and better "decent work" in women-owned enterprises. As the two organizations shared the vision of women entrepreneurs contributing to employment creation, poverty reduction and sustainable development, they endeavoured to identify the most appropriate means of enhancing the enabling environment for women to start and grow their own enterprises. The integrated framework, as developed for Atlantic Canada, provided the essential ingredients for a thorough assessment of enabling environments for women entrepreneurs, and this framework was adapted and applied in the African context. The framework is currently being reviewed so that it can more fully reflect the core concerns of both the ILO and AfDB, and eventually will be rolled out as a joint AfDB-ILO assessment instrument.

## 4. Role of Entrepreneurship in Reducing Poverty in the LDCs

Entrepreneurship is the active process of recognizing an economic demand in an economy, and supplying the factors of production (land, labour and capital) to satisfy that demand, usually to generate a profit. High levels of poverty combined with slow economic growth in the formal sector have forced a large part of the developing world's population into self-employment and informal activities (World Bank Group, 2000). But this is not necessarily negative; micro-enterprises contribute significantly to economic growth, social stability and equity. The sector is one of the most important vehicles through which low-income people can escape poverty. With limited skills and education to compete for formal sector jobs, these men and women find economic opportunities in micro-enterprises as business owners and employees (IDB, 2004). If successful, entrepreneurship is likely to result in a small- to medium-enterprise (SME). They include a variety of firms—village handicrafts makers, small machine shops, restaurants, and computer software firms—that possess a wide range of sophistication and skills, and operate in very different markets and social environments. In most developing countries, micro-enterprises and small-scale enterprises account for the majority of firms and a large share of employment. In Ecuador, for example, firms with fewer than 50 employees accounted for 99 percent of firms and 55 percent of firms in 1980; in Bangladesh, enterprises with fewer than 100 workers accounted for 99 percent of enterprises and 58 percent of employment in 1986 (Hallberg, Kristin, 1986). Finally, it has been noted that, "SMEs constitute the most dynamic segment of many transition and developing economies. They are more innovative, faster growing, and possibly more profitable as compared to larger-sized enterprises (The World Bank Group, 2001)." Hence, the role of entrepreneurship in reducing poverty in LDCs is promising.

It has already been identified that entrepreneurship is a major contributing factor to economic growth, however, entrepreneurial ability and leadership tend to be relatively lacking in LDCs. Collier and Batty (http://www.gdrc.org/icm/micro/guy_sust-micro.pdf) have identified five primary reasons for the shortage of entrepreneurs in LDCs. Firstly, this includes the limited profit opportunities which exist in LDCs as a result of lower per capita incomes and limited markets. Secondly, poorly developed capital markets make it difficult for potential entrepreneurs to borrow the funds needed to establish new businesses and take advantage of new investment opportunities. This ties in closely with the role of microfinance in empowering entrepreneurship. Thirdly, poorly developed infrastructures hinder the development of new commodity and resource markets as well as inhibiting the efficient operation of existing ones. Fourthly, sometimes social, cultural and religious beliefs and attitudes attach little importance to monetary gain, restrict economic and social mobility, or assign very low status to entrepreneurs. And fifthly, an unfavourable economic and political climate might discourage the development of entrepreneurial talent and initiative. It is often argued that in light of these barriers, governments hold the key in opening doors to aspiring entrepreneurs in LDCs.

The governments of LDCs can play an important role in improving the quantity and quality of entrepreneurs in a number of ways. Cole et al. (1991) suggested a number of policies to reduce the shortage of entrepreneurs in LDCs, such as the establishment of specialist educational institutions offering courses in business management and administration, and the establishment of specialist government agencies and departments to provide advice and assistance to local entrepreneurs about to take up a business venture are likely to aid the process. Additionally, tax relief, subsidies, investment allowances and other incentives may encourage entrepreneurial activities, similarly, the provision of credit facilities to finance appropriate new business ventures might help. And finally, the attempted maintenance of an economic, social and political climate, which is favourable to entrepreneurs, is essential. It has also been suggested that official policies often make business difficult for micro-entrepreneurs. Improved business regulations, tax regimes, licensing requirements, financial sector reform and bank supervision will promote better conditions for micro-enterprise development (IDB, 2004). A final optimistic suggestion, according to economic theory, implies that the income expenditure multiplier effect may also help to create chain reactions through developing economies, thus helping to break the cycle of poverty. Most of the growth in the microfinance industry over the last ten years has taken place in the absence of specific financial sector policies for microfinance. Today, about 40 million low-income entrepreneurs, mainly in the developing countries, have access to microfinance (Development Gateway, 2004).

In Bangladesh, where about one-third of the world's estimated 30-40 million micro-borrowers reside, the growth has come from specialized microfinance NGO's and Grameen Bank. What began with a few small grants and loans from international donors has now provided over 100 million dollars in loans. The most distinctive feature of the credit delivery system is the absence of middle men between the credit supplier and end user. The bank's cumulative recovery rate is an astounding 98 percent (Yunus, Muhammad, 1994, 2004). Grameen Bank has its own special legal structure, and does not fall under regulatory oversight of the central bank. The bank also aims to raise health and environmental consciousness. Each of its members must plant at least one sapling a year as part of an afforestation programme. Grameen is perhaps the only bank in the world that encourages birth control, sanitation and a clean environment as part of its lending policy (Yunus, 2001).

In Bolivia the microfinance revolution emerged in the 1990's. Large-scale commercial credit is provided there by BancoSol, a privately owned bank for micro-entrepreneurs, and by a number of competitors following hotly on BancoSol's heels (and profits). By 1997 BancoSol, financed by a combination of domestic and international commercial debt and investment and locally mobilized voluntary savings, provided loans profitably to more than one quarter of Bolivia's clients (Robinson, Marguerite S., 2002). *The Wall Street Journal* (15 July, 1997) notes, "The real measure of its success is that BancoSol has spawned a slew of competitions."

In India, despite the large size and depth of its financial system, the majority of the rural poor do not have access to formal finance and financial services. For this reason, innovative microfinance initiatives pioneered by non-governmental organizations strove to create links between commercial banks, NGOs, and informal local groups to create the "SHG Bank Linkage" (The World Bank, 2003). The success of SHG Bank Linkage has been largely attributed to good policy and strong leadership, in conjunction with facilitating government policy and legal framework. India's approach to microfinance—making it profitable and so widely available—helped the country reduce the incidence of poverty from about 40 percent of the population in the mid-1970's to about 11 percent in 1996 (Robinson, 2002). Members of SHG recognize that "several challenges lie ahead", but still believe it has "the right ingredients to be scaled-up into offering mass access to finance for the rural poor while improving sustainability" (The World Bank, 2003).

The economic benefits of sustainable micro-entrepreneurship in LDCs are compelling, and its potential effects on the development process are equally promising. In terms of development and social impact, the microfinance industry allows significant improvements in quality of life for the micro-entrepreneurs of LDCs around the world. They can now stabilize the cash flow of their economic activity, bringing security to the enterprise. This allows them to better manage spending, which often generates savings; and this provides better standards of living to their family, and dependents in terms of housing, nutrition, health and education. Finally, an access to banking and increased security promotes a sense of entrepreneurship, and thus their self-esteem and reputation increase. The initial small loan of usually less than $100 can eventually reintegrate these entrepreneurs into formal networks of the economy and foster the structural and sustainable development of local communities. Furthermore, estimates indicate that today only 5 percent of the micro-credit demand is fulfilled, thus, the microfinance industry is expected to grow significantly in coming years. Despite several challenges ahead, this emerging industry, and the process of sustainable micro-entrepreneurship combine to offer a potential alleviation solution to the poverty crisis of the 21st century, and into a sustainable future.

## 5. Commercialization of Microfinance: A 'New Road' to Traverse

Microfinance (MF) has been globally established as a leading development tool to combat poverty and more specifically aimed at economically empowering the poor and releasing their entrepreneurial potential. It was not prominent before the 1970s but after the emergence of microfinance in Bangladesh, it expended very rapidly in the world. From this modest beginning, more than 3,000 microfinance institutions now operate around the world, with the Microfinance Summit Campaign Report estimating that microfinance institutions serve 128.2 million poor people in developing countries (Reed, 2011). However, with the creeping commercialization of the microfinance sector most discussion now rotates around profitability, 'sustainability' and risk minimization. It is being increasingly forcefully argued that commercialization allows greater opportunity for MFIs to fulfil their social objectives which increase access to a range of demand driven microfinance products and services to the poor (Charitonenko et al., 1998). The onset of commercialization of microfinance has created two camps that represent broadly two different approaches to microfinance: Welfarist and Institutionalist. Those in favour —Institutionalists—argue that microfinance must operate on a commercial (profitable) footing as subsidized lending is not sustainable, funding restrictions limit potential and an absence of market discipline means increased costs. Commercialization, they claim, offers a win-win position in increasing outreach and sustainability while delivering social benefits. Welfarists oppose commercialization because they believe it results in institutions drifting away from their original mission of poverty alleviation. As microfinance moves along a 'new road' with the creeping commercialization of the microfinance sector, most discussion now rotates around profitability, 'sustainability' and risk minimization. We can say that commercialization refers to the 'movement of microfinance out of the heavily donor dependent arena of subsidized operations into one in which microfinance institutions manage on a business basis' as part of the regulated financial system (Christen and Drake, 2002).

Bank Rakayat Indonesia was one of the very first institutions that moved in this new direction, adopting a 'financial system approach' (Bateman, 2010). In 1984, the end result was the establishment of Unit-Desa (BRI-UD) which was wholly profit-oriented organization and was designed to offer 'Kupedes' microloans which were based on the market interest rate (*Ibid.*). This institution rapidly grew and by the end of 2004 it had 30 million savers and 3.1 million borrowers (Robinson, 2001). A drastic shift came in the microfinance paradigm during the early 1990s when PRODEM, the leading microfinance NGO in Bolivia, transformed into a regulated financial bank (BancoSol) in order to move its funding base into financial markets (Christen and Drake, 2002). BancoSol's remarkable success prompted donors and investors to change their approach towards the sustainability of MFIs. Cost control, operational efficiency and commercialism, 'market' or 'businesslike' approaches have all been promoted, and the emphasis is now on providing 'demand-driven' financial services to the poor (Charitonenko, 2003). The remarkable growth of this industry has captured the attention of various practitioners, academics, economist and latterly intermediaries and investors of institutional finance. For investors "one obvious attraction was its safety, reduced volatility, and high returns compared to other sectors" (Bateman, 2010). So, for potential investors it seemed a win-win situation, poverty reduction while making money (Morduch, 2000), appealing to those who found it hard to reconcile their investments with the objectives of long-term human and environmental sustainability. This challenge—of aligning economic growth and human needs with environmental conservation—has created an awareness of sustainable development among leading actors worldwide. Those investors have created a demand for "triple bottom-line" investments (people, planet, profit).

The entry of conventional finance into microfinance has developed two strands of thought: welfarist and institutionalist (Woller, Dunford and Woodworth, 1999), Institutionalists, who favour commercialism, regard a business-oriented approach as necessary step in order to provide high 'quality' financial services to the poor. This group believes that the success of microfinance, both in terms of poverty reduction, through reaching a maximum number of poor households, and in terms of its sustainability, depends on its ability to adopt principles of commercialization in all its operations (Robinson, 2002 and 2004). Moreover, institutionalists note that funding agencies have limited resources compared to the potential demand from poor households. In order to encourage a greater inflow of financial resources, the sector has to attract private capital. This, in turn, requires that the sector can show a reasonably high return on investment, covering both operational and financial costs. A key principle behind commercialization is that 'poor households demand access to credit, not "cheap" credit' (Morduch, 2000). Therefore, MFIs can charge high interest rates without losing outreach.

A competing *welfarist* approach argues that the introduction of the profit motive into microfinance necessarily distorts the actual mission of microfinance institutions—namely reducing poverty—and potentially 'degrades an organization's commitment to the very poor, who will be crowded out by less poor clients' (Christen and Drake, 2002). Welfarists believe that many of the poor households who participate in microfinance programmes are not capable of bearing the burden of commercial loans which carry market interest rates—especially since market rates for the target sector can be excruciatingly high. Thus, it is not possible to achieve two opposing objectives simultaneously.

First, ensuring profitability on the part of MFIs through charging an interest rate which could cover all operational and financial cost and provide profits as well and, second, ensuring poverty reduction. As a result, the profit motive will take priority over the service motive if profitability is emphasized more than the outreach and poverty eradication on the part of microfinance institutions (Woller et al., 1999). According to welfarists, subsidies and donor funding are the only way to accomplish the poverty-reduction objective (Ledgerwood, 1999).

## 6. Microfinance for Micro-Enterprises: An Impact Evaluation of Self-Help Groups

A Research study on "Microfinance for Micro-Enterprises: An Impact Evaluation of Self-Help Groups" conducted by NABARD aiming at understanding the impact of micro-enterprises on SHG beneficiaries in Andhra Pradesh, Gujarat, Jammu & Kashmir and Himachal Pradesh (NABARD, 2010). Microfinance and micro-enterprise development play a crucial role in alleviating poverty and generation of self-employment. In India, 92 percent of the workforce is in the informal sector and micro-enterprise is the main source of livelihood for many of them. Under SHG Bank Linkage programme promoted by NABARD, some of the SHG members have graduated to become micro-entrepreneurs from the status of micro borrowers. It is important at this juncture to understand the impact of these micro-enterprises on the livelihood of SHG members. The study was conducted by NABARD in Andhra Pradesh, Gujarat, Jammu and Kashmir and Himachal Pradesh. The study covered 155 SHGs and 632 members of these SHGs. The selection of SHGs was based on the stratification of SHGs based on their age. SHPIs like banks, NGOs, Farmers Club and GOs were studied to understand their role in promoting SHG members from micro borrowers to micro-entrepreneurs. The reference year for the study was 2005-06.

With regard to main criterion used in formation of SHGs, it was observed that majority of the SHGs in AP, Gujarat and J&K, were formed on the basis of homogeneity criterion in terms of economic status. In HP it was the proximity criterion. Average size of the SHGs ranged between 12 and 14. More than 50 percent of the total sample SHGs belonged to the age category of 'four to six years'. Around 75 percent of total SHGs had conducted regular SHG meetings. To reduce the absenteeism, SHGs had decided to impose fine on absentees and the fine varied between ₹ 2 to ₹ 10. The attendance was more than 90 percent in 54 percent SHGs. Interestingly, in HP attendance was 100 percent in 60 percent of sample SHGs and this phenomenon was rarely found in other States.

Across the four States, SHGs did not change their leaders. In 70 percent of the total SHGs, leaders maintained SHG records. NGOSHPIs helped 20 percent of the total SHGs to maintain the records. Very few SHGs took the help of outsiders of the groups like family members, literate person of the locality and members of other groups to main records. The amount of savings varied across the SHGs. The saving rate varied from ₹ 10 to ₹ 150 per member per month in the surveyed SHGs. In more than 50 percent of the surveyed SHGs across all the age categories, members saved ₹ 50 per month. SHGs mobilized resources from different sources such as, group savings, interest income from internal lending, bank loans, revolving fund and other receipts in the form of donation and money collected through fines and penalties for not attending meetings and defaults in paying regular savings and loan installments. Bank loan constituted more than 59 percent of financial support in SHGs across all the age groups, followed by savings and RFA.

Around 46 percent of the total SHGs were linked to the bank within six to eight months. Branches of commercial banks, RRBs and cooperative banks provided credit linkage to SHGs. It was found that most of the commercial banks (76%) provided the linkage within six to eight months, whereas most of the cooperative banks provided linkage after one year. Totally, SHGs had borrowed ₹ 7,98,880 from the banks as on the date of the survey. Out of this total loan amount, 68 percent loans were taken for productive activities. Maximum number of loan linkages in the study area varied from four to six linkages. Majority of the sample households in Gujarat and J&K were engaged in mixed economic activities. In AP and HP majority of SHG members were engaged in farm activity. Around 78 percent of members had attended secondary level of education in HP followed by J&K (46 percent). In AP majority of the members could only sign (31.6 percent) and majority of members in Gujarat had attended primary level of education (36.7 percent). Around 61 percent members belonged to households that had four to six members.

The largest proportion of the sample SHG members was in the age group 36-55 years in J&K, whereas in Gujarat and Andhra Pradesh, majority of the members were in the age group of 26-35 years. Around 50 percent SHG member households belonged to SC and ST category. Across the States and across the age group, members of households of marginal farmers and landless agricultural labourers constituted a major share (more than 75 percent) of membership in the SHGs. Comparatively, more number of members from the households of agricultural labourers was covered under SBLP in AP than the States of Gujarat and HP. Around 70 percent households stated that the value of assets owned by them increased in the "post SHG" joining period. In HP, no members reported that the value of their assets decreased after joining the SHGs. In J&K, only two percentage of members reported that the value of their assets had decreased in post SHG period. Overall, the change in value of assets was to the tune of ₹ 58,668.79. Most of the SHGs owned milch cattle, poultry and work animals. With regard to movable assets, there was a sharp increase in percentage of members with new movable assets in the range of ₹ 5,001 to ₹ 10,000 after joining the SHGs in AP and HP. In case of Gujarat, the highest range, the percentage of member-households with movable assets of more that ₹ 15,000 had doubled in post SHG period. In AP, the percentage change in the member households in the immovable assets category of ₹ 30,000 to ₹ 50,000 was 13 percent. However, in Gujarat there was no change in pattern of immovable assets across all the ranges. In Himachal Pradesh, the percentage of member households having immovable assets of more than ₹ 70,000, had increased from 1.58 percent to 13.19 percent.

Strategies adopted by NABARD in promoting SHG-Bank Linkage Programme (SBLP) NABARD is the lead agency promoting SBLP in India. It plays a strategic and promotional role to promote SBLP through formal banks in India. The strategies adopted by NABARD cut across different stakeholders engaged in SBLP. NABARD's activities are related to forming strategic linkages and expanding the range of formal and informal agencies which can work as Self-Help Group Promoting Institutions. Providing crucial capacity building by promoting and conducting different training programmes and workshops with the help of Government and Non-Government Agencies for Bankers, SHPIs and SHG members is also NABARD's important role. Further, removing the existing regional imbalances in SBLP by adopting region specific strategies and interventions is an important aspect of NABARD's role. NABARD also plays an important role as financial agency by providing refinance facility to formal banks in order to promote SBLP. The following Table 1 below gives a summary of the financial and promotional supports of NABARD to promote SBLP.

**Table 1:** Financial and Promotional Supports offered by NABARD under SBLP

| Role of NABARD | Programmes | Supports |
|---|---|---|
| Providing Financial Suppor | Refinance Support of Banks | NABARD provides refinance support to banks to the extent of 100% of the bank loans disbursed to SHGs. In 2008-09 the total refinance disbursed to banks for SBLP was ₹ 2,620.03 crore. |
| Promotional Support | Microfinance Development and Equity Fund (MFDEF) | This fund is created to facilitate and support systematic growth of the microfinance sector through diverse modalities. A corpus of ₹ 200 crore is set up and out of this ₹ 80 crore is contributed by NABARD. The major components of this fund include promotional grant assistance to Self-Help Promoting Agencies, training and capacity building for microfinance clients and |

*Contd...*

| Role of NABARD | Programmes | Supports |
|---|---|---|
| | | stakeholders of SBLP, funding support to MFIs, providing Management Information System (MIS) for MFIs, and research on microfinance. |
| | Training and Capacity Building | Every year NABARD organizes training programmes and exposure visits for SHGs, NGOs, Bankers and government agencies to strengthen their effectiveness for implementation of SBLP. During 2008-09, total amount of ₹ 6.10 crore was disbursed as a fund for capacity building, exposure and awareness building, During this year, 6,278 training/capacity building programmes were conducted for 2,83,998 participants. |
| | Grant Support to partner agencies for Promotion and Nurturing of SHGs | NABARD provides grant support to NGOs, RRBs, DCCBs, Farmer's Clubs and Individual Rural Volunteers for nurturing of quality SHGs. During 2008-09, NABARD provided grant of ₹ 1,7689.58 lakh to 331 partner agencies functioning as Self-Help Promoting Institutions. |
| | Pilot project on SHG-Post Office Linkage Programme | The objective of this pilot project is to examine the feasibility of utilizing vast network of Post Offices in rural areas for credit disbursement to rural poor through SHGs. As on 31st March 2009, 2,835 SHGs have opened zero interest saving accounts with select Post Offices in Tamil Nadu and 889 SHGs were linked with loan amount of ₹ 2,13.11 lakh. NABARD has sanctioned ₹ 3 crore RFA to Department of Posts, Tamil Nadu and ₹ 5 lakh to Post Offices in Meghalaya for lending to 50 SHGs in East Khasi Hills. |

*Contd...*

| Role of NABARD | Programmes | Supports |
|---|---|---|
| | Support to SHG Federations | NABARD provides grant-support to the SHG Federation in terms of training, capacity building and exposure visits of SHG members under all of the NABARD's existing promotional schemes. |
| | Special Initiatives for Scaling up SHGs/SHG Federation | Along with Rajiv Gandhi Charitable Trust (RGCT) and Society for Elimination of Rural Poverty (SERP), NABARD has taken special initiatives to promote credit linkages of SHG federations in Andhra Pradesh and Uttar Pradesh. The project envisages promotion and credit linkage of 22,000 SHGs, 1,100 cluster level associations and 44 block-level associations in UP. As on 31st March 2009, in AP 7,808 SHGs were promoted of which 3,972 SHGs were credit linked. 273 village level and 14 block level SHG federations were formed. |
| Support to micro-enterprise development | Micro-Enterprise Development Programme (MEDP) for skill Development | The objective of this programme is to enchance the skill of the members of the mature SHGs to set up micro-enterprises. The duration of the programme varies between 3 to 13 days and budget of ₹ 30,000 per training programme is allocated. During 2008-09, 879 MEDPs were organized on both farm and non-farm activities and 41,479 members of the mature SHGs attended these training programmes. |
| | Support to Activity-based Groups (ABG) | NABARD introduced a new scheme for supporting small scale activity-based groups in terms of capacity building, and supports to production, investments and market related activities. This scheme has both grant and a loan component. Grant component covers the costs of SHG formation and training, extension services establishing market linkages, etc.; bank loan cover the investment and working capital needs of the SHGs enterprise. |

*Contd...*

| Role of NABARD | Programmes | Supports |
|---|---|---|
| Promotional Supprort-MFI Bank Linked | Rating of Microfinance Institutions (MFIs) | NABARD launched a scheme for providing financial assistance by way of grant to Commercial Banks, Regional Rural Banks and Cooperative Bank to avail the service of accredited credit rating agencies for rating MFIs subject to a maximum of ₹ one lakh. |
| | Capital / Equity Support to MFIs | A scheme titled 'Capital/Equity Support to MFIs' was introduced in 2007-08. Under this scheme NABARD has provided capital/ equity supports to various type of MFIs to enable them to leverage commercial and other funds from banks. During 2008-09, capital support of ₹ 11.75 crore was sanctioned to 13 agencies. |
| | Revolving Fund-Assistance to MFIs | NABARD provides Revolving Fund Assistance (RFA) to select MFIs. RFA helps MFIs to access credit facilities through the regular banking channels. These MFIs use RFA for on-lending to SHGs. RFA has a service charge ranging between 6.5% and 9.5% to be repaid within a stipulated period of three to seven years. During 2008-09, RFA of ₹ 6.25 crore was sanctioned |

*Source*: NABARD Annual Report 2008-09; NABARD (2010).

From the above table it can be seen that NABARD has taken several initiatives in promoting SBLP and assisting the poor to set up micro-enterprises (MEs) or take up income generation activities (IGAs). In the next section we analyse the performance of SBLP by looking at the outreach achieved under SBLP so far.

### *Models of SBLP*

Initially, SBLP was operational under three different delivery models for providing microfinance services. The details are included in Table 2 below:

**Table 2:** Delivery models of microfinance under SBLP

| Model | Description |
|---|---|
| Model I | Banks facilitate SHG formation and provide savings and credit linkage directly to SHG |
| Model II | NGOs or other SHPIs facilitate the SHG formation and banks provide the savings and credit linkage to SHG |
| Model III | Banks lend to MFIs and MFIs facilitate the group formation and on lend to SHGs |

While banks and NGOs facilitate SHG formation, the reporting of credit linkage of SHGs is under SHG Bank Linkage Model and MFI-Bank Linkage Model since 2007-08. From the year 2006-07, SBLP follows a two models strategy where the focus is on credit linkage to SHG. The reporting was carried out under following two models (Table 3).

**Table 3:** Credit linkage models under SBLP introduced in 2006-07

| Model | Description |
|---|---|
| Model (i) | SHG-Bank Linkage Model: SHGs are directly financed by the banks |
| Model (ii) | MFI-Bank Linkage Model: Banks lend to MFIs for on-lending to SHGs |

It was further observed that majority of the SHGs were linked under the Model II under SBLP up to 2006. It appears that NGOs and other SHPIs have helped banks to increase the outreach under SBLP. The overall the outreach was growing at rate of 124 percent per annum during the period from 2001-2006. After 2006, however, it can be seen that majority of the SHGs are linked under newly defined Model I where banks linked the SHGs directly. Overall, the number of credit linked SHGs is increasing at the rate of 15 percent per annum during 2006 to 2009. In case of MFI-Bank Linkage Model, four types of MFIs are considered. These are NGO-MFIs (registered under Societies Registration Act, 1860 and/or Indian Trust Act, 1880), Cooperative MFIs [registered under State Cooperative Societies Act or Mutually Aided Cooperative Societies Act (MACS) or Multi-State Cooperative Societies Act, 2002], NBFC-MFIs (registered under Section 25 of Companies Act, 1956 (Not for Profit) and NBFC-MFIs incorporated under Companies Act, 1956 and registered with RBI.

Micro-enterprises and microfinance have proven to be successful in rural villages to improve the quality of life of the rural community. The main objective of this study was to investigate the impact of microfinance on rural micro-enterprise development by using economic variables of development. To select the sample of the study, Multi Stage Sampling Technique was used and it included both microfinance client entrepreneurs and microfinance non-client entrepreneurs. As the study mainly depended on primary data, a field survey was carried out in ten Grama-Niladhari Divisions within Kuliyapitiya-West Divisional Secretary Division. Based on the objective of the study, five hypotheses were developed for economic variables of business income, household income, household expenditure, employment generation and savings. After the statistical testing, the hypotheses that were developed for business income, household income and household expenditure revealed that there was a significant difference between microfinance client entrepreneurs and non-client entrepreneurs but no such difference for employment generation as those micro entrepreneurs were mainly sole proprietors and highly depended on family labour. However, the variable of savings was not tested statistically because both groups of entrepreneurs were reluctant to give their savings data and it was analyzed qualitatively. Accordingly, client entrepreneurs' objective of saving was to improve their businesses whereas non-client entrepreneurs' objective of saving was to support their family matters.

About 90 percent of the people in developing countries lack access to financial services from institutions, either for credit or savings (Robinson, Marguerite, 2002), which further fuels the "Vicious Cycle of Poverty". If the people of LDCs have a limited capacity to invest in capital, productivity is restricted, incomes are inhibited, domestic savings remain low, and again, any increases in productivity are prevented. A lack of access to financial institutions also hinders the ability for entrepreneurs in LDCs to engage in neither new business ventures, inhibiting economic growth, and often, the sources and consequences of entrepreneurial activities are neither financially nor environmentally sustainable (existing for continuing future use).

Microfinance serves as a means to empower the poor, and provides a valuable tool to assist the economic development process. However, unavoidably, various barriers and obstacles limit the roles of microfinance, entrepreneurship and sustainability in reducing poverty in LDCs around the world.

## REFERENCES

Afrane, S. (2002), "Impact Assessment in Ghana and South Africa: A Synthesis of Major Impacts and Lessons", *Journal of Microfinance*, Vol. 4, No. 1: 38-58.

Ajzen, I. (1991), *The Theory of Planned Behavior*. The Organizational Behavior and Human Decision Processes, 50: 179-211.

Akanji, O.O. (2006), Microfinance as a strategy for poverty reduction, Central Bank of Nigeria, *Economic and Financial Review*, 39(4).

Akinyi, J. (2009), The role of microfinance in empowering women in Africa. Retrieved January 10, 2010, from *The African Executive Magazine*: http://www.google.com

Antoncic, B. (2006), Impacts of diversification and corporate entrepreneurship strategy making on growth and profitability: A normative model. *Journal of Enterprising Culture*, 14(1): 49-63.

Barnes, C. and E. Keogh (1999), An Assessment of the Impact of Zambuko's Microenterprise Program in Zimbabwe: Baseline Findings. Washington DC, Management Systems International.

Basargekar, Prema (2012), Measuring Effectiveness of Social Capital in Microfinance: A Case Study of Urban Microfinance Programme in India. *International Journal of Social Inquiry*, Volume 3, Number 2 (2010): 25-43.

Bateman, M. (Ed.) (2011), Confronting Microfinance: Undermining Sustainable Development, Sterling VA: Kumarian Press.

Bates, J.O. (2005), "Micro-entrepreneurship and Job Creation". *Journal of Microfinance*, Vol. 7, No. 2, winter.

Bharti, N. and H.S. Shylendra (2011), Microfinance and sustainable micro-entrepreneurship development, Institute of Rural Management, Anand, Gujarat.

Bourdieu, P. (1985), The Forms of Capital, Handbook of Theory and Research for the Sociology of the Education, Richardson, J.G. (Ed), Greenwood, New York, pp. 241-58.

Brana, S. (2008), Microcredit in France: Does gender matter?, 5th Annual Conference-Nice, European Microfinance Network.

Brata, A.G. (2004), Social capital and credit in a Javanese village. University of Atma Jaya, Yogyakarta, Indonesia: Research Institute.

Charitonenko, Stephanie; Richard H. Patten; and Jacob Yaron (1998), Indonesia: Bank Rakyat Indonesia: 1970-1996, Sustainable Banking with the Poor Case Studies in Microfinance—Long Version, World Bank, Washington, D.C.

Charitonenko, Stephanie (2003), Commercialization of Microfinance: Philippines, Asian Development Bank Regional Technical Assistance No. 5952, Asian Development Bank, Manila.

CGAP (2002), Helping to Improve Donor Effectiveness in Microfinance: Microfinance and the Millennium Development Goals. Retrieved from http://www.cgap.org/gm/document-1.9.2422/DonorBrief_09.pdf

Cheston, S. and L. Kuhn (2002), Empowering women through microfinance, A case study of Sinapi Aba Trust, Ghana. USA: Opportunity International.

Chowdhury, A.J.M. (2009), Microcredit, micro-enterprises, and self-employment of women experience from the Grameen Bank in Bangladesh, Unpublished information.

Christen, R.P. and D. Drake (2002), Commercialization. In *The Commercialization of Microfinance: Balancing Business and Development*, edited by D. Drake and E. Rhyne. Bloomfield, CT: Kumarian Press.

Cole, David C.; Philip A. Wellons and Betty Slade Yaser (1991), 'Financial Systems Reforms: Concepts and Cases', in M. Roemer and D. Perkins, *Reforming Economic Systems in Developing Countries*, Cambridge, Mass.: Harvard University Press, 1991.

Coleman, J. (1988), Social Capital in the Creation of Human Capital. *American Journal of Sociology*, Supplement 94. pp. 94-120.

Copestake, J., S. Bhalotra, S. Johnson (2001), Assessing the impact of Microcredit: A Zambian Case Study, *The Journal of Development Studies*, Vol. 37, No. 4. 81-100.

Coyle, M. (2003), Microenterprise and Microfinance: Presenting a Global Perspective, Conference Report, www.stfx.com

Crisp, R.J. and R.N. Turner (2007), *Essential Social Psychology*, London: Sage Publication.

Cunha, M.P. (2007), Entrepreneurship as decision-making: Rational, intuitive and improvisational approaches. *Journal of Enterprising Culture*, 15(1): 1-20.

Development Gateway (2004), Microcredit and Micro-business Development, July 8, 2004, www.developmentgateway .org/ microfinance (accessed 5 September 2004).

Diagne, A. and M. Zeller (2001), Access to Credit and its impacts in Malawi. Research Report No.116, Washington DC.

EDA Rural System Pvt Ltd., SIDBI Foundation for MicroCredit (2005), The Maturing of Indian Microfinance: Findings and policy implications from the national study, SIDBI, 2005.

Elle, Serge Messomo (2012), Microfinance and Entrepreneurship in Cameroon, University of Buea-Cameroon. *Journal of Asia Entrepreneurship and Sustainability*: http://www.asiaentrepreneurshipjournal.com/2012/JAES/JAES2012/JAESMay2012.pdf#page=121

Ghate, P., E. Ballon, V. Manalo (1996), Poverty alleviation and enterprise development: The need for a differentiated approach. *Journal of International Development*, Vol. 8, Issue 2: 163-78.

Gobbi, Maria Sabrina De, Nara Hari Dhakal and Syed Tahir Hijazi (2005), Micro-finance and microenterprise development: Their contribution to the economic empowerment of women, Social Finance programme, ILO, Geneva.

Gomez, R. and E. Santor (2001), Membership has its privileges: The effect of social capital and neighbourhood characteristics on the earnings of microfinance borrowers. *Canadian Journal of Economics*, Vol. 34, No. 4: 943-66.

Green, Christopher, J. Kimuyu, Peter Manos, Ronny, Murinde, Victor (2002), How do small firms in developing countries raise capital? Evidence from a large-scale survey of Kenyan micro and small scale enterprises, Loughborough University, Kenya: https://dspace.lboro.ac.uk/dspace-jspui/handle/2134/363

Hallberg, Kristin, A Market-Oriented Strategy for Small- and Medium-Scale Enterprises, World Bank Washington D.C., International Finance Corporation Discussion Paper Number 40.

Harrison, R.T. and C.M. Mason (2007), Does gender matter?, Women business angels and the supply of entrepreneurial finance. *Entrepreneurship Theory and Practice*, 31(3): 445-72.

Heidhues, F. (1995), Rural Finance Markets—An Important Tool to Fight Poverty. *Quarterly Journal of International Agriculture*, Vol. 34(2): 105-08.

Hietalahti, J., M. Liden (2006), Socio-economic Impacts of Microfinance and Repayment performance: A Case Study of the Small Enterprise foundation, South Africa, *Progress in Development Studies*, 6, 3: 201-10.

Hossain, M. (1988), Credit for the alleviation of rural poverty, The Grameen Bank in Bangladesh. *IFPRI* http://www.ilo.org

Ibru, C. (2009), Growing microfinance through new technologies, Federal University of Technology, Akure, Nigeria.

IDB (2004), The IDB and Microenterprise: Promoting Growth with Equity, "What is a Microenterprise?" www.gdrc.org/icm/micro/what-is.html (accessed 4 September, 2004).

International Finance Corporation (IFC) (2007), Gender entrepreneurship markets, GEM country brief. Afghanistan: GEM.

Iganiga, B.O. (2008). Much ado about nothing: The case of the Nigerian microfinance policy measures, institutions and operations. *Journal of Social Sciences*, 17(2): 89-101.

Iheduru, N.G. (2002), Women entrepreneurship and development: The gendering of microfinance in Nigeria, 8th International Inter-displinary Congress on Women. Makerere University, Kampala, Uganda. *IIMB Management Review*: http://www.iimahd.ernet

Ismawan, B. (2002), Micro-Finance, Poverty, and Social Capital—A Case Study on the Impact of Economic Intervention, a paper presented at the Asian Regional Conference jointly organized by INASIA and CDF on The Potential and Limitations of Economic Initiatives in Grassroots Development—Current Issues—an Asian experiences from 27th-30th Nov. 2002 at the BRAC Centre for Development Management (BCDM), Rajendrapur, Bangladesh.

Jill, K.R., P.C. Thomas, G.K. Lisa and S.D. Susan (2007), Women entrepreneurs preparing for growth: The influence of social capital and training on resource acquisition. *Journal of Small Business and Entrepreneurship*, 20(1): 169-81.

Kabeer, N. (2001), Conflicts over credit: Re-evaluating the empowerment potential of loans to women in rural Bangladesh. *World Development*, 29(1): 63-84.

Karnani, A. (2007), Microfinance misses its mark; Retrieved February 18, 2009, from Standford Social Innovation Review:http://www.ssireview.org/articles

Kessy, S. (2009), "Microfinance and enterprises performance in Tanzania: Does gender matter"?; *J. Glob. & Sci. Issues*, Vol. 1, Issue 1 (March, 2013).

Koontz, H. and H. Weihrich (2006), *Essentials of Management* (6th Ed.). Tata McGraw-Hill Publication Co.

Kuzilwa, J. (2005). The role of credit for small business success: A study of the National Entrepreneurship Development Fund in Tanzania. *The Journal of Entrepreneurship*, 14 (2), 131-61.

Lakwo, A. (2007), Microfinance, rural livelihood, and women's empowerment in Uganda, Retrieved August 3, 2009, from African Studies Center Research Report 2006: http://www.google.com

Lawal, J.O., B.T. Omonona, O.I.Y. Ajani and O.A. Oni (2009), Effects of social capital on credit access among cocoa farming households in Osun State, Nigeria. *Agricultural Journal*, 4(4): 184-91.

Ledgerwood, J. (1998), Manuel de Microfinance-Une perspective institutionnelle et financière. Banque Mondiale, Washington.

Ledgerwood, J. (1999), Microfinance Handbook: Sustainable Banking with the Poor, The World Bank.

Mahjabeen, R. (2008), Microfinance in Bangladesh: Impact on Household, Consumption and Welfare [J]. *Journal of Policy Modeling*, (30): 1083-92.

Martin, T.G. (1999), Socio-economic impact of microenterprise credit in the informal sector of Managua, Nicaragua. Retrieved January 21, 2009, from http://scholar.lib.vt.edu/thesis/

May, N. (2007). Gender responsive entrepreneurial economy of Nigeria: Enabling Women in a Disabling Environment, *Journal of International Women's Studies*, 9(1).

Mayoux, L. (2001), Tackling the Down Side: Social Capital, Women's Empowerment and Micro-Finance in Cameroon, *Development and Change*, 32: 421-50.

Mkpado, M. and C.J. Arene (2007), Effects of democratization of group administration on the sustainability of agricultural microcredit groups in Nigeria. *International Journal of Rural Studies*, 14 (2): 1-9.

Morduch, J. and Haley, B. (2002), Analysis of the Effect of Microfinance on Poverty reduction, NYU Wagner, Working Paper No. 1014, New York University, NY.

Morris, S.S., W.P. Woodworth and S.R. Hiatt (2006), The value of Networks in enterprise Development; Case Studies of Eastern Europe and South-West Asia. *Journal of Developmental Entrepreneurship*, Vol. 11, No. 4 (2006): 345-56.

Muktar, M. (2009), The role of microfinance banks in the promotion and development of entrepreneurship in semi-urban and rural areas, Department of Economics, Bayero University Kano. P.M.B 3011, Kano-Nigeria.

NABARD (2010), Microfinance for Micro Enterprises: An Impact Evaluation of Self Help Groups, An Occasional Paper-55, NABARD, Mumbai, 2010.

Ojo, Olu (2009), Impact of Microfinance on Entrepreneurial Development: The Case of Nigeria, the International Conference on Economics and Administration, FAA, Bucharest, 14th November 2009.

Okpukpara, B. (2009), Microfinance paper wrap-up: Strategies for effective loan delivery to small scale enterprises in rural Nigeria. *Journal of Development and Agricultural Economics*, 1(2): 41-48.

Oksan, B. (2008), Mahmmad Yunus, Grameen Bank and the Nobel Peace Prize: What Political Science Can Contribute to and Learn From the Study of Microcredit. *International Studies Review*, Sept. Vol. 10, Issue 3: 525-47.

Olajide, O.A. (1980), Financing enterprises in Nigeria through cooperative, Nigerian institute of social and economic research (NISER), Ibadan, Nigeria.

Olaniyi, O.J. (2011), Effect of Microfinance Organization on Small and Medium Scale Enterprises in Nigeria, International Entrepreneurship Forum, Tamkeen, Bahrain.

Olomola, A.S. (2002), Social capital, microfinance group performance and poverty implications in Nigeria. Ibadan, Nigeria: Nigerian Institute of Social and Economic Research.

Otero, M. (1999), Bringing development back into microfinance. Latin America: ACCION International, Pakistan. *The Journal of Entrepreneurship*, 17(1): 59-72.

Peterson, Rein and Klaus Weiermair (1988), Women Entrepreneurs, Economic Development and Change, In Harvey Leibenstein and Dennis Ray (eds), *Entrepreneurship and Economic Development, Journal of Development Planning*, No. 18, United Nations, NY, pp. 195-12.

Popoola, S.O. (2010), Management Perceptions of Internet-based Banking Services in Nigerian Commercial Banks; African Research & Documentation; http://www.faqs.org

Porter, E.G. and K.V. Nagarajan (2005), Successful women entrepreneurs as pioneers: Results from a study conducted in Karaikudi, Tamil Nadu, India. *Journal of Small Business and Entrepreneurship*, 18(1): 39-52.

Putnam, R. (2000), "Bowling Alone: The Collapse and Revival of American Community", Simon.

Raftus, M. (1998), The Impact of Microcredit on the Business, The Entrepreneur and the Household: A Tanzanian Case Study, an unpublished MS dissertation submitted to Faculty of Graduate Studies of the University of Guelph, Canada.

Reavley, M.A. and T.R. Lituchy (2008), Successful women entrepreneurs: A six-country analysis of self-reported determinants of success-more than just dollars and cents. *International Journal of Research Report*, 65.

Reed, Larry, R. (2011), State of the Microcredit Summit Campaign Report 2011; Micro-credit Summit Campaign, Washington, USA: http://www.microdinero.com/files/noticias/3298_SOCR_2011_ReporteGlobal.pdf

Robinson, Marguerite S. (2002), "The Microfinance Revolution: Sustainable Finance for the Poor", p. 34, Washington D.C.: World Bank Office of the Publisher (May 1, 2001).

Robinson, P. and S. Malach (2004), Multi-disciplinary entrepreneurship clinic: Experiential education in theory and practice. *Journal of Small Business and Entrepreneurship*, 17(1): 317-31.

Roomi, M.A. and G. Parrot (2008), Barriers to development and progression of women entrepreneurs in Pakistan. *The Journal of Entrepreneurship*, 17(1): 59-72.

Ronchi, P. (2004), Microfinance: A New Way of Development?, http://www.microfinancegateway.org/files/26525file MEMOIRE english.doc, 1-90.

Rowlands, J. (1997), "Questioning Empowerment: Working with Women in Honduras", Oxfam.

Sabrina, G.D.M. (2005), Nepal and Pakistan Micro-finance and microenterprise development: Their contribution to the economic empowerment of women, International Labor Organization 2005 SEED Working Paper No. 69.

Salman, A. (2009), How to start a business: A guide for women. Pakistan: Center for International Private Enterprise, Institute of National Endowment for Democracy, affiliate of the USA Chamber of Commerce.

Shane, S. (2003), A general theory of entrepreneurship: The individual-opportunity nexus. UK: Edward Elgar.

Ssewamala, F.M., M. Lombe and J.M. Curley (2006), Using individual development accounts for microenterprise development. *Journal of Developmental Entrepreneurship*, 11(2): 117-31.

Swedberg, R. (Ed.) (2000), Entrepreneurship: The social science view, Oxford: Oxford University Press.

Tata, J. and S. Prasad (2008), Social capital, collaborative exchange and microenterprise performance: The role of gender. *International Journal of Entrepreneurship and Small Business*, 5(3/4): 373-85.

Tazul, I. (2007), *Microcredit and poverty alleviation*. Hampshire, England: Ashgate Publishing Limited.

The World Bank Group (2001), Microfinance and Small- and Medium-Sized Enterprises: www.worldbank.org/wbi/banking/microfinance/ (accessed 4 September, 2004).

Tokman, V. (1996), Regulation and the informal economy: Micro-enterprises in Chile, Ecuador, and Jamaica. Boulder: Lynne Rienner Publishers.

Tonelli, Marcello and Carol L. Dalglish (2011), Entrepreneurial becoming: An educational pathway out of poverty. 3rd International Social Innovation Research Conference (ISIRC) 2011, 12-13 September, 2011, London South Bank University.

Tripathy, T. (2005), Microenterprise: A Step towards Rural Women Empowerment. *The ICFAI Journal of Agricultural Economics*, Vol. II, Issue 4: 83-93.

UNCDF/UNDP (2003), Microfinance Program: Impact assessment (2003) based on case studies in Haiti, Kenya, Malawi and Nigeria. United Nations Capital Development Fund in conjunction with United Nations Development Programme.

Versluysen, E. (1999), Defying the odds—Banking for the poor. USA: Kumerian Press.

Vob, R. and C. Muller (2009), How are the conditions for high-tech start-ups in Germany? *International Journal of Entrepreneurship and Small Business*, 7(3): 285-311.

Vonderlack, R.M. and M. Schreiner (2001), Women, microfinance and savings: Lessons and proposals. Washington University, St. Louis, USA: Center for Social Development, Washington, D.C.

Woodworth, W. (2008), Reciprocal Dynamics: Social Capital and Microcredit, *ESR Review*, Fall. pp. 36-42.

Woller, Garry, M.C. Dunford and W. Woodworth (1999), Where to Microfinance? *International Journal of Economic Development*, 1(1): 29-64.

World Bank Group (2001), Microfinance and Small- and Medium-Size Enterprises: www.worldbank.org/wbi/banking/microfinance/ (accessed 4 September, 2004).

World Bank (2003), India: Scaling-up Access to Finance for the Rural Poor (accessed on 5/9/04): http://www.gdrc.org/icm/micro/guy_sust-micro.pdf

World Bank (2004), "Afghanistan: Pioneering Donor Coordination for Microfinance", February 4, 2004, www.worldbank.org (accessed 4 September, 2004).

Wydick, B. and Kevan (2001), Micro Enterprise Lending to Female Entrepreneurs: Sacrificing Economic Growth for Poverty Alleviation?; *World Development and Cultural Change*, 47(4): 853-69.

Yehuala, S. (2008), Determinants of Smallholder Farmers Access To Formal Credit: The Case of Metema Woreda, North Gondar, Ethiopia: Accessed from: http://cgspace.cgiar.org/handle/10568/691

Ying, L.Y. (2008), How industry experience can help in the teaching of entrepreneurship in Universities in Malaysia? *Sunway Academic Journal*, 5: 48-64.

Yudelman, Sally (1987), The integration of women into development projects: observations on the NGO experience in general and in Latin America in particular, *World Development*, Vol. 13 (Autumn).

Yunus, Muhammad (1994), Grameen Bank: Major Uses of Loan Funds in Bangladesh and Extracts from the keynote address delivered at 85t Rotary International Convention held in Taipei, Taiwan, on June 12, 1994.

Yunus, Muhammad (2001), Yunus Centre: Sacrificing Microcredit for Mega-profits. Muhammadyunus.org. Retrieved 10 March, 2011.

Yunus, Muhammad (2004), Grameen Bank, www.grameen-info.org (Accessed on 5/9/04).

Zahid, Mustafa Z. and N. Ismailov (2008), Entrepreneurship and Microfinance—A tool for empowerment of poor—Case of Akhuwat Pakistan, School of Sustainable Development of Society and Technology.

Zaman, H. (2000), Assessing the Poverty and Vulnerability Impact of Micro-Credit in Bangladesh; A Case Study of BRAC; Retrieved from http://wwwwds. worldbank.org/external/default/WDSContentServer/IW3P/IB/1999/09/10/000094946_99082405303974/Rendered/PDF/multi_page.pdf

# 6

# Emerging Gender Sensitivity Issues in Microfinance Development Programmes

Microfinance is promoted as a mechanism for triggering or sustaining social and economic development by supporting entrepreneurial activities. Microfinance can have multiple spin-off benefits, including the potential to be a component of poverty reduction strategies, thus contributing to the Millennium Development Goals (MDGs). Whilst clients who use microfinance services differ according to age, income, ethnicity and whether they access microfinance services as individuals or in groups, typical microfinance clientele in many parts of the world have been resource poor female entrepreneurs.

Microfinance programmes contribute to the MDG by giving low-income rural women and men a chance to develop both their on and off-farm income generating activities. An increase in women's income has been shown to have positive effects for children's nutrition, education and well-being, which also supports other MDGs. Although responding to major development challenges cannot be based solely on simply improving access to financial services, microfinance is an effective tool if used in conjunction with other development approaches and policies. In this regard microfinance institutions themselves are quite diverse ranging from large commercial banks to smaller NGOs. Microfinance institutions also differ greatly in terms of their methodologies; client base and numbers; range of financial products; average loan size; terms of loans; repayment incentives; savings requirements; interest rates and fees; collateral requirement; reliance on donors or other external funding; governance and management; communication capabilities and the non-financial products and training they offer.

Expanding microfinance programmes more often begin with consultations with community officials and villagers in order to brief them on the microfinance institution and its policies. In other cases, microfinance services evolve from NGOs existing in the community who begin to offer more professional financial services. When the latter is the case, the NGO often legally separates any types of welfare service provision from its microfinance work. Other microfinance programmes grow from groups (especially the self-help groups) that are already established in the community such as informal savings groups, guarantee groups or cooperatives. These groups evolve when there are individuals with relevant financial skills and experience in formalizing and organizing such groups. The end result should ideally be democratic membership-based organizations that provide financial services to its members.

Knowledge about gender issues amongst those involved in providing microfinance services will vary depending on the type of microfinance institution. While the staff of many NGOs involved in microfinance may have a comparative advantage regarding knowledge of gender issues, the lack of business skills among staff within the NGO sector may also limit their ability to sustainably deliver microfinance services to poorer clients. The heterogeneity of microfinance institutions (and microfinance clients) poses challenges for the delivery of microfinance in a manner that is gender equitable. In this context, gender sensitivity can be considered both in terms of:

- Whether the programmes, policies and services that microfinance institutions offer their male and female clients are appropriate and respond to their needs.
- The gender issues in the actual organizational structure and functioning of the microfinance institution.

Gender refers to the social, economic and cultural roles and relations between women and men; taking into account the different responsibilities of women and men in a given culture or location and in different population groups (children, aged people, ethnic groups, etc.). Gender mainstreaming is a process by which a microfinance institution considers gender equality issues in all its activities, programmes and policies. So rather than having the focus only on women, the relative conditions of men and women in access to financial services and improving their entrepreneurial activities, are examined in order to highlight differences. Once such differences are identified, something can be done about these inequalities, or links to other organizations that can help redress inequalities can be made.

Women made up 66 percent of microfinance clients funded by the U.S. Agency for International Development (USAID) in 2004. USAID targets women at a higher rate than men because of the empirical evidence that "cash surpluses controlled by women are more likely to be invested in the well-being of children and the household than are surpluses controlled by men", as well as the "higher rates of social and economic exclusion" that women experience (USAID, 2004). The Micro-credit Summit Campaign estimates that the number of very poor women with access to micro-loans reached 55.6 million in 2004 (www.microcreditsummit.org). This represents 83.5 percent of the poorest clients and not the total clients. The Micro-credit Summit Campaign recognizes that it has failed to report on total women clients to date, and expects to remedy that soon. In many MFIs, women have become preferred clients because more of their income benefits their families through improved nutrition, health, education and well-being, because they have higher repayment rates, and because women work better in the group lending programmes that make reaching the poor efficient. On many levels, the microfinance industry has embraced best practices in reaching women clients, but understanding of how best to provide services for women could be much deeper within many MFIs. As the industry grows, even basic knowledge about the nature of women's businesses and the best ways to provide financial services to support them is sometimes ignored or lost in the face of new contexts and new pressures.

Looking only at the microfinance institutions (including those practicing in Northern countries), an average of 36 percent of board members were women; an average of 44 percent of managers were women; and an average of 49 percent of field officers were women. Women on boards ranged from a high of 40 percent in sub-Saharan Africa to a low of 27 percent in Asia. The United States spiked with women managers at 62 percent whereas Western Europe had a low of 34 percent—and all others fell between 40 and 52 percent. The total of women clients among the organizations participating was 63 percent. These figures are skewed as a result of the impressive participation of CEE and the NIS in the survey, which had an average of 48 percent women clients (with Western Europe only slightly higher at 50%). As might be expected, Asia had the highest percentage of women clients (86%) followed closely by Sub-Saharan Africa (83%) and Latin America (80%). Field officers in this survey do not generally reflect the customer base. Field officers for all regions hovered between 41 percent and 49 percent, with the exception of Latin America (64%), and the United States and Canada (76%).

Knowledge about gender issues amongst those involved in providing microfinance services will vary depending on the type of microfinance institution. While the staff of many NGOs involved in microfinance may have a comparative advantage regarding knowledge of gender issues, the lack of business skills among staff within the NGO sector may also limit their ability to sustainably deliver microfinance services to poorer clients. The heterogeneity of microfinance institutions (and microfinance clients) poses challenges for the delivery of microfinance in a manner that is gender equitable. In this context, gender sensitivity can be considered both in terms of:

- whether the programmes, policies and services that microfinance institutions offer their male and female clients are appropriate and respond to their needs.
- the gender issues in the actual organizational structure and functioning of the microfinance institution.

Gender broadly refers to the social, economic and cultural roles and relations between women and men; taking into account the different responsibilities of women and men in a given culture or location and in different population groups (children, aged people, ethnic groups, etc.). Gender mainstreaming is a process by which a microfinance institution considers gender equality issues in all its activities, programmes and policies. So rather than having the focus only on women, the relative conditions of men and women in access to financial services and improving their entrepreneurial activities, are examined in order to highlight differences. Once such differences are identified, something can be done about these inequalities, or links to other organizations that can help redress inequalities can be made.

Promoting "gender-sensitive" entrepreneurship via microfinance institutions puts the onus on the institution itself to be 'gender sensitive'. But, what do we mean by "gender sensitive"? Being gender sensitive would mean that the gender-based differences between men and women clients/staff are acknowledged and transparent. Once acknowledged, staffs from microfinance institutions take into consideration how such differences affect the ability of microfinance clients to avail of microfinance services and how such differences affect their entrepreneurial activities. Through this process issues that help or hinder men and women clients (or staff) are identified. Very often women face particular constraints in developing their entrepreneurial activities, so the focus of being gender sensitive is frequently on women 'catching up'. On top of their entrepreneurial activity, rural women usually have a heavy domestic workload that is unpaid, leaving them less time to expand their small businesses. Another constraint is that in some regions women's mobility is constrained. They may not then realize the market potential or profitable adjustments they could make to their products.

Gender sensitivity in microfinance institutions would imply that the institution acknowledges gender-based constraints that affect women in their entrepreneurship activities and plan services accordingly. At the very least, the microfinance institution can try to ensure that it does not worsen or perpetuate inequalities between women and men by ignoring gender-based constraints, or expecting women's business to operate exactly like men's. Microfinance institutions should consider how their services can help women to operate in an often 'male-dominated' business world. Promoting gender-sensitive entrepreneurship via microfinance institutions does not mean a focus only on women. Instead the microfinance institution needs to examine the relative conditions of men and women. Without comparing women and men and indeed different categories of women clients, it is not possible to highlight and address gender-based inequalities. Approaches to increasing gender sensitivity thus are analytic tasks, requiring an assessment of the way in which gender (among other factors) contributes to shaping a particular trend in being a successful entrepreneur.

It is important to stress that neither women nor men (nor poorer women and men) are a homogenous group, and should not be treated as such in microfinance programmes. Women that are 'targeted' for microfinance can be widowed, single, newly married, pregnant, young girls, living with HIV, unemployed, employed, rural, urban, etc. Likewise, men can be categorized by their marital status, age, income level, ethnicity, health status and so on. The different categories of women (and men) often have different needs for financial services. For example, savings are very important for both low-income women and men. Savings can provide a safety net for single-mothers or women who face an uncertain future. On the other hand, in many parts of Asia, whilst women are often considered better at saving, rather than focus only on women, it would be better to encourage men in savings groups for more harmonious household financial management (Uma Murray, 2005).

This chapter discusses at length some emerging issues of microfinance development especially in the context of the relevant gender sensitive issues needing special attention to gender mainstreaming for better empowerment. It also reflects the desirability of issuing new guidelines to help promote wider participation of women, relative to men in the microfinance development initiatives. Addressing Gender Concerns in Microfinance Institutions (Development and Regulation)

Draft Bill 2011 has been discussed in detail. The need for greater women's empowerment for better Microfinance access to Financial Services is also briefly touched upon for gender sensitization to this programme.

## 1. A General Guide to Gender Sensitive Microfinance

Microfinance as a business sector emerged when it was realized that low-income people can pay back loans on time and can save money, provided they are able to access tailored financial services. So, why is it important to ensure that microfinance policies and programmes are gender sensitive? Experience has shown that the most effective (and efficient) microfinance programmes for low-income people must be highly personalized explicitly taking into account the needs of such clients (i.e. a 'Client First' approach to microfinance). Prudent business practice stresses client responsiveness. Socio-economic and gender analysis can greatly assist in helping to disaggregate clients and determine if there is a neglected market niche for the services offered by a specific microfinance intermediary. In addition, microfinance delivery must be gender-sensitive because a new source of income can change intra-household relationships and has differential impacts on women and men depending on who controls the new source of finance. An analysis of gender issues at the planning stage of microfinance activities helps to guarantee that programmes and projects are more likely to reach their objectives. Many microfinance institutions (MFIs) are increasingly aware of the importance of gender concerns in their activities. This is particularly true when outside donor funding is contingent on a social and gender audit of a proposed programme. Nevertheless, gender issues are often prominent in the rhetoric of microfinance intermediaries, but absent in practice.

Indeed, there are microfinance viewpoints which assume a lack of gender issues simply because microfinance has become a sector that caters predominantly for women. However, having exclusively male or exclusively female projects does not mean that there are no gender issues. There may still be important gender issues and a gender bias may exist in service delivery. For instance, some members of the community or society may be adversely affected and excluded by a microfinance programme but may not be vocal or powerful enough to express their needs. This Guide takes the approach that it is not sufficient only to cater to women clients to solve gender issues. A gender-sensitive approach is inclusive rather than exclusive. Taking into account the needs and constraints of both women and men when designing and delivering finance, helps to ensure gender sensitivity. Gender analysis is a powerful approach to assess the impact of microfinance on the various stakeholders regardless of whether they are direct or indirect beneficiaries.

Another reason for concentrating on microfinance and gender is because socioeconomic and gender issues are now firmly on the agenda of many governments, international donors and bilateral founders. In the widely accepted Beijing Platform for Action at the Fourth World Conference for Women, 1995, (http://www.rlc.fao.org/en/publications/gender-sensitive-microfinance/) governments pledged to; "promote and support women's self-employment on appropriate terms equal to those of men and review, reformulate if necessary and implement policies to ensure that they do not discriminate against micro, small and medium-scale enterprises owned by women in rural and urban areas" (UNDP, 1995a & b). Gender sensitive microfinance policies provide the supporting framework for an enabling environment. The promotion of women's self-employment often requires the transformation of existing policies with a gender perspective to ensure that women have equal rights to obtain financial services in their own right (Jahan, 1995).

This Guide was developed as a practical aid for those involved in microfinance programmes to ensure that socioeconomic and gender issues are taken into account when starting or developing a microfinance programme, when designing national policies for microfinance and for disaggregating microfinance markets to find out more about clients. Such an approach can minimise risk and improve efficiency by drawing on lessons learned regarding socioeconomic and gender concerns that can help microfinance institutions become sustainable (Johnson, 1999, 2005). The Guide draws upon the Food and Agriculture Organization's

(FAO, 1984) Socioeconomic and Gender Analysis (SEAGA) framework. The aim of the SEAGA programme is to increase awareness of gender issues, as well as to strengthen the capacity of development specialists to incorporate socioeconomic and gender analysis considerations into development planning. SEAGA emphasizes the socio-cultural, economic, demographic, political, institutional, and environmental factors that affect the outcome of development initiatives and the linkages between them from a gender perspective. Furthermore SEAGA examines the linkages among these factors at three levels—macro (programmes and policies), intermediate (institutions) and field (communities, households and individuals).

The Guide structures questions that can be asked by microfinance intermediaries in attempting to ensure that their operations are gender sensitive. There are suggestions in the Guide for ensuring that policy or macro level microfinance planning is gender sensitive. Questions are also posed for finding out more about gender relations at the microfinance client level. Overall, this Guide should serve as a reference point to ensure that microfinance activities reach their intended socioeconomic target group.

## 2. Potential Benefits of Rural Microfinance with focus on Gender Mainstreaming

The expansion of microfinance since the 1990s has significantly increased women's access to facilities for small loans and savings. This increased access to microfinance has been seen as contributing not only to poverty reduction and financial sustainability, but also to a series of 'virtuous spirals' of economic empowerment, increased well-being and social and political empowerment for women themselves, thereby addressing goals of gender equality and empowerment. Some of the dimensions of and interlinkages among the various virtuous impact spirals identified in the literature are shown in Fig. 1. First, increasing women's access to microfinance services can lead to their economic empowerment (the linkages in the centre of the figure). Women's roles in household financial management may improve, in some cases enabling them to access significant amounts of money in their own right for the first time. This might enable women to start their own economic activities, invest more in existing activities, acquire assets or raise their status in household economic activities through their visible capital contribution. Increased participation in economic activities may raise women's incomes or their control of their own and household income.

This, in turn, may enable them to increase longer-term investment in and productivity of their economic activities, as well as their engagement in the market. Second, increasing women's access to microfinance can increase household well-being (the linkages on the left in the figure). This is partly the result of economic empowerment, but may occur even where women use microfinance services for the activities of other household members, for example husbands or children. Even where women are not directly engaged in income earning activities, channelling credit or savings options to households through women may enable them to play a more active role in intra-household decision-making, decrease their own and household vulnerability, and increase investment in family welfare. This situation may benefit children through increasing expenditure on their nutrition and education, particularly for girls. It can also lead to improved well-being for women and enable them to bring about changes in gender inequalities in the household. It is also likely to benefit men as a result of the increased household income.

Third, a combination of women's increased economic activity and increased decision-making in the household can lead to wider social and political empowerment (the linkages on the right in the Fig. 1).

Women, themselves, often value the opportunity to make a greater contribution to household well-being—giving them greater confidence and sense of self-worth. The positive effects on women's confidence and skills, their expanded knowledge and the formation of support networks through group activity and market access can lead to enhanced status for all women in a community. In some societies where women's mobility has been very circumscribed and women previously had little opportunity to meet women outside their immediate family, there have been very significant changes. Individual women who gain respect in their households may then act as role models for others, leading to a wider process of change in community perceptions and men's increased willingness to accept change.

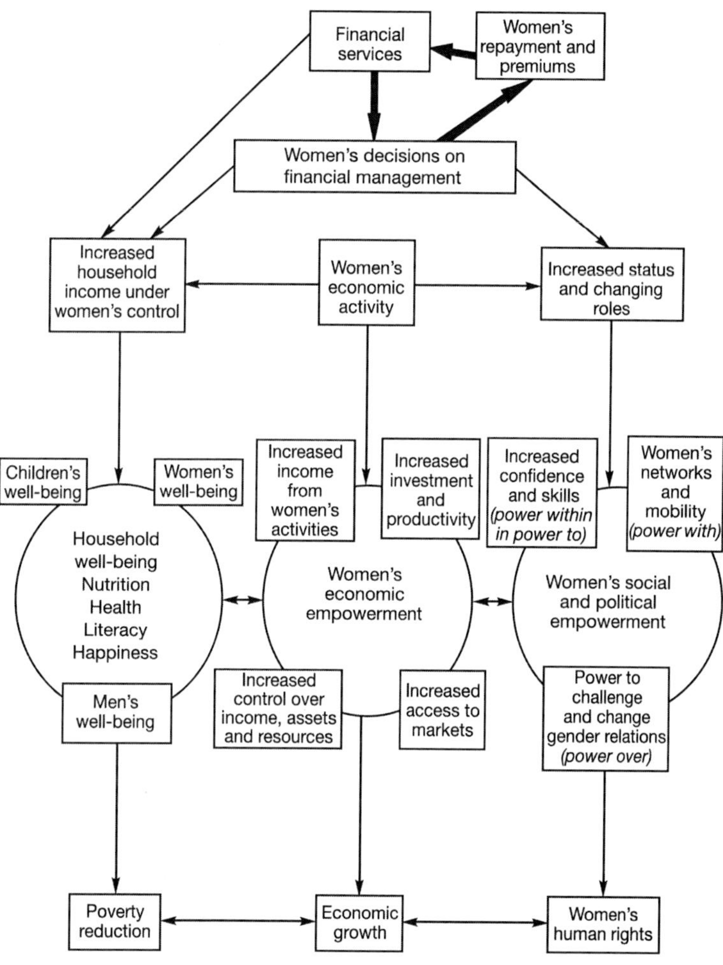


**Fig. 1:** Microfinance to stimulate wider Social and Political Empowerment

*Source*: Mayoux, L. and M. Hartl (2009).

Most microfinance providers can cite case studies of women who have benefited substantially from their services —both economically and socially. Some women who were very poor before entering the programme have started an economic activity with a loan and have built up savings, thereby improving their own and household well-being, as well as relationships in the household, and becoming more involved in local community activities (Cheston and Kuhn, 2002; Kabeer, 1998, 2001; and Rajagopalan, 2009). Some women show enormous resourcefulness and initiative when provided with a loan or given the chance to save without interference from family members. Impact studies that differentiate by poverty level generally find benefits to be particularly significant for the 'better-off poor', who have some education and contacts on which to build in conducting a successful enterprise (Ashe and Parrott, 2001). Finally, women's economic empowerment at the individual level (the linkages across the bottom of the figure) can make potentially significant contributions at the macro level through increasing women's visibility as agents of economic growth and their voices as economic actors in policy decisions. This, together with their greater ability to meet the needs of household well-being, in turn increases their effectiveness as agents of poverty reduction. Microfinance groups may take collective action to address gender inequalities within the community, including such issues as gender violence and access to resources and local decision-making. Higher-level organization may further reinforce these local changes, leading to wider movements for social and political change and promotion of women's human rights at the macro level. Some NGOs have used microfinance strategically as an entry point for wider social and political mobilization of women around gender issues. Savings-and-credit groups have at times become the basis for mobilizing women's political participation. Moreover, these three dimensions of economic empowerment, well-being and social and political empowerment are potentially mutually reinforcing 'virtuous spirals', both for individual women and at the household, community and macro level.

### *2.1 Importance of Gender Mainstreaming: Potential Vicious Circles*

Despite the potential contribution of microfinance to women's empowerment and well-being, there is a long way to go before women have equal access to financial services in rural areas or are able to fully benefit from them. This is partly because of contextual differences in the gender division of labour. Although there are significant differences among and within regions in the types of crops and other economic activities in which they are involved, women tend to be restricted to subsistence food crops and the marketing of lower-profit goods. Although there are significant differences in household, family and kinship structures, women are also almost universally disadvantaged in access to and control of incomes (from their own or household economic activities) and assets (particularly land). These differences and inequalities affect the types of financial services they need and also the ways in which they are able to use and benefit from them. This does not mean that microfinance should cease attempting to target women. They have a right to access all types of financial services and to the removal of all forms of gender discrimination among financial service providers. The right of women to equality is enshrined in agreements and conventions on women's human rights signed by most governments.

Rather, these gender differences and inequalities mean that gender-blind product design and service delivery are not enough, and that gender dimensions must be as integral to financial service provision as are poverty and financial sustainability concerns. Most of what follows is based on the evidence for credit. Despite some advances, women's access to microfinance is still unequal. Statistics on client or membership numbers, even when gender disaggregated, say very little about the quality of the services accessed by women compared with those for men. Women generally receive lower loan amounts, and this cannot be completely accounted for by demand factors. Some women have extremely good business ideas requiring larger loans, but they face discrimination in accessing such loans, with the result that their businesses collapse because they are forced to purchase inferior equipment or materials. Most programmes to which women have access do not give them sufficiently large loans to purchase assets such as land and housing. Many require assets as collateral or the signature of a 'male guardian'. In many rural village banks and credit-and-savings cooperatives, women are the majority of savers, but men receive the majority of loans. The exceptions are women-only organizations or those having an effective gender policy. Because men form the majority in decision-making bodies, the interest rates are fixed in favour of borrowers, leading to lower levels of financial sustainability.

In some cases, and particularly for poor women, microfinance may undermine existing informal systems, such as crisis funds in rotating savings-and-credit associations (ROSCAs), if better-off women divert ROSCA funds as loan-interest payments to MFIs (Mayoux, 2001). Availability of credit may also reduce the willingness of patrons and relatives to give interest-free loans or access to more charitable forms of credit from traders. Moreover, a recent study has found that women's access to loans decreases compared with that of men as NGOs transform into formal institutions and become more profitable and 'mature' (Cheston 2006; Frank, Lynch and Schneider-Moretto, 2008). The degree to which women are able to benefit from minimalist financial services that do not take gender explicitly into account depends largely on context and individual situation, and may also change over time. However, none of the expected linkages between women's access to financial services and empowerment can be assumed to occur automatically. First, women's programme membership, numbers and size of loans and repayment data cannot be used as indicators of actual access or proxy indicators of empowerment.

Registration of loans in women's names does not necessarily mean participation even in decisions about loan applications. Men may take the loans from women or directly negotiate loans in women's names with male credit officers, as an easier way of getting access to credit. Loans may be repaid from men's earnings, through women forgoing their own consumption, or from income or borrowing from other sources. High demand for loans by women may be more a sign of social pressure to access outside resources for in-laws or husbands than of empowerment. Second, the contribution of financial services to increased income varies widely. Evidence suggests that, particularly in South Asia and parts of Latin America, most women use loans for their husband's. In Harper's study of the Aga Khan Rural Support Programme, out of 31 micro-enterprise loan-takers interviewed, only seven loans were controlled by women and by men and women had not been involved in the loan process (Harper, 1995). In a further eight cases, women did not even know the loan had been taken out. Appropriation of loans by men was also noted in Port Sudan (Amin, 1993) and three Agency for Cooperation and Research in Development (ACORD)-Uganda programmes (ACORD, 1996).

In the Bangladesh Rural Advancement Committee (BRAC), 10 percent of women respondents reported no personal income. The women relied on family and friends for weekly cash repayments (Montgomery, Bhattacharya and Hulme, 1996) activities. Even where they use loans for their own activities, women's choice of activity and the ability to increase their incomes are seriously constrained by gender inequalities in access to other, supplementary resources for investment; responsibility for household subsistence expenditure; lack of time due to unpaid domestic work; low levels of mobility; and vulnerability—all of which limit women's access to profitable markets in many cultures. The rapid expansion of loans for poor women may saturate the market for 'female' activities or products and cause profits to plummet, affecting even more those poorer women with no access to credit. The degree to which credit contributes to increased incomes for women (as well as for men) also depends largely on how well the delivery of credit is adapted to the economic activities being financed.

Agricultural loans that arrive late or are not large enough to pay for inputs may simply burden a woman with debt that she cannot repay from the proceeds of the activity she wished to finance. Compulsory savings and insurance premiums may constitute a further drain on resources for investment, unless they are designed in the interests of the borrower and not just to limit risk and increase financial sustainability for the financial institution. Third, women's increased contribution to household income does not ensure that women necessarily benefit or that there is any change in gender relations within the household. Although women do, indeed, often feel more in control and have a greater sense of self-worth, these subjective perceptions are not necessarily translated into actual changes in well-being, benefits or gender relations in the household. Although in some contexts women may seek to increase their influence within joint decision-making processes, rather than seek independent control of income, neither of these outcomes can be assumed to occur. Evidence indicates that, in response to women's increased (but still low) incomes, men may withhold more of their contribution to the household budget for their own luxury expenditure. Men are often very enthusiastic about women's savings-and-credit programmes because their wives no longer 'nag' them for money.

Small increases in access to income may come at the cost of heavier workloads, increased stress and diminished health. Women's expenditure patterns may replicate rather than counter gender inequalities, and may continue to disadvantage girls. Without substitute care for small children, the elderly and the disabled, and services to reduce domestic work, many organizations report that women's outside work adversely affects children and the elderly. Daughters, in particular, may be withdrawn from school to assist their mothers. Although, in many cases, women's increased contribution to household well-being has considerably improved domestic relations, in others it has intensified tensions. This problem affects not only poor women, but women from all economic backgrounds, indicating Goetz and Sengupta's study of 275 women in Bangladesh found that women had full control of loans in only 17.8 percent of cases, and in as many as 21.7 percent they had no control (Goetz and Sengupta, 1996). A survey of 26 women in Samajtantrik Chhatra Front (SCF)-Bangladesh found that 68 percent of loans had been used by the husbands or sons—and all, except one, were first-time loans (Basnet, 1995). Similar patterns of use of loans by men (and sometimes even higher proportions) were reported by most programmes attending the South Asia and Latin America regional workshops facilitated by the author, even where women are explicitly targeted. Kabeer (1998) has discussed this ambiguity in detail for Bangladesh.

In Pakistan, a recent respected impact assessment found that, for all six organizations studied, there was actually a significant decrease in women's empowerment in the household across a whole range of indicators of decision-making. The reasons for this are unclear (Zaidi et al., 2007). The impact of micro-financing to women on men's contributions to the household has not been part of most research questioning. However, this is a frequent finding of in-depth, qualitative interviewing by the author in gender evaluations of microfinance in all contexts. That this is occurring on a relatively large scale is confirmed by anecdotal evidence from practitioners at workshops in Africa, Asia and Latin America. In some cases, this other expenditure includes the costs of marriage to second and third wives or upkeep of families from other relationships. Because of the significant implications for poverty creation and intensification, this is an area in which much more research is needed (Mayoux, 1999). This problem was reported on a significant scale by many programmes in all the regional workshops facilitated by the author that the empowerment process must have effective strategies to work with men on changing attitudes and behaviours.

The economic empowerment of individual women and their participation in group-based microfinance programmes are not necessarily linked to social and political empowerment. Earning an income and finding time to attend group meetings for savings-and-credit transactions may take women away from other social and political activities—and experience suggests that where meetings focus only on such transactions, women commonly want to decrease the length and frequency of group meetings over time. Women's existing networks may come under serious strain if their own or others' loan-repayment or savings contributions become a problem (Rahman, 1999). The contribution of financial services to women's social and political empowerment depends very much on other factors, such as staff attitudes in interacting with women and men, the types and effectiveness of core training (for savings, credit and group formation) and other capacity-building, the types of non-financial support services or collaboration with other organizations.

Where women are not able to significantly increase incomes under their control or negotiate changes in intra-household and community gender inequalities, they may become dependent on loans to continue in very low-paid occupations with heavier workloads while enjoying little benefit. For some women, microfinance has been positively disempowering:

- Credit is also debt. If credit is badly designed and used, the consequences for individuals and programmes can be serious. Debt may lead to severe impoverishment or abandonment and put serious strains on networks with other women.
- Savings and pension instalments are forgone consumption and investment. In many contexts, particularly where inflation is high, depositing cash with financial institutions may not be the best use of poor peoples' resources, compared with investing in other assets or directly in livelihoods.
- Insurance premiums, in addition to representing forgone consumption and investment, may be lost when a crisis prevents poor people from continuing payments.
- Remittance transfers reduce the funds available to migrants in the host country, and may distort local markets and consumption patterns in the recipient country without leading to local economic development.

The contribution of microfinance alone appears to be most limited for the poorest and most disadvantaged women (Ashe and Parrott, 2001). Where repayment is the prime consideration or where the main emphasis of programmes is on existing micro-entrepreneurs, all the evidence suggests that these women are the most likely to be explicitly excluded by programmes and peer groups. Finally, very little research has been done on the gender impact of financial services for men. Any financial intervention available to any household member has the potential to reinforce or challenge existing inequalities in ways that may contribute to or undermine the poverty and potential of other household members. As noted earlier, research suggests that financial services targeted at men contribute less to household well-being and food security. When financial services automatically treat men as heads of household, they may reinforce what are often only informal rights that men have over household assets, labour and income. In other words, they may seriously undermine women's informal rights. The exclusionary practices of groups and their impacts on social capital are discussed in detail in Pairaudeau (1996) and Van Bastelaer (1999). Women's exclusion of particularly disadvantaged women is described in Pairaudeau, and this is often an explicit policy of MFIs in client selection. Development, such outcomes may have consequences not only for the women and households involved, but for the effectiveness of the intervention and the sustainability of the institutions.

There is a need for much greater understanding of the ways in which different types of products and services affect women and men from different backgrounds and in various contexts. The generic question 'Does microfinance empower women?' is not very useful or meaningful. The identification and weighting of standardized SMART indicators (specific, measurable, attainable, realistic, timely) can be controversial because of the complexity of empowerment itself and the frequent trade-offs between its various dimensions, e.g. between levels of income earned and time available for other activities, and between women's autonomy and the effort they have to put into changing abusive relationships. Women's own goals and preferences vary significantly with context and between women even within the same context.

The main justification for in-depth impact assessment is to improve practice, and this requires careful attention to the high degree of variation in financial services and the institutions delivering them. In many contexts, information is likely to be unreliable because of the clients' incentives to alter their responses depending on the actual or perceived consequences of those responses for their future access to credit. The gender of both the respondents and the interviewer affect responses even from members of the same household (Cloke, 2001). Given the costs of credible research and impact assessment, it is the view of the author that more systematic market research that includes information on impact is the most useful approach, though current methodologies need to be more effectively designed in terms of their ability to collect qualitative and quantitative information on empowerment, particularly the dimensions important to clients.

### *2.2 Definition of Gender Mainstreaming*

Gender mainstreaming as a strategy to achieve gender equality was also identified by governments at the Fourth World Conference on Women, held in 1995 in Beijing. Recent reviews and evaluations in a range of development organizations and agencies have demonstrated that gender mainstreaming had not been well understood or supported and thus has not been effective in translating policy commitments on gender equality into resources and implementation. Recommendations toward increased effectiveness include adopting a more strategic approach that analyses and identifies priority opportunities and entry points, rather than attempting to do everything, everywhere; strengthening institutional supports and accountability mechanisms for gender equality mainstreaming; paying attention to the internal/human resource policies as well as operational/programmatic dimensions of an organization's work; and providing the resources to support proper analysis, implementation, monitoring and evaluation.

> "Mainstreaming a gender perspective is the process of assessing the implications for women and men, of any planned action, including legislation, policies or programmes, in any area and at all levels. It is a strategy for making the concerns and experiences of women as well as of men an integral part of the design, implementation, monitoring and evaluation of all policies and programmes in all political, economic and societal spheres, so that women and men benefit equally, and inequality is not perpetuated. The ultimate goal of gender mainstreaming is to achieve gender equality."
>
> —United Nations Economic and Social Council, 1997

### *2.3 Organizational Gender Mainstreaming*

A concern with gender issues in financial services is not new. Nor can it be dismissed as a Western or donor-imposed agenda. From the early 1970s, women's movements in a number of countries, notably India, became increasingly interested in the degree to which women were able to gain access to and benefit from poverty-focused credit programmes and credit cooperatives. The problem of women's access to credit was highlighted at the first International Women's Conference in Mexico in 1975, leading to the setting up of the Women's World Banking network. In the wake of the second International Women's Conference in Nairobi in 1985, there was a mushrooming of government and NGO-sponsored income generating programmes for women, many of which included savings and credit. Then, in the 1990s, microfinance programmes such as the Grameen Bank and some affiliates of the Foundation for International Community Assistance (FINCA) and ACCION International increasingly began to target women, not only as part of their poverty mandate, but also because they found women's repayment rates to be significantly higher than men's.

A range of different types of institutions currently provide rural financial services. Some target women mainly or exclusively, or have a written or informal gender policy. The variations among organizational models can significantly influence gender outcomes and have implications for the most effective ways in which gender can be mainstreamed. In all types of institutions, the most cost-effective means of maximizing contributions to gender equality and empowerment is to develop an institutional structure and culture that is woman-friendly and empowering, and that manifests these traits in all interactions with clients. A full discussion of frameworks and methodologies for institutional gender mainstreaming is outside the scope of this guide. Some key elements that could be included in microfinance organizations of all types are however given in Box 1 and Box 2.

## BOX 1

## Mainstreaming gender: Elements of a strategy in minimalist rural microfinance institutions

**Mainstreaming women's language**

Conceptually—in terms of understanding and valuing women's activities, strategies, priorities and challenges and mainstreaming these understandings throughout the organization's practice.

Literally—in terms of making all information accessible in local languages and visual forms that women are more likely to speak and understand.

**'Walking the talk': Organizational gender policy**

Ensure that the staff of the organization, women and men, are able to interact with women on the basis of respect and equality and also promote a vision of women's empowerment in their interactions with men (see chapter 2).

**Participatory market research**

Design products from the client perspective through participatory market research (see chapter 3).

**Gender mainstreaming in non-financial services**

Ensure that women have equality of access to all non-financial services. Even very basic staff interactions with clients, such as application processes, can promote a vision of gender equality empowerment (see "Integration and inter-organizational collaboration to provide non-financial services" in chapter 4).

**Building on group activities for action learning**

Core group mobilization for savings and participatory action learning, which the groups can continue themselves (see "Participation and collective action" in chapter 4).

**Macro-level focus and advocacy**

Many organizations, even banks, are increasingly interested in value chain finance and specialize in financing particular types of businesses or sectors. These can include activities in which women are concentrated, with the organizations studying ways to develop such activities through marketing and supply chains. A particular area for further investigation is promotion in service markets used by women, for example child care or domestic services.

## BOX 2

## Organizational mainstreaming: Some key strategies for financially sustainable organizations

**Vision and institutional culture**

Institutional culture is expressed in the way an organization chooses to promote itself. What sorts of messages does it sent through the images in its offices, through its advertising, and through the consistency of its gender aims in the community with its internal gender policy? The institution's routinely issued promotional leaflets, calendars and advertising are a very powerful means of presenting alternative models and challenging stereotypes. These can be made available for clients to view while they are waiting to see staff. There should be no extra cost in ensuring that promotional materials achieve these goals. It is just a question of vision—and of ensuring that the designers of the materials understand and share that vision.

**Equal opportunity policies for staff**

As a human rights issue, such policies set an appropriate example for programme participants and increase programme effectiveness in reaching and empowering wormen. They require family-friendly working partices for women and men, and ensuring that women's specific contributions to the job are fully valued (e.g. their better understanding of women, multitasking abilities), and their specific constraints due to contextual factors (e.g. greater vulnerability to violence) are taken into consideration in job requirements, facilities and pay.

**Recruitment, training and promotion policies**

Gender awareness and sensitivity are criteria for recruitment, as essential requirements of a professional service.

Gender sensitivity is an integral part of all staff training.

Perfomance on gender equity is recognized in criteria for promotion.

A gender focal point is appointed and other staff time allocated to work on gender issues. Failing this, the consultant services of a gender expert should be sought to fully institutionalize these basic principles.

**Information systems**

Gender and empowerment indicators are integrated into existing programme management information systems, including 'social performance management'.

Gender disaggregation and gender analysis are done for all studies.

Information on women is maintained and disseminated both to staff and outside the organization.

**Using forms of communication accessible to women**

All information is accessible in local languages, together with visual information accessible to those many women who cannot read or write.

In many developing countries, official ownership of assets (land, housing, etc.) by women is limited due to legal and cultural norms. Ownership titles are often critical requirements to access loans, limiting women's access to affordable financial services. In addition, in many cases women cannot open bank accounts or access loans, unless these are shared or underwritten by their husbands. This can lead to continued appropriation of the wife's income or credit for unproductive or alternative uses by the husband.

In reality, generating income is not always a priority for poor rural women: their priorities are meeting food, education or health needs of the household. Many women are mostly involved in household or farm chores and lack the time and necessary entrepreneurial skills to identify income-generating opportunities or to start or expand business activities. Practitioners that provide credit without accompanying its provision with other services such as business skills development to help women use credit productively cannot expect credit to lead to improved income-generating capacities of households. Many interventions are designed to be sensitive to gender issues or include specific gender components in programming, products or service delivery. In contrast, gender mainstreaming goes beyond this point by fully integrating gender considerations in rural finance interventions.

Mainstreaming gender is not only aimed at providing financial services to women specifically or to empower them, but aims for financial service delivery that is sensitive to local power relations, legislative contexts and cultural norms in order to provide access to both women and men. Contrary to benefiting women only, gender mainstreaming aims to make microfinance less gender specific by mainstreaming the gender dimension as an integral part of financial service provision.

### *2.4 Critical Success Factors for Gender Mainstreaming*

To avoid 'one-size-fits-all' approaches and top-down rural finance, interventions should give way to more participatory methods that build on cultural and legal norms, local socio-economic realities and existing social networks. In this way, interventions can cater more closely to the specific needs and expectations of beneficiaries. The Gender Action Learning System (GALS) is a tool with a proven track record of a successful participatory method. Sensitizing men builds awareness of the importance of empowering women and takes away the fear that female empowerment leads to male disempowerment or gender discrimination. Sensitization can for example be achieved by assigning both female and male members of savings and loan groups' decision-making power or leadership positions. Involving men in such groups enables women to be more open about their needs and aspirations in wider society, and creates more acceptance among men of women being in leading positions. Many poor women lack basic education or business skills—often related to division of labour and unequal schooling of boys and girls—which can lead to inappropriate use of credit and over-indebtedness. Gender mainstreaming therefore also requires that interventions are accompanied by other services such as business skills development, labour-saving technologies and education on gender.

### *2.4.1 Gender Action Learning System*

The Gender Action Learning System (GALS) is a community led empowerment system that aims at 'constructive economic, social and political transformation' in gender relations. Its main goals are:

*2.4.1.1 Individual livelihood planning*: GALS allows women and men, including those who cannot read and write, to determine what empowerment means to them and to create their vision for change in gender relations. Members create concrete action plans on how to reach those goals.

*2.4.1.2 Institutional awareness-raising and changing power relations*: GALS is used to communicate members aspirations and strategies to financial service providers for staff to reflect on and learn. More respect for the views and interests of poor men and women is created, while challenging current gender behaviour. It also aims to provide more voice to women in institutional decision-making.

*2.4.1.3 Collective action and gender advocacy for change*: Individual visions and strategies developed in workshops are shared in discussions with microfinance staff, development agencies and government officials to develop collective strategies for gender mainstreaming. GALS has been used successfully to mainstream gender in rural finance interventions. It has allowed beneficiaries to determine how empowered they are and to set up goals on how to reach gender equality through the intervention. As the system uses tools such as pictorials and symbols, persons without formal education get the opportunity to participate in this learning system.

GALS has been used successfully to mainstream gender in rural finance interventions. It has allowed beneficiaries to determine how empowered they are and to set up goals on how to reach gender equality through the intervention. As the system uses tools such as pictorials and symbols, persons without formal education get the opportunity to participate in this learning system. Staff in microfinance institutions without training on the topic can be insensitive towards gender issues.

*2.4.1.4 Sensitizing microfinance staff on gender through discussion and training* is a successful method to improve service delivery to women. Topics to discuss include improved awareness of bottlenecks to women face in accessing finances, which can lead to changes in loan application requirements but also in practical issues such as adjusted opening hours or outreach at specific events where many female community members are likely to be present.

## 2.5 Critical Failure Factors for Gender Mainstreaming

### 2.5.1 Rural women are not a homogenous group

Their position in society differs between ethnicities, cultures and religions in many areas. When the local context is ignored there is a likely chance that gender mainstreaming in rural finance interventions will fail.

### 2.5.2 To access financial services, collateral or a male cosignatory is often required

As many women have little access to assets, they have limited access to financial services. Institutions should therefore consider ways of adapting requirements that allow women who do not legally own any property to benefit from service provision or ways that take better stock of assumed mutual support that should exist in a marriage or partnership.

*2.5.3 Project costs*

Mainstreaming gender by including additional services or programme components on gender with separate targets, budget lines and monitoring and evaluation requirements can greatly increase costs of rural finance interventions. It is therefore important that gender mainstreaming is conceived as an integrated service in rural finance interventions.

Criteria for selecting financial intermediaries should include:

- Possess or be willing to develop appropriate credit packages suitable for small-scale producers
- Have the capacity to scale up and to serve rural clients engaged in the agricultural sector
- Be profitable, have a high outreach serving more people and reaching more of the under-served
- Have the capacity for resource mobilization and the appropriate legal status of operations
- Should include poor farmers even if it is a modest percentage of the institutions business, as institutional sustainability requires a certain level of diversity of both clients and risk
- Have a poverty outreach, i.e. offering products and services that are pro-poor such as minimum balances for basic deposit products and loan sizes for loan products. Terms and conditions of engagement should include requirements for transparency and disclosure on the pricing structure of credit, terms and conditions of financial products.

To successfully mainstream gender in rural finance interventions, it is necessary to sensitize staff as well as female and male beneficiaries on issues of gender equality, empowerment and power relations. A proven way of mainstreaming gender in rural finance is the use of participatory methods where local communities and individuals are invited to participate in contextualizing local gender relations and setting out their own future actions, without requiring separate programme components in interventions.

### 3. Addressing Gender Concerns in Microfinance Institutions (Development and Regulation) Draft Bill 2011

The Microfinance Institutions (Development and Regulation) Draft Bill, 2011 represents a step forward in the Government of India's (GoI) engagement with the Microfinance (MF) Sector. The Bill, prepared by the Ministry of Finance, has been put up on its website, inviting feedback and comments from various stakeholders and microfinance practitioners. The Indian Microfinance Sector has seen a diverse array of microfinance providers [e.g. Non-Banking Financial Companies (NBFC), Microfinance Institutions (MFIs), Cooperatives, Non-profits, Trusts] proliferating over the past two decades. However, a few practices of microfinance institutions such as high interest rates, short repayment schedules, coercion to ensure timely repayment have come under the scanner due to an increasing over-indebtedness of women. This led the Government of Andhra Pradesh to pass an ordinance to control such practices. The need for regulation of MFIs thus gained ground. At the same time, MFIs felt that they had not been able to grow due to stringent regulations imposed on banking and non-banking companies. For this reason, they have also been lobbying for a special regulation for MFIs. In view of the criticism of the provisions of the Bill, the first Draft Microfinance (MF) Bill which was released in March 2007 was referred to a Parliamentary Standing Committee. However, due to the end of the term of the Parliament, the provisions of the Bill could not be deliberated. The Bill was therefore drafted once again in 2011. It defines microfinance services broadly—financial services in small amounts including micro-credit, collection of thrift, remittances, pensions, insurance and so on—and brings all organizations—except cooperatives only accepting deposits from their members, under the purview of one regulator—the Reserve Bank of India (RBI). It was felt that regulations of the Bill should take into account the concerns of the poor while promoting the microfinance sector. There are also ongoing discussions on how to bridge the two kinds of gaps in the sector—development gap (financial exclusion of large sections of the population) and regulation gap (lack of regulation of many MFI/NGOs operating in the informal sector to provide financial services).

### *3.1 Consultation on the Draft Microfinance Bill, 2011*

It is well recognized that the Draft Bill, 2011 is about regulating microfinance as an activity and institutions that implement microfinance as a business; this is not a women empowerment Bill. However, it cannot be negated that women are the major participants in the microfinance sector. In this regard, it becomes imperative that the current Bill addresses the goals of MF in a gender-just framework and encourages institutions to look beyond profits to address the goals of financial inclusion and poverty alleviation. The enactment needs to foster equitable and gender sensitive practices to prevent malpractices that led to the crisis in Andhra Pradesh from recurring. The Consultation brought together experts on microfinance, gender and livelihood from across the country, who deliberated on critical questions such as what are the key provisions of the Bill that have gender implications (e.g. implications on SHGs, women's responsibility to repay, etc.); what will be the impact on women's economic empowerment, their access and control over their own money (e.g. access to savings, taking equity contribution from women, etc.); what will be the implications for women owned and managed financial institutions such as SHGs and cooperatives; and what will be the implications on women's indebtedness. Further, the group discussed the impact of the Bill on financial inclusion agenda, particularly for women, given the Reserve Bank of India's call for financial inclusion.

### *3.2 Key Gender Issues Identified in the Draft Microfinance Bill, 2011*

While some experts viewed the Bill as a positive and desirable measure to regulate the sector, especially in the context of the recent crisis in Andhra Pradesh, others called it redundant. However, the majority thought it important to introduce this initiative as an Act after thorough analysis of its provisions from the perspective of the women who are the primary stakeholders in this sector. The expert group identified following gaps in the Bill from a gender perspective—

(i) *Preamble and Content of the Bill*: do not reflect the current Bill as a step towards development and regulation of MFIs to address goals of poverty alleviation and women's empowerment. This limits the scope of the proposed enactment. It was noted that the Bill was focused more on the regulation aspects than on the developmental. Further, the blueprint for financial inclusion mentioned in the preamble of the Bill was not enunciated. The regulatory aspects too need further strengthening as they do not include cap on interest rates or regulations for making women's savings more secure in addition to other aspects.

(ii) *Absence of Focus on Women*: More than 90 percent of the borrowers and clients in the MF sector are women. However, the Bill renders them almost invisible by making a reference only in clause 4(g) (i.e. providing for nomination of at least two members in the MF Development Council). In this case also, only women who have experience in rural credit, banking, and microfinance or are representatives of MFIs or other banks are included. No clear reference is made to the inclusion and incapacitation of women as clients into the decision-making processes. Further, it refers to SHGs [clause 2(p)] in an instrumentalist context of deriving their thrift as deposits for MFIs.

(iii) *Thrift Issues*: These have not been understood from the perspective of poor women. It is women's thrift in the form of deferred consumption that has enabled them to save, however meagerly, to rotate their resources for inter-lending, to retain access to these resources as well as to the interest earnings from them. Also, Section 12 (1) (c) which relates to a minimum net owned fund by MFIs before they can be granted the certificate of registration, is likely to affect the availability of savings to women when they need it.

Women's movements have for long contested the collection of savings of women by MFIs on the ground that it causes greater harm to women than good. Additionally, current provisions of the Bill fail to include measures that ensure women's access to and control of their savings. The Bill is, in fact, creating a regulation gap by reducing women's access and control over their own resources through the collection of thrift by organizations, that are, at times unfit for deposit-taking.

(iv) *Depositor Safety* at five lakh rupees is undercapitalized. It will render poor women's thrift collection unsafe, and also allow easy access of unscrupulous elements to such activity.

(v) This Bill leaves lending gaps unregulated such as the interest rate cap issue as well as the sharing of profits earned from lending, while addressing access issues which can as well be addressed by existing institutions if impediments to women's access to mainstream institutions are taken care of.

(vi) *Institutional Scale* and *Type* impinge upon women's access and control over resources. It is important that regulatory frameworks themselves address the interests of clients, majority of who are rural, illiterate, poor women with little or no asset security and who are incapable of impacting decisions in their favour. Large centralized, complex structures and regulatory frameworks also increase the vulnerability of women and expose them to exploitation by unscrupulous elements.

(vii) *On Registration* [Section 10]: Concerns were also expressed at the ambiguities surrounding the status of several types of institutions:

- Status of such organizations that undertake multiple activities for socioeconomic development along with microfinance.
- Status of Community-Based (CB) MFIs that are predominantly owned and controlled by grassroots

women is not clear in the context of the proposed enactment. Such institutions need to be kept out of the purview of this Act.

- There are a large number of cooperative institutions functioning as Mutually Aided Companies (MACs) that already have a streamlined process of regulation and operational principles. This should not be disrupted by the new legislation. In addition, many organizations such as the cooperatives do not find the compulsion to register under the Companies Act or as a Section 25 company motivating. Other means of their regulation may be explored.

  It was also noted that institutions with wider outreach and greater finance that dominate the MF sector and pursue a profiteering agenda are highly inaccessible for women because they cannot exercise their influence or assert their interests in such institutions. These are more likely to instrumentalize women (and were seen to be more errant in the recent crisis that hit the sector). On the contrary, institutions that are decentralized offer more accessibility and control to women.

(viii) The Bill marks a welcome step in explaining financial services as inclusive of savings, micro-credit, money transfer, pension, insurance, etc. However, it only makes provision to regulate credit, for other services, the reference is inadequate. Women's experiences also reveal that it is the burden of interest and premiums on the package of services such as insurance that render them more vulnerable. These clients, most of whom are marginalized women, require greater flexibility, for instance, in the repayment scheduling, etc. Profit and profitability cannot remain the main criteria for determination of these terms and conditions. It is important that operational guidelines for savings products are provided with sufficient safeguards. Systematic studies should also be carried out in understanding the costs involved in mobilising low ticket savings and designing appropriate products. (There is also the need for evolving norms for deposit taking MFIs. Policy advocacy measures are needed to promote deposit insurance coverage for the deposits mobilized by MFIs).

(ix) *Dichotomous Pathways pursued in Government Policies*: Participants also observed a kind of dichotomy in the government's policies with the Bill for Development and Regulation of Microfinance Institutions clearing the way for MFIs to pursue profits and function legitimately in the country on the one hand and the promotion of the National Rural Livelihoods Mission scheme on the other hand, wherein the SHG and federation formation processes are encouraged to achieve the goals of poverty alleviation and women's control over their resources and institutions.

(x) *The concept of Ombudsman* incorporated in the Bill is gender blind. It is not ambiguous and needs elaboration, and lessons for other such realms need to be taken to enable it to function efficiently and effectively.

(xi) *Interest Caps*, an issue that is of utmost importance to women borrowers finds no mention in the Bill. To ensure protection of women's interests against any unscrupulous parties, the Bill should also make provisions for the regulation of interest rates.

(xii) While the group was appreciative of the provision of the *Grievance Redress Mechanisms*, it did express concern over the ways these would be accessed by women. The primary issue that these mechanisms need to address is that of over-indebtedness.

(xiii) The provision of a *MF Development Equity Fund* should be viewed as a means to enhance the developmental initiatives of the sector. The issue of high cost of registering with the Credit Bureau was also raised by the participants. The structure of the Bureau as a private entity was also questioned and it was suggested that it be kept as a public goods/services entity instead.

(xiv) *Role and Powers of the RBI* contained in the Bill include—

- Regulating size of loan number of clients [Section 24(2)(b)]
- Purpose of loan [Section 24(2)(c)]
- Periodicity of repayment of loan [Section 24(2)(c)]
- Facilitating institutional development of all entities, including groups engaged in MF services, theory training and CB [Section 23(g)]
- Promoting their customer education [Section 23(h)]
- Documenting and disseminating fair practices for thrift [Section 23(k)]
- Membership of credit information bureau [Section 24(2) (g)]
- Applying MF Development fund for loan, grant, and seed capital but to categorically mention SHG Federation [Section 30(3)].

The above primarily refer to RBI's role in defining the norms and practices for the MFIs and their operations. It is necessary that these are oriented and designed to address the needs of the women given their importance to the sector and to the goals of poverty alleviation and women empowerment.

### 3.3 Addressing Gender Concerns in the Draft Microfinance Bill, 2011: Key Recommendations

Research and experience have shown that "Empowering Microfinance is that which respects and promotes women's agency, safeguards poor women's savings and ensures their access, empowers them for decision-making at all levels, and grants them the rights that all customers of mainstream banks have, including the right to be fully informed." Keeping this perspective in view, the expert group made the following recommendations to weave gender concerns into the fabric of the Draft MF Bill, 2011:

(a) *Engendering the Preamble*: The preamble of the Bill needs to explicitly incorporate commitments to gender equality and address the concerns of the poor and marginalized people, especially women, who are the primary stakeholders of the sector and in whose interest and by whose efforts of managing frugal resources (for family survival and well-being), the sector evolved in the first instance. In fact, the entire structure of the sector depends on the women, and it is therefore, only appropriate to reflect the right to financial inclusion for women and the role they play in the sector in the preamble and subsequent sections of the proposed Act. The preamble of the Bill makes mention of financial inclusion and of "providing the rural and urban poor and certain disadvantaged sections of the people access to financial services by promoting the growth and development of microfinance institutions as extended arms of the banks and financial institutions and for the regulation of microfinance institutions and for matters connected therewith and incidental thereto". Specific references to women must also be made in various sections of the Bill to indicate their importance, to ensure they have access to and control over their own resources and to enable them to have decision-making powers within the framework of MFIs. Thus the preamble must be modified 'keeping in view the fact that women are the majority customers of microfinance'.

(b) *Security of Savings and Deposits*: Instead of establishing an alternate structure with substandard norms for security of people's resources, efforts are needed to strengthen existing institutions such as the mainstream banks and their services to the poor, and post office services for savings, among others. The Bill should not be silent on measures that ensure security of women's deposits. In an indirect way, the Bill is promoting thrift collection by private microfinance institutions (apparent in the definition of 'microfinance services'), but this Bill is not addressing accountability issues, nor is it defining mechanisms to keep women's savings safe, secure and under their own control.

(c) *Institutional Framework engendering the institutional framework*: is necessary to ensure that these institutions work in women-friendly ways and address women's concerns as their priority. For this, the following measures are considered necessary:

- Increase the number of women in the Microfinance Development Council (MFDC) at the central and State Council levels to at least 60 percent; making it inclusive of women engaged and experienced in the sector and with expertise of working with MF; and/or women's organizations, as well as women from the client groups to ensure that their views and needs are represented and heeded in the MFI.
- Women should be represented on the boards of MFIs at least to the extent of 50 percent.
- Ensure that a majority of women are borrowers; that women with experience in the sector are appointed as ombudspersons and as members of the grievance committees and those women's voices and demands are strengthened and their issues heard.
- Norms for such appointments need to be formulated in such a way that it allows grassroots organizations' women, who have been members and leaders, to come forward and take up challenging roles.

(d) *Registration*:

- The organizations should be allowed to register under any of the legislative frameworks available—as a cooperative or under the Companies Act or as a Section 25 company Not-for-profit organizations must also have the space and support to function as MFIs.
- Status of Community-Based MFIs needs to be clarified; while many felt that these be kept outside the ambit of the Bill; it was agreed that other methods may be considered to ensure their transparency and accountability to all members.

(e) *Profit Sharing*: The norms for profit sharing should also be elucidated, and the goals set in the proposed Bill should also be tailored to ensure that women borrowers are increasingly encouraged to become owners and stakeholders in the institutions.

(f) *Financial Inclusion*: The conceptual framework and strategies for financial inclusion need elaboration with a focus on promotion of gender equality, financial literacy for women and enhancement of their decision-making and leadership skills as well as of their capacities as borrowers and clients. While the Bill provides for client protection, women are less literate than men. They have limited knowledge of products and its features and even their rights as clients. The Bill should include the provision of minimum financial literacy training by MFIs to their clients.

(g) *Interest Rate Cap*: The law needs to be clear in its provisions on usurious rates of interest which most affect the women borrowers. The group made the following recommendations in this regard:

- A limit be set for interest rates (subject to change by a regulation if need be)
- Provision be made for MFIs to adopt a differential rate of interest depending upon their own cost of credit and outreach, notwithstanding the prescribed upper limit
- The cost of loans and other relevant information be communicated by MFIs to their clients to enhance transparency and to enable women to exercise their right of choice
- Base rates need to be prescribed for MFIs
- Provisions in Section 25(2) relating to annual percentage rates and margin: such disclosure should be made in a way that is easy to understand for women with clear demarcations between cost and charge components. The inclusion of measures to regulate the spread/margins was also suggested

so that usurious interest rates are not charged. Considerations of geographical spread need to be taken into account, as costs vary across regions. Measures for incentives for going to underserved areas should also be considered.

(h) *Grievance Mechanisms*: The expert group was appreciative of the provision for Grievance Redress Mechanisms and deliberated on how this could be appropriately designed for rendered accessible to women. Following measures were suggested:

- Care needs to be taken while designing the grievance redress system to include the needs of women, most of whom are illiterate
- Design the system in accordance with the needs of women and based on the experiences of women-centered institutions
- Ensure that mechanisms are in place to identify the problem of indebtedness which compels most women to take extreme steps
- Encourage women to join the grievance redress structures
- The issue of over-indebtedness should also be addressed.

(i) *Ombudspersons*: The concept of Ombudsman should also be made gender sensitive, starting with a change in the term itself to "ombudsperson" or "ombudswoman"; to the inclusion of women from the client groups; as well as ensuring that strategies adopted for their functioning are engendered. Systems of Ombudspersons functioning in the consumer protection cells may be examined for their adaptation to this context. Grievance redressal mechanism will also need to bring women clients in its committee when the scheme is made.

(j) On the *Issue of State Acts and Supervision versus central supervision*, many preferred the latter to avoid any interference from local vested parties.

(k) *Role and Powers of the RBI*

- RBI as the regulator is appreciated
- Reservations were, however, expressed about Section 38(1), which reverses this provision in specific cases. It stipulates that "The Reserve Bank may, with the previous approval of the Central Government delegate any of its powers conferred under this Act to the National Bank in respect of any microfinance institution or a class of microfinance institutions generally, by issue of a notification in the Official Gazette." This move of empowering those entities that are themselves actors in the MF sector was seen by many as the one that may cause conflict of interests. The RBI should instead expand its own capacities and institutional strength to undertake the role of regulation. Only the RBI should be allowed to regulate MFIs, and set standards that do not distinguish between different categories of depositors
- It was also agreed that RBI needs to expand the outreach and enhance the capacities of women-centered and owned institutions
- Reservations were also expressed over Section 41 which provides for exemptions from application of this Act to specific institutions or groups of institutions
- It was also recommended that RBI take specific measures, apart from the provisions of the Bill, to regulate MFIs whose usurious practices have led to the crisis
- The Code of Conduct proposed should refer to the ethical framework for institutions serving poor marginalized women. It should, therefore, be formulated and issued by the RBI and not left to the institutions

- It was suggested that the RBI make aspects of purpose of loan, periodicity of repayment of loan flexible to allow women to repay their debts without any stress
- The group welcomed the measures to facilitate institutional development of all entities, including groups engaged in MF services, theory training and capacity building [Section 23(g)] and suggested they be designed keeping women's roles and needs in mind.

(l) *Section 13(1)*: In the event of a cease and desist order, some measures are necessary to ensure that women have access to their resources deposited with the MFI.

(m) In addition to the financial rating processes already included in the Bill, measures to incorporate social rating and audit should also be included in order to ensure that women borrowers are not adversely affected by MFI operations. Additionally, apart from measures to monitor operational aspects, steps to monitor the MFIs themselves and their adherence to norms and regulations as a women-friendly workspace will also need to be incorporated.

(n) *The MF Development Equity Fund*

- With regard to the Fund proposed in the Bill, some of the members of the expert group were of the view that instead of using it for the growth of MFIs, it should be utilized for the growth and capacity development of women in the sector
- Training and capacity building of women in the sector would contribute towards strengthening the transparency, democratic functioning of these institutions and enhancing their accountability to women
- Funds from the MF Development Equity Fund could also be used to enable small scale, women-owned MFIs to register themselves with the Credit Bureau and gain access to resources for expanding and enhancing poor women's control over MFIs.

Alternatively, the Credit Bureau could be converted into a public utility and such fees waived for not-for-profit institutions

- However, development of women's capacities and of Community-Based MFIs (CB-MFIs) should continue at the same time
- Funds can also be used to develop capacities of CB-MFIs, and to develop social rating processes, etc.
- A National Development Policy for the sector was also suggested in place of addressing gender and equity agenda through MFIs, many of whom are known to be in the profit making sector
- The underlying principle should be to utilize the fund for women's capacity development and promotion of linkages of CB-MFIs as a developmental goal rather than to subsidize the operations and resources available to profit making microfinance operations.

While acknowledging the positive efforts made by the Ministry of Finance, the Government of India (GoI) to strengthen the MF legislation by redrafting the MF Bill that will include a regulatory framework for the MF sector and promote financial inclusion, it was reiterated that the regulatory mechanism for the MF sector must protect and promote the interests of the poor, in particular women from the marginalized communities. The expert group acknowledged that issues would arise in the details of the Bill and the guidelines for its enactment in terms of the final decisions of the Central Government (with RBI consultation). The group, therefore, urged that the Bill be whetted from a gender lens by considering the above mentioned suggestions to ensure that critical issues are addressed and adverse implications for women are averted. The expert group also urged that while it was desirable to have a Bill soon to regulate the sector, it was also necessary to ensure that it addressed marginalized women's needs. The Bill must ensure that adequate measures are taken to incorporate gender concerns into the Bill and that its implementation processes address the issue of poor women's access to and control over their resources. It should also ensure that institutions dealing with these issues pave the way for the advancement of women along with their own development.

### *3.4 Solution Exchange for the Gender Community*

The Gender Community promotes gender equality and women's empowerment in India, focusing on increasing development effectiveness to improve the gender and girl child situation, promote a rights-based approach to development, and ensure gender mainstreaming. Solution Exchange helps members of this Community increase the effectiveness of their individual efforts to promote gender equality and address challenges to women's involvement in development—increased access, capacity, and equality in women's social, economic and political endeavours, by tapping into their collective knowledge and collaborative actions.

#### *Issues Covered*

- Gender Based Violence (GBV) including Prenatal Sex Selection, Human Trafficking, Domestic Violence
- Issues of tribal, dalit and marginalized women
- Child Rights and Protection
- Issues of Sexual Minorities
- Social Security Issues (including the elderly, women headed households)
- Engendering policies, programmes and institutions (e.g. gender budgeting, sexual harassment at work place, gender mainstreaming)
- Gender Equality and Empowerment of Women (e.g. economic, political)
- Gender gaps and disparity (e.g. education, health, governance, access to resources).

## 4. The Millennium Development Goals and Gender Equality

Gender Equality is a core development issue on the agenda of the international community. A number of agreements and conventions are now in place trying to address the gap that exists among men and women on the social, economic and political levels. These include the Convention on the Elimination of All Forms of Discrimination against Women (CEDAW), the Beijing Platform for Action and the Millennium Development Goals (MDG). Therefore, governments, civil society and donor organizations work towards achieving Gender Equality goals.

Eight of the key commitments set out in the Millennium Declaration came to form the MDGs. The third goal of the MDGs is "to promote Gender Equality and empower women". Furthermore, Gender Equality continues to be a cross cutting issue for the rest of the MDGs. As stated in the Human Development Report for 2003, "Gender Equality is at the core of whether the Goals will be achieved". Links have also been established between Gender Equality and the Millennium Development Goals on Poverty, Education, Health and Nutrition, as well as the Environment.

| **Millennium Development Goals** |
|---|
| 1. Eradicate extreme poverty and hunger |
| 2. Achieve universal primary education |
| 3. Promote gender equality and empower women |
| 4. Reduce child mortality |
| 5. Improve maternal health |
| 6. Combat HIV/AIDS, malaria and other diseases |
| 7. Ensure environmental sustainability |
| 8. Develop a global partnership for development |
| *Pathway to Gender Equality: CEDAW, Beijing & the MDGs, p. 6* |

The MDGs have become the yardstick for development organizations to measure their achievements towards human development. The Millennium Declaration and the MDGs have directed the attention of the global community to the possible link between gender inequalities and the persistence of poverty despite the vast poverty reduction efforts. Accordingly, all development organizations, donors and governments are expected to report regularly on their contribution to the MDGs.

### *4.1 Gender Equality and Women's Empowerment in the MDGs*

Gender is defined as a social construct that defines and differentiates roles, rights and responsibilities and obligations of women and men in a context of unequal power relationships. Gender norms and biases affect both men/boys and women/girls. Yet, the focus is primarily to redress the most common gender-based inequalities mostly faced by women/girls (UN Millennium Project: Task Force on Education and Gender Equality, 2005, pp. 31, 140). The term is however often equated with women and/or increased focus on women which in turn creates conceptual confusion. Gender Equality means that women and men enjoy the same status. GE means that women and men have equal conditions for realizing their full human rights and potential to contribute to national, political, economic, social and cultural development and to benefit from the results. GE is therefore the equal valuing by society of both similarities and differences between women and men and the varying roles that they play.

| **Gender Equality** |
|---|
| Gender equality means that women and men enjoy the same status. Gender equality means that women and men have equal conditions for realizing their full human rights and potential to contribute to national, political, economic, social and cultural development, and to benefit from the results.<br><br>Gender equality is therefore the equal valuing by society of both the similarities and differences between women and men, and the varying roles that they play.<br><br>*Excerpt from: CIDA's policy on Gender Equality March 1999, p. 6* |

The task force on the MDGs has adopted an operational framework for understanding GE that has three main domains (UN Millennium Project: Task Force on Education and Gender Equality, 2005):

- *The Capabilities domain*: This refers to basic human abilities as measured by education, health and nutrition. The attainment of those capabilities is seen as essential to the overall well-being.
- *Opportunities*: This refers to the equality in opportunity to use or apply basic capabilities through access to economic assets and resources as well as

political opportunity. Economic [assets] in this context refers to access to land, property, credit, income, employment while the political refers to representation in political bodies and community participation. Unless women have access and opportunity in the economic and political sphere they will not be able to use their capabilities to promote their and their families' well-being.

- *Security*: This refers to reduced vulnerability to violence and conflict. Unless individuals are free from physical and psychological harm, they will not be able to utilize their capabilities or offered opportunities. It is assumed that with increased capabilities and opportunities, women and girls are less vulnerable to violence and conflict (however, the opposite is sometimes the case).

The three domains are closely interlinked and mutually reinforcing. Development interventions need to address the three domains in order to ensure contribution to MDG #3 on GE and Women's Empowerment. Focusing on only one domain might have negative implications to the other two (e.g. Focus on economic opportunity to women only could lead to their increased vulnerability to violence).

According to the MDG Task Force, empowerment is closely linked to GE but distinct from it. To be empowered women must not only have equal capabilities (e.g. Health and education) and equal access to resources and opportunities (e.g. Credit, employment), but they must have the agency to use those rights, capabilities, resources and opportunities to make strategic choices (e.g. Leadership opportunities and participation in political/community organizations). Security and protection from violence are necessary prerequisites to exercise agency (UN Millennium Project: Task Force on Education and Gender Equality, 2005).

### 4.2 Empowerment

Empowerment is about people—both women and men—taking control over their lives: setting their own agendas, gaining skills, building self-confidence, solving problems, and developing self-reliance. It is not only a collective, social and political process, but an individual one as well—and it is not only a process but an outcome too. Outsiders cannot empower women: only women can empower themselves to make choices or to speak out on their own behalf. However, institutions, including international co-operation agencies, can support processes that increase women's self-confidence, develop their self-reliance, and help them set their own agendas.

### *4.3 CIDA's Policy on Gender Equality Discussed in March 1997*

It is noteworthy however, that equality of opportunity does not necessarily lead to an equality of result. No intervention is neutral when players do not start as equals. Even if project intends to treat women equally, the ability of men and women to use and respond to services offered will differ in practice by virtue of their gender roles. This is referred to as equality of opportunity and equality of results. Other important concepts in GE are Practical needs and Strategic Interests. As denoted by the titles, the first refers to immediate needs of food, shelter, sanitation..., etc. The latter, however refers to more long-term interests that also relate to the relative status of women and men within society.

### *4.4 Gender Concerns in Microfinance*

MF provision is about designing and delivering MF products and services to the poor people, both men and women. With increasing competition among MFIs, and with the increasing interest of banks to invade this market, the key success factor for any MFI has become the provision of demand-driven MF services and products. Therefore, careful assessment of the target clients' needs, and continuous monitoring of their degree of satisfaction with the current services/products are crucial for the growth and expansion plans of any MFI. In this context, it is important to study and analyze the different needs and characteristics of both men and women clients, and accordingly modify existing products or introduce new ones.

MF is the provision of financial products and services to the poor people, who are described as moderate or extreme poor and not destitute. Poor women—particularly the heads of households—are considered one of the main categories of clients to whom MF services are provided as a tool to help them increase their income and accordingly fulfill their needs. Therefore, MF is about the design of financial products and services, which are both demand-driven and accessible by the target clients. Furthermore, Gender Sensitive MF means that "all MF initiatives must consider the relevance of gender to the services offered the different needs, constraints and concerns, and gender equality is ensured when the design equally meets the needs and addresses the barriers facing both men and women. Therefore, while designing a MF product/service, gender equality should be considered in determining the loan size, the repayment period, the frequency of installments, the delivery mechanism of the loan, the collection mechanism of the installments, the collateral requirements, the required documents for loan disbursement, the outreach mechanism, and the selected staff. The design of a loan product should be based on gender-sensitive market research and should be periodically evaluated in a scientific manner to accommodate any occurring changes in the clients' needs.

On another hand, as MF is one of the tools employed to alleviate poverty, the social impact resulting from the provision of MF services—increased income, improved living conditions in terms of health care, access to education and better nutrition—gives an indication on whether the provision of MF has achieved the expected impact. Therefore, it is very important to measure the impact of the loan provided on the target clients, and document the achieved impact in order to address any gaps or negative impact resulting from the implementation of the programme. On a macro level, this impact should be measured using certain indicators to monitor the contribution of the MF programmes to the achievement of the MDGs. A range of socio-economic factors and gender issues affect the ability of MFIs to successfully deliver their services to targeted clients. Both men and women clients are likely to work with an institution when services provided are suitable for them and their businesses. Thus by identifying and addressing the socioeconomic and gender issues in their specific contexts, MFIs can significantly improve the functioning and effectiveness of their activities. This is the primary concern of conducting this gender assessment to the implementing partner MFIs to the USAID EMF project. As literature and best practice suggests, institutionalizing gender equality into operations of MFIs requires interventions on both the institutional and operational levels. As mentioned earlier, this assessment has examined both institutional and operational gender issues in the interviewed MFIs.

The MFIs included in this study provide two main loan products, including individual loans (IL) and Group Loans (GL). The IL mainly addresses the small enterprises that have a minimum level of formality (i.e. a business premise that has a rental/ownership contract and an electricity bill after the name of the client), while GL target poor women with a very small scale/informal economic activity. Following is a presentation of the main findings of the study that reflect on the extent to which the MFIs have integrated gender equality into their institutions and operations.

## 5. Women and Microfinance in Mediterranean Countries: A Case Study

Since the beginning of the 1990s microfinance programmes specifically targeted to women have been one of the principal strategies for poverty alleviation by international community of donors, mainly because of the assumed financial self-sustainability of Microfinance Institutions (MFIs). MFIs aim to provide financial services to low income households, even the extremely poor, in a participatory and non-paternalistic development approach to the great interest of the donor community, policy-makers, development researcher and practitioners. According to the so-called 'win-win' proposition MFIs should combine the social goals, such as poverty alleviation and women's empowerment, with operational and financial self-sufficiency based on access to international financial markets independently from international development agencies. Both the financial self-sustainability of microfinance programmes and the growing empirical evidence of the high return on loans of women clients have convinced international development agencies to support the access of women to microfinance. The stated goal of MFIs in development is to generate a virtuous circle of increased family income and improved social and economic conditions for the whole community. Nevertheless, the impact analysis of microfinance intervention on women has shown controversial results, even within the same MFI. Some studies have confirmed the women's economic and social empowerment whereas others have argued that women's participation in MFI programmes has only served to strengthen patriarchal behaviours (Kabeer, 2001).

Similarly, concerns have been raised on the impact of microfinance programmes on economic and social inequalities for women because of the donor to turn Development of the microcredit programmes in self-sustaining projects (Morduch, 2002). This pressure can lead to a minimalist approach and the exclusion of the non-financial components such as healthcare, sanitary and educational literacy, which are necessary for the participation of poorest people, particularly for women. This trend also confirms the existence of a possible trade-off between social and financial goals (Morduch, 1999). In the following we analyze these recent criticisms of MFI programmes by looking at microfinance women engaged in the Mediterranean countries.

### *5.1 A Gender Perspective on Microfinance*

Approximately, 500 million economically active poor people worldwide are operating micro-enterprises and small business (Women's World Banking Global Policy Forum, 1995). The vast majority of them have no access to the formal banking system because of lack of collateral, high transaction costs per loan for small-scale projects, and the high risk of operating in the informal sector. Microfinance is a unique tool in development interventions, pursuing the goal of poverty alleviation in low income countries in a sustainable way, even if most MFIs still rely on subsidies (ArmendaŁ riz de Aghion and Morduch, 2005).

Microfinance covers a wide range of financial services, including loans and savings facilities, insurance, transfers payments and even micro-pensions to people excluded from the formal financial sector. Microfinance reach a wide range of beneficiaries, typically self-employed, low-income entrepreneurs in both urban and rural areas. Many MFIs provide also social intermediation services such as group formation or development of self-confidence, enterprise development services such as business management and bookkeeping training, and social services such as education, nutrition training and health care. MFIs' clients therefore use financial services not only for business investments but also to finance health and education, for household consumption, household emergencies and to meet other cash needs.

MFIs assume a different legal status according to local regulatory frameworks: they can be non-governmental organizations (NGOs), savings and loan cooperatives, credit unions, government banks, commercial banks, or non-bank financial institutions. The most common scheme used is the solidarity group scheme. Group lending contracts make borrowers jointly liable of each group partners' loan, mitigating informational asymmetries problems through peer selection and peer monitoring, and social enforcement. Microfinance programmes also introduce other innovations: dynamic incentives such as increasing loan size amounts upon satisfactory repayment with a focus on more creditworthy and reliable women clients (assuming women's culturally programmed behaviour to be reliable); regular repayment schedules starting almost immediately after loan disbursement, as a means to screen out undisciplined borrowers; and collateral substitutes such as compulsory savings, emergency and group fund, providing insurance in case of default or additional funding to group members (Morduch, 1999, 2002).

Microfinance is assumed to be a gender-sensitive development tool. Early and successful programmes such as Grameen Bank in Bangladesh and BancoSol in Bolivia serve mostly women beneficiaries. Recent studies support the assumption showing overwhelming shares of women clients among major micro-lenders (Mody, 2000; Microcredit Summit Campaign, 2005). The focus on women is reinforced by empirical studies reporting higher repayment rates (Khandker et al., 1995; Hulme and Mosley, 1997) and greater social and economic impact of lending to women rather than to men (Khandker, 2003).Women are deemed to be more conservative about their investment decisions because of limited labour mobility. This implies the possibility of effective monitoring by peer borrowers in-group lending schemes and more effective social sanctions. Serving women clients is also associated with a more positive impact on households, as women are more concerned about children's health and education (Blumberg, 1989). In general, household improvements on nutritional status, housing conditions, savings behaviour and agricultural productivity are associated with women's control of funds and income generating activity (Thomas, 1994; Udry, 1996; Khandker, 2003).

Microfinance capacity to facilitate gender empowerment is strongly debated. Some advocates argue that women enjoy a greater bargaining power within the household when participating in micro-credit programmes. They point to a reduction of domestic violence due to a third party scrutiny provided by peer pressure of other group members. Empirical evidence indicates a mixed picture however of the impact of microfinance on domestic violence. Hashemi et al. (1996) reports a decrease in domestic violence in Bangladesh, and Kabeer (2001) argues that women more likely share loans and benefits of programmes access with other household members, reducing intra-household gender inequalities. On the other hand, Rahman (1999) reports an increasing degree of violence in households because women participating in the Grameen Bank are perceived as a threat to men traditional supremacy.

Most studies indicate that just giving women financial services alone can just reinforce existing social norms; it is the integrated approach which is empowering for women (Rankin, 2002). Opening up restricted working opportunities to poor women and encouraging skills accumulation through non-financial services provision along with micro-credit schemes does the most to empower women (ArmendaŁ riz de Aghion and Morduch, 2005).

### *5.2 Micro-credit in the Mediterranean*

On the occasion of the International Year of Micro-credit and with the financial support of Fondazione Risorsa Donna as a member of the Italian National Committee for the Year, we carried out a project on the social and economic impact that microfinance programmes have on women in the Mediterranean countries. With the help of elected local MFIs, we prepared a questionnaire in order to interview women in Morocco, Tunisia, Egypt, Jordan, Lebanon, Bosnia, Croatia, Kosovo, Albania, France, Spain and Italy. The choice of women to interview was random and largely dependent on the needs of local MFIs (Fig. 2).

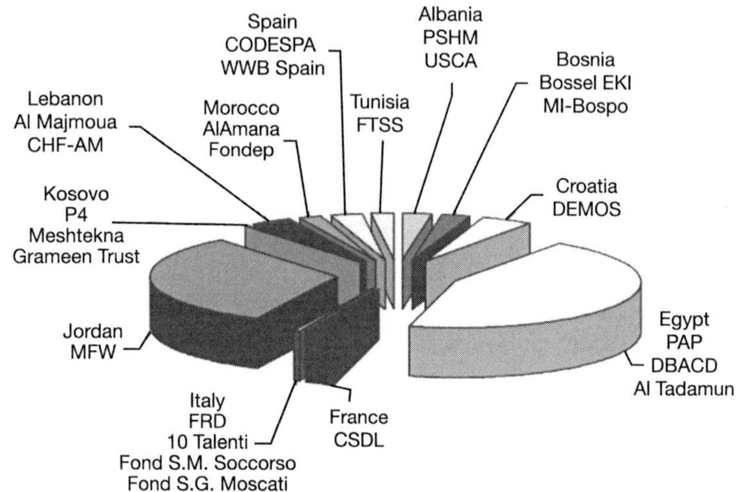


**Fig. 2:** MFIs involved in delivering Microcredit to Women in the Mediterranean

*Source*: Corsi et al. (2006).

The MFIs involved had different kinds of programmes classified according to the range of services offered. These services ranged from minimalist to integrated, they were delivered in both urban and rural areas and to individuals or through groups. The study is based on the MFIs' personnel interviewing 4,323 women, between April and September 2005. The large majority of interviewees were married, between 35 and 45 years old, with low literacy rate (especially in Egypt and Morocco). Most women declared themselves as self-employed in the trade sector; however, in some relevant cases they were employed as salaried workers (e.g. in Albania and Lebanon). In

Jordan, there were a strikingly high percentage of housewives involved in the microcredit programme (64 percent).

It is interesting to note that the interviewees were on the average receiving lower loans than the overall MFI average for women clients, with the exceptions of Egypt, Kosovo, Lebanon and Spain. As commonly assumed in the microfinance industry, average loan balance can be used as a proxy of MFIs depth of outreach. This implies that most of the MFIs selected poor beneficiaries to interview. About 20 percent of interviewees have been facing difficulties in repaying loans, mainly in Croatia, Italy and Spain, but in few cases difficulties are due to the failure of the financed activity; in most cases they are related to the contract terms (i.e. expiry date of payment). Loan amounts have been mainly used to improve an existing activity. The participation of other household members varies among countries. There is a high participation of other family members in Balkan countries and in Morocco, while lower in Egypt and Italy, and very low in Tunisia and Spain. As an overall effect, credit seems to have stabilized household consumption in 85.5 percent of the cases, with the exception of Italy and Spain.

Women's participation in microfinance programmes seems to affect deeply their savings behaviour. The amount of savings increases in all countries when women enters the programme. Coherently with assumptions about women's deeper concern about household needs, savings have been used by a major share of clients for family-related expenses (56.5%), and also in a very significant amount of cases to invest in an already existing activity (29.3%). Furthermore, a considerable share of interviewees who were facing difficulties in providing daily meals before having access to microfinance, succeeded in overcoming food problems, particularly in Croatia, Jordan, Kosovo, Morocco and Spain where 20 percent of pre-existent food problems were solved. House improvements were reported mainly in Kosovo, Jordan and Tunisia where more than 70 percent of clients managed to improve dwelling conditions since they entered the programme (Albania and Bosnia it was about 60 percent), improving their standard of living. Much less house improvements were undertaken elsewhere.

### *5.3 Women Empowerment*

In the project, the impact of microfinance on women empowerment has been assessed by taking into consideration seven dimensions of women social and civic life:

- Mobility outside the family home;
- Role within the reference community;
- Participation in social and civil life;
- Ability to undertake purchases;
- Participation to decisions concerning investment;
- Bargaining power;
- Capacity to reconcile work with family life.

In order to be able to give a total evaluation of the empowerment provided by the micro-credit programme, appropriate indexes were built which considered the results of the seven indicators. As the computed results are arrived at it indicates mobility, that is the possibility of going out of the family home, is considered as an advantage especially in Morocco, Italy, France and Kosovo. This indicator aims to measure the freedom that women have in going out of the house, but in some cases the result has been negative due to the fact that the interviewee has much less spare time after having received the loan, even if she gained more freedom: this could be the reason of the negative impact in Spain. Finally, microfinance programmes seem to have an important impact on women's chances to go out, but in almost all cases for reasons concerning their job.

The ability in doing purchases (without asking permission of the husband) is considered the main advantage for interviewees in Egypt and Albania, while the regional outcome of this dimension appears the highest in the Arab countries and in the Balkans. Women in Tunisia, Bosnia and Croatia attribute great importance to the possibility of increasing the participation in the decision taken inside the family regarding big purchases, repairing of the house or rents. In Jordan, Spain and Bosnia women perceive the most relevant change to be the increase in their bargaining power inside the family.

## 6. Women's Empowerment for Microfinance and Access to Financial Services

The focus on women's empowerment in the context of microfinance brings to light the significance of gender relations in policy development circles more prominently than ever before. Women are vaunted as a 'weapon against poverty' (DFID, 2006). The rationale for providing women access to microfinance services is that gender inequalities inhibit economic growth and development (World Bank, CIDA, UNDP, and UNIFEM). Hence, the Canadian International Development Agency (CIDA) provides "increased access to productive assets (especially land, capital, and credit), processing, and marketing for women" (CIDA, 1999). The alternative perspective emphasizes that women's empowerment emerges: (i) as a result of cultural, economic and other changes, such as the availability of new technologies in their lives (e.g. mobile phones and satellite television); (ii) as women's current opportunities and constraints; and (iii) as a process in time, across generations (Cornwall and Edwards, 2010). Since the context of women's lives matters and the same interventions are not effective everywhere, most of the policies remain ineffective (Abdullah, Aisha and King, 2010; Sardenberg, 2010a). The experiences of empowerment and disempowerment are related not just to material means and interventions, but also to social relationships (Kabeer and Haq, 2010; Sardenberg, 2010b), narratives (Priyadarshani and Rahim, 2010), voice (Goetz and Nyamu Musembi, 2008), choice (Kabeer, 2008) and negotiations (Huq, 2010; Johnson, 2010). This critique is well reflected in the three paradigms of women's empowerment through microfinance: (i) feminist empowerment paradigm; (ii) financial self-sustainability paradigm; and (iii) poverty alleviation paradigm (Mayoux; 2005, 2006; Mayoux and Hartl, 2009).

Women's World Banking (WWB) provides support, advice, training and information to a global network of 40 microfinance institutions and banks that offer credit and other financial services to more than 24 million low-income people—80 percent of whom are women—in 28 countries worldwide (Microfinance —India Summit, 2010). The wide array of carefully targeted, professional services that WWB provides to strengthen its member organizations is unique in the world. Also unique are the personal relationships and guidance that WWB offers to small, grassroots organizations and women's groups as they grow to become successful, financial entities committed to serving the poor, especially women. WWB is a pioneer in setting performance standards in the microfinance industry. The organizations in our network are held to a high standard of performance, encouraging them to excel, to grow and to embrace innovation. Currently, WWB network members are growing their financial resources (and hence their customer base) at a rate of 30 percent per year, and have an outstanding loan portfolio of over $5.5 billion. Our global presence allows us to share best practices across regions and increase the speed of learning across the globe. WWB helps create new ways of banking for the poor, as the microfinance field matures and clients require a greater variety of products and services. We also act as a catalyst to mobilize major banks to enter the microfinance market in profitable and responsible ways.

The initial motivation for microfinance roughly 30 years ago was, to a great extent, gender neutral. The pioneering microfinance institutions (MFIs) sought to provide credit to poor entrepreneurs who had no assets to pledge as collateral and, consequently, were denied access to capital by the formal banking sector. It quickly emerged, however, that women entrepreneurs invested the profits from their businesses in ways that would have a longer-lasting, more profound impact on the lives of their families and communities. The woman entrepreneur as the gateway to household security became a fundamental premise of the microfinance business model and the success of microfinance as a poverty alleviation tool. The microfinance industry has recently moved into the commercial mainstream, reducing its reliance on subsidized donor funding. This commercialization has decidedly shifted the focus of MFIs away from low-income populations in general and poor women in particular. While this trend is worrying, WWB believes its effects can be significantly mitigated by another important development: the movement by MFIs away from a strictly credit-led approach toward providing a broad array of financial products and services, including savings and insurance. The key to success for the MFIs of the future will be offering financial products and services that are designed to meet clients' needs, motivations and desires. WWB's research confirms that the key economic priorities for poor women—to a far greater extent than for men—continue to be health care, the education of their children, and housing. All MFI clients, but particularly women, seek a safe place to save the assets they have created and the means to protect them from catastrophic loss.

### *6.1 ACCESS Development Services—The Parent Institution*

ACCESS Development Services (also referred to as ACCESS) was instituted jointly by CARE and DFID in March 2006, as an exit strategy to build on the expertise and experiences of a large scale successful programme called CASHE (Credit and Savings for Household Enterprises), one of the most successful programme of DFID with a value of GBP 10 million (DFID, 2006).

#### *Vision*

"ACCESS is a global partner of choice providing inclusive and innovative livelihood solutions enabling the poor to overcome poverty and live with dignity."

#### *Mission*

"To build the capacity of community based institutions that deliver relevant financial and livelihood development services to the poor and unreached households."

ACCESS Development Services is a national technical services company with focus on supporting the up-scaling of the microfinance sector in India as well incubating innovations for sustainable enterprise development of the poor. ACCESS is structured uniquely, to work at all levels of the sectoral value chain—implementing programme on the ground, working with Civil Society organizations, Government Departments, Corporate sector, and Multilateral/Bilateral agencies as also undertaking a few national initiatives. Although ACCESS has a national concern, given the scenario of low penetration of development services in certain regions of the country, ACCESS focuses its efforts in the more underserved regions.

### *6.1.1 ACCESS has broadly defined its initiatives under two verticals i.e. microfinance and livelihoods*

*Microfinance*

At the ground level, ACCESS provides technical assistance and mentoring support to new/nascent and grown-up NGOs/ MFIs which have the potential to transform to full-fledged sustainable microfinance operations through its Microfinance Resource Centres spread across six regions. Prior to providing the technical assistance and mentoring support, a qualitative and quantitative assessment is done of the NGOs/MFIs through the Institutional and Capacity Assessment Tool (ICAT). Based on the results of this assessment, customized technical services are provided to the institutions.

At the meso-level, ACCESS has established the ACCESS Microfinance Alliance (AmFA) spread across the country and covering around 4 million clients. The partners in the network are provided various services including structured technical support, linkages with financial and non-financial institutions and learning opportunities by ACCESS.

At the national level, as supporting sector building, we have structured a slew of initiatives under the banner of "Microfinance India" where we organize the Annual Microfinance India Summit, release the annual State of the Sector Report, organize policy retreats and work with stakeholders to develop a state vision document in an underserved region.

*Livelihoods*

Besides, executing over 20 livelihoods (enterprise development as called in India) initiatives across the country and impacting the livelihoods and incomes of over 100,000 primary producers; ACCESS has been successfully organizing one of the significant initiatives since last 6 years i.e. the Micro-Finance India Summit. The summit is participated over 1000 by global resource persons and experts. This has been established as global platform for microfinance in India. Besides the MF

India Summit, ACCESS has also been successfully organizing the Livelihoods India Conference, with specific focus on livelihoods and enterprise development issues and challenges the poor face.

Under the Livelihoods (Enterprise Development) initiatives, ACCESS impacts the lives of the poor by developing sustainable solutions for improving their incomes and improving various income generation activities. To optimize its resources and maximize the results of its interventions, ACCESS believes in partnering with key stakeholders in the sector in order to develop mutually reinforcing strategies, bring convergence of competencies and build consensus on key issues.

ACCESS operates on a pan India basis, but focuses on building local capacity in more underserved regions. Headquartered at New Delhi, ACCESS has operational offices in 7 States and closely works with respective State Government Departments and Central Govt. Ministries and Departments. ACCESS has engaged with a host of other donors/stakeholders, including UNDP, Ford Foundation, SDC, IFC, SEEP Network, Trehan Foundation, Citibank Foundation, Rabobank Foundation, and ABN AMRO.

### *6.2 Integration and Inter-organizational Collaboration to Provide Non-Financial Services*

For some women, well-designed financial products delivered by a gender-aware organization may be sufficient to significantly improve their livelihoods and help them change the gender inequalities that constrain achievement of their aspirations for themselves and their families. Evidence suggests that this is particularly the case for 'better-off' poor women and those in reasonably dynamic market contexts, where access to capital or safe savings facilities is the main constraint on economic activity, and where the political context is supportive of gender equality.

For many others, particularly poorer women, and even for women exporters and large-scale entrepreneurs, this is not the case (World Bank, 2003, 2006, World Bank, FAO and IFAD, 2008). Even if rural finance (including microfinance) increases women's access to financial services on a large scale, markets may become distorted or saturated with a narrow range of economic activities, and indebtedness may be high. Unless women's incomes increase, they are unlikely to find sufficient money for savings, insurance or other financial services. Unless there are investment opportunities in the local economy, women will probably not use remittance transfers to invest in local economic activities. This means that rural microfinance services need to look beyond product design to find ways of increasing women's livelihood skills and empowerment. This does not necessarily mean adding on 'empowerment components' such as non-financial services and organizational development, although these also have their place, as discussed in this section and the following one on "Participation and collective action". Even in minimalist organizations, there are ways of mainstreaming a gender equality and empowerment vision into existing core activities—again, at minimal cost beyond those of the initial design and an inception phase.

Rural microfinance is a cost-efficient means of delivering, or at least linking, a wide range of development interventions, as well as enhancing client—and hence organizational—financial sustainability. Apart from their savings-and-credit initiatives, many NGOs and an increasing number of MFIs provide a range of other, separately funded interventions for women and men. None of these recent developments is necessarily gender sensitive, yet there are ways in which they can take gender dimensions into account. It is crucial to integrate women fully into training, extension and other interventions, regardless of whether such interventions are conventionally viewed as being of interest only to men—especially technical training for new agricultural crops and technology and other livelihood development programmes.

There are a number of ways in which cost-efficient complementary services could be offered more effectively and sustainably:

- Mutual learning and information exchange within groups could meet many basic training needs if systems are properly set up and funded initially. This training does not substitute for professional (and expensive) training, but it enables such training to be targeted to those areas where it is really needed, and it builds peoples' capacities to absorb, benefit from, and disseminate such training.

- Implement a cross-subsidy: charge better-off clients (including men) for some services, such as business services and business registration, or charge clients for more advanced training after they have taken subsidized basic courses. GALS is made sustainable in Uganda through funding from cooperative funds.
- Encourage loans for service provision by microfinance clients or larger private firms. Examples include loans to midwives and health practitioners to buy equipment to provide better service, or loans to set up child-care facilities or waste management services on a commercial basis.

Financial institutions lacking the scope to introduce non-financial services themselves can collaborate with other service providers. By developing formal or informal links with providers of other services, microfinance programmes can increase their contribution at minimal cost and give providers of other services ready access to a sizeable, organized constituency of poor women, which would in turn contribute to the sustainability of their own services. Inter-organizational collaboration between microfinance programmes and specialist providers of other types of services could take several forms. A microfinance programme could advertise complementary services available from other organizations, such as advice and information on legal rights offered by local women's movements. This could be done simply through putting leaflets on the counter for clients to read, or could take a more direct form of collaboration in promotion. A microfinance programme could refer clients to other organizations or make special arrangements for programmes, groups or individuals to pay for particular services. Collaboration could also take the form of sharing the costs of developing training programmes and innovations for conducting research.

In microfinance programmes targeted at reducing poverty, group-based savings and credit have been seen as key innovations, combining efficiency with empowerment (Otero and Rhyne, 1994). Many types of group-based delivery have evolved, with varying degrees of control and function. For example, groups may be responsible for client identification, savings collection and loan disbursal, loan follow-up and repayment, mutual guarantees for loans, product design, more cost-effective service delivery, and pressuring peers to establish and maintain credit discipline. Most group-based microfinance programmes focus on women—or, conversely, most rural finance services directed at women are group-based MFIs. Rural cooperatives are an exception since membership is based on the assumption that households are headed by men. Rural financial institutions targeting men are much more likely to give loans to individuals, because experience suggests that men are generally less likely to favour group loans and group activities in general.

Although MFIs clearly benefit from providing savings-and-credit services to women's groups, the benefits for women are not so obvious. Groups can be a powerful force for change at the local level and for lobbying and advocacy at the national level, yet participation does not necessarily guarantee empowerment. Many rural finance programmes provide groupbased services offering small loans, mostly to women, concurrently with services offering larger, individual loans, mostly to men. Men have other options and may not be interested in group-based finance (Cheston and Kuhn, 2002). It is crucial to track gender differences in applications and subsequent approval for the whole range of financial services—and to take appropriate steps to ensure equal access for men and women if inequalities are found. The benefits of economic collaboration should not be assumed. Collaboration needs to be based on a sound economic rationale, supported by appropriate management and technical training and assistance.

## REFERENCES

Abdullah, H.J., A.F. Ibrahim and J. King (2010), Women's voices, work and bodily integrity in pre-conflict, conflict and post-conflict reconstruction processes in Sierra Leone. *IDS Bulletin* 41(2): 37-45.

ACORD (1996), Background material, East Africa Credit workshop, Bakuba, Tanzania, Nairobi: Agency for Cooperation and Research in Development (ACORD).

Amin, S. (1993), Port Sudan and Red Sea field trip report, Port Sudan, Agency for Cooperation and Research in Development (ACORD).

ArmendaŁ riz de Aghion, Beatriz and Jonathan Morduch (2005), *The Economics of Microfinance.* Cambridge, MA: MIT Press.

Ashe and Parrott (2001), Gender impact assessments rarely distinguish among women by poverty level, but see, for example, the study of Pact's Women's Empowerment Programme in Nepal.

Basnet, P. (1995), Trip Report to Bangladesh, Dhaka, Save the Children.

Blumberg, Rae (1989), Entrepreneurship, Credit, and Gender in the Informal Sector of the Dominican Republic, Women in Development: AID's experience, Washington, DC: USAID.

Cheston, S. (2006), "Just the Facts, Ma'am: Gender Stories from Unexpected Sources with Morals for Micro-finance." Micro Credit Summit, from http://www.microcreditsummit.org/papers/Workshops/28_Cheston.pdf

Cheston, S. and Kuhn, L. (2002), Empowering women through microfinance, A case study of Sinapi Aba Trust, Ghana. USA: Opportunity International.

CIDA (1999), CIDA's Policy on gender equality, Quebec, Canada: Canadian International Development Agency.

Cloke, J. (2001), The gendered household: Who really knows what's going on?, Mimeo, University of Loughborough, Leicestershire, UK.

Cornwall, A. and J. Edwards (2010), Introduction: Negotiating empowerment. *IDS Bulletin* 41(2): 1-9.

Corsi, Marcella, Febrizio Boti, Tamaso Rondinella and Giulia Zachhhia (2006), Women and Microfinance in Mediterranean Countries, *Development*, 2006, 49(2), 67-74.

DFID (2006), Making governance work for the poor, DFID White Paper. London: Department for International Development.

FAO (1984), Promotion of Women's Activities in Marketing and Credit, Rome, Food and Agriculture Organization of the United Nations (FAO), Rome.

Fourth World Conference for Women 1995 (http://www.rlc.fao.org/en/publications/gender-sensitive-microfinance/)

Frank, C., E. Lynch and L. Schneider-Moretto (2008), Stemming the tide of mission drift: Microfinance transformations and the double bottom line. New York: Women's World Banking.

Goetz, A.M. and C. Nyamu Musembi (2008), Voice and women's empowerment: Mapping a research agenda. Pathways Working Paper 2. Brighton, UK: Pathways of Women's Empowerment Research Programme Consortium.

Goetz, A.M. and R. Sengupta (1996), Who Takes the Credit?, Gender, Power and Control over Loan Use in Rural Credit Programmes in Bangladesh, World Development 24(1): 45-63.

Harper, A. (1995), Providing women in Baltistan with access to loans: Potential and problems. Lahore, Pakistan: Aga Khan Rural Support Programme.

Hashemi, Syed M. et al. (1996), 'Rural Credit Programs and Women's Empowerment in Bangladesh', World Development 24(4): 635-53.

Huq, S. (2010), Negotiating Islam: Conservatism, splintered authority and empowerment in urban Bangladesh. *IDS Bulletin* 41(2): 97-105.

Hulme, David and Paul Mosley (1997), *Finance Against Poverty*, London: Routledge.

ILO (1999), Gender and the Access to Financial Services: J:\ilo_data\public\english\employment\finance\download\wp23.wpd

Jahan, R. (1995), *The Elusive Agenda: Mainstreaming Women in Development*. London: Zed Press.

Johnson, S. (1999), Gender and Microfinance: guidelines for good practice, Centre for Development Studies, University of Bath, UK.

Johnson, S. (2005), Centre for Development Studies, University of Bath, U.K. "Making MFIs and financial markets work for poor women", Paper for the Consultation on 'Gender in Microfinance' held by FWWB, Ahmedabad, India, September, 2005.

Johnson, P. (2010), Unmarried in Palestine: Embodiment and (dis)empowerment in the lives of single Palestinian women. *IDS Bulletin* 41(2): 106-15.

Kabeer, N. (1998), Money Can't Buy Me Love'?; Re-evaluating Gender, Credit and Empowerment in Rural Bangladesh. Brighton, *IDS Bulletin*.

Kabeer, N. (2001), Conflicts over Credit: Re-evaluating the empowerment potential of loans to women in rural Bangladesh, World Development, 29(1): 63-84.

Kabeer, N. (2008), Paid work, women's empowerment and gender justice: Critical pathways of social change. Pathways Working Paper 3. Brighton, UK: Pathways of Women's Empowerment Research Programme Consortium.

Kabeer, N. and L. Huq (2010), The power of relationships: Love and solidarity in a landless women's organisation in rural Bangladesh. *IDS Bulletin* 41(2): 79-87.

Khandker, Shahidur et al. (1995), Grameen Bank: Performance and sustainability, World Bank Discussion Paper No. 306.

Khandker, Shahidur (2003), Microfinance and Poverty: Evidence using panel data from Bangladesh, World Bank Policy Research Working Paper 2945.

Mayoux, L. (1999), Questioning Virtuous Spirals: Micro-finance and women's empowerment in Africa. *Journal of International Development*, 11: 957-84.

Mayoux, L. (2001), Tackling the Down Side: Social Capital, Women's Empowerment and Micro-finance, in Cameroon, Development and Change Retrieved 3, 32, from http://www.microfinancegateway.org/files/18143_Tackling_the_Down_Side_Cameroon_.pdf

Mayoux, L. (2005), Women's empowerment through sustainable micro-finance: Rethinking 'best practice' sustainable micro-finance for women's empowerment. (www.genfinance.info/.)

Mayoux, L. (2006), Women's empowerment and microfinance: A 'think piece' for the microfinance field, Sustainable Micro-finance for Women's Empowerment. www.genfinance.info/.

Mayoux, L. and M. Hartl (2009), Gender and rural microfinance: Reaching and empowering women—a guide for practitioners, IFAD Report: International Fund for Agricultural Development, Rome.

Microfinance India Summit (2010), Round Table on Gender Diversity for Microfinance, ACCESS and Women's World banking.

Microcredit Summit Campaign (2005), State of the Microcredit Summit Campaign Report 2005, Washington (www.microcreditsummit.org.)

Mody, Priti (2000), Gender Empowerment and Microfinance, mimeo, Evans School.

Montgomery, R., D. Bhattacharya and D. Hulme (1996), Credit for the poor in Bangladesh, In *Finance Against Poverty*, ed. D. Hulme and P. Mosley, London, UK: Routledge.

Morduch, Jonathan (1999), The Microfinance Promiset. *Journal of Economic Literature* 37:1569-614.

Morduch, Jonathan (2002), 'Microfinance without Trade-offs', paper given at the third international conference on 'Finance for Growth and Poverty Reduction', University of Manchester.

Otero, M. and E. Rhyne, eds. (1994), *The new world of microenterprise finance: Building healthy financial institutions for the poor*. London, UK: IT Publications.

Pairaudeau, N. (1996), Savings and Loan Use Survey and Gender, Impact Assessment of Uong Bi Savings and Credit Scheme, Hanoi, Action Aid Vietnam.

Priyadarshani, A. and S.A. Rahim (2010), Women watching television: Surfing between fantasy and reality. *IDS Bulletin* 41(2): 116-24.

Rahman, A. (1999), Micro-credit initiatives for equitable and sustainable development: Who pays? World Development 27(1): 67-82.

Rajagopalan, S., ed. (2009), *Microfinance and Women's Empowerment: A Critical Assessment*. Hyderabad, India: Icfai University Press.

Rankin, K. (2001), Governing Development: Neoliberalism, Microcredit, and Rational Economic, Woman. *Economy and Society*, 30(1): 18-37.

Sardenberg, C. (2010a), Liberal vs. liberating empowerment: A Latin American feminist perspective on conceptualising women's empowerment. *IDS Bulletin* 39(6), December: 18-27.

Sardenberg, C. (2010b), Family, households and women's empowerment in Bahia, Brazil, through the generations: Continuities or change? *IDS Bulletin,* 41(2): 88-96.

Thomas, Duncan (1994), Like Father like Son, or, like Mother like Daughter: Parental education and child health. *Journal of Human Resources*, 29(4): 950-88.

Udry, Christopher (1996), Gender, Agricultural Production, and the Theory of the Household. *Journal of Political Economy*, 104(5): 1010-46.

Uma Murray (2005), Promoting gender-sensitive entrepreneurship via microfinance institutions, Natural Resources Management and Development Department, FAO: Accessed from http://www.fao.org/sd/dim_pe1/pe1_050401a1_en.htm on 25 April, 2005.

UNDP (1995a), The Beijing Platform for Action, Fourth World Conference on Women.

UNDP (1995b), The Human Development Report. New York, UNDP.

UN Millennium Project (2005), Task Force on Education and Gender Equality, UNMP, 2005: 31, 140.

United Nations Development Programme (2010), Bangladesh: A Baseline for Needs Assessment and Costing. A Situation Analysis Report on Poverty and Hunger (MDG 1). Retrieved from http://www.undp.org.bd/projects/prodocs/PRS_MDG/Situation%20analysis_poverty %20and%20Hunger.pdf

USAID Microenterprise Results Reporting for 2004, Arlington, VA: Weidemann Associates, 2004.

Van Bastelaer, T. (1999), Imperfect Information, Social Capital and the Poor's Access to Credit, mimeo.

Women's World Banking Global Policy Forum (1995), The Missing Links: Financial Systems That Work for the Majority, Women's World Banking, New York.

World Bank (2003), Rural financial services: Implementing the Bank's strategy to reach the rural poor. ARD Report No. 26030. Washington, DC: World Bank.

World Bank (2006), Gender equality as smart economics: A World Bank Group gender action plan (fiscal years 2007-2010). Washington, DC: World Bank.

World Bank, FAO and IFAD (2008), Gender in agriculture sourcebook. Washington, DC: World Bank.

Zaidi, S.A., H. Jamal, S. Javeed and S. Zaka (2007), Social impact assessment of microfinance programmes. Islamabad: European Union-Pakistan Financial Services Sector Reform Programme.

# 7
# Regulatory Dimensions of Microfinance

In the past two decades, many developing countries have witnessed a rapid growth of microfinance activities. The trends on the investment side have included increasing attention from socially responsible and capital markets investors. From an institutional set-up, commercial banks are downscaling, MFIs are moving up market and convergence is happening between the so-called finance for growth and finance for all. Recognizing that microfinance is more and more integrated in the mainstream financial system brings calls for regulation to set up the rules of the game in this industry (CGAP, 2009). The general tendency toward regulation is even reinforced by microfinance institutions' own self-interest. Since regulation remains a precondition for deposit mobilization in many countries, more MFIs seek to transform into regulated entities to access cheap and local currency deposits. Regulation opens also the door to a variety of funding opportunities and helps to reduce the overreliance on subsidies. Donors and microfinance practitioners are well aware that micro-lenders need to prepare for the day when subsidies disappear as donors choose to move on (Armendariz and Morduch, 2005). Understanding how regulation affects performance matters. On one hand costs of designing and enforcing regulatory policies to address the specific challenges of microfinance are substantial (Hartaska and Nadolyak, 2007). On the other hand, complying with supervisory requirements is costly. A microfinance institution acquires permission to lend through registration. Each legal structure; such as the one for Microfinance institution, has different and unique formation requirements and privileges.

Given this background scene, this chapter attempts to put together the various structural and operational aspects relating to the regulatory dimensions of microfinance. Broadly this entails building a Conceptual Framework for Regulation of Rural Finance and MFIs, recent initiatives taken in the Field of Microfinance Regulation, Microfinance regulatory structure in India, Model Microfinance regulations covered under the recently introduced Microfinance Regulation Bill, impact of Legal and Regulatory framework/structure on Sustainable Microfinance development.

## 1. Conceptual Framework for Regulation of Rural Finance and MFIs

The aim of a supportive regulatory framework is to build strong regulated and unregulated institutions of all types—(a) to provide services on a sustainable basis under uniform, common, shared performance standards, and (b) to encourage the regulatory authority to develop appropriate prudential regulations and staff capacity that are tailored to the institutions' operational and risk profiles. This objective requires defining different tiers of financial institutions with different degrees of regulatory requirements. The requirements could vary from (a) simply registering as legal entities, to (b) preparing and publishing periodic reports on operations and financial results, to (c) observing non-prudential rules of conduct in business operations, to (d) securing a proper license and being subject to prudential regulation by a regulatory authority, prudential supervision, or both by a central supervisory authority. Lower-tiers institutions serving the lower end of the market can enable non-bank micro-lenders to seek greater formalization without actual licensing.

As the rural finance and microfinance sector grows, adding a licensing tier that permits MFIs to legally mobilize savings and other commercial sources of funds can encourage capacity building and innovation that are aimed at self-sufficiency and greater outreach. Another approach that has been used is to open a special window for micro-lending as a product that enables commercial banks, as well as alternative specialized institutions, to benefit from different cost and regulatory structures. Licensing of rural and community banks can also facilitate the emergence of new types of MFIs that serve specific markets.

However, the premature creation of special tiers with easy entry may result in weak institutions, may affect the development of the commercial financial system, and may risk overwhelming inadequate supervisory resources. Thus, the licensing of MFIs should be designed to balance promotional and prudential objectives. The main potential threats pertaining to deposit-taking MFIs are that (a) deposit-taking MFIs could collapse, thus adversely affecting the commercial system, and that (b) prudential regulation of deposit-taking MFIs could prove to be an administrative burden that distracts supervisors from adequately protecting the safety and soundness of the main financial system.

*Microfinance Consensus Guidelines* (Christen, Lyman, and Rosenberg, 2003) takes a balanced view, arguing that deposit taking on a small scale may essentially go unsupervised—especially where the deposits consist of only forced-savings components of the lending product, so that most depositors are net borrowers from the MFI at most times. This approach would leave the supervisory apparatus unencumbered from having to deal in-depth with a profusion of tiny MFIs.

A consensus on the framework for the regulation of rural finance and microfinance institutions has evolved on the basis of country experiences in recent years. This framework (summarized in Table 1) identifies different categories and tiers of institutional providers of microfinance, and it specifies the thresholds of financial intermediation activities that trigger the need for progressively stronger types of regulation and supervision. The legal and regulatory framework for banking and finance in many countries may not include lower tiers for rural finance and microfinance banks. Some countries may be in the process of establishing the legal and regulatory framework specifically to create new tiers for rural finance or microfinance banks, which usually have a limited geographical coverage specified by law. Regulation of microfinance activities and institutions may take three main forms: (a) simple registration as a legal entity; (b) non-prudential regulations that provide standards of business operations and oversight, such as operating and financial reports to be submitted, to protect the interests of clients or members; and (c) full prudential supervision. Global experience illustrates that the benefits from regulating microfinance may be limited when commercial banking standards are applied to MFIs without adequate consideration of microfinance methodologies. Non-bank finance companies and other types of registered institutions providing rural finance and microfinance services are not subject to statutory prudential regulation and supervision by a central supervisory authority, because they do not mobilize retail deposits from the public and intermediate those deposits into loans and investments. Nevertheless, such institutions should observe and adhere to a set of rules and standards with respect to the conduct of their business operations to provide protection for their borrowing customers and for third-party providers of wholesale commercial funds, even though commercial fund providers and institutional investors are presumed to be well informed and to be capable of any required due diligence.

### 1.1 Assessment of Regulatory Framework Issues for Rural Finance and Microfinance Institutions

The assessment of the regulatory framework for the rural finance and microfinance sector covers both the institutional aspects and the benchmarks used to evaluate the sector's performance and soundness. The considerations include (a) assessing the need for prudential supervision versus non-prudential regulation and for the technical capacity for supervision, as well as the costs of that supervision; (b) determining which agency should carry out the supervision or regulation, and whether delegated or auxiliary supervision may be warranted or justified; and (c) establishing benchmarks and standards for evaluating outreach and for financial performance and soundness. In addition, certain cross-cutting issues—taxes that may obstruct more effective outreach and costs, and credit

**Table 1:** Tiered Structures and Regulatory Triggers by Type of MFI

| Type of microfinance (MFI) | Activies that trigger regulation | Forms of external regulation | Recommended regulatory authority |
|---|---|---|---|
| Informal saving and credit groups funded by members fees and saving | None | None required | None required |
| Category A: Non-governmental organizations (NGOs) funded by donor funds | | | |
| Category A1: Funding only from grants | None, if total loans do not exceed donated funds, grants, and accumulated surplus | Registration as a nonprofit society, association, or trust | A registrar of societies or self-regulating body, if any |
| Category A2: Funding from donor grants and from commercial borrowings or securities issues | Generating liabilities through borrowings to fund micro-loan portfolio and operations. | Registration as a legal corporate entity; authorization by a banking authority or securities commission | A registrar of companies, banking authority, or securities agency |
| Cotegory B: Financial Cooperatives and credit unions funded members' money and saving | Accepting deposits from and making loans to members | Registration as a financial cooperative | A registrar of cooperatives or banking authority |
| Category C: Special-licensed banks and MFIs funded by the public's money (deposits, investor capital, and commercial borrowings) | Accepting wholesale and retail public deposits for intermediation into loans and investments | Registration as a corporate legal entity; licensing as a finance company or bank (with full prudential requirements) | A registrar of cooperatives or banking authority |

information sharing systems that can help MFIs manage loan delinquencies and reduce costs—need to be considered. Also, PSBs and CFIs—though significant components of the rural finance and microfinance sector—are often excluded from the scope of the regulatory framework. However, an analytical evaluation of their outreach, operating performance, and financial soundness—as well as the primary problems they face or may pose to the rest of the sector—may be an important aspect of the assessment of adequacy of access.

Some key questions in assessing the regulatory framework of rural finance and microfinance institutions include the following:

- Is there a need to regulate (but not prudentially supervise) those other institutions?
- If so, what is the scope of the regulation?

Very often the distinctions between broad regulatory oversight (sometimes called non-prudential regulation) and detailed prudential supervision are ignored in a number of countries. Inappropriate regulatory approach has led to the misallocation of scarce supervisory and staff resources in the attempt to impose prudential standards and requirements on rural finance and microfinance institutions that are not engaged in mobilizing and intermediating public deposits, a step that poses a systemic risk. Prudential supervision involves the regulatory authorities' verifying the compliance of institutions with mandatory standards—such as minimum capital levels and adequacy, liquidity management ratios, and asset quality standards—as measures for financial soundness. Prudential supervision of deposit-taking category C institutions is aimed at protecting public savings that are being mobilized and lent out or intermediated, which puts public savings at risk of being lost if loans are not repaid. In contrast, for various categories of institutions—institutions in category A2 and similar institutions in category B—may require only non-prudential supervision or regulatory oversight.

### *1.2 Regulatory Framework of Microfinance*

The financial regulatory framework in a given country can have a huge impact on even the viability of microfinance. The forms of legal organization an institution has available to them, registration requirements, interest rate caps, capitalization, etc. are all determined by the legal framework or lack thereof. Although Microfinance regulation is still a heavily debated topic and is not yet well understood, it is integral to any study that endeavours to understand the costs and benefits of different institutional forms.

### *1.2.1 Legal basis for Regulation*

Banks in India are regulated and supervised by the Reserve Bank of India (RBI) under the RBI Act of 1934, Banking Regulation Act, Regional Rural Banks Act, and the Cooperative Societies Acts of the respective state governments for cooperative banks. NBFCs are registered under the Companies Act, 1956 and are governed under the RBI Act. There is no specific law catering to NGOs although they can be registered under the Societies Registration Act, 1860, the Indian Trust Act, 1882, or the relevant state acts. There has been a strong reliance on self-regulation for NGO MFIs and as this applies to NGO MFIs mobilizing deposits from clients who also borrow. This tendency is a concern due to enforcement problems that tend to arise with self-regulatory organizations. In January 2000, the RBI essentially created a new legal form for providing microfinance services for NBFCs registered under the Companies Act so that they are not subject to any capital or liquidity requirements if they do not go into the deposit taking business. Absence of liquidity requirements is concern to the safety of the sector.

### *1.2.2 Regulation and Constraints on NGO-MFIs*

One of the main constraints of NGO-MFIs is the ability to mobilize deposits in order to diversify their funding sources and grow. This constraint stems from the RBI Act which states that no unincorporated bodies are allowed to accept deposits from the public. Therefore, the right to collect deposits from the general public is restricted to regulated institutions, and only cooperatives and NBFCs are subject to prudential regulations (Bhattacharya and Stachen, 2004). This means that NGO-MFIs may collect deposits only from their members, but are not subject to prudential regulation. Greater supervision of NGO-MFIs has therefore been recommended in the interests of protecting small savers, ensuring proper terms of credit and financial discipline, and the institution of a proper reporting system. The concern over protecting small savers stems from the fact that it is legal for

NGOs to mobilize savings from their clients but not the greater public, which requires a bank license (Bhattacharya and Stachen, 2004). MFIs not mobilizing savings but only lending are and may only be required to provide periodic statements of financial operations after their initial registration. Microfinance activities of NGO-MFIs are not expressly stated as one of the "charitable purposes" in the preamble to the Societies Registration Act. Therefore, the carrying out of lending activities and charging interest could easily lead to the denial of charitable status, although this has not widely happened as of yet. Therefore, a major concern for NGOs that might affect their decision to transform to an NBFC is the loss of charitable status which entitles them to a tax exemption on interest collected. Lastly, NGOs face the regulatory constraint of not being able to receive shareholder contributions, leaving them with the options of donor and government funds (Bhattacharya and Stachen, 2004).

### *1.2.3 Requirements for Operating as an NBFC*

The transformation from NGO to NBFC is difficult when the minimum start-up capital requirement for registering as an NBFC being ₹ 20 million or US$ 450,000, often too large an amount for most NGO MFIs (Basu and Srivastava, 2006). The main problem with the minimum capital requirement is that MFIs are restricted to bringing in the capital as fresh money, meaning that NGOs are not allowed to invest capital in a non-charitable institution. This restriction makes transformation more difficult and might be the reason we mainly see transformation of large NGO MFIs with better access to capital. Along with the minimum capital requirement for a license, another major regulatory constraint that NBFCs face is the restriction on foreign equity investments. NBFCs face a foreign equity investment ceiling of 51 percent and a minimum equity amount of US$ 500,000. This restriction has impeded equity contributions to microfinance NBFCs by foreign investors. Lastly, for all MFIs there is a strong concern that interest rate caps can be introduced by state governments under existing state legislation. The introduction of interest rate caps for any MFI, but especially NBFCs which need to generate a profit, could prohibit ongoing operations if the imposed interest rate cap does not cover the cost of lending. All of these issues impact the decision an MFI makes when it decides to transform from an NGO to an NBFC because they represent benefits and costs to transformation (Basu and Srivastava, 2006).

### *1.2.4 Some Cross-cutting Issues Affecting Rural Finance and Microfinance Institutions*

Tax issues may present obstacles to rural finance and microfinance institutions from more effectively providing access to financial services. The legal and nonprofit status of non-bank NGO MFIs may sometimes be questioned by tax authorities on the grounds that the credit services they are providing to their clientele are priced at commercial rates, rather than at "charitable" levels, as in the case of NGO MFIs in India. In other instances, licensed specialized banks and non-bank finance institutions may not be permitted by tax accounting laws and regulations to expense provisions for possible loan losses, in spite of prudential regulations issued by the central supervisory authority, as in Tanzania, which creates an unnecessary real economic burden to such specialized banks and non-bank finance institutions. A related problem stems from the requirement by tax authorities that delinquent loans may be written off only when the sale and disposition of collateral securing such a defaulted loan results in recovering a monetary value that is less than the value of the collateral, as in the case of Kenya.

Credit registries allow borrowers to build up a credit history and can assist lenders in assessing risk, thereby reducing the cost of lending and improving access. Credit registries that give easy and reliable access to a client's credit history can dramatically reduce the time and costs of obtaining such information from individual sources and, therefore, can reduce the total costs of financial intermediation. Credit reporting makes borrower quality much more transparent, which benefits good borrowers and increases the cost of defaulting on obligations. It helps borrowers build up a credit history and eases access to credit. Credit registries are especially important for SMEs, because their creditworthiness is more difficult to evaluate and because they have less visibility and transparency relative to large enterprises. Often, current regulations may provide for the sharing of only negative information (i.e. information on non-performing loans). It is preferable that regulations allow for sharing of both positive and negative information to improve reliability of credit risk evaluation and to increase competition. Reporting positive information significantly increases the predictability of rating and scoring models used by lenders, thereby translating into lower loss rates, higher acceptance rates of credit applicants, or both (Stachen, 2003).

Sharing positive information will also allow borrowers to build their credit history, which can especially benefit small borrowers, because it will allow them to establish a good borrowing reputation and to improve their chances to increase borrowings as their business grows. Regulations governing information sharing should also allow for adequate consumer and data protection mechanisms. Allowing all finance providers to share both positive and negative information on their borrowers will allow small business to participate in the process of reputation building and generation of credit history. It would help facilitate the process of borrowers' graduating from microfinance to bank finance as their business develops. Information sharing among all finance providers could contribute significantly to reducing segmentation and increasing competition.

## 2. Recent Initiatives in the Field of Microfinance Regulation

A number of recent initiatives have dealt with the issue of microfinance regulation. This can be taken as a sign of growing interest in the field. Below, some of the most important initiatives are briefly summarized. Furthermore, some of the regulatory changes triggered by this debate are listed.

### *2.1 The NABARD Task Force*

In the late 1990s, it was felt that a suitable national policy framework was essential for the orderly development of the microfinance sector in the country. Various critical issues such as ways to scale up microfinance programmes in India, the division of roles between existing mainstream financial institutions, development banks and newly emerging microfinance institutions (MFIs) and the need for an appropriate policy and regulatory framework for their operations were engaging the attention of microfinance practitioners, the Government and the RBI. It was at this juncture that in November 1998 that a high-powered Task Force on Supportive Policy and Regulatory Framework for Microfinance (henceforth referred to as the Task Force) was set up by NABARD at the instance of RBI (NABARD, 1999). The Task Force comprised senior officials from GoI, RBI, NABARD, banks and chief executives of prominent NGOs implementing various microfinance models in the country. The objectives of the Task Force were, among others, to come up with suggestions for a regulatory framework that brings the operations of the MFIs into the mainstream, to assess the possible role of self-regulatory organizations and to explore the need for a separate legal framework for microfinance. To date, this has been the most comprehensive study about legal issues for microfinance.

The Task Force (1999) made various recommendations, based on which RBI issued a number of important instructions to microfinance practitioners. For the first time, a definition of microfinance was agreed upon. The definition is broad enough to allow for different types of institutions offering various types of financial services.

With regard to the hitherto unregulated microfinance NGO sector, setting up a system of self-regulatory organizations (SROs) features prominently among the recommendations. The Task Force recommends a classification of MFIs according to the question of whether deposit facilities are offered or not and if so, what kind of facilities these are. Both the amount of savings mobilized (below or above a predetermined cut-off limit) and the origin of savings (from clients or from the general public) determine the extent of external control by a supervisory authority. The strong reliance on self-regulation even for NGOs mobilizing deposits from the public does not go in line with more recent recommendations from other international experts, who stress the enforcement problems of a self-regulatory framework and the potential conflicts of interest of the SROs. Basing the extent of regulation on the origin of savings is similar to Christen Robert Peck et al. (2003) approach of looking at the liability side of the balance sheet to determine the need for external regulation (Christen Robert Peck, and Richard Rosenberg, 2000; Christen Robert Peck et al., 2003).

### 2.2 Other Working Groups on Regulatory Issues

Following a meeting at the Prime Minister's Office in October 2001, seven working groups comprising government, NGOs and banking sector representatives were set up, one of them with the mandate of exploring the legal and regulatory challenges currently faced by the microfinance sector in India. In December 2002, the reports of six of the seven working groups were finalized. The Indian microfinance association Sa-Dhan—as one of the members of the group looking into regulatory issues—prepared a report summarising the group's results (Sa-Dhan, 2002a). This report gives clear recommendations regarding how to make the current legal framework more microfinance-friendly. Some of these need immediate attention; some are for the longer term. In addition, the document indicates a way forward for the debate with a strong emphasis on gathering information about the sector as a precondition for better regulation.

RBI has continuously watched the progress of microfinance. In October 2002, the RBI constituted four informal groups for addressing various aspects of microfinance including regulatory arrangements and funding issues. Senior bankers, NGOs and prominent microfinance practitioners and all stakeholders are represented in these informal groups. The recommendations of these informal groups have recently been made public. They are of great importance as some of the changes favoured by a number of stakeholders require the attention and involvement of the RBI. Major recommendations of these informal working groups are to create a separate category of non-deposit taking NBFCs with a lower capital requirement of ₹ 2.5 million (US$ 56,000), and to require NGOs and federations of SHGs either to wind up their savings business and transform into Section 25 companies or to transform into NBFCs or MACS. It is important to note here that the Reserve Bank of India often issues very comprehensive notifications in circular letters giving detailed instructions, explaining its policy or stipulating regulations. To give an example, between 1998 and today the RBI has published 35 notifications regarding NBFCs alone.

### 2.3 Mainstreaming of SHG-Bank Linkage Model

A Working Group on NGOs and SHGs set up by RBI in 1995 looked into various aspects of the linkage between informal SHGs and banks. According to the model, formal banks lend either directly or through an intermediary such as an NGO or an SHG federation to groups of poor people, mostly women. Based on the recommendations of the Working Group, RBI in 1996 issued instructions to the banks to treat the SHG-bank linkage model as part of their mainstream lending. According to the circular, lending to SHGs or to NGOs for on-lending to SHGs is taken as part of their directed lending. Furthermore, SHGs are allowed to open savings accounts with banks. The operational guidelines, earlier issued by NABARD in 1992 for lending to SHGs, envisaged complete flexibility for the banks in regard to lending norms like interest margin, amount to be lent, use of collateral security, repayment period, etc. These guidelines are well accepted by the banking system for providing financial services to the poor. Over the years, the linkage programme has made very good progress. In April 1999, RBI set up a 'Micro Credit Special Cell'. This demonstrates RBI's increased interest in the microfinance sector.

### 2.4 Identification of Potential Risks with the SHG-Bank Linkage Model

The strong growth of the linkage-banking model is a relatively recent phenomenon. Some people argue that the current impressive results cannot simply be extrapolated into the future.

The following were mentioned as potential risks:

- Some interviewees expressed reservations about the quality of new groups promoted in certain states. It is feared that the rapid growth in the linkage programme may hamper the quality of the groups as all high quality groups have already been linked to banks. Essential group processes like the holding of regular meetings, continuous saving by group members and the exertion of group discipline might suffer.

- Some experts saw the present macroeconomic environment as being exceptional. According to this view, the interest rates are the lowest in years, which makes other investment opportunities less attractive. Most banks have excess liquidity and access capacity, so that even a relatively labour-intensive lending methodology with a low return becomes attractive.

Some other reservations have been expressed with regard to the future potential of the SHG-bank linkage model:

- A number of experts expressed doubts as to whether direct linkages with SHGs can ever attract the interest of commercial banks for prolonged periods. In their view, it is more likely that most of the commercial banks may henceforth rely on indirect linkages via NGOs or SHG federations. Thus in the future it will be much more important to look at regulatory problems on this level (Harper, 2002; Sa-Dhan, 2000b; APMAS, 2003; NABARD, 2003; Reddy and Prakash, 2003).
- Some regard the SHG-bank linkage model as inherently constrained. While they acknowledge its success in reaching previously unserved customers, they point out that the form of a SHG quickly becomes constraining. Diversification of risks on this level is rather limited. The potential for growth is restricted as the groups are not allowed to grow beyond 20 members. Individual loan amounts are rather small. New products such as bank cards, health and sanitation finance, and contractual savings for old-age, etc. may not be easy to introduce in SHGs. Again, SHG federations (a growing number of whom is registered as MACS) and NGOs will gain in importance. The corollary is that in the future more attention should be drawn to the appropriateness of regulation on this institutional level.
- There are different estimates of the costs of promotion of SHGs. They are in the range of ₹ 1,500 (NABARD, 2009-10) up to ₹ 10,000 and more (Dhan Foundation) depending upon the philosophy of the promoter

(US$ 30 to 140). Creating a comparable number of SHGs in all states of the country would require substantial resources or a strong increase in self-promoted SHGs.

- Even though the linkage model has spread rapidly in many states, it is yet to fully cover the poor in all states of the country. Currently, the model is geographically concentrated in the South and West of India. There are various reasons for the slow growth in other regions, such as unsatisfactory law and order and difficult socio-economic conditions. The argument goes that linkage banking alone cannot meet the demand in other areas of the country.

None of the respondents held the view that the SHG-bank linkage model does not play a very important role in serving poor people. Yet some were of the opinion that, in view of the uneven growth of the SHG-bank linkage model in the country and the vast number of unreached poor, it is appropriate to encourage all models, particularly the initiatives of MFIs pursuing divergent models.

Some respondents raised the point that the use of federations as intermediaries between banks and SHGs creates additional costs. An interesting case was a federation in Madurai, which prefers to charge an additional service fee on top of the interest payments for loans to SHGs. The rationale is that group members would not understand that they are charged a higher rate for loans from federations than for direct bank loans.

### 2.5 Addressing Regulatory Issues of the SHG-Bank Linkage Model

As already said, the SHG-bank linkage model makes use of the existing, prudentially regulated banking sector. Only minor regulatory issues were mentioned with regard to SHGs. As regards SHGs, they are conceived as informal under the linkage-banking model. As SHGs are not required to be incorporated under any Act, their operations are flexible and can remain simple. Their informal character is seen as one of the strengths of SHGs. The group can, through a simple power of attorney, bind the members both jointly and severally as regards dues to outside institutions, and thus it appears fairly clear that a creditor can proceed against any individual member of the group to recover its dues. From a regulatory perspective, the informality of the groups, their limited size of maximum twenty members, and their collective decision-making guarantee strong internal control and low systemic risk. External regulation therefore seems neither practicable nor necessary.

This view is widely shared among practitioners in the microfinance sector. The RBI made it very clear in its credit policy of November 3, 2003, that the group dynamics of SHGs may be left to themselves and that SHGs need neither be regulated nor formal structures imposed upon them. Further, the procedures for bank linkage should be simple and easy, suited to local conditions. Some people, however, have taken the position that the absence of any legal endorsement of SHGs under any Act may question their legality. It is feared that the lack of an appropriate legal status of SHGs may, in future, hamper the recovery of overdues. One suggestion, therefore, was that SHGs could be appropriately referred to under any of the Acts and their non-incorporation may be duly recognized to avoid any legal difficulty in the future.

The following extract from the statement of the Governor of the RBI on the Mid-Term Review of Monetary and Credit Policy for the year 2003-04, was made on November 3, 2003: "RBI constituted four informal groups to examine various issues concerning microfinance delivery. On the basis of the recommendations of the groups, it is proposed that: (i) banks should provide adequate incentives to their branches in financing the Self-Help Groups (SHGs) and establish linkages with them making the procedures absolutely simple and easy while providing for total flexibility in such procedures to suit local conditions; (ii) the group dynamics of working of the SHGs may be left to themselves and need neither be regulated nor formal structures imposed or insisted upon; (iii) the approach to microfinancing of SHGs should be hassle-free and may include consumption expenditures to enable smoothing of consumptions as needed relative to time-profile of income flows" (Sinha et al., 2003 and 2004).

Some interview partners were concerned about a possible major handicap of informal and unincorporated SHGs in regard to the mobilization of deposits. In their view, a critical issue is the legal definition of deposits as stated in Section 45S, RBI Act. According to this Section of the Act, unincorporated bodies are prohibited from accepting deposits from the public. However, this issue has been dealt with by the stated policy of the RBI and, lately, through the Governor's policy statement. The savings circulating within the SHGs are to be regarded as quasi capital, with both ownership and management of savings with SHGs. In approving the regulatory guidelines issued by NABARD in November 1992, it has been recognized by the RBI that the provisions of Section 45S are by implication not applicable to SHGs, and that SHGs' savings operation are the indispensable starting point for linkages with banks. An issue mentioned was the interest rate cap for loans below ₹ 200,000, which may not exceed the prime lending rate. According to some experts, this rate is too low to allow for profitable lending to SHGs (NABARD, 1999). Others talked of a "social cap on interest rates" meaning that even if interest rates were fully liberalized, there would still be social pressure not to raise the rates above a certain limit.

### *2.6 Exemptions for Non-Deposit-Taking Section 25 Companies*

As regards Non-Banking Financial Companies, the RBI issued instructions on 13th January 2000 to the effect that if NBFCs are engaged in 'microfinancing activities', registered under Section 25 of the Companies Act, 1956, and not accepting public deposits, they would be exempt from the purview of Section 45-IA (registration and minimum net owned funds), 45-IB (maintenance of liquid assets) and 45-IC (transfer of profits to reserve fund) of the RBI Act, 1934 (RBI Notification Ref. DNBS.(PD). CC.No.12 /02.01/99-2000 dated January 13, 2000 (available at http://www.rbi.org.in/sec14/14935.pdf).). These instructions essentially created a new legal form for providing microfinance services without having to comply with the strict regulatory requirements for NBFCs. Section 25 companies are not subject to any capital or liquidity requirements. According to Section 25 of the Companies Act, they must use potential profits for promoting its objects (Sec 25(1) lists describes such a company as an association "formed as a limited company for promoting commerce, art, science, religion, charity or any other useful object"). Although they are not explicitly exempted from supervision by the RBI, in practice they only report to the Registrar of Companies. The price for this is that they are not permitted to go into deposit-taking business.

### *2.7 Allowing More Flexibility for Banks Offering Microfinance Services*

In a circular letter to the banks dated 18th February, 2000, RBI recognized the definition of microfinance as proposed by the Task Force (vide RBI Circular RPCD.No.PL.BC. 62/04.09.01/99-2000 dated February 18, 2000). The central bank advised that for mainstreaming microfinance and to enhance the outreach of microfinance service providers, banks are free to choose their own model for extending microcredit. Further, microcredit extended by banks to individual borrowers directly or through any intermediary would be taken as part of their priority sector lending. Banks are expected to make microcredit an integral element of their corporate credit plans, which are to be monitored by the central bank. To increase micro-lending, the RBI recommended simplification of loan documentation and decentralization of the loan decision by delegating more power to branch managers. Other than for small loans given directly by banks to small borrowers, the interest rate for loans to MFIs and for MFIs lending to the ultimate borrower were fully liberalized (RBI Circular RPCD.No.PL.BC 94/04.01.01/98-99 dated April 24, 1999).

### *2.8 Amending the Existing Legislation for MFIs*

According to scenario 2, more competition from the MFI sector would benefit the poor. The scenario starts from the assumption that the SHG-bank linkage model alone cannot satisfy the huge demand for financial services, and that there is also a role to play for MFIs in the future, particularly in the areas where bank branches are few and far between. A figure frequently quoted originates from the All India Debt and Investment Survey of the Government of India (1992).

According to this source, the formal financial sector in the early 1990s provided credit support to about 64 percent of rural indebted households, while informal sources such as landlords, moneylenders, relatives and friends accounted for the rest of the credit needs. This might have changed in the meantime, as the growth of the linkage model only took off later. A view that emerged strongly out of the discussions was that there has been a fall in the percentage of banks' lending to the poor and that the number of loan accounts below ₹ 25,000 (US$ 560) has come down considerably over the years. No one the consultants talked to questioned that there is still a huge unmet demand for microcredit. As regards savings, the World Bank in a 2001 report on microfinance came to the conclusion: "The demand is nowhere near being met, particularly for small and frequent savings.". The biggest savings collector in India is Sahara India Financial Corporation Ltd. (SIFCL), a Residuary Non-Banking Company (RNBC). It has around 51 million depositors, an asset base of more than US$ 7 billion and around 1,700 branch offices all over India. As an RNBC, at least 80 percent of its deposit liabilities must be invested in high quality securities as specified by the central bank.

It is felt that there is scope for microfinance models other than the SHG-bank linkage model as some of the MFIs have been very successful in various parts of the country. This goes in line with the instructions issued by the RBI in the wake of the Task Force recommendations, which provide for growth of all viable microfinance models. Some people the consultants talked to recommended having a diversity of institutional models competing with each other. Each of these models could have its own comparative advantage, e.g. serve a specific market niche, offer unique products and services, etc. The starting point for a scenario, in which MFIs play an equally strong role in the provision of microfinance services as the SHG-bank linkage model, must be the analysis of the current state of the microfinance sector and potential constraints by its legal environment. The MFIs we are talking about are mainly replicators of the Grameen model, NBFCs financing joint liability groups, cooperatives and individuals, credit unions, SHG federations, etc.

### 2.9 Exploring Potential Ambit of a Special Microfinance Law

An important aspect of a regulatory framework for microfinance is the clear definition of the lower and upper boundaries of the prudentially regulated microfinance tier (cf. Christen, Lyman, and Rosenberg, 2003). Evidence from other countries shows that in Uganda a separate law has been made only for deposit-taking MFIs, while a separate law for all kinds of MFIs has been promulgated in Kyrgyzstan. Such all-encompassing microfinance law usually distinguishes between several tiers, which are subject to different degrees of external regulation. Judging from the current discussions in India, it seems not yet to be clear which MFIs should be covered under the legislation—only the deposit-taking MFIs, Section 25 companies and NGO-MFIs or even banks' with microfinance portfolios. It is doubtful whether the commercial banks, RRBs and the cooperative banks, as important players in the microfinance sector could in any beneficial way be covered under the Act. Going for a functional regulation—i.e. a new law which covers all microfinance activities irrespective of the institutional form under which it is offered—the first step would be to clearly define microfinance from a regulatory point of view. International experience shows that this is a multi-dimensional task (Staschen, 2003b). The outcome could be to introduce a tiered structure of MFIs with different levels of sophistication, different numbers of products to be offered (credit-only, term deposits, savings, insurance, etc.) and varying degrees of regulatory oversight. According to some discussants, it is feared, however, that the proposed new legislation will further complicate the already complex legal environment for microfinance. It was stressed by some people that there is no lack of laws in India—enforcement of the laws and clear separation of legal frameworks are the real issues. In this regard an important question will be whether the new Act supersedes existing laws, or just adds another law those already existing.

It is important to stress that regulatory arbitrage is nothing illegal, but simply a way to use the existing laws in a way, which suits the business to be undertaken best. This brings the added advantage of having a much smaller number of shareholders of the NBFC. Instead of having thousands of clients as shareholders, it is only a small number of, for example, Mutual Benefit Trusts, which are shareholders of the NBFC.

As of now, it appears that both the Government of India (GoI) and the RBI are not very keen to introduce a new Act. Experience from other countries shows that the introduction of totally new legislation of this type requires political conviction and a lot of staying-power. In view of this complex legal and political process, there was a feeling among some interviewees that the addition of a few provisions on microfinance in some of the existing Acts, as described in scenario 2, could be a better alternative. In Bolivia and Indonesia, special microfinance-specific statutory regulations have been brought in under the already existing general banking law. An important aspect will be the definition of MFIs to be covered and thus the number of institutions to be regulated under this new Act, as legislating for only a few NBFCs is seen as a burdensome task. The Task Force recommended a new chapter in the RBI Act on MFIs. This has not found favour with RBI. Instead, the RBI through its instructions dated 18th February 2000 has recognized microfinance as part of the lending activities of the banks with the message that savings services would be provided by the banks and other incorporated approved institutions.

There is a sense of insecurity particularly among those NGO-MFIs who are implementing the Grameen model and are mobilizing savings from their clients. Regulation in any form, either through a separate law or an additional chapter in any Act, would provide them with much-desired recognition of their activities. Finally, there is currently the Financial Companies Regulation Bill (Bill No. 196 of 2000) pending before Parliament, which was introduced in the Lok Sabha (the Lower House of Parliament) on December 13, 2000 (The Bill is available at : http://www.microfinance-mitrabharathi.com/nbfc_financomp_regu_bill_2000_1.htm). This Bill will for the first time introduce a separate Act for NBFCs and thereby streamline legal provisions for NBFCs. It remains to be seen how the final Act will look like. The fact that this is still only a Bill might even open the opportunity to include some microfinance-specific provisions under this Act.

## *2.10 Supervision and Regulation of Banks and MFIs in India*

### *2.10.1 Banking Sector*

The Banking Regulation (BR) Act, 1949 provides legal framework for regulation and supervision of the formal banking institutions. The financial institutions includes 80 Commercial Banks (CBs), 86 Regional Rural Banks (RRBs), 1770 Urban Cooperative Banks, 4 Development Finance Institutions (DFIs), 12739 NBFCs, 31 State Cooperative Banks (SCBs), 370 District Central Cooperative Banks (DCCBs). In terms of the B.R. Act, together with certain provisions of RBI Act, 1934, the RBI assumes powers to prescribe standards and liquidity, solvency and soundness of the regulated institutions so as to ensure that interests of depositors are protected. The Commercial Banks, Urban Cooperative Banks and For Profit NBFCs (registered with RBI) will be subject to supervisory and regulatory jurisdiction of RBI, while RRBs and SCBs/DCCBs will be under the supervisory jurisdiction of NABARD, without dilution of the regulatory and supervisory powers of RBI. The supervisory and regulatory policy and practices for these entities have been developed and matured over the years. While the Board of Financial Supervision (BFS) in RBI provides direction and guidance to exercise regulatory and supervisory powers, the Board of Supervision (BOS) in NABARD extends policy guidance in supervision of SCBs/DCCBs and RRBs.

The Asset classification and provisioning norms, supervisory rating standards, liquidity, disclosure norms, Risk Management System, audit and accounting principles, exposure limits, codes of standards and fair practices, on-site inspection processes, Off-site Surveillance System (OSS), statutory reporting and compliance through Prompt Corrective Action (PCA) trigger points, preventive action through warning signals and punitive action through regulatory directions/penalty/prohibitions/ cancellation of license, Grievance Redressal Mechanism, internal checks and control system, entry barriers, supervisory and regulatory guidelines, fit and proper criteria for Board and

Directors, Corporate governance standards, Branch Licensing Norms, Financial Performance Standards, etc., have been put in place, as a matter of regulatory and supervisory architecture. CBs have been asked to comply with Basel II norms within the stipulated time-frame. The banks which provide microfinance are required to undertake those safeguards and obligations. Although, RRBs and cooperative banks have not been called upon to comply with various principles of Basel Principles of I/II supervision, specifically within any time-frame, they have been facilitated to implement/comply with various principles of supervision as enshrined by Basel Committee. NABARD has adopted CAMELSC approach (Capital, Asset Quality, Management, Earnings, Liquidity, Systems and Compliance) with regard to inspection process and supervisory rating of RRBs and Cooperative Banks. NABARD, apart from making suitable recommendations to RBI for licensing and regulatory action and providing inputs from time to time, has evolved and implemented suitable supervisory best practices pertaining to RRBs and Cooperative Banks. There has been steady progression in this direction.

### *2.10.2 Regulation of MFIs*

NBFCs have played significant role in the Indian Financial Sector in providing outreach to the small clients. With the objective of integrating NBFCs with the financial mainstream, the RBI brought them under its regulatory arm by way of amendment of RBI Act, 1934 in 1996. This paved the way for mandatory registration of companies undertaking financial services with the RBI, compulsory credit rating of deposit taking NBFCs and their compliance to prudential norms. As per Section 45-IA of the BR Act, no NBFC can commence or carry on the business without obtaining certificate of registration from the RBI and having Net Owned Funds (NOF) (Share-holders' equity + internally generated reserves) of ₹ 20 million. All NBFCs have to comply with the provisions of Companies Act relating to Board of Directors, Share Capital, Management Structure, audit, maintenance and publication of books of accounts and general conduct, etc., in addition to the requirements of RBI. Important prudential norms to be complied include Capital

Adequacy Ratio (CAR) based on the risk weight of assets (15%), income recognition, accounting standards, asset classification, provisioning for bad and doubtful debts, disclosures in balance sheet, ceiling on concentration of credit/investment, etc. Not less than 15 percent of their deposits should be invested in specified securities and approved securities (Govt. Securities and Bonds Guaranteed by Govt.) NBFC are required to notify RBI of their intention to open branches. However, only the NBFCs taking public deposits have to comply with prudential norms on CAR, ceiling on concentration of credit/investment/quantum of deposits, etc. Thus, RBI is empowered to give rigorous policy prescriptions and regulatory directions to NBFCs having requisite NOF and accepting public deposits. However, by loan volumes, 77 percent of the MFI Sector is under RBI's direct regulation; but 75 percent of the MFIs are functioning outside regulation. The prudentially unregulated entities are: MACS, Trusts, the Registered Societies which are having a small client base and limited volumes of business.

## 3. Microfinance Regulatory Structure in India—Overview and Limitations

### *3.1 Legal Structures of MFIs*

A MFI in India acquires permission to lend through registration (Table 2). MFIs are registered as one of the five types of entities (NABARD, 2003; 2009-2010) as shown in table 2 below:

**Table 2:** Legal Structure of MFIs

| Category | Type of MFI | Registration |
|---|---|---|
| Not for Profit | NGO MFIs: Societies & | Registerad under Societies Registration Act, 1860 and/or Indian Trust Act, 1882 |
| | Section 25 Companies (10) | Section 25 of Companies Act, 1956 |
| Mutual Benefit | Cooperatives (100) | Registered under State Cooperative Act or Mutually Aided Cooperative Societies Act (MACS) or Multi-State Cooperative Societies Act, 2002 |
| For-Profit | NBFC (50) | Companies Act, 1956 and registered with RBI |
| | NBFC-MFI | RBI Circular, May 2011 |

*Source*: M-CRIL Microfinance Review 2010, www.m-cril.com/Backend/ModulesFiles/NewsEvents/M-CRIL-Microfinance-Review-Nov2010.pdf

The functionality of the various legal structures may be stated as follows:

*NGO MFIs*: There are around 500 NGOs that provide microfinance services and operate as non-profits, although many of these NGO MFIs perform non-financial operations as well. NGO MFIs can be registered as a Society under the Societies Registration Act of 1860 or as a Trust under the Indian Trust Act of 1882.

*Cooperative Societies*: Approximately 100 MFIs in India operate as Cooperatives, registered under the Cooperative Societies Act of the respective state, the Central Multi-State Cooperative Act, 1984, or the new state-level MACS Act. The MACS Act was pioneered by Andhra Pradesh, which sought to prevent political interference in cooperative societies' operations. Some large cooperatives have acquired a banking licence from the RBI to operate as cooperative banks.

*Section 25 Companies*: Many NGO MFIs achieve a more formal corporate structure by registering under the Companies Act, 1956, as a Section 25 Company. These companies offer a structure that can more easily transform into an NBFC. They can accept equity investments, though they cannot offer dividends, and equity investments cannot be withdrawn at the closing of the company. Thus, these institutions often have difficulty attracting equity investments.

*NBFCs*: The mainstream financial sector in India is divided primarily into two categories, banks and NBFCs. Banks adhere to much more stringent regulation than NBFCs because they are all permitted to accept public deposits, and are considered to have consequent systemic risk. The NBFC encompasses many different types of financial companies, which are all subject to the same regulation requirements. Many MFIs have recently registered as NBFCs to take advantage of access to capital markets. NBFCs account for the great majority of the microfinance market in India, with about 50 NBFCs responsible for 80 percent of all microfinance portfolios.

*NBFC-MFIs*: For-profit institutions that qualify for priority sector lending funds are registered as NBFC-MFIs. This NBFC sub-category was created by RBI in May 2011 to classify NBFCs operating as MFIs which meet certain requirements. Currently, it is unclear how many NBFCs will elect to register as NBFC-MFIs, and how many will continue to operate as NBFCs. At this point, only priority sector funding requirements have been made applicable for NBFC-MFIs, though it seems that all existing NBFC regulations also apply to NBFC-MFIs.

### 3.2 Current State of MFI Regulations

This is a very uncertain time for microfinance regulation, since there exist a significant amount of pending regulation. The Malegam Committee recommendations have been 'broadly accepted' by the RBI, though the specifics of the regulation have only been released for items relating to priority sector lending status. The draft of the Microfinance Regulations Bill 2011 has been released as well, and though the bill has been generally well received by practitioners and policy-makers, its passage is still awaited. As sectoral regulation stands now, all the legal structures listed in the previous section face minimal regulatory requirements, except for NBFCs and NBFC-MFIs. Annexure A tabulates the major regulations applicable to NBFCs as stipulated by the RBI. Major regulatory aspects discussed include priority sector lending, deposit mobilization, access to capital, the Money Lending Act, and state level regulations.

*Priority Sector Lending*: Priority sector lending is a government initiative which requires banks to allocate a percentage of their portfolios to investment in specified priority sectors at concessional rates of interest. Currently only MFIs registered as NBFC-MFIs are designated as a priority sector. The number of priority sectors has recently been reduced, which suggests that banks will be relying more heavily on lending to MFIs to meet the priority sector requirements. In order to register as a NBFC-MFI, an institution must meet requirements specified by the RBI.

RBI requires that a minimum of 75 percent of a NBFC-MFI's loan portfolio must have originated for income-generating activities. Additionally, an NBFC-MFI must have 85 percent of its total assets as qualifying assets (excluding cash, balances with banks and financial institutions, government securities and money market instruments). A qualifying asset is a loan which meets the following criteria:

- Borrower's household annual income does not exceed INR 60,000 or INR 1,20,000 for rural and urban areas respectively
- Maximum loan size of 35,000 (first cycle) and INR 50,000 (subsequent cycles)
- Maximum borrower total indebtedness of INR 50,000
- Minimum tenure of 24 months when loan exceeds 15,000
- No prepayment penalties
- No collateral
- Repayable by weekly, fortnightly or monthly instalments at the choice of the borrower.

An NBFC-MFI must also adhere to the following pricing requirements:

- Margin cap of 12 percent
- Interest rate cap of 26 percent Only three pricing components
- Interest rate
- Processing fee (maximum 1 percent)
- Insurance premium
- No penalty for delayed payment
- No security deposit or margin can be taken.

Banks are responsible for ensuring that the institutions receiving priority sector funds adhere to these requirements, with verification through a quarterly Chartered Accountant's Certificate. Securitized assets may also qualify as priority sector assets if an institution meets these requirements. It is assumed that NBFC-MFIs must also adhere to general NBFC requirements.

*Deposit Mobilization*: Regulation stipulates that only NBFCs and Cooperatives are permitted to accept public deposits, though NBFCs must adhere to additional stringent regulations (Manual on Financial and Banking Statistics, Chapter VI, Reserve Bank of India, http://rbidocs.rbi.org.in/rdocs/Publications/PDFs/78928.pdf), and Cooperatives are only permitted to accept deposits from its members. There also exists what is called a deposits limited for NBFCs linked to the institution's Net Owned Fund (NOF). No MFI registered as an NBFC currently accepts deposits because regulation requires that institutions must obtain an investment grade rating, which no MFI has obtained so far.

*Access to Capital*: MFIs in theory can raise capital through various methods, including borrowing from domestic and foreign debt markets, obtaining grants and loans from subsidized lending funds, attracting foreign equity investment from capital markets, though legal structure of MFIs may restrict capital acquisition from some of these sources.

*NBFCs can receive both equity and debt investments*: NBFCs can raise foreign equity investment, though a minimum investment restriction requirement of US$ 500,000 applies, also with a cap of not more than 51 percent stake in the institution. Grants and subsidized onward-lending funds from domestic and foreign sources are not restricted, provided that the foreign grants do not exceed the ceiling of US$ 5 mn per year.

*Section 25 companies* have difficulty attracting equity investments because they are unable to offer dividends and exit opportunities are difficult to predict. They can access External Commercial Borrowing (ECB) up to US$ 5 mn, though the amount that institutions will lend to a Section 25 company is dependent on existing equity. Due to this leverage restriction, many Section 25 company's end up borrowing significantly less than the US$ 5 mn limit.

MFIs can also access priority sector lending funds. Banks are required to lend 32-40 percent of their net credit to priority sectors identified by RBI at a rate lower than the prime lending rate. Microfinance businesses qualify for priority sector lending, and can mobilise this capital much more freely than banks.

*Money Lending Act*: The Indian Moneylenders' Act, 1918 has been adapted by various state governments to restrict interest rates charged by moneylenders. Although the primary purpose of this Act is to protect vulnerable section from the usurious interest rates that moneylenders charge, some states have applied the Act to Societies and Trusts to restrict their lending activity. Other states have applied the Money Lending Act to other forms of MFIs. Gujarat, for example, applied the Money Lending Act to NBFCs in early 2011. Different states have made different provisions while adapting the Act, often restricting interest rates and requiring licences for conducting a moneylending business.

*State Level Regulation*: In late 2010, the Andhra Pradesh government enacted the Andhra Pradesh MFIs (Regulation of moneylending) Ordinance, which was later enacted into Act, to regulate the activities of MFIs. The Act stops MFIs from collecting old loans and originating new loans until the institution registers with the district authorities where they operate. The Act also mandates an interest rate cap such that the total interest charge cannot exceed the principal amount of the loan. The Act also entrusts a great deal of discretionary power to the registering authorities and imposes restrictions on collection practices.

In a perception survey carried out under this project, a semi-structured questionnaire-based survey of key stakeholders/ experts in the sector was conducted, selected from the industry, academics/consultants and policy practitioners, through in-person interviews/meetings and telephonic Consultations. The interviewees were asked to rank, among other things, the regulatory impediments to competition and growth in the sector. The majority of stakeholders (68%) were of the opinion that MFI sector in India needs to be regulated. To control the ongoing problem of over-borrowing and unsustainable debt of MFIs (as MFIs in India give multiple loans to borrowers), majority of the respondents (63.7%) in the perception survey suggested that the creditor should conduct an ability to pay before extending multiple loans.

### 3.3 Competition Analysis

This section provides a brief analysis of competition assessment of the current regulations. Ensuring fair competition in markets is very important for the sector's development of a country like India. Yet the government policies, rules and regulations often pose a threat to fair competition. Anti-competitive practices and policies prevailing in both public and private sectors must be addressed to ensure fair competition. The objective of 'competition assessment' is to examine the potential harm/benefit that might be caused to competition by the rules and regulations laid down by regulatory agencies.

### 3.4 Limitations of Current MFI Regulations

An important limitation of current regulations is the lack of clarity on Central and state regulatory jurisdiction. During late 2010 and early 2011, following the early 2010 eruption of the microfinance loans related deaths and the resultant furor, both Andhra Pradesh and Gujarat passed legislation barring specific microfinance practices within the state, requiring specific consumer protection policies and capping interest rates. States currently have great discretionary power as to how to interpret the Money Lending Act. Stability and confidence will elude the sector until this regulatory ambiguity is resolved. Lack of consumer protection regulation is another limitation of the current structure. There is no regulation that has resulted in a functioning redressal procedure for borrowers to provide feedback on improper collection practices and abusive lending techniques. More than 57 percent of stakeholders in the perception survey agreed that the sector/consumers suffer because of the coercive practices and high interest rates charged by the creditors. Furthermore, standard regulation that explicitly defines appropriate customer protection rights and penalties for violations does not exist.

A major problem in the industry today is over-indebtedness of the customer. A functioning credit information system would be the best way for MFIs to predict a customer's ability to pay. There are several initiatives to start credit bureaus, and some existing microfinance credit bureaus are rapidly expanding their information base, however no regulation requires or incentivises institutions to submit information to credit bureaus. Lack of diversification of funding is also problematic for MFIs due to current regulation on access to capital. Regulation allows NBFCs to raise capital from foreign equity investment, however the minimum investment is very high, and the minimum investment cannot account for more than 51 percent of the company. This requirement excludes a large number of foreign investors that may want to direct their funds to the sector. The restriction on ECB for NBFCs also greatly reduces funding options for MFIs.

Finally, the inability for MFIs to take deposits from the public is a missed opportunity for the sector. Accepting deposits is a service to both clients and institutions. Clients will have a more convenient way to accumulate funds, which will benefit them for emergency protection and saving purposes. Institutions accepting deposits will have a cheap source of funding, thus allowing for potentially lower costs for customers and extension of services to underserved areas. Regulation should allow for qualified institutions to accept public deposits while meeting strong prudential requirements.

## 4. Model Microfinance Regulations and Evaluation of the Microfinance Regulation Bill

The following are some of the pertinent and emerging areas and issues that are associated with the Model Microfinance Regulations (both Prudential & Non-Prudential) and Evaluation procedures and practices of the Microfinance Regulation Bill.

### *4.1 Regulatory Issues that Microfinance Sector Needs to Address*

Regulation of the financial sector is commonly divided into two categories: prudential and non-prudential. Regulation is prudential when it intends to protect the financial system from systemic risk, and to protect deposit safety. Prudential regulation by nature requires a regulator with sophisticated financial knowledge and experience, and one that is comfortable addressing issues such as capital adequacy, liquidity, reserves, and treatment of assets, in order to ensure the soundness of financial institutions. Non-prudential regulation addresses issues relating to the behaviour of financial institutions with respect to their conduct of business. These principles are equally applicable for the microfinance sector. For this analysis, selected prudential and non-prudential areas for regulation from a study conducted by the CGAP are relevant.

### 4.2 Prudential Regulations

*Minimum Capital*: There are often minimum capital requirements to attain normal bank licences to ensure that institutions have a base level of capital that will allow them to cover fixed costs. Investors and donors that support MFIs may not be able to contribute enough to attain a normal bank licence, thus these requirements may be adjusted to suit MFIs accordingly.

*Capital Adequacy*: Capital adequacy refers to the amount of capital that is held relative to the assets of the institution. The microfinance model differs greatly from traditional banking methods, so regulators must decide how much capital institutions should hold based on the unique challenges of the industry, such as high repayments but greater and unknown risks and shorter history of operation.

*Loan Documentation*: Requiring MFIs to follow the same loan documentation process as commercial banks would greatly burden institutions. Documentation requirements thus must strike a balance between useful and constraining, with regulation considering the lack of personal documents of borrowers, lack of financial statements for businesses, and structure of microfinance loans and repayments.

### 4.3 Non-Prudential Regulations

*Permission to Lend*: Sometimes lending is permitted because it is not explicitly outlawed. In such circumstances, an institution would have permission to originate and service microfinance loans. In other legal systems, a system cannot lend unless it is given permission to do so. Regulation directly or indirectly needs to address the institution's ability to lend.

*Consumer Protection*: The two primary consumer protection issues in microfinance that regulation should address are abusive lending and collection practices, and truth in lending. Abusive lending practice refers to abusive loan techniques, where the collector unfairly intimidates, harasses, threatens, or harms the customer. Abusive lending practice also applies to lenders which induce customer over-indebtedness, either intentionally or through lack of repayment assessment.

Truth in lending regulation relates to the transparency of products being provided by institutions. Often multiple fees and different interest rate computation methods make it difficult for consumers to understand the risks of products, and to compare a product to other products, or similar products provided by other institutions.

*Credit Reference Services*: Often called credit bureaus, credit reference services collect financial information on clients' status and history and supply this information to institutions to improve risk analysis and mitigation. Regulation may create a credit bureau, or require participation from MFIs and merchants. Customer privacy must be made a priority, and a customer's access to his own information should be permitted to ensure data accuracy.

*Interest Rate Limits*: MFIs charge much higher interest rates than commercial banks, citing higher administrative costs, higher service costs, and greater risk. However, regulators at times set interest rate limits for loans. These limits can differ based on institution specifics such as size of the institution, registration of the institution, demographic the institution serves, and institution cost of funding.

The existing regulatory structure that applies to MFIs in India currently does not adequately address all of these points.

### 4.4 Global Best Practices

The microfinance sector has unique challenges, which are distinct from the challenges of the traditional consumer and commercial financial sectors. Microfinance services are often provided to people who do not have any collateral security to offer, and who may lack identifying documentation and credit history. Transaction costs are also much higher than the traditional sector, since agents need to meet customers at all hours and at unorthodox locations as they extend financial services to areas that previously had none. A country which implements successful microfinance regulation does not simply enforce existing financial regulation, but designs regulations factoring these unique challenges.

Microfinance practices and challenges also vary between countries. There is no one set of regulation that can be considered as an all-encompassing answer to the needs of the sector. Every country may confront similar issues, however how these issues are dealt with will vary, based on the financial environment and priorities and goals of the sector. Many countries have a substantial number of people without access to formal financial services, though microfinance models vary greatly. Further, many countries have formal microfinance programmes, though some countries have primarily non-profit institutions, some have a sector dominated by for-profit institutions, and some have government-led initiatives. MFI models vary from country to country as well, even varying greatly within some countries. In the global best practice section, regulatory issues are examined that every country must address, and look to other examples around the world for successful regulatory implementation.

#### *4.4.1 Prudential Regulations*

Prudential regulation almost always only applies to MFIs that accept deposits, since MFIs are not large enough to pose systemic risk to the financial system of a country. Applying prudential regulation to institutions that do not take deposits results in unnecessary costs for both regulators and institutions.

*Minimum Capital Requirement*: Nearly all countries that enforce prudential regulations have a minimum capital requirement to ensure that institutions have capacity to cover the fixed costs associated with deposit taking, such as additional reporting and risk management required. Regulators also use the minimum capital requirement to roughly control the number of qualifying institutions. Bolivia used the minimum capital requirement for MFIs well in this regard, initially requiring a relatively small minimum capital amount, and then increasing this amount as MFIs grew in size and maturity. Currently, Bolivia's minimum capital requirement is US$ 6 mn, which is significantly higher than most countries with a less-developed microfinance sector. The minimum capital value is most often determined by a regulator, the central bank, or legislators, depending on the country's preferences. The entity which controls the minimum capital requirement must set and adjust the amount according to the number of qualifying institutions and to keep par with economic measures, such as inflation and foreign currency rates.

Minimum capital requirements can differ within a country as well, as in Pakistan and Indonesia. Pakistan requires minimum capital based on whether the institution operates within a district, within a province, or nationwide, with different requirements for different districts and provinces (Ahmed and Shah, 2007). Honduras bases minimum capital requirements on urban agglomeration. These approaches allow for more growth potential and privileges for MFIs that are serving underserved or rural areas.

*Capital Adequacy*: Capital adequacy requirements are used by nearly all countries to reduce the leverage and thus risk of MFIs that are subject to prudential regulation. The actual percentage of assets required varies amongst countries, though the requirement is almost always higher or equal to those of domestic commercial banks. Countries that have higher requirements often contend that microfinance banks have a shorter track record, and that microfinance portfolios are riskier than commercial bank portfolios. It may be noted that exact definitions of terms must be examined for each country for a full understanding of the implications of the requirements and their impact.

In all the countries except Ethiopia, MFIs must hold at least the recommended 8 percent capital. Uganda clearly has the tightest requirement with 15 percent for core capital (the Basel Committee recommends 4 percent for this) and 20 percent for total capital. An interesting case is Nepal, which uses both a leverage ratio and a capital adequacy ratio. The aggregate amount of all deposits and advances from members of cooperative societies has been limited to ten times the amount of core capital. Such a ratio does not rule out the possibility of increasing leverage by borrowing money, as it does not include debt. This ratio is a more crude measure than the capital adequacy ratio, as it does not use risk-weights to reflect the differences in risk associated with different kinds of assets. Indonesia's BPRs are subjected to a rather low CAR of 8 percent. To give BPRs an incentive to hold more capital, a current proposal is to reward a higher CAR of, say, 12 to 15 percent with a better overall soundness rating and permission to open new branches (Stachen, 1999, 2003a and b).

### *4.4.2 Non-Prudential Regulations*

*Permission to Lend*: Permission to lend is granted through registration in countries with more advanced regulatory frameworks. Many countries offer a special microfinance window for registration of MFIs, which allow regulation and legislation to be specific to these MFIs. Some countries offer multiple windows to allow for different types of institutions. Nepal has three windows which separate microfinance NGOs, cooperative societies, and development banks. Ghana's registration allows for nine different types of institutions, with several offering microfinance services. Each country will have a different approach, but best results have come when regulation is able to address the specific challenges associated with institutions offering microfinance services. For lending business, some countries stipulate a maximum loan size, expressed as a percentage rate of capital or as an absolute amount. The two extreme cases are Ethiopia and Indonesia. Ethiopia's MFIs are only allowed to lend up to a fixed amount of US$ 600 to a single borrower, while the same limit for Indonesia's BPRs is currently at 20 percent of total capital (which is likely to be reduced in the future).

In addition, BI is considering placing an aggregate limit (on total capital or on total loans outstanding) for the largest borrowers. In some countries, the limit depends on the kind of security available. Honduras' FPDOs may grant loans of up to 2 percent of equity capital if secured by a surety and up to 5 percent of capital if secured by other means. In Ghana, rural banks can lend up to a limit of 25 percent and 10 percent of capital in the case of secured and unsecured loans respectively.

In Uganda, the loan size limit depends on whether the loan is granted to an individual (1 per cent of core capital) or to a group of borrowers (5%). The rationale is that group loans are typically larger and that the regulatory framework should not favour one lending technology over the other. Nepal allows for larger consecutive loans with the second loan being double the amount of the first, and the third and all following loans being again double the size of the second. Even though such a requirement takes the graduation principle of many MFIs into account, it might be difficult to control for the supervisor. Finally, Pakistan limits the size of loans to a single borrower to a fixed amount of US$ 1,725 irrespective of the size of the microfinance institution/bank.

*Consumer Protection*: Successful consumer protection regulation levels the information gap between institutions and consumers. Regulation must protect consumers and allow for innovation, while not imposing excessive costs. Regulators in several countries provide consumers adequate information and allow for consumer complaints to be heard and addressed. Cambodia, Peru, Ghana, and many countries in Eastern Europe and the former Soviet Union have recently implemented new price disclosure rules that strive to ensure these objectives (Brix and McKee, 2010). Peru is an example of a country who has implemented a successful consumer protection policy. In Peru, the financial regulatory authority puts policies and procedures in place regarding how institutions receive, manage, and resolve consumer complaints. In 2008, approximately 99 percent of 400,000 consumer complaints were handled by this financial regulatory authority. Consumers may also take their complaints to the courts, the banking association's financial ombudsman, or a consumer protection agency. Peru combines these opportunities with adequate supervision and financial literacy campaigns and projects. Off-site supervision of institutions assures that relevant and adequate information is disclosed. As a result of these policies, consumer complaints dropped by 32 percent since 2004 (Alliance for Financial Inclusion, 2010).

Malaysia also focuses heavily on consumer education and response to consumer complaints. Financial information is disseminated to schools, community groups, and through various media sources to develop financial literacy. Financial institutions are required to have a complaints unit, with services targeting youth, involvement of the financial industry, credit counselling, and debt resolution. The central bank also receives complaints and offers advice (Conroy et al., 2009).

According to the CGAP Access to Finance Survey 2010 (CGAP, 2010), Regulators most frequently require countries to have plain-language, to provide documentation in the local language, describe recourse rights and processes. For deposit products, regulators can require that institutions provide annual percentage yield and interest rate, method of compounding, minimum balance requirements, fees and penalties, and early withdrawal penalties. For credit products, regulators can require that institutions provide an annual percentage rate using a standard formula, all applicable fees, computation methods, and required insurance.

*Credit Reference Service*: The great majority of countries believe that credit reference services would improve conditions for both customers and institutions. However, regulation will determine what is required for these bureaus. Some countries require financial institutions to submit customer information. Peru initially required submission of information on borrowers with loan amounts greater than US$ 5,000, which excluded micro-loans. However, regulation was later amended so that customer information is required to be submitted for all loans. Thus, institutions can check for credit history when extending a micro-loan.

*Interest Rate Caps*: Interest rate caps, though intended to protect the poor, often results in a reduction of financial services to the poorest of the poor and to those in rural areas. The costs of making very small loans and servicing rural areas is greater than making larger loans and servicing more urban areas, thus when an interest rate cap is implemented, MFIs in many countries have reduced these services to maintain profitability. Interest rate caps can also result in less product transparency, since institutions may try to add charges or penalties that make it more difficult to understand product risk (Helms and Reille, 2004).

When an interest rate cap of 27 percent was implemented in South Africa, institutions immediately withdrew from rural areas and focused on less expensive areas to serve. Nicaragua's MFIs' portfolio annual growth fell to 2 percent from 30 percent when an interest rate cap was introduced in 2001 (CGAP, 2004, 2010). An UK's Department of Trade and Industry policy paper (UK's Department of Trade and Industry, Policies, 2004) shows that even in a developed country like the US, interest rate caps restrict the diversity of products offered and the ability of lenders to offer products to different segments.

## 5. Regulatory Approaches and Initiative in MFI Sector—International Experiences

Although the regulation of MFI Sector has been of recent origin, the regulation per se of banking sector is established, well documented and evaluated over the years. The following are accepted as attended advantages and benefits of regulation and supervision of banks/MFIs:

(i) Protects the interest of the depositors;

(ii) Put in place prudential norms, standards and practices;

(iii) Provides sufficient information about the true risks faced by the banks/MFIs;

(iv) Promoters systemic stability and thereby sustains public confidence in the banks/MFIs;

(v) Prevents a bank's/MFI's failure/potential dangers through timely interventions;

(vi) Penalises the violations, misconducts, non-compliance to the norms of behaviour;

(vii) Provides invaluable advisory inputs for problem-solving and overall improvement of the banks/MFIs;

(viii) Promoters safe, strong and sound banking/MF system and effective banking/MF policy; and

(ix) Promotes and enhances orderly economic growth and development.

### *5.1 Genesis, Trends and Practices of Regulation—International Perspectives*

During the 1990's, many countries started to supervise and regulate the nascent microfinance sector. The earliest initiatives to bring microfinance under formal regulation and supervision were undertaken in Latin America. Around the world, microfinance has been on the agenda of policy-makers, regulators and supervisors. Over 50 countries have implemented or are considering specific arrangements for regulation and supervision of microfinance either as a separate new law or as amendments to the existing legal and regulatory framework. In certain countries, Central Bank has assumed the supervisory and regulatory role, while in others separate authority (existing authorities or newly created authority/networks) has been empowered and delegated powers of regulation/supervision. In some countries Self-Regulatory Organization (SRO) has been tried, particularly for non-prudential regulation. The principles define regulation as set of statutory rules that apply to MFIs while supervision is the process of implementing and enforcing compliance with these rules. A clear distinction between prudential and non-prudential regulation is also established.

Prudential regulation mandates capital adequacy requirements, loan loss provisioning, financial solvency, etc., for protecting the depositors. Non-prudential regulation covers enabling aspects like business operation, performance monitoring, credit information services, transparent reporting and disclosure, codes of fair practices and system, consumer protection, fraud prevention, etc. There have been differences in the extent and application of regulations—some have extended prudential to only deposit-taking MFIs. In recognition of uniqueness of MFIs and small, mostly uncollateralized loans, lower minimum capital, higher capital adequacy, lower unsecured lending limits, more aggressive loan loss provision, simpler loan documentation, lower physical security and branching needs, lower frequency and content of reporting, lower reserve against deposits, ownership suitability and diversification requirements are suggested. Most of the countries use a combination of quantitative and qualitative indicators to assess soundness of

MFIs. The regulatory rating indicator of ACCION CAMEL has been suitably adapted to MFIs. The rating agencies like planet rating, M-CRIL, Micro-Finance, Moody's, Standard and Poor, etc., have also developed suitable rating norms and could be useful tools for regulators/supervisors. There have been also attempts to evolve social performance rating standards by integrating economic and social rating, by the Social Performance Task Force (SPTF), CERISE, CGAP—Grameen Ford, FINCA's FACT Tools, Planet, M-CRIL, etc. Although, guiding principles on Regulation and Supervision of Microfinance issued in 2003 by Consultative Group to Assist the Poor (CGAP, 2004) indicates certain consensus, there has been divergence in trends and practices across the world.

The following are certain broad experiences and lessons internationally, in microfinance regulation:

(i) Microfinance has been conceived with a wider spectrum and perspectives.

(ii) Microfinance has been driver to building inclusive sector.

(iii) Regulatory framework is tailored to the national circumstances.

(iv) Regulation is directed towards activities rather than institutions.

(v) Regulation should be proportionate to the expected benefits.

(vi) Elements for an enabling framework are to encourage microfinance activities and increase the level of access to finance.

(vii) The regulation is to encourage linkage and partnership between banks, Microfinance Organizations (MFOs) and other retail outlets.

(viii) Regulation is to ensure consumer protection-prohibition of deceptive and unfair practices in lending and collection, to ensure disclosure of full costs, fees and terms of products and services, supply clients with accurate, full, accessible, comparable and transparent information.

(ix) Microfinance regulatory framework should find ways to pressure the social objectives of microfinance transactions.

(x) Regulation is to set performance standards portfolio management, MIS, internal control system and governance.

(xi) Regulation ensures registration, reserves, compliance with prudential norms, directions in reporting needs.

(xii) We need not regulate those which we cannot supervise.

The international experience of microfinance regulation clearly indicates that in several countries in Asia and Africa that microfinance could be central to achieving overall social objectives and that a conducive environment including a relevant legal framework needs to be provided for the sector to grow in orderly and systematic manner.

### *5.2 New Direction for providing Microfinance Services: International Best Practices*

The late 1970s witnessed a growth in financial services targeted to the poor, through initiatives spearheaded by NGOs such as Grameen Bank in Bangladesh and the affiliates of ACCIÓN International in Latin America. These initiatives were followed in the 1980s by major efforts of ACCIÓN and other NGO networks such as Women's World Banking. In addition, the Foundation for International Community Assistance (FINCA), the Bangladesh Rural Advancement Committee (BRAC) and the Bank Rakyat Indonesia (BRI) Unit Desas (village banks) were reporting success in reaching the poor with financial services. During this period of growth in the number and range of MFIs, various myths about providing the poor with financial services were dispelled—including that the poor cannot save and cannot afford non-subsidized interest rates. In the 1990s, best practices in microfinance as outlined below made important strides in such areas as key indicators for measuring an institution's success, particularly outreach and financial sustainability (refer to Box 1).

**Box 1**

**Lessons Learned from the Global Experience on Microfinance**

- The financial systems approach is important for sustainable microfinance with outreach. The approach emphasizes an enabling environment for policy and regulation and supportive financial infrastructure. The approach also depent on developing a range of financial intermediaries committed to achieving financial sustainability within a reasonable time, and to providing a variety of financial services other than credit.
- The diversity of demand for microfinance services requires a broad range of strong financial intermediation institutions which can expand outreach to household in different layers of poverty and in resource-poor urban and rural areas.
- The primary concern of microfinance clients is access to microfinance services compatible with their requirements, rather than the cost of such services. Demand for savings services by poor households may be as strong as demand for credit facilities. Thus, expanding the access to savings services can have a significant impact on an institution's sustainability.
- Financially viable microfinance institutions limit their operational focus to providing only financial services. It is important to distinguish between and to separate financial intermediation (through microfinance) *vis-à-vis* social intermediation (through social safety nets) in the design of support programmes.

The global experience demonstrates that MFIs change and develop as the scale and scope of their operations grow beyond delivery of credit services to include savings, deposit and other financial services. In addition, that growth prompts innovative approaches to achieving and maintaining financial sustainability. Expanding outreach requires increasing funding resources and exposes the limits to grants and donor funds. Commercial funding sources can usually be accessed when the policy and legal environment are appropriate, and only if the MFI has the appropriate legal status and financial standing.

In Bolivia, the microfinance NGO Fundación para la Promoción y Desarollo de la Microempresa (PRODEM) sought to scale up and transform into a licensed commercial bank in order to fund microfinance operations from retail and wholesale deposits. Through BancoSol PRODEM was able to quickly expand its client base from 14,300 active/repeat borrowers in four PRODEM branches/offices in 1991 to more than 80,000 active loan accounts and 50,000 savings deposit accounts in more than 3 dozen branches/offices of BancoSol by 1998. BancoSol [Banco Solidario, S.A. (Bolivia)] has captured about 20 percent of Bolivia's potential market for microfinance. The PRODEM/Bancosol experience induced several developments that have been beneficial for Bolivia's poor households and its microfinance industry.

- First, the Bolivian bank regulatory authority recognized the importance of the regulatory environment on microfinance development and made room for new category of regulated MFIs—the Private Finance Fund.
- Second, BancoSol's success in the banking industry induced other commercial banks to adjust their market positioning and product offerings in order to compete with BancoSol.
- Finally, the successful experience encouraged other Bolivian NGO-MFIs such as AgroCapital and ProMujer to develop their own institutional transformation to regulated institutions.

The successful transformation achieved by PRODEM/ BancoSol served to encourage other NGO-MFIs around the world like K-REP (Kenya), ADEMI and ADOPEM (Dominican Republic) to design their own transformation to gain the capability to fund expansion by mobilizing deposits and accessing the capital markets. Transformation has enabled a Philippine NGO, the Center for Agriculture and Rural Development (CARD), to move its client base of 23,000 women in rural villages into its CARD Rural Bank subsidiary which has expanded outreach on a sustainable basis to almost 40,000 repeat borrowers and savers in less than four years.

The Bangladesh MFI Grameen Bank has a very extensive outreach. Equally well known is the unit desa network of BRI. While BRI is a state-owned commercial bank, the unit desa microfinance operation has had the management and operating autonomy typically found only in private sector owned banks—there are no subsidies from the central government, and no cross-subsidies from BRI's other commercial banking operations. The unit desa microfinance system has more than 2 million active loan accounts and more than 12 million depositors. In many respects, Egypt has a similar approach and experience with the microfinance programme of its National Development Bank. In both the cases of Indonesia and Egypt, it is important to note that (i) the microfinance programmes in the state-owned institutions were given management and operating autonomy more commonly associated with private sector-owned institutions; and (ii) the government institutions and the policy that informed the microfinance operations eschewed subsidy mechanisms. A principal lesson from the experience of successful MFIs in other countries is the importance of sequencing. In this context, the priority area to address is the policy environment, legal system and regulatory framework for microfinance. When the vision and strategy for microfinance are well defined and articulated, the capacity development needs of different microfinance players are more easily identified and an action programme for building up the institutional capacity crafted. These prior steps facilitate the entry of donors who can focus their technical assistance programmes to the identified needs of players with the potential for outreach and financial sustainability.

## 6. Impact of Legal and Regulatory Framework on Sustainable Microfinance

The insufficient provision of financial services to micro- and small enterprises has been identified as a common problem in many parts of the world, including countries whose financial systems are well developed. Traditionally, micro-enterprises have relied on informal mechanisms, such as moneylenders and rotating savings and cooperative associations (ROSCAs) in order to finance their operations. Due to high administrative cost, inadequate collateral, and lack of trained personnel, banks mostly decline to serve this sector. Over the last ten years however a large number of microfinance institutions (MFIs) emerged in order to deliver financial services to this sector (Campion and White, 1999). As microfinance has become increasingly popular among many developing counties, the international financial community has had an increased interest in the regulation and supervision of microfinance institutions (MFIs). Today, thousands of MFIs operate in countries around the world; however, the majority of these institutions are still not subject to government regulation (Staschen, 1999). The theoretical discussion of the role and effects of the regulation of MFIs is at an early stage and there is limited empirical work on the subject. Furthermore, the theoretical and empirical literature does not address the question, whether the regulated MFIs will still be able to serve the same client base, or will they be forced to behave like banks, i.e. lend to larger size enterprises by increasing the size of the loans that go beyond the absorptive capacity of micro-enterprises.

Improving the access of low-income producers and the poor to basic financial services is viewed as an ingredient of the World Bank's efforts to promote economic growth and reduce poverty. The World Bank's approach emphasizes a market-driven approach in which the financial sustainability of financial intermediaries becomes paramount. In many cases that market approach is possible because of the use by MFIs of group lending and other techniques to offset borrowers' lack of collateral. The World Bank's overall strategy for helping countries develop micro, rural and small and medium enterprise (SME) finance includes a number of key measures in the overall legal and regulatory framework, in building up institutional capacity and in the introduction of financial systems infrastructure (Refer Box 2).

**Box 2**

**The World Bank's Financial Sector Priorities for Developing Microfinance**

- Removing legal provisions (e.g., interest ceilings) or adapting regulatory provisions (e.g. banking regulations) inconsistent with financially sustainable rural and microfinance.
- Establishing registration and titling systmes and foreclosure laws to allow the use of assets (lands, crops, cattle, small equipment) owned by rural and poor urban households as loan collateral.
- Continuing the development of specialized nonbank financial intermediaries (e.g., microfinance institutions, leasing companies, private equity funds) for SME finance.
- Harnessing modern technologies (electronic banking, credit and payment cards) and/or non-financial institutions (postal service) to provide basic, innovative payment and financial services for rural areas, micro-enterprises and SMEs.

*Source*: "Strategy for the Financial Sector", Financial Sector Board, The World Bank, Washington, DC, February 2000.

The regulation and supervision of MFIs should be an integral part of a strategy to develop a market based financial system. Microfinance is not limited to borrowing, but also includes other financial services such as savings, insurance, transfer facilities, etc. Savings facilities are a particularly important question when considering prudential regulation of MFIs because the prospective microfinance target group is usually many times larger in deposit business than in lending.

A clear and transparent regulatory framework is necessary because MFIs' traditional fund sources usually cannot keep pace with their lending business, and thus need to have access to external finance to complement their own resources and those from donors in order to reach as many prospective borrowers as possible. Possible sources of funds are loans from other financial institutions, private savings or—in an advanced microfinance sector—securities issues on the formal capital market. MFIs could thereby advance from credit-only institutions to fully-fledged financial intermediaries. Heretofore, mobilization of savings from the general public has almost always been contingent on MFIs complying with existing banking law. Access to the capital market, in turn, is contingent on MFIs complying with securities regulations (Stefan Staschen, 1999).

### *6.1 The Rationale for Regulation and Supervision of MFIs*

A primary reason for regulating and supervising traditional financial institutions is consumer protection for public depositors in financial institutions. Moral hazard issues arise because the interests of financial institutions *vis-à-vis* the interests of consumers per se are not necessarily compatible. Individual depositors and investors may not be in a position to judge the soundness of a financial institution (the issue of asymmetric information), much less to influence that institution's management. Thus, an impartial third party which such as the state or one of its agencies is required to regulate and control the soundness of a country's financial institutions. Since bank failures and problems tend to be contagious and affect other banks regardless of their soundness, the protection of the whole banking and payment system becomes an additional objective of regulation and supervision.

A country's legal framework and governing principles of financial intermediation define the roles of its banking and financial sector regulatory authorities (such as the central bank, ministry of finance, or bank superintendence), setting out rules for entry and exit of financial institutions, determining and limiting their businesses and products, and specifying criteria and standards for the sound and sustainable operation of the industry. Regulation (which usually refers to non-prudential regulation but may include prudential supervision in its broad general meaning) is not limited to rules set by the state alone. Regulation may include forms of auxiliary regulation and self-regulation by governing boards of financial institutions, their networks and associations, or apex organizations. Prudential supervision encompasses all measures by which regulators enforce compliance by licensed financial institutions with a given legal and regulatory framework, because licensing implies that the financial authority is vouching for or is prepared to assume responsibility for the soundness of the regulated financial institution which the public may be dealing with.

As Chavez and Gonzalez-Vega (1992) defines it, .regulation refers to a set of enforceable rules that restrict or direct market participants, altering as a result the outcomes of those actions.. Whereas, supervision refers to the systematic oversight of financial services providers to make sure that they comply with the rules, risk is minimized, and weak institutions are either improved or closed down.

The need for regulation is often motivated by the different objectives of those involved. Some MFIs need more funds to lend out through their micro-credit operations. They would want to be regulated in order to be allowed to offer bank accounts to hold their savings. Some other NGOs believe that regulation will promote their business and improve their operations. Others want to be licensed in order to expand the range of services they can provide to the poor.

The international donors that have helped to create some of the MFIs may have the expectation that government regulation will lead the way to sustainability for microfinance institutions through the mobilization of client savings that can be used to increase the volume of loans made by MFIs. In order to reach as many prospective borrowers as possible MFIs need to have access to an external source of finance in addition to the reinvested surplus of the MFIs and the financing obtained from donors. However, it is generally accepted that financial institutions that collect public deposits should be subject to prudential regulation and supervision for two main reasons: (i) to protect depositors, particularly small depositors, from loss of their savings if the financial institution becomes insolvent, and (ii) to ensure the financial system as a whole does not become unstable through a loss of confidence as a result of major financial institutions becoming insolvent (Christen and Rosenberg, 2002).

It is well known that taking deposits is a serious responsibility and requires strong and capable institutions. When institutions providing microfinance services fail to demonstrate full financial self-sufficiency (i.e. they are losing money), it would be irresponsible to license them to take deposits. When MFIs become regulated, savers view this to be a signal that the government is taking some implicit and perhaps explicit responsibility for the safety of their deposits. Hence they are more willing to put their money in these financial institutions, even if these financial institutions are fundamentally not very healthy. There is an asymmetry of information between what that saver believes to be the situation and the actual financial health of the MFI. Churchill (1997) states that once MFIs are regulated entities, depositors may not adequately evaluate their risk. Therefore it is argued that only the large MFIs which achieve a significant scale and degree of sustainability should be regulated.

Savings mobilization is a particularly difficult issue for central banks and other regulators to deal within the context of MFIs. On the one hand, low income individuals desperately need savings facilities that will provide them with a safe place to accumulate funds. Having a safe, liquid, stock of savings will enable poor people to undertake economic activities that will enable them to reduce their level of poverty. On the other hand, mobilizing savings places a big responsibility on an institution to ensure that the savings of their clients are not at risk. Savers neither have sufficient information nor do they have control over the operations of financial institutions. Therefore regulation needs to limit the danger of opportunistic behaviour by MFI that would lead to excessive risk taking. It should ensure that financial institutions have enough capital and earnings to cover the risks of intermediation and at the same time maintain enough liquidity to meet their clients.

Another reason for regulating and supervising microfinance institutions is to protect the safety and soundness of the financial system which is a logical follow up of the first argument. There is always the danger of a 'bank run' panic leading to the withdrawal of all deposits, forcing the institution into an inevitable bankruptcy. However, because of their very small size MFIs are not likely to threaten the stability of the financial systems in which they operate. This suggests that MFIs do not need be subject to prudential regulation and supervision unless they accept savings.

### 6.2 Global Experience in Regulating Microfinance

Banking laws in many countries compartmentalize and segment markets and institutions, constraining innovations and making MFIs' institutional development difficult. While the global experience demonstrates the potential for operational growth of MFIs, the range of institutional channels is segmented by the legal and regulatory environment. The framework for banking laws should be structured to provide MFIs a clear view of the thresholds to attain on the path to institutional development and transformation—even if not all MFIs choose to follow that path.

The vast majority of NGO-MFIs will remain as retail delivery channels for microfinance programmes and a few may reach sustainability without ultimately transforming into a licensed bank. Some MFIs may be better off remaining as low-leverage, slow-growth but effective service institutions linked to larger institutions in meeting the needs of their existing clients (Cuevas, 1996). Cuevas points out that entry into the regulated financial sector (through institutional transformation) depends on the nature and extent of existing incentives and deterrents in the MFI environment and on the MFI's perceived potential and actual ability to reach the market "niche" by becoming regulated.

Any decision to transform, evolves, or maintains a status quo is dependent on an MFI's strategic plans for its future. However, the experience of microfinance practitioners in many different settings throughout the developing world underscores the proposition that the future for sustainable microfinance lies in a regulated, licensed environment—because there is no other environment that will permit massive, sustainable delivery of an increasing variety of financial services to the poor to effectively link them to the more developed sectors of an economy (Christen and Rosenberg, 2000). Table 3 below on the operational characteristics of sustainable MFIs serves to illustrate this point further.

**Table 3:** Selected Characteristics of 64 Financially Self-sufficient MFIs (In %)

| Organizational formats | Capital/ assets | Operating self-sufficiency | Dollar average loan | Depth* | External funds/ loans F |
|---|---|---|---|---|---|
| Bank | 21.0 | 118.6 | 527 | 62.5 | 166.6 |
| Non-bank | 27.4 | 110.4 | 958 | 62.4 | 70.3 |
| Credit union | 42.1 | 122.5 | 1,306 | 91.6 | 88.6 |
| NGO | 58.5 | 130.8 | 490 | 38.8 | 26.6 |

* Depth = Average loan balance per borrower/GNP per capita.

F External funds/loans = Borrowed funds @ commercial rates/ average loan portfolio.

*Source*: *The Micro-Banking Bulletin, Issue No. 6 (April 2001), Tables C and D.*

MFIs have large numbers of clients but low overall account balances compared with traditional financial institutions. While MFIs' share in total assets of the financial system is relatively small, direct measurements of MFIs' relative position in the overall financial system do not take into account the sector's volume of deposits in total banking system deposits, since MFIs maintain their operating accounts and clients' deposits in the banks. Their outreach, measured by the percentage of the population doing business with MFIs, can be quite large. As the clients belong to poor segments of the population a bankruptcy of either the MFI or its depository bank would have adverse consequences. The argument that regulation and supervision in microfinance are less important because of its small place in the financial system misjudges the exceptional receptiveness of this segment and its possible contribution to financial systems development.

The existing legal and regulatory frameworks in many of the World Bank's client countries have been unable to support the sustainable growth and commercial integration of microfinance programmes into the formal financial system. In addressing this problem, a number of governments have begun to address the issue of a transparent and inclusive regulatory framework under which micro-credit can be legitimately provided by MFIs, and so that a continuum of MFIs can be developed and strengthened. These governments have realized the advantages and benefits of a "tiered" banking and financial system (including its regulation and supervision), which facilitates the establishment of smaller, specialized MFIs.

The countries which have moved towards a tiered financial and regulatory structure include Bolivia and Peru in Latin America; and Uganda, Ghana and Zambia in Africa. A number of countries in Eastern Europe—e.g. Albania, Bosnia and Georgia—are restructuring their banking laws and prudential regulations to establish a tiered approach to accommodate specialized financial institutions with capitalization requirements much lower than those for regular commercial banks. In Southeast Asia, the Philippines and Indonesia have had tiered banking structures, although the existing regulatory framework still does not make it possible for a range of MFIs to be integrated into the regulated financial sector. India also has in place basic statutes that would permit the establishment of smaller regulated financial institutions with a regional focus. However, it is important to consider the benefits versus the costs associated with establishing and implementing a regulatory framework for microfinance. Regulation and supervision entail costs, not only for the regulator but also for the regulated institution. For instance, BancoSol's management estimates that complying with the bank superintendence's reporting requirements during its first year of operations generated a cost equivalent to 5 percent of the loan portfolio, even though this had declined to about 1 percent of loan portfolio as of last year FENACREP are enough to inspect only 40 of its 130 member credit unions each year (Glenn Westley, 2001).

Thus, the price of regulation has to be carefully adjusted to the benefits it is expected to produce. Over-regulation may result in financial repression, limiting the efficiency of financial intermediation and increasing costs for consumers. The growing research and literature on microfinance regulation highlight the importance of a clear regulatory framework to support sustainable microfinance, and call attention to some important considerations especially of timing and phasing. First, not all MFIs need to be regulated and supervised, as can be seen in the tiered structure for MFIs and for regulation, based on their intermediation activities. Second, there needs to be a critical mass of institutions suitable for prudential regulation/supervision, to justify the commitment of public resources to the undertaking. Third, the approach to regulation differs from country to country, and there is no single universal regulatory model that should be adopted because of different macroeconomic environments and stages of microfinance development.

### *6.3 Financial Intermediation Activities as the Basis for Regulation*

Differences in the organizational and operating characteristics of the various types of MFIs leave them vulnerable to certain risks. The risk-based approach to financial regulation shows that while there may be no major variances in the structure of their assets, MFIs are differentiated by the structure of their liabilities—i.e. how their assets and operations are funded and the adequacy of capital in leveraging additional resources to fund operations. Linking the wholesale funding, limited deposit-taking and unrestricted deposit-taking activities to an institution's qualifying capital base results in *limits* to the asset build-up that MFIs can prudently undertake, without having to instruct them on how to carry out their businesses. The authorization to mobilize funds from the public in turn carries related requirements to comply with prudential standards and guidelines on certain asset side activities, e.g. limits on concentration in loan exposure to sectors, restrictions on insider and related-party loans, provisions for possible loan losses, etc.

Regulation based on typology of financial institutions rather than on intermediation activities creates incentives for *regulatory arbitrage*. Organizers of financial institutions seek out licensing categories which requiring the least initial capital commitment and the lowest degree of mandatory regulation. All participants in the financial system including microfinance stakeholders benefit from a transparent regulatory framework which establishes the continuum where MFIs can progressively evolve into formal financial institutions. The regulatory framework model identifies thresholds of financial intermediation activities which would trigger a requirement to satisfy external or mandatory regulatory guidelines (Greuning, et al., 1999). As financial institutions, it would be prudent for all of the different types of MFIs to observe internal or voluntary guidelines for risk management.

Table 4 illustrates the key features of the regulatory framework model, identifying the fund generating activities that trigger a need for mandatory external guidelines and summarizing the proposed regulatory measures and agencies to carry them out.

**Table 4:** Regulatory Thresholds for Activities of Microfinance Institutions

| Type of institution | Owership | Main source of funds for operations and loans | Activities that trigger regulation | Form of external regulation | Regulatory authority |
|---|---|---|---|---|---|
| Informal Community-based Thrif and Credit Self-Help Group-funding from community members and loans from NGOs and MFIs | Community and village residents | – Fees and assessments on members<br>– Members' saving deposited with SHG | None | None | None |
| Category A: Other People's Money (NGO)—Funding from donor funds | Local and foreign donors through a Trust | Grants and donated funds | None—provided micro-finance loans do not exceed donated funds | Registration as Non-Profit Society or Trust | Registrar of Societies and/or Trust |
| Category A: Other People's Money (Microfinance NGO)—Added funding via commercial loans/ securities issues | Grants and donations converted to share capital | – Grants and donated funds<br>– Concessional and commercial borrowings (wholesale deposit instruments) | – Generating liabilities from commercial<br>– Concessional sources to fund operations and loan | – Registration as limited liability company<br>– Rating by Credit Rating Agency<br>– Licensing by bank authority as non-bank finance company | – Registrar of companies<br>– Central bank authority or superintendency<br>– Securities regulatory agency |

*Contd...*

| Type of institution | Owership | Main source of funds for operations and loans | Activities that trigger regulation | Form of external regulation | Regulatory authority |
|---|---|---|---|---|---|
| Category B: Members' Money-funding from members' contributions | Members joined by recognized closed common bond | Share capital contributed and savings deposited by members | Accepting deposists from members, and making loans to members | Registration as a financial cooperative<br>[Large institutions may fall under jurisdiction of Banking law] | – Registrar of Cooperatives, or of Societies<br>or<br>– Central bank authority/ superintendency for larger cooperative institutions |
| Category C: The Public's Money-funding from retail public deposits | Individual and institutional investors, and shareholders | – Contributed share capital<br>– Commercial borrowings<br>– Wholesales deposits<br>– Retail public deposits | – Accepting wholesale<br>– Retail public deposits for intermediation into loans and investments | – Registration as limited-liability company<br>– Licensing by banking authority as NBFI, or limited-service or full-service bank | – Registrar of companies<br>– Central bank authority, or superintendency |

*Source*: Adapted from Chart 1 and Table 2, H. van Greuning, J. Gallardo, and B. Randhawa (1999), A Framework for Regulating Microfinance Institutions, World Bank Policy Research Working Paper No. 2061, Washington, DC, February, 1999.

### 6.4 Regulation and Supervision of MFIs to match International Standard

Regulation and supervision of the formal banking institutions is well organized under various Acts, viz. B.R Act, RRBs Act, Cooperative Societies Acts, and RBI Act. While the RBI supervises commercial and urban cooperative banks and NBFCs, NABARD has been authorised to supervise RRBs and cooperative banks on behalf of RBI. As regards MFIs, none except those registered as NBFCs and cooperatives are presently treated as part of the financial sector. As most of them are registered as societies or trusts, the question of their supervision and regulation from the financial angle had not arisen. Except submission of annual accounts and a report on their operations to the authorities under the Acts of their registration, these agencies are not under any statutory compulsion to comply with specified norms or instructions in respect of their microfinance activities encompassing mobilization of savings and granting of loans.

The Task force on MFIs in India (NABARD, 1999) noted that the Societies Registration Act was essentially enacted to formalize voluntary associations of like-minded people for promotion of literature, science, fine arts or for the diffusion of useful knowledge, political education or for charitable purposes. With the passage of time, the field of social and developmental interventions has widened, and a large number of such institutions with a wide range of objectives directed towards social and economic upliftment of the people in the lower strata of the community have started functioning. Some of these organizations, as part of their overall objectives, have started providing certain types of financial services in a limited way.

Sa-Dhan (2002b)—a voluntary association of community development finance institutions (CDFIs) started its operation during July, 1999 provides a platform to disseminate and publish sound financial practices to strengthen the capacities of CDFIs and also to negotiate with different government forums to influence the policies related to microfinance development in India. They first published the core values for microfinance, voluntary mutual code of conduct for microfinance institutions to abide by these values and process of compliance for all member microfinance institutions in order to establish a common minimum regulation and supervision standard. In order to facilitate the transparency and public reporting, Sa-Dhan's work with the Institute of Chartered Accountants of India (ICAI) has yielded the accounting standards for Microfinance Institutions, which was published during 2008.

## REFERENCES

Armendariz de Aghion, Beatriz and Jonathan Morduch (2005), *The Economics of Microfinance*, Cambridge, Ma: MIT Press.

APMAS (2003), National Workshop on SHG Federations: A Report, June 20-21, at Hotel Taj Residency, Hyderabad.

Basu, Priya and Srivastava, Pradeep (2006), Scaling-up Microfinance for India's Rural Poor, World Bank Policy Research Working Paper 3646, June 2005; Accessed Jan. 2006, Available from: http://www.worldbank.org

Bhattacharjee, B.R. and Staschen, Steven (2004), Emerging Scenarios for Microfinance Regulation in India: Some Observations from the Field, (Eschborn: GTZ, 2004). Accessed 03/30/2006. Available from: http://www.gtz.de. p. 7.

Brix, L. and McKee, K. (2010), Consumer Protection Regulation in Low-Access Environments: Opportunities to Promote Responsible Finance, CGAP Focus Note 60. Washington, DC: CGAP, February 2010.

Campion, Anita and Victoria White (1999), Transformation of Microfinance NGOs into Regulated Financial Institutions. The Microfinance Network occasional Paper No. 4.

Chaves, Rodrigo A. and Claudio Gonzales-Vega (1992), Principles of Regulation and Prudential Supervision: Should They Be Different for Microenterprise Finance Organizations? Economics and Sociology Occasional Paper No. 1979, Columbus, Ohio: Ohio State University.

CGAP (2004), *The Impact of Interest Rate Ceilings on Microfinance*, May 2004.

CGAP (2009), Overview of Microfinance-Related Legal and Policy Reform in Sub-Saharan Africa.

CGAP (2010), CGAP Access to Finance Survey, 'Financial Access 2010: The State of Financial Inclusion through the Crisis', Washington, DC: CGAP and the World Bank Group.

Christen, Robert Peck and Richard Rosenberg (2000), The Rush to Regulate: Legal Frameworks for Microfinance, Occasional Paper 4. Washington, DC: CGAP.

Christen, Robert P. and Richard Rosenberg (2002). The Rush to regulate: Legal Frameworks for Microfinance. CGAP Occasional Paper No. 4, April 2002.

Christen, Robert Peck, Timothy R. Lyman, and Richard Rosenberg (2003), Microfinance Consensus Guidelines: Guiding Principles on Regulation and Supervision of Microfinance. Washington, DC: CGAP.

Churchill, Craig (1997), Regulation and Supervision of Microfinance Institutions: Case Studies, Occasional Paper No. 2, The Microfinance Network.

Conroy, J., J. Parrenas and W. Manupipatpong (2009), Promoting Financial Inclusion through Innovative Policies, Asian Development Bank Institute, April, 2009.

Cuevas, Carlos E. (1996), Enabling Environment and Microfinance Institutions: Lessons from Latin America, *Journal of International Development*, 8, March-April 1996.

Glenn, D. Westley (2001), Can Financial Market Policies Reduce Income Inequality? Technical Papers Series, MSM-112, Washington, DC: Inter-American Development Bank, October 2001.

Greuning, H. van, J. Gallardo and B. Randhawa (1999), A Framework for Regulating Microfinance Institutions, World Bank Policy Research Working Paper No. 2061, February 1999, Washington, DC.

Harper, Malcolm (2002), Promotion of Self-Help Groups under the SHG Bank Linkage Programme in India. Paper read at Seminar on SHG-Bank Linkage Programme, November 25-26, at New Delhi.

Hartaska, Valentina and Denis Nadolyak (2007), Do regulated Microfinance Institutions Achieve Better Sustainability and Outreach?; Cross-Country Evidence, *Applied Economics* 39(10-12): 1207-22.

Helms, B. and X. Reille (2004), Interest Rate Ceilings and Microfinance: The Story So Far, CGAP Occasional Paper 9, September, 2004.

Manual on Financial and Banking Statistics, Chapter VI, Reserve Bank of India, http://rbidocs.rbi.org.in/rdocs/Publications/PDFs/78928.pdf

NABARD (1999), Task Force on Supportive Policy and Regulatory Framework for Microfinance: Report. Mumbai: NABARD.

NABARD (2003), Working Group on Guidelines for Financial SHG Federations/MACS/MFIs: Summary of Recommendations. Hyderabad: NABARD Regional Office, Hyderabad.

NABARD (2009-2010), Status of Microfinance in India (2009-2010), NABARD, www.nabard.org/pdf/Status%20of%20Micro%20Finance%202009-10%20Eng.pdf

Reddy, C.S., and L.B. Prakash (2003), Status of SHG Federations in Andhra Pradesh: Apmas Assessment Findings. Paper read at SHG Federation Workshop, at Hyderabad.

Sa-Dhan (2002a), Microfinance in India: Report for the Empowered Committee Headed by Shree S.K. Purkayastha, Addressing the Legal and Regulatory Challenge, New Delhi: Sa-Dhan.

Sa-Dhan (2002b), Report of National Workshop 'Strengthening Access to Financial Services for the Poor: Role of Community Based Organizations', December 3, at India Habitat Centre, New Delhi.

Sinha, Sanja, et al. (2003), The Outreach/Viability Conundrum: Can India's Regional Rural Banks Really Serve Low-Income Clients? Gurgaon, India: Micro-Credit Ratings International Ltd.

Sinha, Sanja and Prakash Bakshi (2004), *Crossfire Small Enterprise Development* 15 (2): 4-7.

Staschen, Stefan (1999), Regulation and Supervision of Microfinance Institutions in South Africa, Eschborn, Germany: Deutsche Gesellschaft für Technische Zusammenarbeit (GTZ).

Staschen, Stefan (2003a), Possible Mechanisms to Regulate Tier 4 MFIs in Uganda (with Contributions from Michael Akampurira), FSD Series No. 11. Kampala, Uganda: Financial Systems Development (FSD) Programme.

Staschen, Stefan (2003b), Regulatory Requirements for Microfinance: A Comparison of Legal Frameworks in 11 Countries Worldwide. Eschborn, Germany: Deutsche Gesellschaft für Technische Zusammenarbeit (GTZ).

UK's Department of Trade and Industry, Policies, London, 2004.

World Bank (2000), "Strategy for the Financial Sector", Financial Sector Board, The World Bank, Washington, DC, February 2000.

# 8
# Governance Aspects of Microfinance

Governance is about achieving corporate goals. For the MFI, multiple goals exist. The fundamental goal is to contribute to development. This involves reaching more clients and poorer population strata, the so-called main outreach 'frontier' of microfinance (Helms, 2006; Johnson et al., 2006). A second goal is to do this in a way that achieves financial sustainability, preferably independence from donors. While Rhyne (1998) considers these two main goal areas to be a 'win-win' situation, claiming that those MFI institutions that follow the principles of good banking will also be those that alleviate the most poverty, Woller et al. (1999) and Morduch (2000) think that the proposition is far more complicated. Governance of microfinance institutions has only recently surfaced as an essential component of long-term institutional success. Its importance is highlighted by the juncture at which we find microfinance—a field poised to become part of national financial systems with links to international financial markets. At no other time has the competence and commitment of governance bodies of microfinance institutions appeared more pressing. In the microfinance field, governance has assumed increasing importance for several reasons. First, as microfinance institutions (MFIs) grow in their outreach, the size of their assets, as reflected in their portfolio, also grows to considerable size. Ensuring effective management of this growth requires added input and involvement by a board. Additionally, increasing numbers of MFIs are becoming regulated and assuming the responsibilities and challenges of a regulated entity. Capturing deposits from savers and investors is perhaps their most important challenge and requires the greatest oversight. Finally, MFIs are operating in increasingly competitive markets, and maintaining or increasing market share has become an important component of their strategic objective.

Bearing in mind the strategic importance of rendering good governance to microfinance institutions, together with appropriate regulatory structure and operational framework put in place, this chapter attempts to discuss some of the important aspects of microfinance governance. This includes: the basic principles of good governance for Microfinance entities, ownership and the relevant governance issues of MFIs, impact of good governance on Microfinance performance, governance structure and organizational issues in Microfinance delivery systems, mechanisms of measuring governance quality in Microfinance with the help of some case studies.

## 1. Principles of Good Governance for Microfinance Entities

Governance has assumed increasing importance for several reasons. As microfinance institutions grow in their outreach, the size of their assets, as reflected in their portfolio, also grows to considerable size. Ensuring effective management of this growth requires added input and involvement from the board of directors. The increasing numbers of MFI's are becoming regulated and assuming the responsibilities and challenges of a regulated entity. Capturing deposits from savers and investors is an important challenge and requires the greatest oversight. MFI's are operating in increasingly competitive markets, and maintaining or increasing market share has become an important component of their strategic objectives.

Good governance leads to a number of positive consequences, including: Trust, Clear vision, mission, and direction, relevant values, connection to the stakeholders, Sustainable financial stability. The perception of Kofi Annan, Former Secretary General, and the United Nations about Good Governance may be illustrated as follows: "Good Governance is perhaps the single most important factor in eradicating poverty and promoting development."

Good Governance is about both achieving desired results and achieving them in the right way. Since the "right way" is largely shaped by the cultural norms and values of the institution, there can be no universal template for good governance. Each institution must tailor its own definition of good governance to suit its needs and values. There are, however, some universal norms and values that apply across cultural boundaries. The United Nations published a list of characteristics of good governance. Good Governance models include all of the principles. Defining the principles of good governance is difficult and controversial. The United Nations Development Programme enunciates a set of 5 principles that, with slight variations, appear in much of the literature (Table 1). There is strong evidence that these UNDP-based principles have a claim to universal recognition. In grouping them under five broad themes, we recognize that these principles often overlap or are conflicting at some point, which they play out in practice according to the actual social context, that applying such principles is complex, and that they are all about not only the results of power but how well it is exercised.

**Table 1:** United Nations Five Good Governance Principles

| Principles | |
|---|---|
| 1. Legitimacy and Voice | **Participation**—all men and women should have a voice in decision-making either directly or through legitimate intermediate institutions that represent their intention. Such broad participation is built on freedom of association and speech, as well as capacities to participate constructively.<br>**Consensus orientation**—good governance mediates differing interests to reach a broad consensus on what is in the best interest of the group and, where possible, on policies and procedures. |
| 2. Direction | **Strategic vision**—leaders and the public have a broad and long-term perspective on good governance and human development, along with a sense of what is needed for such development. There is also an understanding of the historical, cultural and social complexities in which that perspective is grounded. |

*Contd...*

| | |
|---|---|
| 3. Performance | **Responsiveness**—institutions and processes try to serve all stakeholders.<br>**Effectiveness and efficiency**—processes and institutions produce results that meet needs while making the best use of resources. |
| 4. Accountability | **Accountability**—decision-makers in government, the private sector and civil society organizations are accountable to the public, as well as to institutional stakeholders. This accountability differs depending on the organizations and whether the decision is internal or external.<br>**Transparency**—transparency is built on the free flow of information. Processes, institutions and information are directly accessible to those concerned with them, and enough information is provided to understand and monitor them. |
| 5. Fairness | **Equity**—all men and women have opportunities to improve or maintain their well-being.<br>**Rule of Law**—legal frameworks should be fair and enforced impartially, particularly the laws on human rights. |

*Source*: Institut Sur la Governance (2014), IOG Principles of Good Governance: http://iog.ca/about-us/iog-principles-of-good-governance/

Governance is a process by which a board of directors, through management, guides an institution in fulfilling its corporate mission and protects the institution's assets. Governance has become an important topic as evidence mounts on the critical role it plays in determining societal well-being. Not surprisingly, governance as a term has progressed from obscurity to widespread usage, particularly in the last decade.

### *1.1 Fundamentals of Good Microfinance Governance*

Fundamental to good governance is the ability of individual directors to work in partnership to balance strategic and operational responsibilities. Effective governance occurs when a board provides proper guidance to management regarding the strategic direction for the institution, and oversees management's efforts to move in this direction. The interplay between board and management centers on this relationship between strategy and operation, both of which are essential for the successful evolution of the institution. For example, in exercising their governance responsibilities, board members must consider the perspectives of numerous external actors. Depending on the legal status of the MFI, these actors can include providers of capital such as donors, governments, depositors or other financial institutions; regulatory bodies such as the superintendence of banks; and other stakeholders, including clients, employees, and shareholders.

In its governance role, the board also is accountable to all these stakeholders and must assess continually which of these are the most important for the institution. All board members must follow basic codes of conduct in carrying out their governance roles and responsibilities in good faith. Not all boards maintain the same level of involvement in the institution. At one end of the continuum of board involvement is a rubber-stamp board, which is generally reactive to management. At the other end is a hands-on board, which provides excessive oversight and engages directly in operations. In the middle are representational boards, made up of highly influential individuals who are not necessarily experts in microfinance. These boards resemble rubber-stamp boards except that board members' access to sources of power and funds is exercised to the benefit of the institution. Multi-type boards balance representational members with those that have microfinance expertise, and generally are better equipped to make informed decisions on a timely and efficient basis.

The relationship between the board and the executive requires clarity about the roles and responsibilities of each, and about the complementarity of these roles. The board should exercise this responsibility by (1) maintaining distance from daily operations; (2) drawing on the institutional memory of the directors; and (3) making binding decisions as a group. Application of these factors results in a process of decision-making that empowers the board and adds significant value to the management of the institution. Major board responsibilities can be grouped into the following four categories:

- The board has legal obligations that revolve around ensuring compliance with the institution's bylaws, procedures, and other legal requirements. The board may be held liable for the institution's activities.

- The board must ensure management accountability by hiring competent professionals, establishing clear goals for these executives and closely monitoring their performance, and confronting weaknesses when they surface.
- The board is responsible for setting policy and providing strategic direction to the MFI. The board must work closely with management in carrying out this role to ensure congruence between the institution's strategic thinking and its operations.
- The board must assess its own performance on a regular basis. It is the board's responsibility to maintain continuity or "institutional memory" in its ranks, to renew its membership with new directors, and to evaluate its own processes for decision-making. Diligence in fulfilling these roles and responsibilities does not in itself ensure effective governance. Other essential factors are the commitment of the directors to the institutional mission; directors' skills and expertise; attributes of the chairperson; the presence, structure, and function of committees; clearly defined board policies and procedures; and a climate that allows for critical self-evaluation.

As the field of microfinance continues to grow and develop, the issue of governance is receiving increased attention, and the role of effective governance is assuming even greater importance. The following microfinance trends reflect the need for enhanced governance:

- MFIs around the world are expanding their outreach and assuming responsibility for increasingly large sums of money, challenging the capacity of their management to maintain high standards of performance, and necessitating increased input and involvement by the board to ensure effective management.

- An increasing number of MFIs are becoming regulated, assuming the responsibilities and challenges of a regulated entity. Their decision to capture deposits from investors and savers, many of whom are low income persons, demands meticulous oversight to ensure the safety of those deposits.
- MFIs are operating in increasingly competitive markets. Maintaining or expanding market share is becoming an important strategic objective. The achievement of this objective demands a sharper focus and more vigilant monitoring of operational efficiency, profitability, outreach, institutional stability, capital mobilization, and other economic outcomes.
- MFIs often operate in unstable financial environments, which are causing stakeholders (donors, lenders, and owners) to require more transparency and communication of information. Only effective governance can assure the desired level of accountability.

Clearly, the governance context for the microfinance field is complex. This complexity makes the act of effective governance even more difficult and challenging than in traditional non-governmental, financial or corporate institutions. In essence, therefore, the Microfinance institutions should be able to make sure that the foundation for good governance is in place. This foundation should ideally be made up of six fundamental elements:

- A shared strategic vision;
- A reliable and quick management information system to make decisions and aid monitoring;
- Decision-making processes that are clear, well-adapted and coherent with the governance structure;
- A level of staff training, capacity and involvement that ensures decisions are executed;
- An efficient monitoring system;
- Ability to prevent and overcome internal and external crises.

Observers of microfinance are increasingly pinpointing improved corporate governance as a key to enhance MFIs' survival and growth. A recent report identified corporate governance as a principal risk facing microfinance, threatening its role as both a business and a social service (CSFI, 2008). However, studies by Mersland and Strøm (2008a & b) and Hartarska (2005) find that best practice governance mechanisms from regular firms in mature markets do not generally have much influence on the performance of the MFIs. Thus, there is a need for a different and more original approach to identify and better understand the governance mechanisms that can enhance MFIs' long-term survival.

## 2. Ownership and Governance Aspects of MFIs

Closely linked to the issue of governance is the issue of ownership. The board of directors either consists of owners or represents the interests of owners. Aligning the interests of individual directors with the interests of the institution is key to realizing effective governance. Creating this alignment depends on understanding the issues associated with each of the four corporate structures of MFIs—public, nonprofit, for-profit, and credit unions. The specific corporate structure does not in itself define effective governance. For each, however, factors exist that may strengthen or undermine a board's ability to fulfill its roles and responsibilities.

Corporate structure does not define effective governance, but for each type of microfinance institution—non-profit, profit, credit union—factors exist that may strengthen or weaken a board's ability to fulfill its roles and responsibilities. The characteristics and the perspectives of owners who exercise the governance role are perhaps the most important factors related to effective governance. Coming to the specific question of ownership structure and mission, an institution's mission and the choices it makes in terms of institutional type and ownership structure are closely linked and influence each other mutually. Indeed, the ownership structure can be influenced by the mission and *vice versa*. There is not necessarily a link between an institution's mission and its legal status. An institution that is subsidized or generally "supported" (nationally or internationally) will more likely be forced to pursue a mission of public interest than one that is financed by private investors. Similarly, private investors expecting dividends will not have the same demands as e.g. private social investors affiliated with an international organization. Congruence between the mission, target public, products offered and the ownership structure are necessarily linked to the institution's history and its environment. The interrelationship between Social Mission and Commercial Mission as well as between the roles of Public and Private Stakeholders is depicted in Fig. 1 below:

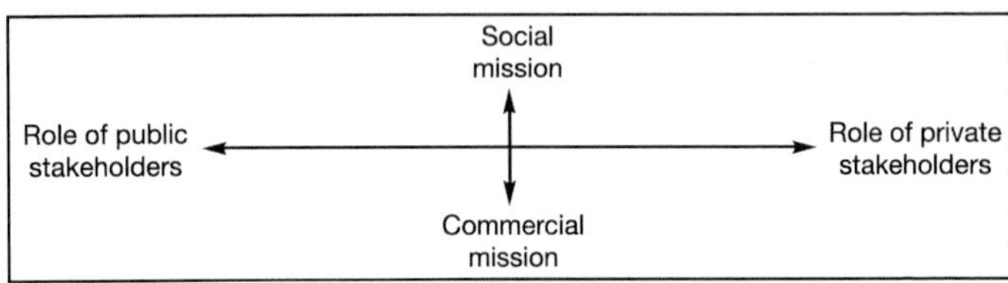


**Fig. 1:** Interrelationship between Social and Commercial Mission and between the Roles of Public and Private Stakeholders

*Source*: Cécile Lapenu (CERISE) and Dorothée Pierret (IRAM)/IFAD (2006)

The interrelationship between the institutional mission and the ownership status of the stakeholders is shown in more explicit terms in Table 2.

As Rosengard (2004) observed, sustainable microfinance proves that commercial banks as well as non-profit organizations can combine financial and social success instead of opposing them: both types of institutions can create social value and apply banking principles very unconventionally ("downscaling" in the case of banks, "up scaling" in the case of non-profit organizations). Yet despite this possibility, non-commercial microfinance still plays an important role. There are many models for microfinance (bank, finance company, cooperative, non-profit) and it is fundamental that the model matches the mission. Sometimes, the most appropriate model is a rural cooperative if significant gains can be made from the financing of collective storage and marketing activities. If the activity is very high risk, for example, targeting extremely marginalized

**Table 2:** Interrelationship between Institutional Mission and Ownership status of Stakeholders

| | Social mission | Commercial mission | Definition of the mission |
|---|---|---|---|
| Non-profit organizations | +++ | + | The mission will likely be primarily socially-oriented. |
| Cooperatives | ++ | ++ | The mission of a cooperative is, above all, to offer the best service at the best price to its members. Its social nature will therefore depend on its members. The democratic principles that guide the functioning of cooperatives make it possible to defend the interests of the majority. |
| Private company | + | +++ | The mission will depend on the type of investors: commercial investors (who might seek to maximize profits) or social investors (who might include non-financial criteria in their objectives). |
| Public entity | ++ | + | Direct or indirect subsidies widespread in public entities are usually provided based on non-commercial objectives. However, public institutions can fail if they do not balance public interest with commercial objectives. |

*Source*: Cécile Lapenu (CERISE) and Dorothée Pierret (IRAM)/ IFAD (2006).

populations, a subsidized non-governmental organization (NGO) might be the most suitable model. The guiding principles [to match the appropriate institutional model with the MFI's mission] should be institutional diversification, product differentiation, and market segmentation.

One of the most challenging tasks facing boards of all institutional types is balancing the dual objectives of social mission and profitability. Particularly in regions where the microfinance industry is underdeveloped, conventional wisdom asserts that these are mutually exclusive objectives. Microfinance best practice has shown, however, that these objectives are complementary. The social and profit objectives reflect the same tradeoffs any business faces when trying to balance short- and long-term goals. The social and profit objectives are aspects of the same business philosophy, each one reinforcing the other. Social mission, expressed in conventional business terms, is an MFI's orientation toward a specialized market niche, where actors must be innovative to serve the market efficiently and profitably. The profit objective, expressed in social terms, is an institution's search for permanence. It is tied to the social objective because institutions that do not achieve permanence will fail to achieve their social mission over the long-term.

A single MFI is likely to evolve through several phases in its life-span, during which its balance of objectives will assume different forms. In its early stage, an MFI may aim to demonstrate that it can provide financial services to a previously unbankable market in a sustainable manner. In a second stage, it might expand its outreach to serve more people in the target market in a permanent, profitable manner. In a third stage, when the institution achieves profitability and attracts competitors, the MFI may develop new products oriented to clients' needs, or restructure its costs to reduce interest rates. At a later stage, it may even return to the first objective, and seek to reach even poorer market segments still considered unprofitable.

Acknowledging the existence and feasibility of these dual objectives, the task of balancing them on a daily basis can still be daunting. In doing so, MFIs should consider the following guidelines:

- The institution must focus on the specialized market niche that defines its social mission. For it to achieve both objectives, it must understand the characteristics of its target market and design its services accordingly. Simultaneously, the board must be aware of the MFI's stage of evolution and set profit objectives accordingly.
- The MFI should embrace the dual objectives in its mission statement and ensure that its institutional policies and procedures follow from that statement.

- The board should seek out additional training and/or temporarily cede to management's discretion if it does not have sufficient experience during certain phases of its existence to implement the balancing process effectively. A solid partnership between board and management is particularly crucial to success in a microfinance institution given the need to provide unified leadership in the face of a challenging balancing act.
- A balance in the composition of the board may enable it to balance the two objectives effectively. However, MFI boards should avoid polarization by avoiding candidates who see the issue from only one perspective. Ideally, board members should consider both objectives important, although they may have a natural bias toward one or the other.

Observers, Policy-makers as well as the practitioners of microfinance in India are increasingly pinpointing on improved governance as a key to enhance MFIs' survival and growth. Thus, there is a need for a different and more original approach to identify and better understand the governance mechanisms that can enhance MFIs' long-term survival. MFIs, whether non-profit or for profit, are institutions that combine a social mission—provision of financial services to the low-income population—with a financial objective that drives the institution to achieve self-sufficiency. Importantly, well-run and well performing MFIs are attracting private sources of capital, including deposits and commercial loans for on-lending. Many of them upgraded themselves to become regulated institutions. That is a very positive aspect of the new horizons of microfinance, which will open the window for development of a robust micro, small and medium enterprise focused financial market in India. The extent to which microfinance institutions seek to maintain the dual focus of profitability and outreach to poor clients is directly shaped by the promoters, composition of the boards of directors and the top management, and by the priorities established by them.

Ownership is rights over property, while governance relates to the management structure and accountability, which exists between the owners and stakeholders. Microfinance in India is currently provided through diverse organizational types as we have observed which can be distinguished by their ownership structures: private capital, state owned enterprises and non-profits. Nonetheless, these are not homogeneous clusters and significant variance can be observed within each institutional grouping with respect to: ownership composition, strategy, operations, sustainability, impact and outreach. Besides member-owned cooperatives, the microfinance industry in India is dominated by NBFCs, not-for-profit (refer Section 25 Companies) and the non-governmental organizations (NGOs). The NBFCs are currently regulated by the Reserve Bank of India and the systems and procedures are streamlined due to its existence for a longer period, which also takes care of the issues related to governance. Several stakeholders influence a not-for-profit organization, but no particular group or person can legally claim ownership or receive residual earnings from it. Majority of stakeholders at a Round Table meet on microfinance organized by the Indian Institute of Economics (IIE) here have favoured the adoption of governance and regulation for an orderly, healthy and sustainable growth of micro-finance sector (Business Line, 2006). Due to the diversity of ownership structures, the separation of ownership from management (whether in a public, private or cooperative form of organization), as well as dispersion in ownership, introduce important problems of governance (Mersland, 2008). One challenge in the governance of not-for-profit organizations is the fact that managers serving as agents are supervised by either the funding organizations or the lending organizations which calls for more transparency of the systems and procedures and should be separated from ownership.

Glaeser (2002) observed that due to the fact mentioned the traditional board governance may be less effective in not-for-profit MFIs. Issues related to the ownership and governance structures and their impact on outreach, financial sustainability and institutional stability are yet to be addressed and the correlation among these issues are required to be found out. The Governance of the majority of the MFIs in India is driven by the vision of the promoters and the management committee or the board has very little say on the future direction of the organization. They generally do not have written documents on various issues and policies being followed by them. The organizational structure and roles are also not much defined and followed. This enables the Promoter/CEO to change the policy and direction according to the need of the organization, which has always a negative impact on the field level workers and managers. The major drawbacks of the MFIs in India are not differentiating the ownership and governance and they are in fact run and manage by few people and not by the system of governance. Like other organizations, resolving the conflict of ownership and governance will play an important role in the growth, development and sustainability of the MFIs. It has now become imperative to transform and restructure the governance of the MFIs in India to enhance their efficiency and to handle large portfolio and client base.

### *2.1 Factors of Good Governance of MFIs*

As we have already discussed about the impressive growth of the MFIs in India in terms of handling increased business volume and large number of clientele, it is necessary for them to adopt good governance to improve their efficiency, acceptability and building image in the society to sustain the growth they have already registered. Good governance in the perspective of MFIs can be defined as the process by which a board of directors/top management, working through management principles, guides MFIs in fulfilling its mission and at the same time protecting the institution's assets and goodwill. Good governance occurs when a promoter/board provides proper guidance to management regarding the strategic direction for the institution, and oversees management's efforts to move in that direction to achieve the short-term, medium-term and long-term goals. This article tries to find out few important factors of good governance in relation to MFIs operating in India.

(a) *Board Membership*: The composition of MFIs Board/ Top management has to be considered from several perspectives, e.g.

- Skills and characteristics of board members—The members should have set of skills to understand the microeconomic aspects of rural financial market, development finance, rural entrepreneurship, etc.
- Commitment to the dual mission of microfinance: The dual mission of microfinance is very crucial for its growth and the board members should be committed to achieve this.
- Ability and willingness to fulfill the duties of care loyalty and obedience towards the mission, vision, goals and objectives of the Institution.
- Commitment to develop knowledge and skills of new and existing members.
- Size of the board should match the volume of business and should be flexible to induct new members but unnecessary crowding should be avoided.
- Clear-cut guidelines on terms of membership, removal of inactive members and performance evaluation of each member should be put in place to avoid confusion.

(b) *Operating Procedures*: The MFIs in India operates through various windows and best suited procedures available in the locality of their operation. Barring few MFIs who have all India characteristics, most of them operate in the State/District of their origin. They are the best persons who know about the challenges of the local people and their requirement. However, a standard operating system can be devised to get a better performance and efficiency of the MFIs. The use of a common platform of information and communication technology will further improve the efficiency parameter.

(c) *Policies and Documents*: Well drafted policies on loan appraisal, recovery management, HR management, Customer service, Monitoring of loan accounts, delinquency management, etc. are very much essential to run MFIs effectively. The policies should also be revisited on a regular interval to update and make necessary changes according to the suggestions received from the field level functionaries.

(d) *Fiduciary Responsibility of Microfinance Institutions*: In general, the fiduciary responsibility of the board of any financial intermediary is considered higher than that of other corporate entities, since financial organizations are entrusted with the public's money in the form of deposits. We should note here that a non-profit/NGO-MFI unregulated microfinance institution is not technically a financial intermediary. It can take deposits from members only as part of a loan guarantee scheme but not deposits as liabilities. Still the MFIs in general have additional public responsibilities of maintaining goodwill in the market and building faith of the investors.

(e) *Risk Assessment Capacity in Microfinance Institutions*: The board of the MFIs must be able to assess risks associated with the provision of financial services. The growth in the client base and asset structure of a microfinance institution, combined with significant increases in banking competition, and the creation of regulated microfinance institutions, require greater ability on the part of the board to assess risk. Vishwanatham and Gupta (2006) have defined good governance as the board and executive processes and systems that enable the institution to identify the risks affecting its performance and to manage them to achieve the promised returns to its various stakeholders. They also argue that single most critical factor that will aid best governance practices to emerge would be the evolution of a healthy and effective relationship between the executive management and the Board.

(f) *Systems of Rating of MFIs*: The Board/Management of the MFIs should insists for rating of their organization by the external rating agencies (e.g. CRISIL-leading rating agency in India and M-CRIL, a specialized rating agency for the MFIs) at a regular interval to assess different aspects of their operation and to improve their operational efficiency.

The microfinance industry is dominated by not-for-profit, non-governmental organizations (NGOs—Marshland, 2008). Similarly, most of the savings banks are not-for-profit organizations. A not-for-profit organization is influenced by several stakeholders, but no particular group or person can legally claim ownership or receive residual earnings from it (Hansmann, 1996, Mersland and Storm, 2008a & b). Thus, savings banks and not-for-profit MFIs are similar, both legally and economically. The corporate governance mechanisms affecting one type of organization may therefore affect the other.

### 2.2 Public Ownership/Government Corporate Structure

With the one conspicuous exception of the government-owned Bank Rakyat Indonesia (BRI), public ownership of financial institutions chartered to service low-income populations historically has been a failure worldwide. In the best cases, well-intended, yet misguided, development policies have severely distorted the market by directing credit to micro-entrepreneurs at subsidized rates. The result has been unsustainable levels of borrower delinquency and a severe undermining of public confidence in government development initiatives. In addition, political interference and corruption have further undermined performance standards and confidence (Robinson, 1994 and Churchill, 1998).

Although the model that prevailed in the last three decades has failed, public ownership of MFIs may be successful with economically sound credit policies and mechanisms to protect the institutional assets from political manipulation. Moreover, the extensive branch infrastructure of many government-owned banks, and the significant financial resources that the public sector brings to a given microfinance project, merit understanding the elements that make public sector involvement in microfinance successful. Several nascent efforts are worth noting as examples of new approaches; however, their early stage of development prevents drawing conclusions.

One example of government participation is found in South Africa in the public-private partnership, KHULA, which is providing funds for the micro-enterprise sector. Created in 1996 as a public company, KHULA is currently capitalized with public funds and provides the following products:

- Business loans to MFIs;
- Start-up loans for emerging MFIs;
- Technical assistance to MFIs;
- Equity investment in businesses; and
- A guarantee fund that allows MFIs to borrow from commercial banks.

KHULA adheres to market principles in its operations. The government has board representation. Once the fund demonstrates significant returns and attracts private investors, the government's participation is supposed to decrease. Whether this occurs will be a true test of the ability to depoliticize government involvement in microfinance in a highly charged political atmosphere.

Banco del Nordeste in Brazil, a government-owned bank that is entering the microfinance field, presents another example of government participation. The bank has an extensive branch network and approximately 180 branches, and it understands the key methodological elements that have resulted in success in this field (i.e. market rates, ever-increasing loan size, and so on). Provided the bank is able to insulate itself from political pressure from the government—in terms of targets for numbers of clients reached, for example, which might be politically advantageous but result in unmanageable growth—Banco del Nordeste's involvement in microfinance has much promise. At the other end of the spectrum of government participation is the example of the newly created micro-enterprise bank, MIBANCO, in Peru. President Alberto Fujimori announced the creation of this bank at the Micro-credit Summit in February 1997; in April 1998, MIBANCO was formally established. In this case, the Peruvian government played a key role in facilitating the necessary processes for establishing the bank and in bringing together potential investees to ensure that it would be wholly privately held. For example, the government helped bring Banco Wiese and Banco de Credito to the table, both of whom took a 6.5 percent ownership interest in the bank. The remaining shares are held by the NGO ACCION Comunitaria del Peru (ACP), which sold its micro-enterprise portfolio to MIBANCO (60%); by PROFUND (20%); and by ACCION International (7%). ACP has five board members, with the other shareholders having one board member each, to total nine board members. The Peruvian government has no equity participation in MIBANCO; instead, there is an invited representative of the President for a two-year period, giving the government a voice but no vote.

In contrast to the MIBANCO example in Peru, the government of Argentina made US$ 40 million available for investment in microfinance. FONCAP, S.A., a private sector corporation under a fiduciary agreement with the Argentine government, was created in 1997 to wholly manage the resources made available by the Argentine government. FONCAP's goal is to help create the infrastructure necessary to increase financial services to Argentina's micro-entrepreneurs. FONCAP will help develop NGOs and other MFIs offering credit to Micro-entrepreneurs by providing financial and non-financial services to MFIs. The structure of this entity, in which the government holds a minority position and the fact that it is managed by a private entity, helps to ensure that the programme does not become politicized. The above examples demonstrate an evolution in the approach some governments are taking toward public ownership of MFIs. Recent initiatives reveal various mixes of public and private ownership, mechanisms to depoliticize the institutions, and an increased adherence to market principles. Although these efforts are relatively new—conceived and initiated in the last three years—if successful, they will open the door for more approaches by other governments.

### 2.3 Skills and Characteristics of Microfinance Board Directors

Effective governance depends primarily on the skills and characteristics of the individual directors. Collectively, these attributes should represent a diverse set of experiences, backgrounds, areas of expertise, ethnicity, and gender. Although the main prerequisite for effective governance of a financial institution is a solid business sense, an MFI board can provide additional guidance to the institution if its members have expertise in microfinance. Of equal value is expertise in law, marketing, or information technology, which are particularly relevant to microfinance. The level of board members' experience and influence in their respective fields may vary significantly in a board that combines members able to dedicate greater time and energy to the board with those who can play more of a representational role. The following skills are important assets to any MFI board:

- *Business sense*: A microfinance board must have solid business sense, with some financial expertise in two areas. The first area is financial analysis, which allows the board to understand and measure the performance of the institution in the key areas of capital adequacy, asset quality, profitability, and liquidity management. The second area is financial auditing, which provides the board with the capacity to adequately assess the strength of the institution's internal control mechanisms.
- *Microfinance experience*: Given the relative newness of MFIs, there are not many experts in this field. However, including individuals with some experience in this area on the board can be very valuable to the institution.
- *Financial markets expertise*: Individuals who understand the local financial markets and know the players, as well as understand or have experience in international financial markets, can be important contributors as MFI board members.
- *Legal and regulatory expertise*: All MFIs, but especially those that have entered the regulated financial sector or are considering such a change, will benefit from

individual directors who bring legal expertise to their boards.

- *Marketing expertise*: With increasing competition, MFIs are being required to more aggressively "sell" their products to micro-enterprise customers. Because marketing is still a relatively new area for MFIs, directors with expertise in this field and in product development can provide guidance to MFIs.
- *Public relations*: MFIs must be concerned with the image they project to the client and to the public at large and must be able to conduct outreach campaigns.
- *Technological expertise*: Increasing competition, emphasis on cost reduction, and the increasingly complex nature of microfinance operations (e.g. savings mobilization and diversified products) require that institutions enhance the information technology they use. Integrated and automated information technology systems enable the institution to better evaluate its performance at any given moment, as well as reduce operating costs. Boards will benefit from individuals with technological expertise.
- *Fundraising*: For the non-profit MFI, board members are expected to play an active role in fundraising. Individuals with prior experience and contacts represent a significant asset.

## 3. Impact of Good Governance on Microfinance Performance

Considerable research efforts have been dedicated to microfinance. Especially the possible impact from getting access to microfinance (Claessens and Feijen, 2006; Littlefield et al., 2003), the economics of group lending (Besley and Coate, 1995; Ghatak and Guinnane, 1999; Paxton et al., 2000), the building of inclusive financial sectors (Helms, 2006; United Nations, 2006) as well as the development of theory (Armendariz de Aghion and Morduch, 2005) has motivated researchers. Linked to the schism debate is the study of the performance of microfinance organizations. Here the Mix-market and the Micro-banking Bulletin (www.mixmarket.org) have provided the industry with important knowledge and benchmarks. Nevertheless, empirical progress on better understanding of the corporate governance mechanisms influencing performance is still held back by the lack of reliable cross-country data. Thus, by introducing a unique dataset to link MFI and performance at the individual MFI level our paper complements the existing research in the microfinance field. The results show that financial performance is improved when the roles of CEO and chairman are split, when the CEO is a woman, and when loans are made to individuals. Stronger competition reduces financial performance. One finds little evidence of internal governance in outreach. Outreach is improved with group lending. There is no difference in SHFs and NPOs in outreach. The risk regressions show few significant results.

Even though we are far from having inclusive financial services for the poor in India with all its components, the microfinance sector has come a long way in the last decade. It is facilitating microfinance (to face the present in the area of poverty) and facilitating micro insurance and micro pension (to face the future, in the area of vulnerability and social security). So far, our discussion goes the factors of good governance have direct bearings on the growth and development paradigm of MFIs in the emerging scenario of financial market in India. The impact of the good governance is visible both in the financial and non-financial areas of operation.

In financial areas, the funds received by the MFIs in the form of donations, loans and VC/PE investments has direct correlation with their governance of structures. Probability of getting funds for their microfinance operation is more in case of an organization with all well-defined systems and procedures put in place and no conflict on the ownership and governance. The Commercial banks in India which happens to be the major source of funds, appraise the MFIs based on certain factors and governance has been given maximum (>60%) weightage for sanctioning of loans. Even the small MFIs are getting better ratings by the rating tools adopted by the banks due to their governance structure. Some other financial factors, e.g. recovery rate, portfolio at risk, etc. are also considered by the funding agencies at the time of their appraisal that are again directly related with the governance architecture of the MFIs. It was reported that some of the commercial banks have almost decided to pull out of financing MFIs, which did not follow governance norms stipulated by the bank, irrespective of the levels of profitability of the MFIs. Apparently, over 90 percent of the MFIs in that bank's portfolio showed one problem or the other with respect to its governance structure.

In the non-financial front, the governance issues of MFIs focus is usually on balancing social and commercial interests, which is now at the crossroad. Nevertheless, in the area of non-financial indicators to sustainability, governance is the key and the board provides proper guidance to the management regarding the strategic direction for the organization and oversees the management effort to move in this direction. Governance sometimes conceived as a virtuous cycle that links the shareholders to the boards, to the managements, to the staff, to the customer and to the community at large (CGAP, 1997). Adoption of technology will also play an important role in the non-financial front of governance in MFIs. In Standard & Poor Report (Nov. 2008) Venkataraman and Raj Sekhar (2008) of CRISIL termed governance-related issues are the biggest challenge to the sustainability of Indian MFIs and point out that NGO-MFIs are likely to be floundering on this front, in their quest to balance the transition from a charitable entity to a commercial one (CGAP, 2006).

### 3.1 The Way Forward

Effective governance is one of the critical factors for success of any microfinance institution in India. It is, therefore, imperative for all stakeholders give this important issue the highest attention and few relevant issues are highlighted hereunder:

*Separation of Responsibilities*: In most of the MFIs in India, it was observed that the promoter/chairperson/CEO is the same person that in real terms hampers the basic chemistry of the Governance architecture and transparency of operation. The chairperson cannot play this role effectively if the same person is also running the daily operations as CEO/MD. It was strongly advocated that splitting responsibilities between the CEO and the chairperson/promoter would bring more transparency of the system. This view has been proved correct in some of the big MFIs in India, which registered their success after splitting the position of Chairperson and CEO. This view has been corroborated by international studies that the professional CEOs in MFIs can bring the desirable success and balance both the social objectives and the profitability (IFAD, 2005).

*Formation of Committees*: Creating and utilizing well-defined board committees/subcommittees to address key issues of different aspect of operation can be useful. Board meetings should not be taken up by work that can best be done in a board committee/sub-committees. The effectiveness of the committee structure, like that of the full board, depends on the clarity of the committees' responsibilities, the dedication of its members, which can include non-board members, and leadership. For this purpose, the clarity of the role of the Board and the committee and the CEO has to be documented as per the best practices notwithstanding the size of the MFIs.

*Framing Appropriate Procedures*: A well-defined and clearly drafted procedures are essential for the execution of effective microfinance governance. Even the most committed and highly qualified individuals cannot discharge their roles effectively without following well-documented procedures. Proper documentation set out in accurate board minutes, up-to-date articles of incorporation and by-laws, and a board policy manual on lending, recovery, risk management, etc. are essential.

*Policy on MFIs and Enabling Environment*: Now in India, there is an urgent need of a well-accepted Microfinance policy supported by regulatory and supervisory framework, which is still missing at the cost of the stakeholders. The Microfinance Bill, 2006 is a milestone event for expanding the provision of financial services to the poor, which is yet to get its legal shape. The Reserve Bank of India (RBI) has increased the capital requirements of NBFCs from the existing 10 percent to 12 percent by March 2009 and 15 percent by March 2010. Many practitioners felt this measure would increase their cost of funds and will hamper the scalability of this sector. The MFIs should also be encouraged to take up all the three areas of activities: financial services (micro-credit, micro insurance, micro pension, etc.); non-financial services (classes on literacy, nutrition, health, environment, etc.); and business development.

*Interest Rate*: The experts in microfinance expressed serious concern over the exorbitant interest rates and favoured evolving methods to bring down the cost of funds of microfinance institutions (MFIs) through funding, subsidies or savings products so that the needy sections of the society get access to low cost finance. The long-term future of the microfinance sector in India depends on MFIs able to achieve operational, financial and institutional sustainability and good governance. The need for MFIs to rope in domain experts, professionals and independent directors on their boards in the larger interest of all stakeholders has now been surfaced. The importance placed on microfinance as a development instrument, combined with the increasing inflow of capital/funds to the industry, indicate a need to better understand governance systems for MFIs. Further studies and research are needed in the microfinance space with special reference to governance issues to find out the correlation of good governance and performance of microfinance institutions in India.

## 4. Governance and Organizational Structure Issues in Microfinance

The following are identified to be some of the contemporary and emerging issues relating to good governance aspects and organizational structure issues relating to microfinance industry:

### *4.1 The Dual Mission: Balancing Social Impact with Financial Objectives*

MFIs are defined as institutions that combine a social mission—provision of financial services to the lowest-income population possible—with a financial objective that drives the institution to achieve self-sufficiency. Some sophisticated MFIs have attracted private sources of capital, including deposits, and have become regulated institutions. The extent to which microfinance institutions seek to maintain the dual focus of profitability and outreach to poor clients is directly shaped by the composition of the boards of directors and by the priorities established by the board. This paper argues that these two objectives are not mutually exclusive, and that boards, through their strategic decisions and policies, can move institutions in the direction of achieving superior profitability and reaching an expanding clientele of low-income entrepreneurs.

### *4.2 Ownership of Microfinance Institutions*

Traditionally, the board of directors either consists of owners or represents the interest of owners. Aligning the interests of individual directors with the interests of the institution is key to realizing effective governance. Creating this alignment within the microfinance industry depends on understanding the issues associated with each of the four corporate structures of MFIs: public (government), nonprofit (NGO), for-profit, and cooperative (credit unions). The specific corporate structure does not in itself define effective governance. For each, however, factors exist that may strengthen or undermine a board's ability to fulfill its roles and responsibilities.

### *4.3 Public Ownership vis-à-vis Government Corporate Structure*

With the exception of Bank Rakyat Indonesia, public ownership models for microfinance from the past three decades have failed because of misguided policies that distorted markets through targeted subsidized credits, political interference, and corruption. In the past three years, however, some governments have taken new approaches to public ownership of MFIs. These approaches range from various mixes of public and private ownership, mechanisms to depoliticize the institutions, and an increased adherence to market principles. Because these efforts are still nascent, it is not possible to draw conclusions about their success.

### *4.4 Nonprofit NGO Corporate Structure*

Because non-profits have no owners, commitment to the institutional mission is what drives NGO board members to fulfill their duties responsibly. Failed governance in NGOs has occurred where power has been concentrated in the hands of an executive who does not receive proper oversight from the board, as evidenced by the collapse of Corposol in Colombia. The NGO model has yielded important successes when individual board members have strongly identified with the institutional mission and possessed the ability to guide the MFI strategically and hold management accountable to performance objectives.

### *4.5 Profit-oriented Corporate Structure*

There are two types of for-profit MFIs. The first includes commercial banks and finance companies that moved down market to serve the micro-enterprise sector; the second type includes NGO-established regulated financial institutions. While profitability primarily motivates the owners of the former, the motivation of owners in transformed NGO-MFIs varies with the mix of capital. Rather than pure, private capital, four principal sources of social capital typically are provided: NGOs, public entities, specialized equity funds, and limited private investors. Each of these potential investors has its own set of concerns and brings different experiences to the institution. In planning for the participation of various parties on an institution's board, balance should not be put ahead of individual ability and commitment. The key is to have clarity in the requirements for effective governance, and to determine the willingness and capability of potential investors to perform the duties required.

#### *4.5.1 Credit Union Corporate Structure*

In credit unions, where owners are also the institution's clients, three critical lapses in governance arise: (1) a misalignment of priorities among elected directors, contracted management, and member-owners; (2) unequal representation of the interests of the two categories of clients—net savers and net borrowers—generally in favour of borrowers; and (3) a lack of regulation and supervision of credit unions. Successful governance of the credit union corporate structure requires a balance between savers and borrowers; this balance can be achieved by reorienting the services of the institution to attract more savers. In addition, specific rules should be in place to guard against excessive risk-taking by the board. These include rules to enforce the fulfillment of board roles and responsibilities, compliance with external auditor requirements, controls on insider operations and loan risk, and the exercise of prudent discipline.

### *4.6 Fiduciary Responsibility of Microfinance Institutions*

In general, the fiduciary responsibility of the board of any financial intermediary is considered greater than that of other corporate entities. Besides maintaining the solvency of a financial institution, boards of MFIs have three additional issues to consider. Low-income micro-entrepreneurs, as borrowers and savers, lack multiple sources of financing and are at greater risk than middle-income savers if their savings are lost. An insolvent microfinance institution, in most countries, means the end of a client's access to capital at commercial rates. Additionally, microfinance boards incur a responsibility with donors, in the case of NGOs, but this fiduciary responsibility increases when the MFI intermediates funds by borrowing from a bank, mobilizing deposits, or floating an instrument in the local securities exchange. Finally, the insolvency of any large-scale microfinance institution that is considered a "success" around the world would have an effect on the domestic and international microfinance sector. It is likely that lenders and other investors would become concerned about the viability of this field and withdraw or curtail the financial resources to microfinance. Hence, boards of advanced MFIs must understand that their fiduciary responsibilities extend beyond their governed institution and can affect the wider microfinance industry.

### *4.7 Risk Assessment Capacity in Microfinance Institutions*

In its role as corporate fiduciary, the board must be able to assess risks associated with the provision of financial services. The growth of microfinance institutions, combined with significant increases in competition, and the creation of regulated microfinance institutions require greater ability on the part of boards to assess risk. The paper covers these factors that make risk assessment an essential board responsibility and discusses effective integration of personnel in NGOs that hire private sector (usually banking) staff to strengthen their financial and banking expertise.

### 4.8 Board Membership Modality

The composition of the board has to be considered from several perspectives: skills and characteristics of microfinance board members; directors' commitment to the dual mission of microfinance; directors' ability and willingness to fulfill the duties of care, loyalty, and obedience; the board's commitment to develop the knowledge and skills of new and existing members; the size of the board; and finally, board member terms, removal of inactive members, and board performance evaluations.

### 4.9 Government Structure

There are three mechanisms a board establishes to operate effectively: (1) the separation of the role of the board chair and that of the managing director or chief executive officer (CEO); (2) the role of the board chair in relation to other board members; and (3) the use of board committees. The paper calls for the splitting of responsibilities between the CEO and the chair and discusses the important role a chair plays in ensuring ample discussion, debate, and the achievement of consensus among board members. Creating and utilizing board committees to address key issues in preparation for consideration by the full board can be useful. The effectiveness of the committee structure, like that of the full board, depends on the clarity of the committees' responsibilities.

### 4.10 Legal Procedures

Well-defined and clear procedures are essential for effective governance. Even the most committed and highly qualified individuals cannot discharge their roles effectively without following well-documented procedures. Proper documentation—in accurate board minutes, up-to-date articles of incorporation or by-laws, and a board policy manual—is essential.

### 4.11 Issues for Future Research

The following three areas related to effective governance that requires further analysis:

1. Conflicts of interest, such as the ability to fulfill the duty of loyalty and the practice of reciprocal board service;

2. Ownership considerations on microfinance boards, which comprise diverse types of people and are becoming ever more diverse; and
3. The effect of rapid change in the microfinance field—caused by competition, a movement toward the commercial model of microfinance, and increased participation by governments—on MFIs' board composition, incentives, function, and leadership.

### *4.12 Issues of Dealing with Difficult Situations*

In an atmosphere of rapid growth and frequent change, issues become more complex and challenging. Preventive rather than prescriptive measures are usually best for addressing difficult situations. Listed below are ten common situations that present difficulties for boards and recommended guidelines for addressing or preventing them (Campion and Frankiewicz, 1999).

*(a) Low staff morale and high turnover*

- Sponsor social activities where board members and staff can interact to become acquainted and gain appreciation of each others' perspectives;
- Bring in an outside specialist to do an organizational climate evaluation under an ad-hoc board committee;
- Identify the problem and mandate that the managing director responds quickly.

*(b) Incomplete or manipulated information*

- Require third-party diagnosis (CAMEL, rating agency review, special audit) reporting directly to a permanent board committee;
- Train staff and management so they understand their responsibility for maintaining the integrity of information: they should not alter information or cover up problems;
- In a crisis, bring the case to the general assembly or larger body of shareholders.

*(c) Fraud*

- Institutionalize a regular internal auditing process so that an audit is seen as normal and does not create mistrust;
- Establish strong system of internal control with regular audits;
- Form an audit committee that receives and reviews reports, and supports management in taking appropriate actions;
- Prosecute those who commit fraudulent acts.

*(d) Manipulation of information by or collusion between managing director and chair*

- Create an executive committee of the board that meets more frequently than the full board;
- Ensure that responsibility for decision-making is not concentrated in the chair or managing director;
- Request the resignation of both parties if guilty of intentional deceit.

*(e) Staff and board recommendations for microfinance loans*

- Clearly prohibit in the institution's policies and procedures; in exceptional cases, the board might agree to issue a loan with a 100 percent written guarantee from the staff/board member who advocated for the client.

*(f) Board unable to reach consensus*

- Ensure the existence of policies that clarify the role of the chair in such cases;
- Maintain an odd number of directors.

*(g) Differing vision, board versus management*

- Establish a board committee to work out issues.

*(h) Institutional culture clash between for-profit and non-profit philosophies during a transformation*

- Create a committee for transformation consisting of board members and staff that oversees staff training, a key component of transformation;

- Bring "bankers" onto the board and train other members in the financial and business skills required for commercialization;
- Make sure "bankers" are aware of the social concerns and non-profit philosophy of other members;
- Make sure board members share a common vision and mission.

*(i) Law suit*

- Establish a policy on this issue. For example, the MFI could agree to cover legal expenses if behaviour was deemed to be in line with the proper fulfillment of institutional responsibilities; if behaviour was deemed improper, the board member would be asked to resign and legal expenses would not be covered;
- All major litigation issues should be reviewed jointly by board and management with an ad hoc committee;
- The board should have legal counsel, either represented among its membership, or externally contracted.

*(j) Deteriorating portfolio quality*

- Board and senior management must address immediately;
- Utilize early warning systems to detect and react as soon as possible;
- Ensure that the latest industry advancements and findings are collected and reported on a regular basis;
- Bring in outside consultant if necessary to resolve problem.

## 5. Measuring Governance in Microfinance: Initial Findings from a Pilot Project

Until recently, corporate governance has been a subject of secondary interest in analyses of the microfinance industry. However, the recent economic downturn in some markets and the risk exposure of some microfinance institutions (MFIs) to bailout has led many in the industry to identify good governance as the primary differentiating factor between those institutions that overcome crises and those that do not. To enhance understanding of MFI Board structure, policies and activities, Microfinance Information Exchange (MIX) tested a new set of governance indicators in 2011 among a sample of 162 MFIs across 57 countries. These indicators were selected by the Institutional Governance Working Group of the World Microfinance Forum of Geneva.

Reporting on these indicators showed a positive correlation among factors such as the presence of risk management functions, internal auditing, and Board committees, suggesting that good MFI governance procedures do not exist in isolation from each other. MFIs of different sizes and geographic locations showed high levels of Board independence and diversity of experience/qualifications among Board members. It was observed that reasonable levels of review in key policy areas and most MFIs appear to have risk management and auditing functions in place. Nevertheless, no significant correlation was found between governance and financial performance in the sample, possibly due to the small sample size and/or the lack of historical governance data. The analysis is also enriched with findings from a separate, older effort on the part of MIX to collect governance indicators related to social performance management. These indicators show that social performance management is a concern among MFI Boards but that serious commitment to the topic, as measured by the presence of a social performance Board committee, is not yet widespread. While more in-depth research is needed to identify best practices for governance, our initial results reveal that some of these pilot indicators could provide useful analytical insights if tracked over time.

In any industry, good governance is a necessary component to securing long-term sustainability and to aligning policies and strategies with an institution's mission or goals. Thus, in order to determine the best practices for MFI governance, we need to understand the relationship between corporate governance and performance. While some efforts have been made to collect and analyze data on governance, there are no large-scale data sets that allow a detailed analysis of what works best in microfinance governance. To gain a better understanding of the current state of governance in the industry, the World Microfinance Forum Geneva created an Institutional Governance Working Group to identify a set of easy-to-measure governance indicators. The Working Group selected 10 such indicators and asked MIX to include them in a pilot survey administered in late 2011. The purpose of the survey was to gather information on MFI Board structures and to learn basic facts on how MFIs manage risk, change policies, and implement actions through the work of committees.

### 5.1 Using Governance Indicators

MIX collects and analyzes financial and social performance data from MFIs around the world, relying on validated data and source documents (e.g. audits) whenever possible. In 2011, MIX created a pilot survey to test 22 new indicators, 10 of which focused on governance as designed by the Institutional Governance Working Group. The governance questions were assessed using two main criteria: which yielded sufficiently reliable data to include in standard data collection and whether any showed a meaningful link to MFI performance. Since an MFI's Board of Directors is the nexus between stakeholders and governance, the 10 governance questions in the survey focus mainly on Board structure and characteristics, Board activity and engagement, and risk management.

#### 5.1.1 Board structure and characteristics

- *Indicators: Number of Board members, Board member qualifications, number of independent Board members, number of Board committees*

A good Board should encompass a range of expertise and experience as well as represent key stakeholders and maintain a significant degree of independence. The Board of Directors, through its members and advisors, should have the collective knowledge and experience necessary to meet strategic demands faced by MFIs (mainly dependent on the mission, the institutional development stage, and the external environment). As MFIs grow in scale and complexity, we expect their Boards to grow similarly. This assumption led us to test indicators related to Board size as well as to the qualifications and independence of its members. In addition, the bulk of the Board's work is often done at the committee level. Therefore we also gathered information on the presence of Board committees.

### 5.2 Board Activity and Engagement

- *Indicators: Frequency of Board meetings, Board meeting attendance, Board policy changes*

To assess Board activity and commitment towards an MFI, we included questions regarding meeting frequency and attendance. To evaluate Board effectiveness in developing policies addressing key business drivers, we asked MFIs which Board policies had changed within the last fiscal year.

### 5.3 Risk Management

- *Indicators: Separation of Chairman and CEO, funder voting rights on committees, presence of risk management and audit functions*

As an organization increases in complexity, separating the CEO function from the Chairman function serves to reduce negative effects of power concentration and the risks associated with losing a key person ("key person risk"). It is important to keep in mind, however, that such separation may not be apparent in fast-growing MFIs. Similarly, collecting information on voting rights allows us to assess the extent of power concentration at the Board level. A widely accepted factor of good risk management is establishing an independent risk management and internal audit function. Hence, the Working Group included the presence of such functions as an indicator in the survey.

### 5.4 Sample Description

MIX sent the survey to 1,000 MFIs, 162 of which responded. MFIs that responded comprised mainly of institutions more active in reporting both financial and social performance information to MIX. Thus, we may consider them to be MFIs committed to information transparency, and we therefore acknowledge self-selection bias in our sample results. The respondent MFIs were located in 57 countries. Table 3 lists the countries with the most respondents.

**Table 3:** Countries with highest number of MFI respondents

| Country | Number of respondents |
|---|---|
| India | 21 |
| Ecuador | 11 |
| Philippines | 9 |
| Colombia | 8 |
| Peru | 7 |
| Nicaragua | 6 |
| Bolivia | 6 |

The vast majorities of reporting MFIs was from Latin America and were NGOs and NBFIs. The median outreach of the respondent MFIs' was 17,000 active borrowers, ranging across a very wide range (from 200 clients to 8 million). The majority of individuals responding to the survey were CEOs/Executive Directors, followed by Heads of Financial Departments/ CFOs, and Heads of other departments (e.g. Research, HR, etc). In order to reduce the burden on MFIs filling out the questionnaire, the survey was structured such that it asked all MFIs only those questions considered most relevant, while the remaining questions were spread out among smaller groups. All MFIs received questions related to Board size and qualifications, Board independence, and frequency and attendance of Board meetings, while the remaining questions were divided among specific MFI groupings.

#### *5.4.1 Basic Findings*

Starting with Board composition, respondent MFIs have a median of seven Board members, with a minimum of three and a maximum of 15. On average, MFIs of all sizes and geographic locations report Board independence and diverse Board experience/qualifications. More than 80 percent of MFIs separate the CEO role from the Chairman of the Board role. Independent members make up 67 percent of the median Board. The majority of MFIs have Board members with multiple qualifications, with finance/microfinance and business experience being the most common (Table 4).

**Table 4:** An Analysis Report of Board members the following required number of qualifications

| Category | Yes | No | I don't know | No Response |
|---|---|---|---|---|
| Formal financial qualification | 145 | 6 | 2 | 9 |
| Formal legal qualification | 95 | 42 | 11 | 14 |
| More than 10 years' experience in banking | 111 | 30 | 8 | 13 |
| More than 10 years' experience in business | 130 | 16 | 4 | 12 |
| More than 7 years' experience in microfinance | 134 | 13 | 4 | 11 |
| More than 5 years' experience in market research | 85 | 38 | 24 | 15 |
| More than 2 years' experience in SP measurement and management | 95 | 32 | 19 | 16 |

The majority of Boards in the sample meet with reasonably high frequency during the year. Legal charter seems to matter for this indicator, as the majority of credit union and bank Boards tend to meet with higher frequency than Boards of NGOs and NBFIs. Size does not appear to correlate with meeting frequency. Eighty-four percent of Board members attended meetings. Half of the MFIs sampled for this question reported having three or more Board committees, while 18 reported none. The most common committees were "executive", "risk" and "audit". Younger MFIs—those established after 2001—have a median of four committees, while older MFIs have a median of only two. This suggests that the perceived need to establish and maintain committees might be more common among younger MFIs and that more established MFIs do not feel as strongly. No significant relationship was found between MFI size and the number of Board committees. The vast majority of MFIs have funders whose representatives do not sit on the MFIs' Boards of Directors (Table 5).

With regard to risk management, 58 percent of MFIs reported having a risk manager or a team dedicated to risk management, while 77 percent reported having an internal auditor or a team dedicated to internal auditing. Both functions tend to report to the CEO contrary to accepted best practice. Finally, concerning policy changes, MFIs show high levels of review/decisions in key policy areas (especially regarding internal controls, client protection, compliance, and funding sources) and 63 percent reported having changed five or more areas over the past year.

**Table 5:** Composition of the Board Committees

| Committee | Yes | No | No Response |
|---|---|---|---|
| Executive committee | 52% | 38% | 10% |
| Risk commitee | 48% | 40% | 12% |
| Audit committee | 63% | 25% | 12% |
| HR committee | 36% | 52% | 12% |
| Remuneration committee | 34% | 49% | 17% |
| Ethics committee | 26% | 57% | 17% |
| Funding committee | 39% | 45% | 16% |
| Transformation committee | 18% | 64% | 18% |

*Source*: MIX data collection 2009-2011.

### 5.5 Results from Correlation Analysis

MIX tested for correlations between governance indicators and MFI financial performance. The analysis revealed:

- No significant correlation between most governance indicators and financial performance. The presence of executive, risk and audit committees does appear positively correlated with staff productivity (number of borrowers per staff) but not with other performance indicators.
- Positive correlations were found among various governance indicators, showing the importance of having certain governance policies and procedures in place. MFIs that change policies more often show a positive correlation to the number of skills represented on the Board and the presence of an internal auditor. A strong correlation also exists between MFIs with executive, risk and audit committees, and the existence of risk management functions.
- Board size, possibly beneath some limiting value, does not seem to be associated with the presence of other

governance indicators. Instead, we found correlation among indicators related to Board structure: the presence of committees and the variety of skill sets.

MIX further explored the possible relationships between financial performance and governance indicators through regression analysis and did not find any statistically significant results. In particular, we focused on productivity (number of borrowers per staff), efficiency (operating expenses as a percentage of loan portfolio and cost per borrower as a percentage of GNI per capita), and portfolio quality (PAR > 30 days and write-off ratio). On the governance side, the indicators selected were Board independence, number of Board members, number of Board skills, number of committees, and the existence of auditing and risk management functions.

### *5.6 Measuring Governance and Social Performance*

For the past three years, MIX and the Social Performance Task Force (SPTF) have collaborated on identifying a set of governance indicators tailored to monitor social performance management at the Board level. These indicators identify whether members of an MFI's Board of Directors have been trained in areas relevant to social performance management and whether a formal Board committee exists to monitor social performance.

MIX data show that, across a sample of 405 MFIs, 77 percent ensured that social performance issues were identified as components of an MFI's strategic and business plans (Table 6). As for more in-depth commitment, 45 percent of MFIs reported organizing staff and client visits for Board members, while just 21 percent of MFIs reported having a standing social performance committee that regularly reviews social performance issues. Thus, while a growing number of MFIs include social performance assessment into their operations agenda, it is not yet common to have Board committees that specifically monitor social performance. Furthermore, one should keep in mind that this particular sample exhibits self-selection bias: it contains only those MFIs serious enough about social performance monitoring to complete the rather lengthy (and now defunct MIX/SPTF Social Performance Standards Report.

**Table 6:** Governance indicators related to Social Performance Management

| Governance Indicators/MFIs reporting by legal status | Banks (33) | Cooperatives (42) | NBFIs (157) | NGOs (160) | Rural Banks (13) | Total (405) |
|---|---|---|---|---|---|---|
| MFIs with a standing social performance committee that regularly reviews social performance issues | 21% | 19% | 22% | 21% | 23% | 21% |
| MFI that organize staff and client visits to help Board members understand how operations are achieving the mission | 48% | 24% | 47% | 46% | 62% | 45% |
| MFIs that ensure that social performance issues are identified as components of the MFI's strategic and business plans | 73% | 76% | 76% | 81% | 46% | 77% |

*Source*: MIX data collection 2009-2011

Given the possible linkages between social and financial performance, any further survey or case studies aiming at identifying best practices in governance should also take into account the capacity of the Board to "protect" the social mission of the institution over time. In the same vein, it would be helpful as well to consider the relationships between governance indicators and the level of information an MFI has at its disposal regarding client and staff satisfaction, and the poverty level of its clients. The strength of institutional corporate governance cannot be adequately measured by a questionnaire concerning a single time period. Only through systematic, longitudinal time series analyses that repeatedly capture indicators before and after governance procedures have been introduced will indicative assessments concerning institutional performance be made. At the same time, in-depth interviews with Boards and management can help elaborate on the quantitative information captured through surveys.

While the results of this pilot should take these limitations into account, we can already conclude that some indicators are worth full integration into MIX's annual data collection, as they show the potential to provide useful insights for the holistic assessment of a MFI if tracked over time. Indicators that showed the strongest correlation with each other are: number/ type of committees and existence of auditing/risk management functions. In addition, any further test of governance indicators or case studies should take into consideration the relationship between governance and social performance management to allow an evaluation of whether a Board effectively monitors social performance targets in the same way that it regularly monitors financial performance.

## 6. Regulatory Supervision of MFIs: Case of Peru and Indonesia

Regulated MFIs must learn how to maintain positive relationships with regulators, adhere to regulations, prepare for and pass inspection, and work with rating agencies. The three key concerns of becoming a regulated institution are (1) sufficient amounts of equity, (2) preparedness for the high costs of regulation, and (3) the ability to manage information, such as balance sheets, collateral calculations, and loan provisions, which all require an efficient management information system. Peru and Indonesia are two countries that have highly developed regulatory systems for microfinance.

### *6.1 The Case of Mibanco, Peru*

Mibanco transformed from the non-governmental organization Acción Comunitaria del Perú (ACP) in 1998, after ACP, a financial intermediary, had managed various projects related to community development for thirty years. In the early 1980s, ACP developed its first strategic plan directly related to micro-enterprise development. In May 1998, ACP became the majority shareholder and operative manager of a new venture called Mibanco (Banco de la Microempresa S.A.). Peru's first for-profit, fully regulated commercial bank dedicated to micro-enterprise. Mibanco's initial $16 million in capital came entirely from the private sector. Sixty percent came from ACP's client base and loan portfolio. Other investors included ProFund, the ACCIÓN Gateway Fund, Banco Wiese Sudameris, and Banco de Crédito del Perú. In November 1999, the Corporación Andina de Fomento became a shareholder of Mibanco. The non-profit ACP continues to offer non-financial social services.

The formal division between micro and commercial banks in Peru is characterized by micro-banks extending credits of less than $20,000 and commercial banks lending $20,001 and more. As a regulated financial institution, Mibanco is now subject to taxes on net income (the NGO was tax-exempt), loan provisioning requirements, reserve requirements, and reporting requirements. Like other institutions, it faces a capital requirement of $8 million. The MIS must track personnel, staff, and all funds. Furthermore, Mibanco must undergo a thorough annual external audit, at the bank's expense. This audit focuses on an analysis of the loan portfolio as well as a review of procedures and regulations. In addition to the yearly external audit, all regulated financial institutions must have an internal audit department. In the case of Mibanco, the internal audit department reports directly to the board. Beyond the annual auditing visits, Mibanco must present updated reports monthly to the superintendence, either by disk or via the Internet. The following list is an overview of the reports required by the superintendent:

- Daily report on interest charged
- Semi-monthly report on reserve position
- Monthly financial statement
- Monthly report on effective equity level and risk-weighted assets
- Monthly report on principal debtors
- Trimester report classifying debt quality to establish credit rating
- Annual report.

The information from these reports is made available to the general public. In addition to annual audits and superintendency reports, Mibanco is obligated to contract, at its own expense, other institutions to supervise specific aspects of its operations. This includes the evaluation and classification of risk. Mibanco also undertakes special market research when it plans to open a branch in a new location in order to evaluate business prospects in that area. While the organization has at times found it difficult to classify loans and manage the many different requirements for information that must be documented for each loan, it is felt that the costs associated with such supervision is minimal when compared to the aggregate value derived from close regulation. Before entering into the phases of transformation, the NGO microfinance institution must consider the supervisory requirements and weigh them against the benefits of becoming a regulated institution. In some cases, an NGO would be better off remaining unregulated, because the benefits may not outweigh the costs. Mibanco became regulated for the following reasons:

1. In Peru, an NGO cannot leverage its capital in the same way a bank can. Mibanco can leverages up to 11 times its capital.
2. Bank status allows access to capital markets, as long as the bank demonstrates efficiency, a strong loan portfolio, and a strong history in delivering financial services.
3. Regulators give the institution enhanced credibility.
4. Only a regulated bank can capture deposits from the public.

Under the current organizational structure, the shareholders and the board of Mibanco are personally responsible should the bank face a crisis. Their personal property is at stake, and they could face incarceration if the problems are serious enough. Despite the inherent risks that accompany bank status, Mibanco recognized the financial benefits of having access to capital markets, incentive enough to accept the increased responsibilities. Table 7 shows the incremental growth of Mibanco's portfolio and micro-lending profile.

**Table 7:** Programme Growth of Mibanco's Portfolio and micro-lending profile

| Year | Active Portfolio | Amount Disbursed | New Clients | Active Clients | Average Loan Balance | Percentage of Women Clients |
|---|---|---|---|---|---|---|
| 1994 | $2,281,094 | $15,375,336 | 6,518 | 9,023 | $376 | 58% |
| 1995 | $6,707,755 | $39,358,665 | 15,150 | 19,120 | $485 | 57% |
| 1996 | $9,673,051 | $58,788,658 | 17,500 | 26,225 | $527 | 59% |
| 1997 | $12,456,976 | $62,358,787 | 18,253 | 31,877 | $530 | 61% |
| 1998 | $12,137,442 | $59,942,102* | 19,189* | 33,858 | $526 | 62% |
| 1999 | $19,273,855 | $58,130,077 | 19,755 | 41,344 | $528 | 62% |
| 2000 | $36,925,607 | $85,700,610 | 29,747 | 58,088 | $636 | 59% |

## *6.2 The Case of Indonesia*

### *6.2.1 Background*

Microfinance in Indonesia is provided by the formal and informal sectors. The formal sector agents for microfinance include commercial banks (BRI Unit Desa), the rural banks (BPR), savings and credit cooperatives (Koperasi Simpan Pinjam/Kosipa), village credit boards (Badan Kredit Desa/ BKDs), village fund and credit institutions (Lembaga Dana Kredit Pedesaan/LDKPs), and village unit cooperatives (Kredit Unit Desa/KUDs). The informal sector agents include various sorts of non-governmental organizations (Lembaga Swadaya Masyarakat/LSMs) and self-help groups (Kelompok Swadaya Masyarakat/KSMs), moneylenders, local sources of trade and consumer credit, and mutual credit arrangements, like rotating savings and credit associations (ROSCAs).

Microfinance institutions in Indonesia have experienced a number of difficulties. The low quality of human resources has made it hard for institutions to find experienced staff. Bad corporate governance has threatened the stability of the institutions and insufficient infrastructure has impeded the growth of microfinance institutions. As of September 2000, approximately 35 percent of rural banks (BPRs) had unsound conditions; 260 of these were certain to be closed and liquidated. Another significant problem has been the lack of legal framework for some MFIs, such as village fund and credit institutions (LDKPs). With technical and financial assistance from international institutions, Bank Indonesia has been initiating efforts to restructure the rural banking industry, setting up a legal framework for informal MFIs, building up infrastructure for MFIs, and undertaking training and courses with certification for the staff of rural banks.

### *6.2.2 Regulation of MFIs*

The Table 8 describes the current legal and regulatory framework for MFIs in Indonesia.

**Table 8:** Legal and Regulatory Framework of Indonesian Microfinance Institutions

| Type of MFIs | The Law | Regulator and Supervisor | Regulation |
|---|---|---|---|
| BKD | The Banking Act No. 10 of 1998 | BRI for and on behalf Bank Indonesia | Asset quality, area of operations. |
| BPR | The Banking Act No. 10 of 1998 | Bank Indonesia | Licensing and management, capital adequacy ratio, legal lending limit, provision for bad debt. |
| BRI-Unit | The Banking Act No. 10 of 1998 | BRI and BI for BRI as a whole | – |
| Cooperatives; | The Cooperatives Act | State Ministry of | Licensing, management, capital. |
| Loan and saving Unit | No. 25 of 1992/ Government Decree No. 9 of 1995 | Cooperatives and Small Medium Enterprises | – |
| LDKP | – | Regional Government/ Regional Development Bank (BPD) | – |
| NGO | – | – | – |
| ROSCA | – | – | – |

*Source*: GTZ-GTZ, Regulatory Requirements for Microfinance: A Comparison of Legal Frameworks in 11 Countries Worldwide: http://www.bu.edu/bucflp/files/2012/08/Regulatory-Requirements-for-Microfinance.pdf

Table 8 shows that village fund and credit institutions (LDKPs) are only regulated by the regional government and do not have any legal status, even though they collect funds from the public. According to the law, every party that collects funds from the public must get a license from Bank Indonesia. Due to the funding of domestic micro-financial markets by international financial markets, there is an urgent need for the proper legal and regulatory frameworks for MFIs. One additional justification for granting MFIs legal status is the fact that MFIs weathered the 1998 financial crisis much better than the commercial banks. Such a legal status might encourage the government to place MFIs as a priority programme. This would, in turn, allow the MFIs to expand their outreach and increase their financial resources through mobilization of deposits and commercial loans.

Currently in Indonesia, the same organization that supervises commercial banks also supervises MFIs. However, the supervisory body experiences high costs with MFI supervision, and is often constrained by a lack of a specialized understanding of the needs of MFIs. Some of the smaller rural banks at present are supervised by BRI, which is in return paid by the Bank Indonesia. However, this is a rather limited arrangement. Two solutions have been proposed to address this issue: (1) a section of the provincial government or a central ministry would handle the supervision, or (2) an association or similar group would handle some self-regulation, perhaps in association with an insurance function. Whatever the final arrangement, the primary burden for rural bank supervision and technical assistance should be borne by the networks with which many of them are connected and the supervision institution should set standards and investigate problem cases. In particular, it has been recommended that resources be concentrated in a compliance unit for cases where legal requirements are not being met.

Costs for regulation and supervision can be high. Government funds are limited and banks are unlikely to want to use their own funds for the purpose of regulation and supervision. Rural banks themselves may be asked to bear some of the costs of supervision, but their resources are also quite limited, and any passing of costs to their customers will affect their competitiveness. Given the severe constraints on cost, it is important to determine the minimum set of supervision requirements and procedures consistent with prudent banking. This process may be assisted by a further automation of reporting and off-site supervision, with a periodic on-site supervision sufficient to guarantee the processes integrity. Two key issues are as follows:

- *Appropriate standards for accounting, reporting, and personnel*: This can be standardized and automated so that the cost is minimized and utility to banks and supervisors is maximized. A series of studies on actual practice and recommendations for its improvement is nearing completion.
- *Appropriate standards for loan classification*: This is one of the most critical issues and has been considered by several of the groups working on reforming supervision.

### 6.3 BRI-Unit Desa System

BRI is a major state bank with a profitable "micro-banking" division called BRI-Unit. BRI more than meets the common criteria used to measure performance of rural financial institutions, i.e. self-sustainability and outreach. Micro-borrowers appear to value their access to BRI's credit and savings services very highly. They are reluctant to break their banking relationship with the BRI units even if they have to squeeze their consumption to make their loan repayments on time. BRI has been careful to keep the micro-credit window open so that those who pay on time are able to borrow again if their enterprise justifies it. BRI branches supervise BRI Units, and the cost of the supervision is charged to the Unit. The supervising manager is required to visit the Unit once a week to verify their reports. Units have to report daily (trial balances), weekly (liquidity reports), monthly (progress report, balance sheet, income statement), quarterly (personnel report), semi-annually (past performance indicators), and annually (balance sheet and income statement) to the supervising branch, regional and head office. Bank Indonesia supervises BRI as a whole. It must maintain a certain capital adequacy ratio, adhere to legal lending limits requirements and publish its balance and income statement showing the amount of such loans quarterly both in newspapers and at a location on its premises. In addition, BRI must have officers who meet minimum requirements in education and professional experience. Detailed rules govern bank accounting and how charges and loan arrears are handled and each bank gets a AMEL rating.

### *6.4 Credit Fund Institutions (Lembaga Perkreditan Desa/LPDs)*

LPDs, which are owned by the traditional village (desa adat), are one type of LDKP in Bali. These LPDs are designed not only to serve the pure economic goals but also to contribute to maintain the desa adat and its system of associated temples. LPDs rely on savings and deposits rather than credit and grants as their source of refinancing. BPD Bali acts as the banker of the LPDs, absorbing over-liquidity and providing credit when needed. Similar to the other LDKP, LPDs offer saving accounts and deposits at market rates. Although owned by traditional villages, the government continues to play an important role in LPD development. To fulfill its guidance, supervisory and auditing role, the government has installed a guidance and supervisory body for LPDs at provincial, district and sub-district level. BPD Bali has undertaken technical guidance and supervision by analyzing monthly LPD reports and by carrying out on-site visits. There is no systematic supervision procedure or standard and the supervision conducted depends on the characteristic of its LDKP, the policy and the capability of each provincial government and BPD.

### *6.5 Rural Banks (Bank Perkreditan Rakyat/BPR)*

There are two types of Rural Banks (BPR), BPR-BKD (Village Credit Board) and BPR-Non-BKD. According to the law, all BPR are supervised by Bank Indonesia. Since there are many BKDs, and since they are not mobilizing deposits from public, Bank Indonesia decided that BPR-BKD should be supervised by BRI on behalf of Bank Indonesia. The other rural banks-BPR Non-BKD—are supervised directly by Bank Indonesia. At present there is a system of both on-site and off-site inspection, using a modified CAMEL for calculating BPR Rating. They also have to meet certain banking standards such as maintaining the minimum capital adequacy ratio and legal lending limits. The present system for rural banks is lacking on several grounds. Both the cost and the number of unsound rural banks are excessive. Bank Indonesia is now restructuring the BPR industry and is in the process of reforming the regulations.

### *6.6 Current Regulation and Strategic Planning*

Public law influences firms, and bank regulation has the potential to seriously affect the performance of a bank or an MFI. However, developing economies suffer from very weak institutional frameworks, imperfect markets, and incomplete information. Regulatory ability and public trust are generally weak under such conditions (Todaro and Smith, 2006). When regulation is weak, mutual banks attract smaller customers and take on less risk than stock banks (Rasmussen, 1988). Weak regulatory ability is therefore a major reason for the existence of not-for-profit organizations like savings banks and MFIs. While privately-owned banks have strong incentives to invest in risky projects, a not-for-profit bank is less likely to employ depositors' money in risky endeavours (Hansmann, 1996). Hansmann (1996) argues that, since regulatory ability was weak in the nineteenth century, savings banks were not-for-profit organizations in order to protect their customers from exploitation.

Under current regulation, rural banks need to submit several monthly reports, an annual business plan, and annual balance sheet and income statement reports. Bank Indonesia is now undertaking steps to simplify the current report of BPRs in order to give more focused supervision and to better grasp structural problems of particular BPRs. Bank Indonesia with technical assistance from GTZ has been working on matters such as improving regulation and supervision referring to international standards, working out BPR restructuring by establishing the Deposit Insurance Scheme and Pooling Fund, proceeded by an industry clean up and setting up a legal framework for non-bank MFIs. The draft legal framework for non-bank MFIs is planned to be finished at end of this year with subsequent proposal to the House of Representatives. The draft defines and presents the characteristics of non-bank MFIs, owners, management, outreach, licensing, minimum capital requirements, supervisory agency and prudential regulation.

Microfinance in Indonesia has a long history that can be traced back to the Dutch colonials, when microfinance services were provided by formal and informal agents such as BRI Unit, BKDs, BPRs, LDKPs, cooperatives, and other informal agencies (NGO, moneylenders, and ROSCA). The success of BRI-Unit is primarily due to strong networking, maintenance of a good information system, saving products development, innovative and flexible loan terms, close monitoring of loan performance, and good quality, professional human resources. Microfinance in Indonesia is still facing structural problems that need to be resolved. In this case, Bank Indonesia is undertaking a study to formulate new regulations and supervision for BPR; building up infrastructure for MFIs, especially BPR through consultation and technical assistance, training and education; setting-up a deposit insurance scheme; and providing a legal framework for non-bank MFIs.

## REFERENCES

Armendariz de Aghion, B. and J. Morduch (2005), *The Economics of Microfinance*, Cambridge: MIT, USA.

Besley, T. and S. Coate (1995), Group lending, repayment incentives and social collateral. *Journal of Development Economics* 46(1): 1-18.

Business Line (2006), Round Table meet on Microfinance; July 03 issue (http://www.thehindubusinessline.com).

Campion, Anita and Cheryl Frankiewicz (1999), Guideline for the effective governance of Microfinance Institutions, Microfinance Network, Occasional Paper No. 3.

Cécile Lapenu (CERISE) and Dorothée Pierret (IRAM) (2006), Handbook for the analysis of the governance of microfinance institutions; IFAD/GTZ, 2006.

CGAP (1997), Effective Governance for Microfinance Institutions, Focus Note No. 7, CGAP, 4 p. (http://www.cgap.org/docs/FocusNote_07.pdf)

CGAP (2006), Transforming NGO MFIs: Critical Ownership Issues to Consider. (http://www.cgap.org/gm/document-1.9.4213/OccasionalPaper_13.pdf)

Claessens, S. and E. Feijen (2006), *Financial Sector Development and the Millennium Development Goals*. New York: World Bank.

CSFI (2008), Microfinance banana skins—Risk in a booming industry, In Hilton, A. (Ed.), *Banking banana skins report*. New York, Centre for the study of financial innovation.

Ghatak, M. and T.W. Guinnane (1999), The economics of lending with joint liability: Theory and practice. *Journal of Development Economics* 60: 195-228.

Glaeser, E.L. (2002), The Governance of Not-For-Profit Firms. http://search.epnet.com/login.aspx?direct=true&db=ecn&an=0715210&loginpage=login.asp National Bureau of Economic Research, Inc, NBER Working Paper: 8921.

GTZ, Regulatory Requirements for Microfinance: A Comparison of Legal Frameworks in 11 Countries Worldwide, Economics & Employment Promotion Department (42), GTZ: Accessed from: http://www.bu.edu/bucflp/files/2012/08/Regulatory-Requirements-for-Microfinance.pdf

Hansmann, H. (1996), *The ownership of enterprise*. Cambridge, Massachusetts, The Belknap Press of Harvard University Press.

Hartarska, V. (2005), Governance and Performance of Microfinance Institutions in Central and Eastern Europe and the Newly Independent States, World Development, 33: 1627-43.

Helms, B. (2006), Access for All: Building Inclusive Financial Systems. Washington: CGAP: http://www.standardandpoors.com/ratingdirect

IFAD (2005), Handbook for the analysis of the governance of microfinance institution, Guidebook for the microfinance institutions, IFAD, Rome, Nov. 2005.

Institut Sur la Governance (2014), IOG Principles of Good Governance: http://iog.ca/about-us/iog-principles-of-good-governance/

Johnson, S., M. Malkamaki, and K. Wanjau (2006), Tackling the 'frontiers' of microfinance in Kenya: The role for decentralized services, Small Enterprise Development 17, 41-53.

Littlefield, E., J. Murduch, and S. Hashemi (2003), Is microfinance an effective strategy to reach the millennium development goals? CGAP: Focus Note 24.

Mersland, R. (2008), The Governance of not-for-profit microfinance institutions: lessons from history, Paper presented in the first International workshop on "Microfinance Management and Governance" 2-3 June 2008, Kristiansand, Norway. (Website: http://papers.ssrn.com/sol3/papers.cfm?abstract_id=1298613)

Mersland, R. and Storm, R.Ø. (2008a), Microfinance Mission Drift Working Paper, Kristiansand, Norway, University of Agder.

Mersland, R. and Storm, R.Ø. (2008b), Performance and trade-offs in microfinance institutions—Does ownership matter? *Journal of International Development*, 20, 598-612.

Morduch, J. (2000), The microfinance schism, World Development 28(4): 617-29.

Paxton, J., D. Graham, and C. Thraen (2000), Modeling group loan repayment behavior: New insights from burkina faso. *Economic Development and Cultural Change* 48(3): 639-55.

Rasmussen, E. (1988), Mutual Banks and Stock Banks. *Journal of Law and Economics* 31: 395-421.

Reserve Bank of India (2008), Report on Trend and Progress of Banking in India 2007-08, Reserve Bank of India Publications, Mumbai, India.

Rhyne, E. (1998), The Yin and Yang of microfinance: Reaching the poor and sustainability. *MicroBanking Bulletin* 2: 6-9.